Naples

timeout.com/naples

Published by Time Out Guides Ltd, a wholly owned subsidiary of Time Out Group Ltd.
Time Out and the Time Out logo are trademarks of Time Out Group Ltd.

© Time Out Group Ltd 2005
Previous editions 2000, 2002

10 9 8 7 6 5 4 3 2 1

This edition first published in Great Britain in 2005 by Ebury
Ebury is a division of The Random House Group Ltd,
20 Vauxhall Bridge Road, London SW1V 2SA

Random House Australia Pty Limited, 20 Alfred Street, Milsons Point, Sydney, New South Wales 2061, Australia
Random House New Zealand Limited, 18 Poland Road, Glenfield, Auckland 10, New Zealand
Random House South Africa (Pty) Limited, Endulini, 5A Jubilee Road, Parktown 2193, South Africa

Random House UK Limited Reg. No. 954009

Distributed in USA by Publishers Group West
1700 Fourth Street, Berkeley, California 94710

Distributed in Canada by Penguin Canada Ltd
10 Alcorn Avenue, Toronto, Ontario, Canada M4V 3B2

For further distribution details, see www.timeout.com

ISBN 1-904978-31-2

A CIP catalogue record for this book is available from the British Library

Colour reprographics by Icon, Crowne House, 56-58 Southwark Street, London SE1 1UN

Printed and bound in Germany by Appl. Papers used by Ebury Press are natural, recyclable products made from wood grown in sustainable forests.

Time Out Guides Limited
Universal House
251 Tottenham Court Road
London W1T 7AB
Tel + 44 (0)20 7813 3000
Fax + 44 (0)20 7813 6001
Email guides@timeout.com
www.timeout.com

Editorial

Editor Ros Sales
Consultant Editors Anne Hanley, Fergal Kavanagh
Deputy Editors Christi Daugherty, Jan Fuscoe
Listings Checker Fulvia Angelini
Proofreader John Pym
Indexer Jonathan Cox

Editorial/Managing Director Peter Fiennes
Series Editor Ruth Jarvis
Deputy Series Editor Lesley McCave
Business Manager Gareth Garner
Guides Co-ordinator Holly Pick
Accountant Sarah Bostock

Design

Art Director Mandy Martin
Deputy Art Director Scott Moore
Senior Designer Tracey Ridgewell
Designer Oliver Knight
Junior Designer Chrissy Mouncey
Digital Imaging Dan Conway
Ad Make-up Charlotte Blythe

Picture Desk

Picture Editor Jael Marschner
Deputy Picture Editor Tracey Kerrigan
Picture Researcher Ivy Lahon, Monica Roche

Advertising

Sales Director Mark Phillips
International Sales Manager Ross Canadé
Advertising Sales (Naples) MAD & Co. International
Advertising Assistant Lucy Butler

Marketing

Marketing Director Mandy Martinez
US Publicity & Marketing Associate Rosella Albanese

Production

Production Director Mark Lamond
Production Controller Samantha Furniss

Time Out Group

Chairman Tony Elliott
Managing Director Mike Hardwick
Group Financial Director Richard Waterlow
Group Commercial Director Lesley Gill
Group Marketing Director Christine Cort
Group General Manager Nichola Coulthard
Group Circulation Director Jim Heinemann
Group Art Director John Oakey
Online Managing Director David Pepper
Group Production Director Steve Proctor
Group IT Director Simon Chappell

Contributors

Introduction Ros Sales. **History** Anne Hanley. **War & Peace** Simon Pocock. **Naples Today** Stefano de Stefano (*Scooterville* Mark Walters). **Painting in Naples** Victoria Primhak. **Architecture** Victoria Primhak. **Where to Stay** Michele Mastronardi. **Sightseeing: Introduction, Royal Naples & Monte Echia, The Port & University, Centro Storico, Via Toledo & La Sanità, Capodimonte, Vomero, Chiaia to Posillipo, Suburbs & Elsewhere** Simon Pocock (*Blood rites, The good doctor, Maria Francesca, Skulls & bones* Raffaella Malaguti); **Campi Flegrei** Mark Walters. **Restaurants** Adrienne Harrison. **Cafés, Bars & Gelaterie** Chris Rose. **Shops & Services** Jane Ritter. **Children** Simon Pocock. **Film** Victoria Primhak. **Galleries** Chris Rose. **Gay & Lesbian** Michele Mastronardi. **Nightlife & Music** Chris Rose (*Sounds of the city* Fergal Kavanagh). **Performing Arts** Chris Rose. **Sport & Fitness** Fergal Kavanagh. **Around Naples: Introduction** Anne Hanley. **Capri** Raffaella Malaguti, Lee Marshall (*Capri dips, Artistic licence* Raffaella Malaguti). **Ischia** Victoria Primhak. **Procida** Victoria Primhak. **Pompeii & Vesuvius** Mark Walters (*Madonna dell'Arco* Raffaella Malaguti). **Sorrento & Around** Chris Rose. **The Amalfi Coast** John Moretti, Lee Marshall (*Once were warriors, Squeezing manna from a stone, Vietri ceramics* John Moretti). **Further Afield** Mark Walters. **Directory** Fergal Kavanagh.

The editor would like to thank Rosario Canadé.

MAD & Co. Advertising & Marketing Director: Margherita Tedone Tel +39 06 3550 9145, Fax +39 06 3550 1775. **Sales executive (Naples)** Dario Di Cesare.

Maps LS International, via Sanremo17, 20133 Milan (lsinigaglia@geomaker.com).

Photography by Jonathan Perugia except: page 10 The Art Archive/Museo di Capodimonte Naples/Dagli Orti; pages 13, 19, 25, 91 Corbis; pages 16, 90 Bridgeman Art Library; page 20 National Museums Liverpool (Lady Lever Art Gallery); page 22 Getty Images; page 95 Tom Sneddon; page 161 Oreste Lanzetta; page 166 Kobal; page 233 Tony Gibson; page 251 Giovanni Rinaldi

Contents

Introduction

The first glimpse of the Bay of Naples is like seeing a well-known picture for the first time. It's famously familiar: the round Bay, the blue Mediterranean, Vesuvius looming. This was the scene the Grand Tourists loved, and painted.

By the mid 20th century, however, the port was all that most visitors saw. Travellers with tickets to romantic places who passed through Naples did not dally here. The city itself had become nothing more than a jumping-off point for destinations whose names dripped with glamour, like Capri and Sorrento. Devastated by World War II and saddled with seemingly insoluble social and economic problems, Naples was not a pretty sight.

The gloom started to recede in the 1990s. Under new leadership, the city began to move forward, albeit in fits and starts, but with enough certainty to give residents – probably for the first time in the city's history – real faith in the power of their local government to work on solving some of Naples' chronic problems. The city cleaned itself up: *piazze* that had been used as car parks became *piazze* again; streets were cleaned, and buildings were restored.

Much of this guide is devoted to covering the region's incomparable ancient sites (Pompeii, Herculaneum, Paestum), its sun-drenched islands (Capri, Ischia and Procida) and its stunning coastline and hinterland (Sorrento, the Amalfi Coast). These places, for many, represent the quintessential southern Italy.

But Naples today has become a destination in its own right once again, and the boom in hotels and upmarket bed and breakfast accommodation attests to this. Dilapidation remains; this is still a city with problems of poverty and unemployment. But it is also a city awash with churches, art, ancient sites and museums. It is a city with a vibrant cultural life, from opera performances at the Teatro San Carlo to distinctive Neapolitan popular music styles; with justified pride in a fine cuisine deeply rooted in the region; and with a lively café society.

But the real essence of the Neapolitan experience is a visible, individual daily life, lived largely outside for all to observe and enjoy. Don't come to Naples expecting a homogenised Euroland city; history has made Naples a highly singular place. Enjoy it for what it is.

ABOUT TIME OUT CITY GUIDES

Time Out Naples is one of an expanding series of travel guides produced by the people behind London and New York's successful listings magazines. Our guides are all written and updated by resident experts who have striven to provide you with all the most up-to-date information you'll need to explore the city, whether you're a local or first-time visitor.

THE LOWDOWN ON THE LISTINGS

Above all, we've tried to make this book as useful as possible. Websites, telephone numbers, transport information, opening times, admission prices and credit card details are all included in our listings. And, as far as possible, we've given details of facilities, services and events, all checked and correct at the time we went to press. However, owners and managers can change their arrangements at any time. Before you go out of your way, we'd strongly advise you to call and check opening times, dates of exhibitions and other particulars. While every effort has been made to ensure

the accuracy of the information contained in this guide, the publishers cannot accept responsibility for any errors it may contain.

PRICES AND PAYMENT

We have noted whether venues such as shops, hotels and restaurants accept credit cards or not but have only listed the major cards – American Express (AmEx), Diners Club (DC), MasterCard (MC) and Visa (V). Some businesses may take other cards and euro travellers' cheques issued by a major financial institution (such as American Express).

The prices we've supplied in this guide should be treated as guidelines, not gospel. Fluctuating exchange rates and inflation can cause charges, in shops and restaurants particularly, to change rapidly. If prices vary wildly from those we've quoted, ask whether there's a good reason. If not, go elsewhere. Then please write and let us know. We aim to give the best and most up-to-date advice, so we always want to know if you've been badly treated or overcharged.

THE LIE OF THE LAND

Naples is bustling and chaotic, so for ease of use we have divided many chapters by district. Within easy reach of the city are the islands of Capri, Ischia and Procida, as well as resorts such as Sorrento and the Amalfi Coast, and archeological wonders like Pompeii and Herculaneum. All these destinations are covered in this guide.

TELEPHONE NUMBERS

The area code for Naples is 081. To dial numbers in this book from abroad, use your country's exit code (00 in the UK, 011 in the US), followed by the country code for Italy (39). When within Italy, all telephone numbers now require that the area code is dialled as part of the number, whether you are in the relevant area or not. For more details on phone codes and charges, *see p294*.

Advertisers

We would like to stress that no establishment has been included in this guide because it has advertised in any of our publications and no payment of any kind has influenced any review. The opinions given in this book are those of Time Out writers and entirely independent.

ESSENTIAL INFORMATION

For all the practical information you might need for visiting the city – including visa and customs information, disabled access, emergency telephone numbers, a list of useful websites and the lowdown on the local transport network – turn to the Directory chapter at the back of this guide. It starts on p282.

MAPS

At the back of this guide (and within the Around Naples section) you'll find maps of Naples and the towns, areas and islands featured, as well as plans of major archeological sites. We've included a series of fully indexed colour street maps to the city at the back of this guide – they start on p311 – and, where possible, we've included a grid reference for all venues that appear on the maps.

LET US KNOW WHAT YOU THINK

We hope you enjoy *Time Out Naples*, and we'd like to know what you think of it. We welcome tips for places that you consider we should include in future editions and take notice of your criticism of our choices. You can email us on guides@timeout.com.

There is an online version of this book, along with guides to over 45 other international cities, at **www.timeout.com**.

In Context

Features

History

Saints and sinners, kings and paupers.

In the eighth century BC a small band of adventurers from the Greek island of Euboea set up a trading station near what is now Lacco Ameno (*see p201*), on the island they called Pithekoussai (Ischia). Ischia's volcanos were rumbling at the time, driving some of the less courageous newcomers across the bay to Cuma (*see p106*) on the mainland. There, they soon got down to the crucial business of improving trade links around the Mediterranean basin.

Infinitely more sophisticated and organised than the tribes that had long populated the lush hinterland and sparser mountain region beyond, the Greeks soon made Cuma the area's most powerful city. The addition of a sibyl – a prophesying voice of the gods – in her cave deep inside the town added to the clout of the new settlement. Confident in their control of the area, the Cuman Greeks spread down the coast, founding Parthenope (near Pizzofalcone, *see p62*) in c680 BC, Dikaiarchia (Pozzuoli, *see p100*) in c530 BC and Neapolis ('New Town') in 470 BC. Today the original Greek plan of Neapolis can still be made out in the grid pattern of the streets in central Naples.

Yet as the Cuman Greeks were extending their sphere of influence, so were those who would prove the first real challenge to Greek power: the Etruscans. From their power base in Tuscany, these highly advanced people spread southwards from the ninth or eighth centuries BC, establishing their southern capital at Capua in about 600 BC. They rapidly absorbed the extraordinary culture imported into the region by the Greeks, adding their own particular twists to it. Conflict was inevitable between two such dynamic groups, and battles were fought at Cuma in 524 and 474 BC, both won by the Greeks, but both exhausting the strength and reserves of the rivals, and leaving them prey to the encroaching Samnite hill people.

Shepherds and fighters, the Samnites took Capua in 424 BC and Cuma in 421 BC. Into this scenario stepped another tribe with a mounting lust for land and power: the Romans. Around 340 BC the Romans began the job of bringing the Samnites to heel. By 328 BC they had turned on Neapolis, laying siege to the city; it held out for two years before grudgingly handing itself over to the conquerors.

THE BEAUTIFUL SOUTH

The city's flourishing trade suffered a setback as it was forced to supply ships and men for Roman naval battles. Its assimilation into greater Rome sent its economy into a depression that was to last for centuries.

Neapolis continued to grow in population and culture, while still clinging to its Greek identity and language. As all things Hellenic became fashionable in republican Rome, wealthy Roman offspring were often dispatched to the southern city for their education, while their parents soaked up the balmy climate in holiday villas along the coast from Cuma to Sorrento. To make communication and transport easier, the Appian Way (via Appia), the first major Roman highway, was begun in 312 BC.

Of course, the idyll suffered the occasional brutal interruption: in the Second Punic War (218-201 BC), the Romans battled Hannibal's Carthaginian forces back and forth across the plains of the Neapolis hinterland; during the Roman Civil War (88-82 BC), Sulla occupied Neapolis, and massacred a large proportion of its inhabitants during his triumphal march on Rome, where he was to rule as dictator from 82 to 79 BC; while, in 73 BC, runaway slave Spartacus established the headquarters of his slaves army on the slopes of Mount Vesuvius, from where he set out on his rampages up and down the Italian peninsula.

But by the time the Roman Empire was established in 27 BC, Neapolis was once again a centre of learning, attracting writers, teachers and holidaymakers. Virgil lived here for many years, composing his Georgics, and ultimately died here; the sybaritic General Lucullus built a home where Castel dell'Ovo now stands.

If the city flourished under the Empire, not so the surrounding region, where agriculture was hit hard by imports of cheaper grain and oil from Rome's new possessions in Africa and Spain. In the largely abandoned areas around the Volturno estuary to the north of the city and Paestum to the south, malaria was rife. By the time Vesuvius erupted furiously in AD 79, burying many surrounding towns beneath a layer of lava and ash, Pompeii was already little more than a ghost town.

As the Empire declined, so did Naples and its environs, which from the early fifth century were prey to Goth and Vandal attacks. The latter razed Capua in 456 and the former won and lost Naples itself several times during the fifth century, despite works to strengthen the walls in 440. It was in Naples that the Western Roman Empire (*see p12* **Age of empires**) truly came to an end, when the last emperor, Romulus Augustulus, imprisoned by the Goth King Odoacer, died in 476.

DUCHY LIVES ON ITS WITS

Over in Byzantium (Constantinople), the Eastern emperor Justinian was keen to assert his power over Italy. In the 530s he dispatched his prize general, Belisarius, to do the job.

In 536, Naples' walls held Belisarius out for three weeks. Then one of the general's men spotted a water conduit leading into the city, and a handful of crack fighters crawled inside. Attacked from within and without, Naples fell and many Neapolitans were slaughtered.

The Byzantines continued to harry the increasingly demoralised Goths until 553 when the last Goth ruler was killed. The following year, Naples became a Byzantine-controlled duchy, with dukes, magistrates and military leaders appointed by the Eastern emperor's Italian representative, the Exarch of Ravenna. (By 645, this tight rein had been loosened, and a Neapolitan by the name of Basilio became the first native duke of the city, with the blessing of the emperor himself.)

With its population of 40,000, Naples was flourishing once again, its importance growing in inverse proportion to that of declining Capua. But marauding foreigners would continue to threaten the area.

'Naples played Machiavellian games to keep the wolves from the door.'

In 568, the Germanic *longobardi* (Lombards) swept across the Alps, taking northern Italy without too much of a struggle and moving swiftly down the peninsula. Their sieges of Naples – in 581, 592 and 599 – were largely unsuccessful, though much of the surrounding Campania region, including Capua and, in 625, Salerno, fell to them. At the same time, Naples was beset from the sea by Saracens. In the ninth century came the Franks, who were allies of the Pope (generally speaking) but sworn enemies of the Neapolitans.

Uninterested in territorial aggrandisement, the little duchy was content to ensure its own independence by playing its conflicting allies (Byzantium and the Pope in Rome) and foes (Lombards, Franks and Saracens) off against each other, sealing secret pacts, and balancing loyalty against distance, coherent policy against tactical advantage.

While Naples played Machiavellian games to keep the wolves from the door, inside the walls the city was growing in beauty and wealth. Churches were built, schools were founded; artists and goldsmiths worked

Age of empires

Roman Empire – the Roman Republic (509-27BC) gave way to the Empire when Octavian was crowned Emperor Augustus in 27 BC, bringing extraordinary stability to a realm that extended over much of the known world. The Roman Empire would continue – through glory days, a slow implosion and the onslaught of barbarian hordes – until the death in Naples of the last emperor, Romulus Augustulus, in 476.

Eastern Empire – also known as the Byzantine Empire, this was the eastern half of the Roman Empire and was to outlive its western counterpart by almost 1,000 years. The empire of the Romans was split in AD 396 when Emperor Theodosius gave Rome to one son, and richer, more urbane Constantinople – the eastern capital – to another. When the Ostrogoths overran Rome in 476 Constantinople came to the fore. After that, successive emperors launched unsuccessful campaigns to win back the western bit; as time passed, the cultures and the religions of Rome and Byzantium drifted further apart, the eastern and western churches agreeing on a schism in 1054. Constantinople suffered constant harrying both from Venetians and from the Turks, who finally breached its virtually impregnable walls in 1453.

Holy Roman Empire – this was conceived by Pope Leo III as the reincarnation of the empire of ancient Rome – he conceived of a power led by a strong Pope-friendly figure who would make papal writ law across Europe. To that end, Pope Leo sprang a surprise coronation on Frankish King Charlemagne in 800. Over the centuries relations between the Holy See and the Holy Roman Emperor were to lurch from hand-in-glove to very sour indeed. The title remained firmly in German hands until it finally died out in 1806. Well before its demise, it had become an empire in name only, with the independent states of Christian Europe not even paying lip service to their nominal overlord.

furiously to decorate the proud duchy. In the mid tenth century, with Saracens attacking from the sea and disgruntled Byzantines besieging from the landward side, Duke John III still found time to dispatch monks to libraries around Christendom to copy manuscripts

sacred and profane to enrich his own splendid collection. Industry and trade flourished, as Neapolitan textiles were in demand all around the Mediterranean basin.

Beyond Naples and the lands directly under its control, things started to look up for the Lombard-dominated territories after the Germanic overlords converted to Roman-style Christianity in the seventh century. Firmly settled in their southern dominions, the Lombards themselves embarked on a bout of building and learning, especially in their capital at Benevento (*see p274*). By the eighth century, however, divisions were appearing in the united Lombard front, as Salerno grew in importance and wealth. In 849, the Lombard centres of Benevento and Salerno split, which severely weakened the Lombard position. Capua, too, became a separate Lombard principality in the tenth century.

Not many miles from Salerno, Amalfi had emerged as a law unto itself, resisting Lombard encroachment, slipping out of the control of the Duchy of Naples (though highly active in the duchy's mercantile activities) and continuing to swear fealty to Byzantium, which was gradually becoming an invaluable trading partner for this growing sea power.

THE NORMAN CONQUEST

This fragmented state of affairs was soon to come to an end. In a final show of strength in 1027, the Lombard Prince Pandolf IV of Capua seized power in Naples, helped by Neapolitan barons keen to oust the reigning Duke Sergio IV. Holed up in Gaeta, Sergio turned to an unruly band of Normans who had strayed into southern Italy shortly before. He married his sister to their leader, Rainulf Drengot, and then made him the Count of Aversa. The combined Neapolitan and Norman force soon drove the Lombards out of Naples.

With Aversa – a small town north of Naples – as a power base, the Normans grew in number as more compatriots arrived from France, grew wealthier thanks to their mercenary activities, and became increasingly power-hungry.

In 1062, they took Capua, in 1073 Amalfi. In 1077 Lombard Salerno fell to Robert the Guiscard ('the Crafty') – a member of the powerful Hauteville (Altavilla) family – who made the city his mainland capital. Around this time Salerno was a boomtown, famous throughout Christendom for its extraordinary and respected medical school.

The Normans besieged Naples for two years to no avail. Robert turned his sights on Byzantium, but died in his bid to oust the Eastern emperor. His brother Roger concentrated his efforts on southern Italy,

Ashes to ashes: **Pompeii**. *See p11.*

most of which was firmly under Norman control by 1130, the year when his son was crowned Roger II, King of Sicily.

The Norman monarch demanded that Duke Sergio VII of Naples recognise him as sovereign. Sergio obliged, then retracted, joining an anti-Norman League that scored numerous bloody victories against the French interlopers. Having identified Naples as the centre of opposition, Roger laid siege after siege to the city, but he was driven back by weather and disease and the unhealthy exhalations from the volcanic areas surrounding it.

Sergio, having made another one of his temporary pledges to support Roger, died fighting for the Normans in October 1137. The Neapolitan people turned to the anti-Norman Pope Innocent II for help, holding out against the Norman king for a further two years. When Innocent was taken prisoner by the Normans, however, Naples was left with little choice; in August 1139, a delegation vowed to support the Sicilian crown in Benevento.

Despite the lengthy struggle, the capitulation was not an unpopular one. When Roger visited Naples in autumn 1140, 30,000 joyous people turned out to greet him. Within walls over 4.5 kilometres (2.8 miles) in circumference, Roger was impressed by the great houses and lavish churches. Outside the walls, trade flourished in two separate ports.

But with its incorporation into the Kingdom of Sicily, Naples moved backstage and was overshadowed by Palermo. A model of stability and efficiency, the Norman kingdom was also highly centralised, leaving little scope for independent action by its constituent parts. The Neapolitan nobility – for centuries a thorn in the side of the ruling dukes – swore fealty to the Norman crown in exchange for feudal land and privileges. That Norman conquest coincided with a period of high agricultural production in the Campanian countryside, and with explosive growth in the shipping trade, though this boom was thanks mainly to canny immigrants from Amalfi, Pisa and Genoa, rather than to Neapolitan activity as such. Relative peace and prosperity meant a livelier market for the city's artisans.

This general well-being (which ended, coincidentally, with the Norman line), may explain Naples' loyalty to Roger's vacillating grandson Tancred when his throne was contested by the more dynamic Henry Hohenstaufen of Swabia, the son of Holy Roman Emperor Frederick Barbarossa and son-in-law of Roger (*see p12* **Age of empires**).

After Tancred's death in 1194, Henry became king of Sicily and punished Naples by ripping down its walls. However, Henry, too, was to die three years later, leaving a three-year-old heir, Frederick. Still smarting from its punishment, Naples entered into the dynastic struggles of the German emperors, wholeheartedly backing the claims of Otto IV of Brunswick over those of the baby king Frederick II. The city decided to recognise Otto as sovereign, sticking by him through papal excommunications and various routs on the battlefield.

It was a wonder, then, that the victorious Frederick, when he was safely on the thrones of the Holy Roman Empire and southern Italy in 1214, decided to invest so much in Naples and treat it with such munificence. Though his brilliant, learned and artistically astonishing court remained in Palermo, he rebuilt Naples' walls and fortifications, and made the city an intellectual centre of his Italian kingdom.

Naples' new university – the Studium – was established to promote *ghibelline* (pro-Holy Roman Empire) teachings in contrast to the *guelph* (pro-papacy) advocacy of the great university at Bologna.

Nothing, however, could erase Naples' historic hatred of the Hohenstaufen family. In 1251, after the death of Frederick II, the city rose up against attempts by his son Conrad to assert control. With the backing of Pope Innocent IV, it declared itself to be a free commune, resisting sieges laid by Conrad's Italian representative, who was his illegitimate brother Manfred. In 1253, however, imperial forces broke through.

When the emperor died the following year, the commune was re-established briefly. In 1258, Manfred became king of Naples but the Neapolitans seized the first possible opportunity to offload their Hohenstaufen sovereign. Charles of Anjou had hardly completed his invasion of Sicily in 1265 when the city rushed to pledge its loyalty to the newly arrived French dynasty.

ANJOU'S CAPITAL, ARAGON'S ACQUISITION

To set themselves apart from their predecessors, the Anjous (*see p15* **Family affairs**) moved the capital of their Italian kingdom from Palermo to Naples, though the realm continued to be called the Regno di Sicilia. New buildings went up, and merchants and craftsmen from all around Mediterranean Europe flocked to the booming city. Charles I (who reigned over all southern Italy 1265-82) had the Castel Nuovo built, and a new, wealthy, well-planned and salubrious quarter grew around it.

In Sicily, things did not go so smoothly for the Angevin kings. Resentful at the removal of the capital from their soil, as well as at harsh taxes imposed by the newcomers, Sicilian barons began plotting with Peter III, king of Aragon, to overthrow Charles. The rebellion went into top gear on Easter Monday 1282, when French soldiers were killed after vespers outside a Palermo church; over the following night, in a riot that became known as the *vespri siciliani,* 2,000 French people were killed.

The ensuing Vesper Wars dragged on until 1302, raging through Sicily, and up and down the southern mainland, until Charles finally acknowledged that Sicily was lost and was reduced to ruling the southern Italian mainland.

Naples thrived as the Anjous sought to make the city a fitting capital for their dynasty. Under the third Angevin king, Robert (reigned 1309-43), the Castel Sant'Elmo (*see p93*) was built. However, the city's growing wealth and population caused lasting harm to the area

around it. Naples' port expanded exponentially, sounding the death knell for one-time naval powers such as Amalfi, Gaeta and Salerno. And while the primarily agricultural regions immediately surrounding the city capitalised on the food demands of the growing populace, the foothills of the Apennines became increasingly poor and more depopulated, and diseases such as malaria flourished in the marshy districts around the mouth of the Volturno, and in the Sele valley south of Salerno.

Naples' relationship with its French rulers was loyal, though never unquestioningly so. When Andrew of Hungary, husband of the beautiful and highly intelligent Queen Joan I (reigned 1343-81), was murdered in 1345, the Neapolitan people caught and wreaked their vengeance on his suspected murderers. King Louis I of Hungary suspected, however, that Joan might have had something to do with his brother's demise, and invaded Naples in 1348. Joan remedied the situation by fleeing to her county of Provence, and selling her city of Avignon to the Pope in return for absolution for any misdemeanours she might have committed. In 1352 she returned to Naples to a rapturous welcome. Thirty years later, when Joan backed the anti-Pope Clement VII, her own people rose up to overthrow her in favour of her cousin Charles III of Durres (reigned 1381-86), a champion of Pope Urban VI.

'With his leech-like crowd of Catalan followers, Alfonso failed to ingratiate himself.'

When Charles's son Ladislas (reigned 1386-1414) died, the Neapolitans defended his sister, the promiscuous Joan II (reigned 1414-35), against her second husband Jacques de Bourbon, who tried to wrest power away from her. They also backed Joan's designated heir, her cousin René of Anjou (Good King René of Provence) against the claims of Alfonso 'the Magnanimous' of Aragon (King Alfonso V of Sicily), whom she had adopted, then disinherited, previously.

But Alfonso was more than a match for René, whom he drove out of Naples shortly after Joan's death. Southern Italy was one kingdom again, and a long period of Spanish control had begun. With his leech-like crowd of Catalan followers, Alfonso (reigned 1442-58) failed to ingratiate himself with his Neapolitan subjects, despite his lenient treatment of a city that had fought tooth and nail to prevent him taking its crown. His illegitimate son Ferdinand (reigned 1458-94) won some hearts when he ejected the overbearing freebooters and championed the arts and trades of the expanding city.

Naples' powerful barons, however, continued to oppose the Aragonese presence; some even persuaded France's King Charles VIII to occupy the city in 1494. But the Neapolitan people rose up against French domination, reinstating King Ferrante's grandson, Ferdinando II (known as Ferrandino) to the throne.

On Ferrandino's premature death in the following year, the people pressed for the crown to be given to his young widow Joan, sister of Spain's King Ferdinand 'The Catholic'. The barons, on the other hand, conspired to place Ferrandino's uncle Frederick (reigned 1496-1501) on the throne. This solution enraged both France and Spain, which marched together on Naples in 1501.

ENTER THE HABSBURGS

When the French arrived first, Frederick hoped to salvage something for himself by agreeing to hand over Naples and part of his realm to its King Charles VIII. But when the great Spanish General Consalvo di Cordoba appeared at the city walls in 1503, the people promptly let him in, and Spain's King Ferdinand, of the Habsburg family (*see below* **Family affairs**),

Family affairs

Anjou (adj. Angevin) – in the 12th century this French family provided England with a royal house that would become known as the Plantagenets, though this line lost the province of Anjou itself to the French crown in 1206. A new line – the Capet-Anjou – was born in 1246 when the French king, Louis IX, made his brother Charles count of Anjou. This Charles was granted the crown of Naples and Sicily in 1266, and some of his descendents would go on to rule Poland and Hungary in the 14th century.

Aragon – descended from Ramiro I of Aragon (1035-63), members of this dynasty ruled in Aragon, Catalonia, Majorca, Sicily, Naples, Sardinia, Athens, Valencia and swaths of southern France at various times during the Middle Ages and early Renaissance. After his marriage in 1469 with Isabella of Castile, Aragonese King Ferdinand II became joint king of Castile as Ferdinand V or Ferdinand the Catholic. His grandson, Charles I (later Holy Roman Emperor Charles V) succeeded him and merged the houses of Aragon and Castile with that of Habsburg.

Bourbon – one of the great ruling houses of Europe, the Bourbons descended from Louis I, Duke of Bourbon, grandson of the French king, Louis IX (ruled 1226-70). Louis IX was a Capet; this line died out in 1328, to be replaced by the Valois line of the family; the Valois insisted on the imposition of the Salic Law – in which only first-born males could inherit a title – and therefore when the Valois themselves reached the end of the line in 1589, the Bourbon line took over. Bourbons were kings of France from 1589-1792, and from 1814-48; kings of Naples and/or the Two Sicilies from 1734-1808 and from 1816-60; dukes of Parma from 1731-35 and 1748-1802; and monarchs of Spain from 1700-1808, from 1814-1868, from 1874-1931 and from 1975 to the present.

Farnese – statesmen and soldiers, the Farneses hailed from northern Lazio, north of Rome, becoming dukes of Parma and Piacenza when Pope Paul III – aka Alessandro Farnese – detached these lands from the papal territories and made his illegitimate son Pierluigi duke in 1545. The duchy remained firmly in Farnese hands until 1731 when it passed to Don Carlos (Naples' King Charles III), the eldest son of King Philip V of Spain and of Elisabetta (aka Isabella) Farnese.

Habsburg – by a brilliant series of strategic marriages from the Middle Ages onwards, the Habsburg dynasty became rulers of much of Europe and – through the Spanish crown – of the New World too. Counts of Habsburg are recorded in the 11th century, with a Habsburg – Rudolf I – becoming king of Germany in 1273. He bestowed Austria on his sons, thus founding a realm that would remain in the family without interruption until 1918. In 1452 the Habsburg king of Germany, Frederick V, was crowned Holy Roman Emperor Frederick III; Habsburgs would retain that (increasingly meaningless) title until it was done away with in 1806. Frederick's son Maximilian I acquired the Netherlands, Luxembourg and Burgundy through marriage in 1447; his descendants would inherit Spain, Naples, Sicily and Sardinia. Habsburgs were kings of Hungary and Bohemia from 1526-1918, and of Spain and its empire from 1504-1700. The Habsburgs were at their most powerful in the 16th century under Charles I of Spain/Holy Roman Emperor Charles V. But Charles found himself with too much on his imperial plate, keeping Spain to himself and giving first Austria, then the title of emperor, to his brother Ferdinand.

Europe's finest theatre, **Teatro San Carlo**. *See p17*

added the Neapolitan crown to his already impressive list of titles (he reigned 1503-16 under the title Ferdinand III).

Ferdinand visited his new acquisition during 1506, conferring privileges on both the nobles and the *piazza* – the people – and leaving behind him the first of a long succession of viceroys who would be feared, hated and mistrusted over the next two centuries.

With the arrival of the viceroys, the locals' say in running of their own affairs diminished greatly. The parliament, in which nobles and the people were represented, served almost exclusively to rubber-stamp inaptly named *donativi* – not in fact donations, but crippling taxes. Even the barons were deprived of their near-omnipotence. During his term of office, Pedro di Toledo (viceroy from 1532 to 1553) had no qualms about imprisoning or even executing nobles who before then had impunity.

And although violent Neapolitan protests halted attempts to introduce the Spanish Inquisition, and the city reaped some benefit from the viceroys – especially from Toledo, who was responsible for vast redevelopment to improve living standards in the city, building the Quartieri spagnoli (*see p83*) – on the whole, Spanish rule did little to improve Naples' lot.

In the very early days, the city did profit from the extraordinary economic boom resulting from the Spanish conquest of the New World. Still, the ensuing inflation-fuelled slump hit hard in a city with no strong trade infrastructure (trade had long been dominated by transient merchants from Genoa, Amalfi and Pisa). The slump was accentuated by short-term administrators who had little interest in stamping out the endemic corruption in the realm's bureaucracy, and by chronic crime levels in the unpoliced countryside (which regularly failed to produce enough food to feed the population).

Yet it was on this depressed part of its dominions that Spain depended to finance its European wars. Taxes were levied on just about every commodity or transaction: on flour and bread, on tobacco, on rents, on hemp and on imported metals. Even ransoms paid to free Neapolitans from Turkish pirates were subject to tax. But the levy most certain to set the city aflame was the one on fruit and vegetables.

This tax sparked the worst uprising to hit Spanish-controlled Naples. In 1647, Neapolitans rallied behind a 27-year-old fisherman from Amalfi called Tommaso Aniello (known as Masaniello), who headed a bloody revolt until his assassination. Masaniello was pro-king but anti-levy. His task of leading the undisciplined mob was rendered all the more difficult by a vacillating viceroy, the Duke of Arcos. He promised to suspend the tax but didn't, armed the people then sent his troops to gun them down, and pledged greater clout in parliament to the masses while stationing troops to cover the retreat of the barons' henchmen after they had murdered Masaniello. By April 1648 the Neapolitans had grown tired of the upheaval. Endlessly optimistic, they settled for a new viceroy – the Count of Oñate – and a promise of more reasonable taxes in the future.

At the beginning of the 17th century, Naples was Europe's biggest city, with a population of over 300,000. The plague that ravaged the area for six months in 1656 left three-quarters of the population dead. But the rest of Europe, sinking deeper into dynastic struggles and into its own wars of succession, had little time to worry about the devastation caused by disease in this poverty-stricken outpost.

SPANISH SUCCESSION, POLISH SUCCESSION

When it became clear that the last of the Spanish Habsburgs, Charles II (Charles V of Naples, reigned 1665-1700), would die childless, various crowns needed to be reassigned.

England, France and Holland agreed that Spain and the Spanish Netherlands should pass to the Austrian Habsburg Archduke Charles (younger son of the Holy Roman Emperor, Leopold I), with Naples and Sicily going to France. But Charles II rejected this arrangement: he had been persuaded by his Bourbon brother-in-law, King Louis XIV of France, that only a Bourbon would keep Spanish dominions intact.

On Charles' death in 1700, Louis' grandson Philip of Anjou became Philip V of Spain, sparking a continental conflict that would last from 1701 to 1714. When France backed Philip and invaded the Spanish Netherlands, Britain, Holland and Austria formed an anti-French alliance. But when Archduke Charles unexpectedly became Holy Roman Emperor Charles VI in 1711 after the death of his older brother, the allies baulked at extending his power and dominions still further.

Sick of the succession of Spanish viceroys, and hoping for their own independent monarch in the shape of a minor Habsburg, Neapolitan nobles sought Austrian victory in the War of Spanish Succession. The Neapolitan people, as much at loggerheads with their nobles as ever, were happy to support Spain's new Bourbon king, and Philip V was given a tumultuous welcome when he visited the city in 1702.

In 1707, however, Austrian forces occupied southern Italy, and Naples once again found itself with a series of Habsburg-appointed viceroys at its helm.

Succession in Poland caused the next major European shake-up (1733-35), pitting Russia and Habsburg-controlled Austria (in favour of Augustus III) against the Franco-Spanish Bourbon alliance (which backed Stanislav I, father-in-law of France's Louis XV).

A CITY WORTHY OF THE TIMES

When the War of Polish Succession broke out, the squat, ugly but likeable Spanish Infante Don Carlos, younger son of Philip V and the scheming Elisabetta Farnese (*see p15* **Family affairs**), was in Florence, amusing himself (according to the British envoy of the time, Horace Mann) by shooting the eyes out of birds in the Gobelins tapestries in the Pitti Palace and whisking courtiers' wigs off with strategically placed hooks and lines. Elisabetta had sent her teenage son, with a 40,000-strong army, to occupy her family's dominions in Parma and Piacenza. He was also to take over Tuscany on the death of Gian Gastone Medici, the last of his line and a Farnese relation.

> **'Shortly after his 18th birthday, Elisabetta ordered her son to take "the most beautiful crown" in Italy.'**

But when the Bourbons entered hostilities with Austria, Elisabetta set her sights higher. Shortly after his 18th birthday, she ordered her son to mobilise his army, and to take 'the most beautiful crown in Italy'.

Charles's procession south was largely good-natured and mostly unimpeded. Austria failed to reinforce its embittered, over-taxed city of Naples and Charles entered the city in triumph in May 1734. In July 1735, having expelled the Austrians from the whole of southern Italy, he was crowned Charles III of the Kingdom of Sicily. Though the Peace of Vienna (1738) obliged Charles to cede Parma, Piacenza and most of Tuscany to Austria, he was confirmed as king of an independent southern Italian realm. Finally, Naples was a capital again, with a king it could call its own. It welcomed the Spanish newcomer, and Charles reciprocated.

With the Age of Enlightenment in full swing, the king (supported, from 1737, by his wife Maria Amelia of Saxony, upon whom Charles doted) transformed his capital into a city worthy of the times. No opera lover, he built Europe's finest theatre, the San Carlo (*see p67*); although he was no scholar, he established the

Biblioteca Nazionale. Under Charles's rule, the excavation of Herculaneum and Pompeii got under way. The 16th-century Palazzo Reale was extended and refurbished. To pursue his passion for hunting, Charles had magnificent palaces built at Portici, Capodimonte and Caserta. To house the city's poor, he built the Albergo dei Poveri (see p86), the largest edifice in southern Europe.

The death of the Austrian emperor in 1740 plunged Europe into war again. Unwillingly, Charles was prevailed upon to back the Franco-Spanish-Prussian alliance contesting the accession of the late emperor's daughter Maria Teresa to the Austrian throne. Once the redoubtable empress had secured her crown (and Naples had been forced to capitulate in humiliation to her British allies, who threatened to bombard the city from the sea in 1742), Charles could settle back down to the business of running his kingdom, or of choosing very able men to do it for him.

In 1759, Charles abdicated and returned to Spain, to succeed his father as King Charles III. As he did, he left eight-year-old Ferdinand under the jealous tutorship of his most trusted adviser, the honest and highly competent Tuscan lawyer Bernardo Tanucci. Tanucci had been instrumental in seeking to introduce bureaucratic and fiscal reforms into Charles's shambolic state. The continued power of the feudal barons limited his success there. Even more resounding was his failure to provide Ferdinand monarchial education.

When the highly educated, highly cultured and strong-willed Maria Carolina, daughter of the Austrian empress, arrived in Naples to marry the young king in 1768, she was shocked. He played with toys, talked coarse local dialect, enjoyed rough games with low-class youths, and abhorred anything to do with books or learning. Ferdinand was, however, terribly impressed by his intelligent young wife, whose orders – especially in matters of state – he soon accepted unquestioningly.

With the birth of her first son in 1777, Maria Carolina entered the Council of State, as was stipulated in her marriage contract. From this position of strength, she was able to engineer the downfall of her arch-enemy Tanucci.

In 1778, she adopted as her favourite John Acton, a wandering British naval hero, who may have become her lover. Born in France, Acton had made vast improvements to the Tuscan navy before being summoned to modernise Naples' neglected fleet.

In Spain, King Charles was furious that a subject of his enemy Britain should be gaining influence in his former realm. Indeed, Acton was apt to pass classified information from

the queen's lips to the British ambassador, Sir William Hamilton (see p20 **William, Emma... & Horatio**), and he steered Naples into an iron-clad alliance with Britain. He also served Naples faithfully, however, displaying exceptional honesty and organisational powers in the midst of ministers who were known for their inefficiency and graft.

He may also have attenuated the worst excesses of the queen's hysteria following the outbreak of the French Revolution. For the reactionary Maria Carolina, the revolution was shock enough, but the execution of her sister Marie Antoinette in 1793 was too much.

Naples entered enthusiastically into the anti-French alliance. A Neapolitan army of 60,000 troops occupied French-held Rome on 27 November 1798, with the triumphant King Ferdinand at its head. But Karl Mack, the Austrian general who led the Neapolitan forces, proved to be a bungling fool. When France's General Championnet marched back into Rome 11 days later, the Neapolitans fled, with the French on their heels.

ROYAL EXILE

In Naples, news of the defeat was greeted by the fiercely royalist masses with ferocious attacks on those Neapolitan liberals who had championed French ideals of liberty and equality. The massacre ended only as the French entered the city, and the Repubblica Partenopea was declared in January 1799.

The royal family, with Acton, fled to Sicily on board Admiral Horatio Nelson's ship the *Vanguard*. In Naples, efforts – confused and bungled – by Republican leaders to introduce pro-equality reforms failed to impress the poor, who took advantage of the early withdrawal of the French military to rise up and force liberals to take refuge in the city's forts.

Further south, the queen's envoy Cardinal Fabrizio Ruffo led his raggle-taggle Christian Army of the Holy Faith up the boot of Italy, in a bloody campaign to oust the French and their sympathisers. In June, the Republican leaders agreed to a capitulation, the terms of which were promptly ignored by Nelson and King Ferdinand. More than 200 executions – which included those of the royalist-turned-rebel Admiral Francesco Caracciolo and aristocratic child prodigy Eleonora Fonseca di Pimental – were carried out.

Naples was a minor player on the European chessboard, and easily sacrificed by allies in general disagreement over how to cope with the vast Revolutionary and then Napoleonic armies descending on them. When France beat Austria at Marengo in 1800, becoming the dominant European power on land and debilitating

Saints alive *La reginella santa*

Maria Cristina, daughter of King Vittorio Emanuele I of Sardinia and Piedmont, had no wish to be married; she wanted to devote her life to God. But not even vocation can stand in the way of dynastic ambition and Vittorio Emanuele despatched this mystically minded 20-year-old to Naples in 1832 to marry Ferdinando II and become queen of the two Sicilies.

Ferdinando, too, was a religious type, to the point of bigotry. But his wife's brand of spirituality did not appeal to the king, who treated her with contempt and made her married life a calvary. To compensate, perhaps, she went all out in an effort to gain the affection of her subjects who were, reportedly, split between those who loved and those who loathed the saintly (or sanctimonious) monarch. Maria Cristina believed that work was good for the soul, and so sponsored craftsmen of all kinds, including the renowned silk-makers of San Leucio near Caserta.

She was also a tireless advocate for the abolition of the death penalty, and succeeded in persuading her spouse to commute many death sentences before she herself expired while giving birth to the future Francesco II in 1836. A cult grew up around her after her death and her tomb in Santa Chiara (*see p75*) became a place of pilgrimage for those who remembered her as the *reginella santa* (holy little queen). She was beatified in 1872. Her husband, who remarried less than a year

after her death, showed no such devotion. In a burst of centenary enthusiasm, supporters made moves to have her canonised in 1936, but the short-lived queen has yet to receive the Vatican's top honour.

Naples' chief ally, the kingdom bartered its independence for those parts of Tuscany that still belonged to the Neapolitan crown. Only Britain – still Europe's greatest sea power – stood by the little kingdom; but with French troops poised in Rome, this friendship was more a red flag to a bull than any guarantee that there would be no invasion.

In 1805, Austria suffered another crippling defeat on the battlefield at Austerlitz, and French forces under Joseph Bonaparte occupied Austria's ally Naples on 14 January 1806. The royals fled to Sicily, and Joseph was declared king of Naples, to be replaced on the throne by Napoleon's brother-in-law Joaquin Murat in 1808 when Joseph was crowned king of Spain.

Try as they might, the Napoleonic rulers failed to win the hearts of the fiercely royalist southern Italians. The reforms introduced under French rule were numerous and, on the face of

it, very much to the advantage of the people: feudalism was abolished and land redistribution begun; absolute power was wrested from the hands of the Neapolitan aristocracy and the towns of Campania grew in status and importance. Murat, moreover, gave the city its Orto Botanico (botanical garden, *see p89*) and made efforts to stamp out southern Italy's endemic banditry.

Though their weak-willed ex-monarch Ferdinand dithered in Palermo – thoroughly under the thumb of British ambassador Lord William Bentinck, who first forced Ferdinand to promulgate a democratic constitution, and then to send his by now fanatically scheming wife Maria Carolina into exile in Austria in 1811 – the Neapolitan masses remained doggedly hostile to the French, rising up against them on innumerable occasions in mostly minor protests up and down the mainland provinces.

William, Emma… & Horatio

is a genius and yet he has ended by marrying a mere girl, who was clever enough to make him fall in love with her. Such a misfortune often comes to clever men in their old age… he is bound to pay dearly for his folly; and if his wife is amorous of him, she will kill him,' he wrote.

But beautiful, buxom Emma was not the type to kill a husband with too much affection, and in 1798 her attention was diverted when the hero of the Nile, Admiral Horatio Nelson, returned to Naples having already met Emma there in 1793 when he'd been a mere captain. An affair soon blossomed, and William – knowingly or not – swiftly became the third in Europe's most famous *ménage à trois*.

British visitors to the Kingdom of the Two Sicilies expressed shock and horror at the set-up, and the Admirality was so outraged that Nelson was ordered first to Minorca (he refused to go) and then back to a desk job in London, Sir William, on the other hand, gave little indication that he thought anything was amiss. Not only did he allow Nelson to live in his home, but he and Emma accompanied the hero on his triumphal procession homewards across Europe in 1800.

Former army officer Sir William Hamilton (1730-1803) had been British envoy to the Neapolitan court for 18 years when his wife died in 1782. Over the years he had built himself a reputation not only as a fine diplomat but also as an acute observer of the antics of Vesuvius and Etna, his treatises on which were widely admired.

His collection of ancient artefacts – from Pompeii, Herculaneum and the other sites being excavated at the time – was famous; parts of it would later make their way into the British Museum. But it's likely he felt the most precious item in his collection was a certain Emma.

This blacksmith's daughter, who began her life in Cheshire as Amy Lyon, was 31 years William's junior. Mistress of Hamilton's penniless nephew Charles Francis Greville, Emma was despatched to Naples in 1786 to cheer up the elderly uncle who, Greville hoped, would pay his debts in return. In 1791 Hamilton married her, to the admiration of some and the contempt of others, including libertine Giacomo Casanova. 'Mr Hamilton

It was only once back in England that he began to show signs that he was actually disgruntled by his wife's blatant flaunting of her relationship with the nation's darling. And if he had any lingering doubts about what was really going on, they were dispelled when Emma became pregnant and gave birth to a daugher whom she subtly named Horatia. One can only wonder whether or not Hamilton was well pleased that Nelson rushed to London to say farewell when the diplomat lay on his death bed in 1803. But two years later Horatio was dead too, at Trafalgar. After that, Emma was alone. She spent her last ten years ostracised, squandering her inheritance. She died in poverty in Calais in 1815.

They were also singularly unimpressed by Murat's efforts to create a united Italy when Napoleon's star waned.

During ten years of French rule, Naples' rightful monarch spent much of his time hunting in the Palermo hinterland, while the British – the only power that could have reinstated him in his capital – used Sicily as their Mediterranean power base.

At the Council of Vienna in 1816, Europe's victorious conservative monarchies confirmed Ferdinand as Naples' ruler; he took the new title of King Ferdinand I of the Kingdom of the Two Sicilies. The old king received a rapturous welcome when he returned to Naples. But he and his successors misjudged the changing times, and the enthusiasm would soon wane.

Ferdinand responded to the demands of the shadowy Carbonari liberal reform movement by promulgating a parliamentary constitution in 1820. However, he then stood by contentedly as his reactionary ally Austria sent troops into his kingdom to quash these dangerous signs of anti-absolutism.

Ferdinand died in 1825. His successor, Francesco I, had shown early signs of liberal leanings, but these soon disappeared when he took the throne.

Ferdinand II, who became king in 1830, managed to bring Naples' huge public debt under control, helped the poor on the orders of his first wife, the saintly Maria Cristina of Savoy (*see p17 La reginella santa*), and initiated a series of important public works, including the completion of the Portici railway, Italy's first, which opened in 1839. But the king was just as fully committed to absolutism as his predecessors had been. Liberal movements were watched by an efficient spy network, and all revolts were ruthlessly put down, sometimes before they even began.

In 1847-8, when the city of Naples joined the more openly rebellious Sicily in demanding a constitution, Ferdinand granted it, but then played moderate and extreme liberal camps off against each other until he could justify dissolving the bickering parliament in 1849.

A UNITED ITALY

Ferdinand II's son Francesco II (reigned 1859-60) came to the throne in mid-Risorgimento, as Piedmontese troops fought to oust the Austrians from northern Italy. Each victory for these Italian unification forces was greeted with joy in Naples, but the new king still could not see that he his harsh repression of liberalism could not continue. It was becoming clearer – even to those who had backed the Bourbons so enthusiastically – that Italian unification could only bring change for the better.

With unification troops having taken Sicily and much of the southern mainland, Francesco agreed to the introduction of a constitution in June 1860. It was too little, too late. The city's residents turned out en masse to welcome unification General Giuseppe Garibaldi, with an enthusiasm boosted by the fact that he had established his credentials as a royalist, rather than a republican. When Garibaldi entered Naples on 7 September 1860, banners hanging from every window showed the cross of the Piedmontese royal family, the Savoys. On 21 October the city voted overwhelmingly in favour of joining a united Italy ruled by Victor Emanuel II of Savoy.

It was to be ten years before the Unification of Italy was complete – with the capture of Rome. For Naples, integration into the national fabric meant that any faint glory that still clung to the once-flourishing capital evaporated. It was Rome that the Unification leaders aspired to, and Rome was now to be designated capital of the newly united realm. Meanwhile, Naples loss importance. Despite some housing reforms instituted after a devastating cholera epidemic in 1884, on the whole Naples languished in growing neglect and poverty.

DEVASTATION

Naples' importance – as a port, and as the gateway from southern to northern Europe – was only fully recognised once again during World War II; this time, though, it was much to the city's detriment. Aerial bombardments ripped out much of its historic centre and waterfront; and its incomparable state archive, perhaps the richest in Europe, was destroyed by the city's German occupiers.

The Germans were ejected in an uprising known as *Le Quattro giornate napoletane* (the four days of Naples). Between 27 and 30 September 1943, residents of Naples paved the way for the arrival of the Anglo-American forces. When the Allies finally entered the city's blackened shell, they found Neapolitans barely eking out the most pitiful of livings. The injection of Allied food and funds – coupled with Allied reliance on underworld figures to get things done – served more to fuel the black market and crime than to put the city back on its feet. Reconstruction was carried out in an unregulated, lawless fashion; in the early 1970s, an official enquiry found that almost none of the post-war buildings in the Naples area – a large majority of them horrendous eyesores – had acquired planning permission. Beset by local government corruption, high crime and unemployment rates, and decaying urban infrastructure, Naples had entered one of its worst dark ages.

The war-torn ruins of **Montecassino**.

War & Peace

The road to national reconciliation has been a hard one.

When Anglo-American forces entered Naples on 1 October 1943 they found a city on its knees. Over the years, Allied air raids had claimed more than 20,000 lives. Transport networks, utilities and thousands of buildings had been destroyed. Retreating German troops had sabotaged what was left in the scorched-earth policy they implemented throughout the region.

'It is astonishing to witness the struggles of this city so shattered, so starved, so deprived of all those things that justify a city's existence, to adapt itself to a collapse into conditions which must resemble life in the Dark Ages,' wrote Norman Lewis in his wartime diary, published as *Naples '44*.

It is generally reckoned that the first major episode that finally brought home the truth about the war to the Neapolitan population took place on 4 December 1942. A large formation of US B-24 Liberator medium bombers, armed with the new Norden bomb sights, took the city's air defences by surprise while the entire

Southern Italian fleet was standing at ease, celebrating the feast of St Barbara, patron saint of gunners, miners and fire-fighters. Italian losses that day, including the sinking of the heavy cruiser *Muzio Attendolo* along with other smaller vessels, and the destruction of two crowded trams in via Monteoliveto, near the Central Post Office (*see p292*); the day ended with a death toll of around 900.

The first eight months of 1943, in particular, saw daily (US) and nightly (British) Allied air-raids on a city that was poorly protected by antiquated anti-aircraft batteries. With such little resistance, the city had taken a terrible battering. In addition to the loss of life, there was huge damage to property. The port area, the old railway terminal in piazza Garibaldi (*see p68*), the industrial infrastructure in the eastern suburbs of the city around San Giovanni a Teduccio and the steelworks in Bagnoli (*see p100*) were all badly damaged, with a dire effect on post-war recovery. Among many churches and other historic buildings that were damaged, Santa Chiara (*see p74*) took a direct hit on 4 August 1943; the resulting fire raged out of control for six days (though, in a rare happy ending, the subsequent rebuilding may have improved on what was destroyed); during the same raid the San Lorenzo Maggiore (*see p80*), the Girolamini and San Pietro a Maiello were also damaged.

On 28 March 1943 the Italian munitions ship *Caterina Costa* caught fire and exploded while loading troops and arms bound for the North African front. The force of the explosion hurled debris as far as Capodimonte. More than 500 people, many of whom had been watching the pyrotechnics from behind the safety of the iron railings separating via Marittima from the port, lost their lives; thousands more were injured. The tragedy – coming, as it did, shortly before the collapse of the Rome–Berlin axis, the fall of Mussolini from power and the end of the Italian military adventure – was etched indelibly in the minds of the city's populace.

'The sadly reduced contents of the city's aquarium appeared at a dinner to welcome General Clark.'

Despite untold privations during this period, a threat from Nazi occupiers to deport the city's young male population caused dampened spirits to flare up in what became known as *Le Quattro giornate napoletane* (the four days of Naples). In a series of spontaneous uprisings – mainly centred on the Vomero district – from 27 to 30 September 1943, motley bands of Italian ex-servicemen and young Neapolitan patriots kept the German garrison so busy that it was unable to concentrate on rebuffing the advancing Allies and was forced to speed up its retreat from the city, leaving behind a trail of blown-up buildings.

Later, during the dark days of autumn 1943 when Allied forces were pushing on across the Volturno plains towards the Winter Line and Montecassino, a sour note was left in many smaller communities, especially in the area around Caserta, when retreating German soldiers carried out barbarous acts of retaliation at the expense of some local communities, held responsible for aiding the Allied war effort. The two small villages of Bellona and Caiazzo saw a total of 76 people, mainly old men, women and children, machine-gunned, bayoneted or blasted to death in episodes that have only recently been restored to their proper place in the collective consciousness; Caiazzo,

for example, has now been twinned with Ochtendung, home town of the German NCO held responsible for the massacre.

THINGS CAN ONLY GET BETTER?
The arrival of the Allies was greeted with relief as liberation meant respite from bombs and, it was hoped, starvation. Before long, however, the city's million-odd population was swelled by the influx of 100,000 Allied soldiers. Then there were the remnants of Mussolini's disbanded forces, unable to return to their homes in German-occupied northern Italy and exiled in Naples. Hopes for a quick return to peacetime normality faded fast as the city struggled on through more air raids – German this time. Malnutrition (food was still in extremely short supply) and outbreaks of typhoid and other serious diseases were the rule rather than the exception. To cap it all, Vesuvius erupted in spring 1944.

There were, however, lighter moments during the Allied occupation of Naples, as recorded by Lewis in *Naples '44* and Curzio Malaparte in *La Pelle* (*Skin*): both relate how the sadly reduced contents of the city's aquarium appeared on plates at a dinner staged to welcome American General Mark Clark; both spread the city's unfortunate reputation for kleptomania, with accounts of entire military vehicles disappearing, piece by piece, overnight.

But Malaparte, and John Horne Burns in *The Gallery*, also provide heart-wrenching snapshots of the prevailing sense of despair. These writers dispelled the city's ruffianly, somewhat romantic image in favour of a grimier, sleazier portrait of ragged *scugnizzi* (street urchins) and *segnurine* (girls forced into prostitution). It was an image exported around the post-war western world by Allied ex-servicemen and correspondents. For 50 years this was to be the Neapolitan stereotype, reproducing itself with such tedious monotony that, until very recently, Naples seemed trapped in an air-bubble dated 1943.

THE PHYSICAL LEGACY OF WAR
Generally speaking, unlike in Normandy, nearly all traces of the battle on the Salerno beaches have long since disappeared, partly due to the far more improvised nature of the German and Italian coastal defences, and partly because the area has since undergone such widespread development. However in other places, such as along the Cuma coastline north of Naples and around the Campi Flegrei, it is possible to see the occasional decrepit-looking concrete bunker, the only signs of hastily assembled Italian coastal defence installations.

Elsewhere, on lonely mountain sides all over the region, walkers straying from the beaten track might come across the remains of fox-holes, slit-trenches and bomb craters, testimony to a bitter struggle fought out against a backdrop of some of the most beautiful and idyllic landscapes in the world. This is particularly true of the whole of the Volturno valley, the low Picentino mountains south-east of Salerno, and the Appenine ridge that runs westwards to the coast north of Caserta, and which formed the western extremity of the German Winter Line, along which opposing forces locked horns in a brutal war of attrition for the winter of 1943-44.

Some of the damage caused from the air is still visible today, directly or indirectly. The area around the railway marshalling yards, port installations and industrial suburbs to the east of the Naples still bears signs of destruction, while, despite much recent activity, some buildings along the via Marina waterfront are still awaiting demolition or redevelopment. Although most of the city's important monuments, such as the completely remodelled Santa Chiara, have long since been repaired, others, such as the Girolamini were still awaiting restoration when the earthquake of 1980 struck, thereby adding to the bill. Careful examination of buildings around the Museo Nazionale Archeologico (*see p84*), and Piazza Trieste e Trento will yield signs of shell and grenade damage, a permanent record of the street fighting that took place there at the end of September 1943.

Subsequently, thousands of residential buildings were levelled, to be replaced by cheap modern constructions. There are few streets without an ugly modern block, standing out inelegantly between the stately *palazzi*.

The same traces can be found all over the region; the Old Court House, struck by a British naval shell, still stands gutted in the middle of Nocera Inferiore, near Salerno. In Ferrari, a small hamlet outside Avellino, a heap of ruins marks the spot where an American bomb fell, destroying the house and its occupants.

NATIONAL RECONCILIATION

The legacy of the war years was not restricted to physical damage. Beneath the joyous scenes of spontaneous jubilation when a town or village was liberated by Allied forces, lurked social, economic and psychological scars that would take generations to heal.

As the days and weeks passed, economic conditions remained bitterly hard, creating conditions where perceptions of political right and wrong became blurred. Initially, there was a kind of collective amnesia at a national and and individual level. How else to deal with an immediate past that had seen Italians fighting

each other in several cities, including Naples? During this period former combatants – both those who had stuck with Mussolini and those who had gone over to the Allied side in 1943 – were trickling home from POW camps, German labour camps and military service under the Nazi occupiers in northern Italy.

But the country could not put off reflection forever. Italy's surrender to Allied forces on 8 September 1943 had paved the way for peace, but it also triggered a process of self-examination that would lead to social and generational fragmentation as some people asked the difficult questions: how could Italians have been party to an alliance that had been responsible for the Nazi death camps? To what extent was it possible to be a good fascist one day and a good democrat the next? Could Italian soldiers really have fought alongside Germans one day and Americans the next, without becoming a laughing stock in the eyes of the international community?

THE TRUE COST OF FASCISM

With the approach of the 60th anniversary of the end of World War II it might be well to remember just how costly Italy's 20-year dalliance with fascism was, not only in the enormous loss of human life and property during the war itself, but also the Herculean post-war task of rebuilding the country's shattered political, social and economic morale.

Anti-fascist 'purges', the abdication of the Italian monarchy, a series of ultimately elusive boom-and-bust economic miracles, the rise of a series of dangerously violent unelected right- and left-wing groupings, and a long unbroken string of unstable yet scandal-besmirched Christian Democrat governments can all be viewed in the context of a failure to achieve real national reconciliation and unity.

Nowhere was the attempt at this process so slow, and the cumulative sense of abject despair so strongly felt, as in the south of Italy, and in Naples and the region of Campania in particular. In these backwaters Mussolini's strict control of local government, via a network of centrally appointed *podestà* instead of locally elected mayors, had at least capped corrupt practices. But with the arrival of the Allied troops in October 1943, and, more importantly, with the setting up of the efficient but short-sighted provisional Allied Military Government, local mobsters saw a heaven-sent opportunity to set the gravy trains rolling once more.

An acute shortage of food and other prime necessities fostered a thriving black market; indeed, with so few legitimate goods to sell, there was virtually no other market to speak of. On to this black market went thousands

A family at war: civilians suffered huge levels of deprivation.

of tonnes of Fifth Army supplies then being shipped through the hastily repaired port of Naples. An estimated 40 per cent of throughput went AWOL.

'According to the Psychological Warfare Bureau,' wrote Norman Lewis, '65 per cent of the per capita income of Neapolitans derives from transactions in stolen Allied supplies.' Allied indifference to (and in some cases collaboration with) the local wheeler-dealers led to the creation of a system-within-a-system. From it arose a new political and business class, its well-being dependent on the art of turning a blind eye.

The whole topsy-turvy system that was thus engendered came of age in the late 1950s and '60s with the unauthorised transformation of large tracts of splendid countryside on the Vomero hill into cheap second-rate housing estates; ironically much of this land was around the Collana Stadium, where young Neapolitan patriots had been involved in running street clashes with German soldiers during the *Quattro giornate*.

A careless disregard for the past was demonstrated in Caiazzo, where the memorial gravestone of 22 civilian martyrs of Nazi retaliation was moved to make way for that of a local potentate, while in Santa Maria Capua

Vetere, as members of the old fascist hierarchy trickled back into local politics, several young men who had been actively engaged in skirmishes with retreating Nazi and Fascist forces were hauled up in front of the courts to answer charges of murder and damage to property. In other cases – still extremely sensitive – people who had resisted German occupying troops, thereby incurring retaliation subsequently meted out by the Germans often in collaboration with local fascist sympathisers, were subsequently drummed out of communities by relatives of the victims.

The model of local government based on nods, winks and reciprocal back-scratching went quite unchallenged for decades, mirrored at national level, where southern politicians were often involved in the most complex political scandals. It was not until the *Mani pulite* (clean hands) anti-corruption enquiries in the mid 1990s, coinciding with the 50th anniversary of the war years and also with the election of a new left-wing local administration in Naples itself, that any serious attempt was made to interfere with the process. It may be too early to say whether the process has really been halted or whether it has simply led to the creation of an even more cynical and arcane ruling class.

With TIM you can access your home operator services by the usual short codes, and get all the local information you need.*

With TIM you can continue using your local service numbers to access voice mail, customer care, etc. without the international dial code. In Italy, our **TIM 412 FindEverything** service assists you with information on restaurants, transportation, open pharmacies, directory assistance, and much more. For further information on the services visit **www.visitors.tim.it**

*Short codes and 412 are payment services. For further information on the costs, contact your operator's Customer Service.

Members of *freemove* alliance

Make yourself at home.

GSM

TIM national coverage, Italy (March 2004) - GSM: 94.6% country, 99.8% population.

TIM

Living without borders

Naples Today

A tale of two cities.

Ten years have passed since Antonio Bassolino beat Il Duce's granddaughter Alessandra Mussolini to become mayor of Naples. With his left-wing city council, Bassolino turned over a new leaf in Neapolitan politics, and ushered in a new era for this beleaguered city.

The preceding decade – the 1980s – had seen Naples worn down and worn out by the worst misgovernment in its recent history; political instability worthy of a banana republic meant that mayors rarely lasted more than six months. These were the *Tangentopoli* ('Bribesville') years, when public services were moribund, politicians didn't appear to be doing the job they were elected for and ordinary people suffered. And nowhere in Italy was Tangentopoli fallout felt more than in Naples.

Just 300 clapped-out buses served more than one million Neapolitan transport-users. Rubbish often lay uncollected on city pavements for days and days. A very few policemen tried to instill order into increasingly chaotic traffic – hours each day spent in jams was the norm for the city's long-suffering residents.

REBIRTH

Small wonder, then, that the new course ushered in by the Stakhanovite Bassolino and his administration was baptised – with true southern brio – the 'Neapolitan Renaissance'. A member of the post-Communist Democratic Left Party, Bassolino wisely devoted his energies to changing Naples' abysmal reputation in Italy and further afield. In this he was given a huge helping hand by the 1994 G7 meeting, held in Naples on the express wishes of Italian President Carlo Azeglio Ciampi.

The meeting was a brilliant propaganda coup for the new, improved city. Even if, at the time, it was the notification that he was under investigation handed to Prime Minister Silvio Berlusconi during the summit that made headlines. But in the longer term, what remains in the popular memory are images of the world's most powerful leaders – including Bill Clinton and Boris Yeltsin – sitting down to an official dinner at the spectacular Reggia in Caserta (*see p275*)… and Clinton tucking into a chunk of pizza during a walkabout along the Spaccanapoli, the city's *decumanus*, in the heart of ancient Neapolis. As the G7 leaders talked and strolled in the shadow of Vesuvius, the world was treated to stunning images of a freshly scrubbed-up city, restored to its former dignity and every bit the image of a

magnificent old European capital. From that moment on, everything changed. The G7 summit was the most effective international advertising that the most important city of southern Italy could have hoped for.

Ten years later, Bassolino's efforts are still paying dividends. Visitors continue to flock to Naples and the region of Campania, drawn by its natural beauty, matchless archeological remains and excellent cuisine.

But is everything really so rosy? Unfortunately not. Bassolino – now governor of Campania – continued to work successfully on the city's image and began to tackle the less popular, more ingrained social issues that shape the city's darker side. With so many problems to resolve, he was barely able to scrape the surface. In 2001 he was replaced by Rosa Russo Jervolino, Naples' first-ever woman mayor, who has striven valiantly, though with mixed success, to carry his work forward.

Scooterville

Southern Italians have had to cope with high noise levels for millennia: several tough laws were passed in ancient times to ensure quiet streets at night. However, with its army of two-stroke scooters – known to the Italians as *motorini* – 21st-century Naples seems to have evolved backwards. Souped up with engine tampering and driven at breakneck speed around the more populous areas of the city, *motorini* are recognised by most as a severe environmental hazard. Given the lack of serious enforcement, the recent introduction of mini-driving licences for 14-year-olds, tighter crash helmet legislation and the sale of newer, less polluting scooters have made little headway. In some parts of the city (like the inappropriately named Sanità area) motorcyclists have been dissuaded from wearing helmets by residents involved in crime, as they could be mistaken for potential hitmen operating away from home.

Thankfully, pedestrianised areas are catching on, but a words of warning still needed: when crossing a one-way road, always look both ways just in case a scooter is tearing up the wrong way. If on a pedestrian crossing or at traffic lights, don't assume that just because a car has stopped that motorbikes will do the same. And remember, about 50 per cent of all bag-snatching is done from scooters, especially by pillion riders. So in general, give those scooters a wide berth.

With a centre-right government in Rome, Jervolino's centre-left adminstration does not always receive the support it needs. But it is the complex social and economic situation in this city of 3.5 million people that makes her task particularly difficult.

THE DARK SIDE

Since the collapse in the late 20th century of Naples' iron and steel industry – the only real major employer in the city – no proper alternative has presented itself. A boom in the service and IT sectors has certainly helped, but only to a limited degree. Naples has an unemployment rate of 24 per cent compared to an Italian national average of nine per cent. And among the 15 to 24 age bracket, this rises to a whopping 58 per cent. For the young people affected, the chances of getting a proper job in the foreseeable future are slim to non-existent, and the city's very high truancy rates show there's little cultural inclination to view education as a solution. Many of these young people join an underclass that is unable to participate legally in the city's economic life.

'In the space of a decade, the city has built itself a cutting-edge metro.'

But Naples' youth have all the same aspirations, or maybe more, than young people elsewhere in this era of consumerism. If the lucky ones with jobs can purchase what they aspire to, many of the jobless – concentrated in the hard, run-down, crime-ridden outer stretches of the city – opt to obtain as much, or maybe more, in their own way. In Naples' mean streets, flashy cars, fast motorbikes, shiny Rolexes and the very latest mobile phones are essential status symbols; drug dealing and extortion are quick ways to get them. The most 'successful' parade their yachts around the bay of Naples and throw wild parties… all in the worst possible taste of the criminal parvenu and much to the dismay of the city's respectable majority.

Until not so many years ago, the crime situation in Naples was serious but relatively 'simple': illegal activity was firmly in the hands of the big Camorra families – much along the lines of Sicily's Mafia: rake-offs from public and private works contracts, major trafficking and blanket control of their territories were the main concerns of the old-style criminals. Remove the head of one of these clans and you'd struck a major blow at the whole organisation.

Nowadays, things are infinitely more complex. The phenomenon of *microcriminalità*

– a host of tiny gangs, insidious, uncontrollable, ruthless and answerable to no one – makes cracking down a nightmare.

AND YET…

All this in a city with an artistic heritage and a contemporary arts scene – not to mention a highly cultured middle class – which is second to none. Naples is full of ambiguities.

In the space of a decade, the city has built itself a cutting-edge underground metro that is not only one of Europe's most comfortable mass transport systems, but has stations that are galleries of contemporary art in their own right (*see p153* **Underground art**). Capodichino airport is smart and efficient (and, incidentally, run by Britain's BAA).

Against a backgroup of three incomparable castles – Sant'Elmo, dell'Ovo and Maschio Angioino – the stunning bay and the smouldering hulk of Vesuvius, the most highly acclaimed international artists exhibit frequently.

The San Carlo, one of Europe's oldest opera houses, has recently staged intriguing, innovative versions of such favourites as *The Barber of Seville* and *The Flying Dutchman*. The 18th-century Teatro Mercadante has been revamped as the city's new showcase for traditional Neapolitan theatre and avant-garde productions. In clubs around the city centre, local jazz and rock musicians fuse the latest sounds with Neapolitan roots (*see p160* **Sounds of the city**).

… BUT ON THE OTHER HAND

Yet Naples is also the city that let the next America's Cup slip through its fingers (it'll be held in Valencia). There's speculation that Naples was passed over because the Bagnoli area (former home of the city's steelworks), where the Cup would have been based, is still the subject of haggles over a long-promised revamp, and site selectors weren't confident the area would be ready on time. This is also the city that allows rubbish to pile high on its streets as it fails to find a solution for having nowhere to dispose of it. Protest marches block its streets and its railway tracks. And, worst of all for the city that worshipped at the feet of Diego Armando Maradona (*see p172* **The CalcioNapoli file**), a declaration of bankruptcy meant that Naples' football team was demoted to the third division in 2004 after a dispiriting display of bad management and lack of enterprise.

Whether Bassolino's clean sweep can be carried forward, or whether the 'renaissance' of this intriguing, confusing, infuriating, yet entrancing city will be halted by social problems and political infighting remains a question that has yet to be answered.

Titian's *Portrait of Cardinal Pietro Bembo.*

Painting in Naples

A city with a huge appetite for art.

The vicissitudes in Naples' fortunes and history – coupled with the extraordinary violence of the nature that surrounds it – have left their mark on Neapolitan painting. From the arrival of the Angevin dynasty in the 12th century to the unification of Italy in the 19th, great artworks were commissioned and then lost (the most notable example being Giotto's frescos in the Castel Nuovo; *see p66*) as tastes and rulers changed.

For much of the city's history, the Church and the monastic orders were the foremost patrons of art. Down the centuries, the paintings in Neapolitan churches have been neglected, painted over, destroyed, bombed, stolen or damaged by earthquakes. In some cases only what was buried or hidden for centuries underground or beneath layers of paint has survived. Only in recent decades has there been a gradual restoration of what remains of Neapolitan religious art in situ. The hidden glories of the medieval city, for centuries overwhelmed by the dramatic baroque art so typical of Neapolitan churches, have been brought to light.

Foreign rulers, too, had a hand in encouraging Naples' artistic output. In the 17th century, for example, Spanish viceroys developed an immense lust for local works – though many of these left Naples with their owners. During his four-year term, Count Olivares amassed sufficient paintings and antique sculpture to fill 40 ships on his return to Spain; much of his collection now graces the Prado in Madrid.

Naples' great families put together private collections over generations, many of which were broken up as noble fortunes declined in the 19th century. In a few lucky cases, they were left to the State (and can now be found in Museo di Capodimonte and the Certosa-Museo di San Martino, *see p93*) or religious institutions (*see* Pinacoteca Girolamini and Pio Monte della Misericordia, *both p80*).

CLASSICAL ART

Naples and the Campania region are home to some of the world's greatest examples of classical art. Much of it – including mosaics from Pompeii and marble and bronze statues from Herculaneum – can be seen in the Museo Nazionale Archeologico (*see p84*).

Where the art's at

Caravaggio
Seven Acts of Mercy: Pio Monte della
Misericordia (*see p80*).
Flagellation: Museo di Capodimonte
(*see p90*).
Pietro Cavallini
*Scenes from the Lives of Christ and
John the Baptist*: San Domenico Maggiore
(*see p75*).
Last Judgment and *Bible Scenes*: Santa
Maria Donnaregina (*see p82*).
Donatello
Tomb of Cardinal Rinaldo Brancaccio:
Sant'Angelo a Nilo – Cappella Brancaccio
(*see p74*).
Artemisia Gentileschi
*Judith and Holofernes, Annunciation,
San Gennaro Tames Animals in the
Amphitheatre, Adoration of the Magi*

and *Saints Procolo and Nicea*: Museo
di Capodimonte (*see p90*).
Masaccio
Crucifixion: Museo di Capodimonte
(*see p90*).
Michelangelo
Cartoon of Three Soldiers: Museo di
Capodimonte (*see p90*).
Raphael
Farnese family portraits and *Cartoon of
Moses*: Museo di Capodimonte (*see p90*).
Rembrandt
Judith and Holophernes and *Nathan and
David*: Museo di Capodimonte (*see p90*).
Titian
Portrait of Pierluigi Farnese: Palazzo
Reale (*see p67*).
Farnese family portraits, *Danaë* and *Mary
Magdalen*: Museo di Capodimonte (*see p90*).

But there's plenty still in situ (or nearby).
The frescoed slabs from the Tomba del
Tuffatore (480 BC), now in the museum in
Paestum (*see p270*), are the only surviving
examples of classical Greek painting in Magna
Grecia. The detail of two male lovers intent on
their conversation in the banquet scene, and
the image of the diver – symbolic of the sudden
passage from life to death – have come to
symbolise Greek culture.

The heights of Roman figurative art can be
seen in the wall paintings in Pompeii (at Villa
dei Misteri and Casa dei Vettii; *see p222*), with
their warm, intense tonalities, dominated by the
russet-brown colour known as Pompeian red.

CHRISTIANITY AND CAMPANIAN ART

It is difficult, however, to spot a truly local
tradition in these classical examples. Only
with the coming of Christianity did Campanian
art really take off, in the frescos and mosaics
decorating the catacombs of the city. The
paintings in the catacombs of San Gennaro
(*see p90*) date back to the second century
AD, when Christianity was a clandestine cult;
they mix classical decoration with Christian
symbolism. The lack of a gold background,
the use of classical elements and the figures
collocated in space, differentiate the local early
Christian art from the Byzantine tradition,
although gradually the Byzantine influence
and classical tradition mingled.

Outside the city, late classical elements, mixed
with Byzantine iconography and elements
introduced by the Lombards (*see p11*), continued

to influence religious painting; the late 11th-
century frescos in Sant'Angelo in Formis near
Caserta (*see p275*) show the maturity of the local
artists in realistic, figurative art.

The domination of Naples by foreign powers
was inevitably reflected in art. The arrival of the
Anjou dynasty in the 13th century (*see p14*) led
to an initial decline in local art as painters and
architects were imported first from France and
then from other parts of Italy to make Naples
a centre of creative fervour. **Pietro Cavallini**
was brought from Rome; his refined use of
colour and calm naturalism can be seen in
the frescos (1309) that decorate the Brancaccio
chapel in San Domenico (*see p75*) and the church
of Donnaregina Vecchia (*see p82*).

Giotto arrived from Florence and worked
as court painter from 1328 to 1334, decorating
Castel Capuano (*see p76*), Castel Nuovo (*see
p66*) and Santa Chiara (*see p74*). Though
only traces of his own work remain, Giotto
influenced many local painters. His Neapolitan
pupil **Roberto di Oderisio** (active 1340-70)
continued Giotto's experimentation with space
and perspective in the fresco cycle of Old
Testament stories in Santa Maria Incoronata
(1340-43; *see p65*). In the same church, Oderisio
offers an arresting glimpse of Angevin court
life in *The Sacraments* and *The Triumph of
the Church* (1352-54) with their scenes of
fashionably dressed Neapolitan nobles.

Power struggles in the late 14th century
halted the innovations in Neapolitan art. Few
examples remain from the period, in which the
late Gothic style prevailed; the most notable

are frescos in San Giovanni a Carbonara (*see p76*) by **Leonardo da Besozzo** and **Perinetto da Benevento**.

The Renaissance swept into Naples around 1450, with the advent of Alfonso 'the Magnanimous' of Aragon (*see p14*), who brought Aragonese/Catalan culture to the city.

Niccolò Antonio Colantonio (active in Naples 1440-70), the most important Neapolitan painter of the 15th century, was to fuse the Flemish and Burgundian traditions left over from the last of the Anjous with the new Renaissance spirit. His extraordinary capacity for reproducing Flemish painting in its microscopic detail can be seen in the *St Jerome in his Study* (1445) in Capodimonte. During his artistic development, Colantonio was the first to bring the spatial innovations of Piero della Francesca to Naples, in the representation of *San Vincenzo Ferrer* for the church of San Pietro Martire (1462; *see p70*).

In the early 16th century, Naples' Spanish viceroys were little more than transient bureaucrats, uninterested in commissioning artworks. The task of patronising the arts fell to the new monastic orders that arrived in the city from the 1530s. In new monasteries, and refurbished older ones, emotional and tortured Mannerism dominated. The Mannerist style of the Sienese **Marco Pino** (c1525-c1587) can be seen in the brilliance of the twisted figure of Christ in San Domenico (1564; *see p75*); however, his paintings for Santi Severino and Sossio (1571-77; *see p69*) were tempered by his knowledge of Spanish figurative painting.

GOLDEN AGE

Counter-Reformation fervour and immense sums spent on building and decorating churches and monasteries provided a fertile climate for the golden century of Neapolitan art. Religious commissions were a counterpoint to a troubled

Caravaggio's *Flagellation of Christ.*

period scourged by earthquake, volcanic eruption, epidemics, famine and riot, and subject to a repressive regime under the Spanish viceroys.

Strangely, few of the founders of the so-called Neapolitan School were Neapolitan. Michelangelo Merisi da **Caravaggio** (c1571-1610), the most influential, fled to Naples after killing a rival tennis player in Rome in 1606 and remained for little more than a year. His theatrical intensity, stark naturalism and vivid contrasts struck a chord with the local passionate temperament. His flesh-and-blood *Flagellation* (in Capodimonte) and *Seven Acts of Mercy* for the Pio Monte della Misericordia (*see p80*) revolutionised the tired Mannerist tradition. He paved the way for the enthusiastic reception of new painters.

'With the growth of Romanticism, increasing numbers of foreign painters were drawn to lyrical, emotional Naples.'

Caravaggio's follower **Jose/Jusepe/Giuseppe de Ribera** (c1588-1652) was born near Valencia. His sensational style and bold originality quickly caught on among the Spanish viceroys and religious orders, and his sadistic martyrdoms became the last word in religious taste. Immensely ruthless and ambitious, he formed a tyrannical cabal with Greek-born **Belisario Corenzio** and Neapolitan **Battistello Caracciolo**: only with the group's consent could other artists work on religious commissions in the city. When it came to securing the plum job of decorating the Cappello del Tesoro in the Duomo, for example, the cabal's competitors soon suffered: Guido Reni's assistant was badly wounded; Domenichino (a sensitive soul) was hounded out of the city in a state of collapse. Ribera's malice was boundless – he deliberately ruined Massimo Stanzione's *Dead Christ* at the entrance of San Martino under the pretext of cleaning it.

Ribera's taste for vivid narrative was sometimes grotesque, as in the *Drunken Silenus* (Capodimonte), but he gradually developed an extreme pictorial elegance with refined colours, which can be seen in the *Pietà* (1637) in the Certosa-Museo di San Martino. In contrast, from the 1630s there was a move towards a neo-Venetian painterliness and Bolognese classicism, evident in the intimate works of **Massimo Stanzione** (c1585-1656), who was to decorate the most important Neapolitan churches, including the Certosa-Museo di San Martino, Gesù Nuovo (*see p68*) and San Paolo Maggiore (*see p76*).

Artemisia Gentileschi (1593-1652/3), who lived in Naples from 1630 until her death, experimented with dramatic chiaroscuro effects. Her *Judith and Holofernes* (Museo di Capodimonte) had a great impact on Neapolitan painting. (The victim of a well-publicised rape, Artemisia was inclined to dwell on the theme of female vengeance.) In later life, she adopted Bolognese classicism in her religious works; this is visible in three large altarpieces made for the cathedral at Pozzuoli (*see p98*; in storage at the time of writing).

Bernardo Cavallino (1616-56), the major Neapolitan painter of the 1640s, represented the transition from lucid Caravaggio-esque naturalism to more refined painterliness in delicate, intimate work, influenced by Gentileschi and Stanzione. **Giovanni Lanfranco** (1582-1647), after initial success in Rome, had been eclipsed by the leading artists of the papal court and jumped at the chance to work for the Jesuits in Naples in 1634. He was the most successful fresco painter in Naples for the next 15 years; his warm colours and chiaroscuro contrasts can be seen in the Gesù Nuovo, the Certosa-Museo di San Martino, Santissimi Apostoli (*see p82*) and the Cappella del Tesoro.

The flourishing, passionate atmosphere of the city affected its artists: naturalistic still-life paintings by **Giovanni Recco** (c1615-c1660) and **Paolo Porpora** (1617-c1680) were juicier and fleshier; larger-than-life **Salvatore Rosa** (1615-73) – artist, poet, actor and musician – painted romantic battle-pieces, *banditti* and the poetic landscapes that were particularly popular in 18th-century England.

The plague of 1656 raged for six months, exterminating nearly half the population and many artists, including Stanzione. **Micco Spadaro** (1609-75) chronicled the event in his precise *Piazza Mercatello in Naples during the Plague of 1656* (now in San Martino).

Those Neapolitan artists who survived the plague embraced the baroque wholeheartedly. **Mattia Preti** (1613-99) brought new life to the city in his four-year stay, by his use of light as the basis of composition. His extraordinary use of colour, light and shadow is best seen in the *Stories of the Life of San Pietro Celestino and Santa Caterina di Alessandria*, painted for the vault of the nave of San Pietro a Maiella (*see p76*).

Local boy **Luca Giordano** (1634-1705), moving from airy, baroque visions to iridescent rococo, dominated the scene for nearly 50 years. Known as *Luca fa presto* ('Luca does it quickly'), he was a prolific painter; in his seventies he completed frescos in the Certosa-Museo di San Martino in just a few days. **Francesco Solimena** (1657-1747) merged naturalism and the influence of Preti and Lanfranco.

Smart art

In an effort to make life easier for visitors as they explore the art and museums of Naples and Campania, the local authority has introduced the **Campania artecard**. The cards offer free and reduced-price admission to sights, with free use of city transport and shuttle buses to some sights. They're good value – as long as you're determined to get round a lot of sights. It's easiest to buy the card once you arrive in Naples: they are available from the airport, port, stations, major sites and some travel agencies.

The card comes in three versions. The first covers Naples and the Campi Flegrei, and includes free entry to the first two sites visited and half-price entry to the rest, transport to the Campi Flegrei (the Archeobus Flegreo, operating Friday-Sunday, public holidays), the Alibus (*see p282*) from the airport to the centre of town, and one return trip on the MM1 Metro del Mare running from Bacoli to Sorrento (*see p284*). Naples venues included in the offer are: Museo Archeologico Nazionale, Capodimonte, San Martino, Castel Sant'Elmo, Palazzo Reale, Castel Nuovo, Città della Scienza, sites at Campi Flegrei. The card costs €13 (€8 18-25s, with all sites free).

The three-day card with access to publicly owned sights in the whole of Campania is the best bet for those who want to venture further afield. It includes free access to two sights and half-price admission to the rest – so it makes sense to visit the most expensive first (Pompeii, Herculaneum, Paestum, the Museo Archeologico in Naples). Free transport is also part of the deal: the Archeobus Vesuviano and the bus to Paestum from Salerno make the card good value for money if you don't stop for breath. A trip on the Alibus airport bus is also included as well as a return trip on the MM1 Metro del Mare during the summer months. Costs €25 (€18 18-25s, with all sites free).

The seven-day card offers free entry to all Campania's publicly owned sights, but no transport concessions. Costs €28 (€21 18-25s).

Holders of all three versions of the card are also eligible for a range of discounts on private museums, cultural events and other attractions in the region.

For more information, check website: **www.campaniartecard.it** or phone 800 600 601 (toll free) or 06 399 67 650.

The Certosa-Museo di San Martino is a magnificent example of Neapolitan baroque splendour. Artists vied for commissions from the fabulously rich but famously stingy Carthusian monks. With works by Caracciolo, Stanzione, Ribera, Lanfranco and Giordano, the chapel forms a unique gallery of 17th-century Neapolitan painting.

LANDSCAPE PAINTING

Landscape painting reached the height of its popularity in the 18th century, when the taste for the picturesque, the classical and the sublime made the spectacular scenery around Naples, the bay islands and the classical sites a must for the Grand Tourist. The most popular image was the panoramic or bird's-eye view of Naples from the sea. Vibrant, lustrous portraits of the city painted in 1700 by **Gasper Van Wittel** (1652/3-1736) – a few of which remain in the Certosa-Museo di San Martino – revolutionised landscape painting, with their synthesis of naturalism and the Dutch School. The warm Neapolitan light and local colour inspired him to combine reality and humanity in scenes like *Largo di Palazzo* and *Galleys in the Port*.

With the growth of Romanticism, increasing numbers of foreign painters were drawn to lyrical, emotional Naples. Vesuvius fast became a favourite theme, personifying the heroic and diabolic in a blend of the picturesque and the sublime. Frenchman **Pierre-Jacques Voilaire** (1729-1802) captured this spirit in his dramatic *Eruption of Vesuvius with the Bridge of the Maddalena*, now in Capodimonte.

Not all collectors wished to experience such strong emotions. A market grew for sentimental standardised images of Naples in gouache. The situation improved in the 19th century, with artists expressing their individual, contemplative interpretations of the Bay of Naples.

Dutchman **Antonio Pitloo** (1791-1837) infused his real-life landscapes (some now in the Certosa-Museo di San Martino) with natural colour and life, inspiring the Posillipo school. **Giacinto Gigante** (1806-76), many of whose works are in Capodimonte, was the leader of this school, where impressions of an idyllic landscape are expressed in delicate, romantic fashion. **Filippo Palizzi** (1818-99) continued to experiment, contrasting natural colours, light and contours (in the Certosa-Museo di San Martino).

Castel Nuovo
See p37.

Architecture

Naples' buildings tell the city's story.

Earthquakes, unscrupulous property developers and World War II bombs combined to give this ancient city a battering in the 19th and 20th centuries, the effects of which are still all too evident. But a recent drive to revamp decrepit baroque churches and *palazzi*, and to reconvert once-stately *piazze* from car parks to elegant gathering places is begining to change the face of this long-suffering city.

Even before the modern age, Naples had some serious problems, architecturally speaking, the chief of which was lack of space. Until the mid 16th century the residents of one of Europe's most populous cities were crammed into a tiny walled area. Great houses, grandiose civic buildings and convents with extensive gardens left little space for the *popolo*. Successive enlargements of the walls failed to solve the problem (especially since construction outside the walls was strictly limited). Unable to build outwards, Neapolitans built upwards instead – up to four and five storeys – using the area's volcanic tufa stone and incorporating inherited architectural elements, often from the Roman era. What green there had been – sweeping convent

gardens and orchards – was rapidly built over. To ease overcrowding, in the mid 16th century Spanish viceroy Pedro de Toledo extended the walls again to increase the city area by a third.

Within the crowded city, class stratifications governed the height that people lived at. Within a single tenement, the poorest lived in tiny ground floor *bassi*, where rooms open directly on to the street, while the upper classes enjoyed the light and airiness of first- and second-floor apartments called *piano nobile*.

Naples' *palazzi* were structures upon which each successive age and architect left a mark. By the 18th century, low-ceilinged top storeys had been added, then decorated according to the latest fashion. Inside, courtyards, windows, façades and arches were altered in the name of 'modernity'; from the end of the 19th century, jutting-out loos were tacked on to corners in tiny towers or on loggias. As late as the 1960s, jerry-built extensions and flats – invisible from street level – were crammed on to historic rooftops.

These odd juxtapositions remain: grandiose portals dominate dark, narrow alleys; and tall, freshly restored *palazzi* stand next to buildings in desperate need of repair.

TRACES OF GREECE AND ROME

The temples in **Paestum** (*see p271*) and the sanctuary of the Sybil in **Cuma** (*see p104*) testify to the existence of thriving Greek communities in Campania. Nothing remains of the original settlement of Paleopolis, but the chequerboard plan of Neapolis (the new city founded by the Greeks around the seventh century BC) can still be seen clearly from the belvedere of **San Martino** (*see p93*). The Roman *decumani* (main roads) – now **via Anticaglia**, **via dei Tribunali** and **Spaccanapoli** (*see p72*) – intersected north–south by *cardines*, followed the original Greek layout. The Greek *agorà* (marketplace, later the Roman forum) stood by today's piazza San Gaetano. Small sections of the Greek walls can be seen just a metre below the current street level in **piazza Bellini** (*see p78*).

Centuries of construction have hidden the remains of the Roman city from view. They're still there, though: there's a fascinating glimpse of market life beneath the church of **San Lorenzo Maggiore** (*see p80*) and the **Duomo** (*see p79*), while an area of Roman baths has been incorporated into the museum behind the church of **Santa Chiara** (*see p74*).

Some of what didn't end up underground found its way into later buildings: two columns and marble bases from a temple to Castor and Pollux can be seen in the late 16th-century façade of **San Paolo Maggiore** (*see p81*).

The kind of prosperous town planning that passing centuries obscured in the city is very much in evidence at **Pompeii** (*see p213*) and **Herculaneum** (*see p216*). But the Campania Felix of the Romans is dotted with other smaller reminders of the extent to which this region, with its mild climate and spectacular landscape, was beloved and adorned in ancient times: there are sumptuous homes in **Capri** (Tiberius's **Villa Jovis**, *see p185*), **Castellammare di Stabia** (*see p224*) and near **Sorrento** (*see p228*); temples at **Baia** (*see p104*); and a four-tier amphitheatre in **Capua Vetere**, a model for the Colosseum in Rome.

CHRISTIAN BUILDERS

When Emperor Constantine embraced the cult of Christianity in AD 313, its followers came out of hiding and built places of worship near the burial sites of their early saints. Taking the Roman basilica (a meeting place with columned porticos outside) as their model, the Christians turned them inside out, putting the columns in the interior to form side aisles. Paleo-Christian basilicas can still be seen above the catacombs of **San Gennaro** (*see p90*), and in the fourth-century Santa Restituta, incorporated into the **Duomo** in the 13th century.

During the early Middle Ages the real stratification of the city began, with new constructions going up above the Greek and Roman ones around the *agorà*/forum in piazza San Gaetano. These, in their turn, made way for later buildings; nothing remains of the civic architecture of the period. Further south, the early Middle Ages are better represented: the religious architecture along the Amalfi coast, in **Ravello** (*see p260*) and **Salerno** (*see p269*) is a harmonious mix of Byzantine and Romanesque styles. Near Caserta, the tenth-century basilica of **Sant'Angelo** in Formis has 11th-century mosaics of clear Byzantine influence.

EARLY RENAISSANCE

In the 11th century, the Normans made Palermo the capital of their southern Italian kingdom, and Naples became a quiet political backwater. But the city expanded west towards **Castel dell'Ovo** (*see p64*) when Roger II made the castle his fortified Neapolitan citadel and inland: when Roger's son William built **Castel Capuano** (*see p76*) to house his humanist court, peopled by artists and architects from Catalonia. The *Tavola Strozzi* (1474), a painting of the city now in the Certosa-Museo di San Martino, affords a glimpse of how Naples looked at the time. The city walls were enlarged yet again, and provided with towers and gates; the fortress of the **Carmine** (*see p70*) marked the city's eastern limit.

'Unable to build outwards, Neapolitans built upwards.'

The new king chose **Castel Nuovo** (*see p66*) as his home, sending for the Majorcan Guillermo Sagrera in 1449 to oversee alterations. Sagrera produced a trapezoid plan with five huge towers, inspired by similar buildings in Provence and Catalonia. He designed the Sala dei Baroni, with its magnificent 28-metre (93-foot) high vaulted ceiling. But the crowning glory of the early Renaissance in Naples was the **Arco di Trionfo**, a double arch flanked by Corinthian columns, celebrating the virtues and power of the Aragon dynasty, between the two high towers of the entrance to the Castel Nuovo. Its style is clearly Tuscan, showing just how quickly Sagrera's Catalan-Majorcan manner became interwoven with Italian influences.

The same Tuscan flavour was popular with Neapolitan nobles: **Palazzo Maddaloni** (via Maddaloni 6), for example, has a Renaissance portal and a smooth rusticated yellow and grey tufa façade (contrasting with late Gothic elements such as the low arches in the courtyard, the vestibule and arch behind); the diamond-pointed rustication of the façade of the church of **Gesù Nuovo** (see p74) was originally the front of a palace. The Tuscan influence reached its apex in the **Palazzo Gravina** and the Brunelleschi-style chapels in the church of **Sant'Anna dei Lombardi** (see p83) next door. The Tuscan Renaissance form of the ideal city was in reality little different from the Greek *polis*, with the same elements of town-planning.

SPANISH STYLE

The arrival of troops from the recently united Kingdom of Spain in 1503 changed the face of the city. The fortifications of Castel Nuovo were beefed up, a task that took 30 years; a new city wall with polygonal bastions was built around the city, from via Foria to Castel Sant'Elmo, and along the seafront to the east to protect Naples from the continuing threat of attack from the sea.

In 1540, the most avid builder of all the Spanish viceroys, Pedro de Toledo, ordered a new palace, complete with formal gardens, more or less where today's Palazzo Reale stands. To cope with a chronic lack of housing (the population had almost doubled to 220,000 inhabitants in 50 years), he extended the walls to increase the city area by one third. Illegal shanty towns that had spread west (towards Pizzofalcone) and north (from via Monteoliveto up the hill towards Sant'Elmo) of the new palace were razed to make way for new quarters. An impressive thoroughfare, **via Toledo** (see p83), was created to link the old and new parts of town, and noble palaces sprang up along it. Immediately to the west of via Toledo, a network of intersecting streets sprawling up the hill known as the **Quartieri spagnoli** (see p84) was built to house Spanish troops; as demand for housing grew, the original single-storey dwellings rose to four or five floors.

THE BAROQUE

The highly decorative flourishes of the baroque appealed to the Neapolitan imagination, and few employed them more extensively than Cosimo Fanzago (1591-1678), the city's most prolific church architect, who dedicated 33 years to revamping the **Certosa-Museo di San Martino** (see p93). The extraordinary **Guglia di San Gennaro** (see p73) epitomises his decorative exuberance; the gruesome bronze skulls on the façade of the church **Santa Maria del Purgatorio ad Arco** (see p80) show him in glummer Counter-Reformation mood.

The advent of the Bourbon dynasty in 1734 produced a rash of imposing civic buildings that gave Naples a veneer of modernity but failed to impose any true order on its architectural chaos.

Fernando Fuga (1699-1781), Giovanni Antonio Medrano (born 1703) and Luigi Vanvitelli (1700-73) designed the immense, official palaces of the kings; Domenico Antonio Vaccaro (1678-1745) and Ferdinando Sanfelice (1675-1748) were responsible for many of the city's private and religious buildings.

Only one-fifth of Fuga's over-ambitious design for the **Albergo dei Poveri** (see p86) poorhouse was ever completed, but even so it was Europe's largest civic construction. The newly restored central section provides a tantalising glimpse of his dream. Medrano designed the **San Carlo** opera house (see p67) that made Naples one of Europe's musical capitals, and the **Palazzo Reale** at Capodimonte (see p90) to house Charles III's spectacular art collection. Vanvitelli gave the city the imposing Foro Carolino, today **piazza Dante** (see p84).

'Sagrera's Catalan-Majorcan manner became interwoven with Italian influences.'

But it was the Bourbon love of the countryside (and its potential for hunting) that allowed these architects their most grandiose scope. Medrano began work on Reggia at **Portici** (see p215), later to be replaced by both Fuga and Vanvitelli; the royal palace sparked a building boom along the coast south of Naples, as noble families constructed luxurious homes on the so-called **Miglio d'Oro** (see p213) near Charles' favourite palazzo. Here, country villas were built with two aspects – one up to the live volcano and the other down to the sea, with beautifully designed gardens. Vanvitelli's crowning glory – and perhaps the finest product of the Neapolitan baroque – was the Reggia at **Caserta** (see p275), its internal vistas, ceremonial staircase and octagonal vestibule ensconced in a garden where fountains and waterfalls feature as fully fledged architectural elements. Sanfelice devoted his talents to the city palaces of the nobility.

His work was an organic but lively blend of decorative stucco and stonework that was imitated all over the city. His staircases in **Palazzo Sanfelice** (see p86), **Palazzo Serra di Cassano** (see p64) and **Palazzo dello Spagnuolo** (see p86) are simply spectacular. Vaccaro's touch is best seen in the cloister of Santa Chiara, a splendid tiled garden in shades of blue and yellow.

SPECULATION AND 'RENEWAL'

In the 19th century, urban renewal projects – originally designed to impose some order on Naples' haphazard urban development – degenerated into wholesale destruction of poorer, more dilapidated but nonetheless historic areas of the old city centre.

Early in the century, the city's French rulers introduced neo-classical touches in **piazza del Plebiscito** (*see p64*). This style was continued by Ferdinand I, on his restoration, in the church of **San Francesco di Paolo** (*see p67*), which was designed by Pietro Bianchi. Nobles fled the crowded centre, building seafront palaces along the **Riviera di Chiaia** (*see p97*). The simple two-storey **Villa Floridiana** (*see p94*), with its English-style irregular garden design, was built for Lucia Migliaccio, the morganatic wife of King Ferdinand.

But the Consiglio Edilizio (building council), set up with the best intentions in 1839, soon became a vehicle for rampant speculation. Clearance of the city's ancient slums started in via Duomo, radiating out to the bay. An entire nave of the basilica of **San Giorgio Maggiore** (*see p75*) was destroyed in the process. Plans to hack a road through the 15th-century **Palazzo Cuomo** (*see p74*), with its rusticated façade, sparked a protest campaign; philanthropist Prince Gaetano Filangieri financed the rebuilding of the façade 20 metres (66 feet) further back, designing the interior to house his art collection.

The eclectic, revivalist style of British architect Lamont Young dictated the fashion in the late 19th century. His creations range from the neo-Gothic Palazzina Grifeo (Parco Grifeo 37) to the pseudo-Tudor Castello Aselmeyer (Corso Vittorio Emanuele 166). Young's sense of the weird and wonderful caught on. Neo-medieval and Chinese-style villas can still be seen along via Posillipo, while art nouveau decoration flourished in buildings for the new, rich professional classes in **Vomero** (*see p92*) and **via dei Mille**.

A cholera epidemic in 1884 gave unscrupulous speculators further scope. With the excuse of making Naples a healthier city, the Società per il Risanamento, owned by northern bankers, built straight 'clean' streets by ruthlessly razing not only insalubrious slums, but 57 historic *fondaci* (merchants' yards, shops and lodgings) and medieval and Renaissance buildings. (Before destruction, the slums were recorded for posterity by painter Vincenzo Migliaro; his works can be seen in the Certosa-Museo di San Martino.)

Between the two world wars, Naples recieved its fair share of the rational design favoured by the country's Fascist regime. The **Palazzo delle Poste** (*see p83*) with its curved façade and rectangular steel windows is a good example, as is the **Mostra d'Oltremare** (*see p108*), a mixture of gardens, water features and exhibition spaces, now being restored to former glory.

THE FINAL BLOW

Allied bombs did immense damage to Naples' Centro storico during World War II. Ironically, painstaking post-bombardment restoration work gave the city such gems as the church of Santa Chiara, rebuilt to its original specifications without later baroque trappings.

Elsewhere in the city, however, bomb sites gave way to a haphazard concrete jungle of devastating ugliness. Naples' sole skyscraper – standing out unhappily just off piazza Municipio – was permitted by Mayor Achille Lauro in the 1950s. The havoc wreaked by construction magnate Mario Otieri inspired film director Francesco Rosi's searing indictment, *Le Mani sulla città* (Hands over the City, 1963).

Cloister of **Santa Chiara**. *See p37*.

Palazzo dello Spagnuolo. *See p38.*

Unregulated and unchecked, the concrete sprawl spread beyond the city limits, making the fortunes of ruthless property developers. Eighteenth-century villas in Portici were engulfed by modern apartment blocks (blithely built in the shadow of an active volcano, Vesuvius). Huge council estates, built in the 1970s outside Naples to house the city centre's poor, became crime-ridden no-hope ghettos. Meanwhile, the coastline and islands have been riddled by unlicensed villa development for holiday homes.

CLEANING UP THE CITY

Gradually, the tide is turning as local authorities are greening what is left or promoting ambitious renewal projects. The most futuristic complex of all – named Le Vele ('the sails') after the sail-like shape of the buildings – has now been knocked. A concrete eyesore hacked out of the cliffs on the Amalfi coast (the never-completed Hotel Fuente) was finally demolished in 1999.

Naples was wounded still further by the 1980 earthquake – some historic buildings are still shored up with iron chains.

HOPE FOR THE FUTURE

So tight was space in the 1980s that an ambitious project got under way to extend the city eastwards; but the **Centro Direzionale**
(*see p107*), designed by Japanese architect Kenzo Tange, was unappealingly isolated on marshy land near the city's prison and a derelict industrial area. Now housing offices, law courts and homes, it has yet to be completed.

Sustainable town planning is the buzzword for 21st-century Naples. The wall that separated piazza Municipio from the port was demolished in May 2000. The lift linking the galleria Vittoria tunnel near the port to Piazza Plebiscito has been reopened after 20 years. Abandoned industrial buildings and warehouses on the seafront are being converted. Funds have been made available for restoration in the Centro storico, and the underground railway is being extended and embellished (*see p153* **Underground art**).

An ambitious project to convert the abandoned steelworks at **Bagnoli** into a museum park, leisure park and marina (*see p100*) is limping slowly forwards as the final buildings are demolished and the brownfield site cleared. And the abandoned factories along the coast just east of the port are to become a new university campus and tourist harbour. But true to tradition, progress continues to be hampered by continual flouting of building regulations; and chronic air pollution still threatens Naples' historic buildings.

Where to Stay

Where to Stay

Old-style luxury, period conversions and spruced-up B&Bs.

BAR IL PAVONE

The **Hotel Santa Lucia** is all about traditional-style luxury – and amazing views. *See p53.*

Naples is one of the few Italian cities that has yet to be struck by the mass tourism that has changed the soul of gems like Florence and Venice. As a result, it still has elements of challenge – and surprise – for visitors. There has been an explosion in B&B accommodation in the city: if you have a sense of adventure and the time to investigate possibilities, you may be lucky and find yourself an inexpensive antique-filled room in a historic palazzo tucked away in the most unexpected *vicolo* (little street). Ask caretakers, bar staff or tourist information offices (*see p296*) for tips. *See also p50* **Bed & breakfast**.

Urban planning has never been a strong point in Naples; as a result, the city has developed in haphazard fashion, with each *quartiere* acquiring its own distinctive architectural and social flavour. This is reflected in the range of accommodation available in the city. The latest development is that a host of old *palazzi* in the **Centro storico** (*see pp72-82*) have been converted into new hotels. There's no doubt that this is the best place to be if you're seeking full

immersion in Naples' culture, nightlife and countless everyday instances of true *napoletanità*.

The foreshore from via Partenope in the **Santa Lucia** district (*see p67*) along the **Chiaia** seafront (*see p97-101*) to **Mergellina** (*see p98-100*) has splendid views and good nightlife, and tends to attract well-heeled, international clientele, but it has less of a local atmosphere than the Centro storico. It's handy for the hydrofoil dock (Mergellina) and the ferry port, if you're planning a quick getaway to the islands. The swishest four-stars and some of the more pleasant *pensioni* are here.

After a full day of sweaty trudging, you might want to retire to the less chaotic, more residential **Vomero** (*see p92-96*). Situated on a hill above the centre, it has easy, efficient access to all the downtown area by means of three funicular railways (though the Montesanto funicular is closed until July 2005), the new ultramodern metro with its sculptures and modern art (*see p153* **Underground art**) and a variety of buses (which are best avoided at rush hour).

The area around **Stazione Centrale/ piazza Garibaldi** (see p68) is very noisy by day and very dodgy by night. If you're staying in cheap accommodation around here there's a pretty good chance that your fellow guests will be renting rooms by the hour. It's an interesting area in that it's the only truly multi-ethnic part of Naples, but this doesn't really make up for its general unsavouriness.

Public transport has improved greatly of late, but, nevertheless, think very carefully about where you want to be and what you plan to do before booking accommodation. A more central, expensive hotel could save on taxis in the long run.

PRACTICALITIES

Many hotels, especially expensive ones, offer special deals for weekend stays, in low season and for large groups: check websites and ask when booking. Prices quoted below include breakfast unless otherwise stated. Bed & breakfasts tend to give out vouchers for a nearby bar, where you can have the usual Italian breakfast of coffee or cappuccino and *cornetto* (croissant).

If you are travelling with children, most hotels will put another bed in the room – for which they should charge no more than 35 per cent extra. If you want a single room and are put in a double, you should be charged no more than the highest single rate, or 65 per cent of the price of a double.

High season is Easter, April, June to October, and Christmas and New Year. If you're travelling in May, you should book well in advance: the Maggio dei Monumenti (see p77 **Monuments in May**) attracts many visitors as the doors of churches, historical sites and private chapels that are usually firmly closed to the public are thrown open.

Italian hotels are classified according to a star system (running from one star for a cheap pensione to five stars for high-end facilities). Naples' top hotels, like the **Vesuvio** (see p225), are truly luxurious. If you're looking at the other end of the market, you'll have no trouble at all finding budget accommodation.

Standards vary wildly, however, from the clean-and-simple to the cockroaches-and-louche-neighbours. It's a good idea, therefore, to ask to see the room you'll be expected to sleep in before registering: you don't want to have to negotiate with a desk clerk who's already taken possession of your passport and credit card.

For destinations outside Naples, see individual chapters in the **Around Naples** section. The **Associazione Albergatori** has listings of many of the area's hotels on its website www.campaniahotels.com.

Royal Naples

Note that all seafront hotels along via Partenope have been included in the **Chiaia to Posillipo** section that begins on p97.

Expensive

Miramare

Via Nazario Sauro 24 (081 764 7589/fax 081 764 0775/www.hotelmiramare.com). Bus C25. **Rates** €146-€212 single; €202-€272 double; €291-€314 double with sea view. **Credit** AmEx, DC, MC, V. **Map** p315 1-2A.

The Hotel Miramare was converted in 1944 from an aristocratic art deco villa built in 1914. Small and nicely kept with a welcoming atmosphere,

The best Hotels

For a slice of history

Nineteenth-century British travellers felt quite at home at **Grand Hotel Parker's** (see p51), while **Miramare** (see p43), originally an art deco villa, drew famous Italian and international singing stars for performances in the 1950s.

For rooms with a view

Villa Capodimonte (see p50) high on Capodimonte hill, has glorious views over the bay. The **Jolly Hotel** (see p45) may be known as an eyesore, but you can see for miles from its upper floors, while the **Hotel San Francesco al Monte** (see p52) makes the most of its Vomero views with a sun roof and panoramic terraces.

For legendary luxury

The **Excelsior** (see p52) has hosted royals and film stars, while the **Vesuvio** (see p53) was the choice of Enrico Caruso and Bill Clinton. Both have restaurants famed for their views.

For style and comfort on a budget

Caravaggio Hotel di Napoli (see p47) has creamy decor and open brickwork. **Il Convento** (see p49), once a convent, has white walls wood-beamed ceilings. Some of the stylishly furnished rooms at the home-like **Parteno** (see p53) have views towards Capri.

For an unusual location

Agriturismo Il Casolare di Tobia (see p55) is in an (inactive) volcanic crater.

the hotel sprang to fame in the 1950s when its restaurant/piano bar, the Shaker Club, drew top-name Italian and international singing stars for live performances. Breakfast is served on the roof-garden terrace with breathtaking views over the bay. Guests get a 10% discount at nearby restaurants La Cantinella (*see p112*) and Il Posto Accanto. Special deals at weekends (minimum of two nights) and in January, February, August and over Christmas.
Hotel services *Bar (1). Concierge. Parking (€15-€21). Room service. TV: satellite.*

Moderate

Albergo S Marco

Calata San Marco 26 (081 552 0338/fax 081 552 0338/www.sanmarcohotelnapoli.it). Bus C25, C55, C57. **Rates** €90-€115 single; €120-€140 double; €135-€150 triple; €160 quadruple. **Credit** AmEx, DC, MC, V. **Map** p313 2C.
Very conveniently located in piazza Municipio, near the main port and within a stone's throw of practically everything. All rooms are double-glazed and air-conditioned.
Hotel services *Bar (1). Concierge. Parking (from €12). Restaurant. TV: satellite.*

Chiaia Hotel de Charme

Via Chiaia 216 (081 415 555/fax 081 422 344/ www.hotelchiaia.it). Bus C22. **Rates** €122-€142 single; €140-€160 double. **Credit** AmEx, DC, MC, V. **Map** p315 1A.
Part of Marchese Nicola Lecaldano's newly restored home, and two minutes from the Palazzo Reale (*see p67*), this is the place to stay if you hanker after a touch of old-fashioned aristocratic class. Most rooms have their original furniture and are named after ancestors of the marquis who lived in them. There are jacuzzis in 9 of the rooms. Staff are most professional.
Hotel services *isabled-adapted rooms (2). Internet access (dataport). TV: satellite.*

Jolly Hotel

Via Medina 70 (081 410 5111/fax 081 551 8010/ www.jollyhotels.it). Bus C25, C55, C57. **Rates** €142-€205 single; €162-€245 double. **Credit** AmEx, DC, MC, V. **Map** p313 2C.
With thirty floors and 224 rooms, the Jolly rises incongruously above the city centre like a monument to 20th-century capitalism; a green neon sign completes the horrible effect. Built in the wake of World War II by a property developer apparently devoid of any aesthetic sense, it looms over Naples' as one of its worst eyesores. Inside, however, it's another story. The air-conditioned rooms are small and rather impersonal, but they do have all the comforts that you'd expect of a hotel in this class, and the views from the top floors are breathtaking. The Jolly is well located for the major shopping streets, the port and the Centro storico, and its restaurant is not at all bad.

A touch of class at **Chiaia Hotel de Charme**.

Hotel services *Bar (1). Business centre. Concierge, Disabled-adapted rooms. Internet. No-smoking rooms. Parking (€23/24). Restaurant (1). Room service. TV: satellite.*

Mercure Napoli Angioino Centro

Via Depretis 123 (081 563 5906/fax 081 552 9509/www.accorhotels.com). Bus C25, C55. **Rates** €135-€152 single; €160-€180 double. **Credit** AmEx, DC, MC, V. **Map** p313 2C.
The modern, comfortable Mercure is situated close to the Centro storico as well as being just five minutes from the port – which makes it ideal for a quick getaway to the islands or Amalfi coast. There are 85 air-conditioned rooms, a meeting room and undercover parking.
Hotel services *Bar (1). Business centre. Concierge. Disabled-adapted room (1). No-smoking rooms (22). Parking (€14). Room service. TV: pay, satellite.*

Port & University

Moderate

Cavour

Piazza Garibaldi 32 (081 283 122/fax 081 287 488/www.hotelcavournapoli.it). Metro Piazza Garibaldi/bus CD, CS, C30, C40, C55. **Rates** €75-€110 single; €110-€154 double; €200 suite. **Credit** AmEx, DC, MC, V. **Map** p311 3E.

The 17th-century exterior of the **Caravaggio Hotel di Napoli**. *See p47.*

This comfortable, long-established, three-star hotel has been refurbished tastefully. The down side? Its location on the insalubrious (particularly after dark) piazza Garibaldi.
Hotel services *Bar (1). Concierge. Internet (€5/hr). Parking (€15). TV: satellite.*

Executive

Via del Cerriglio 10, off Via San Felice (tel/fax 081 552 0611/081 552 8363/081 552 3980/www.sea-hotels.com). Bus CD, CS, C25. **Rates** €83-€145 single; €114-€180 double; €140-€238 suite. **Credit** AmEx, DC, MC, V. **Map** p311 3A.

Hidden in a tiny side street off a busy thoroughfare, the Executive's simple entrance gives on to an oasis of comfort and peace (as long as you keep the double-glazing firmly shut). The rooms are comfortable if somewhat anonymously modern. The port and Centro storico are close at hand. Breakfast is served on the sunny roof terrace.
Hotel services *Bar (1). Internet access. Parking (€15). TV: satellite.*

Starhotel Terminus

Piazza Garibaldi 91 (081 779 3111/fax 081 206 689). Metro Piazza Garibaldi/bus CD, CS, C30, C40, C55. **Rates** €111-€219 single; €131-€239 double; €121-€359 triple. **Credit** AmEx, DC, MC, V. **Map** p311 3E.

Right opposite the Stazione Centrale, this modern hotel attracts a mostly business clientele. Despite its 168 rooms, it manages to feel cosy and relaxed. The restaurant's roof garden has a view of Vesuvius. The major drawback is the location: piazza Garibaldi is no place for a stroll after dark.

Hotel services *Bar (1). Business centre. Concierge. Disabled-adapted rooms. Gym. Internet. No-smoking rooms. Restaurant (1). Room service. TV: cable, satellite.*

Suite Esedra

Via Cantani 12, off Corso Umberto I (tel/fax 081 553 7087/081 287 451/www.sea-hotels.com). Bus CD, CS, C55. **Rates** €73-€145 single; €93-€180 double; €120-€310 suite. **Credit** AmEx, DC, MC, V. **Map** p311 3D.

What it lacks in history (it opened in 1997), the Suite Esedra makes up for in atmosphere. The cosy, well-equipped rooms are individually decorated with astronomy motifs; the Venus suite, with its private rooftop plunge pool, is a delight. There is also a fitness room. Handy for the Centro storico, the port and the railway station, the Suite Esedra has only one drawback: it's just off the thundering, smog-filled and definitely insalubrious Corso Umberto I.
Hotel services *Bar (1). Gym. Parking (€10). Room service. TV: satellite.*

Budget

Europeo & Europeo Flowers

Via Mezzocannone 109 (tel/fax 081 551 7254/ www.sea-hotels.com). Bus CD, C58, E1. **Rates** *Europeo* €42-€62 single; €55-€93 double. *Europeo Flowers* €65-€110 double; €89-€130 suite. **Credit** AmEx, DC, MC, V. **Map** p311 3B.

Close to the Spaccanapoli, the university district and the Centro storico, the Europeo hotels are surprisingly cheap. They're rather basic, but have modern rooms and those at Europeo Flowers have air-conditioning. Five of the Europeo rooms are also frescoed. The hotels don't serve breakfast. You can book rooms online.

Hotel services *Concierge. Parking (€15). TV: satellite.*

Centro storico

Moderate

Costantinopoli 104

Via S Maria di Costantinopoli 104 (081 557 1035/ fax 081 557 1051/www.costantinopoli104.it). Metro piazza Dante. **Rates** €145 single; €170 double; €165-€190 suite. **Credit** AmEx, DC, MC, V. **Map** p311 1B-2B.

It may be in the midst of the crowded, hectic centre of town and close to the social hub of piazza Bellini, but Costantinopoli 104 is a quiet oasis of elegance and comfort, converted from a late 19th-century palazzo and hidden in a neo-classical courtyard. Each room has individual charms: the terrace rooms, where guests can breakfast al fresco; and the garden rooms which are right next to the small but attractive pool. The Villa suite is on two floors, with a private terrace. Its huge outdoor jacuzzi is more like a mini swimming pool. There is a free supply of limoncello and *nocino* for guests.

Hotel services *Bar (1). Business centre. Concierge. Internet access. Parking (from €20). Pool (outdoor). Room service. TV: satellite.*

Budget

Caravaggio Hotel di Napoli

Piazza Cardinale Sisto Riario Sforza 157 (081 211 0066/fax 081 442 1578/www.caravaggiohotel.it). Bus CS. **Rates** €80-€85 single; €80-€150 double; €140-€170 triple; €160-€180 suite. **Credit** AmEx, DC, MC, V. **Map** p311 2C.

The Caravaggio opened in December 2001 in a restored 17th-century building. Facilities and decor are modern – creamy colours and plenty of open brickwork give it an airy feel – but the conversion has managed to respect the building's age. Rooms are comfortable and nicely furnished; some have a jacuzzi. There is also a small garden. The hotel is just behind the Duomo; from its windows you can see the spire of San Gennaro and Pio Monte della Misericordia, home of Caravaggio's *Seven Acts of Mercy*.

Hotel services *Bar (1). Business centre. Concierge, Disabled-adapted rooms. Internet access. No-smoking rooms. Parking (from €20). TV: satellite.*

Hotel des Artistes

Via del Duomo 61 (081 446155/fax 081 211 0403/www.hoteldesartistesnaples.it). Bus E1, R2. **Rates** €70-€90 single; €90-€110 double. **Credit** AmEx, DC, MC, V. **Map** p311 C1.

Traditionally decorated and comfortable, and housed in an old building previously divided into flats, the three-star Hotel des Artistes is a good bet for the area. It's just a few metres away from the Duomo, and all the main Centro storico sites are just a walk away. It's nice and quiet too.

Hotel services *Bar (1), Concierge. Parking (from €15). TV: satellite.*

Neapolis

Via Francesco del Giudice 13, off Via Tribunali (081 442 0815/fax 081 442 0819/www.hotelneapolis.com). Metro Dante/bus CD, E1, 47. **Rates** €80-€100 single; €100-€120 double; €120-€140 triple; €140-€160 quadruple. **Credit** AmEx, DC, MC, V. **Map** p311 2B.

In the heart of the Centro storico, close to the buzzing piazza Bellini and surrounding nightlife, this hotel has all the traditional services, plus a PC with free internet access in all rooms. The hotel also provides special software with which you can design your

The conveniently located **Oriente**. *See p49.*

San Francesco al Monte. *See p52.*

own itinerary of the city. An additional bed is provided free of charge for families of four staying in triple rooms.

Hotel services *Concierge. Disabled-adapted room. Internet access: PC in rooms. No-smoking rooms. Parking (€20). Restaurant (1). Room service. TV: satellite.*

Toledo & Sanità

Expensive

Mediterraneo

Via Ponte di Tappia 25 (081 797 0001/fax 081 2552 5868/www.mediterraneonapoli.com). Bus C25, C55, C57. **Rates** €210-€270 single; €270-€325 double; €490-€1,140 suite. **Credit** AmEx, DC, MC, V. **Map** p313 2C.

Centrally located with a roof-terrace restaurant. Though a touch impersonal and business-like, this is somewhat compensated for by the bustling atmosphere once you step outside the front door.

Hotel services *Bar (1). Business centre. Concierge. Disabled-adapted rooms. No-smoking rooms. Parking. Room service. TV: satellite.*

Moderate

Hotel del Real Orto Botanico

Via Foria 192 (081 442 1528/fax 081 442 1346/ www.hotelrealortobotanico.it). Bus 47, 182, 3S, R5

Rates €97-€130 single; €162 double; €188 suite. **Credit** AmEx, MC, V. **Map** p311 1D-1E.

As the name suggests, this hotel is right beside the botanical gardens, which hold rare species and offer valuable peace and quiet. On the other hand, it's on via Foria, one of the busiest streets in Naples (and about ten minutes' walk from the Archaeological Museum). Step inside the hotel, however, a nd you will find a quiet and relaxed atmosphere and well-appointed rooms, which will help you recover from the chaos outside.

Hotel services *Bar (1). Concierge. Internet access (€3/hr). Restaurant (1). Room service. TV: satellite.*

Oriente

Via A Diaz 44 (081 551 2133/fax 081 551 4916/ www.oriente.it). Bus CS, C57, R1, R3, R4, 24. **Rates** €90-€180 single; €135-€310 double; €195-€390 suite. **Credit** AmEx, DC, MC, V. **Map** p313 1C-2C.

Close to the Centro storico and a short walk from the shops in via Toledo, the Oriente has a very modern marble façade that makes it look severe and cold. Once inside, however, the decor is welcoming, with a touch of personality and style. The surrounding area is off the beaten nightlife track, making it either dreary or pleasantly tranquil, depending on your mood.

Hotel services *Bar (1). Business centre. Concierge. Disabled-adapted room. No-smoking room. Internet (dataport). Parking (€19). TV: satellite.*

Toledo

Via Montecalvario 15 (081 406 871/fax 081 406 800/www.sea-hotels.com/www.hoteltoledo.com). Bus CS, C57, R1, R3, R4, 24. **Rates** €70-€145 single; €85-€180 double; €120-€320 suite. **Credit** AmEx, MC, V. **Map** p314 2A.

Neapolitans shudder at the very idea of staying in the Quartieri spagnoli (*see p83*), but this area's reputation for crime far outstrips reality and (as long as you don't parade your diamond tiara about after dark) you're unlikely to see anything but the pulsating, colourful side of life here. The three-floor 17th-century palazzo that houses the Toledo has been restructured. The roof garden gives a view over Certosa-Museo di San Martino and the Castel Sant'Elmo. The pedestrianised shopping precinct of via Toledo is just a few steps away.

Hotel services *Bar (1). Concierge. Internet. Restaurant. Parking (€16). Restaurant (1).*

Budget

Il Convento

Via Speranzella 137/A (081 403 977/fax 081 400 332/www.hotelilconvento.com). Bus CS, C57, R1, R3, R4, 24. **Rates** €68-€145 single; €83-€180 double; €99-€210 triple; €115-€230 suite. **Credit** AmEx, MC, V. **Map** p313 1A.

Housed in a former convent dating from 1600, just off the shopping street of via Toledo, this hotel has been restored with an accent on the monastic (but with ample comfort for its modern secular guests).

Wood-beamed ceilings, plain creamy-white walls and grey stone floors dominate. Rooms (or 'cells', as they're known) are spacious; some have a small terrace. The hotel is handy for the port, the Royal Palace, Teatro San Carlo and all main sights. Discounts for family groups.
Hotel services *Bar (1). Concierge. Disabled-adapted room. Internet access. No-smoking rooms. TV: satellite.*

Capodimonte

Expensive

Villa Capodimonte
Via Moiariello 66 (081 459 000/fax 081 299 344/ www.villacapodimonte.it). Bus 110, 137. **Rates** €175-€195 single; €200-€220 double; €276-€320 suite.
Credit AmEx, DC, MC, V. **Map** p312 1C.
Built in 1995, on Capodimonte hill (*see p90*), the hotel has glorious views over the bay, a small manicured park and rooms with terraces. If the hectic

pace and hellish traffic down in the centre bewilder you, the Villa Capodimonte will seem an oasis of perfect peace.
Hotel services *Bar (1). Business centre. Concierge. Disabled-adapted room. No-smoking rooms. Internet (€5/hr). Parking (free/€15). Restaurant. Room service. TV: satellite.*

Moderate

Hotel Villa Ranieri
Corso Amedeo di Savoia , trav Via Cagnazzi 29, (081 741 6308/081 743 7977/fax 081 743 7978/ www.villaranieri.it). Bus 178, C64, R4. **Rates** €100-€150 single; €135-€190 double; €170-€220 triple.
Credit Amex, DC, MC, V. **Map** 312 1C.
A beautiful 18th-century villa, now a charming four-star hotel with mature gardens where a buffet breakfast is served in summer. It's well furnished, in an antiquey style, but there's no lack of modern comforts. Discounts for families with children.
Hotel services *Bar. Parking. Disabled-adapted room. TV.*

Bed & breakfast

Bed and breakfast establishments (B&Bs) are popping up all over the place in Naples. They are filling a niche in the market, catering to those who aren't on a very large budget, but aren't tempted by the city's limited budget offerings either – or those who simply want somewhere more unusual to stay or enjoy a less hotel-like environ-ment. When booking, try to ascertain precisely what's on offer. At worst, you could find yourself in a poky room far from the centre with over-inquisitive hosts. At best – and the best can be very good indeed – you may get lucky in a room with frescoed ceilings in a Centro storico palazzo of the kind usually only visible to the public in Maggio dei Monumenti openings (*see p77*), with charming hosts who make your stay into something really special.

The tourist office in piazza dei Martiri (*see p97*) has a list of room-renters, and the following agencies will also fix you up with well-vetted places to stay.

Agencies

Associazione
Cupa Camaldolilli 18, Vomero Alto (no phone/ www.bbnaples.it). Bus C44 from piazza Medaglie d'Oro. **Rates** from €30 per person.
No credit cards. Map p314 1A.

Contactable by email or in person only, this association has three types of accommodation available in various parts of town: rooms with shared bathrooms, rooms with private bathrooms, and flats. All hosts are carefully selected by the association itself.

My Home Your Home
Via del Duomo 196 (tel/fax 081 282 520/ 081 1956 5835/outside opening hours 348 731 9244/fax 081 289 780/www.myhome yourhome.it). Bus R1, R2. **Open** 10am-2pm, 3.30-6.30pm Mon-Fri. **Credit** AmEx, MC, V. **Map** p311 1-3C.
Rents rooms, flats and villas in and around the Naples area.

Rent a Bed
Vico d'Afflitto 16 (tel/fax 081 417 721/ www.rentabed.com). Funicular Centrale to Augusteo/bus R2. **Open** 10am-6pm Mon-Fri. **Rates** €25-€60 per person. **Credit** MC, V. **Map** p313 2A.
This agency started out renting rooms around the city, but has expanded its activity into B&B and apartment rentals. There's a large choice, both in Naples and around the region, including accommodation on the Amalfi Coast, Capri and other islands, plus farmhouses in the Neapolitan hinterland. Contact by email if possible (via the website).

Vomero

Deluxe

Grand Hotel Parker's

*Corso Vittorio Emanuele 135 (081 761 2474/
081 663 527/www.grandhotelparkers.com).
Funicular Chiaia to corso Vittorio Emanuele/bus
C27, C28.* **Rates** €215-€230 single; €325-€360
double; €570-€1,300 suite. **Credit** AmEx, DC, MC,
V. **Map** p315 1B.
A mecca for 19th-century British travellers,
Parker's was closed for many years. A restoration
returned it to its original large-scale grandeur:
crystal chandeliers, period furniture, antique
paintings and statues abound. It also houses a
library of antique volumes. The rooms are tastefully, rather lavishly, furnished and comfortably
equipped. The two restaurants, one on the roof garden, serve good international food. There is a luxurious spa on the premises too. Specify when
booking if you want a room with a view.

Hotel services *Bar (1). Business centre. Gym.
Internet. No-smoking rooms. Parking (€13-€20).
Restaurants (2). Room services. Spa. TV: satellite.*

Moderate

Britannique

*Corso Vittorio Emanuele 133 (081 761 4145/
fax 081 660 457). Funicular Chiaia to corso
Vittorio Emanuele/metro Piazza Amedeo/bus
C28, C16.* **Rates** €92-€150 single; €170-€190
double; €220 suite. **Credit** AmEx, DC, MC, V.
Map p315 1B.
Built as a private villa at the end of the 19th
century, this palazzo was bought by a Swiss company when tourism became a major industry in
Naples. It was converted into a hotel for an international (and in particular British) crowd relaxing
after their strenuous tours of the Amalfi Coast,
Capri and Pompeii. The Britannique's understated
elegance has the air of a long-gone colonial era
and it's a very far cry from the more characterless
chain hotels around.

B&Bs

Carafa di Maddaloni

*Via Maddaloni, 6, via Toledo (081 551
3691/fax 081 551 3691/bbcarafa@bb-
carafa.com). Metro Dante/bus 201, C55,
R1, R3, R4.* **Rates** from €62-€90 double;
€72-€110 triple. **No credit cards.**
Map p312 2C.
Right on Spaccanapoli, the long road with
changing street names bang in the city
centre, the Carafa di Maddaloni is housed
in a palazzo built by the dukes of Maddaloni
(it dates back to the 16th century). The
somewhat decrepit building still conveys a
sense of its original grandeur and the power
of its owners. Spacious rooms and original
frescos add to the charm.
Services *Internet access.*

Mergellina Bed & Breakfast Hotel

*Via Giordano Bruno, 115, Mergellina (081
248 2142/www.hotelmergellina.it). Metro
Mergellina/bus 140, C9, C12, C18, C19,
C24, R3.* **Rates** €80 single; €110 double/
triple. **Credit** DC, MC. V. **Map** p313 2C.
Handy for island connections and observing
locals promenading on the seafront, the
Mergellina has well-furnished rooms with a
touch of classic style.

Services *Internet access. Parking.
TV: satellite.*

Morelli 49

*Via Domenico Morelli 49, Chiaia (081 245
2291/338 357 6314/www.bedmorelli49.it).
Metro Mergellina/bus C9, C10, C12, C18,
C19, C24, C25, R3.* **Rates** €55-€65 single;
€85-€95 double; €110-€120 triple; €140-
€150 quad. **No credit cards. Map** p313 1A.
Centrally located, on the first floor of a period
building in via Morelli, a cobbled antique
shop-lined street. The apartment has been
refurbished in keeping with the style of the
building but has modern facilities. Rooms are
spacious and well-furnished with terracotta
floors and traditional Vietri ceramics. It's a
hop and a skip from the seafront.
Services *Internet access. Parking
(from €15). TV.*

Plebiscito

*Via Chiaia, 216 (081 423 8202/fax 081 411
221, 081 410 272/prestigiocasa@libero.it
or fulviolaardaro@liberto.it). Bus C22.* **Rates**
€80 single; €150 double. **No credit cards.**
Map p313 1A.
Just 50 metres from the Royal Palace, and
on one of the city's main shopping thoroughfares, this elegant B&B is housed in a
fascinating 18th-century building.
Services *TV.*

Excelsior.

Hotel services *Bar (1). Business centre. Concierge. Internet. Parking (from €13). Restaurant (1). Room service. TV.*

Hotel San Francesco al Monte

Corso Vittorio Emanuele 328 (081 423 9111/fax 081 251 2485/www.hotelsanfrancesco.it). Funicular Centrale to corso Vittorio Emanuele/bus C16. **Rates** €255 single; €220-€285 double. **Credit** AmEx, DC, MC, V. **Map** p315 1A.

This hotel was converted from the Santa Lucia al Monte convent, founded in 1557 by the Minori Conventuali monks. All the beautifully furnished rooms – once monks' cells – have views over the bay. A sun roof and panoramic terraces add to the charm and the big back garden climbing up the Vomero hill offers breathtaking views and an open-air restaurant. A free hotel bus runs to and from the centre of town every 30 minutes.

Hotel services *Bar (1). Disabled-adapted rooms. Internet (dataport). Parking (€18). Pool (outdoor). Restaurants (2). Room service. TV: satellite.*

Budget

Margherita

Via Cimarosa 29 (tel/fax 081 556 7044). Funicular Montesanto to via Morghen, Centrale to piazzetta Fuga or Chiaia to via Cimarosa/bus C28, C31, C32, C36. Closed 2wks Aug. **Rates** €37 single without bath; €65 double without bath. **Credit** MC, V. **Map** p314 2B.

The Margherita is basic and has rather dreary rooms, but it's in a very safe part of town, near the Certosa-Museo di San Martino (*see p93*), and just a short funicular ride away from the centre of the action. No services to speak of.

Chiaia to Posillipo

Deluxe

Excelsior

Via Partenope 48 (081 764 0111/fax 081 764 9743/www.excelsior.it). Bus C25, 140. **Rates** €280-€310 single; €340-€400 double; €550-€2,000 suite. **Credit** AmEx, DC, MC, V. **Map** p315 2A.

The Excelsior has seen royals, film stars and jet setters of all ilks walk through its luxuriously decorated halls and corridors. A landmark in the Neapolitan *dolce vita*, its fascination remains – helped by its enviable position overlooking the bay, with Vesuvius in the background and the Borgo Marinaro right opposite. Every room is different, though all share a *fin-de-siècle* atmosphere. The top-floor restaurant, La Terrazza, enjoys breathtaking views. The bar on the ground floor is open to non-residents.

Hotel services *Bar (1). Disabled-adapted rooms. Internet (dataport, €20 for 30 mins). No-smoking rooms. Parking (from €20). Restaurant (1). Room service. TV: pay/satellite.*

Santa Lucia

Via Partenope 46 (081 764 0666/fax 081 764 8580/ www.santalucia.it). Bus C25, 140. **Rates** €209.99-€249.99 double; €359.99-€389.99 double with sea view; €469.99-€1,599.99 suite. **Credit** AmEx, DC, MC, V. **Map** p315 2A.

Overlooking the bay, this long-established hotel, renovated in 1998, enjoys marvellous views. It's traditionally furnished, the atmosphere is relaxing and the staff are very professional. It is situated opposite the Castel dell'Ovo (*see p64*) and the Borgo Marinaro with its many bars and restaurants.
Hotel services *Bar. Restaurant. Room services.*

Vesuvio

Via Partenope 45 (081 764 0044/fax 081 764 4483/www.vesuvio.it). Bus C25, 140. **Rates** €330-€380 single; €410-€470 double; €600-€4,000 suite. **Credit** AmEx, DC, MC, V. **Map** p315 2A.

Built in 1882, when the Santa Lucia seafront was created in a huge redevelopment, the Vesuvio was completely destroyed during World War II and rebuilt in 1950 with the addition of two extra floors. On the top floor is the roof garden restaurant, named after Enrico Caruso, who was a favoured guest. The restaurant is famous for its view. The hotel's luxury and comfort are legendary and have attracted royalty and world leaders down the years, including Guy de Maupassant, Queen Victoria, Grace Kelly and Bill Clinton. An outdoor pool is planned for next year.
Hotel services *Bar (2). Business centre. Disabled-adapted rooms. Gym (in spa). Internet (dataport). No-smoking rooms. Parking (€21). Restaurants (2). Room service. Spa. TV: pay/satellite.*

Expensive

Majestic

Largo Vasto a Chiaia 68 (081 416 500/fax 081 410 145/www.majestic.it). Metro Piazza Amedeo/ bus C22, C25, C28. **Rates** €170-€210 single; €210-€240 double; €370 suite. **Credit** AmEx, DC, MC, V. **Map** p315 1B.

The Majestic is perfectly located in a quiet side street in the heart of the smart via dei Mille shopping area. The Villa Comunale (*see p98*) and the seafront are a stroll away. Its rooms are furnished with a sober elegance; some, on the upper floors have sea views.
Hotel services *Bar (1). Concierge. Disabled-adapted rooms. Internet. Parking (from €20). No-smoking rooms. Restaurant. Room service. TV.*

Palazzo Alabardieri Hotel

Via Alabardieri 38 (tel/fax 081 415 278/www. palazzalabardieri.it). Tram 1, 4/bus C9, C10, C12, C18, C19, C24, C25, R3. **Rates** €275 double; €390 suite. **Credit** AmEx, DC, MC, V. **Map** p315 1A.

An impressive building, which has been recently refurbished. A first-floor gallery surrounds the marble-floored lobby area, giving a palazzo-like feel (the building dates from 1870). Rooms are well furnished and staff are professional and friendly. Suites have jacuzzis.

Hotel services *Concierge. Disabled-adapted rooms. Internet access. Parking (from €20). Room service. TV: plasma screen, satellite.*

Royal Continental

Via Partenope 38-44 (081 245 2068/081 764 4636/ 081 764 4800/fax 081 764 5707/081 764 4661/ www.hotelroyal.it). Bus C25, 140. **Rates** €143-€211 single; €179-€300 double; €300-€500 suite. **Credit** AmEx, DC, MC, V. **Map** p315 2A.

You won't find marble staircases or chandeliers in this simple, modern hotel in Chiaia (it was built 30 years ago, and a wing was added more recently). But it's functional and perfectly comfortable, and much favoured by busy business people who may or may not take time out to appreciate its wonderful location on the seafront overlooking the Castel dell'Ovo, roof garden, and view. There is also a swimming pool.
Hotel services *Bar (1). Business centre. Concierge, Disabled-adapted rooms. Gym. Internet. No-smoking rooms. Parking (from €15). Pool (outdoor). Restaurant. Room service. TV.*

Moderate

Paradiso

Via Catullo 11 (081 761 4161/fax 081 761 3449/ www.bestwestern.com). Bus C21. **Rates** €105-€118 single; €160-€199 double. **Credit** AmEx, DC, MC, V. **Map** p315 2C.

The beautiful – indeed, aptly named – Paradiso is situated high on the hill of Posillipo, away from the hustle and bustle of the city. From this idyllic perch, you can watch the traffic hell below and heave a sigh of relief that you're not in it. The rooms are airy and bright.
Hotel services *Bar (1). Business centre. Concierge. Internet. No-smoking rooms. Parking (€15). Restaurant (1). TV: satellite.*

Parteno

Via Partenope 1 (081 245 2095/fax 081 247 1303/ www.parteno.it). Bus 140, C24, C25, C28, R3/tram 1, 4. **Rates** €80-€130 single; €100-€139 double with sea view. **Credit** AmEx, MC, V. **Map** p315 2A.

Though this is officially a hotel, the Parteno has a cosy, warm, B&B ambience – you'll feel like the personal guests of the charming owners. The few rooms – each named after a flower – are stylishly furnished; some have windows or balconies with a view towards Capri. It's a 15-minute walk from the main port and hydrofoil port at Molo Beverello and five minutes from the designer boutiques on via Calabritto and piazza dei Martiri (*see p97*). The entire hotel is no-smoking.
Hotel services *Concierge. Internet. No-smoking rooms. TV.*

Pinto-Storey

Via G Martucci 72 (081 681 260/fax 081 667 536/ www.pintostorey.it). Metro Piazza Amedeo/bus C24, C25, C27, C28. **Rates** €75-€96 single; €116-€175 double. **Credit** AmEx, MC, V. **Map** p315 1B.

With its charming Liberty (art nouveau) entrance and convenient location near the via dei Mille shopping area, the Pinto-Storey is an ideal hotel in this price range, especially if you're seeking to avoid the hustle of the Centro storico. The rooms, all recently restored, are very pleasant.

Hotel services *Bar (1). Internet. Parking (€20).*

Splendid

Via A Manzoni 96 (081 645 462/fax 081 714 6431/ www.hotelsplendid.it). Bus C21, C27, C31. **Rates** €90-€115 single; €117 double; €140 double with sea view.* **Credit** AmEx, DC, MC, V.

On the top of Posillipo hill (*see p100*), far from the smoke of the exhaust pipes, the Splendid looks away from the centre, towards Pozzuoli, the Campi Flegrei and Capo Miseno (*see p106*), from where Pliny wrote his terrifying account of the eruption of Vesuvius in 79 BC. Unless anodised aluminium is your thing, you might find the interior decor a little disappointing, but the rooms are pleasant nonetheless. It's a bit of a hike to the centre.

Hotel services *Bar (1). Business centre. Concierge. Disabled-adapted rooms. Internet. Parking. Restaurant (1). Room services. TV: satellite.*

Budget

Canada

Via Mergellina 43 (081 680 952/fax 081 681 594/tel & fax 081 682 018/www.sea-hotels.com). Metro Mergellina/bus R3, 140. **Rates** €60-€104 single; €70-€104 double.* **Credit** AmEx, DC, MC, V. **Map** p315 2C.

Facing the Mergellina seafront by the chalets (*see p127* **Chalet society**), at the base of the Posillipo hill, the Canada is buzzing throughout the summer. It's conveniently located near the Mergellina hydrofoil port for quick transfers to the islands, and the airconditioned rooms are furnished with unpretentious elegance.

Hotel services *Concierge. Parking (from €15). TV.*

Cappella Vecchia 11

Vico Santa Maria a Cappella Vecchia 11 (Piazza dei Martiri) (081 240 5117/www.cappellavecchia11.it). Tram 1, 4/bus C25, R3. **Rates** €90-€110 double.* **Credit** AmEx, MC, V. **Map** p315 1A.

Six rooms and a breakfast/reading room. Furnishings are modern, lines are clean and the place is comfortable. A strong point of this hotel is its location: Cappella Vecchia is just off the 'Bermuda triangle' of designer shops and antique dealers, in the elegant Chiaia quarter.

Hotel services *Internet access. Parking (€18-€24).*

Crispi

Via F Crispi 104 (tel/fax 081 668 048/www.hotel crispi.it). Metro Piazza Amedeo/bus C24, C25, C28. **Rates** €45-€54 single; €81-€90 double.* **Credit** MC, V. **Map** p315 1B.

Once a flophouse, the Crispi has cleaned up its act somewhat, though the rooms remain glum. But it's very central and quite cheap, and there are lots of good restaurants and bars in the area – Chiaia – which is one of the safest in Naples. Not a service in sight (parking facilities aside).

Hotel services *Parking (from €11).*

Le Fontane al Mare

Via N Tommaseo 14 (081 764 3811/fax 081 764 3470). Bus C12, C18, C19, C24, C25, C28, 140. **Rates** €50 single without bath; €60 single with bath; €70 double without bath; €90 double with bath; €100 double with sea view.* **Credit** AmEx, DC, MC, V. **Map** p315 2A.

One of the cheapest places to stay along the Chiaia seafront. Le Fontane al Mare is central, and has the advantage of a small terrace with a beautiful view. Decent enough for the price.

Hotel services *Bar.*

Hotel & Residence Villa Medici

Via Nuova Bagnoli, 550, Posillipo (081 762 3040/ fax 081 570 1934/www.hotel-villamedici.com). Campi Flegrei metro then C9 bus or Cumana line to Agnano. **Rates** €70-€181 single; €80-€181 double; €110-€207 suite.* **Credit** AmEx, MC, V.

Villa Medici is a charming, converted, Liberty (art nouveau) style villa, well connected to the Centro storico by public transport. There's a variety of rooms and apartments, many with kitchenette, plus a garden and pool. Special seasonal offers and discounts for family groups.

Hotel services *Bar. Parking. Concierge. Disabled-adapted room. Internet access. No smoking rooms. Pool. TV: DVD.*

Ostello Mergellina (Youth Hostel)

Salita della Grotta a Piedigrotta 23 (081 761 2346/ 081 761 1215/fax 081 761 2391). Metro Mergellina/bus C12, C16, C18. **Rates** €14 per person in dorm; €16 double.* **No credit cards.** **Map** p315 2C.

Centrally located in the Chiaia area, the rooms at this youth hostel are very clean, with light wood furniture, and the reception areas are spacious and welcoming. Double rooms are available as well as dorm space. The hostel is popular and booking is obligatory in July and August. The restaurant serves full evening meals for €8.50. The reception closes at 12.30am and there is a curfew.

Hotel services *Bar (1). Internet. Parking. Restaurant.*

Ruggiero

Via Martucci 72 (081 663 536/fax 081 761 2460). Funicular Chiaia to piazza Amedeo/metro Piazza Amedeo/bus C24, C25, C28. **Rates** €60 single without bath; €70-€80 single with bath; €80 double without bath; €90 double with bath.* **Credit** DC, MC, V. **Map** p315 1B.

If you're after a cheap room in a very central location, and aren't too fussed about the appearance of it, this is the place for you. The whole central area is reachable on foot from here.

Hotel services *Bar (open for breakfast only). Parking (€20). Room services. TV (in Italian).*

Campi Flegrei

See also p55 **Camping**.

Budget

Agriturismo Il Casolare di Tobia

Contrada Coste di Baia, via Selvatico 12, Bacoli (081 523 5193/www.datobia.it). Bus SEPSA 1 from piazza Garibaldi to Bacoli. **Closed** 2wks Dec-Jan; 2wks Aug. **Rates** €55-€65 double. **No credit cards**.

A 19th-century farmhouse offering accommodation (*agriturismo*) in a volcanic crater (inactive, thankfully, for the last 10,000 years), Il Casolare di Tobia is nothing if not bucolic. It's surrounded by vineyards and the gardens in which vegetables used in the *agriturismo*'s excellent and well-known restaurant (*see p125*) are grown. Only four rooms are available, each with two or four beds, as well as communal cooking facilities for breakfast and an open terrace with a view over the fields. Children aged up to two stay for free; there are discounts for groups.

Hotel services *Parking (free). Restaurant (closed Sun dinner, Mon).*

Suburbs & elsewhere

Moderate

Holiday Inn

Via Centro Direzionale, Isola E6, Centro Direzionale (081 225 0111/fax 081225 0683/www.hotel-invest.com). Metro Piazza Garibaldi/bus C30, C40, C58, C61, C81, 191. **Rates** €185-€222 single; €195 double; €227 suite. **Credit** AmEx, DC, MC, V. **Map** p312 2A.

Located in the Centro Direzionale business area , this Holiday Inn is handy for Capodichino airport and the main railway station, but very far removed (in spirit, though not geographically) from the city's sights. As a result, it attracts mostly people doing business in the Centro Direzionale. It's not a nice place for strolling around, especially at night. Like the district, the Holiday Inn is strong on mod cons and weak on atmosphere. The gym and pool are currently being refurbished.

Hotel services *Bar (1). Business centre. Concierge. Disabled-adapted rooms. Gym. Internet (dataport). Parking (€13). Restaurant (2). TV: satellite.*

Camping

There are no camping facilities within easy reach of the city centre: most are located in beautiful green spots, mostly in the Campi Flegrei area (*see pp102-106*) in western Naples.

The ones listed below are well organised. They are also handy for the sea, but don't expect an azure, inviting Mediterranean.

Chiaia's **Pinto-Storey**. *See p53.*

Averno

Via Montenuovo Licola Patria 85, Arco Felice Lucrino, Pozzuoli (081 804 2666/fax 081 804 2570/www.averno.it). Bus M1 (from piazza Garibaldi). **Rates** €6.50 per person; €6.50 per camper van or tent pitch; €2.50 per car. **Credit** AmEx, MC, V.

Big and well equipped, this campsite in the Campi Flegrei is a fair hike from Naples but only 2km (1.25 miles) from the beach.

Services *Bar. Disco. Gym. Internet. Parking. Pools (2). Reception (open 24hrs). Restaurant.*

Vulcano Solfatara

Via Solfatara 161, Pozzuoli (081 526 7413/ www.solfatara.it). Metro Pozzuoli/bus SEPSA 1 from piazza Garibaldi. **Closed** Nov-25 Dec, 9 Jan-Mar. **Rates** €7-€8.70 per person; €4.10-€6 per tent pitch; €7-€8.70 per camper van. **Credit** AmEx, DC, MC, V.

Just 800m (933yds) from the Pozzuoli metro stop, this is the most convenient campsite for visiting Naples and surrounding areas. It's less than an hour into town on the metro, and handily placed for the ferry port at Pozzuoli. Moreover, it's right on the fringes of the bubbling, hissing Solfatara crater (*see p104*). There are bungalows for rent too: one for four people costs from €37 to €95 for a deluxe model in high season.

Services *Bar. Disabled-adapted bathroom (1). Internet (€1.50 per hour). Parking (from €5.20). Pool. Reception (open 24hrs). Restaurant).*

Londoners take when they go out.

EVERY WEEK

Sightseeing

Introduction

Life's never dull in this treasure-packed living theatre.

The facelift that Naples has been undergoing during the past ten years or so continues apace: well-thought-out redevelopment schemes; pedestrianisation; improved road, rail and air links; the list is endless. Whether this process has genuinely reversed the city's decline, or whether political in-fighting will erode the delicate process and return the city to its traditional paralysis is an open question. In the meantime, thankfully, Naples' unique treasures are still there for all to see.

The origins of Naples' very endearing peculiarities become clear only by considering the history of this strikingly beautiful city, with its bay, distant mountain ranges and volcano on the horizon. The place has attracted intense competition over the centuries, both from outside (a succession of foreign rulers have left ample traces) and, more importantly, from within. For centuries Naples was, as a European royal described it (*see p17*), 'Italy's most beautiful crown'; and it has all the artistic and architectural glories befitting a city of such importance. Its museums and churches are among the world's finest, and will keep any visitor busy and culturally satisfied no matter how long the stay.

At the same time, competition for living space, employment, power and personal attention has always been intense here. Moreover, a succession of lackadaisical, corrupt foreign governors taught Neapolitans to shift for themselves; sloth and extravagance at high levels were countered by a frantic struggle for survival among the great majority. That sense of struggle still makes Naples what it is: the Neapolitan people are its most outstanding feature and each is a player in a living theatre. Observe the daily drama of city life as it unfolds and you too will be assigned a role: that of *'o straniero* (the foreigner). You may be offered all forms of Mediterranean hospitality (although your role demands that you normally refuse). Never forget that behind the scenes, real life in Naples can be hard.

A densely populated city of over a million inhabitants, Naples has its fair share of petty crime. Be wary, without being frightened. Avoid flashy jewellery and carry the minimum amount of cash necessary. Large backpacks are the best indicators of hapless visitors/easy prey. Avoid deserted alleys. Bag-snatchers generally whip by on scooters. If you fall victim to them, don't go in for heroics; you may find that keeping calm will unnerve the thieves, most of whom are kids who specialise in picking on panicky Neapolitan ladies in furs. Remember that if you're prepared for the worst, you can safely expect the best. *See also p293* **Safety & security** and *p294* **Emergency numbers**.

Sightseeing

PALAZZI

Naples' *palazzi* (and their inner courtyards and gardens) are the city's best-kept secrets. Nearly all are in private hands, carved up into flats. Though most of those mentioned in this guide have memorable exteriors, and some have wonderful courtyards (usually visible by walking confidently through the door from the street), chances of visiting interiors are rare and should be grasped unhesitatingly if they arise; the *piano nobile* (main floor) of even the dowdiest building often contains a *salone* with a beautifully frescoed ceiling. If you're here in May, watch out for one-off Maggio dei Monumenti openings (*see p77* **Monuments in May**).

CHURCHES

Naples is awash with churches, be they bustling places of worship, deconsecrated buildings used for non-religious purposes, or firmly boarded up for '*restauro*' (which can be active or dormant, begun recently, after the floods in 2001, the earthquake in 1980 or in the wake of World War II). Over 50 per cent of the city's churches fall into the boarded-up category.

The 17th-century Counter-Reformation was the golden period for Neapolitan churches, vast numbers of which owe their current appearance to baroque treatment administered at that time. Many churches, however, pre-date their façades, which hide much older interiors.

Though churches are best visited in sober attire, all but the most indecent extremes of exposure are generally tolerated from tourists. To avoid giving offence, use common sense: don't visit during mass unless there are empty side aisles where you can blend quietly into the shadows. Most priests are only too happy to talk about their churches; don't expect exhaustive historical knowledge, though.

MUSEUMS AND GALLERIES

Naples boasts some of the world's finest museums: the **Museo Nazionale Archeologico** (*see p273*) is second to none, while the art collections at the **Museo di Capodimonte** (*see p90*) and the **Certosa-Museo di San Martino** (*p93*) are spectacular. Due to low staffing levels (and union touchiness), even museums of this calibre will close some rooms on a rotating basis. Be prepared to make more than one trip to any given museum if you are determined to see it all.

ANCIENT SITES

Buried and built over by space-starved citizens down the ages, what remains of Greek and Roman Naples is almost exclusively underground. Comparatively little has been excavated; still less is open to the public. That said, there are glimpses beneath the churches of **Santa Chiara** (*see p74*), **San Lorenzo** (*p80*), **Santa Maria in Purgatorio ad Arco** (*p80*), and the **Duomo** (*p79*). Thanks to the unflagging commitment of the Napoli Sotterranea association (081 296 944/368 354 0585/www.lanapolisotterranea.it), other sites should be visitable in the not-too-distant future, while recent building work on the new underground railway uncovered an ancient Roman harbour and boats in Piazza Municipio (*see p65*).

OPENING TIMES

Traditionally, Monday is lock-out day in Naples, but the situation has improved since the four biggies (Palazzo Reale, Museo Nazionale, Museo di Capodimonte and the Certosa-Museo di San Martino) began staggering their closing days.

Though every effort has been made to get opening times right in this guide, they can change without warning; these changes are often for the better, including late-night summer openings for major galleries and sites. Ask at tourist information offices for latest updates, or phone ahead.

Churches are a case apart. As flocks – rather than tourists – are the Church's main concern, visiting times are more fluid, often depending

Galleria Umberto. See p67.

Sightseeing

on the prior engagements or whims of a single priest and a dwindling band of ageing volunteers. Accordingly, some churches now actively discourage sightseeing on Sundays. Far from grumbling about their unpredictable time-keeping, we should probably be thankful they are there at all.

Maggio dei Monumenti (*see p77* **Monuments in May**) is a special treat for visitors, who should seriously consider planning their visit at this time – though finding out what's on and when can be difficult: City Hall, which organises the event, is remarkably unwilling

(or unable) to provide programme information. Try the EPT (*see p296* **Tourist information**) instead. Even the most secretive of properties usually open their doors for at least one Sunday, and there are walks, talks and even guided snorkling trips too.

TICKETS AND ADMISSION
We've given the prices of full adult tickets. At state-owned sites, EU citizens under 18 and over 65 are admitted free; some places offer further reductions for groups, full-time students and so on. Keep a range of ID with you at all

A city walk

The square outside the Museo di San Martino is a great place to start a Naples walk. The low wall of **Largo San Martino**, favourite noctural haunt of canoodling teenagers, affords an unparalleled view over the old city, stretching away as far as the eye can see, along the arrow-straight Spaccanapoli, past the vast green roof of Santa Chiara, the bulk of the Albergo dei Poveri, the Tangenziale ring-road and the airport, to the Matese mountains in the background, often snow-capped in the winter. (This world-class view is equally sumptuous at night, by the way.) A cup of caffè espresso and a warm cornetto in one of the square's bars will put a spring in your step.

From the Largo di San Martino, walk down the steps, the Pedamentina, at the north of the square. Follow the steps as they snake down to corso Vittorio Emanuele. Turn left along the corso, past the **Montesanto funicular station** on your left, until you get to the recently renovated flight of steps on the right, the scala Montesanto, leading down into the heart of the city.

They will take you past the Cumana railway station on your left. Shortly afterwards you will come to the head of a chaotic market – the **Pignasecca** – if you're there in the morning it will be packed with commuters, school kids and market-stall owners bawling out their wares. Turn right into the market – the street here is via Portamedina. Where the street forks at the small piazza Pignasecca, take the right fork – via Pignasecca.

When you get to the modernist Piazza Carità, turn left up the rather less fashionable part of via Toledo. Turn right into via Pasquale Scura, crossing over via Santa Anna di Lombardi, until you reach piazza Gesù Nuovo. From here, you can do

as much wandering in the Centro storico as you like, taking **Spaccanapoli** (the series of streets that run in a straight line through the Centro storico) as your main axis. Spaccanapoli is dotted with interesting churches: **Santa Chiara**, **San Domenico Maggiore**, **Gesù Nuovo**, **San Giorgio Maggiore**. For all, *see p72-82*.

Return to piazza Gesù Nuovo, and from there take calata Trinità Maggiore to piazza Monteoliveto and then via Monteoliveto. Turn right on to via Diaz, walk past the modernist **post office**, and then left on to the more upmarket southern section of **via Toledo**. Enjoy the shops on via Toledo, and then turn into **Galleria Umberto I** on your left, emerging opposite the **San Carlo Opera House** (notice the Castel Nuovo further down to your left). From San Carlo turn right up into piazza Trieste e Trento and piazza Plebiscito, dominated by the imposing **Palazzo Reale** on one side and the impressive church of **San Francesco di Paola** on the other.

From here you can either return to the Vomero by way of the Funicolare Centrale (from piazza Duca d'Aosta), maybe finishing with a stroll round **Villa Floridiana**, or alternatively continue through piazza Plebiscito down via C Console to the **seafront**. Here, you have arrived at the location of a classic Naples stroll: past the luxury hotels, the **Castel dell'Ovo** and along into the **Villa Comunale**.

Stop for well-earned refreshment in one of the bars along the way, cross to the Villa when you come to the **Acquario** and turn up into via San Pasquale, through the upmarket but relaxed district of Chiaia. When you reach piazza Amedo, you will be ready to take the Funicolare di Chiaia back up to the Vomero.

times: you never know when you might qualify for cheaper tickets. Ticket prices at sites not owned by the state – including many smaller museums and galleries – vary, but rarely exceed €3. In 2002 the city council introduced the Campaniartecard, which combines free and reduced-price entry to a number of sites with free use of city transport. A Naples-only version costs €13 (€8 for those aged 18 to 25). For more information, *see p35* **Smart art**.

Ticket sales and the bookshops at Capodimonte, the Museo Nazionale Archeologico, Castel Sant'Elmo, the Certosa-

Museo di San Martino, Villa Pignatelli and the Museo Nazionale della Ceramica Duca di Martina are operated by a private company called **Pierreci**. For information, consult the website www.pierreci.it. For details in English, or to book guided group visits in advance, phone 848 800 288 from landlines within Italy, or 06 3996 7150/081 741 0067 from cellphones or (putting 00 39 first) from abroad.

For information on public transport, *see p282-6* **Getting around**. For suggestions for Naples most unmissable sights, *see p63* **The best sights**.

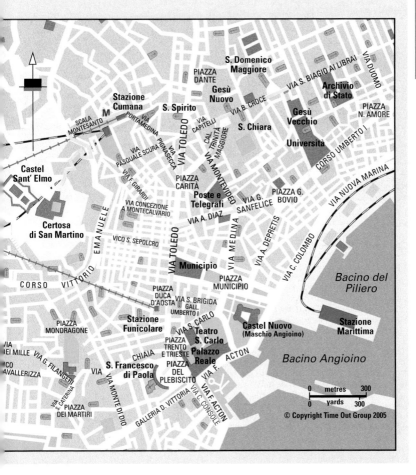

Royal Naples & Monte Echia

Naples' birthplace and one-time hub of power.

Classical good looks: **Royal Naples**. *See p64*.

It was on the tiny island of Megaris, where the imposing bulk of the Castel dell'Ovo now sits, that Naples was founded more than 2,500 years ago. According to legend, passing sailors found the body of the siren Parthenope: jilted by Ulysses, the heartbroken mermaid had drowned herself. The mariners buried her on the rock and thus the original settlement of Parthenope or Paleopolis ('old town') was established.

Archaeology may not confirm the legend, but it does verify the location, for the island of Megaris, and Monte Echia towering above, were settled as a trading colony in 680 BC by Greeks who came from nearby Cuma (*see p105*). Two centuries later the settlers moved inland to found Neapolis ('new town'). There are two focal points for this very old 'new' area, which is now a mishmash of government offices, historical sites, exclusive shops and low-rent housing: **piazza del Municipio** and **piazza del Plebiscito**.

For over a thousand years this district was the centre of monarchic power. With the post-war demise of Italy's royal family and the relocation of many government offices to the new Centro Direzionale (though City Hall remains in piazza Municipio), it has acquired something of a shop-window role for visitors.

Monte Echia

Rising to the south-west behind piazza del Plebiscito is Monte Echia, the remains of the crater rim of an extinct volcano (the island of Megaris is another chunk) and the site of ancient Paleopolis. In the first century BC, the Roman general Lucullus owned an extensive villa here, surrounded by an estate that stretched from the top of the hill down to the shoreline and as far as Mergellina.

It's a 20-minute walk from piazza del Plebiscito up via Egiziaca a Pizzofalcone and salita Echia to the scruffy public gardens on top of Monte Echia. From the terrace of the gardens, note the sinister observation posts of the modern police head-quarters and bask in a rather obstructed but still glorious view of one of the cradles of Western civilisation. On the

Sightseeing

The best Sights

So much to see and so little time? Here, we offer graded suggestions for some of the city's most interesting sights, streets, parks and views, with estimates of how long you might want to spend at each.

Churches

★★★★ **San Lorenzo Maggiore** (including underground archaeological site). Allow an hour and a half. See p80.

★★★ **Cappella Sansevero**. Allow an hour and a half. See p78.

★★★ **Duomo** (including archaeological site). Allow an hour and a half. See p79.

★★★ **Santa Chiara** (including archaeological area). Allow an hour and a half. See p74.

★ **San Domenico Maggiore**. Allow half an hour. See p75.

★ **Gesù Nuovo**. Allow half an hour. See p74.

★ **Sant'Eligio**. Allow half an hour. See p71.

Castles

★★★ **Castel dell'Ovo**. Allow one hour. See p64.

★★★ **Castel Sant'Elmo**. Allow one hour. See p93.

★★★ **Castel Nuovo** or Maschio Angioino (including the Museo Civico). Allow one and a half hours. See p66.

Palazzi

★★★ **Palazzo Reale**. Allow two hours. See p67.

Museums

★★★★ **Museo Nazionale Archeologico**. Allow two hours. See p83.

★★★★ **Museo di Capodimonte** (art collection and park). Allow half a day. See p90.

★★★★ **San Martino** (including monastery and garden). Allow half a day. See p93.

★★ **Città della Scienza**. Allow half a day. See p147.

Underground sites

★★★ **Catacombe di San Gennaro**. Allow an hour and a half. See p90.

★★ **Catacombe di San Gaudioso**. Allow an hour and a half. See p87.

★★ **Grotta di Seiano**. Allow one hour. See p101.

Streets

★★★ **Via Pignasecca**. Naples' biggest street market. See p84.

★★★ **Via Toledo**. A busy pedestrianised shopping street. See p83.

★ **Via Scarlatti**. A quieter shopping street in Vomero.

Parks

★★ **Floridiana**. See p94.

★ **Parco Virgiliano**. See p100.

★ **Villa Comunale**. See p98.

Views

★★★ **Certosa-Museo di San Martino**. Eastwards over old Naples and Vesuvius. See p93.

★★★ **Castel Sant'Elmo**. A 360° view eastwards over old Naples and Vesuvius and westwards towards Campi Flegrei). See p93.

★★ **Parco Virgiliano**. Westwards towards Fuorigrotta and Campi Flegrei, eastwards towards Castel dell'Ovo and Vesuvius. See p100.

★ **Via Orazio** in Mergellina. Has views eastwards and southwards over Chiaia, Mergellina and Capri.

northern side of the hill (also reachable by lift, free of charge, from the eastern end of via Chiaia), the Pizzofalcone district contains more military and police establishments, including the **Nunziatella** military academy with its baroque church, and the melancholy-looking **Palazzo Serra di Cassano**.

Pizzofalcone is home to the early 17th-century churches of **Santa Maria degli Angeli** (open 7.30-11.30am, 5-7.30pm Mon-Sat; 8.30am-1.30pm, 6-7.30pm Sun) and **Santa Maria Egiziaca a Pizzofalcone** (open 9-10am, 5-7.30pm Mon-Sat; 9am-1pm, 5-7.30pm Sun). The former has an enormous dome, not immediately visible from the

road, while its interior features a splendid barrel-vaulted ceiling and two delicate marble reliefs by Tito Angelini in the first chapel on the right.

From Monte Echia, the rampa di Pizzofalcone zigzags down towards the **Castel dell'Ovo**. On the seafront, via Partenope and via Sauro skirt the Santa Lucia district (see p67), then pass by Pietro Bernini and Michelangelo Naccherino's **Fontana dell'Immacolatella** (1601) and back to piazza del Plebiscito (see p64). Savour Naples' briny side as you inhale seafood smells wafting from the extractor fans of the waterfront restaurants and admire the yachts packed into the marina at the island of Megaris.

Castel dell'Ovo

Via Partenope (081 240 0055). Bus 140, C24, C25, C28, R3/tram 1. **Open** *9am-sunset Mon-Sat; 9am-1.30pm Sun.* **Admission** *free.* **Map** *p315 2A.*

The castle you see today is the result of 1,000 years of military occupation beginning in Norman times. The Aragonese gave it its present look in the 16th century. Prior to that, in the Middle Ages, a monastic community lived here; even earlier, it was part of the estate of Roman general Lucullus. When the poet Virgil stayed here in the first century BC, local legend says he buried an egg (*uovo*) in the ground, predicting that when the egg broke disaster would happen – hence the name of the castle.

After crossing the bridge, pass through the main portal and either climb straight on up to the right, or bear left along to the far end of the *mole* (breakwater), where the gun emplacements used to stand – this is a strangely deserted spot with Naples very close, yet completely hidden from view by the castle. Some of the rooms leading off the long climb up the ramp inside the castle itself are offices, while others are exhibition areas; yet others are currently being excavated and restored, and for the moment are only visible through glass.

La Nunziatella

Via Generale Parisi 16 (081 764 1520/www.esercito. difesa.it/professio/nunziatella/index.htm). Bus C22. **Open** *9am-10am Sun for Mass; by appointment at other times.* **Map** *p315 2A.*

Fork-lifting **Fontana di Nettuno**. *See p65.*

This pocket-sized baroque jewel belongs to the adjacent military academy founded by the Bourbon royal family in 1787. It took its name from the church of the Annunziata, designed by Ferdinando Sanfelice in 1737. Notice the unusual tiled flooring and striking 18th-century marble altar by Giuseppe Sammartino.

Palazzo Serra di Cassano

Via Monte di Dio 14 (081 245 2150). Bus C22. **Open** *by appointment only.* **Map** *p315 1A.*

You'll find it hard to get a proper view of the trim façade of this immaculately kept 18th-century palazzo, as it's hemmed in by other buildings. One of the high points in Ferdinando Sanfelice's (*see p38*) architectural career, it has a no-nonsense double stairway in cool grey volcanic stone with a beautifully cut marble-pillared balustrade. The apartments feature fine frescos and original furniture. The main entrance in via Egiziaca was closed in 1799 by the Prince of Cassano in mourning for the death of his son Gennaro, one of the leaders of the short-lived Parthenopean Republic (*see p10*). Gennaro was beheaded in piazza del Plebiscito, and the entrance, which at the time enjoyed an unobstructed view of the Royal Palace, remained closed until bicentenary celebrations in 1999. The palazzo is now the headquarters of the Italian Institute for Philosophical Studies.

Royal Naples

Start at the vast, traffic-free neo-classical **piazza del Plebiscito**. Until 1994 the piazza was a grimy oil-streaked expanse of tarmac used as a bus depot and car park. One of the most splendid *piazze* in Italy, if not Europe, it has now been restored to its former glory, including a new surface of local volcanic cobblestones. This is traditionally the site for large city events: concerts, political rallies, New Year's Eve parties and so on. The piazza is dominated by the church of **San Francesco di Paola** (*see p67*) and **Palazzo Reale** (*see p67*). The semicircular colonnade with Doric columns adoring this stately piazza was begun in 1809 under French ruler Joaquin Murat; San Francesco di Paola was added later by the restored Bourbon monarchy in thanks for the end of the French occupation. The bronze equestrian statues of Bourbon kings Charles III and Ferdinand I are by Antonio Canova.

Adjoining piazza del Plebiscito to the north-east, piazza Trieste e Trento is home to Naples' most elegant watering hole, the **Gambrinus** café (*see p129*), from where guided tours to the underground 16th-century water system, the **Acquedotto Carmignano** (*see p66*), depart.

Also in the square is the church of **San Ferdinando** (open 8am-noon Mon-Fri; 8am-noon, 5.30-6.30pm Sat; 9.30am-1pm Sun), which has fresco scenes from the lives of illustrious Jesuits on its ceiling and

Once an Angevin stronghold. **Castel Nuovo.** *See p66.*

some fine 19th-century marblework by Tito Angelini and the Vaccaros in the chapel in the left-hand transept.

Leading west out of the square, via Chiaia is a street of high-density clothes shops that vary enormously in price and quality. Amorous athlete and supreme self-publicist Giacomo Casanova and the infinitely more serious German poet Johann Wolfgang von Goethe both stayed at the imposing **Palazzo Cellamare** (No.149; not open to the public) in the 18th century (though not at the same time).

Pedestrianised via Toledo – with more shops – leads north from the square. A couple of hundred metres along the road on the right is the entrance to the magnificent **Galleria Umberto** (*see p67*).

Heading east out of piazza Trieste e Trento, via San Carlo leads past the illustrious **Teatro San Carlo** opera house (*see p67*), the gardens of the **Palazzo Reale** (*see p67*), and into the heavily congested **piazza Municipio**.

At the northern end of the piazza, the early 19th-century **Palazzo San Giacomo** was built to house the massive bureaucracy of the Bourbon monarchs. Today, it's the headquarters of Naples city council, and a magnet for all kinds of protesters. An easily missed door on the right of the palazzo leads to the charmingly royalist 16th-century church of **San Giacomo degli Spagnoli** (restoration work currently in progress; open 10.30am-2pm Sun); behind the altar, the tomb (1570) of Spanish viceroy Don Pedro di Toledo (*see p16*) sits amid the crumbling remains of a very theatrical chapel; if you can find him, ask the sacristan for the keys.

The centre of piazza Municipio is not enhanced by the presence of a large construction site, under which work has been continuing furiously for the last two years on the new Naples underground

line. Excavations have, however, revealed the remains of an old Roman harbour, including the wrecks of three boats. This amazing find has thrown the construction schedule into disarray. The site is not open to visitors now, but when the new station opens it will incorporate some of the treasure trove.

Via Medina is the new home to the impressive **Fontana di Nettuno** (fountain of Neptune), brought here in 2001 from its previous site in nearby piazza Bovio (currently cluttered beyond recognition with another building site for the underground). Almost opposite the fountain stands the deconsecrated church of **Santa Maria Incoronata** (currently closed to the public, with no reopening date set). The church was adapted from a court house in the second half of the 14th century to commemorate the coronation of Angevin Queen Joan. It was reputedly much loved by Petrarch, Boccaccio and Giotto; restored frescos inside by Giotto's pupil Roberto Oderisi show scenes from the coronation in 1352.

On the opposite side of the street, the **Pietà dei Turchini** church (open 7.15am-noon, 5-7.30pm Mon-Fri; 8.30-11.30am, 5-7.30pm Sat; 9.30am-1.30pm Sun) started life as a poorhouse where children were dressed in turquoise shifts. The imposing police headquarters at the end of the street on the left dates from the fascist period.

On the southern side of piazza Municipio rise the massive towers of the 13th-century **Castel Nuovo** (*see p66*). Beyond it is the port. Ferries for Sicily, Sardinia, North Africa and the islands leave from the Stazione Marittima (1936). From here a tram heads west past the military harbour and public gardens, and through the smoggy **Galleria della Vittoria** tunnel; hop out at the end by the offices of *Il Mattino,* Naples' paper, and head into the Santa Lucia area (*see p67*).

A steel and glass pleasure dome: **Galleria Umberto**. *See p67*.

Acquedotto Carmignano

*Vico Sant'Anna di Palazzo 52 (081 400 256/www.lana
polisotterranea.it). Bus 24, C22, C82, R2.* **Open**
Guided tours only (Bar Gambrinus, via Chiaia 1-2) 9pm
Thur; 10am, noon, 6pm Sat; 10am, 11am, noon, 6pm
Sun. **Admission** €7. **No credit cards. Map** p315 1A.
Naples' historic infrastructure extends for miles
beneath the city centre at a depth of 40m (130ft) and
more. A maze of water ducts and cisterns tunnelled
into the rock during the 16th and 17th centuries, the
Carmignano drainage system was developed as part
of the expansion of the city under the Spanish
viceroys. It can be visited on hour-long tours. The
tunnels were in use until the disastrous cholera epidemic of 1884, and again as air-raid shelters in World
War II. The volcanic tufa rock that was extracted
was used to build the houses above. Excavation is
still in progress. Not for the claustrophobic. Booking
is not necessary. *See also p96* **What lies beneath**.

Castel Nuovo (Maschio Angioino)

*Piazza Municipio (081 420 1241). Bus C25, E3, R1,
R2, R3/tram 1.* **Open** *June-Mar* 9am-7pm Mon-Sat.
Apr, May 9am-7pm Mon-Sat; 9am-2pm Sun. Ticket
office closes 1hr earlier. **Admission** €5. **No credit
cards. Map** p313 2C.
Called *nuovo* (new) to distinguish it from the older
Castel dell'Ovo, this castle is better known locally as
the Maschio Angioino (Angevin stronghold). It was
built in 1279 by Charles of Anjou and used by subsequent Angevin monarchs as a royal residence and
fortress. It also became a centre of arts and literature, attracting such illustrious characters as
Petrarch, Boccaccio (some of the best tales of the

Decameron are set in a very realistic Naples)
and Giotto, who, in around 1330, frescoed the main
hall and chapel of the castle.
    Unfortunately, little of Giotto's work remains. The
castle's current appearance is the result of radical
alterations carried out by Aragonese monarchs in
the mid 15th century; the splendid triumphal arch
was added for the entry into the city of Alfonso I 'the
Magnanimous' of Aragon in 1443, a scene depicted
in the relief above the portal.
    In the back left-hand corner of the courtyard, stairs
lead up to the Sala dei Baroni, probably named after
the mutinous barons murdered here by King
Ferrante in 1486. Giotto's frescos have disappeared;
not so the unusual umbrella-vaulted ceiling that now
looks down upon the lively proceedings of Naples
City Council meetings.
    The plain yet elegant Cappella Palatina, also shorn
of its Giottos (except for tiny traces in the embrasure
of the right-hand apsidal window), is the only section
that still remains from the Angevin period. An ambitious restoration project – well under way as this guide
went to press – includes the addition of a lift to the top
of the north-eastern tower (which has three floors from
the original Angevin structure, and a terrace walkway
on top). The dungeons are also to be opened to the public: one room features glass-covered tombs containing
bones (probably the barons'); the other room, known
as Fossa del Coccodrillo, is believed to be where a
gigantic crocodile would emerge from a drain (now
covered with a grating) to devour prisoners.
    In the far left-hand corner of the inner courtyard,
a large area has been given imaginative glass flooring to enable visitors to examine some very recent

finds. These include the foundations and cemetery areas (replete with skeletons) of a convent that long pre-dates the building of the castle itself.

The first and second floors host the *museo civico* and art gallery, containing works of dubious quality but much local colour. Also housed here is the fine bronze door commissioned in 1475 by the Aragonese to commemorate their victory over the Angevins; the embedded cannonball probably dates from a sea battle off Genoa in 1495 when the door was being removed to France. There are fine views over the bay from the terrace walkways.

Galleria Umberto

From piazza Trieste e Trento to via Toledo. Bus 24, C22, C82, R2, R3. **Open** 24hrs daily. **Map** p315 1A.
This steel and glass-covered cross-shaped arcade was completed in 1890, and generally compares favourably to its slightly older counterpart, the Galleria Vittorio Emanuele II in Milan. (Unlike its Milanese twin, the mosaic bull under the central dome in Naples has no testicles.) The somewhat sleazy air of the place tends to distract attention from the elaborate neo-Renaissance decorations and fine engineering. During a World War II air raid, all the glass was blown out of the massive dome.

Palazzo Reale

Piazza del Plebiscito (848 800 288 followed by 0). Bus 24, C22, C82, R2, R3. **Open** 9am-8pm Mon, Tue, Thur-Sun; ticket office closes 1hr earlier. **Admission** €4. **No credit cards**. **Map** p315 1A.
Work on the Royal Palace was started in 1600, under the rule of the Spanish viceroys, by Neapolitan architect Domenico Fontana. The bulk of the palazzo was completed in two years, although a number of features (such as the magnificent staircase) were added 50 years later. The Bourbon monarchs had the building extended eastwards in the mid 18th century, when niches were added to the façade. Under French rule in the early 19th century the interior took on its current neo-classical appearance. The hanging gardens were created mid 19th century, while the statues of Naples' kings date from the late 19th century.

It's easy to miss the poorly marked ticket office to the left of the main entrance. Access to the 30 royal apartments is from the top of the staircase. The apartments overwhelm more by size and number than by content. There's an unremarkable collection of paintings (though some are interesting for their portrayal of Neapolitan rulers and customs), frescos, tapestries, chandeliers and furniture from the 17th to the 19th centuries; the gilt-and-stucco ceilings are impressive; and the Teatrino di Corte (1768) is a gloriously ornate private theatre. In contrast, the hanging gardens are in a sad state of dilapidation. However, plans are afoot to restore them to their 17th-century glory.

The Palazzo Reale houses the Biblioteca Nazionale (national library) with its impressive reading rooms, collections of manuscripts and musty books, some dating to the fifth century. There's also a poorly signposted tourist office (081 252 5711; open 9am-3.20pm Mon-Fri) on the first floor (take the lift), stocked with excellent handouts in many languages for a number of sites in Naples, though not for the palazzo itself. Note that the Palazzo Reale is open until 11pm on Saturday at certain times of the year; consult tourist information offices for details.

San Francesco di Paola

Piazza del Plebiscito (081 764 5133). Bus 24, C22, C82, R2, R3. **Open** 8am-noon, 3.30-5pm Mon-Sat; 8am-1pm Sun. **Map** p315 1A.
One of Naples' neo-classical rarities, San Francesco is surprisingly unpopular with the locals. This plain yet majestic imitation of the Pantheon in Rome was erected in 1817 by King Ferdinand in thanks for the repossession of his kingdom after the period of French rule. It was named after a saint who, conveniently, came from the town of Paola in Calabria, near to where Joaquin Murat – Napoleon's brother-in-law and Naples' king from 1808 to 1815 – had been shot by Ferdinand's police after an ill-fated attempt to lead an Italian uprising. The apex of the cool grey dome stands 53m (185ft) above the ground.

Teatro San Carlo

Via San Carlo 98F (081 797 2412/081 797 2331/ www.teatrosancarlo.it). Bus 24, C22, C82, R2, R3. **Open** Guided tours organised by Itinera (081 664 545/347 634 1483/www.itineranapoli.com) 9am-7pm daily. **Admission** €5. **Map** p315 1A.
The original San Carlo theatre was built in 1737 in just eight months to a design by Giovanni Medrano. It was rebuilt in less than a year after it burned down in 1816. Second in prestige only to Milan's La Scala, the San Carlo has lavish decor with acres of red velvet and intricate gilded stucco moulding, plus an unusual revolving clock in the vault of the proscenium arch. A century and a half ago, foreign tourists complained of the noise level during performances; in the boxes, the local aristocracy would chat, eat meals and play cards. Twenty-minute guided tours are available daily, subject to rehearsals and performances. Alternatively, put on your poshest togs and catch a performance.

Santa Lucia

Via Chiatamone and via Santa Lucia wind through Santa Lucia, where the rambling backstreets of the old fishermen's quarter, the **Pallonetto**, rise up towards Pizzofalcone. To the left of the altar in the tiny church of **Santa Maria della Catena** at via Santa Lucia 102 (open 8-11am Mon, Tue, Thur-Sat; 10am-noon Sun) is the tomb of Francesco Caracciolo, one of the leaders of the Parthenopean Republic (*see p10*); Caracciolo was hanged on the orders of Admiral Nelson (*see p20* **William, Emma… & Horatio**).

The church of **Santa Lucia** (open 7am-noon, 5-8pm Mon-Sat; 7.30am-1pm, 5.30-8pm Sun) was rebuilt after its 19th-century predecessor was bombed during World War II; a church has stood on the site since the ninth century.

The Port & University

Congestion, connections and an ancient seat of learning.

It is ironic that it was the brutal, arrow-straight corso Umberto I, built in 1884 in an attempt to isolate the city from the cholera-ridden port, that has ultimately threatened to engulf the rest of the city in traffic. All day long cars, buses and vans thrash for space along this dangerous four-lane highway – from the functional 1960s Stazione Centrale railway station, past the resurrected port area and the ancient university. The situation is not likely to improve until the completion of the new underground metro system some years down the line, which will link the station area to the rest of the city and thus relieve much of the pressure on the city's road network.

Corso Umberto & the Università

Corso Umberto I (also known as *il Rettifilo*) runs from piazza Garibaldi to piazza Bovio. The former is a vast, rectangular and rather sleazy car and bus interchange – also home to the Stazione Centrale train station – with an early 20th-century monument to Giuseppe Garibaldi (*see p20*). Piazza Bovio is usually the pretty home to the fine **Fontana di Nettuno** (*see p65*), built in the late 16th century by several artists, including Domenico Fontana and Pietro Bernini, and placed here in 1889. But at the moment the whole piazza, like much of Naples, is a building site for the new underground line, and there's not much to see.

At first glance, corso Umberto seems little more than an array of tacky clothes shops and street vendors, but there's plenty to see along the way: from the university area at the piazza Bovio end of the street, to the ill-famed Forcella district and the extraordinarily colourful street market around the Porta Nolana by the station.

The **Università di Napoli Federico II** was founded in 1224. Its faculties (including law, which has 40,000 registered students) are now scattered around the city, but the nucleus is still in the area north of piazza Bovio. Also here is the headquarters of the 16th-century **Università Orientale**, so-called because its first students came from China. Around the two universities is a host of churches – many of them perpetually closed for renovation – and plenty of splendid *palazzi*, some of them, alas, quite derelict.

On via Monteoliveto, north-west of piazza Bovio, **Palazzo Gravina** (No.3; open during university term) is now the architecture faculty; its 16th-century façade was restored after being destroyed by Swiss troops trying to flush out Italian patriots in 1848. Next to the hideously busy crossroads overlooked by the Questura (police station), **via Santa Maria La Nova** leads to the church of the same name (closed indefinitely for restoration). Its Renaissance façade matches that of Palazzo Gravina; its cloister can be seen at No.43.

Via Santa Maria La Nova continues to piazzetta Monticelli, where the petite early

On the waterfront: Naples' **Port**.

Santissima Annuziata's bell towers.
See p70.

15th-century **Palazzo Penna** (No.11; not open to the public) is one of Naples' few surviving houses from that era.

In largo San Giovanni Maggiore, the small chapel of **San Giovanni Pappacoda** has a splendid early 15th-century ogival portal, a rare example of Gothic decoration in Naples. The church is now deconsecrated and only opens for university functions. Opposite stands **Palazzo Giusso** (No.30; open during university term), seat of the Università Orientale. The church of **San Giovanni Maggiore** (No.29; closed indefinitely for restoration) was built over the ruins of a pagan temple in the fourth century, then rebuilt in the 17th and 18th centuries.

The main entrance to the Università di Napoli is on corso Umberto, but a side entrance in via Mezzocannone gives easier access to the fascinating **Centro Musei Scienze Naturali** (see below).

Through the university buildings in via Paladino, the church of **Gesù Vecchio** (No.38; open 7am-noon, 4-6pm Mon-Sat; 7am-noon Sun) dates from the late 16th century.

In piazza Grande Archivio, the **Archivio di Stato** (No.5) was once the convent of the adjoining church of **Santi Severino e Sossio** (which is closed indefinitely for restoration).

Near the station, the 13th-century church of **San Pietro ad Aram** (see below) stands guard over the notorious **Forcella** district. More than any other downtown area, Forcella lives up to the stereotype of lowlife Naples: racketeering, rip-off joints, petty crime, legendary cases of gangland honour and solidarity, but above all a long history of crushing poverty and neglect. Here, unwanted children, or those their parents could not afford to care for, ended up in the infamous wheel of the foundling hospital beside the church of **Santissima Annunziata** (see p70), and women were saved in the convent of **Santa Maria Egiziaca** (via Egiziaca a Forcella 31; now the Ascalesi Hospital). Even today, there's often a sense of uneasy tension on the streets around here.

Centro Musei Scienze Naturali

Via Mezzocannone 8 (081 253 7516/www.musei. unina.it). Bus 14, CD, E1, R2. **Open** 9am-1.30pm, 3-5pm Mon, Thur; 9am-1.30pm Tue, Wed, Fri; 9am-1pm Sat, Sun. Closed Aug. **Admission** *Each museum* €1.50, €4.50 family ticket. *All museums* €3.50. **No credit cards. Map** p311 3B.

These four delightful little museums – known collectively as the Centro Musei Scienze Naturali – are all in and around the large rambling Università di Napoli Federico II. Although the main entrance is on corso Umberto, the easiest access to the museums is from via Mezzocannone. The four museums (in order of appearance) are: the splendid Mineralogy and Geology Museum; the refurbished Anthropology Museum (on the first floor across the courtyard); the Zoology Museum (kids love this one); and the Palaeontology Museum, in the magnificent ex-Basilian convent and cloisters (largo San Marcellino).

San Pietro ad Aram

Corso Umberto I 292 (081 286 411). Metro Garibaldi/bus R2/tram 1. **Open** *Church* 7-11.30am, 5-7pm Mon-Sat; 7am-1pm, 5-7pm Sun. Crypt closed indefinitely for restoration. **Map** p311 3C.

In the first century AD, the sea reached almost to the current site of the Stazione Centrale, lapping against what would later become the huge estates of the convent of San Pietro ad Aram. It was here, according to local tradition, that St Peter was driven ashore by a storm that stopped him from reaching Pozzuoli in AD 44. Undaunted, Peter seized the

Santa Maria del Carmine.

Foundling wheels are by no means unique to Naples, and were once common throughout Italy and Spain. Women would place their unwanted newborn babies here and, at least in Naples, there was never a shortage of childless or good Christian couples to adopt them. Astonishingly, this particular wheel remained in use until the 1980s. The wheel (*ruota*) is not a tourist attraction for Neapolitans. It's a reminder of very recent, very harsh times; don't mistake the stoicism with which this symbol is borne for indifference.

On the waterfront

On the southern side of corso Umberto, via Nolana leads to **Porta Nolana**. Just before this graceful 15th-century city gate (the Circumvesuviana railway station is beyond), the whole world explodes into a seething mass of colour and smells as you enter **via Supramuro**, the length of which is occupied by the most vibrant and chaotic street market in Europe. Open Monday to Saturday (mornings only), it has produce and fish spilling out of shops and stalls, as well as stores dealing in specialist merchandise such as leather or fabrics.

Via Marina (also known simply as La Marina) cuts along the port past piazza del Mercato. Now a massive car park, the piazza lives up to its name, with shops selling cheap toys, cheap furniture, cheap mattresses, cheap clothes and cheap underwear. The southern prospect over the sea is obstructed by a hideous modern construction; there is little to indicate that this was the site of the public burning, hanging and beheading of wrong-doers down the ages, including King Corradino of Swabia in 1268 and the leaders of the Parthenopean Republic (*see* p10) in 1799. But it is. The executions took place beside the easternmost obelisk, and the names of the Parthenopean leaders are listed in sombre fashion just inside the church of **Santa Maria del Carmine** in the adjacent piazza of the same name. Traffic streams to and from the motorway exit past the two remaining piers of the 14th-century **Porta del Carmine** gate (white with black piperno stone highlights) and the two towers from the same period – all that's left of the fifth castle in Naples' medieval defence system. The rest was demolished in 1906.

Naples' waterfront was subjected to heavy bombardment during World War II, and only two splendid and little-known churches – **Sant' Eligio** and **San Giovanni a Mare** (for both, *see* p71) – remain amid the juxtaposition of derelict, ramshackle structures and new office blocks.

Off via Marina in via Porta di Massa, the Faculty of Letters occupies the ex-convent of **San Pietro Martire** (open during university term), with its fine cloisters and church. Built in the late 13th century as a bulwark against

opportunity to convert Asprenus (who became the first bishop of Naples) and Candida, both of whom were eventually canonised. The first reliable written reports of a church on this spot were in 877. However, the so-called altar of St Peter that stands immediately to the left inside the church's vestibule dates back no further than the 12th century. Most of the building we see today was constructed in the second half of the 17th century on top of the early Christian basilica, which is now incorporated into the crypt, along with some catacombs.

Santissima Annunziata

Via dell'Annunziata 34 (081 2542 608). Metro Garibaldi/bus R2/tram 1. **Open** *Wheel* 8am-noon Mon-Sat. Closed 2 wks in August. **Admission** free. **Map** p311 3D.

The church owes its current appearance to a design by Carlo Vanvitelli in the mid 18th century. However, the whole Annunziata complex including the church dates back to the 14th century. The complex includes a fine courtyard and fountain, the revolving wheel for the acceptance of foundlings, and the adjoining orphanage (now a hospital) set up for their care. At 67m (235ft), the dome of the recently reopened church is one of the highest in the city. The main entrance to the old hospital is from via Annunziata, next to the church. Dominated by a large bell tower with a majolica clock by the same hand as the tiled courtyard in Santa Chiara (*see* p74), the entrance features a splendid carved marble portal (c1500) by Tommaso Malvito; in the apex, a loving yet unsentimental Madonna gathers children under her cloak. The fine wooden doors (by Belverte and Da Nola) are also from the early 16th century.

portside vice, the church was remodelled in the 18th century. The area south of corso Umberto, between piazza Bovio and piazza Nicola Amore, is known as **I quattro palazzi**, after its four fine fin-de-siècle buildings. Within this area, the **Borgo degli orefici** (goldsmiths' district) still features an age-old community of silversmiths and goldsmiths, and *orefice* (goldsmith) features often in street names.

Via Marina continues past the container port. Further west, opposite the 16th-century church of **Santa Maria di Portosalvo** (closed indefinitely), the Immacolatella quayside area – between the 18th-century **Capitaneria di Porto** (harbour master's office) and the fascist-era **Stazione Marittima** – has all been earmarked for redevelopment, but the area still lacks identity and remains a hotch-potch of lorry, bus and car parks, bollards and chains, makeshift ticket offices and swathes of tarmac. Thankfully, **Dolcezze Siciliane** (*see p129*), the tiny portside shop selling delicious Sicilian specialities off the Palermo ferry, is still standing safely inside the Ports's original Customs' area.

The ferry port facilities on the western **Molo Beverello** dock – once a decidedly seedy place – are now clean, sailing times are clearly indicated and there are a couple of fairly priced bars to hang out while you wait for your boat.

San Giovanni a Mare

Via San Giovanni Maggiore 8 (081 5538 429). Bus 14, CD, R2/tram 1. **Open** 9am-noon daily; afternoons by appointment. **Map** p311 3B.
So-called because the sea (*il mare*) used to wash up against its walls, this 12th-century building is the only surviving Norman church in Naples. The foundations of the original apse can now be viewed through glass at the junction of the nave and the transept (a 13th-century addition). The first side altar on the left – the one with an unusual cambered arch – contains a small photographic exhibition of restoration work recently carried out. If you can't find anyone to let you into the church, call at the Sant'Eligio (*see below*).

Sant'Eligio

Via Sant'Eligio (081 553 8429). Bus 14, R2, CD/tram 1. **Open** 8.30am-12.30pm Mon-Wed; 8.30am-12.30pm, 5-7pm Thur-Sat; 9.30am-1.30pm Sun. **Map** p313 1B.
This extraordinary 13th-century church was badly damaged in 1943, and restoration work uncovered much of the original building. Sant'Eligio was the first church built in Naples by the Angevin monarchs. The fine archway and bell tower are from the 15th century; the clock may date from the 16th century.

Santa Maria del Carmine

Piazza del Carmine 2 (081 201 196). Bus 14, CD, R2/tram 1. **Open** 7am-12.30pm, 5-7.30pm Mon-Sat; 6.30am-2pm, 5-7.30pm Sun. **Map** p313 1B.

San Giovanni a Mare.

Part of a complex including a convent (which can be visited by appointment), the Carmine has a colourful past and present. The pre-12th century church was rebuilt in the 13th century thanks to the mother of Corradino of Swabia, who was executed some years previously in the adjacent piazza Mercato. In return for a cash donation, the church allowed her to bury her son's ashes here. They are believed to be under, or in, the pedestal of the monument to Corradino in the transept, erected in 1847. One thing is sure: they aren't in the statue itself. SS agents sent by Hitler in 1943 searched in vain for the remains of that earlier German leader who failed to conquer Italy. Opposite the monument is the pulpit where Tommaso Aniello (aka Masaniello; *see p16*) delivered a fiery speech in 1647, calling on the people to rise up against the Spanish occupiers. He was later murdered in the convent and buried in an unidentified tomb here. Many notables from the failed 1799 revolution also lie here.

Tradition has it that during a siege in 1439, a cannonball pierced the wall of the church and headed straight for the 14th-century wooden crucifix in a tabernacle under the transept arch. The statue's head miraculously ducked, the eyes closed and the hair (which had previously been brushed back) all fell on to one side. Impressed, King Alfonso ordered the shooting to stop, but his brother Pietro continued, only to be mortally wounded in the head a few minutes later. On conquering the city, Alfonso went to pay his respects to the image. Popular devotion focuses, however, on the 14th-century image of the Madonna della Bruna, behind the main altar, which has been associated with many miraculous events. Crowds flock to the church on 16 July, when the magnificent bell tower is lit up in a blaze of fireworks.

Centro Storico

Centuries of history line the Centro's ancient streets.

It's a paradox: those who live or work in the Centro storico (or even visit it as tourists) may pray for a day when something will be done to halt the decline into which this lovely old area is steadily sinking, but it is precisely that decline that makes the area what it is.

The Angevins concentrated their initial construction fervour here when they made Naples the capital of their realm in the 13th century, and soon huge churches soared above lowly houses. Today the area is thronged by bands of kids dodging the *liceo* (high school) in what appears to be mass truancy, and by tourists clambering amid stalls selling joss-sticks, second-hand books and religious articles, necks craning upwards towards the detail of decrepit *palazzi*. By night, the sounds and smells of southern Italian nightlife waft out of ventilation shafts. And if you happen to be here around Christmas time you'll find that the

A quiet corner...

crush is unbearable as locals flock to via San Gregorio Armeno to purchase figures for their nativity cribs (*see p80*).

The streets the Centro storico is built on form a regular grid based on the city's ancient Greek and Roman roads: three *decumani* (main roads) run arrow-straight east to west, intersected from north to south by *cardines*. The main street here – the ancient *decumanus inferior* at the heart of Greek and Roman Neapolis – is known as Spaccanapoli, and incorporates vie Benedetto Croce, San Biagio dei Librai and Vicaria Vecchia.

Spaccanapoli

Spaccanapoli runs straight through the heart of old Naples, the streets changing their name along its route. Because it divides the district in a long clean line it was given its collective name, which means 'splitting Naples'. Most of the Spaccanapoli is now pedestrianised, packed with tourists and students toing and frozing between historical sights and schools and university departments, and stopping along the way at its shops: bookshops and bookbinders; musical instrument stores (especially along via San Sebastiano, which runs up towards the Conservatory of San Pietro a Maiella); jewellers, and establishments selling religious articles, pictures and frames, fried food and souvenirs.

Towards the western end of Spaccanapoli, piazza del Gesù has a towering rococo obelisk, the **Guglia dell'Immacolata** (1747-50).

The piazza is surrounded by elegant *palazzi* (including the private **Palazzo Pignatelli di Monteleone** at calata Trinità Maggiore 53, where Edgar Degas was a frequent visitor) and is overlooked by the unusual façade of the church of the **Gesù Nuovo** (*see p74*) and the lopped-off bell tower of **Santa Chiara** (*see p74*).

The short stretch of Spaccanapoli called via Benedetto Croce, after the Neapolitan philosopher and historian (1866-1952), is crammed with prestigious *palazzi*. Croce's own home, **Palazzo Filomarino** (No.12) has two 14th-century arches walled into the left-hand staircase, while the portico in the courtyard is from the 16th century (the *portiere* is fierce but won't bite if you go in). The **Palazzo Carafa della Spina** (No.45) has an unusually high doorway from the late

Sightseeing

off a busy street: **Spaccanapoli**.

16th century; a pair of weather-beaten marble lions sit patiently in the smog (their blackened mouths were used to snuff out torches), and lively fauns frolic above the portal.

Work on the elaborate obelisk, the **Guglia di San Domenico**, in piazza San Domenico, was started in 1658 in thanks for the end of a plague epidemic, but only completed 99 years later. The piazza itself is dominated by several fine 16th- and 17th-century *palazzi* (none of which is open to the public), including the red-ochre **Palazzo Corigliano** (No.12), now owned by the university, **Palazzo Casacalenda** (No.16) and **Palazzo Sangro** (No.9), in addition to the 13th-century church of **San Domenico Maggiore** (*see p75*), erstwhile home of St Thomas Aquinas.

Before becoming via San Biagio dei Librai, Spaccanapoli crosses piazzetta Nilo, which contains the little church of **Sant'Angelo a Nilo**, which houses the only work by Donatello in Naples (*see below*). The statue in the small square by the church portrays the Nile god reclining. It dates from Roman times when worship of the Nile was commonly practised by the Egyptians who lived in this area.

Further down via San Biagio is **Palazzo Marigliano** (No.39), with a well-preserved and recently renovated façade from 1513, and a fine coat of arms; steps at the back of the courtyard lead to a small 'invisible' garden (open 10am-2pm Mon-Fri). At No.114, the **Monte di Pietà chapel** (open 9am-7pm Sat; 9am-2pm Sun) has statues of Safety and Charity by Pietro Bernini in the façade, and a 17th-century frescoed ceiling by Belisario Corenzio.

The massive bulk of the church of **San Giorgio Maggiore** (*see p75*), dates from the fourth century, and stands where Spaccanapoli crosses via Duomo. To the north on via Duomo is the **Museo Civico Filangieri** (*see below*), which has been closed for several years now for restoration. It holds an extensive collection of industrial and applied art, plus suits of armour, weapons and sculpture.

Around the museum, Spaccanapoli becomes via Vicaria Vecchia, and passes the pretty church of **Sant'Agrippino** (No.86; still closed following flood damage in 2001). It was almost totally destroyed during World War II, but the delicate, original 13th-century arches in the apse have been salvaged, and much of the furnishings of the utterly derelict church of **Santa Maria a Piazza** (via Forcella 12), which stands opposite, have been moved here, including the 13th-century crucifix. There's also a fine carved wooden door from the late 15th century inside.

In an ignobly litter-strewn pit at the centre of nearby piazza Calenda you'll find a chunk of ancient Greek city wall.

Gesù Nuovo

Piazza Gesù Nuovo 2 (081 551 8613). Metro Montesanto or Dante/bus E1, R1. **Open** 7am-12.30pm, 4-7pm Mon-Sat; 7am-1.30pm, 4-7pm Sun. **Map** p311 2A.

The façade of this extraordinary church is not that of a church at all. The diamond-shaped ashlar work dates back to a 1470 palazzo. It was only transformed into a church for the Jesuit order (by architect Giuseppe Valeriani) at the end of the 16th century. The portals, windows and external decorations date from the conversion. Inside is a stupefying barrel-vaulted ceiling, and a dome that has been rebuilt several times. The inner façade has a large fresco (1725) by Francesco Solimena, while the ceilings and walls are a treasury of frescos and paintings, with work by Luca Giordano and Giuseppe Ribera, and marble statues by Cosimo Fanzago.

A large, busy room on the right-hand side of the church is dedicated to Giuseppe Moscati. The ex-votos covering the chapel walls give an indication of local faith in the doctor's miracle-working abilities. *See p81* **The good doctor**.

Museo Civico Filangieri

Via del Duomo 288A (081 203 175). **Bus** E1, R2. **Closed** for restoration and reorganisation as this guide went to press. **Map** p311 1C-2C.

Founded in 1882 by Prince Gaetano Filangieri, this museum was designed for students of industrial design to observe and copy outstanding examples from the fine and applied arts. It contains more than 3,000 items, ranging from suits of armour and weapons to paintings and sculptures from the 14th to the 19th centuries, majolica and chinaware, coins and crib figures. The glass-ceilinged main hall, the Sala Agata, with its mezzanine wooden-balustraded walkway, is a fine exhibit in itself. The 15th-century Palazzo Cuomo, which houses the museum, was dismantled in the 19th century and rebuilt 20m (70ft) further back to allow for road widening.

Sant'Angelo a Nilo

Piazzetta Nilo (081 420 1222). Metro Montesanto or Dante/bus E1. **Open** 9am-1pm, 4-6pm Mon-Sat; 9am-1pm Sun. **Map** p311 2B.

Also known as the Cappella Brancaccio on account of its association with the family of that name, this church contains the fine marble tomb (1426) of Cardinal Rinaldo Brancaccio in a chapel to the right of the altar; it was made in Pisa, and Donatello had a hand in its creation. The fine bas-relief portraying the Assumption on the front of the tomb, the cardinal's head and the right-hand caryatid (a column shaped like a person) are the only works by the Tuscan artist in Naples, although it is unlikely he actually came here. There's a delicate bell tower, but it's difficult to see.

Santa Chiara

Via Benedetto Croce (church 081 552 6280/museum 081 552 1597/www.oltreilchiostro.org). Metro Dante or Montesanto/bus E1. **Open** *Church* 8am-12.30pm,

4.30-7.30pm daily. *Museum & cloister* 9.30am-1pm, 2.30-5.30pm Mon-Sat; 9.30-1pm Sun. **Admission** *Church* free. *Museum & cloister* €4. **Credit** AmEx, MC, V. **Map** p311 2A.

The church and convent of Santa Chiara was built for Robert of Anjou's wife, Sancia, in the early 14th century, and has always been a favourite with local aristocracy. Its original Gothic features were hidden by baroque restructuring in the mid 18th century. A direct hit in an air raid in August 1943 started a fire that raged for six days, destroying everything but the four walls of the main church. During the 1950s, a rose window, the portal, the chapel arches and high mullion windows, exterior flying buttresses and some altars and shrines were salvaged or faithfully copied, and the church was rebuilt along its original Gothic lines. Of the impressive bell tower, set aside from the church, only the base is original. To the left of the church, a door leads into the tiled cloister, a haven of baroque peace. Beyond the cloister, a museum has bits and pieces salvaged from the bomb attack, including some superb 14th-century friezes, bas-reliefs and busts, plus an archaeological area revealing a gymnasium and baths from the old Roman city.

San Domenico Maggiore

Vico San Domenico Maggiore 18/piazza San Domenico Maggiore 8A (081 459 298). Metro Dante/bus E1.
Open 8.30am-noon, 4.30-7pm daily. **Map** p311 2B.
This large castellated building has an extraordinary rear entrance leading up from the piazza by means of a curved double flight of marble steps

Nile reclining, piazzetta Nilo. *See p74.*

under the main altar, but is best entered from the side street, vico San Domenico. There the porticoed entrance with pointed arch dates from the late 13th century when the church was built, incorporating the pre-existing church of Sant'Angelo a Morfisa (right of the altar, closed to the public). The church has been much altered over the centuries. The chapels include some fine works of art: marble tombstones from the 13th century (first chapel on right); 14th-century frescos by the great and unjustly neglected Roman artist Pietro Cavallino (second on right); and a couple of fine paintings by Mattia Preti (fourth on right).

The Neapolitan headquarters of the Dominican order, the monastery hosted the hermeticist philosopher Giordano Bruno (burnt at the stake for heresy in Rome in 1600), who studied here, and St Thomas Aquinas, who stayed in the latter part of the 13th century and to whom the sixth chapel on the right is dedicated. In that chapel is a 13th-century Crucifixion scene in a glass case over the altar; the figure of Jesus is reputed to have spoken temptingly to Thomas, offering him anything he wanted in return for the nice things the saint had written about Him. At which Thomas replied, 'Nothing, if not You'.

The large, luminous sacristy has a fresco by Francesco Solimena on the ceiling and a bizarre collection of coffins; their contents include the decapitated body of a victim of the infamous barons' conspiracy of 1486.

San Giorgio Maggiore

Via del Duomo 237A (081 287 932). Bus E1, R1.
Open 8.30am-noon, 5-7pm Mon-Sat; 8.30am-1pm Sun. **Map** p311 1C-2C.
The original basilica was built in the fourth century by St Severus (364-410) when this area of Naples was occupied by families driven out of their homes around Vesuvius by the AD 79 eruption. Severus's relics are now behind the altar; his splendid marble throne is on the right of the main aisle. The vestibule, with its three Byzantine-Roman arches (at the entrance in piazzetta Crocelle ai Mannesi), was the apse of the original basilica, and the only bit of it to have survived an earthquake in 1640. Subsequently, architect Cosimo Fanzago rotated the floorplan by 180°, placing the 17th-century apse and main altar at the opposite end of the church.

The city walls

Considering the sprawling chaos of modern Naples, it is hard to believe that the city remained neatly confined within its walls from its Greek beginnings until the middle of the 17th century. But those city limits around the edges of the Centro storico remained more or less unchanged for 2,000 years. During the early 15th century, the Aragonese King Ferdinand I had them extended for a few hundred extra metres. In the 16th century, Spanish viceroy Don

Pedro de Toledo beefed up defences still further by stringing walls or ditches between the city's five castles: Carmine (now demolished), Capuano, Sant'Elmo, Nuovo and dell'Ovo.

A few minutes' walk from the eastern end of Spaccanapoli, the impressive **Porta Capuana** gate, with its carved marble triumphal arch and dark towers, dates from 1484. The stretch of wall there dates from Ferdinand's extension of the fortifications.

In nearby piazza de Nicola, **Castel Capuano** (closed to the public) owes its Renaissance appearance to modifications carried out in the early 16th century, when it was changed from palace to law court, but it was actually built in the late 12th century. The façade of this irregularly shaped building contains striking decorative elements in white plaster contrasting with severe black piperno stone. Between castle and gate is the early 16th-century church of **Santa Caterina a Formello** (open 8.30am-7.30pm Mon-Sat; 8.30am-1pm Sun), which many consider to be one of the most beautiful Renaissance churches in Naples.

The street that heads north-east from the church, via Carbonara, got its name because this was once where the city's rubbish was burnt; ten minutes up the street on the right is the rambling, beautiful complex of **San Giovanni a Carbonara**, with its carved treasures (*see below*).

San Giovanni a Carbonara

Via Carbonara 5 (081 295 873). Metro Cavour or Museo/bus 110, E1. **Open** 9.30am-1pm Mon-Sat. **Map** p311 2D.

This 14th-century church stands at the top of a dramatic flight of steps (added in 1707 by Ferdinando Sanfelice) above the modern church of the same name. At the head of the staircase, the chapel of Santa Monica (closed to the public) has a marble Gothic portal. The entrance to the church is to the left of this portal. The church's sculptures are numerous and magnificent. The monument and tomb of King Ladislas (1428) behind the main altar is 18m (63ft) high, and shows Renaissance touches in its mainly Gothic design. The round chapel behind the altar has a complex majolica-tiled floor, 15th-century frescos portraying the lives of the hermits, and the tomb of Gianni Caracciolo (1433), the much-hated lover of Ladislas' sister and successor, Queen Joan II. The whole complex suffered severely in the air raids of August 1943.

Via dei Tribunali

Via dei Tribunali, the *decumanus maior* of Greek Neapolis, has maintained its distinctly commercial flavour intact since ancient times, and is lined with small shops and street markets. The traffic on this street is non-stop and can be infuriating.

At the eastern end of via dei Tribunali, piazza Riario Sforza is home to the monumental **Guglia di San Gennaro**,

San Giovanni a Carbonara.

Monuments in May

Once a year, Naples' hidden historic gems open their doors to public gaze. Maggio dei Monumenti is a glorious cultural beanfeast, still growing in stature, organisational finesse and international standing, despite the goofy-sounding 'themes' that it has been saddled with in recent years.

It all began in 1994, when Naples' new mayor Antonio Bassolino started giving the city a much-needed shake-up, and the term 'Neapolitan Renaissance' was coined. Secondary schools were encouraged to 'adopt' abandoned monuments. There were certainly plenty to choose from; *palazzi*, churches and miscellaneous sites galore were taken in hand by kids who researched their history, cleaned them up, produced information handouts and showed guests around during open days, which were concentrated in May.

The idea took off, and was institutionalised as Maggio dei Monumenti (Monuments in May) and it has become larger and more important over the years. Now even the most reluctant doors are prised open for rare chances to view the city's fascinating, little-known treasures.

From the last weekend in April until the first weekend in June, there are guided tours of monuments and districts, open days, concerts and exhibitions in venues all over the city. The only problem, for both visitors and tourists, is finding up-to-the moment information on the packed programme (most events are at weekends) with sufficient notice to be able to plan your holiday carefully. The city council's website www.comune.napoli.it is a good place to start. Alternatively try Naples' City Council Information Office (081 247 1123).

inaugurated in 1660 when the residents believed that a prompt intervention by the city's patron saint had saved Naples from destruction by an eruption of Vesuvius in 1631. Opposite the monument, the 17th-century church of the **Pio Monte della Misericordia** contains Caravaggio's spellbinding *Seven Acts of Mercy* (1607). In the church's *pinacoteca* (gallery) next door is a small collection, including works by Giuseppe Ribera and Luca Giordano. From here, you cannot miss the **Duomo** (*see p79*), Naples' cathedral. To reach the main entrance turn down via Duomo.

Via dei Tribunali continues up the hill past the white façade of the early 17th-century church of the Girolamini (closed for restoration), attached to the **Pinacoteca** of the same name with its tiny but lovely collection of religious paintings (*see p80*). Across from the Pinacoteca, grimy but timeless plaster statues look down from above the portal of the derelict church of **Santa Maria della Colonna** (No.283; closed for restoration); as they have for nearly 200 years. Beyond, the medieval church of **San Lorenzo Maggiore** (*see p80*) stands. The church lies above one of the most extraordinary archaeological sites in the region, where ancient Naples' streets can be seen in amazing detail.

If you turn left off via dei Tribunali on to via **San Gregorio Armeno** you'll soon find the 16th-century church of the same name where more miracles, it is said, regularly occur (*see p80*). As you'll surely notice, Via San Gregorio

is famous for its Christmas nativity scenes and for selling the necessary accessories for this much beloved Neapolitan artform (*see p140*). Even in midsummer, the unseasonal wares pour out of shops and on to the narrow street, and crowds line up via to buy.

Back on via dei Tribunali, the imposing church of **San Paolo Maggiore** (*see p82*) stands on piazza San Gaetano, which was the *agorà*, and later the forum, of the ancient city. Beside the church is the entrance to the fourth-century BC underground **Acqueduct** (*see p78*).

At No.339 is a palazzo (not open to the public) built in the 13th century for Philip of Anjou; it has its original, sturdy four-span portico and a 13th-century portal. Opposite is the church of **Santa Maria del Purgatorio ad Arco** (*see p81*), famed for its skeletal proclivities. Not far away, the baroque **Santa Maria Maggiore** (closed to the public) has a pretty Romanesque bell tower known as 'the Pietrasanta', probably left from an earlier church. The adjacent **Cappella Pontano** is a Renaissance work from 1492, though the interior is the result of a baroque makeover (open 9am-1pm Monday to Saturday).

Nearby is the small and bare 16th-century church of the **Croce di Lucca** (open 9am-1pm Mon-Sat), which was saved from demolition by Benedetto Croce, when a university wanted to knock it down to make room for more buildings. It still bears an unusual fascist emblem on one external wall.

Just beyond the Croce, vico San Domenico Maggiore then via Francesco de Sanctis lead to the extraordinary funerary chapel, **Cappella Sansevero** (*see below*) with creepy well-preserved corpses.

Back on via dei Tribunali, the splendid church of **San Pietro a Maiella** stands next to the music school, the **Conservatorio**, illustrious producer over the years of such musicians as Scarlatti and Pergolesi.

Finally, the street reaches piazza Bellini, at the centre of which are scant remains of fourth-century BC Greek city walls.

Acqueduct

Piazza San Gaetano 68 (081 296 944/368 354 0585/www.napolisotterranea.org). Metro Dante or Montesanto/bus E1. **Open** guided tours every 2hrs noon-4pm Mon-Fri; 10am-6pm Sat, Sun. **Admission** €9.30. **No credit cards**. **Map** p311 2C.

Wandering 35m (123ft) below street level, these tunnels, aqueducts and chambers date back to the dawn of the Greek city of Neapolis in the fourth century BC. They were gradually incorporated into Naples' labyrinthine water supply system, and remained in use until the cholera epidemic of 1884. The guided tour covers only 1km (0.6 miles) of the almost 450km (270 miles) of tunnels, but lasts about 90 minutes. The group that oversees the site also conducts tours of the recently excavated Roman theatre around the corner in via Cinque Santi – these are included in the price of a tour of the acqueduct.

Cappella Sansevero

Via Francesco de Sanctis 19 (081 551 8470). Metro Dante or Montesanto/bus E1. **Open** *Nov-Apr* 10am-4.40pm Mon, Wed-Sat; 10am-1pm Sun. *May-Oct* 10am-5.40pm Mon, Wed-Sat; 10am-1pm Sun. **Admission** €5. **No credit cards**. **Map** p311 1C.

Saints alive Blood rites

Naples's former mayor Antonio Bassolino once said that the city's patron saint, San Gennaro, should be called 'the mayor of saints' because he had presided over all the city's most important moments. Credited with halting eruptions of Vesuvius and keeping calamities, wars and epidemics at bay, San Gennaro has been an integral part of Neapolitan life, and the object of devotion, down the ages. The Bourbons even awarded him the title of 'captain general' of their army. Naples felt the tumult of the 1960s Second Vatican Council in a very particular way: the Council decided to downgrade Gennaro to a local cult, causing an uproar of protest in the city (graffiti appeared with slogans like '*San Gennaro, futtenne!*' (San Gennaro, don't give a damn!). He was officially reinstated to his position as patron saint by Pope John Paul II in 1980.

The saint met his glorious end in 305, when he was beheaded in the Solfatara after surviving another gruesome attempt to kill him (various accounts have him thrown to the lions, incinerated in a fiery furnace or dragged in chains from Nola to Pozzuoli). His blood was scooped up by his far-sighted nanny Eusebia (other versions of the story simply say a pious old woman) and brought to what was to become the catacombs of San Gennaro (*see p90*). About a century later, the first miraculous liquefaction of Gennaro's dried blood is said to have taken place, although the first official records of the occurrence date back only as far as 1389.

Gennaro's blood bubbles into action in a Duomo chapel three times a year: on the Saturday before the first Sunday in May, on 19 September (his feast day) and on 16 December, each time egged on by hysterical crowds. The September feast day is a real event, covered by national media and attended by dignitaries. A group of women called the *parenti di San Gennaro* (relatives of San Gennaro) accompany the ritual with prayers and chants. The liquefaction is signalled with a white handkerchief.

It usually takes two minutes to an hour for the blood to liquefy, and the amount of time it takes is considered a portent of what lies in store for Naples, its citizens and its football team over the following 12 months. The longer it takes, the more likely the city is to be stricken by disaster. The phials and sumptuous bust of the saint containing bits of what is said to be his skull are exposed for the eight days following the liquefaction, then locked away again.

The liquefaction of saintly blood is something of a Neapolitan theme. Santa Patrizia and San Giovanni Battista both go liquid in **San Gregorio Armeno** (*see p80*). And various other saints liquefy too, or have liquefied in the past. Not for nothing is Naples known as *urbs sanguinum* (city of blood). Neapolitans are generally pretty sceptical about saintly blood, but there's a great affection for the rituals. In any case, why take chances? 'It's not true,' they'll tell you. 'But I believe it anyway.'

Ceiling at the **Duomo**.

The funerary chapel of the Di Sangro family was built in 1590, but took on its current appearance in 1749-66 thanks to the eccentric prince of Sansevero, Raimondo di Sangro, who hired the most important sculptors of the day to decorate it. The high altar is carved in accordance with the then fashionable 'picture hewn out of stone' criteria; the statues have titles like *Domination of Self-will, The Pleasures of Marriage* and *Shyness*. The *Veiled Christ* (1753), by Giuseppe Sammartino, is uncanny in its realism; so impressed was neo-classical sculptor Antonio Canova when he visited the chapel that he tried to purchase the statue. The extraordinary figures in the crypt are not just uncanny: they're downright macabre. Obsessed with embalming, the pseudo-scientist prince carried out experiments on his defunct domestics, injecting their bodies with chemical substances to preserve their inner organs. Local lore has it that they were not always dead when this operation took place.

Duomo

Via del Duomo 147 (081 449 097/www.duomodi napoli.com). Bus E1, R2. **Open** *Church* 8am-12.30pm, 4.30-7pm Mon-Sat; 8am-1.30pm, 5-7.30pm Sun. *Archaeological area & baptistry* 9am-noon, 4.30-6.30pm Mon-Sat; 8.30am-1pm Sun. **Admission** *Church* free. *Archaeological area & baptistry* €3. **No credit cards. Map** p311 1C-2C.

Naples' cathedral can date it's history back to the fourth century when the basilica of Santa Restituta was founded here. At the end of the fifth century the cathedral of Santa Stefania was constructed perpendicular to the original basilica, and at the end of the 13th century the current Duomo was built over Santa Stefania, incorporating Santa Restituta as a side chapel. The bland 19th-century façade (the three portals are from 1407) remains hidden from view in an unprepossessing side street, so little prepares the visitor for the splendours within. The gloom of the 100m-long (328ft) Latin-cross interior fails to conceal the fine gilt coffered ceiling (1621) and the paintings between the windows and arches, by Luca Giordano and his school.

The large chapel on the right is the Cappella di San Gennaro, also known as Il Tesoro. It contains a large number of bronze and silver statues of saints associated with Naples' patron saint, Gennaro; many of them are kept in the sacristy (which is closed to the public) and only put on display here during May and September. The most famous of these is a 14th-century French silver bust and two vials, kept in a strongbox behind the altar. The bust contains Gennaro's skull, while the vials hold his congealed blood. In an annual miracle, the blood in the vials liquefies on Gennaro's feast day, 19 September (*see p78* **Blood rites**).

The chapel has a magnificent gilded bronze gate by Cosimo Fanzago (1668) and fine frescos by Domenichino (1631-43) showing miraculous episodes from the saint's life. San Gennaro emerges unscathed from a fiery furnace in a painting (1647) by Giuseppe Ribera above the right-hand altar.

Back in the main church, to the right of the high altar, the chapel of Sant'Aspreno and the Minutolo family chapel have original Gothic decorations. In the magnificent marble late 16th-century *succorpo* or *confessio* by Tommaso Malvito, beneath the altar, is a fine statue of a kneeling Cardinal Carafa and an altar with urn containing more of San Gennaro's bones. On the left side of the nave is the entrance to the fourth-century church of Santa Restituta (Naples' oldest remaining basilica) and the way in to the archaeological area and baptistry. The painting on the ceiling of Santa Restituta is attributed to Luca Giordano.

In the archaeological area Greek and Roman walls and columns still stand, along with early Christian mosaics, part of the original Santa Stefania cathedral and sections of Greek and Roman roads. The outstanding mosaic decorations on the baptistry ceiling date from the fifth century.

Pinacoteca Girolamini

Via del Duomo 142 (081 449 139). Bus E1, R2. **Open** 9.30am-12.50pm Mon-Sat. **Admission** free. **Map** p311 1C-2C.

From the entrance, a flight of steps leads up to the right and into a splendid cloister encompassing a forest of medlar and lemon trees. This small art gallery is one of Naples' most rewarding. The last two rooms (four and five) are the best, with Battista Caracciolo's superb chiaroscuro *Baptism of Christ* and other works by the same artist, plus Andrea Vaccaro's *Adoration of the Shepherds*, Luca Giordano's stirring *Mourning the Death of Christ*, and five paintings bearing all the typical grotesque features of Giuseppe Ribera's school. Along the side walls are works by Neapolitan stalwarts Paolo De Matteis and Francesco Solimena. The 60,000-volume library is renowned, but closed to all but the most insistent.

Pio Monte della Misericordia

Via dei Tribunali 253 (081 446 944/www.piomonte dellamisericordia.it). Metro Dante or Montesanto/bus E1. **Open** *Church* 9am-1pm Mon-Sat. *Gallery* 9am-2pm Tue, Thur, Sat. **Admission** €5. **No credit cards. Map** p311 2C-2D.

This splendid old art gallery has recently reopened to the public after a lengthy renovation and the restoration of some paintings. At last you can take in its 19th-century furniture and fine paintings, including delicate, satiny oil paintings by the 18th-century Francesco De Mura in the entrance, a St Anthony by Giuseppe Ribera, and a St Agnes by Massimo Stanzione in the Sala del Coretto. The attendant will provide you with a glossy catalogue of the main works of art, and leave you free to roam around on your own.

San Gregorio Armeno

Via San Gregorio Armeno 1 (081 552 0186). Metro Dante or Montesanto/bus E1. **Open** 9am-noon Mon, Wed-Fri; 9am-12.45pm Tue; 9am-12.30pm Sat, Sun. **Map** p311 2C.

Built on the site of a Roman temple to the fertility goddess Ceres, the 16th-century church of San Gregorio owes its unflagging popularity to the cult of St Patricia (*see p78* **Blood rites**), whose relics are conserved here and whose blood obligingly liquefies not only on her feast day (25 August),

when impressive celebrations are held, but also each Tuesday (hence the extended opening times). Patricia might well have been Naples' patron saint had the closed order of nuns that brought her relics from her native Constantinople in the eighth century not kept them shrouded in secrecy in their convent. After many years when only women were allowed to see the relics, they are now on view to all in a chapel to the right of the altar. The nuns also brought relics of San Gregorio, but somehow they never attracted as much attention.

The church is preceded by an unusual vestibule with pillars, and, once inside, the interior is rich with Neapolitan baroque. There are paintings and frescos by Luca Giordano and Paolo de Matteis, and a fine 17th-century marble altar by Dionisio Lazzari.

To reach the adjacent convent and cloisters, continue up via San Gregorio under the arch and turn left into via Maffei; press the intercom at the first gate on the left. Still visible by the entrance are the bronze drums through which supplies were passed to the nuns. The cloisters, with their orange trees and pretty fountain, are a haven of tranquillity (despite the primary school run by the sisters) and have a view over the church's majolica-tiled dome.

San Lorenzo Maggiore (church)

Via dei Tribunali 316 (081 211 0860/www.san lorenzomaggiorenapoli.it). Metro Dante or Montesanto/ bus E1. **Open** 9am-5pm Mon-Sat; 9am-1pm Sun. **Admission** €4. **No credit cards. Map** p311 2C-2D.

Returned more or less to its original 13th-century appearance by post-war restoration work, the vast, stern interior of this much-used church is in stark contrast to the tiny baroque façade (1742) designed by Ferdinando Sanfelice. It was here that Boccaccio fell in love with Fiammetta (as recounted in the *Decameron*); Petrarch stayed in the adjoining convent, which served as the headquarters of the Parthenopean government in 1799.

Some traces of the 17th- and 18th-century baroque treatment have remained inside, most noticeably in the third chapel on the right. A splendid Gothic triumphal arch leads into the delicate ribbed cross-vaulted apse. On the high altar is an early 16th-century relief sculpture of Naples by Giovanni da Nola. Sections of the original mosaic flooring are preserved under glass in the transept. The left-hand transept chapel has two paintings by Caravaggio's follower Mattia Preti.

San Lorenzo Maggiore (archaeological site)

Via dei Tribunali 316 (081 211 0860/www.sanlorenzo maggiorenapoli.it). Metro Dante or Montesanto/bus E1. **Open** 9am-5pm Mon-Sat; 9.30am-1.30pm Sun. Extended opening times May, Dec. **Admission** €4. **No credit cards. Map** p311 2C-2D.

This is undoubtedly one of the most extraordinary archaeological sites in the whole Naples region. Right at the heart of the most densely populated city in Europe, you can stand in silence and feel that you have been whisked back to Graeco-Roman Neapolis. In this confined area under San Lorenzo, excavation work is still under way, but what has been dug up so far are the streets of ancient Naples as they were 2,000 years ago: complete with a butcher's shop, a dyer's, a baker's and a beautiful porticoed arcade.

Santa Maria del Purgatorio ad Arco

Via dei Tribunali 39 (church 081 292 622/Hypogeum 081 296 944). Metro Dante or Montesanto/bus E1. **Open** *Church* 9am-1pm daily. *Hypogeum* 10am-1pm Sat or by appointment. **Admission** *Church* free. *Hypogeum* €2.60. **No credit cards. Map** p311 2C-2D. The three bronze skulls (a fourth was stolen in the 1950s) outside its railings, and its popular name, *cap'e morte* ('death's head'), are clues to why this 17th-century church has such a hold on Neapolitans. This was a centre of a death cult, in which people would adopt and look after the cache of skulls in the church's hypogeum (underground chamber). The Church has officially banned the practice, although it is said to live on. *See p88* **Skulls & bones**.

Inside the church, a winged skull and crossbones overlook the main altar. As well as several baroque paintings, there is a circular *Madonna and Child* attributed by some to Giotto. Beneath the church, the hypogeum still contains a pile of dusty bones. Barely visible through a grating is another area containing more bones.

San Paolo Maggiore

Via dei Tribunali (081 454 048). Metro Dante or Montesanto/bus E1. **Open** *Church* 9am-noon Mon-Sat. *Crypt* 9am-noon, 5-7pm daily. **Map** p311 2C-2D. This lofty magniloquent church, dating from the end of the 16th century, stands on the site of a Roman temple to Castor and Pollux. In front of the façade are two tall, white fluted pillars from the temple. The interior is notable for the colossal size of its Latin-cross

Sightseeing

Saints alive The good doctor

In a poor community, a doctor who cares enough to leave behind a promising academic career and treat the penniless for free, even surreptitiously leaving money under their pillows, will probably be popular. But few can expect to be the subject of such ardour as that felt for Dr Giuseppe Moscati. This good doctor died in 1927 and was canonised in record time in 1987 on a wave of popular support. His story is told in the **Gesù Nuovo** church (*see p74*), where his body is kept under the altar in the Capella della Visitazione and a larger than life bronze statue is an object of devotion (devotees like to rub his hands). Back rooms at the church are devoted to a large collection of ex votos – thousands of little heads, legs, hands, most made in silver, representing individual cures. Many of these come with a thank-you note, often recounting the story of the illness and its resolution in intricate and deferential detail. Two other rooms have reconstructions of Moscati's home and surgery, complete with the saint's own furniture, behind glass panels. Glass cases display memorabilia including such earthly trifles as the doctor's train tickets. Beside the entrance to the display rooms is the shell of a World War II bomb, which, legend has it, landed beside the altar, near Moscati's body (which was brought here from the Poggioreale cemetery in 1930), cracked open, but did not explode.

Grassroots support is important but it doesn't make anyone a saint. For that, the Vatican and its Congregation for the

Causes of Saints need proof in the form of two certified miracles. Moscati's are the healing of a prison guard deemed incurable (the guard's relatives prayed to Moscati, the guard saw the saint in his dreams and the next day he had got over his illness) and the curing of a man with terminal meningitis. For more tales of Moscati's accomplishments see www.gesuiti.it/moscati.

interior, while the sacristy has fine frescos by Francesco de Maria. The adjoining ex-convent at via San Paolo 14 is now an archive containing legal documents from the 15th century onwards.

San Pietro a Maiella

Piazza Luigi Miraglia 393 (081 459 008). Metro Dante or Montesanto/bus R1, R4. **Open** *7.30am-noon, 5.30-7pm Mon-Sat; 8.30am-1pm Sun.* **Map** p311 2B.
Approached from via dei Tribunali, San Pietro looks for all the world like an English country church, with its cusp-shaped spire of tufa stone. Dating from the early 14th century, the interior has many of its original Angevin features. There's a range of round and pointed arches, in stark contrast to the elaborate coffered ceiling adorned with paintings (1656-61) by Mattia Preti and the other lavish works of art, including a fine Madonna Appearing to Celestinus V by Massimo Stanzione in the fourth chapel on the right. Note that, despite the official opening hours, the church is generally closed on August afternoons.

The *decumanus superior*

The third ancient *decumanus* runs parallel with, and north of, via dei Tribunali, starting opposite the church of **San Giovanni a Carbonara** (*see p76*) at via Santa Sofia. It passes the towering church of the **Santissimi Apostoli** (open 9am-1pm, 4.30-7.30pm Mon-Sat; 9am-1.30pm Sun), believed to have been built over a Roman temple to Mercury. The street then changes name to via dei Santissimi Apostoli, passing the baroque church of **Santa Maria Donnaregina** (*see below*). Behind the 17th-century church, up vico Donnaregina, is the original 14th-century church of the same name.

After the church, the street changes its name to via dell'Anticaglia, and if you follow it a brief distance you'll reach two Roman brick archways that used to join a large theatre on the south of the street to baths on the north.

Santa Maria Donnaregina

Vico Donnaregina 26 (tel/fax 081 299 101). *Bus E1.* **Open** *by appointment only; fax a request.* **Map** p311 1D.
A 17th-century portal leads through a dainty porticoed cloister from the same period. On the left is the door to the deconsecrated 14th-century church. It was abandoned from the 1600s to the 1850s, eclipsed by the 17th-century church next door, which probably saved the building from a baroque makeover.

Inside the older building the bare interior has fan-vaults which, like the walls, still bear traces of 14th-century Giotto-style frescos. Tino da Camaino's magnificent marble tomb of Queen Mary of Hungary (1323) is against the left-hand wall. From the altar steps, looking up and back, the nuns' choir with its coffered ceiling and stunning 14th-century frescos by Pietro Cavallino is visible above. Depicting biblical scenes, saints and contemporary nobles, these are the most complete frescoes of their age in Naples.

From 1924 to 1925 the rear wall of the newer building, which had consumed the apse of the old church, was placed on rollers and moved 5m (16ft) back, creating the space between the two churches and revealing the frescos. The old church is home to Naples University's architectural restoration department, and is unofficially open for visits from around 9am to 12.30pm from January to June. To be sure of getting inside, however, fax the number given above at least a week in advance.

Via Toledo & La Sanità

Smart shopping abuts the crowded Quartieri.

Chaotic yet captivating. **Quartieri spagnoli**.

Via Toledo and via Foria run along two borders of the Centro storico, converging at the Museo Nazionale Archeologico. Via Toledo, pedestrianised for much of its length, is generally considered the main street of a city that has no real centre. Its flashy shops and banks mask the forlorn urban reality of the adjacent Quartieri spagnoli. Along its length an astonishing assortment of characters – from bankers to beggars – stroll or struggle their way down the *palazzo*-lined route.

Both streets have recently attracted major investment as part of the renovation of the city centre. Even the traffic-clogged via Foria – behind which lie the Sanità, Miracoli and Vergini districts – has begun to change. The new Museo and Piazza Cavour underground metro interchange and one end of the street, and the ongoing restoration of the massive Albergo dei Poveri at the other will ultimately force the rest of this long street to upgrade.

Via Toledo & the Quartieri spagnoli

Via Toledo was created in the early 16th century by Spanish viceroy, Don Pedro di Toledo (*see p16*), but was rechristened via Roma when Naples became part of the newly formed Italian republic in 1860. A recent return to its original name has led to confusion and you may hear it called both.

Forming a link between the Quartieri spagnoli and the old city to the east, via Toledo was lined with *palazzi* so elegant that it was lauded as one of Europe's most impressive streets by Grand Tourists. Where the homes of nobles and bankers once dazzled visitors, clothing retailers now hold sway. The *palazzi* are still there, though, visible above the shopfronts, and from *cortili* (courtyards) behind impressive portals leading off via Toledo.

Head to the southern stretch of via Toledo to experience the *struscio,* that particularly southern Italian phenomenon in which vast crowds of well-dressed people stroll and strut back and forth along the main drag. Neapolitans of all ages flock here to relax, chat, flirt, see and be seen. The pace is extremely slow – steer clear of via Toledo in the evening if you are in a hurry.

The street's pedestrian area ends at the junction with via Diaz. East along via Diaz, modern piazza Matteotti is dominated by the vast, semicircular and resoundingly fascist façade of the 1930s **Palazzo delle Poste** (post office), while towering over the square from behind the modern **Questura** (police headquarters) is the 30-storey **Jolly Hotel** (*see p45*), one of the most unpopular eyesores ever to receive planning permission from the now-discredited city council of the 1950s.

North of the post office in piazza Monteoliveto, the 15th-century church of **Sant'Anna dei Lombardi** (*see p84*) was originally part of a much larger convent complex. Some of the complex has been incorporated into the adjacent Carabinieri (police) station, scene of controversial investigations ranging from the one that resulted in the execution of the leaders of the Parthenopean Republic in 1799 to the *Mani pulite* anti-corruption enquiries of the 1990s.

Sightseeing

Further north the grim 20th-century façade of the church of **Spirito Santo** (open 9-11.30am Mon-Sat; 10.30am-noon Sun) masks a vast, cool, grey and white interior. The church has one of the largest domes in the city.

The rigidly regular streets on the slope west of via Toledo constitute the **Quartieri spagnoli**, built during Don Pedro di Toledo's flourish of urban development in the 16th century to house troops of the Spanish occupation. Cramped from the start, the Quartieri gradually became home to some of the poorest of Naples' poor; spaces that were scarcely fit for Spanish horses 400 years ago became the damp, exhaust-filled dwellings of wretched human beings. Many still are, and the Quartieri holds some unenviable records: Europe's highest rates of unemployment and respiratory disease are just two of them. Yet there's something fascinating about this warren of streets… for the visitor. One attraction is the delightful via Pignasecca, home to a chaotic street market. With the market in full swing, crowds of people streaming towards the city centre by funicular railway and ambulances screaming around Pellegrini hospital – the swirling inferno is both loud and mesmerising.

Sant'Anna dei Lombardi

Piazza Monteoliveto 14 (081 551 3333). Metro Montesanto/bus E1, R1, R4. **Open** 9am-noon Tue-Sat. **Map** p311 3A.
The church dates from the early 15th century, though it was refurbished in the 17th. Inside are several Renaissance sculptures, including an extraordinary group of terracotta statues entitled *Mourning the Death of Christ* by Guido Mazzoni (1492). The sacristy has a fine ceiling frescoed by Florentine artist Giorgio Vasari in 1544; the unusual inlaid wooden panels along the walls are from the same period. The church is currently undergoing restoration, but visitors are still allowed to see the main sculptural attractions.

Piazza Dante

At the point where via Toledo becomes via Enrico Pessina, piazza Dante – restored to undreamed of elegance for the 2002 opening of its metro station – is dominated by the crescent-shaped **Convitto Nazionale**, originally a state-funded boarding school for poor children from outside Naples. Designed in the mid 18th century by Luigi Vanvitelli, the Convitto has 26 statues representing the virtues of Charles III. At the Convitto's northern end is the **Port'Alba arch**, built in the early 17th century and rebuilt 150 years later. The **metro** station is one of a series containing an impressive collection of modern art. *See p153* **Underground art**.

The **Museo Nazionale Archeologico**, home to some of Italy's greatest treasures, is further north on the smoggy, noisy via Pessina. En route, in via Bellini, stands the **Accademia delle Belle Arti** (Fine Arts Academy, not open to the public), with its mid 19th-century façade in tufa stone. From the northern end of via Bellini, the rather sleazy and generally unloved **Galleria Principe di Napoli** leads to piazza Museo.

Beyond the museum on via Santa Teresa degli Scalzi stands the church of **Santa Teresa degli Scalzi** (No.43), which was built in the 17th century and reworked in the 18th century. The church is largely neglected, its fickle congregation having decamped to the **Gesù Nuovo** (*see p74*). It has recently been taken over by a different order; the new incumbents hope to establish regular opening hours. Unlike the church, the old people's centre and school for the blind attached to St Teresa's are fully functional.

Piazza Cavour, with its busy underground station (complete with art, *see p153* **Underground art**) and scruffy public gardens, leads east out of piazza Museo. The recently restored Porta San Gennaro, with a 17th-century fresco by Mattia Preti, was part of the original 15th-century walls.

Museo Nazionale Archeologico

Piazza Museo 19 (081 564 8941/081 440 166/ www.archeona.arti.beniculturali.it). Metro Cavour or Museo/bus 47, CS, E1. **Open** *Museum* 9am-7.30pm Mon, Wed-Sun. Ticket office closes 1hr earlier. *Gabinetto segreto* Guided tours every 30mins 9.30am-1.30pm, 2.30-6.30pm Mon, Wed-Sun. **Admission** €6.50. **No credit cards. Map** p312 2C.
Built in the early 17th century, the palazzo housing this museum was chosen in 1777 by King Ferdinand I as the perfect home for the immense Farnese collection of ancient artefacts inherited from his grandmother Elisabetta Farnese. Discoveries from Pompeii, Stabiae and Herculaneum were added later, making this one of the world's best archaeological museums.

The museum is distributed over four floors. The basement (Rooms 17-23) holds the Egyptian section, with Egyptian objects imported into Italy during the Roman period and unearthed in excavations in the Campania region and Rome. There's a large collection of obelisks, busts, funerary statues, jewellery, and sarcophagi from the Hellenic and Ptolemaic periods, and the obligatory mummy, once part of the Borgia collection.

On the meandering ground floor is the collection of the powerful Farnese family of Parma (although the paintings are in Capodimonte, *see p90*). Most of the collection was filched from ancient sites in Rome during the 16th century, when Alessandro Farnese ruled as Pope Paul III (1534-49). In Room 1 on the right of the entrance hall are the *Tirannicidi*, the tyrant-killers Armodios and Aristogitones, who did

Saints alive Maria Francesca

The only Neapolitan woman ever to be canonised, Santa Maria Francesca 'of the five wounds', a stigmatic and mystic who died more than 200 years ago, is still going strong in terms of popular feeling. At the heart of her cult is her chair, a reminder of many Neapolitans' faith in the divine powers of saintly relics.

The chair in question is a pretty ordinary-looking wooden one. Placed next to the window of Maria Francesca's tiny house-turned-sanctuary in the Quartieri spagnoli, the holy chair sees a procession of people of all ages sitting on it to ask the saint's intercession in matters ranging from work to exams to financial matters. Above all, it attracts women with fertility problems.

She's at rest here, but it's hardly surprising she looks rather frazzled in most of her statues: pain was a thread running through her life, from childhood with a cruel father (she escaped an early forced marriage to enter religious life), through illnesses, the agony of her stigmata, not to mention the self-imposed pain of hair shirts, severe fasts and other forms of ecstatic self-torture.

Maria Francesca's home, where the nun spent the last 38 years of her life serving the poor, is looked after by the Daughters of Santa Maria Francesca, who may be willing to impart a blessing for those who sit on her chair 'with faith'. The walls of the house – a typical, cramped Quartieri home – are lined with relics of the saint: hair shirts, gloves Maria Francesca wore over her stigmata, and so on. Every year on 5 October, the day before the anniversary of her death, there is a ceremony to bless the children born thanks to the saint's intercession. In the nine days leading to the anniversary and for the entire month of October there are three masses a day (two at weekends) in the little chapel on the ground floor of the house. The anniversary itself is celebrated with a whole day of masses.

Casa e Santuario di Santa Maria Francesca delle Cinque Piaghe

Vico Tre Re a Toledo 13, via Toledo (081 425 011). **Open** 8am-12.15pm daily. On the 6th of every month also open 4.30pm-7pm. **Map** p315 1A.

away with the cruel Athenian rulers Hippia and Hipparchos in 514 BC – a Roman copy of the fifth-century BC Greek original. In the same room is a Roman copy of Polycletus' *Doriforo*. Elsewhere on this floor is a series of busts and statues (see the two fine heads of Caracalla in the un-numbered gallery leading off the entrance hall into Room 8), some of which are simply enormous. There's the powerful *Ercole Farnese* (Farnese Hercules; between Rooms 11 and 12) and the recently restored *Toro Farnese* (Farnese Bull; Room 16), a large marble group from the early third century AD found in the Baths of Caracalla in Rome. In Room 8, the graceful Roman copy of a Greek Venere (Venus) Callipige glances daintily backwards at her reflection in the water as she slips off her clothes.

Room 10 contains the tiny, delicate Tazza Farnese, a small dish made in Egypt during the Ptolemaic period and consisting of four layers of sardonyx agate. Its transparent beauty is renowned; examine it from both sides. The mezzanine floor houses the mosaic collection, including the large scene depicting the battle between Alexander the Great and Darius from the House of the Faun in Pompeii (Room 61). Also here is the Gabinetto segreto, a collection of ancient pornography uncovered at Pompeii and Herculaneum. The collection of explicit paintings and sculptures includes a vast range of phallus talismans – winged ones, jingling ones with bells, others with hats on. One item approaches the subject in pre-Freudian manner, depicting a frantic struggle between the member and its owner. The high (or low) point of the collection is a sculpted Pan, caught in the act with a nanny-goat. This collection has attracted controversy over the ages and was only reopened to the public in 2000. It is off-limits to children under 11.

The first floor, centred around the Sala Meridiana, contains artefacts from Pompeii, Herculaneum and other southern Italian sites, as well as the pre- and proto-historical sections. The vast, echoing room is 54m (189ft) long and 20m (70ft) high. On its walls are paintings on archaeological themes from the Farnese collection. On its floor is a line marking a zodiacal meridian; around noon, an oval bead of light snakes in through a hole high in the top right-hand corner of the room striking the meridian in the appropriate zodiacal sign. To the left as you enter the sala, Rooms 85-89 contain glassware, silver and pottery from Pompeii, while Rooms 66-73 have friezes and frescos from Herculaneum and Stabiae. To the right as you enter the Sala, the first entrance leads to Rooms 114-117, with artefacts from the Villa dei Papiri in Herculaneum; note the lovely bronze Hermes in the centre of Room 117. The second series of rooms on the right (130-140) contains vases, bowls and funerary offerings from Greek and Roman Paestum, and from other sites around Magna Graecia (ancient southern Italy).

The pre- and proto-historical sections are reached from the third corridor on the right. The rather complex layout here features, on the upper mezzanine

floor, Palaeolithic, Neolithic and Early Bronze Age finds from the Campania region (Rooms 148 and 149), including stone artefacts dating back to 100,000 BC. The lower mezzanine floor (Rooms 145 and 146) houses finds from the Middle and Late Bronze Ages. The main section (Rooms 124-127) is arranged according to place not time, and includes Palaeolithic bones and flints (300,000 BC) found on Capri (Room 127); the Iron Age is represented best, with eighth- and ninth-century funerary relics from a number of necropoli from Capua to Ischia.

Be aware that on-going restoration projects within the museum mean that exhibits are often not where they're meant to be.

La Sanità & beyond

Between via Foria, via Santa Teresa degli Scalzi and the hill of Capodimonte is an area made up of three districts: La Sanità ('healthy', because it was outside the city walls), I Miracoli (because of the miracles wrought around saintly inmates of the catacombs) and Le Vergini (named after a pre-Christian no-sex-please Greek religious group). Now densely populated and *folkloristico* (dearly loved Neapolitan comedian Totò, *see p166* **Totò & Eduardo**, was born here at via Antesaecula 109; there's a plaque above the grocery store), the area is also honeycombed with underground burial places: from the early Christian **catacombe di San Gaudioso** under the church of **Santa Maria della Sanità** (for both, *see p87*) and the **catacombe di San Severo** (*see p87*) under the church of the same name to the comparatively recent **cimitero delle Fontanelle** (*see p89*). This part of the city was popular for burials as it remained outside the city walls until the 18th century; burial within the walls was forbidden for public health reasons.

Along with its incredible catacombs, the area contains two archaeological gems (visible from outside only) by 18th-century architect Ferdinando Sanfelice: **Palazzo Sanfelice** (via Sanità 2 and 6), now sadly dilapidated, was the architect's own home; and the truly magnificent 'flying' staircase in **Palazzo dello Spagnuolo** (via dei Vergini 19), which has recently been restored to its former glory. Further east, pine tree-lined piazza Miracoli is home to the 17th-century church of **Santa Maria dei Miracoli** (open 8.30-11.30am, 5-8pm Mon-Sat; 8am-1pm Sun).

Beyond Porta San Gennaro, traffic crawls relentlessly along via Foria, past the **Orto botanico** (botanical gardens, *see p89*), to piazza Carlo III, which is dominated by the fearful bulk of the **Albergo dei Poveri** (closed to the public except for a small central section which hosts some exhibitions), the

The sumptuous interior of **Santa Maria della Sanità**.

largest public building in Europe. Vast as it is (the façade measures 354 metres/1,239 feet; the building covers 103,000 square metres/360,500 square feet), the Albergo is only one-fifth the size of Ferdinando Fuga's original design, commissioned by Charles III to house Naples' destitute and homeless. Construction began in 1751 and was completed in 1829. In 2000, a project to repair serious damage from the earthquake of 1980 and general decay began, and is due for completion in 2006; half the building is currently swathed in what must surely be the largest single piece of assembled scaffold in all Europe.

Via Santi Giovanni e Paolo runs north-east out of the eastern end of piazza Carlo III. The great tenor Enrico Caruso (1873-1921) was born at No.6. A dingy plaque on the wall introduces this as the house 'where the world first heard his voice'. Naples itself heard very little more of it; slated by Neapolitan critics early in his career, he left the city and never came back.

Catacombe di San Gaudioso/ Santa Maria della Sanità

Via della Sanità 124 (081 544 1305/www.santa mariadellasanita.it). Metro Cavour or Museo/bus C51, C52. **Open** *Church* 8.30am-12.30pm, 5-8pm Mon-Sat; 8.30am-1.30pm Sun. *Catacombs* Guided tours 9.30am, 10.15am, 11am, 11.45am, 12.30pm daily. **Admission** €5. **No credit cards**. **Map** p314 1A.
Tunnelled out of the Capodimonte hillside in Roman times for use as water cisterns, the subterranean labyrinth of the San Gaudioso catacombs was a

burial site from the fifth century onwards. The burial here of St Gaudiosus – a North African bishop and hermit – in 452, made the site an important shrine. There are patches of mosaic from the fifth and sixth centuries, and frescos – some from the fifth, others from the 17th and 18th centuries – in the damp, musty caves. A fascinating range of burial techniques is demonstrated. Note the method used from 1620 to 1650: the corpse was walled upright in a niche with its head cemented into the rear wall; after the body fluids had drained away, the headless body was buried (a job carried out by convicts) and the skull was removed, to be repositioned over a frescoed portrait of the illustrious deceased. The remains of St Gaudiosus and the skulls were all transferred to the nearby Cimitero delle Fontanelle (*see p82*) during the cholera epidemic of 1974.

In the 17th century, Dominican friars who had previously tended the chapel of San Gaudioso in the catacombs built the Greek-cross-plan basilica of Santa Maria della Sanità above it. There's a fine Madonna and Child with Saints Hyacinth, Rosa of Lima and Agnes by Luca Giordano over the entrance to the vestry. From the transept, steps lead down to the Cappella di San Gaudioso, which dates from the fifth century but was rebuilt in the tenth and 15th centuries.

The hour-long guided tours leave from the basilica; departure times may vary. Phone ahead to request an English-speaking guide.

Catacombe di San Severo

Piazzetta San Severo a Capodimonte 81 (081 544 1305). Metro Cavour or Museo/bus C51, C52. **Open** *Church* 9.30-11.30am, 5.30-7.30pm Mon-Fri (note: the morning hours are not always adhered to);

Saints alive Skulls & bones

Naples' own version of a cult of the dead involves caring for skulls – *capuzzelle* in local dialect – of the unknown dead. People would 'adopt' skulls in the city's hypogeums, showering the bones with gifts, clothes, pillows and flowers, or even building small wooden houses for them. In gratitude, the souls belonging to those skulls are supposed to grant favours to their carers.

The **Cimitero delle Fontanelle** (*see p89*), a cavern housing thousands of skulls and bones brought from around the city during times of cholera, was once the centre of the cult. The practice was around for centuries, and skyrocketed during World War II, when mothers and wives lavished attention on skulls amid their own anxiety or grief for menfolk away fighting or killed in action. In later years the practice took on a more mercenary hue, with skulls that didn't come up with the goods liable to be smashed. The cemetery has been closed to the public since the 1970s, but the practice survives in places such as the small church of **Santa Maria del Purgatorio ad Arco** (*see p81*).

The modern Church takes a dim view of the cult, and a large notice at Santa Maria del Purgatorio ad Arco warns visitors that it is prohibited. It first forbade the worship of human remains in 1969, and the practice has been on the wane since then. But it hasn't completely died out if the evidence underneath the church is anything to go by.

In the church's hypogeum, open only on Saturdays, are a few skulls and piles of bones surrounded by flowers, plastic jewellery and other gifts. One of them, known locally as Principessa Lucia, wears a white bridal veil. Various stories surround this particular skull. According to one, it belonged to a girl who died on the eve of her wedding. Another maintains that the princess in question was in love with a commoner but her father opposed their marriage and locked her in a convent where she died of a broken heart. Whatever the truth about her origins, she is believed to protect newlyweds and brides-to-be, some of whom have been known to visit the Principessa to seek her blessing.

5.30-7.30pm Sat; 9.30-11.30am Sun. *Catacombs* by appointment only. **Admission** donation expected. **Map** p312 1C.

The church here today was built in 1573, but it stands on the site of a monastery complex around a much earlier church founded by Naples' first bishop, Severus. When Severus's saintly body was moved to San Giorgio Maggiore (*see p75*) in the ninth century, the site lost its importance. On the left side of the nave, steps lead down to a tiny cubicle containing all that is left of the original catacombs. A wall fresco from the late fourth century depicts St Peter and St Paul – the earliest representation of these apostles found in Naples – alongside the city's own San Gennaro and San Severo.

Cimitero delle Fontanelle

Via delle Fontanelle 154 (081 296 944). Metro Cavour or Museo/bus C51. **Open** Currently closed to the public; see review. **Map** p314 1A.

This enormous trapezoidal cavern with side galleries – once a quarry for tufa building stone – acquired importance during the cholera epidemic of 1835, when the authorities decided to move all the city's dead here from their resting places in and around the city. This process was repeated during the outbreak of 1974, when more bones were brought here from the catacombs of San Gaudioso. About 40,000 skulls and bones were subsequently stacked up around the cavern. The place is far from ghoulish: it has all the peace and tranquillity of a cemetery, though some outlandish lighting effects are created as sun filters down through the vegetation-covered air shafts, dancing over the mournful statues and piles of dusty

bones. The Cimitero underwent a popularity boom during and after World War II, when grieving parents took up the practice of 'adopting' a skull in memory of sons killed in action. For Neapolitans, the place evokes painful memories.

This extraordinary place has been closed to the public since the 1970s, but plans are under way to lease management of the site to the Napoli Sotterranea Association (*see p59*) which would arrange guided tours. All enquiries should be addressed to the Association, as it is planning to conduct regular tours at €4 per person.

Orto botanico (Botanical Gardens)

Via Foria 223 (081 449 759/www.ortobotanico. unina.it). Metro Cavour or Museo/bus 14, 15, 47, CD, CS, C51. **Open** by appointment 9am-2pm Mon-Fri. **Admission** free. **Map** p312 1B.

A steep double flight of steps leads up out of the smog and into this shady park lined with a sturdy mixture of plane trees, palms and riotous vegetation. Despite the constant roar of traffic, and the proximity of one end to the vast rat-infested remains of the Albergo dei Poveri, this garden is a haven of peace. Founded in 1807 by Joseph Bonaparte, it now belongs to Naples University's science department.

There's a fine array of palms, aquatic plants, cacti, ferns and shrubs from all around the world. The *castello* at the centre of the park pre-dates the park by about 150 years. On its first floor a dainty, well-kept museum contains fossilised plants and leaves, and plant artefacts from non-industrialised civilisations. The greenhouses and their collections are not open to the public.

Peace, palms and exotic plants at **Orto botanico**.

Capodimonte

Very fine art and some fascinating catacombs.

Although the peace and tranquillity of the northern outskirts of Naples is long gone, shouted down by the constant roar of traffic and of jets approaching Naples airport, Capodimonte is still an oasis of architectural, artistic and environmental beauty. The palace and surrounding park that dominate a hill north of the city centre were created by King Charles III, who saw the area's hunting potential in the 18th century. It remains a verdant haven; beneath it is the fascinating yet unheralded **Catacombe di San Gennaro** (*see below*).

South-west of the park on via Capodimonte, the pseudo-classical 20th-century church of the **Madre del Buon Consiglio** (open 8am-12.30pm, 4.30-7.30pm Mon-Sat; 8am-1pm, 5-7.30pm Sun) is a bombastic imitation of St Peter's in Rome. The **Osservatorio Astronomico** (*see p91*), south-east of the park, bears witness to progress made during the Bourbon Restoration.

On the road curving down from Capodimonte's Porta Grande are the **Ponti Rossi**, the well-preserved remains of an aqueduct built during the reign of the Emperor Claudius (AD 41-54) to bring fresh water to Naples from the mountains near Avellino. Byzantine forces breached the city walls in 536 through this aqueduct, thanks to admirable military espionage.

Catacombe di San Gennaro

Via Capodimonte 16 (081 741 1071). Bus 24, 110, R4. **Open** guided tours only 9am, 10am, 11am, noon Tue-Sun; afternoon tours for groups by appointment only. **Admission** €5. **No credit cards. Map** p312 1C.
From a pleasant garden (entrance to the left of the church) overlooking Sanità, steps lead down into the two-level catacombs with their fascinating – if dilap-idated – second-century frescos. This was a burial rather than a hiding place; early Neapolitan Christians were persecuted in a far less systematic way than their counterparts in Rome. After the body of San Gennaro (St Januarius) was brought here from Pozzuoli in the fifth century, this became an impor-tant pilgrimage centre. Fine arcosolium tombs (sar-cophagi in arched, frescoed niches) fill the upper levels in the main ambulatory, with fifth-century mosaics and frescos from the second century in the vestibule, one possibly portraying Adam and Eve. The lower level has an eighth-century baptismal tub and a chapel dedicated to Sant'Agrippino (closed indefinitely). Tours of the catacombs take 40 minutes.

Regrettably, the early Christian basilica of San Gennaro above the catacombs has also been closed for years and is used as a storeroom by the hospital.

Museo di Capodimonte

Porta Grande via Capodimonte; Porta Piccola via Miano 2 (081 749 9111/www.beniculturali.it). Bus *24, 110, R4.* **Open** Park 8am-1hr before sunset daily. *Museum* 8.30am-7.30pm Tue-Sun. Ticket office closes 1 hr earlier. **Admission** *Park* free. *Museum* €7.50; €6.50 after 2pm. **Credit** bookshop only MC, V. **Map** p312 1C.
When construction began in 1738 on the palace that now houses one of Italy's largest and most artisti-cally rich museums, King Charles III envisaged no more than a hunting lodge. Seduced by plans for something far grander – and hard-pushed to find space for the vast collection he had inherited from his mother, Elisabetta Farnese – a monumental three-storey *palazzo reale* (royal palace) went up at the heart of a magnificent park covering seven sq km (2.5sq miles). Though it would be 100 years before the finishing touches were put to the build-ing, the Farnese collection was moved in by 1759; acquisitions by Charles and later Bourbon monarchs enriched the gallery, while porcelain and weaponry were added in the late 19th century.

Work by Botticelli (*above*) and Carracci (*right*)

Over the years the palace was variously a receptacle for the royal collections, the main seat of the court, and a royal summer holiday home. Recently restored, the second-floor gallery is truly stunning.

The main entrance to the palace is a regal affair. Cool cavernous porticos on the ground floor hide bars and shops. The Farnese collection, with its natural extension the Bourbon collection, is upstairs, as are the smaller Borgia, porcelain and contemporary collections, and the armoury. There's information about the individual works of art (in English) in each room.

Italian art makes up the bulk of the Farnese collection. It starts in Room 2 with ground-breaking portraits by Raphael (of the future Pope Paul III when he was still Cardinal Alessandro Farnese) and by Titian. Titian's masterpiece, *Danaë*, is in Room 11. In it, Danaë, daughter of King Argos, is seduced by Jupiter in the form of golden rain; the courtesan who modelled for the painting was probably the lover of a Farnese cardinal. El Greco's *El Soplon*, a version of a work mentioned by Pliny, is in the same room.

Umbrian and Tuscan schools are represented by Masaccio (the 15th-century Crucifixion from a now-dismantled altarpiece in Room 3 is one of the few additions to the collection since Unification in 1861) and an early work by Botticelli, the *Madonna with Child and Two Angels* (Room 6, pictured). Sixteenth- and 17th-century works from the Farnese family's native Emilia region are plentiful. Works by Correggio include the *Mystic Marriage of St Catherine* (1517) in Room 12; Parmigianino's *Antea* (Room 12) with her virginal look and odd attire is a byword for Mannerism; Annibale Carracci's *Mystic Marriage of St Catherine* (pictured) is in Room 19, his allegorical *Hercules at the Crossroads* is in Room 20; Guido Reni's *Atlanta and Hippomenes* is in Room 22.

The 15th-century Veneto tradition is represented above all by Giovanni Bellini's *Transfiguration* (Room 8; note the blend of religious mysticism and realistic rural Veneto setting), and Andrea Mantegna's *Portrait of Young Francesco Gonzaga* (Room 8) and *St Euphemia* (Room 7). Not to be overlooked in this galaxy of Italian talent are Brueghel's two enigmatic pieces, the *The Parable of the Blind* and *The Misanthrope*, in Room 17.

Also on the first floor are the Royal Apartments, including Queen Maria Amalia's boudoir (packed with Capodimonte porcelain), the magnificent ballroom, the dainty Pompeian drawing room, and a range of French furniture and paintings.

The newly refurbished second floor features works made in Naples from the 13th to 19th centuries. All the greats are here: Simone Martini's *St Ludovic of Toulouse* (Room 65) was originally intended for the church of San Lorenzo; Caravaggio's powerful *Flagellation* (Room 78) influenced generations of Neapolitan painters; Massimo Stanzione's *Moses' Sacrifice* is in Room 89, his *Madonna and Child* in Room 93; Giuseppe Ribera's *St Jerome and the Angel* and the complex allegorical *Drunken Silenus* are in Rooms 90 and 91; Pietro Cavallino's *St Cecilia in Ecstasy* is in Room 94; Luca Giordano's *Madonna of the Canopy* is in Room 103; Francesco Solimena's *Aeneas and Dido* (Room 104) inspired his friend Alessandro Scarlatti to set the classical subject to music in 1696. A third-floor attic houses modern and contemporary paintings.

The area immediately around the palace pulsates with locals, especially on sunny Sundays; the rest of the enormous park is strangely deserted. Laid out in the mid-18th century to a design by Ferdinando Sanfelice, five tree-lined avenues radiate from a hub near the palace. Smaller buildings are dotted about, including the Reale Fabbrica delle Porcellane (royal porcelain factory). Work in the factory came to an abrupt standstill in 1759, as Charles shifted the whole operation to his native Spain when he returned to take that crown; the factory is now a craft school.

Osservatorio Astronomico

Salita Moiariello 16 (081 557 5111/www.na.astro.it). Bus 24, 110, R4. **Open** guided tours only, 9am-1.30pm Mon-Fri; evening tours once a mth (usually Thur); book well in advance by phone 8am-1pm Mon-Fri. **Admission** free. **Map** p312 1C.

This magnificent neo-classical building dates from 1819, and was commissioned by King Ferdinand I. The first observatory in Italy and one of the first in Europe, it contains a fine collection of equipment, historical and modern, some of which may be used during the tour. It also has a superb setting on the Miradois hill overlooking the entire Bay of Naples.

...at the **Museo di Capodimonte**.

Vomero.

The once-green hill is now built over, but monastery and castle still stand guard.

Certosa-Museo di San Martino.
See p93.

The ancient guardians of the city's military and spiritual values, Castel Sant'Elmo and the San Martino monastery, stand high on a bluff over the Centro storico and Chiaia foreshore. The Vomero, the hill dominated by these two remarkable monuments, was once portrayed in landscape paintings as green fields dotted with sheep and trees. Unfortunately, much of greater Vomero – the backdrop to this romantic idyll – now lies buried under an unseemly slag heap of cheap high-rise housing projects. Gone for good, then, are the days when families took the funicular up to what was essentially a hilltop village on Sunday mornings for a picnic in the country. The city put an end to that in the 1970s when the *tangenziale* inner-city ring road was built over and under much of the hill. Since then the rest of the slopes have been enveloped by building projects (including hospitals vital to healthcare for all of southern Italy).

At the heart of the district is piazza Vanvitelli, a round space where the tree-lined via Scarlatti (recently pedestrianised, its *struscio* on summer evenings rivals that on via Toledo) meets via Bernini (traffic hell). With its elegant café tables spilling out on to pavements filled with well-heeled residents, piazza Vanvitelli epitomises the pan-European middle-class air of the Vomero that can alienate as much as captivate. The temperature is a degree or two lower up here than down the hill, and the streets are noticeably cleaner. On summer evenings the square fills to bursting with a vast crowd of teenagers whiling away their time in aimless chatter and endless pose-striking.

Three of Naples' four funicular railways lead up to the Vomero. Before those were built in the late 19th and early 20th centuries, getting to the Vomero involved scaling the long flights of steps from the city centre. The steps are still there, and that's a pleasant way to make the journey down from the Vomero without suffering its traffic (although this is not really advisable after dark). To reach the westernmost flight – the **Calata di San Francesco** – cut through the cool, dreamy **Parco della Floridiana** from its top gate (stopping to take in the magnificent views from its belvedere and to visit its **Museo Nazionale della Ceramica Duca di Martina**, *for both see p94*), then exit on to via Aniello Falcone from the bottom gate.

Heading west along via Falcone, the Calata descends sharply to the left, shortly after passing a splendid art nouveau palazzo on the right. Cut across the corso Vittorio Emanuele and carry on down via Arco Mirelli to get to the Chiaia seafront. A short hike east on corso Vittorio, on the other hand, will take you to **Castel Aselmeyer** in the lower reaches of the Parco Grifeo, home to some of the extraordinary creations of English architect Lamont Young.

From here you can easily get to **Castel Sant'Elmo** (*see below*), part of the city's 16th-century defence system, which offers one the best views to be had in all Naples. (Entry to the castle is by a gateway in via Angelini, about 90 metres (300 feet) on the right before reaching largo San Martino.) **Gradini di Petraio steps** start in via Caccavello and cut down past the austere baroque church of **San Carlo alle Mortelle** (open Sept-July 8.30am-noon, 5.30-8pm daily; Aug 6.30-8pm daily); *mortella* is the dialect word for myrtle, which used to flourish hereabouts. The path then continues through the Quartieri spagnoli.

The Castel Sant'Elmo towers above the recently revamped **Certosa-Museo di San Martino** (*see below*). From the square in front of the museum, the staircase known as via **Pedamentina a San Martino** leads towards the Centro storico.

All three stairways cross the winding, traffic-snarled corso Vittorio Emanuele, which, when it was built in the mid 19th century, opened areas formerly occupied by terraced gardens and vineyards to construction. Today, the corso provides access a few patches of welcome inner-city green. The **via Pedamentina steps** emerge closest to all of them.

Heading north along corso Vittorio Emanuele from the foot of the steps, via Cupa Vecchia on the left leads to the small **Parco Viviani** (open 7am to 1hr before dusk daily), though the main entrance to this green oasis is from Via G Santacroce 15.

Almost opposite the steps on the other side of the corso, vico Trinità delle Monache leads down to the **Parco dei Quartieri Spagnoli** (open Nov-Apr 9am-5pm Tue-Sat; 9am-2pm Sun. May-Oct 8am-7pm Tue-Sat; 8am-2pm Sun). Its creation was a city council project that involved the redevelopment of a one-time military hospital (which started its life in the 17th century as the Trinità delle Monache convent) and much of the surrounding area. The plan for the park calls for the demolition of some of the uglier modern eyesores, and the creation of a garden and park overlooking the old city, while the remaining buildings will, eventually, house a natural history museum, a sports complex and concert areas. The first phase, a public park and play area, featureless save for a planation of magnificent pines, was completed in 2000. Despite ongoing work, mainly demolition or structural consolidation of existing buildings, deadlines for the park's completion were clearly unrealistic, and it may take some time to come to fruition. Still, in summer months the garden area already hosts some fine open-air concerts.

Castel Sant'Elmo

Via Tito Angelini 22 (081 578 4030). Funicular Montesanto to via Morghen, Centrale to piazzetta Fuga or Chiaia to via Cimarosa/bus V1. **Open** 8.30am-7.30pm Tue-Sun (ticket office closes 1hr earlier). **Admission** €2. **No credit cards**. **Map** p314 2B.

Castel Sant'Elmo gets its name from the small church which stood here in the 10th century, called St Erasmus, a name corrupted over the centuries to 'St Elmo'. A castle has stood here since 1329, when King Robert of Anjou modified a pre-existing Norman watchtower incorporating the work of artists, architects and workmen who were then employed on the building of the adjacent monastery of San Martino. It acquired its distinctive six-pointed star shape in the mid 16th century after what amounted to an extensive reorganisation of the city's defences. In 1587 the ammunition warehouse was struck by lightning; the castle was badly damaged and 150 people died.

Over the years, the castle dungeon has held many illustrious inmates, including heroes of the 1799 Parthenopean Republic, and it still served as a military prison as recently as the mid 1970s. That might help to explain why, despite being close to the centre, spacious and airy, the castle has never been a popular destination for Neapolitans. Its unmistakeable bulk has, however, long provided a focal point for pictorial cityscapes, including the extraordinary *Tavola Strozzi*, in the Certosa-Museo di San Martino next door (*see below*). Entry to the castle is by a new gateway in via Angelini. The ground floor is closed, although glimpses of its gloomy interior (including the prisons) may occasionally be snatched through glass panels on the first floor. This, too, is normally closed except during important exhibitions, which allow this magnificently restored area to be shown to its full advantage.

Piazza d'Armi, as the top floor is called, is in fact the castle's roof, and is best reached by lift; the 360° view over Naples from here is arguably the most breathtaking in the city. The walkway around the battlements is splendid. A gently sloping path inside the castle leads you back down across the drawbridge, passing under the coat of arms of Charles V.

Certosa-Museo di San Martino

Largo San Martino 5 (081 558 5942/081 558 6408). Funicular Montesanto to via Morghen, Centrale to piazzetta Fuga or Chiaia to via Cimarosa/bus V1. **Open** 8.30am-7.30pm Tue-Sun. Box office closes 1hr earlier. **Admission** (includes Castel Sant'Elmo) €6. **Credit** (bookshop only) MC, V. **Map** p314 2A.

This Carthusian monastery was founded in 1325, although its present appearance is the result of much reworking at the end of the 16th century. Under the priors' spiritual and, above all, economic management, it gradually became renowned for its priceless architectural and artistic assets. Like most monasteries, San Martino was dissolved under French rule (1806-15); the monks moved back in only briefly before the *certosa* (charterhouse) was wrested from them again in the wake of Italian Unification in 1861. A long period of neglect ended only after World War II, and a seemingly endless restoration programme has been under way ever since.

To the left after the ticket office, the church's late 17th-century façade is by Cosimo Fanzago; it conceals remnants of the Gothic original, such as the pointed arches and cross-vaulted ceiling in the *pronaos* (projecting vestibule), which has frescos (1651-6) by Micco Spadaro depicting the persecution of Carthusians in England in the reign of Henry VIII.

The church's interior contains as complete (and well labelled) a selection of Neapolitan painting and sculpture as you could hope for. Massimo Stanzione's *Deposition* (1638) dominates the inner façade, flanked by two fine portraits by Giuseppe Ribera, who is also responsible for the 12 paintings of prophets (1638-43) tucked into the spandrels of the arches. The delicate 18th-century marble altar balustrade is by Giuseppe Sammartino. The walls and side chapels feature paintings by the Vaccaros, Francesco Solimena and Stanzione. In the vaulted ceiling are frescos (1637-40) by Giovanni Lanfranco: *Ascension with Angels, Apostles and Saints.* Bonaventura Presti used material already prepared by Fanzago for his intricate inlaid marble floor (1664). Don't miss the rooms surrounding the church: the choir features Ribera's *Communion of the Apostles,* Guido Reni's *Adoration of the Shepherds* (1642) and Battista Caracciolo's *Washing of Feet* (1622); the sacristy has some exquisite marquetry (on the recently restored cupboards are 56 panels showing biblical scenes). In the Cappella del Tesoro are Ribera's *Pietà* and frescos by Luca Giordano, while both the *parlatorio* and the chapter room (where there are several works by Battista Caracciolo) are essential viewing.

A long passageway leads left out of the small *chiostro dei procuratori* into the *chiostro grande* (great cloister) – one of Italy's finest. This bright, sunny area was created in the 16th century by Giovanni Antonio Dosio, although the work was completed by Cosimo Fanzago who added the small monks' graveyard (note the fine balustrade and skulls) and the busts and statues above the cool Tuscan-Doric pillared portico.

The *pinacoteca* (art gallery) is beautifully laid out on two floors in the northern, eastern and southern wings of the main cloister, recently reopened to the public in all its splendour. The main bulk of works from the 17th and 18th centuries, originally made for the monastery, is now housed in the prior's quarters in the southern wing (Rooms 17-23) and includes

works by Ribera (Saints Jerome and Sebastian), Lanfranco (*Our Lady of the Rosary*) and Stanzione (*Baptism of Christ*); Spadaro was responsible for the ceilings in Rooms 14, 15 and 16. Room 8 contains a remarkable sculptured group of the *Madonna and Child with the Infant John the Baptist* by Pietro Bernini (father of the more famous Gianlorenzo).

The *certosa,* the Carthusian order and the history of Naples, are constant themes in the works in the *pinacoteca*. In Room 23 are portraits of priors. There are splendid maps (such as the vast one of the city from 1775 by Duca di Noja in Room 45) and landscape paintings, with work ranging from the anonymous *Tavola Strozzi* with its detailed depiction of 15th-century Naples in Room 32, and Didier Barra's bird's-eye view of Naples at the end of the 16th century, to a fine series of late 17th-century paintings by Gaspar Van Wittel in Room 40. On the first floor are 19th-century paintings by local artists.

There's a section devoted to the art of Nativity scenes, including a massive *presepe* (crib) with particularly rare pieces, named after its creator, Cuciniello. You'll also find sections dedicated to theatre, to ships and shipping, and in the former pharmacy, to porcelain and glassware.

Access to some sections, such as the Museo dell' Opera, depends on staff availability. Other sections, such as the one dedicated to 19th-century Neapolitan artists, and the creepy Gothic basements with sculptures and coats of arms, are closed indefinitely.

Parco della Floridiana
Museo Nazionale della Ceramica
Duca di Martina

Via Cimarosa 77 (081 578 1776/081 229 2110). Funicular Montesanto to via Morghen, Centrale to piazzetta Fuga or Chiaia to via Cimarosa/bus E4, V1. **Open** *Park* 8.30am-1hr before sunset daily. *Museum* 8.30am-2pm Tue-Sun (last admission 1.15pm). Occasional guided tours. **Admission** €2.50. **Credit** *bookshop only* MC, V. **Map** p315 1B.

In 1815, King Ferdinand returned to Naples after ten years of French rule, bringing his second wife, with whom he had contracted a morganatic marriage. Lucia Migliaccio, Duchess of Floridia, was given this splendid villa and garden. In the 1920s, the villa and garden were purchased by the Italian government, the park was opened to the public and the villa turned into a museum. The park is a favourite spot for Vomero walkers and joggers; its network of paths, lawns and spinneys makes the Vomero a bit different from the rest of the city, and the view from the terrace at the bottom of the garden is memorable.

The Museum is currently undergoing limited redevelopment, including the addition of a refreshment area, scheduled for completion in early 2005.

The first floor is dedicated to European ceramics: there's an early 18th-century picture frame from Sicily in Room 2; some fine local biscuit pieces, two dishes from the royal dinner service showing costumes of the realm, and the fine *Capodimonte Declaration* by Gricci in Room 5; some splendid Meissen porcelain in

Il Liberty

The opening of the Chiaia and Montesanto funiculars in 1889 and 1891 respectively was the beginning of the end of rural Vomero. Among the early beneficiaries of the area's new accessibility were a few aristocratic families who built dainty art nouveau-inspired villas among the farms. The Italians called the style Liberty; most examples were in the area around what is now piazza Vanvitelli.

Few of these buildings remain, and most that do have long been put in the shade – literally – by high-rise modern developments. There are some examples in via Solimene: the small villa at No.76 and the larger block at No.8 where, admittedly, the Liberty influence is restricted to the sharp and elegant angle of the building's corner, and the dainty hoods above the windows. Nearby, via A Vaccaro has another three buildings in slightly later architectural styles, with Nos.25, 29 and 31 built in neo-Renaissance, neo-Romanesque and neo-classical styles respectively.

Tucked away on the slopes of the hill on the seaward side of the Chiaia funicular top station is a part of Vomero that has managed to escape the ravages of time and grime. Here we can see, in via Toma No.18 and in via Palizzi Nos.19 and 50, beautifully preserved examples of Liberty. There's more Liberty on via Palizzi at No.33, although here the external decor is almost completely worn away.

Another great, if isolated, example of Neapolitan Liberty is on salita del Casale in the Posillipo district. At No.5 the extravagant Villa Pappone reflects an obsession with floral decoration. This was probably a reflection of the original owner's occupation – he was a florist.

The most compact group of Neapolitan Liberty is on via del Parco Margherita in Chiaia, which runs steeply up the hill from

piazza Amedeo. Here young architects created an art nouveau showpiece. Although the cramped perspective and ubiquitous traffic makes it hard to it appreciate properly, the large majolica-tiled building – formerly the Grand Hotel Eden – set back from the road at No.1 still dominates Piazza Amedeo. Villas at Nos.14, 36, 51 and 57 all bear more than passing reference to Liberty: an elegant wrought iron porch or railings here, fine majolica tiling there, and stained glass, crenellated balconies or floral decoration.

All of Naples' Liberty *palazzi* are privately owned, so it's virtually impossible to get a glimpse of their fabulous, often well-preserved, interiors. If you get the chance, though, grab it. Inside there is often quality craftwork, with lavish use of wrought iron, stained glass and tiling.

Room 6; pieces by Ginori (including *Three Putti with a Goat*) in Room 9; china from Vincennes/Sèvres and Saint-Cloud in Room 10; and an intriguing Meissen clock-cum-inkstand in Room 14.

The ground floor has majolica from the Middle Ages onwards: near the entrance in Room 18 is a set of vases showing biblical scenes; Room 21 has an interesting walking stick with a glass top (look inside too see a portrait of King Ferdinand's second wife; wits joked that this was the only way he could get the unpopular lady into the court). In Room 22 is a reliquary casket from Limoges. In the basement are ceramics – China's Ming (1368-1644) and Qing (1644-1911) dynasties are represented, and there's a Tang (618-906) drummer on horseback in Room 24. The Meiping vase in the shape of a phoenix is particularly rare. There are also items of Japanese porcelain, with many items from the Edo period (1615-1867), including a pair of fine octagonal dishes in Room 34.

What lies beneath

Beneath the city of Naples is a whole other world: it has been estimated that 60 per cent of Neapolitans live or work above a natural or artifical underground cavity.

These holes in the ground exist for a variety of reasons. First, the intense volcanic activity to which the Naples area has been subjected over the centuries has given rise to myriad variations and faults in basic rock formation, creating yawning subterranean chasms and pits. Second, the local rock – a yellow tufaceous stone – is porous, crumbling easily under the pressure of underground water courses. Third, the rock has long been in demand for building, and has attracted the insatiable attention of quarriers over the years.

The earliest Greek and Roman water mains under the city were probably extensions of natural underground courses, hewn straight out of the rock in the form of narrow tunnels running for hundreds of metres under what is now the city's Centro storico. During the Spanish period of the 16th century, more channels were built in the Royal Naples area.

To draw water from the channels that ran beneath their homes, Neapolitans began to bore down into the tunnels, usually constructing a well-head in the middle of their courtyard. In some cases, wells were simply adapted from the bore shafts that had been used to access stone for the construction of their own homes. Blamed by the authorities for the spread of disease, most of these wells and underground water courses fell into disuse after the cholera and typhoid outbreaks of the late 19th and early 20th centuries. But they may not be entirely redundant. Neapolitan superstition holds that spirits called *munacielli* roam among old houses, travelling by night along the disused underground water courses, popping up well shafts into houses to make mischief and take advantage of lonely housewives.

Some tunnels were built for military use. The Romans were responsible for the **Grotta di Cocceio** (*see p104*) and **Grotta di Seiano** (*see p101*), as well as the **Crypta Romana**, which runs under the Posillipo hill out towards Fuorigrotta, and is still visible today.

There was more cutting up of the landscape from the fifth century onwards as the hills outside the city walls, around Sanità, were dug up for use as cemeteries and early Christian catacombs, including **San Gaudioso** (*see p87*) and **San Gennaro** (*see p78*).

Meanwhile the hills on the city outskirts – Sant'Elmo, Posillipo, Vomero, Arenella, Scudillo, Capodimonte and San Giovanni Carbonara – were quarried furiously, leaving gaping pits and tunnels. Every time the city walls were extended, or the local authorities revised the town plan, Naples would see a new spate of excavation. The process continued for centuries and was particularly damaging in the 1700s, when frenetic quarrying left large gashes in the Chiaia district (where the Warner cinema complex is today), modern-day Parco Viviani (*see p93*) and the Ventaglieri (an area up the hill from the Montesanto railway station, visible from San Martino, *see p93*).

Tunnelling for transport started in 1855 with the opening of the now disused and little-known Borbonico tunnel, running from Chiaia under the Palazzo Reale down to the port. Parts of the tunnel were used as air raid shelters during World War II, but it was closed immediately after the war because of its dangerous state. The late 19th and early 20th centuries saw the construction of the four funiculars joining downtown Naples to the Vomero and Posillipo hills, while the Quattro Giornate road tunnel (1882-1885) was finally completed in 1940 when Mussolini opened the Mostra d'Oltremare, to link the city to the Mostra. This was followed by more road and rail construction, and, last but not least, the new Naples underground railway.

Chiaia to Posillipo

Naples gets greener: stunning views, cliffs and seafront.

Villa Communale bandstand. *See p98.*

See p98.

As you head down towards the seafront, the hustle and bustle of the Centro storico and via Toledo give way to the quieter and more variegated western districts of Chiaia and Posillipo. The way they look today is still reminiscent of Goethe's romantic descriptions of the Chiaia foreshore, with the pine-clad hill of Posillipo in the background. In reality, though, little remains of the German poet's idyll, though Mergellina harbour still has its fishing community, and some of the narrowest and oldest *vicoli* (alleys) can be found between piazza Amedeo and the Villa Comunale. This area is more aloof than the rest of Naples, with designer shops and elegant Liberty *palazzi* around via dei Mille, and the rarefied upper-class feel to via Petrarca. The long seafront stroll from Santa Lucia around to Mergellina is a classic.

Chiaia

On the northern fringe of Chiaia, piazza Amedeo is a cosy, tree-lined, cobbled square overlooked by splendid art deco *palazzi*. At No.14, **Palazzo Regina Margherita** (not open to the public) has a lovely faded majolica-tiled façade with mullioned windows. South

from piazza Amedeo, via Ascensione – or its parallel via Bausan – is where playwright Eduardo de Filippo (*see p165*) was born: controversy still rages over the exact location. In nearby piazzetta Ascensione, the church of the **Ascensione** (open 8-11am, 5-8pm Mon-Sat; 8am-1.45pm Sun) is a Cosimo Fanzago creation from the mid 17th century.

Heading east out of the square, via Colonna is home to the church of **Santa Teresa a Chiaia** (open 7.30-10.45am Mon-Sat; 7.30am-1.30pm, 5.30-7pm Sun), also designed by Fanzago (1650). It has a striking three-storey façade, and, inside, several works by Luca Giordano. With its gracious double flight of curved steps and semicircular forecourt, it is much loved by its well-heeled parishioners.

Via Colonna becomes via dei Mille and then via Filangieri, where Naples' most exclusive clothes shops are located. At the southern end of this elite drag, piazza dei Martiri is dominated by four stone lions guarding an obelisk celebrating Victory. This monument was constructed in the mid 19th century in honour of the martyrs of the 1799 revolution; one lion is dead, another is turning to dislodge a sword from its side, while the third looks pretty much OK and the fourth is

Find peace in **Parco Virgiliano**. *See p100.*

definitely on the prowl. The piazza is flanked by two splendid *palazzi* (both closed to the public): **Palazzo Partanna** (No.58), where only the portal from the original 1746 construction remains – the rest is 19th-century neo-classical, and **Palazzo Calabritto** (No.30) with a fluted column portal by Luigi Vanvitelli.

Leading out of the piazza, the narrow vico Santa Maria a Cappella Vecchia was once home to British Ambassador Sir William Hamilton, his wife Emma and her soulmate Admiral Horatio Nelson (*see p20* **William, Emma... & Horatio**). An archway nearby dated 1506 leads into the courtyard of what was a Benedictine abbey until 1788, after which it was rented out to a string of notables, including the Hamiltons. Under a second archway (No.31) is the house where Admiral Nelson was introduced to Emma in 1793. The rest, as they say, is history.

Via Morelli leads into the uninspiring via Chiatamone, which was the road closest to the coast until the late 19th century, when the parallel via Partenope, with all of its luxury hotels, was built. Via Chiatamone attracted the best and worst of Neapolitan tourism; in 1770, Giacomo Casanova visited a club in the 17th-century *palazzo* (now Nos.26-30) to drum up business for a smart new brothel on Posillipo run by Irish madam Sarah Goudar.

To the west, the once-picturesque **Riviera di Chiaia** is now sadly synonymous with tyres thrashing over cobbles, threatening life and limb of anyone rash enough to attempt the hazardous crossing to the sole park in this area, the **Villa Comunale**, which is home of the **Acquario** (for both, *see below*), one of Europe's oldest aquariums.

Percy Shelley and his wife Mary stayed at No.250 (the original building was demolished in the 1950s) from 1818 to 1819. During this period they took a child to the church of **San Giuseppe a Chiaia** (open 5-8pm Mon-Sat; 8.30am-1.30pm Sun) to be christened; the child's identity remains a mystery to this day. **Villa Pignatelli** (No.200, *see p99*) was built for Ferdinand Acton, the son of King Ferdinand I's prime minister, Sir John Acton.

A detour north from the Riviera di Chiaia along via **Santa Maria in Portico** leads to the church of the same name (open 8-11am, 5-7.30pm daily), which has a life-size Nativity scene (1647) to the left of the altar.

Stazione Zoologica (Acquario)

Villa Comunale (081 583 3111). Bus 140, 152, C28, R3/tram 1. **Open** *Mar-Oct* 9am-6pm Tue-Sat; 9.30am-7.30pm Sun. *Nov-Feb* 9am-5pm Tue-Sat; 9am-2pm Sun. **Admission** €1.50. **No credit cards**. Map p315 1B.

This aquarium was founded by German naturalist Anton Dohrn in 1872, making it one of Europe's oldest. The ground floor of the two-storey building still contains the original 24 tanks, housing sea creatures from the Bay of Naples: coral, jellyfish, turtles, sea-horses, an octopus or two, lobsters and starfish. Water for the tanks is brought in from 300m (1,050ft) out in the bay. Luckily for the inmates, it's filtered and left to decant before being used.

Villa Comunale

Riviera di Chiaia/via Caracciolo (no phone). Bus 140, 152, C28, R3/tram 1. **Open** *May-Oct* 7am-midnight daily. *Nov-Apr* 7am-10pm daily. **Admission** free. Map p315 1B.

Swathes of historic buildings were demolished in the 18th century to make way for this park designed by Luigi Vanvitelli. It was inaugurated in 1781 as the *giardini reali* (royal gardens) and was originally only open to the public once a year, on the feast of Mary's nativity (8 Sept). It quickly became known as the 'Tuglieria', a tongue-in-cheek comparison to the Tuileries in Paris. The *Toro Farnese* – now in the Museo Nazionale (*see p86*) – stood here until 1825, when it was replaced by a large bowl found in Paestum. Now surrounded by four lions, the bowl is the centrepiece of the Fontana delle Paparelle. The villa was restored for the G7 conference in 1994, when US president Bill Clinton jogged along the newly laid paving. There's a magnificent bandstand, built in 1887, plus the small-is-beautiful Stazione Zoologica (aquarium, *see above*).

Villa Pignatelli

*Riviera di Chiaia 200 (081 669 675). Bus 140, 152,
C28, R3.* **Open** *9am-2pm Tue-Sun.* **Admission** €2.
No credit cards. Map p315 1B.

Built in 1826 for Ferdinand Acton, the son of Naples'
prime minister, Sir John Acton, this villa is a mishmash of styles, with a neo-Doric portico and a neo-
Palladian vestibule. The Rothschild family bought
and enlarged the villa in 1841; it passed to the
Pignatellis in 1867 and to the Italian state in 1952.
On the ground floor are magnificent rooms including the ballroom, dining room, library and series of
'coloured rooms'; the Green Room contains a priceless collection of porcelain and majolica artefacts
from the 17th to the 19th centuries. On the first floor
is the Banco di Napoli collection. Room 1 has works
by 19th-century sculptor Vincenzo Gemito, including charming terracotta and bronze busts of street
urchins and working-class women. Room 2 has the
collection's finest piece, Francesco Guarino's intense
St George (17th century). There are some outstanding 18th- and 19th-century landscapes in Room 6.

The villa also holds occasional temporary exhibitions. The lawns of the English-style garden are a
magnet for mothers and babysitters with children.

Mergellina & Piedigrotta

Further west, the Riviera forks: north of largo
Torretta lies the densely populated district
of Torretta; towards the sea are the elegant
palazzi of viale Antonio Gramsci (renamed
in the 1970s after the founder of the Italian
Communist Party, but still known to locals

Urban dips

Visitors to Naples are often
surprised to find that a city so
famed for its superb climate doesn't
have even a half-decent beach for
swimming. As is the case with many
other Mediterranean ports, the
problem is water quality. The sea
here is certainly cleaner than it was
years back, after improvements
in local sewage treatment, but the
quantities of flotsam and jetsam
and the discharge from hundreds
of boats and ships in the bay makes
swimming here a toxic experience.

Since the prevailing north-westerly
mistral wind tends to carry water-
borne garbage down towards the
industrial coastal towns of Torre
Annunziata and Castellammare
di Stabia, the further north you
go from Mergellina, the cleaner the
water becomes: and by the time you
get to via Posillipo, it is almost inviting.

Three charming, winding lanes lead
down from via Posillipo (and its continu-
ations, via San Strato and Discesa Coroglio)
to the sea, where there are *spiagge libere*
(public beaches). The fact that none of
the approach roads is served by public
transport ensures a degree of peace and
quiet, although the walk back up is a real
challenge. Before motorboat fiends invade
in July and August, this stretch of coast
can usually be relied upon for a relatively
quiet, uncrowded dip.

The first road down, via Russo, passes
Villa Roseberry, the presidential summer
residence, which is almost always closed
to the public (except during the month of
May). At the end is a long rocky breakwater.

Via Marechiaro starts where via Posillipo
meets via Boccaccio; it winds downhill to
a small car park and an overpowering smell
of fried fish. The footpath passes assorted
restaurants and around to the right to **calata
del Ponticello a Marechiaro**, where you can
rent deckchairs and umbrellas in season.

Discesa la Gaiola drops down from
discesa Coroglio. Shortly before the road
ends, a pathway on the left descends
to the pleasant cove of **La Gaiola**, with
a shingle beach and a long quay to swim
off; there are no restaurants here, so bring
provisions for a picnic.

by its old name, viale Elena). Straight ahead, the traffic hell of via Piedigrotta leads to the extraordinary, late-Liberty (art nouveau) Mergellina railway station.

Before the railway bridge is **Santa Maria di Piedigrotta** (open 7am-noon, 5-8pm Mon-Sat; 7am-2pm, 5-8pm Sun). A church has stood since the 13th century on this spot, which is associated with apparitions of Mary. This particular church is the fulcrum of the feast-day celebrations of Mary's nativity on 8 September. The pavement beneath the railway bridge is unpleasant and dangerous, but leads to the very rewarding **Parco Virgiliano** (see below).

Via Mergellina skirts the bay to the area known as the 'Chalets' – not the Swiss kind, but a ramshackle assortment of ice-cream parlours and late-night dives (see p127 **Chalet society**). In largo Barbaia (from where Naples' shortest funicular ascends to the hillside suburbs above), via Orazio climbs up Posillipo hill to Naples' most exclusive residential areas, which have little to offer but fine views and the self-satisfaction of wealth.

Back on the bayfront, the church of **Santa Maria del Parto** (via Mergellina 21; open 5.30-8pm Mon-Sat; 9.30am-1pm, 6-8pm Sun) stands at the head of a long flight of steps (spare yourself the climb by taking the lift at number 9B). The church was built by 15th-century poet Iacopo Sannazzaro (his tomb is behind the altar); its lights guided fishermen home. In the first side chapel on the right, the painting *St Michael Vanquishing the Devil* recalls a 16th-century episode in which the ambitious prelate Diomede Carafa was sorely tempted by a local beauty, Vittoria D'Avalos. When she declared her love for him, he illustrated his quandary by commissioning this work; the realistic faces of the archangel and the serpent are those of Diomede and Vittoria respectively. What she thought of being portrayed as a satanic snake is not recorded.

Via Mergellina becomes via Posillipo at largo Sermoneta, where there is a fountain (1635) by Carlo Fanzago, Cosimo's son, named after the now-buried River Sebeto that flowed through Naples in ancient times, perhaps beneath today's via Toledo.

Parco Virgiliano

Salita della Grotta 20 (081 669 390). Metro Mergellina/bus C16, C24. **Open** 9am-1hr before sunset daily. **Admission** free. **Map** p315 2C.
Fair warning: to do justice to this splendidly peaceful spot you will first need to climb an extremely long flight of steps. For your pains, though, you'll get a view into the Crypta Neapolitana, a first-century AD road tunnel (closed). Stories abound of the atrocious conditions that existed in this primitive borehole as cart-drivers fought to control their

vehicles in the choking dust. (Conditions in the modern tunnel beneath it haven't greatly improved.) At the top of the stairs stands what is controversially known as Virgil's Tomb, looking like a large dovecote. Virgil did live in Naples. He died, however, in Brindisi. Whether he was brought back here for burial is an issue that has spawned thousands of polemical volumes.

Posillipo

Via Orazio becomes via Petrarca and then, at the top of the hill, merges with via Manzoni; if you turn left around there you'll see wonderful views over the Bay of Pozzuoli as well as the site of the former steelworks at **Bagnoli**, now transformed into a vast quadrangle of waste ground, still awaiting development; latest news is that the removal of all industrial waste won't be completed until 2006. The lower reaches of via Manzoni is a preserve of 'courting' couples; newspaper obscures the condensation-soaked windows of many a quivering car tucked in between the graceful pines. Further down the hill, turn right up viale Virgilio to reach the confusingly named **Parco Urbano Virgiliano**, a large, recently restored, horseshoe-shaped park on top of Posillipo Hill, now a pleasant place with sumptuous views over the Campi Flegrei and the islands.

Back up at the junction with via Petrarca, a right turn (uphill) into via Manzoni leads to a Spanish watchtower, the **Torre Ranieri** (1530). Originally this was one of a chain of towers, many of which still stand along the coast; its signals could be seen from Baia.

From largo Sermoneta down in Mergellina, cobbled via Posillipo clatters gradually away from the bathing establishments that nestle along the shoreline, passing the decrepit **Palazzo Donn'Anna** in the piazza of the same name. This rambling, partly derelict building has a long, sad history. The reputed site of Queen Joan II's perverse and cruel amorous pursuits in the 15th century (see p14), the original building was demolished in 1642 to make way for the present *palazzo*, designed by Cosimo Fanzago for an aristocratic couple, but the young wife for whom it was built died within a couple of years of its completion. This is private property, although a polite word at the gatehouse may gain you admission to the porticoed terrace, where the view across the bay is fantastic.

Shortly after the municipal bus depot on the right, the moody grey faux-Egyptian **Mausoleo war memorial** (open 7am-noon Tue-Sun) overlooks the road from its position in a peaceful shady garden dominated by massive pine trees.

Master of all he surveys? Overlooking **Mergellina** seafront. *See p99.*

A dearth of safe bathing in Naples proper is partially offset by the facilities at the end of three charming, winding lanes leading down from via Posillipo (*see p99* **Urban dips**), although they're definitely not for young children or poor swimmers. No buses service these routes so it's a long haul back up again. All are best out of high season.

Via Russo passes the presidential summer residence **Villa Rosebery** (closed to the public except on rare, crowded occasions during the Maggio dei Monumenti).

Via Marechiaro starts where via Posillipo meets via Boccaccio, and winds down to a tiny parking area surrounded by fish restaurants. The Calata del Ponticello a Marechiaro leads round to the right to a romantic spot overlooking a pebbly beach.

Discesa la Gaiola leads off left from Discesa Coroglio. This takes you to the Roman **Villa Pausilypon** (*see below*), with its setting of natural beauty on the Posillipo cliffs. You reach the villa through the extraordinary tunnel known as the **Grotta di Seiano** (*see below*), created in the first century AD by the architect Cocceius.

If you want to get down to the sea, there's a path on the left of the road, just before the villa. It descends to the pleasant cove of **La Gaiola**, with its small shingle beach and a long quay to swim off; there are no restaurants here, so bring your own provisions.

Via Posillipo continues on from the villa, through a cutting in the headland becoming Discesa Coroglio, then dropping sharply down towards the alternative entrance to the Grotta di Seiano and the vast sprawling ex-industrial site of the Bagnoli steelworks, now occupied in part by the **Città della Scienza** (*see p147*).

The island in the distance, Nisida, is home to a NATO naval support base and a reformatory, and is thus very much closed to the public.

Grotta di Seiano

Discesa la Gaiola 36 or Discesa Coroglio (081 230 1030/guided tours 081 795 2003). Bus 140 to Capo Posillipo, then F9. **Open** guided tours only 9.30, 10.30, 11.30am Mon-Sat. **Closed** August. **Admission** free.

This tunnel, which was the private entrance to the ornate Villa Pausilypon, was built by the architect Cocceius in the first century AD; he was also responsible for the Grotta di Cocceio (*see p105*), and the Crypta Neapolitana (*see p100*). The tunnel was strengthened in 1840 by a series of load-bearing arches, and it stretches for 770m (2,526ft) along the coast. En route, galleries provide magnificent views over the small Trentaremi Bay, named after the rowing boats the Romans used to unload stores. The fragile cliff into which the tunnel was bored is prone to landslides, and over the years access to the grotto has been irregular, but for the moment it is open regularly. Guided tours on Tuesday, Thursday and Saturday include the Villa Pausilypon (*below*).

Villa Pausilypon

Discesa Coroglio 36 (081 230 1030). Bus 140 to Capo Posillipo, then F9. **Open** *Guided tours only* 9.30, 10.30, 11.30am Tue, Thur, Sat (jointly with visits to Grotta di Seiano). **Admission** free.

This villa, in an area of stunning natural beauty on the Posillipo cliffs, once belonged to the Roman senator Publius Vedius Pollio. Access was, and still is, through the Grotta di Seiano. Apart from the remains of the villa itself, there's also an amphitheatre, used for occasional open-air concerts, and outstanding views over the small Gaiola island, site of an ugly neo-classical villa last owned by the Agnelli family and reputed to bring bad luck to all who possess it.

Campi Flegrei

A mysterious world of bubbling mud, steaming volcanoes and underwater sites.

The remains of Pozzuoli's **macellum** (market). *See p103.*

The very name Campi Flegrei (Phlegrean Fields) conjures up an area steeped in myth and history. Occupying the coastal strip around Pozzuoli, west of Naples, this is a land of bubbling, steaming volcanic activity, the reputed home of the Sibyl, a Greek prophetess, and the entrance to the Underworld. Here Roman emperors and aristocrats built fabulous summer palaces, and 18th-century aesthetes such as Sir William Hamilton (*see p20* **William, Emma... & Horatio**) were enthralled by the landscape.

Much of the aura of mystery of the Campi Flegrei has now evaporated, however, destroyed by *abusivismo edilizio* – building without planning permission – that has carpeted broad swathes of the countryside with cement. The classical ring to the place names can be deceptive: Arco Felice (happy arch), named after the old Roman arch spanning the road from Pozzuoli to Cuma, is a traffic nightmare; **Lago di Averno** (Virgil's Lake Avernus) and **Lago Lucrino** (the Lucrine lake famed for its oyster beds in antiquity) have unseemly, litter-strewn perimeters.

Some areas have been spared: two volcanic craters (**Monte Nuovo** and **Astroni**) have been transformed into nature reserves; **Pozzuoli** has been spruced up and gentrified, and its extensive underground Roman remains are being gradually opened to the public; Baia has added a new wing to the spectacular museum within its castle walls and increased opportunities for visiting the underwater remains of the ancient town; while **Cuma** – long known as mainly a Greek site – has opened up parts of its Roman heritage to the public.

TICKETS AND TRANSPORT

The highly successful Artecard cumulative museum/transport ticket (*see p35* **Smart art**) has been extended to cover the area's major sites; the Metro del Mare (maritime shuttle service) now calls at Pozzuoli and Bacoli, and the Archeobus – a special bus service linking the areas major archaeological sites – operates from Friday to Sunday.

Astroni

Astroni is one of the natural wonders of the Campi Flegrei: an entire volcanic crater carpeted with Mediterranean vegetation. Tapped by the Romans for its geothermal waters (the baths have never been discovered) and used by Naples' various dynasties from the 15th to 19th centuries as a hunting area, Astroni is now a World Wildlife Fund (WWF) reserve. A gentle pedestrianised road winds down from the entrance at the lip of the crater towards the lakes on the crater floor, through holm oak woodland that changes to deciduous at the bottom. A shady picnic site has been laid out and screened observation walkways have been erected for birders by the lakeside, but much of the area is so dense in vegetation that birdwatching here requires a good pair of ears as well as binoculars.

Riserva degli Astroni

Oasi WWF, Agnano (081 588 3720). **Open** 9.30am-4.30pm daily; ticket office closes 2pm. **Admission** €5 (free for WWF members).

Pozzuoli

Greeks from Cuma founded Dikaiarchia (ancient Pozzuoli) in c530 BC as a bulwark against encroaching Etruscans and Samnites, but there are few traces of the original Greek settlement. The area regained strategic importance in the late third century BC during the Second Punic War when the Romans were anxious to prevent Hannibal reaching the Tyrrhenian coast from nearby Capua. The hill overlooking the port, now known as **Rione Terra**, was definitively colonised in 194 BC and the new settlement (Puteoli) rapidly expanded. In Imperial times Puteoli was a thriving entrepôt port several times larger than Pompeii, and extensive traces have survived – regrettably often suffocated by the modern town.

The seafaring tradition is still strong. Pozzuoli is the closest mainland harbour to the islands of Procida and Ischia, and its ferry port does brisk business. Neapolitans come here in droves to dine on fresh fish and *frutti di mare* (seafood) at considerably lower prices than in Naples. Down near the port is the ancient fish and meat market, the **macellum**, commonly known as the Serapeo (Temple of Serapis). Its columns are visibly perforated by molluscs, showing that the macellum has spent much of its existence submerged in seawater. This is due to a rising and sinking phenomenon called bradyseism, caused by what's going on a couple of kilometres below the earth's surface.

Up on the hill jutting out over the port is the site of the original Roman colony, known as Rione Terra, a warren of ancient roads, shops and habitations in the foundations of 18th-century palazzi. Thanks to a massive injection of public funds, part of the site can now be visited (*see p105* **Rione Terra**).

Located north-east of the port, the 40,000-seater **Anfiteatro Flavio** (Flavian amphitheatre) was the ancient world's third largest, after the Colosseum in Rome and Capua's amphitheatre. Rising above – both literally and figuratively – the congested roads, railtracks and ugly modern apartment blocks that surround it, the amphitheatre was built mostly during Vespasian's rule (AD 70-79), though work may have started under Nero. The impressive *carceres* (cells) in the underground area below the arena indicate that the amphitheatre was used for *venationes*, contests involving exotic animals, shipped in through Puteoli's port from one of the Empire's distant provinces. The large *fossa* (ditch) cutting across the arena may have contained the stage setting, which was raised or lowered depending on the backdrop required. The underground cells are visitable, while the *cavea* (stalls) and the arena are back in use again for slightly more sedate, musical forms of entertainment from June to September (information from the site ticket office or 081 526 6639/azienturismopozzuoli@libero.it).

For a taste of just how 'burning' the Campi Flegrei still are, take a walk across the dormant volcanic crater of the Solfatara to the east of the town centre. From an eerie lunar landscape, hissing wisps of sulphurous steam rise up; here and there mud bubbles. The entrances to a foul-smelling *sudatorium* (built in the 19th century and now partially closed) on the north-eastern side of the crater form weird saunas.

The ancient Romans called it the Forum Vulcani and visited it with the same morbid fascination as modern-day tourists (though the signposting is probably better today; there's a restaurant and campsite as well).

On the via San Gennaro, 200 metres (230 yards) south of the Solfatara, the 16th-century church, the **Santuario di San Gennaro**, marks the spot where Naples' patron saint was decapitated. The deed was done, legend has it, near the second column on the right; the congealed blood on a stone, kept in the first chapel on the right, turns a bright healthy red on the days when a phial-full of San Gennaro's blood liquifies in Naples' Duomo (*see p78* **Blood rites**).

Anfiteatro Flavio

Via Terracciano 75 (081 526 6007). **Open** 9am-1hr before sunset Mon, Wed-Sun. **Admission** (includes Cuma and the museum and site of Baiae) €4. **No credit cards.**

Santuario di San Gennaro

Via San Gennaro Agnano 10 (081 526 1114). **Open** 8am-noon, 4.30-8pm Mon-Sat; 8am-1pm, 4.30-8pm Sun. **Admission** free.

Solfatara

Via Solfatara 161 (081 526 2341/www.solfatara.it).
Open 8.30am-1hr before sunset daily. **Admission**
€5. **No credit cards**.

Baia

From well before the Christian era until well
into the 18th century, Baia (possibly named
after Baios, a companion of Ulysses who,
according to legend, was buried here) was one
of Italy's prime holiday resorts, combining all
those essential ingredients of sea air, health-
giving mineral springs and glorious scenery.

Modern Baia consists chiefly of unattractive
strip development along the main coast road,
with arrays of bars, restaurants and *gelaterie*.

In Roman times, movers and shakers built
splendid villas here. Much of ancient Baiae
now lies under the sea (the *città sommersa* can
be seen from the Associazione Aliseo's glass-
bottomed boat; *see below*), but there's still a
certain opulence about the site and its natural
setting. Emperor Caligula (reigned AD 37-41)
built a causeway of boats and ships across the
stretch of water from Baiae to Puteoli (now
Pozzuoli). According to a second-century
account by Suetonius, 'Caligula is generally
supposed to have built the bridge as an
improvement on Xerxes' famous bridging of the
much narrower Hellespont. Others believed that
he planned this huge engineering feat to terrify
the Germans and Britons into submission.'

The **Parco Archeologico** is arranged in
terraces overlooking the bay. Up at the top,
the view from the Villa dell'Ambulatio gives
a good idea of the layout. At the end of the
ambulatio is the *balneum* (bathroom), a jewel
of stuccoed artistry. The level below contains
a nymphaeum (*see p299* **Glossary**) or perhaps
a miniature theatre; further down on the lowest
terrace stands the Tempio di Mercurio (Temple
of Mercury), a large *natatio* (swimming pool)
with an imposing dome (50-27 BC) that pre-
dates the cupola of the Pantheon in Rome.

Housing some of the archaeological finds
from the area is the **Museo Archeologico dei
Campi Flegrei**, in the atmospheric Castello
di Baia, built late in the 15th century on the
ruins of a Roman fort to improve the area's
defences; the castle was given its present
appearance between 1538 and 1550. There's a
reconstructed *sacellum* (shrine) used for the cult
of the emperors, represented here in flattering
statues of Vespasian and Titus; the bronze
equestrian statue of the unpopular Domitian
was reworked to depict his successor Nerva
after he had been deposed. On the upper level
is a reconstruction of a *nymphaeum* that was
excavated in the 1980s but lies, together with

much of Baiae, under six metres (20 feet) of
water. The statues, though, have been brought
to the surface, and include a headless Odysseus
plying Polyphemus (statue not found) with
wine, a favourite theme of Roman sculptors.
The rest of this castle (few English panels)
is given over to a new display of archaeological
finds from all over the Phlegrean Fields.

North of Baia, the **Lago di Averno** (Lake
Avernus) was where Virgil led Dante down
into the Underworld, but the *sommo poeta*
might think twice about getting his feet wet
in its decidedly uninviting waters today. The
sulphurous belching from beneath the surface
of this crater lake was once said to be potent
enough to stop passing birds dead in mid-flap.
On the north-western shore, the **Grotta di
Cocceio** (closed to the public) leads to a wide,
dead-straight tunnel that runs to the Sibyl's
cave in Cuma. In antiquity, Averno was an
inner harbour, connected by canals to the sea
via the Lago di Lucrino, where stubs of Roman
walls and arches can still be seen.

Città sommersa (underwater city)

*Associazione Aliseo, piazza della Repubblica 42,
Baia (081 8545 784/www.associazionealiseo.it).*
Tours *Mid Mar-early Nov* noon, 4pm Sat; 10.30am,
noon, 4pm Sun. **Tickets** €15; €10 6-12s.
No credit cards.
The Association, which also arranges scuba-diving
trips to Baiae and other underwater sites, organises
weekday trips in a glass-bottomed boat for large
groups by appointment. Tickets are sold on board
the boat, which is moored in Baia harbour. There are
also occasional night tours at 9pm on Saturday and
Sunday from mid June to mid September.

Museo Archeologico dei
Campi Flegrei

Via Castello 39, Bacoli (081 523 3797). **Open** 9am-
1hr before sunset Tue-Sun. **Admission** (includes the
site of Baiae, Cuma and the amphitheatre in Pozzuoli)
€4. **No credit cards**.

Parco Archeologico e
Monumentale di Baia

Via Fusaro 75, Baia (081 868 7592). **Open** 9am-
1hr before sunset Tue-Sun. **Admission** (includes the
museum of Baia, Cuma and the amphitheatre in
Pozzuoli) €4. **No credit cards**.

Cuma

With ample supplies of fresh water and rich
agricultural land, not to mention sweeping
views along the coast, it's not hard to see
what made Euboean Greeks settle around the
Acropoli di Cuma in the eighth century BC.

The history of the Greek colony of Cumae
is little known, but archaeological remains point
to a flourishing settlement that was to have

Rione Terra

Volcanic activity in the 1970s led to the mass evacuation of Rione Terra, Pozzuoli's densely inhabited and somewhat insalubrious 'acropolis' overlooking the modern port. As so often happens in these parts, a human tragedy was turned into an archaeological treasure trove: with a massive injection of regional government funds, archaeologists excavated below the 17th-century *palazzi* and brought to light much of ancient Puteoli. An underground visitors' walkway has been laid out through the dense network of roads and passageways that date, in some cases, from Puteoli's foundation in 194 BC. Much is revealed along the way: *tabernae* (simple eateries), a *cryptoportico* (underground storerooms), a *pistrinum* (bakery), and on a lower level some *ergastula* (cells for slaves) with surprisingly erudite graffiti from Catullus and a frescoed *lararium* (household shrine). Beneath the *decumanus* *maximus* (the main road leading to the forum) is part of the impressive Roman sewage system which channelled wastewater from several sources towards the southern and western edges of the promontory and then – you've guessed – straight into the sea. At the end of the walkway you come out just below the 17th-century cathedral, built around a major Roman temple, its columns revealed by a devastating fire in 1964.

The guided tour (English on request for groups) lasts about an hour, and can be confusing if you don't have a good look beforehand at the site map at the entrance. Admission (9am-7pm Sat, Sun, €3 or €5.50 for a 2-day pass to all sites in the Campi Flegrei) is on a strict quota system, so make sure you book well in advance (information and reservations 848 800 288, or from abroad 39 06 39 967 050, 9am-1.30pm, 2.30pm-5pm Mon-Sat).

Sightseeing

Parco Archeologico. *See p104.*

a considerable influence in Italy throughout the classical period. The settlement had extensive trading contacts with the Etruscans.

The Romans expanded the site, building a forum to the east and linking Cuma by a series of impressive tunnels to the Lago di Averno, an important inland harbour for the Roman fleet.

Virgil recounts (in Book VI of the Aeneid) the fascination exerted by the cave of the Sibyl, a prophetess. With its eerie light shafts (the *centum ostia* – 100 mouths – as the poet called them) in a long, echo-filled gallery, the fascination remains today. It was here that the Trojan Aeneas received his instructions to descend to the Underworld beneath Lake Avernus (*see p102*).

Apollo, the god of light and divination, was worshipped here, as the temple on the lower level of the Acropolis reveals. On the highest level – and it's worth trekking up to the top for the sweeping views through the oak woods along the way – is the Tempio di Giove (Temple of Jupiter), built in the third century BC but manhandled by Roman refurbishers in Imperial times.

South of Cuma, the Acherusia Palus of old, now **Lago Fusaro**, has a *cascina* (lodge) designed in 1782 by Carlo Vanvitelli, joined by a causeway to terra firma. Beyond Lake Fusaro is Capo Miseno (Misenum) from where Pliny the Younger watched Vesuvius erupt in AD 79.

Acropoli di Cuma

Via Montecuma (081 854 3060). **Open** 9am-1hr before sunset daily. **Admission** (includes the museum and site of Baiae, and the amphitheatre in Pozzuoli) €4. **No credit cards**.

Getting there

By bus

Buses M1 and 152 buses from piazza Garibaldi by Naples' Stazione Centrale pass by the Solfatara and the church of San Gennaro, though you'll save time by taking the underground from Piazza Garibaldi to Pozzuoli, and then taking buses or walking.

By car

Take the tangenziale ring road westwards out of Naples (direction Pozzuoli) and peel off at the appropriate exit (for Astroni and Solfatara take exit 11 at Agnano). All sites listed are within a half-hour drive of the centre if traffic isn't too dire.

By train

The Cumana railway (081 551 3328/toll free from Naples only 800 001 616/www.sepsa.it) runs three to four trains per hour to coastal sites in the Campi Flegrei. For Baia, get off at Lucrino and take the bus to the old station in Baia, from where two bus lines depart to Cuma (CD or CS). For Pozzuoli (amphitheatre, Rione Terra and Solfatara) take the Metropolitana (Line 2) to Pozzuoli–Solfatara; there's a one-kilometre walk up to the volcano; for Astroni, the most inaccessible of the sites, pick up a bus outside the Campi Flegrei metro.

Suburbs & Elsewhere

Interesting corners outside the city centre.

Although the cheap cement blocks of post-war urban expansion have pushed the city limits far into the countryside around Naples, leaving very little of its old rustic charm, there are still some places that have been salvaged from the aesthetic devestation wrought in the 1950s and '60s.

North-west

The opening in recent years of the Collinare railway – a considerable feat of engineering – improved access to the city centre from the north-western suburbs, encouraging more construction in what was once Naples' green belt. What is left of the countryside has been preserved in the park around the Eremo di Camaldoli and in the new **Parco Urbano Viale del Poggio**.

Eremo Santissimo

Via dell'Eremo 87 (081 587 2519/eremo.camaldoli @libero.it). Bus C44 from piazza Medaglie d'Oro. **Open** Mass only 5pm Thur; 8.45am, 11.30am, 6pm Sun. **Admission** free.

The chapel built here in 493 by St Gaudosius was replaced in 1585 by the current church and monastery. The monks' cells were little houses, each with its own garden. The belvedere affords a high (458m/1,600ft above sea level), hazy view over the Bay of Naples. Occupied by monks of the Camaldolese order until 1998, by which time only three were left, the site was then taken over by the Sisters of St Bridget; at the time of writing, the long-running, meticulous restoration of the buildings, gardens and walkways had still not been completed. The thriving religious community caters mostly for those on religious retreat, with prayer meetings and simple accommodation. Visitors are welcome, although the estate is not officially open to the public. A courtesy phone call beforehand is recommended in order to avoid disappointment.

Parco Urbano dei Camaldoli

Via Rai (no phone). Bus C44 from piazza Medaglie d'Oro. **Open** 7am-sunset daily.

Founded in 1995, this park is intended to halt the uncontrolled expansion of urban development on the upper reaches of the Vomero hill. A number of paths on both sides of via Rai wander through chestnut-wooded, orchid-strewn slopes and take in breath-taking views over the Bay of Naples.

Parco Urbano Viale del Poggio

Viale del Poggio 60 (no phone). Metro Colli Aminei/ bus C38, R4. **Open** 7am-sunset.

Another brand-new inner-city park, this unusual site opened in 2000 and soon became a local favourite. The park clings to an exposed hillside above the city ring road, offering little protection against sun or heavy rain (a notice at the entrance states the park may close during thunderstorms). There's a dramatic view over the palace at Capodimonte and out across the bay. The park has play facilities, smooth grass, a lake and lots of seating, all of which makes it an excellent place for kids and frazzled parents.

North-east

When they die, most Naples residents will be laid to rest in a vast cemetery region north-east of the centre, towards Capodichino airport. On via Santa Maria del Pianto, the **Cimitero Monumentale** (open 8am-7pm daily) has imposing older graves, while the newer **Cimitero Nuovo** (open 8am-5pm daily) is nearby. On busy days the area outside the graveyards hosts an animated cut-flower market, overseen carefully by the Polizia Mortuaria – flower traders have been known to gather flowers from graves and resell them next day.

A quieter resting-place is near the piazza at the top of via Nuova del Campo; the **British Cemetery** (open 9am-5pm Mon-Fri; 9am-1pm Sat, Sun) is in fact international and inter-denominational. Prior to 1898, foreigners were buried in the Cimitero degli inglesi nearer the centre of town by piazza Santa Maria della Fede (map p312 2B). When that cemetery was closed, the remains of the deceased were either repatriated or dumped in a common burial ground, and the area was reborn as the **Parco ex-cimitero degli inglesi**. The larger tombs remain, however. With its shady trees and friendly gardens, this is a corner of a foreign field that will be forever England.

Centro Direzionale

Just north of the tracks leading into Stazione Centrale (and highly visible from trains to Naples), the gleaming Centro Direzionale district rose in the late 1980s from the ashes of a hideous industrial site. The first fruits of a decades-long administrative battle over redevelopment of derelict eastern Naples, the Centro Direzionale is an incomplete version of a design by Japanese architect Kenzo Tange. The district is dominated by the towering twin

Parco Urbano Vial del Poggio.
See p107.

mirror-glass blocks of the Enel electricity board. Many state and corporate bodies – the regional government, Telecom Italia, the state railways – have relocated here.

In August 1990, the whole of Tower Block A went up in flames in mysterious circumstances during the transfer there of the Central Criminal Court and its archives. Motives suggested for the dramatic arson attack even included speculation about an insurance scam. It was initially thought the whole tower would have to come down. But that was not the case and the courts have since reopened in the building.

The central avenue of the district could have been lined up with Vesuvius for a magnificent view, but instead the volcano is barely visible between the towers, and there's little to take your mind off the barren litter-strewn expanse of windswept concrete.

Fuorigrotta

So-called because of its position outside (*fuori*) the two tunnels into the Mergellina area, the eastern suburb of Fuorigrotta was developed

under the fascist government during the 1920s and '30s. A downmarket residential district, it has wide, regular streets that are rather soulless.

Piazzale Tecchio lies at the heart of Fuorigrotta, which is best reached by taking the metro to Campi Flegrei or the Cumana railway to Mostra. The piazza was given a facelift for the soccer World Cup in 1990.

The gigantic 82,000-seat **Stadio San Paolo** (1959) dominates the scene. On Sundays in season, it's a deafening swirl of sky-blue shirts and scarves, though with Napoli currently languishing in Serie C, the halcyon days of Maradona are a very distant memory. *See also p172* **The Calcio Napoli file**.

Beyond, the **Mostra d'Oltremare** was built in 1939-40 to show off 'achievements' in Italy's African colonies. Heavily bombed during World War II, it was extensively rebuilt as a trade exhibition space in 1952. It is only open for shows and exhibitions, although the quiet tree-lined area is accessible at any time. The **Edenlandia** funfair (*see p148*) is at the far end of the Mostra area.

Eat, Drink, Shop

Restaurants

Fresh, local produce, traditional cooking methods: it's hard to eat badly in Naples.

Sophistication and a smile at **La Bersagliera**. *See p112.*

Neapolitans are always up for a heated gastro-nomic discussion. Food is regarded as something almost sacred, and unorthodox culinary methods can be viewed with horror – as something akin to mortal sin. Some less traditional cuisine is emerging in Naples, but when push comes to shove the traditional wins hands down among Neapolitans. It's difficult to eat badly in this city, although some of the new establishments muscling in on the growing tourist market leave a lot to be desired. On the other hand, the number of restaurants where the food is exquisite is large.

Smart is not necessarily best here; many of Naples' best eating experiences can be had in spit-and-sawdust *trattorie* and *osterie* (the terms are more or less interchangeable), rather than in the plusher restaurants.

HOW TO ORDER

Ordering in a Neapolitan restaurant can be a palaver, but it can be immensely entertaining too. Although restaurants are obliged by law to produce a menu, many fail to do so. If a list of dishes is forthcoming, its contents may bear little

relation to what is being prepared in the kitchen, particularly in smaller *trattorie*. Don't be put off; it only means that the chefs, in their tiny kitchens, are using the best, freshest ingredients available at market that day. Menus may be in dialect (*see p124* **The menu**) or may list dishes named after a former chef or the owner's beloved mamma. You can overcome difficulties by seeing what others are eating and pointing to what you fancy.

The *menu turistico* is best avoided; the *menu del giorno*, on the other hand, is likely to be fresh and tasty. It is perfectly acceptable to order a *primo* (pasta course) but no *secondo* (main course). On the whole, portions tend to be abundant. If you're not up to a full main course, replace it with *contorni* (cooked vegetables such as peppers, aubergines, spinach and courgettes), *antipasti misti di mare* (seafood hors d'oeuvre) or an *insalata verde* (fresh green salad).

VEGETARIANS

In the southern Italian culinary mind, meat does not include ham or pancetta (bacon). Vegetarians should double-check by asking *c'è la pancetta?* ('is there bacon in it?') when they are told that dishes such as *pasta e fagioli* (pasta and bean soup) or *pasta patata e provola* (pasta with potatoes and smoked cheese) are valid veggie options. If your host offers to bring 'a taste of everything' or to select some *antipasti* on your behalf, try to establish just what this will entail economically. For fish-eaters, Naples is heaven, but to avoid a hellish bill, get your host to weigh the fish and quote you a price before it goes in the oven.

PIZZA

Naples credits itself as being the birthplace of the Italian pizza, back in the 16th century, and Neapolitans, through their zeal to maintain their supremacy as producers of the dish, have taken pizza from its origins as the simplest food of the poorest to the status of a gourmet art form.

The Neapolitan pizza is a truly balanced creation; a fairly soft, thinnish base, and medium amounts of topping contained within a thick doughy rim. A genuine Neapolitan pizza must be cooked in a wood-fuelled oven.

Many of the best *pizze* are to be found in places where staff have never heard of a *prenotazione* (reservation) and where queues can be huge. Don't be put off: the turnover is often remarkably quick. Don't neglect, however, to single out the head waiter and book your place in the queue: if you don't, you may be there all night.

WINE BARS

Wine culture in southern Italy dates back to Roman times and beyond; in the south, however, wine is always accompanied by food. Traditionally, both oil and wine were bought in *vini e olii* (wine and oil) outlets, but only the most hardened of drinkers would actually spend time in these places. You'll still find a couple of tiny tables squashed between barrels of oil and *vino sfuso* (wine from the barrel) in some shops; others have become fully fledged restaurants.

Naples missed the 1970s and '80s wine bar boom, which might be lucky, since there are now lovely wine bars of recent origin around the city, with good food to accompany varied modern wine selections, usually featuring local bottles.

Wine lists often appear extensive, but to avoid disappointment and time wasting, it is worth asking which are out of stock before you make your choice. (*Sono tutti disponibili?* 'Are they all in stock?') Local producers can be slow in delivering, so stocks are depleted around October and November. *See p116* **Selecting local wine.**

SNACKS

As in any large city, there are snack bars where you could munch off the floor and others where you wouldn't let your dog eat. The food served in bars is incredibly cheap, with pizzas ranging from €1.50 to €2.50 each and fried foods at 15¢ or 25¢ a piece. Some places have seats and there is rarely an extra charge for these. Generally, snack bars in Naples are fairly hygienic and, as long as the hot snacks haven't been sitting around for too long in a warm display cabinet, you should have no problems. It's worth persisting at the busier bars, where the turnover of food is brisk.

The pavement fried-food stalls (*friggitorie*), where bits and pieces are plunged into oil – sometimes smelling like engine oil – in a large

The best Restaurants

For fish and seafood
La Vecchia Cantina is right next to the fish market (*see p119*); fishy *antipasti* are a meal in themselves at **D'Angelo Santa Caterina** (*see p119*); **Dora** serves fantastic fish in a tiny space (*see p122*).

For views
Try **Ciro** (*p112*), in a beautiful setting below the Castel dell'Ovo; **Caronte** (*see p124*) looks across Lago d'Averna; or, for a stunning Posillipo panorama over the bay, there's **Giuseppone a Mare** (*see p122*).

For eating outside
Il Giardino del Pontano (*see p121*) has tables in a little courtyard/garden; **Féfé** (*see p125*) is on the picturesque port of Bacoli.

For pizza
Da Ettore (*see p113*); **Da Michele** (*see p115*); **Lombardi a Santa Chiara** (*see p116*); **Di Matteo** (*see p116*); **Ciro a Santa Brigida** (*see p119*); **Angolo del Paradiso** (*see p121*); **Piazzeria Cilea** (*see p121*).

For a cheap lunch (not pizza)
Osteria Donna Teresa (*see p121*) serves exemplary traditional food; **La Mattonella** (*see p113*) has fab *antipasti* and spaghetti with squid; at **Cantina della Sapienza** (*see p115*) you'll eat the nearest thing to Neapolitan home cooking you can find in a restaurant.

For top-notch cuisine
Authentic local ingredients make for vivid flavours at **La Stanza del Gusto** (*see p113*); at **Don Salvatore** (*see p122*) you'll have the perfect wine to complement fab *antipasti* and fish and meat dishes; ingredients from around Italy are combined to palate-blowing effect at **Vadinchenia** (*see p123*).

Eat, Drink, Shop

wok-like pan on wheels are almost a thing of the past, which is perhaps not such a bad thing. The ones listed below, however, are reliable.

Stalls selling *o muss'e o per 'e puorc* (pig's muzzle and trotters with salt and lemon: a traditional Neapolitan speciality) in the Pignasecca area are generally clean. But if this dish isn't your idea of a tasty nibble, try something from one of the huge, mobile, nocturnal sandwich stalls that sell an excellent range of doorstop sandwiches; these, too, are usually clean.

On the seafront along via Caracciolo is a line of stalls selling fresh, hot and tasty *taralli* (crunchy pastry/biscuit rings with black pepper and almonds) and *treccine* (the long, plaited version).

WHAT TO DRINK

The house wine served in most restaurants – especially in *osterie* and *vini e olii* (bottle shops with tables) – is local and good. The red is a safer bet than the white between April and November, when the current year's production arrives. Order un *bicchiere di rosso/bianco* (a glass of red/white) or *un quarto* (a quarter-litre carafe) to start, giving you the option of ordering more, or opting for a bottled variety. *See also p116* **Selecting local wine**.

Many *osterie* and restaurants do not serve coffee (or if they do it is likely to be limited to espresso). They do, however, serve post-prandial shots of traditional *digestivi* to facilitate digestion: try the limoncello (*see p233* **LimonHello**), *nocillo* (a hazelnut variety) or *basilico* (made with basil). These are often made in-house and can be potent.

THE BILL AND PRICES

All restaurants charge *coperto* (cover charge), which is generally between €1.50 and €2.50 per person. When the bill arrives, check it carefully (particularly if there was any confusion over your order) and calmly query anything that is unclear. It is customary, though by no means obligatory, to leave a tip (usually around ten per cent), which is a particularly good investment if you intend to return to the restaurant. In theory, restaurants are obliged to issue a receipt; in practice, this is often overlooked.

Average prices given below are for one person consuming a *primo*, *secondo* and a *contorno*, plus a dessert or *antipasto*, without wine. For *pizzerie*, the price covers a pizza and one pre-pizza snack.

Royal Naples

Restaurants

Amici Miei

Via Monte di Dio 78 (081 764 4981/081 764 6063). Bus C22, C25, R2. **Meals served** *Sept-June* 1-3pm, 8-11.30pm Tue-Sat; 1-3pm Sun. *July* 1-3pm,

8-11.30pm Mon-Fri. Closed Aug. **Average** €45. **Credit** AmEx, DC, MC, V. **Map** p315 1A.

A family-run restaurant with excellent cuisine. It's best to come with a good appetite for the likes of palate-blowing *paccheri Amici Miei* (pasta with an aubergine and gorgonzola sauce), excellent chargrilled meat (the lamb is particularly tasty), vegetables and cheeses – there is no fish. Delicious *dolci* are made in the kitchen, including *crema pasticciera* served with brandied chestnuts, and chocolate mousse. There's also a good choice of quality southern wines at very reasonable prices; try the Primitivo di Manduria (red) or the Vigna Caracci (white). If you want a chuckle, take a look at English-language version of the menu.

La Bersagliera

Borgo Marinaro 10-11 (081 764 6016/www.la bersagliera.it). Bus C25. **Meals served** noon-3.30pm, 7.30pm-midnight Mon, Wed-Sun. Closed 2wks Jan. **Average** €50. **Credit** AmEx, DC, MC, V. **Map** p315 2A.

The famous neighbour of Zi Teresa (*see p113*), this restaurant is slightly more sophisticated in terms of decor and clientele. The cuisine, majoring in fish-based dishes, is generally of a high standard. The *taglierini alla Bersagliera* (fine ribbon pasta with baby octopus, black olives and tomato) is highly recommended.

La Cantinella

Via Nazario Sauro 23, Lungomare Santa Lucia (081 764 8684/www.lacantinella.it). Bus C25. **Meals served** *May-Aug* 12.30-3pm, 7.30-11.30pm Mon-Sat. *Sept-Apr* 12.30-3pm, 7.30-11.30pm Mon-Sat. Closed 2wks Aug. **Average** €60. **Credit** AmEx, DC, MC, V. **Map** p313 2A.

There's no denying that this holy of holies among Neapolitan restaurants serves some wonderful food, including *pesce spada affumicato* (smoked swordfish) or *penne con calamaro e cavolo* (pasta with squid and white cabbage). But rich sauces are often added, overpowering the subtle flavour of seafood dishes in particular. The service is professional and the wine list is international, if somewhat pricey.

Ciro

Borgo Marinaro 29-30 (081 764 6006/www.ristorante ciro.it). Bus C25. **Meals served** 12.30-3.30pm, 7.30pm-midnight Mon, Tue, Thur-Sun. **Average** €40. **Credit** AmEx, DC, MC, V. **Map** p313 2A.

In a lovely setting below the Castel dell'Ovo (*see p64*), Ciro offers delightful service and old-fashioned charm. The quality of the food can be inconsistent, though: fish-based dishes, such as *'mpepata di cozze* (steamed mussels with pepper and lemon), are generally tasty; meat is less of a forte. Prices are on the high side, but the view is hard to beat.

Da Angela

Santa Anna di Palazzo 25 (081 401 495). Funicular Centrale to Via Roma/bus 24, C22, C25, C57. **Meals served** 1-3pm, 7.30pm-midnight Tue-Sat. Closed 2 wks Aug. **Average** €25. **Credit** DC, MC, V. **Map** p315 1A.

You'll need to book or arrive early to avoid a wait at this tiny trattoria just off via Chiaia. At lunchtime the turnover is rapid, though, so it's worth waiting. Angela prepares all the tasty *antipasti* and many of the pasta sauces. Try the *paccheri alla pescatrice* (large tube pasta with fresh tomato and fish) or the *siciliana* (with aubergines tomato and mozzarella). The grilled *pesce bandiera* is delicious and the *vino locale* good.

La Mattonella

Via Nicotera 13 (081 416 541). Bus C22, C25, R2. **Meals served** *July, Aug* 12.30-3.30pm, 8pm-midnight Mon-Sat. *Sept-June* 12.30-3.30pm, 7.30-11.30pm Mon-Sat; 12.30-3.30pm Sun. Closed 3wks Aug. **Average** €25. **No credit cards. Map** p315 1A.

This tiny *osteria* takes its name from the strange collection of tiles (*mattonelle*) that decorates its walls. The *antipasti* are great (tiny mozzarella balls and aubergine and cheese rolls), as is the spaghetti with *calamaretti* (baby squid). Good *vino locale* is served in ceramic jugs from Vietri on the Amalfi Coast.

La Stanza del Gusto

Vicoletto Sant'Arpino 21 (081 401 578). Bus 140, C9, C18, C22, C25. **Meals served** 8-11pm Mon-Sat. Closed 3wks July-Aug. **Average** €35. **Credit** AmEx, DC, MC, V. **Map** p315 1A.

This gem-like restaurant hides at the top of a tiny flight of stairs just off the frenzied via Chiaia. The à la carte menu changes regularly. Dishes might include *millefoglie melenzane con baccalà affumicato* (millefeuille with aubergine and smoked cod), *pasta corta con salsiccia e finocchio* (pasta with sausage and fennel), or *stinco di maiale nero all'aglianico* (hauch of pork – *maiale nero* is a semi-wild pig found in the Caserta area – in red wine). There's an extensive international wine list and friendly but professional service. For the *menu degustazione* (€45 including wine), diners select a theme (seafood, mushrooms or lamb, for example) and owner Mario Avallone will personally select seasonal ingredients and come up with a customised menu and accompanying wine; several days' advance booking is required for this.

Trattoria San Ferdinando

Via Nardones 117 (081 421 964). Bus C22, C25, R2. **Meals served** 12.30-3.30pm Mon, Tue; 12.30-3.30pm, 8-11.30pm Wed-Fri. Closed 3wks Aug. **Average** €30. **Credit** AmEx, DC, MC, V. **Map** p315 1A.

The menu changes daily but there is always a choice of seafood, veggie or meat pasta dishes. Firm favourites are *pasta e fagioli* (pasta and beans), *pasta e calamaretti/seppioline* (pasta with baby squid or cuttlefish). There's a good selection of *contorni* and the *secondi* aren't bad either. The grilled squid is particularly flavoursome as is the *scarola* (cooked endive with olives and capers).

Zi Teresa

Borgo Marinaro 1 (081 764 2565/www.ziteresa.it). Bus C25. **Meals served** 12.30-3.30pm, 8-11.30pm Tue-Sat; 12.30-4pm Sun. Closed lunch 1wk Aug. **Average** €50. **Credit** AmEx, DC, MC, V. **Map** p315 2A.

La Mattonella.

With humble beginnings in 1916 as an *osteria* selling beans and mussels, Zi Teresa – now run by Teresa's grandchildren – is a favourite for christening, First Communion and anniversary parties, so expect large groups and cheerful noise. The food is consistently good; try *pasta fagioli e cozze* (pasta with beans and mussels) or *tubetti con fiore di zucca* (pasta with courgette flowers). All the *dolci* are made on the premises, and you can tell: the tiramisù is particularly good. The tables overlooking the port are the most pleasant. Book in advance, especially for Sunday lunch.

Pizzerie

Brandi

Salita Sant'Anna di Palazzo 1 (081 416 928/www.brandi.it). Bus C22, C25, R2. **Meals served** 12.30-3pm, 7.30pm-midnight daily. Closed 1wk Aug. **Average** €30. **Credit** AmEx, MC, V. **Map** p313 1A.

Brandi claims to be the place where the pizza margherita was invented (for Italy's Queen Margherita, in 1889), although there are plenty of contenders for that distinction. Many famous diners have eaten here, including Bill Clinton. The pizza is always good, and there's a decent restaurant menu too, for which you'll pay around €50. Booking recommended.

Da Ettore

Via Santa Lucia 56 (081 764 0498). Bus C25 140. **Meals served** 12.30-3pm, 7.30-11.30pm Mon-Sat. Closed Aug. **Average** €20. **No credit cards. Map** p315 1A-2A.

Although it is a restaurant too, Da Ettore is most renowned for its wonderful pizzas and for its *pagniottiello*, a sort of pizza-bread bap stuffed with delicious fillings. The *fiorilli* (deep-fried courgette flowers) are

great when available, but the *vino locale* is rough: better to opt for a bottled wine. Evening bookings are not taken, so arrive early or be prepared to queue.

Re di Napoli
Piazza Trieste e Trento 7-8, off Via Toledo (081 423 013/4). Funicular Centrale to Augusteo/ bus C25. **Meals served** noon-3pm, 7.30pm-midnight daily. **Average** €15. **Credit** AmEx, MC, V. **Map** p313 1C.
Part of the Sebeto group of pizzerie, the Re di Napoli serves a wide choice of pizze; stick to the classic varieties, and you won't go wrong. Also interesting is the pizza DOC, a hot pizza base topped with fresh mini-mozzarella and tomatoes. The branch below has a lovely view of the Castel dell'Ovo.
Other locations: via Partenope 29-30 (081 764 7775).

Regina Margherita
Via Partenope 19 (081 764 4629). Bus C25. **Average** €15. **Open** noon-4pm, 7pm-1am daily. **Credit** AmEx, MC, V. **Map** p315 2A.
Plenty of pizzerie have sprung up along the seafront overlooking the bay. Of these the Regina Margherita has the best *pizze* and the nicest service. And the *vino locale* is perfectly palatable tooi. Choose your pavement table carefully to avoid being baked under the sun in summer.

Port & University

Restaurants

Taverna dell'Arte
Rampe San Giovanni Maggiore 1A (081 552 7558). Bus C25, R1, R2. **Meals served** 8pm-midnight Mon-Sat. Closed 3wks Aug. **Average** €30. **Credit** MC, V. **Map** p313 1C.
Dell'Arte has that perfect combination of homely atmosphere, good food and wine, and attentive service. The menu is limited, but ingredients are used imaginatively and quality is consistently high. Try the *paccheri ai carciofi* (large tube pasta with an artichoke, pine nut and black olive sauce), *calamaro con patate* (squid cooked with potatoes and a little tomato) or *tagliatelli con funghi porcini* (pasta with porcini mushrooms). Basil sorbet is served between courses to refresh the palate. This place is popular, so booking is usually essential.

Pizzerie

Da Michele
Via Sersale 1 (081 553 9204). Metro Piazza Garibaldi/bus R2. **Meals served** 10am-11pm Mon-Sat (daily Sept-May). Closed 3wks Aug. **Average** €8. **No credit cards. Map** p311 3D.
A seriously minimalist traditional pizzeria: just large marble tables; two types of pizza (margherita or marinara); beer and water. Friendly, fast service and enormous, truly delicious *pizze* at unbelievably low prices. Take a number at the door before joining the queue.

Centro storico

Restaurants

Antica Osteria Pisano
Piazzetta Crocelle ai Mannesi 1 (corner of via Duomo and Spaccanapoli) (081 554 83 25). Metro Dante or Museo/bus R2. **Meals served** noon-4pm, 7-11pm Mon-Sat. Closed 2 wks Aug. **No credit cards. Map** p311 3C.
This trattoria has a limited lunchtime menu and a more elaborate selection in the evening, but it's superb whenever you eat. Traditional favourites like *pasta al sugo* or *alla genovese* are a forte.The *contorni* are abundant and fresh, and make an excellent substitute for a main course. The kitchen opens on to the restaurant, and staff are more than happy for you to have a gander. This place is understandably popular, but tiny – so be prepared to wait.

Bellini
Via Santa Maria di Costantinopoli 79-80 (081 459 774). Metro Dante. **Meals served** *July-Sept* 12.30-3.30pm, 7.30-11pm Mon-Sat. *Oct-June* 12.30-3.30pm, 7.30-11pm Mon-Sat; 12.30-3.30pm Sun. Closed 1wk Aug. **Average** €35. **Credit** MC, V. **Map** p311 1B-2B.
Enormous portions of pasta with seafood as a first and second course in one. Try *linguine ai frutti di mare* (pasta with a mixture of fresh seafood) and *linguine con astice* (pasta with langoustines).

Cantina della Sapienza
Via della Sapienza 40 (081 459 078). Metro Piazza Cavour/bus C57, R4. **Meals served** noon-3.30pm Mon-Sat. Closed 3wks Aug. **Average** €15. **No credit cards. Map** p311 1B.
The nearest thing to Neapolitan home cooking you'll find in a restaurant. The menu changes every day, but favourites include *pasta alla siciliana* (with aubergines, tomato and mozzarella) and *pasta al ragù* (with meat and tomato sauce). The *parmigiano di melanzane* (baked aubergine with mozzarella and tomato) is outstanding. Friendly family service, fine desserts and good *vino locale* (red).

La Cantina del Sole
Via Paladino 3 (081 552 7312). Metro Dante/bus R2. **Meals served** 7pm-midnight Mon, Wed-Sat; 1-3.30pm, 7pm-midnight Sun. Closed Aug. **Average** €35. **Credit** MC, V. **Map** p311 3B.
This little restaurant offers an incredible array of dishes, with many recipes dating back to the 17th and 18th centuries. The *genovesi al sugo di agnello* (pasta with onion and lamb sauce) is hearty. For something light but flavourful, try the *spaghetti alla maccheronata* (fresh tomatoes, lashings of basil and a sprinkling of pecorino cheese – no oil or garlic).

La Locanda del Grifo
Via F del Giudice 14 (081 442 0815). Metro Dante/ bus R4, R1. **Meals served** *Jan-Oct* noon-3.30pm, 7-11.30pm Mon,Wed-Sun. *Nov, Dec* noon-3.30pm, 7-11.30pm daily. **Average** €20. **Credit** AmEx, DC, MC, V. **Map** p311 2B.

Local classics like *spaghetti alla puttanesca* or *pasta alla siciliana* are top-notch at this convenient Centro storico stop-off. Locanda also offers good local wine too (the red is better than the white), and a few tables outside.

Pizzerie

Lombardi a Santa Chiara

Via B Croce 59 (081 552 0780). Metro Dante/ bus C25, R1, R2. **Meals served** 1-3pm, 7.30-11.30pm Tue-Sun (open daily Dec). Closed 2wks Aug. **Map** p311 2A-2B.

Lombardi a Santa Chiara offers good service, excellent pizza and a decent wine list; in fact it's one of the city's best-established pizzerias. But it's popular and there are long queues, especially at weekends, so it's a good idea to book in advance. It also serves a selection of scrumptious *dolci* and has a very good restaurant menu.

Di Matteo

Via dei Tribunali 94 (081 455 262). Metro Dante/bus R1, R2. **Meals served** 10am-midnight Mon-Sat (open daily Dec). Closed 2wks Aug. **Average** €10. **No credit cards.** **Map** p311 2B-2D.

The decor may be unimpressive but the pizzas are fabulous at this highly popular pizzeria. Di Matteo is one of the few places where *ripieno fritto* is to be recommended. Delicious deep-fried bits and pieces (*frittura*) can be nibbled to keep hunger at bay.

Selecting local wine

Campania is one of the rising stars of the Italian wine firmament. A clutch of energetic young producers is finally doing justice to grapes like Aglianico – a red that can hold its own with Tuscany's Sangiovese or Piedmont's Nebbiolo – and rediscovering interesting local varieties such as Piedirosso and Gragnano. Producers from the Cilento and Amalfi coast are also creating some worthwhile new wines, but these can be hard to come by, so grab the opportunity should it arise. Unfortunately, many less scrupulous producers have jumped on to the Falanghina and Aglianico bandwagon, with wines ranging from mediocre to downright awful. Things are further complicated by the tendency of some producers to bottle their very best wines as humble old vino da tavola, thus bypassing the ploddingly restrictive DOC regulations. As a result, the names of wineries and individual crus are always a safer guide to quality than the official classifications. *See also p176* **Wine tourism**.

Reds

Aglianico del Taburno

This full-bodied red ranges from bog-standard to palate-blowing. Cantina del Taburno and Ocone are the best-known producers, but La Rivolta in the Cilento also does a tasty version.

Costa d'Amalfi Furore Rosso

A Piedirosso and Aglianico blend, this delicious full-bodied red from the Amalfi Coast matures well. The Gran Furor (Marisa Cuomo) label is by far the best.

Falerno del Massico

Both this and its white equivalent (*see below*) were known to the Romans, and were drunk on special occasions in ancient Pompeii. They are still going strong today. The best producers are Villa Matilde and Moio.

Gragnano

A slightly fizzy, dry wine that should be drunk young. Grotta del Sole – which specialises in rare local varieties like this one – is the best producer.

Montevetrano

In the hinterland of Salerno, photographer Silvia Imparato has been making one of Campania's most impressive reds for years. It's a blend of Cabernet Sauvignon and Merlot, with a little Aglianico thrown in.

Per'e Palummo

The 'foot of the dove' is a red grape native to Ischia, where it makes for a surprisingly complex wine. Look out for D'Ambra and Pietratorcia (which uses the grape in its Ischia Rosso blend).

Piedirosso

Drink this light and very pleasant wine while it's still young: two years old at the most. Both Ocone and Grotta del Sole are good producers.

Taurasi

Produced around the little village of Taurasi near Avellino, this 100 per cent Aglianico is serious competition for the Brunello of the north. Look for the Mastroberardino, Feudi di San Gregorio and Caggiano labels.

Vigna Camarato

Produced by Villa Matilde, this single cru Aglianico has been attracting serious praise from Italy's wine critics. Try the 1997 or '98.

Trianon da Ciro

Pietro Colletta 46 (081 553 9426). Metro Piazza Garibaldi/bus R2. **Meals served** 10.30am-3.30pm, 6.30-11.30pm daily. **Average** €10. **No credit cards. Map** p311 2D-3D.

There are absolutely no frills at this traditional pizzeria, just long marble tables and a fairly limited choice of *pizze*, all of which are truly delicious. To go with them, there's Coca-Cola, beer and water. That's it. You may be expected to write your own order.

Wine bars

Berevino

Via San Sebastiano 62 (081 290 313). Metro Dante or Montesanto/bus C57, R1, R4. **Open** 11am-2am Mon-Sat, 4.30-8pm Sun. Closed 3wks Aug. **Credit** MC, V. **Map** p311 2A.

This wine bar/shop serves a delicious selection of munchies to accompany your choice of wine from the fairly extensive, though not international, wine list. Big on Campanian wines.

Snacks

Ciao Pizza

Via B Croce 42 (081 551 0109). Metro Dante/ bus R1, R4. **Open** *Mar-Sept* 9am-midnight Mon-Sat; 5.30pm-midnight Sun. *Oct-Feb* 9am-midnight daily. Closed 2wks Aug. **No credit cards. Map** p311 2A-2B.

Tasty, traditional pizza triangles.

Other locations: via San Carlo 3 (081 421 616).

Villa dei Misteri

Italian national heritage Pompei got together with Mastroberardino to recultivate the vines once grown in ancient Pompeii in the archaeological site today. The result is a full-bodied red, Scianscinoso and Piedirosso, called Villa dei Misteri. Sold at auction for the first time in 2003, it is difficult if not impossible to come by.

Whites

Biancolella

An Ischian grape with which the D'Ambra winery does great things. Look out for its Tenuta Frassitelli cru. Pietratorcia blends it with Fiano to produce the superb, barrel-aged Scheria Bianco cru.

Coda di Volpe

A pleasant, light, easy-quaffing white.

Costa d'Amalfi Furore Bianco

This blend of Biancolella (known locally as Biancazita) and Falanghina from the Amalfi Coast really works. Try the Apicella label, or the Fior d'Uva cru turned out in tiny quantities by Gran Furor (Marisa Cuomo).

Falanghina

The name means 'little stick'; in ancient times it was the first vine to be trained over a support. Probably the most popular of the Campanian whites, it's fresh and fruity. Try Villa Matilde, Mustilli, Ocone, Feudi di San Gregorio or Moio.

Falerno

Dry but fruity. As with the red of the same name, Villa Matilde leads the field.

Fiano di Avellino

Another ancient, perfumed, full-bodied white that's worth trying. Again, Feudi di San Gregorio is one of the best producers, closely followed by Terredora and Mastroberardino. A case apart is the fragrant Kratos produced in the Cilento by one-man-band Luigi Maffini; his Kleos and Cenito reds are also worth hunting down.

Greco di Tufo

One of the few whites that can be drunk more than a year after bottling, but still best young. There are many inferior types about; for the best, seek out the Feudi di San Gregorio or Mastroberardino versions.

Eat, Drink, Shop

The sausage season

If you try ordering sausages in a Naples *osteria* in summer, prepared to be told '*non è stagione*' – it's not the season; sausages are traditionally only produced in the cooler months of the year. Neapolitan restaurant menus change with the seasons, and the main reason for this is that dishes rely on fresh, local produce, only available at certain times of year. The high standard of food in Neapolitan restaurants is largely down to this.

Italian cuisine varies widely between regions, reflecting both climatic and agricultural differences. The Campania region is particularly conservative in its culinary traditions and most dishes have a long history. Key ingredients include seafood (supposedly to be eaten only in months containing the letter 'r'), tomatoes, olives (particularly the small, black Gaeta variety), capers, beans, lentils and chickpeas.

The Slow Food movement has been active in promoting the principles of independent, diverse, localised food production. The Italian government, too, has begun to promote traditional production methods. A variety of products are being classified with the DOC/DOP (Denominazione di Origine Controllata/Protetta) quality control system, better known for classifying wines. To qualify for DOC status, the whole production process must take place within the traditional area for that particular product, using tried and tested methods. A DOC certificate guarantees quality, but Italian certification and authorisation processes are painfully complex and time-consuming, and there are a lot of equally good food around that has yet to gain the DOC seal of approval.

Below we list some of Campania's most typical produce, together with some producers who do things the traditional way.

Olive oil

Types of oil (all local), cultivation and pressing methods vary as they have done over the last thousand years. Le Tore DOP is a top-notch organic oil as is Villa Angelina DOP ed extra and Li Portali DOP. Oil tasting is fast becoming the new wine tasting. The producers below also provide *agriturismo* (farm holiday) services and are in rather beautiful locations on the Sorrento peninsula.

La Villanella *via Galatea 16, Massa Lubrense (081 807 5651/347 629 6673).*

Le Tore *via Pontone 43, Massa Lubrense (081 808 0637/www.letore.com).*
Torre Cangiani *via Vigliano 1, Massa Lubrense (081 533 9849/torre cangiani@sirene.it).*

Pasta di Gragnano

This pasta is produced using exclusively *grano duro* (durum wheat) and is dried naturally, to maintain fragrance, nutritional value and consistency during cooking.

Pomodorini del Vesuvio

Tiny slightly pear-shaped tomatoes, grown within the fertile volcanic area of Vesuvius.

Mozzarella di bufala Campana

Mozzare means 'to cut' and this mozzarella is produced in the traditional manner, by hand, using buffalo milk, rennet and salt. It should be eaten between 12 and 24 hours after production. No other so-called mozzarella can compete.

Maiale nero del Casertano

Pork from a special kind of pig from the Caserta area. Incredibly gamey tasting, it makes for very flavoursome stews, particularly when cooked with the local aglianico red wine, or served braised with pan-fried sweet peppers or *papaccelle* (pickled round flattish peppers).

Limone della Penisola Sorrentina e Amalfi

Lemons, lemon flower honey and limoncello made from lemon rind. The use of the rind means that organic lemons (where no pesticides have been used) are a must for limoncello. *See p233* **LimonHello**.
Azienda Agricola Il Gesù *Massa Lubrense (081 808 9419/www.massalubrense.it/ilgesu).*
This ancient lemon grove has been cultivated by many generations of the same family using the same traditional methods. Phone to organise a guided tour.

Other Campania specialities

La Tradizione *Via R Bosco 969, Vico Equense Localita' Seiano (081 802 8869).*
Salvatore and Silvana have a wonderful range of *latticini* (dairy products), cheeses and *salumi* (hams, salamis and so on) from Monti Lattari, and many other regional specialities.

Friggitoria-Pizzeria Giuliano

Calata Trinità Maggiore 33 (081 551 0986). Bus R1, R4. **Open** 10am-11pm Mon-Sat. Closed 3wks Aug. **No credit cards. Map** p311 3A.
Probably the best *pizzette* (snack-sized pizza) in town. Both the *ripieno* and the margherita are exceptional. Potato croquettes and *zeppole* (deep-fried dough balls) are crisp and fresh.

Toledo & Sanità

Restaurants

Hosteria Toledo

Vico Giardinetto a Toledo 78, off Via Toledo (081 421 257). Funicular Centrale to Via Roma/bus C25, R2. **Meals served** noon-3pm, 8pm-midnight Mon, Wed-Sun; noon-3pm Tue. **Average** €30 dinner. **Credit** DC MC V. **Map** p313 2C.
Good traditional fare and palatable *vino locale* are served here. Contorni are fresh and flavoursome.

La Vecchia Cantina

Via San Nicola alla Carità 13-14 (081 552 0226). Metro Dante or Montesanto/bus C57, R1, R4. **Meals served** noon-3.30pm, 8-11pm Mon, Wed-Sat; noon-3.30pm Tue, Sun. Closed 2wks Aug. **Average** €15. **Credit** AmEx, DC, MC, V. **Map** p314 2A.
A little *osteria* serving delicious, traditional food at unbeatable prices. It's next to the fish market; grilled squid and swordfish are good, as is *linguine con polpetti* (pasta with baby octopus).

Timpani e Tempure

Vico della Quercia 17 (081 551 2280). Metro Dante/ bus C57, R1, R4. **Meals served** *Summer* 9.30am-8.30pm Mon-Sat; 9.30am-2pm Sun. *Winter* 9.30am-7pm Mon-Sat; 9.30am-2pm Sun. Closed Aug. **No credit cards. Map** p311 2A.
This place, which mainly caters for takeaways, specialises in traditional dishes (sold by the kilo) such as *timballi* and *sartu' di riso* (baked pasta and rice dishes). A generous portion is around €3.50.

Pizzerie

Ciro a Santa Brigida

Via Santa Brigida 71 (081 552 4072). Funicular Centrale to Augusteo/bus C25, R2. **Meals served** 12.30-3.30pm, 7.30pm-midnight Mon-Sat. Closed 2wks Aug. **Average** €20. **Credit** AmEx, DC, MC, V. **Map** p315 1A.
Ciro is really a restaurant, but *pizze* is what it does best. If you've experienced the usual Naples pizza varieties once too often, try the *pizza ai frutti di mare* (seafood pizza) for a change. Lovely old-fashioned service and a good wine list.

Rosso Pomodoro

Piazza Dante 16 (081 544 7230). Metro Dante/ bus C57, R1, R4. **Meals served** noon-4pm, 7.30pm-midnight daily. Closed 1wk Aug. **Average** €15. **Credit** AmEx, DC, MC, V. **Map** p314 2A.

Seriously good food. **Umberto**. *See p122.*

This branch of the Sebeto group of pizzerias (*see p116* Re di Napoli *and p121* Rosso Pomodoro) is a handy pitstop before or after a visit to the Museo Nazionale Archeologico.

Snacks

Friggitoria Fiorenzano

Piazza Montesanto 6 (no phone). Metro Montesanto. **Open** 8am-10pm Mon-Sat. Closed 2wks Aug. **No credit cards. Map** p314 2A.
A great selection of tasty snacks. Try the deep-fried artichokes (only in season). The owners also have a good pizzeria next door.

Lo Sfizietto

Corner of vico Basilico Puoto & via Pignasecca (no phone). Metro Montesanto. **Open** 10am-10pm daily. Closed 3wks Aug. **No credit cards. Map** p314 2A.
Traditional *pizzette*, oven-baked and fried calzone, and an array of fried snacks.

Vomero

Restaurants

D'Angelo Santa Caterina

Via Aniello Falcone 203 (081 578 9772). Bus C28. **Meals served** 7.30-10.30pm Mon, Wed-Sat; 1-3.30pm Sun. Closed 2wks Aug. **Average** €50. **Credit** AmEx, DC, MC, V. **Map** p315 1C.
Set amid swathes of jasmine and bougainvillea, this peaceful restaurant with its striking views over the city is the ideal spot for a romantic dinner or an extra-special lunch. Service is friendly but profes-

Eat and drink your way around the world

sional and the food is abundant and excellent. The *antipasti* – with delicacies such as deep-fried baby squid, marinated sardines and octopus, sautéd prawns or smoked swordfish – are a meal in themselves. The varied wine list is reasonably priced for a restaurant of this calibre.

Il Giardino del Pontano

Via Luca Giordano 99 (081 658 4699). Funicular Chiaia to via Cimarosa, Centrale to piazza Fuga/bus C28, C31, C32, V1. **Meals served** 1-3pm, 8pm-midnight Tue-Sun]. Closed 2wk Aug. **Average** €30. **Credit** AmEx, MC, V. **Map** p314 2B.

Hidden away in a side street off via Scarlatti, this restaurant is a haven, with tables outside in a little courtyard/garden. There are lots of quality cheeses and *salumi* (hams salamis, and so on) in addition to top-notch fish dishes and fairly good pizzas. The restaurant also hosts frequent gastronomic evenings where food is based on typical regional produce. Service is friendly but this place is very popular so booking is advisable.

La Cantina di Sica

Via Bernini 17 (081 556 7520). Funicular Chiaia to via Cimarosa, Centrale to piazza Fuga/bus C28, C31, C32, V1. **Meals served** 12.30-4pm, 8pm-midnight Mon,Wed-Sun. Closed 1wk Aug. **Average** €25. **Credit** AmEx, MC, V. **Map** p314 2B.

Good, traditional dishes such as *pasta patata e provola* (pasta, potato and smoked cheese) or *pasta alla siciliana* (pasta with aubergines, tomato and mozzarella) at slightly higher prices than the average trattoria. There's an interesting choice of delicious *contorni*; try the *parmigiano di peperoni* (layers of cooked peppers and white sauce). The *vino locale* is fair but pricey at €10 a carafe, so it's probably worth going for a bottled wine. The wine bar downstairs frequently hosts jazz or neapolitan folk music.

L'Osteria del Balconcino

Via F Solimene 73 (081 229 2213). Funicular Chiaia to Via Cimarosa or funicular Centrale to piazza Fuga/bus C28, C31, C32. **Meals served** 1-3pm, 8pm-midnight Tue-Sat, 1pm-3pm Mon, Sun. Closed 2 wks Aug. **Average** €20. **Set lunch** (Mon-Sat) €7.50. **Credit** MC, DC, V. **Map** p314 2B.

Particularly popular with office workers for its fast and efficient low-cost lunchtime service, this tiny *osteria* (built into the ex-atrium entrance to an elegant palazzo) is also a buzzing place in the evening. The food is good, prices are reasonable and it makes a perfect refuelling station on the trek up to the sights of the Vomero hill.

Osteria Donna Teresa

Via Kerbaker 58 (081 556 7070). Funicular Chiaia to via Cimarosa, Centrale to piazza Fuga/bus C28, C31, C32, V1. **Meals served** 12.30-3pm, 7.30-11pm Mon-Sat. Closed Aug. **Average** €18. **No credit cards. Map** p314 2B.

A small menu of exemplary home cooking features here. Try *polpette* (meatballs) in tomato sauce or *salsicce al sugo* (sausages with tomato sauce). The insistent owner will probably force you into eating at least two courses. Good *vino locale* (red).

Pizzerie

Acunzo

Via Cimarosa 60/62 (081 578 5362). Funicular Centrale to piazza Fuga or Chiaia to via Cimarosa/bus C28, C31, C32, V1. **Meals served** 1-3pm, 7.30-11pm Mon-Sat. Closed Aug. **Average** €15. **Credit** MC, V. **Map** p314 2B.

All the usual pizzas are here, but also some unusual specialities such as calzone stuffed with pasta or beans. The house wine is best avoided.

Rosso Pomodoro

Via Cimarosa 144 (081 5568169). Funicular Centrale to piazza Fuga or Chiaia to via Cimarosa/bus C28, C31, C32, V1. **Meals served** noon-4pm, 7.30pm-1am daily. Closed 1wk Aug. **Average** €15. **Credit** AmEx, DC, MC, V. **Map** p314 2A.

This branch of the Sebeto group of pizzerias (*see p116 and p119*) is right bang opposite the Villa Floridiana. It also has a very comfortable bar where newspapers are provided – it's a little pricey but there's no extra charge for use of the tables. Try a take-away pizza for a picnic in the Floridiana park opposite (but watch out for the park attendant).

Angolo del Paradiso

Via Kerbaker 152 (081 556 7146). Funicular Centrale to piazza Fuga or Chiaia to via Cimarosa/bus C28, C31, C32, V1. **Meals served** 12.30-3pm, 7.30-midnight Tue-Sun. Closed Aug. **Average** €18. **No credit cards. Map** p314 2B.

In addition to a fair restaurant menu, staff at Angolo serve top-notch traditional pizzas at fair prices. For something different, try the *cinque gusti* (five small slices with different toppings).

Pizzeria Cilea

Via Cilea 43 (081 556 3291). Bus 181, C31, C32. **Meals served** 1-4pm, 7-11.30pm Mon-Sat; 7.30-11.30pm Sun. Closed 2wks Aug. **Average** €10. **No credit cards. Map** p314 2C.

Delicious pizze and *frittura* at exceptional prices: Pizzeria Cilea does a mean *ripieno* and an excellent *margherita al filetto* (pizza with cherry tomatoes and mozzarella); the *contorni* are also very good. It's a tiny place and extremely popular, so be prepared to queue. The size of the place and waiting times mean that it's not advisable for groups of more than four.

Wine bars

Bocca d'Oro

Piazzetta Durante 1 (081 229 2010). Funicular Centrale to piazza Fuga or Chiaia to via Cimarosa/bus C28, C31, C32, V1. **Open** 12.30-4pm, 8.30pm-2am Tue-Sat; 8.30pm-midnight Mon, Sun. Closed Aug. **No credit cards. Map** p314 2B.

Eat, Drink, Shop

This *vineria* has a good wine list and excellent food to accompany it; we are fond of the *rotelli alle noci* (ravioli with ricotta in a walnut sauce). It also does a nice line in *bistecca fiorentina* (T-bone steak) and serves assorted cheeses and salamis.

Snacks

Friggitoria Vomero

Via Cimarosa 44 (081 578 3130). Funicular Chiaia to via Cimarosa, Centrale to piazza Fuga/ bus C28, C31, C32, V1. **Open** 9.30-2pm, 5-9.30pm Mon-Sat. Closed Aug. **No credit cards. Map** p314 2B.

A great place for breakfast: the *graffe* (light dough-nuts) are wonderful and available from 9.30am. A host of other fried delights are ready from 10am, including mini-potato croquettes, *zeppole* (deep-fried dough balls), courgettes, courgette flowers and aubergines fried in batter. A good stop-off on the way to Castel Sant'Elmo.

Chiaia to Posillipo

Restaurants

Don Salvatore

Via Mergellina 5, Mergellina (081 681 817/ www.donsalvatore.it). Bus 140, C16, C24, R3. **Meals served** 12.30-3.30pm, 7.30pm-midnight Mon, Tue, Thur-Sun. **Average** €40. **Menu degustazione** €32-€50. **Credit** AmEx, DC, MC, V. **Map** p315 2C.

Superb *antipasti* are a highlight here: try *cecinielle* (a tiny transparent fish fried in patties with batter), *polpo ai carciofi* (octopus with artichokes) or *calamaretti con uva passa* (baby squid with sultanas and pine nuts). Fish and meat dishes are excellent too. Hospitable owner Tonino Aversano is passionate about wine; he'll help you choose the perfect bottle to complement your meal from the exceptional, continually updated wine list.

Dora

Via Ferdinando Palasciano 30, Chiaia (081 680 519). Bus 140, C9, C18, C24, C25, C28. **Meals served** 12.30-3pm, 8pm-midnight Mon-Sat. Closed 3wks Aug. **Average** €70. **Credit** DC, MC, V. **Map** p315 1B.

The best fish money can buy in one of the tiniest restaurants in the city; if you don't book, you'll never get in. Try the oysters, *pezzogna* (blue-spotted bream), or the *zuppa di pesce* (fish soup). The char-grilled prawns are exceptional.

Giuseppone a Mare

Via F Russo 13, Posillipo (081 769 1384). Bus 140, then 10mins walk. **Meals served** noon-3.30pm, 7.30-11.30pm Tue-Sat; 1-3.30pm Sun. Closed 2wks Aug. **Average** €50. **Credit** AmEx, DC, MC, V.

This restaurant is a legend. The view over the bay is stunning, decor is luxurious, and service and food

match up. The *antipasti* are flavoursome; *fusilli marinari* (own-made pasta with baby squid, prawns and shellfish) is superb.

Osteria Castello

Via Santa Teresa a Chiaia 38, Chiaia (081 400 486). Funicular Chiaia to Parco Margherita/metro Piazza Amedeo/bus C24, C25, C26, C27, C28. **Meals served** *June-Aug* 8-11.30pm Mon-Sat. *Sept-May* 1-3.30pm, 8-11.30pm Mon-Sat. Closed 3wks Aug. **Average** €30. **Credit** AmEx, MC, V. **Map** p315 1B.

This lively *osteria* attracts all sorts, making it a great place for people-watching. The *pappardelle ai frutti di mare* (long, wide ribbon pasta with seafood) is excellent (when in season) and the *fagotto alla fiamma* (sausage-like meat with cheese and a cream sauce, flambé) is successful too. There's plenty of choice for vegetarians – try *funghi pleos* (pleos mushrooms) or *radicchio alla brace* (barbecued radicchio). The menu is far from clear (plans have been afoot to translate it into English for at least the past ten years), but don't hesitate to ask the head waiter, Alfredo, to explain.

Osteria da Tonino

Via Santa Teresa a Chiaia 47, Chiaia (081 421 533). Funicular Chiaia to Parco Margherita/metro Piazza Amedeo/bus C24, C25, C26, C27, C28. **Meals served** *Oct-May* 12.30-4pm Mon-Wed, Sun; 12.30-4pm, 8-11pm Thur-Sat. *June, July, Sept* 12.30-4pm Mon-Sat. Closed Aug. **Average** €18 lunch; €25 dinner. **No credit cards. Map** p315 1B.

It's one of the busiest *osterie* in town, but dinner at Tonino's is an experience worth queuing for. Try *seppie in umido* (cuttlefish stewed in tomato) or *provola alla pizzaiola* (cheese with a tomato and basil sauce). The *pasta ragù e ricotta* (meat, tomato and ricotta cheese) cannot be faulted.

Trattoria dell'Oca

Via Santa Teresa a Chiaia 11, Chiaia (081 414 865). Funicular Chiaia to Parco Margherita/metro Piazza Amedeo/bus C24, C25, C26, C27, C28. **Meals served** *Apr-Sep* 1-3pm, 8-11.30pm Mon-Sat. *Oct-Mar* 1-3pm, 8-11.30pm Mon-Sat; 1-3pm Sun. Closed 3wks Aug. **Average** €30. **Credit** AmEx, DC, MC, V. **Map** p315 1B.

Decor here may be more northern European than usual, but the food is strictly trad – and it's good too. *Caprino con speck* (soft cheese and smoked ham) makes an interesting antipasto; *penne alla scarpariello* (pasta with fresh tomatoes, pecorino cheese, basil and a touch of chilli) and *tagliata alle erbe* (thinly sliced beef grilled with herbs and olive oil) are delicately flavoured, and service is friendly and efficient. The chocolate soufflé is scrumptious; plan ahead as it has to be ordered in advance.

Umberto

Via Alabardieri 30/31, Chiaia (081 418 555/ www.umberto.it). Bus140, C22, C25, C28. **Meals served** noon-4pm, 7-11.30pm Tue-Sun. Closed 3 wks Aug. **Average** €35. **Credit** AmEx, DC, MC, V. **Map** p315 1A.

Possibly the only restaurant in Naples where you can find gluten-free food and true vegetarian menus, and where special dietary requirements will be taken seriously. There's nothing sombre about the food here, though. Both the restaurant and pizzeria have a wide variety of well-prepared, typical dishes. The restaurant is in the heart of the old Chiaia district and close to the chic retail outlets that line via dei Mille.

Vadinchenia

Via Pontano 21, Chiaia (081 660 265). Funicular Chiaia to Parco Margherita/metro Piazza Amedeo/ bus C24, C25, C26, C27, C28. **Meals served** 8pm-midnight Mon-Sat. Closed Aug. **Average** €35. **Credit** AmEx, DC, MC, V. **Map** p315 1B.

Silvana and Saverio have taken the best ingredients from various parts of Italy and combined them to palate-blowing effect. Favourite dishes include *cavatelli* (a small nut-shaped pasta) in a gorgonzola and pistachio sauce, served in a bowl formed of melted parmesan cheese and beautifully flavoured stuffed squid. *Pecorino con miele e pistacchio* (cheese with honey and pistachio) makes an unusual alternative to a traditional dessert. The wine list excels in local labels. The August closing can be extended into late July and early September. Booking is essential.

Pizzerie

Da Pasqualino

Piazza Sannazaro 77-79, Mergellina (081 681 524). Metro Mergellina/bus 140, C16, C24, R3. **Meals served** noon-4pm, 7pm-midnight Mon, Wed-Sun. **Average** €15. **Credit** AmEx, MC, V. **Map** p315 2C.

This is one of the best *pizzerie* in the piazza and incredibly good value for money, so queues tend to be long. Excellent *frittura*: deep-fried mozzarella, potato croquettes and aubergines. There's a fair restaurant menu too, and the *vino locale* is palatable.

Wine bars

Barrique

Piazzetta Ascensione 9, Chiaia (081 662 721). Metro Piazza Amedeo/bus C24, C25, C26, C27, C28. **Open** 7.30pm-1am Tue-Sun. Closed 2wks Aug. **Credit** MC, V. **Map** p315 1B.

An interesting variety of Italian wines from around Naples and other areas, served with a choice of well-flavoured salami, olives, cheeses and ham. There are also a couple of daily-changing pasta dishes. The place is pleasantly done out in terracotta, with low lighting and the sound of relaxed jazz music.

Enoteca Belledonne

Vico Belledonne a Chiaia 18, Chiaia (081 403 162). Bus C16, C22, C24, C25, C28, R3. **Open** *Sept-May* 6.30pm-1am Mon, Sun; 9am-2pm, 4.30pm-1am Tue-Sat. *June, July* 6.30pm-1am Mon; 9am-2pm, 4.30-1am Tue-Fri; 9am-2pm Sat. Closed 3wks Aug. **Credit** DC, MC, V. **Map** p315 1B.

Just pizza. **Trianon da Ciro**. *See p117.*

Belledonne has an amazing choice of Italian wines, with bottles divided by region on racks around the walls. Wine by the glass is palatable and cheap. Staff are happy to help out with packaging your bottled purchases for shipment home. It gets busy here at weekends, when the little place can get jammed with patrons spilling with the alleyway.

Vinarium

Vico Santa Maria Cappella Vecchia 7, Chiaia (081 764 4114). Tram 1/bus C9, C18, C24, C25, C28, R3. **Open** *Sept-June* 11am-4.30pm, 7pm-1.30am Mon-Sat. *July* noon-4pm Mon-Sat. Closed Aug. **Credit** AmEx, DC, MC, V. **Map** p315 1A.

A fair range of reasonably priced wines are available here. Vinarium is noisy and very busy at weekends, so be prepared to queue. Rather run-of-the-mill risottos and toasted sandwiches are also available.

Snacks

La Focaccia Express

Vico Belledonne a Chiaia 31, Chiaia (081 412 277). Bus C22, C25. **Open** 10am-2am Mon-Sat; 6pm-3am Sun. Closed 3wks Aug. **No credit cards**. **Map** p315 1B.

This place serves the most delicious choice of pizza slices (*pizza al taglio*) and focaccia imaginable. Try the *peperoni e patata* (peppers and potato), *ricotta e salsiccia* (ricotta and sausage) or *margherita al filetto* (with cherry tomatoes and mozzarella). To be sure of a really fresh slice, watch the oven and buy what has just come out. A phenomenal range of beers (over 50, the owner claims) and wine by the glass and bottle are in stock. The TV is usually on; if you're a football fan this is a good place to get involved in a match.

Campi Flegrei

The stretch of land between Lucrino and Capo Miseno in the Campi Flegrei is the garden of Naples – full of vegetable plots, orchards and vineyards, planted in fertile volcanic soil. Among the area's many restaurants are a few gems.

Caronte

Via Lago d'Averno 2, Lago d'Averno (081 804 1429). Cumana rail to Lucrino/Monte di Procida bus from piazza Garibaldi or piazza Municipio, get *off at Lucrino.* **Meals served** 1-4pm, 7pm-midnight Tue-Sun. Closed 2wks Aug, 2wks Dec. **Average** €30. **No credit cards**.
Situated on Lago d'Averna, this family-run snack-bar-turned-restaurant provides a breathtaking view across the lake, and great food too. *Antipasti* servings are copious and packed with flavour. Try the cannelloni or *fagioli con seppie* (beans and cuttlefish). Fish dishes are also good and the *crostone* (toasted sandwiches) with *salsiccia* and *friarielli* or provola cheese are excellent and a meal in themselves. The *vino* is home-produced and palatable.

Il Casolare da Tobia

Via Selvatico 12 (081 523 5193/www.sibilla.net/ ilcasolare/www.datobia.it). Cumana rail to Lucrino then take the Torregàveta bus and get off at first stop; bus SEPSA 1 from piazza Garibaldi to Bacoli.

The menu

Antipasti

Alici marinate: sardines marinated in garlic, chilli and parsley.
Antipasti di mare: a selection of (usually) cold, cooked seafood such as octopus, squid, clams, smoked swordfish, salmon and marinated sardines, or *frittelle di cicinielli*: delicious fried patties of microscopic, transparent fish.
Antipasti misti (or di terra): a selection of salamis, hams, cheeses and olives.
Bruschetta: toast with chopped tomatoes, garlic, basil and oil, or, occasionally, aubergine or olive paste.
Funghi trifolati: cooked diced mushrooms with garlic, chilli and parsley.
Involtini di peperoni: cooked peppers, rolled and filled with cheese and breadcrumbs.
Mozzarella e prosciutto: mozzarella and parma ham.
Prosciutto e fichi: parma ham and figs.
Prosciutto e melone: parma ham and cantaloupe melon.
Saute di vongole: sautéd clams.

Pasta

Alla barese: with broccoli.
Alla genovese: thick onion and meat (pork) sauce.
Alla puttanesca, alla bella donna: with tomato, capers, black olives and a touch of chilli.
Alla Santa Lucia, alla bella Napoli, alla pescatora: with seafood and shellfish.
Alla Siciliana: with tomato, aubergine, basil and mozzarella.
Alla Sorrentina: with tomato and mozzarella.

Alle vongole: with clams (specify *in bianco* if you don't want your clams cooked with tomato).
Al sugo: simple tomato and basil sauce.
Con fagioli e cozze: with beans and mussels.
E ceci: with chickpeas.

Meals served 1-3.30pm, 7-11.30pm Tue-Sat; 1-3.30pm Sun. Closed 1wk Aug, 1wk Jan. **Average** €35. **No credit cards.**
Using lots of organically grown produce from their own vegetable garden, owners Tobia and Elisabetta create seasonal banquets based on traditional recipes. Excellent *vino locale* (Falanghina and Per'e Palummo) is served. It's not great for vegetarians, however, as animal fats and ham are used in most recipes. Don't wear those brand new stilettos for the short, steep path down to the restaurant. There's accommodation too (*see p55*).

Féfé
Via Miseno 137 (new name via della Shoah 15), Case Vecchie, Bacoli (081 523 3011). Monte di Procida bus from piazza Garibaldi or piazza Municipio, get off at last stop. **Meals served**

June-Sept 8.30-11pm Mon-Fri; 1-5pm, 8.30-11pm Sat, Sun. *Oct-Apr* 8-11.30pm Tue-Fri; 1-5pm, 8-11.30pm Sat; 1-5pm Sun. *May* 8.30-11pm Tue-Fri; 1-5pm, 8.30-11pm Sat, Sun. Closed 2wks Dec. **Average** €25. **Credit** MC, V.
On the picturesque port where Roman fleets once moored, this tiny restaurant serves delicious but relatively pricey dishes made from fresh, traditional ingredients. An aperitif, the ingredients of which remain a mystery, is served as you arrive. *Pasta zucchini e cozze* (own-made pasta with mussels and courgettes) and *pezzogna al forno con patate* (bluespotted bream baked with potatoes) are popular, very appetising dishes. Féfé attracts the alternative bourgeoisie of Naples, and everyone seems to know everyone else here. The best tables are outside, but you have to be prepared to queue.

Provola e patata: with smoky cheese and potato.
Ragù e ricotta (alla mammà): tomato and meat sauce blended with soft ricotta cheese.

Carne (meat)
Carne alla pizzaiola: meat served with a tomato and basil sauce.
Carne al ragù: slow-cooked beef in tomato.
Gattò di patate: a shepherd's pie-like dish with mozzarella and ham.
Involtino: a small roll of beef (or aubergine – *involtini di melanzane*) stuffed with ham and cheese.
Polpette: meatballs, usually served in a thick tomato sauce.

Pesce & frutti di mare (fish & seafood)
Calamaro ripieno: stuffed squid.
Mazzancolle: very large prawns.
'Mpepata di cozze: mussels steamed with pepper and served with lemon.
Mussillo marinato: marinated cod-like fish.
Pignatiello: seafood soup served with fingers of toasted bread.
Polipo affucate/affogato: literally 'drowned octopus', cooked in an earthenware dish with a little water and tomato.
Purpietielle/purpo/polpo/polipo: octopus.
Seppie in umido: similar to *polipo affucate/affogato* (*see above*) but with cuttlefish.
Totano: similar to squid, often cooked with potatoes.

Contorni (vegetables)
Carciofi alla giudea: artichokes cooked with olives and capers.

Fagiolini all'agro: cooked green beans with garlic and lemon.
Friarielli: spinach-like greens, unique to the Naples area.
Melanzane a funghetto: diced aubergines cooked in tomato and basil.
Melanzane alla brace: sliced char-grilled aubergines, dressed with garlic, chilli, and parsley.
Peperoncini verdi: tiny sweet green peppers cooked in tomato and basil.
Peperoni in padella: pan-fried peppers (often with capers and black olives).
Scarola 'mbuttit'/'mbuttonat': stuffed endive (usually with capers, pine nuts and olives).

Formaggi (cheese and its uses)
Caprese: fresh mozzarella, tomatoes and basil.
Mozzarella in carrozza: deep-fried, traditionally on a small square of bread, but nowadays in breadcrumbs.
Provola: similar to mozzarella but with a smoky taste.
Provola alla pizzaiola: smoky cheese cooked in a tomato and basil sauce.

Methods of cooking
All'acqua pazza (fish): baked with garlic, parsley and a touch of tomato.
Al sale (fish): cooked under a huge pile of sea salt.
Con pomodoro al filetto: cooked with fresh cherry tomatoes.
In bianco: without tomato.
Macchiato: with a touch of tomato.

Cafés, Bars & Gelaterie

Cake, ice-cream and coffee are nothing less than Neapolitan essentials.

Even a passing knowledge of Italy's rich food culture proves that Naples is not famous for pizza alone – but for its coffee too. Quite why is subject to dispute, but its status as a major port with strong connections to both South America and the Middle East must play a part in the story. Added to this, Neapolitan ingenuity is also credited with inventing a new way of brewing the drink – in the little topsy-turvy stove-top coffeemaker still known as a *napoletana* (these days seen mainly in souvenir shops).

Drinking coffee (or 'taking a coffee' as the Neapolitans phrase it) is a major ritual in the city's social fabric. The phrase *'prendiamo un caffè insieme'* (let's have a coffee together) is far more than a simple polite offer, but rather an invitation to chat, do business, or forge a closer relationship – the Neapolitan equivalent of 'let's do lunch'. Despite this, coffee is rarely drunk at a leisurely pace seated at a pavement café, but usually consumed very quickly while standing elbow-to-elbow at a crowded bar.

If you do sit at a table, wait to be served and expect to pay more (sometimes twice as much). Sometimes you are expected to settle straight away, sometimes on leaving. At the bar (*al banco*) you usually have to pay at the cash desk first, get a receipt, then slap the receipt on the bar with a 10¢ or 20¢ coin. (This process is often repeated ad absurdiam if you also want a cake – in some larger bars you have to queue at the cake counter too). Don't expect the bar staff to ask what you'd like: you may wait all day. Instead, summon up all the assertiveness (though not rudeness) you can muster and say *due cappuccini* or *due caffè* (the likes of 'please' or 'could I possibly have' are unnecessary).

A 'bar' can be anything from a tiny stand-up-only coffee place to a chic hangout. All bars sell hot and cold drinks, alcoholic drinks and sweet snacks. Some have more to offer: a *bar-tabaccheria* also sells cigarettes, bus tickets and phone cards, while a *bar-pasticceria* offers cakes, pastries and often ice-cream, though this last can also be found in a *bar-gelateria*. The *bar-lotteria* has the wherewithal for playing Italy's various lotteries and football pools; most will have a copy of the lottery bible, *La Smorfia*, a manual for converting dreams into winning numbers. Alternatively, look out for the sign saying *'Totocalcio'* and ask for a *schedina* (coupon) if you fancy a flutter on the football.

CAFFÈ COMPLEXITIES

Be warned: Neapolitan coffee is short and very, very strong. A recent local news article recounted the unfortunate tale of a man who drank ten *espressi* in one day and keeled over dead as a result. Three or four over the course of a busy day is an advisable maximum for those who wish to avoid caffeine-induced palpitations. The edge is taken off its bitter strength with sugar. If you don't want your coffee to come already sugared, ask for it *amaro*. To retain your dignity, don't even think of asking for a 'moccacino' or any of the other concoctions served in Anglo-Saxon coffee houses. With all the coffee variations on offer, you probably won't be tempted to anyway. *See p131* **Caffè choices**.

PASTICCERIE

Dolci are a serious business in Naples, and Neapolitans will happily cross from one side of the city to the other to obtain the perfect cake, particularly for special occasions. Should you be invited for Sunday lunch, don't turn up with a bottle of wine but with some finely wrapped cakes. The popularity of the Sunday cake ritual means that large queues can form at top *pasticcerie* on Sunday mornings. If you decide to eat your cake seated at a table at a *bar-pasticceria*, feel free to avoid any misunderstanding or disappointment by accompanying the waiter to the counter and pointing out the pastry you want.

GELATERIE

Neapolitans are endearingly passionate about ice-cream, so you can expect the best. Ice-cream marked as *'produzione proprio'* was made on the premises; this is generally the best quality. *'Produzione artigianale'* means the ice-cream was hand-made (in other words, not mass-produced), but not on the premises.

Before you order decide whether you want a *coppetta* (tub), *cono* (cone) or *brioches* (buns). Prices usually begin at €1, going up for larger sizes. A basic €1 cone allows you two flavours.

When it comes to flavours, most *gelaterie* offer a bewildering array, broken down into *crema* (creamy) and *frutta* (fruit). Some of the most popular among the former include **caffè** (coffee, often combined with hazelnut), **fior di latte** (cream), **nocciola** (hazelnut), **stracciatella** (plain ice-cream with fragments of crunchy chocolate) and **zabaglione** (very sweet ice-cream made with eggs and Marsala wine).

Chalet society

To an English speaker the word 'chalet' sums up at best a chic Swiss skiing resort, or at worst a *Hi di Hi*-style holiday camp. In Italian, however, the word has another meaning. Lining the seafront to the north of the port at Mergellina, you can see a long row of low buildings decorated with gaudy neon signs nestling among the palm trees. These are the 'chalets' of Naples.

During the 1950s, with the first tremors of Italy's post-war economic boom rumbling, everyone felt they were entitled to a piece of the high life they were seeing portrayed on films and advertising hoardings. The port of Mergellina, formerly only for barefoot fishermen, was the starting-off point for international celebs to sail off to Capri. Many Neapolitans, being unable to afford Capri itself, instead hung around on the shore and constructed their own version of the *dolce vita* right there. The existing old kiosks along via F Caracciolo, selling bottles of beer and piles of peppery *taralli* biscuits (some still survive) were upgraded into more exotic-sounding 'chalets': **Chalet Ciro** (*see p132*), **Chalet delle Palme** (no.1/D), **Chalet delle Rose** (no.1/B), **Chalet Primavera** (*see p132*),

Chalet del Mare (no.1/A), and others. Many still remain, preserving their slightly tacky atmosphere of good times past. Immaculately liveried waiters still bring tall glasses of synthetic-looking cocktails to people seated on swing chairs under tasselled umbrellas. Pick of the bunch is the Chalet delle Rose, whose faded red awnings, long, panelled interior and kitschy '50s paintings of Mount Vesuvius are far more reminiscent of old-style Italian restaurants abroad than anything to do with modern Italy. The clientele is still a mix of out of town boys trying to impress their first-date girlfriends, Polish domestic helps on their day off and rather corpulent elderly folk; perhaps they're nostalgic for their youth, perhaps they simply enjoy a drink by the sea, or perhaps they don't realise that the high life has moved on.

And time is moving on – several of the old chalets have been recently remodelled into far more ordinary restaurants or bars, and while the Chalet Ciro retains its reputation for the best ice-cream in the city, there is a feeling that this Neapolitan via Veneto may be on the road to becoming just like anywhere else, more's the pity.

Chalet Ciro.

Let them eat cake

Cakes are a ritual in Naples and locals will travel miles to purchase the right ones for special occasions... even if it's only Sunday lunch with the mother-in-law.

Babà

A much lighter version of what you might recognise as a rum baba – a yeast cake which is soaked in rum. It was, apparently, invented by French chefs in Poland before being brought south; in Neapolitan dialect *tu si 'nu babà* can be roughly translated as 'you're gorgeous'.

Chiacchiere

Icing and sugar covers tongues of lightly fried flour and egg confection. Eaten by Neapolitans at Carnevale in the run-up to Lent. It's occasionally served with heavy *sanguinaccio*, a chocolate sauce that was originally made from a mixture of pig's blood and cocoa, though this concoction is now (mercifully) illegal.

Pastiera

A deep flan filled with a mixture of ricotta cheese and softened cereals flavoured with orange-blossom water. Formerly an Easter cake, it's now sold all year round.

Raffioli

Sponge and marzipan covered in white icing. This is a soft and sugar-heavy treat around Christmas.

Rococò

A teeth-challengingly hard almond biscuit made at Christmas.

Sfogliatella

Sweet, lightly spicy ricotta cheese in either puff pastry (*riccia*) or shortcrust pastry (*frolla*). Omnipresent, and usually excellent.

Torrone

A light, chocolate-based nougat from Benevento, eaten around All Souls' Day (1 November).

Torta caprese

Moist, heavy cake made with chocolate and hazelnuts dusted with icing sugar.

Zeppole di San Giuseppe

Fried or baked choux pastry filled with custard and topped with bitter wild cherries, sold around the feast of St Joseph (Fathers' Day in Italy) on 19 March.

The classic *frutta* combination is *fragola e limone* (strawberry and lemon), but you could try more exotic flavours, such as *fichi d'india* (prickly pear), *limoncello* (lemon liqueur) or liquorice.

Most *gelaterie* offer *sorbetti* (sorbets) and *semifreddi* (a mousse/ice-cream combo), served with or without *panna* (sweet whipped cream).

Then there's *granita di limone*, a rough-cut sorbet found in stalls around the city. An even rougher sorbet is *Grattacheccha*, with ice scraped on demand off a large chunk and doused with flavoured syrup or lemon juice. Though they may not always look very salubrious, these streetside stalls are generally perfectly clean. If in doubt, go to the ones full of locals: Neapolitans are as fussy about food hygiene as they are about flavour.

Royal Naples & Monte Echia

Cafés & bars

Bar del Professore

Piazza Trieste e Trento 46 (081 403 041). Funicular Centrale to Augusteo/bus 24, C22, C25, C57. **Open** 6.30am-midnight Mon-Fri, Sun; 6.30am-3.30am Sat. **No credit cards. Map** p315 1A.

A cheap-and-cheerful next door neighbour to snooty Gambrinus (*see below*), this place has a few somewhat cramped tables outside at which to consume an excellent *caffè alla nocciola* (hazelnut coffee) or *caffè al cioccolato* (chocolate coffee). If you're not put off by the traffic and mass of humanity passing by, this is a good, centrally located stop-off.

Gambrinus
Via Chiaia 1-2 (081 417 582). Funicular Centrale to Augusteo/bus 24, C22, C25, C57. **Open** 8am-1.30am daily. **Credit** AmEx, MC, V. **Map** p315 1A.
Gambrinus' fame has been largely earned by its central location, the impressiveness of its flouncy art deco interior and its distinguished history – it was established over a century ago and clients have included the likes of Oscar Wilde. In truth, it's rather expensive and the service can be far from friendly these days. Its rather racy past is far behind it too: in the 1930s the fascist government closed down some of its rooms that were the haunt of left-wing intellectuals; these days you'll find more fur coats than anti-fascists. Still, it's an extremely convenient meeting place for an *aperitivo* (especially if you're going to San Carlo, just over the road).

Pasticcerie

Pintauro
Via Toledo 275 (081 417 339). Funicular Centrale to Augusteo/bus 24, C22, C25, C57. **Open** 9.15am-8pm Mon-Sat; 9am-2pm Sun. Closed Aug. **No credit cards. Map** p315 1A.
This hole-in-the-wall *pasticceria* serves a traditional but limited selection of delicious *dolci* from its nononsense marble counter. It's most famed for its *sfogliatelle* and *babà* (cake soaked in rum syrup), which are indeed excellent, if somewhat oily. The service has no frills either, with surliness often a feature.

Port & University

Pasticcerie

Attanasio
Vico Ferrovia 2-3 (081 285 675). Metro Piazza Garibaldi/bus R2. **Open** 6.30am-8pm Tue-Sun. Closed July. **Credit** MC, V. **Map** p312 2B.
Hidden in the backstreets around central station, Attanasio is worth hunting out for anyone with the slightest sweet tooth. The reason: *sfogliatelle*. They are the finest in the city, and so the best in the world. Fluffy, sweet and spicy ricotta cheese wrapped in light flaky pastry, hot out of the oven – heaven. The only choice is which type: triangular *millefeuille*-style *riccia* or oval pie-like *frolla*. You don't need anything else.

Dolcezze Siciliane
Piazzale Immacolatella Vecchia (081 552 1990). Bus 24, C25, R3. **Open** 7.30am-7pm Tue-Sat; 7.30am-2pm Sun. Closed mid July-Aug. **No credit cards. Map** p313 2C.
Fresh Sicilian *dolci* come here from Palermo by boat every morning – literally. The shop is actually inside the port; enter from piazza Municipio, turn left and keep walking – it's worth it. The *cannolo* (a crisp horn with sweet filling) has reduced grown men to tears.

Centro storico

Cafés & bars

Gran Caffe Aragonese
Piazza San Domenico Maggiore 5/8 (081 552 8740/ www.grancaffearagonese.it). Metro Museo or Piazza Cavour/bus CS, E1, R2. **Open** 8am-midnight daily. **Credit** AmEx, DC, MC, V. **Map** p311 2B.
A large selection of sweet and savoury food, tables outside, comfortable divans inside (a rarity), friendly service and daily newspapers make this the best bar on this lively piazza. Regulars include everyone from the buskers and beggars who hang out on the square to students and the area's many arty types.

Piazza D'Arte
Piazza Dante 33 (081 564 5076). Metro Dante. **Open** 7.30am-midnight Mon-Fri, Sun; 7.30am-2am Sat. **No credit cards. Map** p311 2A.
Gaining from Piazza Dante's recent makeover and the opening of the metro stop, this place helps to make the formerly tatty square into the chic *salotto all'aperto* it now seems to be. The modish chairs and tables outside and refined marble bar top inside are more Milan than Naples, but with fine coffee, good food and prices, this is certainly no drawback.

Pasticcerie

Scaturchio
Piazza San Domenico Maggiore 19 (081 551 7031/ 081 551 6944). Metro Museo or Piazza Cavour/bus CS, E1, R2. **Open** 7.30am-8.30pm Mon, Wed-Sun. 7.30am-8.30pm daily during Easter, Dec. Closed 3wks Aug. **Credit** AmEx, DC, MC, V. **Map** p311 2B.
Right on bustling piazza San Domenico Maggiore, historic Scaturchio traditionally has had a reputation for serving the best cakes in the city. It's resting on its laurels a bit these days, but the speciality *babà* (cake soaked in rum syrup) is still a fearsome concoction.

Toledo & Sanità

See also p158 **Intra Moenia**.

Cafés & bars

Bar Mexico
Piazza Dante 86 (081 549 9330). Metro Dante/ bus 24, R1, R4. **Open** 7.30am-8.30pm Mon-Sat. Closed 2wks Aug. **No credit cards. Map** p311 2A.
Arguably the best espresso in Naples, but beware – it comes with sugar already added, making it treacly stuff. Bar Mexico also sells a wide range of excellent,

Eat, Drink, Shop

Its racy past may be behind it, but **Gambrinus** still draws the crowds. *See p129.*

freshly roasted coffee in gorgeous '50s-style packaging; try the Harem or Moana blend. The *frappe di caffè* (iced coffee whisked up to pure froth) is a real treat.

Caffè dell'Epoca

Via Costantinopoli 82 (081 402 794). Metro Dante or Museo/bus 24, R1, R4. **Open** 7.30am-10pm Mon-Sat; 7.30am-2pm Sun. **No credit cards**. **Map** p311 1-2B.

The Epoca serves a serious espresso, plus good *cornetti* (croissants) and other pastries. As the café is near the School of Fine Art, it often exhibits students' work. There are a few tables outside during summer months.

Gelaterie

Gelateria della Scimmia

Piazza Carità 4 (081 552 0272). Funicular Centrale to Augusteo/metro Montesanto/bus R1, E3. **Open** *Jan-Mar, Nov* 10am-10.30pm Mon, Tue, Thur Fri; 10am-1am Sat, Sun. *Apr-Oct, Dec* 10am-midnight daily. **No credit cards**. **Map** p314 2A.

One of the city's oldest and most renowned *gelaterie*, this place is sparsely furnished and often very busy. Go for basic flavours and you won't be sorry (strawberry and lemon are an excellent combo). Look out for the intensely sweet chocolate-coated banana on a stick.

Vomero

Cafés & bars

FNAC

Via Luca Giordano 39 (081 2201000) Funicular Chiaia to Cimarosa or Centrale to Vomero/metro Vanvitelli/bus V1. **Open** 10am-9pm daily. **No credit cards**. **Map** p314/p315 1-2B.

So, OK, it is a record/book/electrical goods shop, but FNAC also has a handsome if small café with stylish furniture, clean toilets (by no means a given in this town) and it hosts regular author talks and readings, along with photography exhibitions. This is a good meeting place if you're in Vomero.

Pasticcerie

Bellavia

Via L Giordano 158 (081 578 9684). Metro Collana/bus V1. **Open** 8am-9pm Tue-Sat. Closed Mon. Closed Aug. **Credit** AmEx, DC, MC, V. **Map** p314 2B.

Look for the trail of people carrying large, impressively wrapped packages, and you'll soon find Bellavia. Vomero's best-known cake shop is particularly renowned for its birthday cakes. If you're around at Easter, don't miss the *pastiera* – a traditional cake made from ricotta cheese and rice-like *grano* (wheat grain).

Gelaterie

Otranto

Via Scarlatti 78 (081 558 7498). Metro Vanvitelli/ bus V1. **Open** *May-Sept* 10am-11 Mon, Tue, Thur-Sun. *Oct-Apr* 10am-10pm Mon, Tue, Thur-Sun. **No credit cards**. **Map** p314 2B.

Don't let the minimal furnishings and lack of atmosphere put you off this place: dedicated ice-cream connoisseurs have Otranto down as one of the finest suppliers of the frozen treat in the whole city. It's well worth checking out, even in the middle of winter.

Chiaia to Posillipo

Cafés & bars

Bar Guida
Via dei Mille 46, Chiaia (081 426 570). Metro Piazza Amedeo/bus C24, C25. **Open** 7.30am-9pm Mon-Sat. Closed 1wk Aug. **No credit cards. Map** p315 1B.
Located slap in the middle of this swish part of town, Guida offers a good range of drinks and light lunches (choose your sandwich contents from what's in the food cabinet). There are a few seats where you can rest your weary feet after hitting the shops.

Caffè Amadeus
Piazza Amedeo 5, Chiaia (081 761 3023). Metro Piazza Amedeo/bus C24, C25. **Open** 7am-3am daily. **No credit cards. Map** p315 1B.
There's no space inside, but the large number of year-round tables on busy piazza Amedeo make this a good place for observing the youth of Naples indulging in their customary evening pastimes of posing on Vespas, chatting, and insouciantly causing major traffic congestion.

Caffetteria Colonna
Via Vittorio Colonna 13, Chiaia (081 404 735). **Open** 7.30am-9pm Mon-Sat. 7.30am-9pm daily during Christmas. Closed 2wks Aug. **No credit cards. Map** p315 1B.
This tastefully wood-panelled eatery is popular among local business types. There are large glasses of whipped cream on the bar – help yourself to a dollop for your coffee. It also has miniature cakes for those unable to manage a whole one.

La Caffettiera
Piazza dei Martiri 30, Chiaia (081 764 4243). Bus C25. **Open** 8am-9.30pm Mon-Fri, 8am-10pm Sat, Sun. Closed 2wks Aug. **Credit** DC, MC, V. **Map** p315 1A.
Fancying itself as a rival to Gambrinus (*see p129*), La Caffettiera has the service and decor of the coffee houses of the past, and the well-heeled clientele as well. The canopy-shaded outside tables are surrounded by designer shops, and customers look as if they've either just jumped off a yacht or are about to clinch a mega-buck deal. The blue-rinse contingent lurks inside. Not cheap.

Chalet Primavera
Largo Barbaia 1, Mergellina (081 681 705). Metro Mergellina/bus 140, C24, R3. **Open** *July-Sept* 8.30am-1am daily. *Oct-June* 8.30am-1am Mon-Wed, Fri-Sun. **No credit cards. Map** p315 2C.
This is one of several 'chalets' along this stretch of the seafront. Twenty years ago these places were the height of Neapolitan chic; now they're deliciously retro and tacky (*see p127* **Chalet society**). Admire the stunning views across the bay, incongruously interrupted by large portly families, courting teens, kids hanging out of cars, the old rusty boats in the port and the roar of traffic. This is the essence of Napoli.

Pinterré
Via Partenope 12, Chiaia (081 764 9822). Bus C25. **Open** 9am-3am Mon-Thur, Sun; 9am-5am Fri, Sat. Closed occasional 2wks Aug; phone to check. **Credit** MC, V. **Map** p315 2A.
This large pavement café is packed full of Naples' idle rich (or aspirers to the label), especially during the summer. Its excellent sea view is spoiled only by the busy road between customers and the seafront. Pinterré is an ideal spot for people

Caffè choices

Brasiliano: espresso topped with frothy milk and cocoa, sometimes with a dash of alcohol. Varies from bar to bar.
Caffè: a short, very strong espresso; known as a *ristretto* ('concentrated') further north, this tooth enamel-removing strength is the norm for the south.
Caffè alla nocciola: an espresso with sweet hazelnut froth added.
Caffè americano: something approaching what you might drink in Europe or the US – lots of added hot water and a dash of cold milk.
Caffè corretto (literally 'corrected'): an espresso with a dash of alcohol, usually grappa but you can decide what you want (whisky, rum, Bailey's or the sweet and sickly Vov liqueur).
Caffè d'orzo: a barley-based coffee substitute prepared espresso-style.
Caffè freddo: iced coffee, usually very sweet; only sold in the warm months.
Caffè Hag (or *decaffeinato*): decaf espresso (this one's not always available).
Caffè latte: a milkier version of the cappuccino without cocoa.
Caffè lungo: a slightly less concentrated version of the standard *caffè*.
Caffè macchiato: an espresso with a touch of milk.
Cappuccino (or cappuccio): usually more coffee than milk; specify without sugar (*amaro* or *senza zucchero*) or without cocoa (*senza cacao*) or very hot (*molto caldo*), as there is a tendency to serve it lukewarm to allow customers to drink up quickly and get on their way to work. No self-respecting Neapolitan would be seen dead drinking one after noon.
Cappuccino freddo: a cold cappuccino without froth, often made with sweet iced coffee.
Latte macchiato: hot milk served with a dash of coffee.

Scaturchio.
See p129.

watching and scrutinising the latest in designer gear and affectations. Snacks are fresh and include pizza and good *dolci*.

Pasticcerie

Bar Cimmino
Via Filangieri 12-13, Chiaia (081 418 303). Bus C25. **Open** 7am-10.30pm daily. Closed 10 days Aug. **No credit cards. Map** p315 1A.
Incredibly crowded with lawyers and yuppies, who descend on Cimmino for their post-work *aperitivo*, this is an excellent café (if you can get a seat) for delicious cakes and pastries (try the *mimosa* or *torta al cioccolato bianco*). If you're here for an aperitif, Campari soda or Biancosarti are popular choices.

Moccia
Via San Pasquale a Chiaia 21-22, Chiaia (081 411 348). Bus C25. **Open** 8am-9pm Mon, Wed-Sun. Closed Aug. **Credit** AmEx, DC, MC, V. **Map** p315 1B.
This is one of the most famous cake shops in the city, with prices to match its reputation. Try the *fungo al cioccolato* (a mushroom-shaped choux pastry filled with chocolate), a slice of the excellent *pastiera*, or the delicate *chiacciere* with chocolate sauce if you're here around Carnevale time (late February).

Gelaterie

Chalet Ciro
Via Francesco Caracciolo, Mergellina (081 669 928). Metro Mergellina/bus 140, C24, R3. **Open** 7am-2am Mon, Tue, Thur-Sun. **No credit cards. Map** p315 2C.
This shop is one of the greats of Neapolitan ice-cream: locals will travel across the city just to eat here (*see p127* **Chalet society**). After making

your choice from the apparently infinite selection, sit outside and watch the boats coming and going in the port of Mergellina.

Gelateria Bilancione
Via Posillipo 238B, Posillipo (081 769 1923). Bus 140. **Open** 7am-11pm Mon-Fri; 7am-1am Sat, Sun. **No credit cards.**
This is one of Naples' most traditional *gelaterie*. The fantastically flavoured ice-creams and mouthwatering sorbets ensure the place is always packed. See spectacular views across Naples from the benches.

Remy Gelo
Via Galiani 29, Mergellina (081 667 304). Metro Mergellina/bus R3. **Open** *Apr-Sept* 9am-midnight daily. *Oct-Mar* 9am-midnight Tue-Sun. **No credit cards. Map** p315 2C.
A much-renowned *gelaterie*, although aficionados reckon it has lost ground to Bilancione (*see above*) and Ciro (*see above*) Remy offers a huge range of ice-creams, sorbets, *semifreddi* (a cross between mousse and ice-cream), served in different-sized tubs, pots and cones, all made on the premises. There's also a delicious *babà* (cake in rum syrup) filled with ice-cream.

La Torteria
Via Filangieri 75, Chiaia (081 405 221). Bus C25. **Open** 7am-10.30pm daily. Closed 1wk Aug. **Credit** AmEx, MC, V. **Map** p315 1A.
Sit at the tables across the road, but make sure you go inside to at least look at La Torteria's cakes and ice-cream cakes, produced in limited quantities by a local family company. One of the specialities is unusual fruit-flavoured ice-creams packed into the peel or shell of the fruit itself. Like the artistic cakes, the ice-cream walnuts, apples and mandarins look beautiful and taste even better.

Shops & Services

Small, intriguing and idiosyncratic: Naples shops are a world of their own.

'You can march to kingdom come in these beautiful boots.' Norman Lewis spotted that slogan in a Naples market in 1944. Market placards may not be what they once were, but Naples' markets and many of its shops have managed to maintain their individuality in a globalising world: this city fairly bursts with idiosyncratic stores and exuberant street markets.

If you follow a few simple rules, shopping here can be pleasant. You'll get better value for money and more choice in smaller shops and markets than in the big department stores. For designer gear and top brands, try the shops in the **Chiaia** area. If you are on a tight budget, **via Toledo**, **Corso Umberto** or the **Centro storico** are bursting with bargains all year round, peaking during the sales in January, February and August.

Unless you relish the challenge of elbowing your way through the *passeggiata* crowd, avoid shopping between 6pm and 8pm on a Saturday. Don't carry your wallet or other valuables in your handbag where nimble fingers will too easily find them.

For a touch of old world elegance, take a turn around the **Galleria Umberto** and up **via Toledo**, **via San Biagio dei Librai** and the

Colonnese. See p134.

streets west of **piazza dei Martiri**. Bumping and jostling are all part of the experience here, so throw yourself bodily into it and enjoy.

For less atmosphere, but a decidedly more restful shopping experience, head for **via Chiaia**, or the area around **piazza Vanvitelli** and **via Scarlatti** in the Vomero district.

Wherever you go there'll be bootleggers, their wares displayed on the pavement or on stalls, willing to bargain over their music, bags, clothes and sunglasses. They are alive to the police and ready to bolt in seconds.

LOOK BUT DON'T TOUCH
Naples has three types of shop assistant: the talking clam, the store detective and the lady on the phone who won't deign to notice you. Whichever you encounter, expect a lot of huffing and puffing as you work your way around, fingering the merchandise. '*Sto solo dando un'occhiata*' will alert staff to the fact that you're just looking, which may be all you can do in some shops where trying on clothes is not permitted. Ask to be shown the display items on the shelves ('*potrebbe farmi vedere quello?*' – could you show me that?) or risk incurring the shop assistant's wrath.

In the Centro storico, any attempts to speak Neapolitan will be greeted with unreserved enthusiasm; a simple '*grazie assaije*' ('thanks for your help', pronounced 'gratzee yahsighyah') will warm the cockles of even the surliest shop-keeping heart.

TIME TIPS
The majority of shops close for lunch from about 1.30pm to 4.30pm. Some clothes and food shops are open on Sunday mornings, particularly around Montesanto and the Centro storico. Most food shops still close on Thursday afternoon in winter (November to April) and on Saturday afternoon in summer. The majority of non-food shops are closed on Monday mornings and on Saturday afternoons during summer (May to October). Neapolitans abandon the city in August, so don't be surprised to find many shops closed for the whole month.

QUICK-CHANGE ARTISTS
If the name over the door doesn't correspond with the address given in this chapter, check inside. Chances are it's the same business trading under a different name.

Sweet dreams are made of this

Chocolate with chilli did not start with the film *Chocolat*. This exotic combination is an ancient Maya tradition and it has been part of the **Gay Odin** selection for years. That, and everything else involving chocolate. This temple to the cocoa bean is also famed for its chocolate-coated espresso beans and flaky, milk chocolate *foresta*.

Competitors in the Naples chocolate creativity stakes include **Scaturchio** (*see p129*), where the *ministeriale* chocolate was invented for a banquet in 1861. Each individually wrapped piece resembles a large coin of rich, dark chocolate filled with a rum mousse. And for Easter eggs that resemble works of art, try **Dolce Idea di Gennaro Bottone**, but don't leave it until the last minute – they disappear quickly.

You can't get much more Neapolitan than chocolate artist **Perzechella**. This shop sells '*pulcinella's* balls' (chocolate balls with limoncello, mandarin or aniseed) and traditional nativity scenes – in chocolate – at Christmas. To cap it all, everything you buy is wrapped in classical Neapolitan music scores.

Chocolate consumption changes with the seasons in Naples. In winter, try the *cioccolata calda* in bars around town. This is not the milky hot chocolate found elsewhere, but a thick chocolate syrup. **Gambrinus** (*see p129*), **Bar Mexico** (*see p130*) and **Chalet Ciro** (*see p132*) in Mergellina have some of the best in town.

Around Carnival time (February to March) bars stock tubs of chocolate sauce. Don't let the name – *sanguinaccio* (blood) – put you off. Pigs' blood was originally added to the mix, but it's now illegal to do so. Also appearing around this time are *chiacchere* (gossip) – sweet, fried pastry strips, eaten in the run-up to Lent. The best *sanguinaccio* and *chiacchere* are to be found at **Moccia** (*see p132*).

When the weather heats up there is chocolate ice-cream to savour. Try the wonderful chocolate and nut praline *gianduija* ice-cream from **La Scimmia** (*see p130*), one of Naples' oldest ice-cream makers. **Il Gelatiere** has a mouth-watering selection of chocolates with ice-cream fillings and chocolate cones rolled in nuts. For more places to try Naples' scrumptious ice-cream, *see pp126-32* **Cafés, Bars, Gelaterie.**

Dolce Idea di Gennaro Bottone

Via Solitaria 7, Royal Naples (081 764 2832). Bus R2. **Open** 9.30am-2.30pm, 4-8pm Mon-Sat. Closed mid July-Aug. **Credit** AmEx, DC, MC, V. **Map** p315 1A.

Antiques

There are antiques shops all over Naples, but the best known are in **via Costantinopoli** in the Centro storico and around **piazza dei Martiri** in Chiaia.

Campobasso

Via Carlo Poerio 17, Chiaia (081 764 0770). Bus C25, C28/tram 1, 4. **Open** 10am-1.30pm, 4.30-8pm Mon-Sat. Closed Aug. **Credit** AmEx, MC, V. **Map** p315 1A.
Campobasso specialises in Neapolitan religious arte-facts dating from the 17th century. Items here tend to be a bit OTT: portraits of the Virgin embroidered with precious stones, waxen cherubs reclining in beds of filigree flowers under glass domes, votive offerings and saints' relics.

Iermano Antiquities

Via Domenico Morelli 30, Chiaia (081 764 3913). Bus C25, C28/tram 1, 4. **Open** 10am-1.30pm, 4-8pm Mon-Sat. Closed Mon am in winter. Closed Aug. **Credit** AmEx, DC, MC, V. **Map** p315 1-2A.
This shop specialises in the 18th- and 19th-century pieces, with a good selection of European and local antiques. Staff are very helpful.

Mario Giordano

Via S Maria di Costantinopoli 100-100A, Centro storico (no phone). Metro Dante/bus R1, R2, R3. **Open** 9am-1.30pm, 4-7.30pm Mon-Fri; 9am-1.30pm Sat. **Credit** AmEx, DC, MC, V. **Map** p311 1B.
Mario has a fairly priced range furniture, ceramics, prints and exquisite reproductions of antique Neapolitan furniture made from recycled wood.

Antiquarian books & prints

Bowinkel

Piazza dei Martiri 24, Chiaia (081 764 4344). Bus C25, C28/tram 1, 4. **Open** 9.30am-1.30pm, 4-7.30pm Mon-Fri; 9am-1.30pm Sat. Closed Aug. **Credit** AmEx, DC, MC, V. **Map** p315 1A.
Bowinkel is Naples' most respected dealer in period watercolours, prints and photos. Deliveries can also be made abroad.

Colonnese

Via San Pietro a Maiella 33, Centro storico (081 459 858/www.colonnese.it). Metro Dante or Montesanto/ bus R1, R2, R3. **Open** 9am-1.30pm, 4-7.30pm Mon-Fri; 9am-1.30pm Sat. Closed 1wk Aug. **Credit** AmEx, DC, MC, V. **Map** p311 2B.

Other locations: via San Liborio 2, Toledo
(081 420 3090); Via Bonito 2B, Vomero
(081 556 0563).

Gay Odin
Via Toledo 214, Toledo (081 400 063/
www.gayodin.it). Funicular Centrale to
Augusteo/bus C25, R2. **Open** 9.30am-
8pm Mon-Sat; 10am-2pm Sun. Closed
1wk Aug. **Credit** AmEx, DC, MC, V.
Map p311 2A.
Other locations: via Toledo 427, Toledo
(081 551 3491); via Vittoria Colonna 15B,
Chiaia (081 418 282). *Factory:* Via Vetriera
12, Chiaia (081 417 843).

Il Gelatiere
San Pasquale a Chiaia 15, Chiaia
(081 406 750). Funicular Chiaia
to Parco Margherita/metro Piazza
Amedeo/bus C25, R2. **Open** *Mar-Dec*
10.30am-midnight daily. *Jan, Feb*
10.30am-midnight Tue-Sun.
Map p315 1B.

Perzechella
Vico Pallonetto a Santa Chiara 36,
Centro storico (081 551 0025). Bus
E1, R1. **Open** 9.30am-7pm Mon-Sat;
10.30am-2pm Sun. Closed mid July-Aug.
No credit cards. Map p311 3B.

The owners of this shop are passionate publishers
and collectors of books on the arts, holistic
medicine, magic and history for adults and children.
New publications, photographs and prints vie for
space with old and rare items. Look out for the distinctive Neapolitan tarot and playing cards. Ask
here about literary tours and cultural events.

Books

You'll find the best range of second-hand
bookshops in the Centro storico, around
Port'Alba and between **via Costantinopoli**
and **San Biagio dei Librai**. A growing number
of bookshops stock novels, art history and travel
books in English and other languages.
Along with those listed here, **Eva Luna**, in
Piazza Bellini (in the Centro storico), has a fine
selection of books, antiques and stationery.

FNAC
Via Luca Giordano 59, Vomero (081 220 1000/www.
fnac.it). Funicular Centrale to piazzetta Fuga or Chiaia
to via Cimarosa/metro Vanitelli/bus C36. **Open** 10am-
9pm daily. **Credit** AmEx, DC, MC, V. **Map** p314 1-2B.

The huge French book chain stocks a limited
selection of English books, DVDs and CDs, plus
electronic items such as CD players, DVD players
and digital cameras. You can purchase cinema and
concert tickets here as well.

Libreria Feltrinelli
Piazza dei Martiri, via Santa Caterina a Chiaia 23,
Chiaia (081 240 5411). Bus C25, C28/tram 4. **Open**
10am-10pm Mon-Thur; 10am-11pm Fri, Sat; 10am-
2pm, 4-9pm Sun. **Credit** AmEx, MC, V. **Map** p315 1A.
Naples' biggest bookshop has three floors of
stationery, music, DVDs – and books. It holds a wide
selection of novels in English, along with some of
the latest publications on Neapolitan history and culture. There are theatre and concert booking facilities (a branch of Concerteria, *see p144*). Recharge
your batteries in the café.
Other locations: via San Tommaso d'Aquino 70,
Toledo (081 552 1436).

Universal Books
Corso Umberto I 22, Port & University (081 252
0069). Bus 105, C55, R2. **Open** 9am-1pm, 4-7pm
Mon-Fri; 9am-noon Sat. Closed 2wks Aug. **Credit**
DC, MC, V. **Map** p313 1C.

Step through the courtyard to escape the madding crowd and peruse Universal's selection of literature and non-fiction in English.

Department stores

Coin
Via Scarlatti 88/100, Vomero (081 578 0111). Funicular Centrale to piazzetta Fuga or Chiaia to via Cimarosa/bus C36. **Open** *Sept-June* 10am-1.45pm, 4.20-8pm Mon-Sat. *July, Aug* 10am-1.45pm Mon-Sat. **Credit** AmEx, DC, MC, V. **Map** p314 2B.
Along with all the usual department store stuff, Coincasa on the top floor stocks household goods and furnishings. Regular art and film events are held too.

La Rinascente
Via Toledo 340, Toledo (081 411 511). Funicular Centrale to Augusteo/metro Diaz/bus R1, R2, R4. **Open** 9am-8pm Mon-Sat; 10am-2pm, 5-8pm Sun. **Credit** AmEx, DC, MC, V. **Map** 311 A2.
This is where Naples gets its knickers. Known for its extensive selection of underwear and perfume, La Rinascente also sells clothes for the rest of you, and the usual household goods.

Upim
Via Nisco 11, Chiaia (081 417 520). Funicular Chiaia to Parco Margherita/metro Piazza Amedeo/bus C25. **Open** 9.30am-8pm Mon-Sat; 10am-1.30pm, 4.30-8pm Sun. Closed Sun in Aug. **Credit** AmEx, DC, MC, V. **Map** p315 1B.
A useful store with plenty of cheap clothes, cosmetics, underwear, toys and household goods.

Zip to stylish **Via Calabritto** for designer labels.

Fashion

Every second shop in Naples is a purveyor of fashion, or so it seems. While Neapolitan outposts of large international chains are now springing up, most stores still reflect the individual tastes of their owners. Explore the **Centro storico**, **via Toledo**, the **Chiaia** district and the shops around **via Scarlatti**, and don't forget the markets (*see p140*).

Boutiques

Eddy Monetti
Menswear: *Via dei Mille 45, Chiaia (081 407 064/ www.eddymonetti.it). Funicular Chiaia to Parco Margherita/metro Piazza Amedeo/bus C25.* **Map** p315 1B.
Womenswear: *piazzetta Santa Caterina 8, Chiaia (081 403 229). Bus C25/Tram 1, 4.* **Map** p315 1A.
Both: **Open** 9.30am-1.30pm, 4.30-8pm Mon-Sat. Closed Mon am in winter. Closed 2wks Aug. **Credit** AmEx, DC, MC, V. **Map** p315 1A
Eddy Monetti is not only an institution – it's the first word in quality and timeless style. Neapolitans, who in general wouldn't be caught dead in anything not bought new this season, still wear their Monetti trousers bought 30 years ago.

Designer labels

Naples has all the designer emporia you'd expect in a major Italian city, together with all the usual big price tags. Shops are clustered around piazza dei Martiri (bus C25, C28/tram 1, 4, map p315 1A). You'll find both **Ferragamo Uomo** and **Ferragamo Donna** in the piazza. Tiny **via Calabritto** is home to a veritable galaxy of fashion stars: **Armani**, **Cacharel**, **Gucci**, **Louis Vuitton Italia** and **Versace**. **Max Mara** and **Valentino** are just down the road in via Filangieri. Most designer shops offer tax-free services to non-EU tourists.

Garlic
Via Toledo 111, Toledo (081 5524 4966). Metro Montesanto/bus 24, 105, R1. **Open** 9.30am-1pm, 4.30-8pm Mon-Sat. Closed 2wks Aug. **Credit** AmEx, DC, MC, V. **Map** p311 2A.
Garlic's idiosyncratic range of clothes, shoes and accessories by up-and-coming young designers is aimed at those who are stylish, original or very adventurous. Check downstairs for sales.

Maxi Ho
Via Nisco 20, Chiaia (081 414 721). Funicular Chiaia to Parco Margherita/metro Piazza Amedeo/bus C25. **Open** 10am-1.30pm, 4.30-8pm Mon-Sat. Closed 1wk Aug. **Credit** AmEx, DC, MC, V. **Map** p315 1B.
A collection of designer clothes and shoes that veers towards the avant-garde and includes Dolce & Gabbana and Prada.

Deli delights in **Spaccanapoli**. *See p72*.

Melinoi

Via Benedetto Croce 34, Centro storico (081 552 1204). Metro Dante/bus 137, E1, R1, R3. **Open** *Sept-June* 10am-2pm, 4.30-8pm Mon-Sat; 10am-2pm Sun. *July* 10am-2pm, 4.30pm-8pm Mon-Sat. Closed 2wks Aug. **Credit** AmEx, DC, MC, V. **Map** p311 A2.
For individual, stylish and less conventional clothing, check out Melinoi's range of Italian, French and Spanish labels. Individuality comes at a price, mind.

Discount design

Lo Stock

Via Fiorelli 7, Chiaia (081 240 5253). Funicular Chiaia to Parco Margherita/metro Piazza Amedeo/bus C25. **Open** 10am-1.30pm, 4.30-8pm Mon-Sat. Closed 2wks Aug. **Credit** MC, V. **Map** p315 1B.
If your credit card is crying in pain, head for Lo Stock, a large basement where designer-label end-of-lines can be found at hugely reduced prices. You have to be prepared to rummage and hope they've got your size, as all items are one-offs.

Mid-range fashion

Anna Li

Via dei Mille 17-19, Chiaia (081 423 8033/www. anna-li.it). Metro Piazza Amedeo/bus C25. **Open** 10am-1.30pm, 4.30-8pm Mon-Sat. Closed 3wks Aug. **Credit** AmEx, DC, MC, V. **Map** p315 1B.
Worth visiting just to see the amazing interior. International designer gear abounds.

Diagonale

Via Chiaia 218, Royal (081 411 914). Bus C25, R2. **Open** 10am-8pm Mon-Sat. **Credit** AmEx, MC, V. **Map** p315 1A.
An interesting range of clothes and fashion accessories targeted at women of all ages. Staff are helpful.

Olympus & Olympus

Via dei Mille 59B & 61D, Chiaia (081 413 962). Metro Piazza Amedeo/bus C25. **Open** 10am-1.30pm, 4.30-8pm Mon-Sat. Closed 3wks Aug. **Credit** AmEx, DC, MC, V. **Map** p315 1B.
These Chiaia shops have the latest women's designer brands such as Angela Mele and Patrizia Pepe.

Kids' clothes & toys

Like their parents, Neapolitan children tend to wear their wealth on their backs. From a baby's first public appearance, no expense is spared. If prices in the well-heeled parts of town shock you, don't despair: you'll find the big names and quality copies at the markets (*see p140*), including Pignasecca (*see p142*).

Leonetti

Via Roma 350, Toledo (081 412 765). Funicular Centrale to Augusteo/metro Diaz/bus R1, R2, R4. **Open** 10am-2pm, 3.30-8pm Mon-Sat. **Credit** AmEx, DC, MC, V. **Map** p311 2A.
A monthly visit to Leonetti is a tradition for Neapolitan children. It stocks a fantastic selection of every kind of toy and game imaginable.
Other locations: Via Crispi 82 (081 667 780).

Pupi Stellari

Via Carlo Poerio 54C, Chiaia (081 764 2515). Bus C25, C28/tram 1, 4. **Open** 10am-1.30pm, 4.30-7.30pm Mon-Sat. Closed Aug. **Credit** AmEx, DC, MC, V. **Map** p315 1A-B.
A great collection of fun, well-made and comfortable clothes for kids. Good reductions in the sales.

Siola

Via Chiaia 111-15, Royal (081 412 580/415 036). Bus C25/tram 1, 4. **Open** 10am-1.30pm, 4.30-8pm Mon-Sat. Closed Mon am winter; Sat pm summer. Closed 2wks Aug. **Credit** AmEx, DC, MC, V. **Map** p315 1A.
Siola is the place for elegant maternity clothes and designer children's wear. It stocks top Italian brands such as Giorgio Armani kids and Pinko Pallino, as well as the delightful Japanese brand, Miki House, found only in Naples and Milan.

Fashion accessories

Jewellery & watches

Not known for understatement, Naples' passion for the baroque extends to jewellery as well as architecture. Don't leave without visiting the city's famous cameos (*see p218* for cameo factories in Torre del Greco). For the best deals in antique and modern jewellery, wander along the Spaccanapoli in the Centro storico. For a wider selection, try the **Borgo degli Orefici** area, between via Porta di Massa (Mezzocannone), via Marina, Corso Umberto and via Duomo. This is one of the main goldsmithing and jewellery production areas in Italy, and one of the oldest in Europe (it has been a centre of goldsmithing since the Middle Ages); there are 200 jewellery makers and 100 shops within one square kilometre.

Arte in Oro
Via Benedetto Croce 20, Centro storico (081 551 6980). Metro Dante/bus E1, R1, R2, R3, R4. **Open** 10am-1.30pm, 4.30-7.30pm Mon-Sat. Closed 3wks Aug. **No credit cards. Map** p311 A2.
The Marciano brothers create exquisite copies of classical Roman jewellery in a shop that doesn't seem to have changed since it opened at the beginning of the last century. Unique jewellery and antique items at affordable prices.

Ascione
19 Piazzetta Matilde Serao, Galleria Umberto I, Royal (081 421 1111/www.ascione.it). Funicular Centrale to Augusteo/metro Municipio/bus R1, R2, R4, C25. **Open** 10am-1.30pm, 4.30-8pm Mon-Sat. Closed Mon am in winter. **Credit** AmEx, MC, V. **Map** p315 1A.
For over 150 years the Ascione family has been making jewellery and other ornate pieces in coral in their factory in Torre del Greco. This is their showroom.

Caramanna
Via della Cavallerizza 2, Chiaia (081 423 8352). Bus C25/R3 to Piazza Vittoria. **Open** 9.30am-1.30pm, 4-8pm Mon-Sat. Closed 2wks Aug. **Credit** AmEx, DC, MC, V. **Map** p315 1A-1B.
This family-run business has a good selection of top-name brands and unusual local pieces.

Caruso
7 Piazzetta Orefici, off via E Capocci, Port & University (081 554 4922). Metro Piazza Garibaldi/bus 14, 110, 125, R2/tram 1. **Open** 10am-2p1m, 4-8pm Mon-Fri; 10am-2pm Sat. Closed 2wks Aug. **Credit** AmEx, DC, MC, V. **Map** p313 1C.
Located in the heart of the gold district, the Borgo degli Orefici, Caruso has a quality selection of antique and locally produced items.

Galleria Aurea
Galleria Umberto I 71, Royal (081 417 876). Funicular Centrale to Augusteo/metro Municipio/bus R1, R2, R4, C25. **Open** 10am-1.30pm, 4.30-8pm Mon-Sat. Closed Mon am in winter. Closed 2wks Aug. **Credit** AmEx, MC, V. **Map** p315 1A.
Specialising in silverware, this shop also has a good selection of porcelain and jewellery.

De Nobili
Via Filangeri 16B, Chiaia (081 421 685/www.denobili.com. Bus C25/tram 1, 4. **Open** 10am-1.30pm, 4.30-8pm Mon-Sat. Closed Aug. **Credit** AmEx, DC, MC, V. **Map** p315 1A.

Nobili pays homage to the goldsmiths of the past with its exclusive, limited-edition pieces in gold, precious stones and coral. Its jewellers will make individual pieces on request.

Shoes & leather

The cannier Neapolitan buys his or her footwear and other leather goods from the Pignasecca, Poggioreale or other markets (*see p140* and *p142* **La Pignasecca**).

AG Spalding & Bros/Yien
Via Alabardieri 40/43, Chiaia (081 412 770/www.spaldingbros.com). Bus C25/R3 to Piazza Vittoria. **Open** 10am-2pm, 4-8pm Mon-Sat. Closed 3wks Aug. **Credit** AmEx, DC, MC, V. **Map** p315 1A.
If Italian design is beginning to strike you as a touch production line, step into this shop for a more individual approach to shoes, clothes, jewellery and fashion accessories.

Fratelli Tramontano
Via Chiaia 142-143, Royal (081 414 837/www.aldo tramontano.it).Bus C25, R2. **Open** 10am-1.30pm, 4-8pm Mon-Sat. Closed 2wks Aug. **Credit** AmEx, DC, MC, V. **Map** p315 1A.
Traditional Neapolitan craftsmanship manifests itself in superbly designed handmade shoes and bags.

Furla
Via Filangeri 26, Chiaia (081 414 218). Bus C25/R3 to Piazza Vittoria. **Open** 4-8pm Mon; 10am-1pm, 4.30pm-8pm Tue-Sat. Closed 2wks Aug. **Credit** AmEx, DC, MC, V. **Map** p315 1A.
This national and international chain has a lovely range of shoes, bags and accessories guaranteed to match the latest season's colours. High-quality products at reasonable prices.

Parlato
Via San Pasquale a Chiaia 27, Chiaia (081 406 677/www.parlatopelletterie.it). Bus C28. **Open** 9.30am-1.30pm, 4.30-8pm Mon-Sat. Closed 2wks Aug. **Credit** AmEx, DC, MC, V. **Map** p315 1B.
The Parlato family has been in the leather trade for generations. The shop sells excellent-quality and original designs: jackets, handbags, purses, belts and bags are sold at accessible prices.
Other locations: via Cavallerizza 39, Chiaia.

Food & drink

If you're a foodie, you've come to the right town. All you have to do is shop for food the way the locals do. Neapolitans buy their groceries daily, and they stick to whatever is in season, which may be why everything looks and tastes so good. The best place to find regional delicacies is **Pignasecca market** (*see p142*). One word of caution: don't get caught foodless on Thursday afternoons, when most food shops are closed.

The best mozza in town: **Antiche Delizie**.

Antiche Delizie
Via Pasquale Scura 14, Toledo (081 551 3088).
Metro Montesanto/bus 24, 105, R1. **Open** 8am-8pm
Mon-Wed, Fri, Sat; 8am-3pm Thur; 9am-2pm Sun.
Closed 1wk Aug. **Credit** AmEx, DC, MC, V.
Map p311 1E.
Home of the best mozzarella in town and a mouth-watering selection of meat, cheese and preserves.
Try the aubergine antipasti, *caprignetti* (soft goat's
cheese in herbs) and cheese with *tartufo* (truffles).
There's also a range of local wines, and pasta dish-es (made in-house) to take away. It's not cheap, but
it's friendly and well run.

Enoteca Dante
Piazza Dante 18, Centro storico (081 549 9689).
Metro Dante or Montesanto/bus 24, 105, R1.
Open 9am-8.30pm Mon-Sat. Closed 2wks Aug.
Credit AmEx, DC, MC, V. **Map** p311 A2.
The Annunziata family has specialised in fine wines
for 40 years. Ask to see the range of local Aglianico,
Greco di Tufo, Falanghina and Lacrima Cristi. You'll
also find a wide array of wines, liqueurs and cham-pagne from other parts of Italy and the world.

Supermarkets

The following have a reasonable food selection.

Di Per Di
Via Mezzocannone 99, Centro storico (081 579 2616).
Bus E1, R2. **Open** 8.30am-8.30pm Mon-Sat; 8.30am-1.30pm Sun. **Credit** AmEx, MC, V. **Map** p311 3B.

GS
Via Morghen 28 (081 556 3282). Funicular Chiaia
to via Cimarosa, Centrale to piazza Fuga/metro
Vanvitelli. **Open** 8am-8.30pm Mon-Sat; 9am-1.30pm
Sun. **Credit** AmEx, MC, V. **Map** p314 2B.

Gifts

Drogheria Santa Chiara
Via Benedetto Croce 50, Centro storico (no phone).
Bus E1, R1. **Open** *Sept-May* 10am-2pm, 4.30-8pm
Mon-Sat; 11am-1.30pm Sun. *June, July* 10am-2pm,

4.30-8pm Mon-Fri; 10am-2pm Sat. Closed Aug.
Credit AmEx, DC, MC, V. **Map** p311 A2.
This shop has great gift ideas with a local flavour,
from hand-painted ceramics to candles, limoncello
and grappa, preserves and chocolate-coated figs.
The friendly staff speak English and French.

Napoli Mania
Via Toledo 312-313, Toledo (081 414 120/
www.napolimania.com). Funicular Centrale to
Augusteo/bus C25, R2. **Open** *Jan-Apr, June-Nov*
10am-1.45pm, 4.30-8pm Mon-Sat. *May, Dec* 10am-1.45pm, 4.30-8pm daily. Closed Sun in Aug.
Credit AmEx, DC, MC, V. **Map** p311 2A.
These souvenirs are unique and witty, including
watches, ceramics, gadgets and T-shirts created by
the owners featuring *bons mots* in Neapolitan
dialect. There's also a branch at the airport.

Ceramics

Naples is famous for hand-painted Capodimonte
porcelain. Further south, around the town of
Vietri sul Mare at the southern tip of the
Amalfi coast, craftsmen make beautiful
ceramics reflecting centuries of domination
by the north African Saracens, the Spanish
and the French (*see p267* **Vietri ceramics**).
Neapolitan tile work (*majolica*) rivals that of the
Middle East and is still evident on the cupolas
and in the churches of Campania.

La Bottega della Ceramica
Via Carlo Poerio 40, Chiaia (081 764 2626).
Bus C25/tram 1, 4. **Open** 9.30am-1.30pm, 4.30-8pm
Mon-Sat. Closed Aug. **Credit** AmEx, DC, MC, V.
Map p315 1A-B.
Exquisite handmade ceramics from the south of
Italy, sold at very reasonable prices.

Decumanus
Via Benedetto Croce 30/31, Centro storico (081
551 8095). Metro Dante/bus E1, R1, R3, R4.
Open 9.30am-1pm, 4-8pm Mon-Sat; 10am-2pm
Sun. Closed 1wk Aug. **Credit** AmEx, DC, MC, V.
Map p311 A2.

Souvenirs from **Decumanus**. *See p139.*

Reproductions of Capodimonte porcelain, period ceramics and the types of souvenirs that Grand Tourists might have taken home.

Local craftmanship

Marinella
Riviera di Chiaia 287A, Chiaia (081 245 1182/ www.marinellanapoli.it). Bus C28/tram 1, 4. **Open** 6.30am-1.30pm, 4-8pm Mon-Sat. Closed 2wks Aug. **Credit** AmEx, DC, MC, V. **Map** p315 1B.
For more than 80 years the Marinella family has provided that extra-special sartorial something for the man who has everything. The firm is most famous for its ready-to-wear and made-to-measure ties, but there's also a selection of watches, clothing and shoes.

Merolla e del'Ero
Via Calabritto 20 (081 764 3012). Bus C28/tram 1, 4. **Open** 9.30am-1.30pm, 4-8pm Mon-Sat. Closed Aug. **Credit** AmEx, DC, MC, V. **Map** p315 2A.
According to Oscar Wilde, 'elegance' is concentrated in a gentleman's shirt. This tailor agrees. If you have time for a fitting make sure you order a shirt here. There's a beautiful selection of fabrics to choose from, and mother-of-pearl buttons.

Talarico
Vico Due Porte a Toledo 4/B, Toledo (081 401 979/ www.mariotalarico.com). Funicular Centrale to Augusteo/bus C25, R2. **Open** 7am-8pm Mon-Sat. Closed 2wks Aug. **Credit** AmEx, DC, MC, V. **Map** p314 1B.
Talarico is one of the oldest handicraft shops in Naples. Mario and his nephews, Pietro and Luca, are local leaders in a century-old art that has been handed down from generation to generation.

Nativity figures & religious art

For centuries, **via San Gregorio Armeno** has been home to the Christmas crib. Believer or not, you'll find something to grab your attention – from figurines of priests and politicians roasting in hell to miniature food and animals and sublimely crafted angels.

The street is one long pedestrian gridlock for weeks before Christmas (there's talk of making it a pedestrian one-way thoroughfare around the Christmas season). For a less crowded selection of Madonnas with electric halos and backlit views of Christ levitating over the Bay of Naples, take a stroll round the corner to via San Biagio dei Librai.

Marco Ferrigno
Via San Gregorio Armeno 10 (no phone). Bus E1. **Open** 9.30am-1.30pm, 4-8pm Mon-Sat. Closed 3wks Aug. **Credit** MC, V. **Map** p313 1C.
Marco's terracotta figures of Neapolitan peasants, biblical characters and street markets are sought by collectors all over the world. The shop is a fairy grotto.

Health & beauty

Hairdressers

Italian hairdressers are closed on Monday. You generally don't need to make an appointment, but be prepared to spend a lot of time waiting.

Enrico Canè
Via San Pasquale 13, Chiaia (081 405 613). Bus C25. **Open** 9am-7.30pm Tue-Sat. Closed 2wks Aug. **No credit cards. Map** p315 1B.
A men-only barber where you can get a shave, beard trim, manicure, haircut or use the sunbed facilities. Shampoo, cut and dry costs €15.
Other locations: via Trinità degli Spagnoli 6/7, Toledo (081 422 704).

Jean Louis David
Via E Toti 7, Toledo (081 551 6849). Metro Montesanto/bus 24, 105, R1. **Open** 9am-6pm Tue-Sat. **Credit** AmEx, DC, MC, V. **Map** p313 1C.
Speedy, stylish, hassle-free and reliable haircuts for women and men. Choose a style and colour from the JLD catalogues. Wash, cut and dry from €25 (there's 20% discount for students). English spoken.
Other locations: corso Arnaldo Lucci 135, Port & University (081 282 654).

Manolo Tranchesi
Via V Colonna 14, Chiaia (081 421 678). Funicular Chiaia to Parco Margherita/metro Piazza Amedeo/ bus 25. **Open** 9.30am-6.30pm Tue-Sat. Closed 1wk Aug. **Credit** AmEx, DC, MC, V. **Map** p315 1B.
Manolo will keep you entertained in English and a few other languages, too. Wash, cut and dry from €36. Women only.

Parrucchieri
Vico Due Porte a Toledo 4/C, Toledo (081 658 3314). Funicular Centrale to Augusteo/bus C25, R2.
Open 9am-6.30pm Tue-Sat. Closed 3wks Aug.
Credit MC, V. **Map** p314 1B.
Anna and her sister Maria are famous in the area for their fast and funky trims and colours. A quick wash and blow dry here will cost you €8; a wash, cut and blow dry €15. If you want to indulge yourself totally, you can have a manicure and pedicure done at the same time. And if you're feeling really extravagant, speak to Maria about hair extensions.

Natural healthcare

Most Neapolitan chemists have a wide range of homeopathic medicine – look for *omeopatico* signs. Healthfood and exquisitely packaged herbal remedies, essential oils and beauty products can be found in *erboristerie*.

Il Chiostro Erboristeria
Via Santa Chiara 5, Centro storico (081 552 7938). Bus E1, R1. **Open** 10.30am-2pm, 4.30-7.30pm Mon-Fri; 10.30am-2pm Sat. Closed 3wks Aug. **No credit cards. Map** p311 A3.
Everything for the health-conscious, from herbal remedies to health food, all in a tiny shop next to the church of Santa Chiara.

Helianthus
Galleria Vanvitelli 34, Vomero (081 578 2953). Funicular Chiaia to via Cimarosa, Centrale to piazza Fuga/metro Vanvitelli/bus C36. **Open** 9.30am-1.30pm, 4.30-8pm Mon-Sat. Closed 2wks Aug. **No credit cards. Map** p314 2B.
This lovely shop stocks a large selection of natural remedies, health food and beauty products. The staff are very helpful.

Perfumes & cosmetics

Fusco Profumeria
Corso Novara 1H, Port & University (081 283 421). Metro Piazza Garibaldi/bus 14, 110, 125, R2/tram 1. **Open** 9am-8pm Mon-Sat. Closed 2wks Aug. **No credit cards. Map** p312 2B.
Naples' largest range of cut-price perfumes and cosmetics. At these prices, it's not worth bothering with airport duty free.
Other locations: piazza Amedeo 7, Chiaia (081 682 610).

Officina Profumo – Farmaceutica di Santa Maria Novella
Via S Caterina a Chiaia 20, Chiaia (081 407 176). Bus C28/tram 1, 4. **Open** 10am-1.30pm, 4.30-8pm Mon-Sat. Closed 2wks Aug. **Credit** MC, V. **Map** p315 1A.
The Officina remains faithful to the original recipes of its monkish founders and everything is beautifully packaged. Try the Acqua di Santa Maria Novella cologne to combat shopping fatigue.

Homewares

Frette
Via dei Mille 2, Chiaia (081 418 728). Funicular Chiaia to Parco Margherita/metro Piazza Amedeo/bus C25. **Open** 10am-1pm, 4.30-8pm Mon-Sat. **Credit** AmEx, DC, MC, V. **Map** p315 1B.
The national chain Frette is loved throughout Italy for its sheets, towels and bedspreads.

Spina
Via Pignasecca 62, Toledo (081 552 4818). Metro Montesanto/bus 24, 105, R1. **Open** 10am-2pm, 4-8pm Mon-Sat. Closed 2wks Aug. **Credit** AmEx, DC, MC, V. **Map** p314 2A.
This shop has teapots, pans and kettles but – most of all – coffeepots in every shape, size and colour.

Studio K
Via Cimarosa 81, Vomero (081 556 8240). Funicular Chiaia to via Cimarosa, Centrale to piazza Fuga/metro Vanvitelli/bus C36. **Open** 10am-1.30pm, 4.30-8pm Mon-Sat. Closed 3wks Aug. **Credit** AmEx, DC, MC, V. **Map** p314 2B.
A stylish and friendly shop with a carefully chosen selection of designer tableware, lamps and furnishings.

Laundry & dry-cleaning

Lavanderia Santa Chiara
Via S Giovanni Maggiore Pignatelli, Centro storico (081 551 8460). Metro Dante/bus R1, R2, R3. **Open** 8.30am-1.30pm, 3-8pm Mon-Fri; 8.30am-2pm Sat. **No credit cards. Map** p311 3B.
Will wash (not underwear), iron and dryclean.

Markets

Naples' markets provide high-octane shopping opportunities for bargain hunters who enjoy a challenge and a zesty atmosphere. Neapolitans are passionate market shoppers, and they don't let obstacles – ie other people – get in the way once they've spotted the coveted bargain. Stick out your elbows, mind your wallet and fight for what you want. Leave your credit cards somewhere safe: you won't need them here. *See also p142* **La Pignasecca**.

Bancarelle a San Pasquale
Via San Pasquale, via Carducci & via Imbriani, Chiaia. Bus C25/tram 1, 4. **Open** 8am-2pm Mon-Wed, Fri, Sat. Closed Aug. **Map** p315 1B.
Fruit, vegetables, spices and fish are sold between via San Pasquale and via Carducci. Clothes, underwear and jewellery stalls can be found in nearby via Imbriani.

Fiera Antiquaria Napoletana
Villa Comunale, Chiaia. Bus C25/tram 1, 4. **Open** from 7am last Sun of the mth and occasional Sat. Closed Aug. **Map** p315 1-2B.

This market is as attractive for its setting along the graciously decadent Riviera di Chiaia as for its clutter of furniture, paintings, prints (usually fakes), beautiful antique Nativity figures, jewellery and junk.

Mercatino di Antignano
Between via Mario Fiore and piazza degli Artisti, Vomero. Metro Medaglio D'Oro/bus R1. **Open** 8am-1pm Mon-Sat. Closed Aug. **Map** p314 2B.
A great place to buy kitchenware, bags, clothes, jewellery, shoes, towels and linen. New, end-of-line and secondhand wares are sold, and produce too.

Mercatino di Poggioreale
Via M di Caramanico, off via Nuova Poggioreale. Bus C61, C62/tram 1, 4. **Open** 8am-2pm Mon, Fri, Sat (mostly men's clothes), Sun. Closed Aug. **Map** p312 1A.

Famous for its range of shoes, as well as adult and children's clothes, household goods and fabric. The stock here is all-encompassing; you can find everything from top of the range to tat and tragic seconds.

Mercatino di Posillipo
Viale Virgilio, Posillipo. Bus C27. **Open** 8am-2pm Thur. Closed Aug.
Clothes, shoes and bags. Get there early or you'll miss the bargains.

Mercato di Resina
Via Pugliano, Ercolano. Circumvesuviana rail to Ercolano. **Open** 8am-1pm daily. Closed Aug.
This market in Ercolano, south of Naples, rivals the flea market of Paris, but on a human scale. Everything from ancient theatre costumes to leather jackets

Discovering La Pignasecca

You can find everything under the sun in one of the city's oldest markets: the best fish, vegetables, deli goods, cut-price perfume, fashion, linen and kitchenware.

Begin your tour in piazzetta Montesanto, with its joking vendors, its bustle and colour; this is the essence of Naples. Cars, Vespas and ambulances scream by, but don't let them put you off: these folk have been driving since they were weaned. If it's hot, ask Antonio for a *spremuta* (freshly squeezed fruit juice) at one of the city's oldest *acquafrescaio* stalls tucked away behind the banana and veg stands.

The crowd will carry you along via Portamedina to **Scaturchio** (No.24), where you can have coffee and cake with pyjama-clad patients from the hospital across the road. Look up when you pass the slipper shop at No.18 – the balcony above, decorated with dried fruit and vegetables, belongs to the banana lady in piazzetta Montesanto.

If you blink you'll miss the delightful and tiny **Il Buco** ('the hole') lingerie shop a few doors up. Unless it's Monday, the **Pescheria Azzurra** (No.4) will be shimmering with exotic fish, the like of which you've only seen in a Pompeian mosaic, the enormous head of a swordfish taking pride of place. If you can tear yourself away from the *vongole* (clams), you'll find yourself in piazzetta Pignasecca, the stall-packed home to **Pane** (No.35), a tiny shop bursting at the seams with freshly baked cakes and regional breads. Try a piece of the enormous *montevergine in bianco* (white), *nero* (wholemeal) and *bionda* (mixed); the pointy-ended *sfilatino* (a cousin of the baguette); and *freselle*, a dried bread resembling a sliced

bagel (sprinkle with water and cover with your favourite sandwich fillings).

By this point, chances are **Music Romano** (*see above*) is competing with the traffic and the barking vendors by means of its selection of Neapolitan CDs. To the left of Romano's is via Forno Vecchio, an alley worth exploring for its hole-in-the-wall jewellery shops. Moving towards via Pignasecca brings you to **Salumeria Rognoni** (No.38), famous for nutbread and cheeses. If you can't squeeze in the door, duck down via Pasquale Scura to **Antiche Delizie** at No.14 (*see p139*).

Back among the chaotic tumble of stalls and shops on via Pignasecca, pop into **Profumeria Pantera Rosa** (No.39) for some good deals in big-name brands. Across the road, take note of the triperies and their vendors, all of whom are a whiter shade of pale. At **Egidio** (No.34) fill your bags with lingerie and nighties, then struggle upstairs for exquisitely embroidered bed- and table-linen at bargain-basement prices. For kids' shoes, cross the road to **Giusi Baby** (No.58), which has something for even the fussiest. **Spina** (*see p141*), the last word in kitchenware, is at No.62. For all, *see* **Map** 314 2A. Apart from some listed below, few shops take credit cards.

La Pignasecca
Via Pignasecca and surrounding streets, Toledo. Metro Montesanto/bus 24, 105, R1. **Open** 8am-1pm daily.

Egidio
Via Pignasecca 34 (081 551 8640). **Open** 9am-2pm, 4-8pm Mon-Sat. Closed 2wks Aug. **Credit** MC, V.

and finely embroidered *belle époque* linen nighties can be snapped up. Combine a trip here with a visit to the ancient site of Herculaneum, which is right next door to the market.

Music

The Neapolitan contemporary scene is the result of a resurgence of interest in local culture. The delicate Neapolitan mandarin and other traditional instruments can be bought in shops on via San Sebastiano in the Centro storico.

Fonoteca
Via Morghen 31C/D/E, Vomero (081 556 0338). Funicular Chiaia to via Cimarosa, Centrale to piazza Fuga/metro Vanvitelli. **Open** *Sept-June* 9am-9pm

Mon-Sat; 10am-2pm Sun. Closed Sun in July, Aug. Closed 3wks Aug. **Credit** AmEx, DC, MC, V. **Map** p314 2B.
You may not find the top ten chart albums, but there's an eclectic range that repays browsing. Staff will let you listen before buying. For second-hand CDs and LPs, take a couple of steps down the road to No.14 (081 542 2006).

Music Romano
Piazzetta Pignasecca 18, Toledo (081 552 2343). Metro Montesanto/bus 24, 105, R1. **Open** 8am-2pm, 4-8pm Mon-Sat. Closed 1wk Aug. **Credit** AmEx, DC, MC, V. **Map** p314 2A.
Don't be misled by the name. The Romanos specialise in Neapolitan music, from folk to classical and the latest contemporary artists.

Giusi Baby
Via Pignasecca 58 (081 552 9175). **Open** 9am-2pm, 4-8pm Mon-Sat. Closed 1wk Aug. **Credit** AmEx, MC, V.

Pane
Via Pignasecca 35 (081 552 0299). **Open** 8am-1.30pm, 4-7.30pm Tue, Wed, Sat; 8am-1.30pm Thur. Closed Aug.

Pescheria Azzurra
Via Portamedina 4 (081 551 3733). **Open** *Sept-July* 8am-1pm, 4.30-7pm Tue, Wed, Fri, Sat; 10am-1.30pm Thur, Sun.

Profumeria Pantera Rosa
Via Pignasecca 39 (081 551 9591). **Open** 9.30am-2pm, 4.30-8pm Mon-Sat. Closed 2wks Aug. **Credit** AmEx, MC, V.

Salumeria Rognoni
Via Pignasecca 38 (081 552 0834). **Open** 8.30am-2pm, 4.30-8pm Mon-Sat. Closed 1wk Aug. **No credit cards**.

Scaturchio
Via Portamedina 24 (081 551 3850). **Open** 7am-2pm Mon; 7am-7.30pm Tue-Sat; 7am-7.30pm Sun. Closed 2wks Aug. **No credit cards**.

Opticians

Apetino Ottica
Via G Paisiello 41, Vomero (081 578 6933). Cilea metro. **Open** 9am-1.30pm, 4.30-8pm Mon-Sat. Closed 2wks Aug. **Credit** AmEx, MC, V. **Map** p314 2C.
Helpful staff offer free eye tests as well as a quick glasses replacement service.
Other locations: Via G Bernini 87, Vomero (081 558 6598).

Sacco Ottica
Via D Capitelli 35-37, Centro storico (081 551 2552). Bus 24, 149, E1, R1. **Open** 9.30am-1.30pm, 4-7.30pm Mon-Sat. Closed 2wks Aug. **Credit** AmEx, MC, V. **Map** p311 2A.
Your prescription can be made up in one hour by the friendly staff at Sacco Ottica.

Pharmacies

Pharmacies are marked by green crosses in front of their shops. Those listed here are open every other Saturday. *See also p290.*

Cristiano
Riviera di Chiaia 77, Chiaia (081 681 544). Bus C28/tram 1, 4. **Open** 9am-1pm, 4-8pm Mon-Sat. Closed Aug. **Credit** AmEx, DC, MC, V. **Map** p315 1B.
Service here is very helpful and professional and staff are patient with foreigners.

Farmacia d'Atri
Piazza Municipio 15, Royal (081 552 4237). Bus C25, R2, R3, V10/tram 1, 4. **Open** 9am-1pm, 4-8.30pm Mon-Sat. Closed Aug. **Credit** MC, V. **Map** p313 2C.
Staff here speak English.

Photo developers

Maurizio di Cesare
Via D Capitelli 19, Toledo (081 551 3114). Bus 24, 149, E1, R1. **Open** 8am-1.30pm, 4-7.30pm Mon-Sat. Closed 1wk Aug. **Credit** MC, V. **Map** p311 2A.
Well-organised and friendly service with photos developed in one hour.

Print Sprint
Via Cimarosa 166, Vomero (081 556 4506). Funicular Chiaia to Via Cimarosa, Centrale to piazza Fuga/metro Vanvitelli/bus C36. **Open** 9.30am-1.30pm, 4.30-8pm Mon-Fri; 9.30am-2pm Sat. Closed 2wks Aug. **Credit** MC, V. **Map** p314 2B.
Roberta and Sergio will help with all you developing needs. Digital CDs on request.

Stationery

Stationery shops (*cartolerie*) abound throughout the city. Many of them also provide a photocopy and fax service.

Gambardella
Largo Corpo di Napoli 3, Centro storico (081 552 1333). Bus E1. **Open** 9am-7pm Mon-Fri; 9am-1.30pm Sat. Closed 3wks Aug. **Credit** AmEx, DC, MC, V. **Map** p311 2B.
This mad paperchase of a shop is floor-to-ceiling wrapping paper, boxes, cards, stationery and ribbons, mostly handmade. There are 500 paper creations, many of them devised in-house.

E Graphe
Piazza Miraglia 391, Centro storico (081 446 266/www.egraphe.it). Metro Dante/bus R1, R3. **Open** 9am-2pm, 4-7.30pm Mon-Fri; 9am-1pm Sat. Closed Aug. **Credit** AmEx, DC, MC, V. **Map** p311 2B.
Along with designs in recycled paper, this shop has a wonderful selection of coloured inks in quaint little wax-sealed bottles, and calligraphy pens. There's also a photocopy and fax service.

Penna & Carta 1989
Largo Vasto a Chiaia 86, Chiaia (081 418 724). Bus C25/tram 1, 4. **Open** 10am-1.30pm, 4.30-8pm Mon-Sat. Closed Aug. **Credit** AmEx, DC, MC, V. **Map** p315 1B.
As well as a beautiful selection of top-quality stationery and accessories, and a truly wonderful line in fountain pens, this shop also sells pretty, hand-blown glass pens.

Ticket agents

See also p135 **Fnac** *and* **Feltrinelli**.

Box Office Associazione Culturale
Galleria Umberto I 17, Royal (081 551 9188/fax 081 551 0297/www.boxofficeclub.it). Funicular Centrale to Augusteo/bus 149, R2. **Open** 9.30am-1.30pm, 3.30-7pm Mon-Fri; 9.30am-1pm, 4.40-7.15pm Sat. **No credit cards. Map** p315 1A.
A conveniently central place to pick up tickets for just about everything that happens in Naples.

Concerteria
Via Schipa 23, Chiaia (081 761 1221/www.concerteria.it). Bus C28/Cumana rail to corso Vittorio Emanuele. **Open** 10am-1.30pm, 4.30-7.30pm Mon-Fri; 10am-1.30pm Sat. Closed 3wks Aug. **Credit** MC, V. **Map** p315 1C.
Information about, and tickets for, anything and everything that's going on.

Travel agents

Dedalus Centroviaggi
Piazza Monteoliveto 2, Centro storico (081 551 0643/www.dedaluscentroviaggi.it). Metro Dante/bus R1, R3. **Open** 9.30am-1.30pm, 3.30-7pm Mon-Fri; 9.30am-1pm Sat. Closed 1wk Aug. **Credit** AmEx, DC, MC, V. **Map** p311 A3.
Paride and his English-speaking team make train, ferry, hotel and flight bookings. They can also recommend B&Bs in the area.

Eat, Drink, Shop

Arts & Entertainment

Features

Children

Where kids are seen, heard and spoilt rotten.

The old adage 'children should be seen and not heard' is enthusiastically ignored in Naples, where few dare to demand that *bambini* respect such adult institutions as 'peace and quiet'. Nobody tells these kids not to speak until they're spoken to. Wherever they might be – in restaurants, supermarkets, churches, museums, cinemas or walking down a quiet street on a Sunday morning – Neapolitan children make themselves heard, loud and clear.

This exasperating approach to juvenile freedom is probably Naples' attempt to compensate for the lack of facilities that other western children would take for granted – it is fair to say that, in Naples, it is very hard to find enough running room for a game of hide-and-

seek, much less football. This is actually quite a difficult city for children, and so adults let them make a lot of noise.

Like much of the adult population, Neapolitan children seem to live out on the streets. It's not unusual to see two or three children riding (without helmets, naturally) on the back of mamma's scooter. You get used to seeing too-young children smoking nonchalantly, or to hearing children using startlingly atrocious language (if you don't speak Italian, just be grateful you don't understand them). And children tend to roam the streets in carefree truancy during school hours.

On the other hand, those visiting Naples with children will certainly notice a scarcity of facilities for kids, especially after they reach that point where they finally refuse to even go *near* another church or museum.

Luckily, there are a few public parks around where they can stretch their legs and blow off steam, most noticeably the traditional **Villa Comunale** in Chiaia, which has a magnificent bandstand, dating back to 1887, and also holds the charming **Stazione Zoologica**, Europe's oldest aquarium (for both, *see p98*). There's also the **Parco della Floridiana** in Vomero (*see p94*), with a tangled network of paths for walkers and joggers across its lovely lawns. Alternatively, you could try one of the newer stretches of green in the city's outskirts, such as the child-friendly **Parco del Poggio** (*see p107*), with its enchanting views out across the bay, and its relatively new play-facilities, or **Parco Virgiliano** which also has great views over the city from Posillipo hill (*see p100*).

If trees and grass get boring, the jetties and breakwaters around the port and Mergellina harbour provide long breezy walks and the opportunity to watch the ferries and hydrofoils speed in and out. Or even to take one, if you're feeling energetic.

Along with the parks, there are a few child-oriented sights, such as the splendid **Città della Scienza** (*see below* **Science city**) in Bagnoli, where the multilingual staff help keep kids busy, entertained and learning. At the opposite end of the educational spectrum, but closer to the centre, there's the ageing but reliably amusing **Edenlandia** funfair (*see p148*).

But not all kidstuff is labelled as such. You'll find that plenty of Naples' attractions geared at adults are just as likely to captivate children. The four university museums (*see p69* **Centro Musei Scienze Naturali**) are packed with the kinds of rocks, fossils and stuffed animals that fascinate kids, while the Nativity crib section of the **Certosa-Museo di San Martino** (*see p93*) is a sight to behold. For any child with even a passing interest in medieval fortifications, the **Castel dell'Ovo** (*see p64*) and **Castel Sant'Elmo** (*see p93*) allow plenty of room for martial manoeuvres. The dungeons of **Castel Nuovo** (*see p66*) are pleasantly grim.

Catacombs (*see p87-8*) may appeal to teenagers' sense of the macabre, but they're far too spooky for little children; the underground sites on **Napoli Sotterranea** excursions (*see p59*) are pleasantly spooky, though the otherwise excellent guides tend to be oddly impervious to children's requirements.

Science city

Once little more than a few interesting and kid-friendly scientific attractions, the **Città della Scienza** expanded a few years back into one of the city's best attractions for children.

The vast main exhibition hall is holds a dizzying array of hands-on games, experiments and interactive video booths. No avenue of science has been left un-explored, and special attention has been lavished on properties of the physical world – experiments with hydraulics ('bubbles', really), energy displacement and a hair-raising demonstration of static electricity. One stand features excellent slow-motion footage of objects and liquids caught in the act of breaking and spilling: you can reassemble the video frames to put it all back together again.

Another section caters for toddlers, with beanbags and cushions, lots of games and activities that rely less on reading and more on touching, feeling and smelling.

The most popular display for older kids is the avatar computer puppet called Bip, who appears on screens around the hall, remote-controlled by the helpful and friendly young staff (some of whom speak English).

Exhaustive written explanations (including English) versions are provided for all exhibits. There's also a **planetarium** with regular screenings throughout the day in Italian, (admission €2). For commentary in English, contact the Città in advance, although knowledge of Italian is not essential to appreciate a trip across the Neapolitan sky. You can easily spend the better part of a day here, and there are snack bars and a restaurant for sustenance if you do.

A splendid walkway along the water has views over the bay and, across the road, plans are afoot to resurrect an old nature park. Whatever happens here in the future, the science museum is certainly a good start.

Città della Scienza
Via Coroglio 104, Posillipo (081 372 3728/www.cittadellascienza.it). Metro Bagnoli, then bus C9, C10 to Città della Scienza/bus 140 to Capo Posillipo then F9. **Open** *June-Mar 9am-5pm Tue-Sat; 10am-7pm Sun. Apr-May 9am-5pm Mon-Sat; 10am-7pm Sun.* **Admission** *€7; €6 under-18s; free under-4s. Planetarium €2.* **Credit** *AmEx, DC, MC, V.*

...ile most of Naples' transport system is a nightmare for families with kids in tow, the funicular railways (*see p284*) are fascinating.

OUTSIDE THE CENTRE

The volcanic activity of the Naples area is sure to thrill your offspring. Walk them across the hissing lunar landscape at **Solfatara** (*see p103*), drag them up **Vesuvius** (*see p225*) to peer into the crater, or take a trip to Ischia to see steam gushing from between the rocks on the beach at **Sant'Angelo** (*see p205*).

Pompeii (*see p220*) and other ancient sites can be brought alive with a bit of imaginative role play, while the Pietrarsa railway museum (**Museo Ferroviario di Pietrarsa**, *see p216*) is a true delight, however slight your appreciation of trains might be.

ONCE MORE UNTO THE BEACH

When all this has palled, there's always the beach. City authorities insist that the water along the Naples seafront is getting cleaner, and it may be. But after even a cursory examination you will probably want to put some distance between the city and swimming. The shingly **Posillipo** beaches (*see p100*) are close to the centre and fine for teenagers and older kids, but generally unsuitable for toddlers. **Torre Gaveta** at the end of the Cumana railway and **Licosa** at the end of the Circumflegrea branch of the same railway line have sandy beaches; they have a rather tarnished reputation because they are next to the city's sewage outlet (though the water is properly processed these days). For the best beaches, you have to head out of town.

The beaches on the islands may be short, rocky and/or crowded, but the water will be cleaner than in the city, and the boat ride is guaranteed to be seriously entertaining.

See p196 for the best beaches on **Ischia**, *p209* for the **Lido** on Procida and for various recommendations in the **Capri** chapter *see p178*. Alternatively, try the beaches on the coast around **Sorrento** (*see p228*) or along the **Amalfi Coast** (*see p243*).

SHOPPING

Most main shopping areas have toy shops, but wares tend to be of the unimaginative moulded plastic type. **Feltrinelli** (*see p135*) has the only stock of children's reading material in English. For kids' clothes, *see p137*.

Edenlandia

Viale Kennedy, Fuorigrotta (081 239 4800/www.eden landia.it). Metro to Campi Flegrei, then C2 or C3 bus to Edenlandia/Cumana railway to Edenlandia. **Open** *Apr, May* 2-8pm Tue-Fri; 10.30am-midnight Sat, Sun. *June* 2-9pm, Tue-Fri, 10.30am-midnight Sat-Sun. *Sept* 5pm-midnight Mon-Fri; 10.30am-midnight Sat, Sun. *July, Aug* 5pm-midnight Mon-Sat; 10.30am-

Get the bug... at **Edenlandia**.

midnight Sun. *Oct-Mar* 10.30am-midnight Sat, Sun. **Admission** €2.; day pass to most attractions €10. **Credit** AmEx, DC, MC, V.
Edenlandia is a traditional funfair – it's ageing now, but the kids won't notice – with a Big Dipper, Ghost Train, Dodgems and Canoe Chute. There's also a 3-D cinema with regular screenings, a 40m (131ft) Katapult Tower (both extra at €2.60) and a flight simulator (€1.60). There are snack bars, a good pizzeria and a restaurant within the grounds. Check opening times before heading out, because they change constantly. The adjacent zoo – closed at the time of writing – is due for renovation under new management, while a busy kids' theatre puts on occasional performances in English (*see p167* **Le Nuvole**).

Film

Cinema Neapolitan-style.

Neapolitans love a night out at the movies, but their traditional approach to film-watching is completely different from that in many other countries. In Naples, going to the cinema is a social occasion in which the movie itself isn't always the centre of attention. So audiences chat cheerfully, and phones chirp and twitter as non-Neapolitan film lovers fume.

Films usually start on time, but locals arrive fashionably late, with much fussing about and talking as they settle into their seats. Most films have an intermission so the projectionist can nip out for a cigarette.

As in the US, showings in the afternoon and early evening cost less than those later on in the evening, and midweek nights may be cheaper than weekends.

Tragically, Neapolitans share the national Italian distaste for subtitles. Any British or American films you see here will almost certainly be dubbed. Naples has three cinemas showing films in VO (*versione originale*, also sometimes called *lingua originale*) from October to May: the **Plaza** on Tuesday, the **Amedeo** on Thursday and **La Perla** on Monday.

In warm weather films are shown late at night in the open air, often for free. Usual locations are the **Centro Direzionale** (*see p107*) and the WWF reserve at **Astroni** (*see p102*). There is also a summer season of films at **Castel Nuovo** (*see p66*).

Cinemas

At 4.30pm and 6.30pm showings during the week, tickets are reduced to €6.20. None of the cinemas listed below takes credit cards.

Academy Astra
Via Mezzocanone 109, Port & University (081 552 0713). Bus CD, CS, R2. **Tickets** €7. **Map** p311 3B.
The Astra is something of a Neapolitan institution, offering interesting European films (although rarely in the original language). There are €5 second-run showings on Wednesdays. Stop by the bar outside afterwards and banter with earnest Italian cinephiles.

Amedeo
Via Martucci 69, Chiaia (081 680 266). Metro Piazza Amedeo/bus C24, C25. **Map** p315 1B.
This cinema was closed for renovation at the time of writing. An unusually long, thin space (get there early to get a decent seat), it shows current films in English (usually Hollywood blockbusters) on Thursdays.

Galleria Toledo
Via Concezione a Montecalvario 36B, Quartieri spagnoli (081 425 824/www.galleriatoledo.com). Metro Montesanto/bus E2. **Tickets** €5. **Map** p314 2A.
In the heart of the lively Quartieri spagnoli, the Galleria Toledo is best known as an avant-garde theatre. It occasionally runs well-curated short seasons of arty films (usually in *lingua originale*).

Modernissimo
Via Cisterna dell'Olio 59, Centro storico (081 551 1247). Metro Dante/bus 24, R1, R4. **Tickets** €7.20. **Map** p311 2A.
On the edge of the Centro storico, four screens offer choices ranging from children's cinema (childcare included) on Sunday afternoons to showings of restored classics, occasional blockbusters and oddities that will only ever be seen by a handful of cine-enthusiasts in the living room-sized Sala 4.

La Perla
Via Nuova Agnano, angolo via Kennedy, Fuorigrotta (081 570 1712/www.cinteteatrolaperla.it). Metro Agnano/bus 152, C2. **Tickets** € 3-€5.
Out of town but cheap and well-equipped, this cinema shows original-language films (Monday), runs a cinema club (Tuesday) and a summer season of open-air films in the nature reserve of Montenuovo.

Plaza
Via Kerbaker 85, Vomero (081 556 3555). Metro Vanvitelli. **Map** p314 2B. **Tickets** €4.50-€7.20.
This Vomero cinema shows English-language films in their original version on Tuesday evenings.

Warner Village Metropolitan Napoli
Via Chiaia 149, Royal (081 252 5133/www.warnervillage.it). Bus C25, R2. **Tickets** €4.50-€7. **Map** p315 1A.
Big Hollywood films are the main fare here.

Festivals & summer programmes

Cartoons on the Bay
Venue: Positano beach (information 06 374 98315/www.cartoonsbay.com). **Date** April. **Admission** free.
An international jury judges some of the most innovative filmmakers around in this festival, now in its eighth year. Website has good information in English.

Giffoni Film Festival
Venue: various locations in Giffoni Valle Piana, including Convent of San Francesco and Giardino degli Aranci (information 089 8023001/www.giffoniff.it). **Date** July. **Admission** free.

Held in Giffoni in the province of Salerno, this well-established festival hosts world premieres of unique and moving films made for and about children. In 2004 the top award went to *Planta Cuarta* (Fourth Floor), Spaniard Antonio Mercero's funny and touching story of five teens with cancer. Despite the children's film tag, this is a showcase for gems that would otherwise never be shown in Italy. There's good information in English on the website.

CortoCircuito

Venue: various locations in Naples (information 081 410 4401/www.cortocircuito.it). **Date** Dec. **Admission** free.

Billed as a festival of short audiovisual communication, CortoCircuito is mostly a celebration of short films, but also includes adverts, music videos and video art from around the world. Quality ranges from brilliant to abominable, and subtitles and translations are haphazard. But the great thing about short films is that, even if you hate it, it's over in a few minutes.

Artecinema

081 414 306/www.artecinema.com. **Admission** free.

Organised by the well-established Studio Trisorio gallery (*see p152*), this is an annual three-day marathon of films by artists, and films about art. There's always something fascinating (and in the original language). In 2004 the venue was the Teatro Politeama (via Monte di Dio 80).

Rassegna Duelli cinema all'aperto

Venue: Ospedale Militare, Parco dei Quartieri spagnoli, calata Trinita delle Monache (information 081 551 2701/081 240 0911). Metro Montesanto. **Date** August. **Map** p314 2A.

A good mix of Italian cinema and Hollywood films, including classics and animated films, characterises this festival, which has now had its second season in one of the most fascinating areas of the city. Jazz and world music concerts are also held here.

Villa Pignatelli

Riviera di Chiaia 200, Chiaia (information 081 425 037/www.galleriatoledo.com). Bus C28, R3. **Date** July & Aug. **Tickets** €5. **No credit cards. Map** p315 1B.

A series of lovingly curated double bills of new and old films from around the world (usually in the original language) is shown in this sumptuous villa. Some are much-loved classics or restored versions, others are utterly obscure.

La Colombaia

Via Francesco Calise 130, Forio, Ischia (www. colombaia.org/information from Ischia tourism office 081 507 4231).

Film-maker Luciano Visconti's villa, La Colombaia in Forio, Ischia, has been turned into an arts foundation dedicated to cinema and theatre. The villa houses a documentary library on Visconti, cinema history and films made on the island. A prize in Visconti's name is awarded each September and other arts events are held throughout the year.

It started with Sofia

Naples' nascent film industry first burst on to the international consciousness in the 1950s, when a pizza-making Sofia Loren shimmied and winked her way into cinema history in Vittorio de Sica's *L'Oro di Napoli* (1954). Since then, Naples and the Italian Mediterranean have served as film locations for dozens of Hollywood movies, including *The Talented Mr Ripley*, where a tanned Jude Law and Gwynneth Paltrow lounged on its beaches, and the fourth and fifth *Star Wars* instalments, in which the Reggia in Caserta (*see p275*) serves as Queen Amidala's palace.

The local film industry is strong as well. In the 1980s the stuttering, anxious comedian and actor, Massimo Troisi, became hugely popular for his performances in Naples-based films like *Ricomincio da tre* (1981) and *Non ci resta che piangere* (1984) as Italy's version of Woody Allen. Sadly, after receiving worldwide acclaim for his work in the Oscar-nominated film *Il Postino*, Troisi died in 1994 at 41.

His effect on the local film industry lives on, though, as his success meant that investors were more likely to take chances on Neapolitan films, and a whole generation of young actors and film-makers followed in his footsteps – directors Mario Martone, Pappi Corsicato and Leonardo Di Costanzo among them.

Martone creates intense, finely acted psychological dramas played out against the backdrop of some of the city's toughest suburbs in films like *L'Amore molesto* (1995) and *Teatro di guerra* (1998). His latest work is *L'Odore del sangue* (2003).

Corsicato's first film, *Libera* (1993) won awards at the Berlin Film Festival, letting the world know that it had found a new talent. The comedy, eroticism and portrayals of the lost middle class in his films *I Vesuviani* and *I Buchi Neri* evoke Pedro Almodóvar.

The documentary-maker Di Costanzo spent a year filming in a school in rundown San Giovanni di Teduccio (near the port of Naples) to make *Teachers*, his testimony to those at the tough end of teaching, dealing with difficult pupils who have no inclination to learn (Venice Film Festival winner 2003).

Galleries

The best of Naples' contemporary art is underground.

Fondazione Morra. *See p152*.

The much-vaunted Neapolitan renaissance may be running out of steam, but some of its vital achievements remain. One of the key strategies of the 1990s clean-up campaign of former mayor Antonio Bassolino – along with sweeping the streets and closing some of them to traffic – was to bring contemporary art into the city. Successive regional and local governments have continued to promote contemporary art in Naples, most notably through the annual large-scale installations in piazza Plebiscito every Christmas. The first of these was Mimmo Palladino's *Montagna di Sale* (Salt Mountain) in 1995; later installations have included work by Jannis Kounellis and Mario Merz, Anish Kapoor's huge, dazzling red *Tarantantara*, Joseph Kosuth's illuminated quotation from Neapolitan philosopher Benedetto Croce, Rebecca Horn's eerie blue neon lights and skulls rising from the earth and, in 2004, Richard Serra's elegantly curving spiral maze. There have been accusations of window dressing surrounding these exhibits, but the authorities have also shown their commitment to art with big-name exhibitions in the Castel Sant'Elmo (*see p93*) and the Museo Nazionale Archeologico (*see p84*). Francesco Clemente, Jeff Koons, Anselm Kiefer and Damien Hirst (whose first major retrospective took place in autumn 2004) have all shown here.

That doesn't mean Naples is an easy city for aspiring young artists and gallery owners. There isn't much of a market here: the city still lacks both art collectors and the art-world infrastructure of Rome or Milan. However, some new spaces run by artists themselves or by young enthusiasts have managed to put on consistently exciting exhibitions over the past few years. **T293** – a space run by curator Paola Guadagnino in the heart of the Centro storico – shows mostly up-and-coming Italian artists. **Raucci Santamaria** has recently moved to larger premises and does consistently good work. Recent shows having featured Matt Collishaw, Cathy Wilkes, Padraig Timoney, Peter Doig and Michael Raedecker. **Changing Role** is part way between a gallery and upmarket interior design store. Recent events here have included shows by Simon Periton and Kevin Francis Gray, as well as New York electro-performance duo Fischerspooner.

There's more performance at the **Sintesi Electronic Arts Festival** (www.sintesi.na.it), which features acts working at the boundaries of electronic music, contemporary art and new technologies. The festival takes place in the autumn at deconsecrated churches across the city.

The death of gallery-owner Lucio Amelio ten years ago is still felt on the Naples art scene. Amelio was an amazing presence, best known for organising an exhibition in the wake of the 1980 earthquake that killed 3,000 people. Called **Terrae Motus**, the exhibition is now housed permanently in the Reggia in Caserta (*see p275*). It includes works on the theme of earthquakes by a roll call of some of the late 20th century's major artists: Andy Warhol, Joseph Beuys, Cy Twombly, Keith Haring, Jean-Michel Basquiat, Robert Mapplethorpe, Tony Cragg and Richard Long. Amelio's gallery space on piazza dei Martiri has now been taken over by Alfonso Artiaco.

There's a limited contemporary collection (including Andy Warhol's take on Vesuvius) hidden away on the top floor of the **Museo di Capodimonte** (*see p90*), and a much-talked-about municipal gallery of contemporary art is set to open at Palazzo Donnaregina on Via Settembrini in the Centro storico in 2006.

Meanwhile, the biggest story in Naples contemporary art is to be found underground.

Arts & Entertainment

The city's metro art is Italy's most ambitious state-sponsored project. The metro line (*see* p153 **Underground art**), while nothing special architecturally, has given five of its stations over to a free gallery of everything and everyone from the local art scene in the past 20 years.

LOCAL TALENT

Names to look out for include joker Piero Golia, electronic installation-making duo Bianco Valente, painter Mariangela Levita, Naples' answer to Cindy Sherman – Betty Bee, Pennacchio Argentato, another pair of installationists. International talents such as Ryan Mendoza and Johnny Shand-Kydd have also chosen to take up (semi-permanent) residence in Naples.

A useful website for up-to-date listings (in Italian only) of exhibitions in the area is www.exibart.com, or www.undo.net.

Galleries

Alfonso Artiaco

Piazza dei Martiri 58, Chiaia (081 497 6072/ www.alfonsoartiaco.com). Metro Piazza Amedeo/ bus C24. **Open** 10am-1pm, 4-8pm Mon-Sat. Closed Sat pm summer. Closed Aug. **No credit cards.** **Map** p315 1A.

Recently moved to the central piazza dei Martiri, Artiaco is one of the key galleries in Naples. It has shown high-profile international artists such as Carl Andre and Giuseppe Penone as well as local youngsters Bianco Valente.

Changing Role

Via Chiatamone 26, Santa Lucia (081 195 759 58/ www.changing role.com). Bus 140, 152. **Open** 10am-1.30pm, 5-8pm Tue-Fri. Closed Aug. **No credit cards.** **Map** p315 2A.

Showing decorative works by local and foreign artists, Changing Role is a cross between a shop and a gallery, but none the less enjoyable for that. It also has an 'events space' on its lower floor for video work and live performances.

404 arte contemporanea

Via Santa Brigida 76, Royal (081 552 9169/404/ www.404gallery.com). Bus R2. **Open** 5.30-8pm Tue-Fri. Closed Aug & 2wks Sept. **No credit cards.** **Map** p315 1A.

Now in a new, larger home in the centre of town, 404 still hosts up-and-coming international and local artists. Chat to owner Francesco Annarumma for the lowdown on who's who and what's what on the local arts scene.

Fondazione Morra

Via Vergine 19, Sanità (081 454 064/fondazione@ virgilio.it). Metro Piazza Cavour/bus 201. **Open** 10.30am-1pm, 4-7pm Mon-Fri; by appointment Sat, Sun. Closed 2wks Aug. **No credit cards.** **Map** p312 2C.

Worth visiting for the building alone – it's housed in the stunning Palazzo dello Spagnuolo – this gallery has shown stalwarts of the European avant garde such as Hermann Nitsch, runs a festival of experimental cinema every autumn, and hosts part of the Sintesi electronic arts festival (*see* p151).

Galleria Fonti

Via Chiaia 229, Royal (081 411 409/www.galleria fonti.it). Bus C25, R2. **Open** 4.30-7.30pm Tue-Fri. Closed Aug. **No credit cards.** **Map** p315 1A.

A newish space dedicated to up-and-coming painters and with an emphasis on the modish.

Lia Rumma

Via Vannella Gaetani 12 (081 764 3619/www. gallerialiarumma.it). Metro Piazza Amedeo/Bus C25. **Open** 4.30-7.30pm Tue-Fri. By appointment other days. **No credit cards.** **Map** p315 2A.

One of Naples' historic spaces, these days Lia Rumma tends not to come up with the goods in the way that it used to in days past.

Scognamiglio

Via M d'Ayala 6, Chiaia (081 400 871/www.mimmo scognamiglio.com). Metro Piazza Amedeo/bus C24. **Open** 11am-1pm, 4.30-7pm Mon-Fri; 11am-1pm Sat. Closed Aug. **No credit cards.** **Map** p315 1B.

This gallery near piazza Amedeo holds exhibitions by Italian and foreign artists. Mimmo Scognamiglio personally commissions work, including a cycle of exhibitions inspired by the Capella Sansevero (it featured a stunning show by Anthony Gormley).

Studio Trisorio

Riviera di Chiaia 215, Chiaia (081 414 306/www. studiotrisorio.com). Metro Piazza Amedeo/bus R3. **Open** 11am-1pm, 4.30-7.30pm Mon-Fri; 11am-1pm Sat. Closed Aug. **No credit cards.** **Map** p315 1B.

One of the most active and well-established galleries of international contemporary art in Naples, Trisorio has shown Rebecca Horn and British photographer Martin Parr.

Raucci Santamaria

Corso Amedeo di Savoia 190, Sanità (081 744 3645/ raucciesantamaria@interfree.it). Metro Museo. **Open** 10.30am-1.30pm, 3.30-6.30pm Tue-Fri; 10.30am-1.30pm Sat. Closed Aug. **No credit cards.** **Map** p312 1C.

One of the best young galleries in Naples, Raucci Santamaria devotes consistent effort to finding and nurturing new talent. Excellent recent shows have included Britartist Mat Collishaw and Scandinavian photographer Anne Lislegaard.

T293

Via Tribunali 293, Centro storico (081 295 882/ www.t293.it). Metro Dante. **Open** 4-8pm Tue-Sat. Closed Aug. **No credit cards.** **Map** p313 1C.

A small but dynamic space is in the darkest part of Via Tribunali – follow the dark corridor in to reach the surprisingly light first-floor gallery. Run by curator Paola Guadagnino, it shows consistently thought-provoking work by young artists, and is working on a resident artist programme.

Underground art

Plans for a museum of contemporary art in Naples may still be on the drawing board, but that doesn't mean that the city doesn't provide a round-up of some new Neapolitan, Italian and international art talent. All you have to do is buy a metro ticket.

In an attempt to beautify the stations on Linea 1, five of its stations have been filled with some significant chunks of contemporary art. Most of these stations are in somewhat nondescript residential areas and therefore slightly off the beaten path for the visitor, but it's worth forking out a euro for the 90-minute ticket (*see p282*) and taking the tour.

The best place to start is **Piazza Dante**. This station has the most impressive collection, loosely linked by the theme of 'travel', and featuring some big international names. As soon as you enter the station you're hit by Joseph Kosuth's neon rendition of (appropriately enough) a Dante quotation. *Queste cose visibili* is 15 metres (49ft) long and almost impossible to see all at once. The letters reflect to either side and seem to wriggle as you pass below them on the escalator. Just trying to read them can make your brain wince – trying to work out what they mean will take you the rest of your stay. The quote – as long and as complex as the language-artist Kosuth likes 'em – is taken from Dante's *Il Convivio* (and not from the *Inferno* as some suggested it should have been) and concerns perception and beauty.

Once the escalator ride is done, you're immediately faced with Jannis Kounellis's stunning untitled piece, which covers the entire 25-metre (82ft) span of the wall. Train tracks head across the wall, far from being parallel, squashing abandoned shoes as they go. Like much of Kounellis's work, the piece evokes travel, migration and flight, with an undercurrent that is both faintly comic and somewhat disturbing. Turn and head down the next escalator where one of Michelangelo Pistoletto's signature mirror pieces continues the experience. *Intermediterraneo* has the outline of the Mediterranean sea inscribed on its mirrored surface, making your short escalator trip feel rather like *The Odyssey*.

Skip the Museo station (it contains only a couple of replica statues from the Archaeological Museum – better go visit the originals) and head on to **Materdei**. This was the most recent station on the line to be

opened, and feels like the place where the curators put everything they didn't have space for anywhere else. Sol Lewitt's long corridor, with its bright geometric murals and curvaceous plastic stalagmites, is spacious and luminous and could give you a headache if you have to wait for your train too long. It's worth going up out of the station here just so you can come back in again and experience anew the impact of Luigi Ontani's fantastic mosaic, which gives an impression of something between a grandiose baroque theatre and an old Victorian swimming bath.

Next stop is **Salvator Rosa**, imaginatively floored in pink lino (*rosa* is Italian for pink). The highlight here are Perino & Vele's veiled Fiat 500s, life-size and looking almost rusty enough to be real. The entrances to the station are themselves striking, and have given a much-needed facelift to the surrounding area – covered with two steel-and-glass spires (a postmodern echo of the spires in piazza San Domenico and piazza del Gesù) and lined with coloured mosaics by Gianni Pisani and playful sculptures by Mimmo Paladino and Salvatore Paladino.

Finally, **Via Cilea/Quattro Giornate** shows the cream of current Neapolitan artists, although some of the works are fairly well-hidden in this labyrinthine station. Look out for Sergio Fermariello's *Guerrieri*, hundreds of glyph-like figures who could be cave-painting warriors, or rush-hour commuters. An image of artist Betty Bee peers out of a light box over one escalator, unsure if she's trapped there or just having a look in, while other works by Nino Longobardi, Marisa Albanese and Umberto Manzo lurk round every corner.

Gay & Lesbian

A small scene but lots of action.

Bar-B Discobar.

A gay 'scene' is a relatively new concept in Naples. In fact, until the recent past, very few people would adopt a gay identity, preferring instead to get on with things behind a 'respectable' heterosexual veneer. But despite their po-faced Catholic façade, Neapolitans have tended to be tolerant towards minorities, be they religious, racial or sexual. Indeed, the *femminiello* (a very camp gay) has been an integral part of traditional Neapolitan theatre culture since the 17th century, and is considered cute rather than contemptible. Terms for gay – from the Neapolitan dialect *ricchione*, to the nationally used *frocio*, *finocchio* and *checca* – are rarely meant as insults. The same tolerance informs official attitudes; police raids in gay pubs, discos or cruising areas are virtually unheard of.

The lack of 'scene' has certainly never meant a lack of activity: there were and are a wealth of gay experiences you may come across in a city such as this. If you're on the ball, you'll discover opportunities in the most unlikely places: just keep your gaydar switched on.

Gay men with a penchant for construction workers, taxi drivers or uniforms stand a good chance of scoring. Don't let butch appearances put you off. Just keep your eyes open, use your intuition and remember things can happen any time, any place, anywhere. This is a fertile hunting ground as long as you stick to the rules (he's always 'the man'). Whatever you do, don't be too obvious. Allusion is your best tactic: it gives both parties a chance to pull out with no risk or loss of face.

If a male gay scene is a new concept in Naples, the lesbian scene is an even more recent phenomenon. Unshackled by the preconceptions of more established gay communities, and launching straight into a post-feminist social environment, Naples' lesbians have been quick to find their own identity. Male and female gays share meeting places and events; most of Naples' gay clubs are managed by lesbians. So new is the lesbian scene that terms for the various stereotypes – *bubù* (lipstick lesbian), *severa* (tough), *totora* (butch) – are all neologisms.

On the other hand, any time and anywhere is good for cruising, so keep your eyes peeled.

Bars & clubs

Most places are straight venues, functioning as gay meeting places one day a week. They don't usually charge an entrance fee, but you are obliged to have at least one drink. Any drinks you have are marked on a slip you receive at the entrance and are paid for on leaving. In the summer, the crowds migrate from the stuffy, packed winter nests to open-air places on the cooler hills that surround the city, or to Capri.

Port & University

Bar B-Discobar

Via Giovanni Manna 14 (081 287 681/338 840 7769). Bus CS, R2. **Open** 9pm-3am Mon-Fri, Sun; 10pm-7am Sat. **No credit cards**. **Map** p313 1C.
One of only two dedicated gay venues in the city, Bar B-Discobar is a disco with a darkroom area, video room and a 'labyrint', as the sign says. There are two bars, one with sofas to facilitate socialising. You'll need Ariadne's thread not to lose your way in this intricate three-level maze of small grottos and narrow corridors. Search hard enough, and you may find your Theseus… or your Minotaur. You must spend a minimum €13 on drinks. All types and ages.

Centro storico

Duniaa

Via Atri 36 (081 295 808/338 320 8587). Metro Dante. **Open** 10pm-2am Tue-Sun. **No credit cards**. **Map** p311 2B.
This discobar with darkroom is situated in an underground cavern, in the heart of the Centro storico. It attracts a very mixed crowd at weekends; there are occasional gay events here, usually on a Sunday.

Intramoenia Caffè Letterario

Piazza Bellini 70 (081 290 720). Metro Dante. **Open** 10am-2am daily. **No credit cards**. **Credit** AmEx, MC, V. **Map** p311 2B.
A straight meeting place for Naples' intellectuals, the Intramoenia – and piazza Bellini too – becomes on summer evenings a catwalk for self-confident gays to show off their beautiful tans, well-toned bodies and designer clothes. Sit in the open air and relax among beautiful 18th-century buildings and 21st-century bodybuilders.

Underground

Suerte, via Santa Maria dell'Aiuto 4, off Santa Maria La Nova (349 6748 557). Bus C25. **Open** 10.30pm-2am Sun. **No credit cards**. **Map** p311 3A.
Near the church of Santa Maria la Nova in the Centro storico, Underground plays revival pop and house music on the lower of two levels. There's a fair-sized darkroom. Suerte hosts a party here on Sunday evenings.

Tom Cruising

Via della Veterinaria 72, Sanità (081 780 9578). Metro Cavour or Museo/bus 14, 15, 47, CD, CS, C51. **Open**: 6pm-midnight Tue-Thur; 6pm-2am Fri; 10pm-5am Sat, 9pm-2am Sun. **Admission** €5. **No credit cards**. **Map** p314 1B.

A proper gay club, just like you could find in any large European city, with a darkroom, labyrinth, cubicles, sling, gloryholes – the lot. Not for those of a weak disposition.

Chiaia to Posillipo

Kontatto

Antica Birreria Edenlandia, via Oderico da Pordenone (no number, off viale Kennedy), Fuorigrotta (333 2446 496/vaniajgroup@libero.it). Metro Piazzale Tecchio/bus C14. **Open** 9.30pm-3am Thur. **No credit cards**.
This disco pub with a country American flavour serves pints of beer on wooden tables to a mixed crowd of twentysomethings who are out for a good laugh. The music is revival pop. There's a terrace in the summer.

Elsewhere

Freezer

Via Lauria 6, Centro Direzionale, Isola G6 (081 750 2437/339 210 4142/www.freezerstereobar.it). Metro Piazza Garibaldi/bus R2. **Open** 11pm-4am occasional Fri. Closed Aug. **No credit cards**. **Map** p312 2A.
Always packed with extravagant creatures of the night, Freezer is Naples' hippest discobar. Deep in the incongruous Centro Direzionale, it's light years away from the usual Neapolitan baroque; this postmodern club would not look out of place in Berlin or Amsterdam. The minimalist decor and serious-

Meet friends at **Piazza Bellini**.

Arts & Entertainment

thinking regulars contrast entertainingly with more flamboyant members of the clientele in a typically Neapolitan mixture of extremes. You must spend a minimum €6 on drinks.

Bookshops

Colonnese

Via San Pietro a Maiella 32-33, Centro storico (081 459 858/fax 081 455 420/www.colonnese.it). Metro Dante/bus CD. **Open** 10am-1.30pm, 4-7.30pm Mon-Sat. Closed 1wk Aug. **Credit** AmEx, MC, V. **Map** p311 2B.

In the heart of the Centro storico, this wood-panelled bookshop exudes mystery and witchcraft. Here you might uncover antiquarian books, modern editions (both new and used), prints, postcards, books on Naples and Campania, and gay and erotic literature – not to mention tried and tested potions for impotence, love and jealousy.

Eva Luna

Piazza Bellini 72, Centro storico (081 292 372/ www.evaluna.it). Metro Dante/bus CD. **Open** 9.30am-2.30pm,6pm-midnight Mon-Sat. Closed 2wks Aug. **Credit** AmEx, DC, MC, V. **Map** p311 2B.

Features mostly women's literature, but also has a large choice of prints and postcards. There's also a public payphone inside.

Cinemas

No, these are not arthouse movie houses with erudite gay programming. Cinemas like **Argo** (via A Poerio 4, Centro storico), **Eden** (via Guglielmo Sanfelice, Royal), **Agorà** (via Guanti Nuovi 6) and **Casanova** (corso Garibaldi 14, Port & University) show heterosexual porn but attract gay men. Few see much of the film, though. Most of these places are in bad parts of town, so take care.

Cruising

Centro Direzionale

Map p312 2A.
Around the Holiday Inn; after midnight and only by car. Dangerous.

Via Brin

Map p313 1A.
After midnight, only by car. Dangerous.

Villa Comunale around via Dohrn

Map p312 1A-B.
After midnight, on foot or by car. Fairly safe.

Events & one-nighters

The only two exclusively gay places in town are **Bar B-Discobar** (*see p155*) and **Tom Cruising** (*see p155*). Otherwise, there are

occasional events organised by the following three groups. The scene is a fluid one, so it's a good idea to check with the organisations directly or with **Arcigay** (*see below*) for up-to-date information.

Free Lovers

333 771 7698/333 244 6496/328 944 6753/ www.freelovers.it.
This group usually organises events on a Thursday or a Saturday.

The Other Side

338 617 5071/339 8934 003/www.theotherside.it.

Suerte

496 748 557.
This outfit organises gay parties for younger people, including a regular event at Underground (*see p155*).

Gay associations

Arcigay-Circolo Antinoo

Vico San Geronimo alle Monache 17-20, Centro storico (081 552 8815/fax 081 268 808/ www.arcigaynapoli.3000.it). Bus C25, R1, R2. **Open** 5-8pm Mon, Wed, Fri. Closed Aug. **Map** p311 3B.

The Arcigay organisation (www.gay.it), based in Bologna, is Italy's most serious and highly regarded gay lobby. Its Naples offshoot organises films and events such as poetry readings, often in collaboration with other cultural associations in the city. Welcome sessions are held for new members on Fridays. The premises house a small bar. Up-to-the-minute information on bars, clubs and events is provided. A very young environment.

Arcilesbica-Circolo Le Maree

Vico San Geronimo alle Monache 17-20, Centro storico (081 552 8815/www.arcilesbicanapoli.tk). Bus C25, R1, R2. **Open** 5.30-8pm Tue, Thur, Sat. Closed Aug. **Map** p311 3B.

An information point for lesbian events, bars and clubs in Naples and the surrounding area. There's also a gay and lesbian library and magazine collection, and a small bar.

Saunas

Blu Angels Sauna

Via Taddeo Da Sessa, Centro Direzionale, Isola A7 (081 562 5298). Metro Piazza Garibaldi/bus C58, R2. **Open** 2-11pm daily. **Admission** €11 or €4 with Tessera azzurra (blue card) at €4. **No credit cards. Map** p312 2A.

Naples' first ever sauna, the Blu Angels has a gym, darkroom labyrinth, two Finnish saunas, a Turkish bath, a jacuzzi and numerous masseurs spread over three floors. You'll need to join the Arcigay cultural association (*see above*; €13 at the door) to get in.

Nightlife & Music

Late, late nights and city sounds.

Naples' incredibly noisy streets often seem to make music superfluous, or at least little more than one element in the overall urban soundtrack. Despite the roar, however, Naples earned a reputation as a centre for Italian music during the 20th century. *Il canzone napoletano* (with songs such as 'Turna a Surriento', 'Funiculì, Funiculà', 'O Surdato Annamurato') actually defines Italian music for some people, but such sentimental traditional songs have had little positive effect on the city's contemporary music scene. While there are good artists around, you have to be prepared to seek them out. The live music scene is oddly downbeat – due to the lack of decent venues as much as the lack of bands. However, some energetic local promoters are ensuring that more touring bands get further south than Rome, so keep your eyes peeled for posters and flyers around the Centro storico (still the best source of information), and check newspaper listings.

Rock, roots & jazz

New talent has been slow to make an appearance recently. Local heroes **Almamegretta** (mixing traditional Neapolitan melodies with dub and techno, and impressing Massive Attack and Leftfield along the way) parted company with their charismatic vocalist Raiz in 2003. Both Raiz and the new Almamegretta have produced new records – but do check out their 1995 album *Sanacore* for a taste what they could do when they were together. Raiz regularly guests on other projects. One involves ex-Police drummer Stuart Copeland – called La Notte della Taranta, it is a celebration of the traditional *tarantella*.

A similar fate has befallen **99 Posse**. The once-ferocious political rap outfit seems to have dissolved into a mass of side-projects: chief rapper Zulu is collaborating with the more dubby Al-Mukawama, soundman Marco Messina with the electronic Resina, and singer Meg is making her own poppier solo record). **24 Grana** is still considered the best local rock band, with their energetic wiry post-punk sound, while local megastar **Pino Daniele** has alienated some fans recently by turning to Renaissance music for inspiration.

The most outstanding recent local record has been from **Enzo Avitabile ed i Bottari**

di Portici (a bunch of guys who use large old wine barrels as percussion instruments). Their record '*Salvamm 'O Munn*' ('Save the World') in which they duet with Khaled, Manu Diabango and Hugh Masekela was a hit in world music charts all over Europe. Unclassifiable saxophonist **Daniele Sepe** still performs around the centre's bars, clubs and sometimes even on the streets. Sepe can be found playing traditional Italian music one night, avant-garde jazz the next and Latin American the night after that – or even all on the same night. *Anime Candide* (2003) is as good as any of his eclectic records, featuring Balkan, French, Spanish and – of course – Neapolitan tunes.

The **Nuova Compagnia di Canto Popolare** are stalwarts of the local roots scene (around for nearly 30 years now and still a heady live experience), while **Eugenio Bennato**'s Taranta Power project puts *tarantella* back on to the dancefloor. Finally, **E' Zezi** (and their international offshoot **Spaccanapoli**) are as chaotic, vital, ramshackle, funny, sentimental and downright Neapolitan as music produced in the city should be.

LIVE MUSIC VENUES
Naples suffers from a chronic lack of decent live music spaces. Any big names who make it this far south will probably end up in the

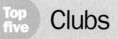

Top five   Clubs

Kinky Bar
Kinky by name but not by nature, *see p161*.

Rising South
Imagine you're in New York City, *see p162*.

S'move
The smartest place in town, but fun too, *see p163*.

Otto Jazz
A legend on the jazz scene, *see p163*.

Velvet Zone
Dark, smoky, claustrophobic, atmospheric, *see p162*.

Palapartenope (via Barbagallo 115, 081 570 0008, www.palapartenope.it): spacious with a cheap bar, but barn-like and utterly devoid of atmosphere. The outdoor **Arena Flegrea** (part of the Mostra d'Oltremare exhibition area, *see p108*), is a better bet. Restored in 2001, it now hosts summer concerts on its pleasant marble terraces. Recent visitors have included Peter Gabriel, Massive Attack, Air and David Byrne. In summer, keep an eye on programmes for the **Neapolis Rock Festival** (various venues), the **Arenile** in Bagnoli, or – best of all – the space beside the Maschio Angioino castle.

The **Ethnos Festival** (081 882 3978, www.festivalethnos.it) has a great range of world music acts (with a heavy emphaisis on the Mediterranean – 2004 saw neo-fado singer Mariza, the Franco-Algerian Orchestre National du Barbes and Natacha Atlas) at the outdoor **Parco degli Quartieri Spagnoli** in June and July. The **Sguardo di Ulisse Festival** (a double bill of a film and a band – see www.sigbloom.it) takes place at the space next to Maschio Angionino in July or September. For details on **Sintesi** (December, various venues), which brings

On the beach

By the middle of June the weather gets so hot in Naples that even the most hardened clubber finds the idea of a dark, sweaty, smoke-filled club as appealing as yesterday's pizza. Until recently, this simply meant that everything closed up for the summer – until someone came back from Ibiza with a great idea...

While Napoli may not rival the Isla Blanca for the quality of its beaches, it can match it for the sheer amount of its coastline. Clubs like Music on the Rocks in Positano have been making use of their spectacular locations for years, and now Napoli has a scene to rival it.

The granddaddy of the movement from the street to the beach is the **Arenile** in Bagnoli (via Coroglio 14/B, 081 570 6035). Originally a fairly scummy beach in the shadow of the decommissioned steelworks, the Arenile was cleaned up as part of the relaunch of the whole area. It didn't have a lot of success as a beach until the owners realised that more people were turning up and hanging around the bar in the evenings to catch the great sunsets. From then, progress was unstoppable, with live indie and dance bands followed by a disco directly on the sand. Success was such that Arenile rapidly went upmarket – the sandy dancefloor has been replaced by an elegant wooden one, the bar now does cocktails instead of bottled beer, and the music is mainstream commerical house and dance, rather than rap, indie and dub. Despite losing some of the spontaneity that made it initially so attractive, this is still the beach club that's closest to the centre, and still a good night out.

Vibes on the Beach (via Miseno 52, Capo Miseno, 081 523 2828) was originally an offshoot of the city centre Vibes bar, until

they realised they were having more fun on the beach and uprooted permanently. Attracting a slightly older crowd than the Arenile, Vibes on the Beach is more about chilling than raving, especially given the frighteningly moreish frozen cocktails the bartenders invent, as well as the downbeat/nu-jazz soundtrack. Great for when you want to preserve that sundown chill-out until sun-up. The nearby **Lido Turistico** (via Lido Miliscola 56, Bacoli, 081 523 5228) feels more like a glorified beach bar – a long space where the sea comes almost right up to the row of tables and chairs. Occasional live bands (they're keen on reggae) complete the atmosphere. **Nabilah** (via Spiaggia Romana, Cuma, 335 527 8189) is the summer version of the S'Move bar and is the other beach clubs' wealthy cousin. Red velvet sofas are carefully arranged around low white tables with designer candles on the beach itself. Sitting on a comfortable sofa with a chilled drink late at night with bare feet on the sand listening to the surf is a wonderfully decadent experience, and worth the steep bar prices.

A tip for all these places – remember that your shoes will get dusty and sandy, and high heels are not great for beaches. If you're really feeling daring, have your swimming cossy on and go for a dip later... though make sure you stay well in the shallows if you've had more than one cocktail.

The major drawback of the beach scene is its inaccessibility to those without transport. The Arenile is reachable by taxi, but to get to the other places, you'll need to get the Cumana train as far as Torregaveta, or the Metropolitana as far as Pozzuoli, then take a taxi or bus from there. As for getting home... well, be prepared to stay late!

together Europe's finest experimental electronic artists, see the website: www.sintesi.na.it.

For smaller and local groups, check out the club scene: **Velvet Zone** and **Rising South** for rock and dance; **Bourbon Street**, **Around Midnight** and **Otto Jazz** for jazz.

TICKETS

Information on – and tickets for – major concerts can be found at **Concerteria** and **Box Office** (for both, *see p144*), **Fnac** or **La Feltrinelli** (for both, *see p135*). It's a good idea to buy tickets for big concerts in advance as there's always a crush on the door.

Turn up at the advertised times – you never know, miracles sometimes happen in Naples – but be prepared for a long wait before there's any on-stage action.

Nightlife

Everything happens later here. You can digest that big dinner slowly while checking out a nice late-night bar, many of which will be open even after the discos have closed. If you're going to a club, there's not much point in turning up before midnight.

WHERE TO GO

Different areas of the city attract different types of people. Students of all ages, would-be artists, intellectuals and alternative types in general haunt the **Centro storico**, which gets extremely lively on Friday and Saturday nights. Make for the areas around piazza Bellini, piazza del Gesù and via Cisterna dell'Olio, or piazza San Domenico Maggiore and via Paladino. In summer, you won't even need to choose any particular bar: grab a beer anywhere, then wander the streets until you find a congenial flight of steps to perch on and hang out.

Arts & Entertainment

Along the bay-front in **Chiaia** and **Mergellina**, Saturday night entertainment is more traditional. What feels like the entire population of Naples and its suburbs take to their cars for a few hours of horn-blowing, minor bumps, scooter-dodging (a necessary skill in Naples) and furious gesticulating. This is usually followed by a 30-minute ice-cream, drink or *passeggiata* (stroll) and then it's back to the cars for the real fun.

If techno and trance is your thing, you'll have to trek out to the Naples–Rome motorway where events – and in particular those

Sounds of the city

The origins of the *canzone napoletana* can be traced back to 7 September 1837, the date of the first official **Piedigrotta Festival**, and its signature tune 'Te Voglio Bene Assaje'. Held around the time of the religious feast of Mary of Piedigrotta (8 September), the festival continued for almost 140 years. Every year music publishers would be inundated with new compositions from aspiring and established poets and musicians for months before the event, and sheet music of the featured songs sold prodigiously. Performances at the festival were in the form of *audizioni*, with the public deciding the winning number.

The song festival lost its relevance with the invention of radio and the jukebox, finally fizzling out in the 1970s, but not before giving us 'Funiculì, Funiculà' (winner of the 1880 festival and promoting the new funicular on Vesuvius) and ''O Sole Mio' (taking second place in 1896), and making Naples the capital of Italian music.

Many credit poet Salvatore Di Giacomo with really inventing *canzone napoletana* as a genre in the latter part of the 1800s. He hit upon the idea of fusing classical arias, chamber music and the voices of celebrated tenors with popular, more traditional, working-class *tarantella* music and dialect to create a distinct Neapolitan sound, a process helped by the inherent suitability of the Neapolitan dialect for the city's music – the clipped words fit perfectly with the rhythm, giving it a unique sound.

This was the beginning of the end for the street musicians, or *posteggiatori*, who had played their mandolins and performed in cafés and *trattorie* throughout the city for at least six centuries. The tenor Enrico Caruso started out this way in 1891, aged just 17. His tomb, in Cimitero Santa Maria del Pianto on via Nuova del Campo, still attracts visitors from all over the world. Here you will also find the tomb of comedy actor Totò (*see p166*), himself responsible for a Neapolitan staple, 'Malafemmena', written in 1951.

Being a port city, Naples has always been open to outside influences, with sailors bringing songs and music from Africa and the Middle East. It was the arrival of the American allies in 1943 that opened the floodgates for the introduction of rhythm, jazz, boogie and swing to Neapolitan music.

The 1970s brought a revival of interest in more traditional folk music, with musicians exploring the traditional *tarantella* and *tammuriata*. These styles, based around the beats of a *tammora*, a large tambourine-type of drum, are accompanied by traditional dances. iIn the *tammuriata* dancers emulate flirtation and sex in three phases: the man courts the woman, they embrace, then roles are reversed. You are very likely to see this dance performed in squares in the Centro storico in the warmer months. It takes its name from a similar dance in Puglia, but Neapolitans will tell you it is quite different. **Nuova Compagnia di Canto Popolare** was the most prolific of a number of groups celebrating this style, and the group still occasion-ally plays together over 30 years later (Eugenio Bennato, a founder member, produced the very successful *Taranta Power* album and tour in 2001). NCCP scored their biggest hit in 1977 with 'Tammuriata Nera', a reworking of a 1944 tune about a girl's encounter with an US officer.

The '70s scene was incredibly vibrant, producing **Napoli Centrale**, led by saxophonist James Senese (son of a North Carolina military officer), who created a fusion of jazz, soul and roots. Edoardo Bennato (Eugenio's brother) became Naples' resident singer-songwriter, experimenting with American rock and his own city's traditions. One of Italy's biggest names, **Pino Daniele**, also began writing and recording at this time – his 1977 album *Terra Mia* was an instant

organised by the Angels of Love crew (329 163 5445, www.angelsoflove.it) – take place in mega-discos. Be warned: you'll never get there without a car.

GETTING IN

Some bars have small dancefloors where you're welcome to get up and shake your stuff should you feel like it. Sometimes a membership card (*tessera*) is required for admission; there may be a small fee for the card, but entry is generally free on subsequent visits.

Most discos charge an entrance fee, which may or may not include one drink. In some places you'll be given a card that is stamped for every drink you purchase. You are required to spend a minimum amount on drinks before leaving.

Unless otherwise stated, admission to the venues listed below is free.

Spaccanapoli.

success, and his rhythm and blues defined the city musically for over two decades. He has now turned his back on the city, with all new material in Italian, claiming to be disillusioned with how the city is run – a topic he first touched upon over 25 years ago in his signature tune 'Napule è' (*Napul'è tutt nu suonn e a sap tut'o munn, ma nun sann a verità*: Naples is a dream and everyone knows it, but nobody knows the truth).

The scene continues to thrive, despite a lack of places to play (although parks and squares become live-music arenas in the summer months). Whether it's rap, ragga-muffin and reggae with **24 Grana**, **Bisca** and **99 Posse**, **Planet Funk**'s dance music; saxo-phonist **Daniele Sepe** and his mix of styles as diverse as *tarantella*, jazz, ska and Irish folk music; violin virtuoso Lino Cannavaciuolo's chill-out sounds; **Almamegretta** with their intriguing mix of dub and techno Neapolitan-style, modern folk musicians **E Zezi** and **Spaccanapoli**, or the latest hunks of *neo-melodici* (*see p164* **I Neo-melodici**), Neapolitan influences are alive and well.

Teatro Trianon – Il Teatro della Canzone Napoletana
Piazza Calenda 9, Port & University (081 225 8285/www.teatrotrianon.it). This theatre specialises in Neapolitan music and song.

Archivio Sonoro della Canzone Napoletana
RAI, Viale Marconi, Fuorigrotta (www.radiorai.it) **Open** 10.30am-1.30pm, 3-6pm Tue, Thur, Sat; Mon, Wed, Fri by appointment. Closed Aug.
One of the world's biggest jukeboxes, this is a collection featuring Neapolitan songs from the 1800s to the present day. If you'd like to experience the collection, email canzonenapoletana@rai.it or leave a message at 081 725 1312.

Conservatorio di Musica
Via San Pietro a Majella 34, Centro storico (081 564 4411/www.sanpietroamajella.it). Naples famous music school has a well-stocked library, holding a museum of manuscripts and rare prints.

Centro storico

Bars, clubs & discos

Intra Moenia
Piazza Bellini 70 (081 290 720/www.intramoenia.it). Metro Dante/bus 24, R1, R4. **Open** 10am-2am daily. **Credit** AmEx, DC, MC, V. **Map** p311 1A.
There's not much difference between most of the bars on this lively piazza, but this one is the largest and also has lots of space inside for the colder months. Intra Moenia also doubles up as a bookshop and small publisher and is a great place for an early morning coffee, meeting friends at any time of day, or that last beer.

Kinky Bar
Via Cisterna dell'Olio 21 (081 552 1571). Metro Dante/bus 24, R1, R4. **Open** 10.30pm-3am daily. Closed mid June-Sept. **No credit cards**. **Map** p311 2A.

Intra Moenia.

Aret' a' Palm. *See p163.*

By its name, you might be expecting a different sort of entertainment, but this little place is actually a reggae bar. Neapolitans like their rocksteady and dub, and this is the best place in town to hear it. A DJ-cum-bartender spins the tunes, there's decent beer and its open until the early hours. In summer the crowd takes over the alleyway outside, much to the discontent of the few drivers crazy enough to attempt to pass.

Rising South

Via San Sebastiano 19 (335 811 7107/www.rising south.com). Metro Dante/bus 24, E1, R1, R4. **Open** 10pm-3am Tue-Sun. Closed June-mid Oct. **No credit cards. Map** p311 1A.

The latest addition to Naples' club scene, Rising South opened with a major word-of-mouth buzz in 2002. It's the best-designed club in the city – leaving the rest of the slightly rundown places behind. A long tunnel-like space with stone walls filled with temptingly comfy-looking sofas and armchairs. Music sticks to a downbeat/nu-jazz/lounge vibe. Good for when you want to leave Napoli behind and pretend you're in NYC.

Superfly

Via Cisterna dell'Olio 12 (347 127 2178). Metro Dante/bus 24, R1, R4. **Open** 7pm-3am Tue-Sat; 7pm-3am Sun. Closed June-Sept. **No credit cards. Map** p311 2A.

This place is tiny with only half a dozen stools to compete for, so be prepared to stand – but it's worth it. The bartender takes care of the fine jazz soundtrack, as well as ensuring both the drinks and snacks are of a high quality. (Avoid the beer – go for the cocktails.) Small photographic exhibitions are held, which are often surprisingly good. Superfly is a great place to meet up for a drink before going to the Modernissimo cinema across the road, the Velvet next door (*see below*), or for winding up a long evening. In warmer weather, everyone piles out on to the street outside.

Las Tapas Bar

Piazzetta del Nilo 36 (333 978 1626). Bus CS, E1, R2. **Open** 7pm-2.30am Mon, Wed-Sun. Closed Aug. **No credit cards. Map** p311 2B.

There's not much space inside here, but several tables outside allow mellow drinkers to enjoy the cool air and the ancient surroundings while Latin-flavoured music emanates from the interior or the record shop next door. This is a good place for a late drink after having eaten somewhere else nearby. Despite the name, however, there are no tapas to be had. The statue of Nilo in this little square is rumoured to whisper indecent suggestions to lone women at night.

Velvet Zone

Via Cisterna dell'Olio 11 (339 6700234). Metro Dante/bus 24, E1, R1, R4. **Open** 11pm-4am Wed, Thur, Sun; 11pm-6am Fri, Sat. Closed June-mid Oct. **No credit cards. Map** p311 2A.

Known to one and all as the Velvet, this warren-like space is dark, smoky, claustrophobic and atmospheric – and your best bet for a night out dancing in the Centro storico. Different DJs spin different sounds (from minimal techno to 1980s revival to downbeat to rock) every night. Occasionally there's live music (usually local or Italian dance-oriented groups). Sit in one of the smaller rooms and chat, or end up getting sweaty on the packed dancefloo. The *tessera* (membership card) is sometimes waived for out-of-town visitors, but you'll be expected to spend at least €15 on drinks.

Live music

Sanakura

Vico Pallonetto a Santa Chiara 5 (339 344 7455/ www.bourbonstreetclub.it). Metro Dante/bus E1. **Open** 10.30pm-4am Thur-Sat. **Admission** €8 for live music events. **No credit cards. Map** p311 3B.

A dark, smoky and subterranean place, Sanakura is popular with the local student population. Despite murky sound and a tiny stage, it occasionally hosts good live bands from Italy, as well as Germany and the UK – particularly from the electronic end of the musical spectrum.

Toledo

Live music

Bourbon Street

Via Bellini 52 (328 068 7221/ 347 051 2211). Metro Dante/bus 24, R1, R4. **Open** 9pm-3am Tue-Sun. Closed July, Aug. **No credit cards. Map** p311 1A.

Bourbon Street is a largeish, centrally located space dedicated to local jazz, with shows every night. It usually gets crowded with a mixture of bright, fashionable young things and slightly older bearded jazz-heads. The red brick decor lends the place a very American feel.

Port & University

Bars, clubs & discos

Aret' a' Palm

Piazza Santa Maria La Nova 14 (339 848 6949). Metro Montesanto/bus R1, R3. **Open** 10am-2pm Mon-Fri; 6pm-2am Sat, Sun. **No credit cards. Map** p311 3A.

Aret' a' Palm being Neapolitan for 'behind the palm', this small but stylish place is – not surprisingly – located by an incredibly tall palm tree on a quiet square right in the centre of town. Well designed, with a comfortingly long bar, it gets pretty crowded inside at weekends. The only live music is when owner Alan Wurzburger gets inspired to take his guitar out, but otherwise DJs spin a soundtrack of jazz and world music so loud that it's audible even if you sit at one of the tables out on the piazza.

Live music

Kestè

Largo San Giovanni Maggiore 26-27 (081 551 3984). Bus CD, CS, R2. **Open** 8am-11pm Mon-Fri. Closed 2wks Aug. **No credit cards. Map** p311 3B.

Situated opposite the Orientale university, the vivacious Kestè is a bar, café, live music venue and restaurant. The interior is attractively designed but very small, though as the tables spill on to the square, you'll usually manage to find a seat. This is

an enjoyable place for a drink at lunchtime or an *aperitivo* before going on to eat elsewhere. On Friday and Saturday evenings, however, it's worth hanging around later into the night for live music.

Chiaia to Posillipo

Bars, clubs & discos

Enoteca Belledonne

Vico Belledonne a Chiaia 18, Chiaia (081 403162). Metro Piazza Amedeo/bus C25, R3. **Open** 6pm-midnight daily. Closed Aug. **Credit** DC, MC, V. **Map** p315 1B.

Wriggle through to the back room to find a seat or stand squashed up at the bar with the rest of the area's lawyers and moneymakers enjoying an after-work *aperitivo*. Despite its clientele, this old-style *enoteca* is wonderfully relaxed and easygoing and has excellent, reasonably priced wines by the glass. It gets packed between 7pm and 9pm.

Marshall Lounge

Vicoletto Belledonne a Chiaia12, Chiaia (081 405 216). Metro Piazza Amedeo/bus C25, R3. **Open** 6pm-2am Tue-Sun. Closed July-Sept. **No credit cards. Map** p315 1B.

A tiny space, but furnished with such minimal elegance you're almost afraid of spilling your drink on the designer furniture. One to pop into for a refresher after having blown your month's paycheck in the designer stores on nearby via Calabritto.

S'move

Vico dei Sospiri 10A, Chiaia (081 764 5813/ www.smove-lab.net). Metro Piazza Amedeo/bus C25, R3. **Open** last 2wks Jun, July 8pm-4am daily. *Sept-mid June* 2pm-4am Mon; 9am-4am Tue-Sat; 7pm-4am Sun. Closed July, Aug. **Credit** MC, V. **Map** p315 1B.

The smartest place in this part of town, S'move boasts upmarket decor (it's a bit like walking into an extremely posh furniture shop) and a crowded, friendly atmosphere. The area's beautiful young things make up most of the clientele, but it's refreshingly unsnobbish. There's no dancefloor as such, but the careful selection of music ranges from Latin to house to techno, which encourages even the glacially cool to end up shaking a limb or two. The management here organise the Nabileh beach venue in the summer.

Live music

Otto Jazz

Salita Cariati 23, Chiaia (081 551 3765/340 294 1006). Funicular Centrale to corso Vittorio Emanuele/bus C16. **Open** 11pm-2am Fri-Sun. Closed July, Aug. **No credit cards. Map** p313 1A.

A historical fixture on the city's jazz scene, this is the place to come to if you like your jazz more trad than acid. Musicians are mainly local and always of

I neo-melodici

Spend time surfing late night Neapolitan TV and you'll come across some strange phenomena. Among the guys flogging carpets and the adverts for soft porn chatlines, you will inevitably also find low-budget music videos featuring a succession of dodgy-looking singers belting their hearts and lungs out against the backdrop of some of the less attractive parts of Naples. This is the only overground manifestation of the strange musical world of the *neo-melodici*.

The *neo-melodici* are a group of singers who have risen to a kind of prominence over the last few years. An intensely localised phenomenon, they tend to be extremely famous in tiny parts of the city. The songs are sung in Neapolitan dialect and the sound is a mixture of traditional Neapolitan song mixed with cheesy electronic keyboards and pumped up bass. The singers have a nasal

crooning style which sounds equal parts Arabic pop and cut-price Tom Jones.

Songs deal with the reality of life in the poorer parts of the city, not only the central areas of the Quartieri spagnoli or the Sanità, but the areas of Casandrino, Cardito, Casalnuovo – the endless housing estates that spread out around the Vesuvian plain.

Stars appear and disappear with amazing rapidity, though Gigi d'Alessio and Nino d'Angelo are leaders of the genre. Classic numbers include Tommy Riccio's 'Nu Latitante', which tells the heartbreaking tale of a fugitive from justice whose only desire is to go back and visit his family at Christmas, while Mimmo Rocco's 'So' Già Spusato' recounts the temptation of a married man. Ciro Ricci is the genre's answer to Ricky Martin, with his 'Chill' Va Pazz' Pe' Te' ('She's Crazy About You') often to be heard banging out of car stereos across the Quartieri spagnoli. Strangest of all is Valentina, a transsexual who had a massive underground hit with her 'Ragazzo Gay' – a song lending support to a boy from a tough neighbourhood having trouble expressing his sexuality.

Arguments abound as to whether the *neo-melodici* are contemporary bearers of an old musical tradition, cheesy rip-offs, an excuse for money laundering, or an authentic subcultural expression of life in the Neapolitan ghetto. Turn the telly on after midnight, venture beyond channel 7, and decide for yourself.

a good standard, with an enjoyable atmosphere guaranteed. Usually only open at weekends, Otto sometimes stages events during the week, including occasional Tuesday evening jazz lessons.

Vomero

Live music

Around Midnight

Via Bonito 32A (081 558 2834/www.around midnight.it). Funicular Montesanto to San Martino /metro Vanvitelli/bus V1. **Open** 8.30pm-1am Tue-Sun. Closed Aug. **No credit cards. Map** p314 2B. Around Midnight is dedicated to live jazz; local musicians, along with combos from across Italy, play standards most nights here. The space is small and can be uncomfortable when it gets crowded, but the atmosphere is unpretentious and friendly.

Elsewhere

Officina 99

Via Gianturco 101 (081 734 9091/www.officina 99.org). Metro Gianturco/bus 81, CS. **Open** (live music) *July-Sept* 10pm-3am Fri, Sat. *Oct-June* 10pm-3am Fri-Sun. **Admission** varies; payment is voluntary, around €5 for live music is typical. **No credit cards. Map** p313 1A.

Naples' most famous *centro sociale* (a semi-legally occupied space), the Officina is located in an abandoned factory in the mean streets south-east of Stazione Centrale. It hasn't spruced itself up like its sibling set-ups the Brancaleone in Rome or the Leonkavallo in Milan, so it remains cold and cavernous, raw and edgy. But there's fun to be had here for all those who have ever pierced unusual parts of their body or walked around with a mangy dog on a piece of string.

Performing Arts

All of Naples is a stage.

Naples' dramatic appearance – like a vast amphitheatre spread around the stage of the bay – makes its natural theatricality seem only logical. Orson Welles' quip that 'there are 56 million actors in Italy and the worst are on the stage' is spot-on here. It often seems a shame to swap the pleasure of people-watching at a café for an earnest piece of intellectually rigorous theatre. Despite having one of the oldest theatrical traditions in the country (the *commedia dell'arte* was born, or, at least, given its greatest impetus here in the 16th century, see *p169*), it has to be said that modern Napoli's theatrical offerings can be a bit heavy-going.

Things are changing, however. The **Mercadante** (*see p167*) has now been set up as a *teatro stabile* (subsidised theatre), with public money helping to attract quality touring productions and nurture good home-grown ones. And, in fact, Neapolitan theatre *can* be quite good, and at times it can also provide a unique insight into this complex city's soul. If you find Luca de Filippo doing a play by his late father Eduardo – who was considered one of theatre's all-time greats by Laurence Olivier – then you're in for a treat. Anything by film and theatre director Mario Martone is unmissable, while works by Enzo Moscato are electric – his intense, heavily Neapolitan mixtures of mime, music and physical theatre are either brilliant or disastrous. Another local star is Renato Carpentieri, who uses money from a starring role in an Italian crime soap opera to fund his Libera Scena Ensemble in experimental productions.

Classical music fans – or those who don't have a penchant for contemporary music – are well served: the **San Carlo** (*see p168*) is still one of the best opera houses in the country. In addition, the **Pietà dei Turchini** (*see below*) organisation puts on a series of exceptional early music events every year.

PRACTICALITIES

You'll probably find that box offices at most smaller theatres rarely open more than half an hour before the show, so if you want to purchase tickets any further in advance (or just guarantee that you'll get a seat on the night) then you're really better off heading for the ticket agencies (*see p144*). Big-name productions, especially those at San Carlo, can sell out months in advance, so book early.

Small musical companies

Associazione Scarlatti

Piazza dei Martiri 58, Chiaia (081 406 011/ www.napoli.com/assocscarlatti). Metro Piazza Amedeo/bus C24, C25. **Open** *Box office* 10am-1pm, 3.30-6pm Mon-Fri. *Performances* 9pm Thur. Closed June-Sept. **Tickets** €13-€25. **No credit cards.** **Map** p315 1A.

The best of the city's resident international artists and frequent visitors can be found in this group's performances of classical chamber music and occasional jazz. The productions are usually held in the Teatro delle Palme (via Vetriera 12; metro Piazza Amedeo, bus C25). The decor's rough – it doubles as a cinema – but the acoustics are quite good and the tickets are fairly priced.

Pietà dei Turchini

Via Santa Caterina da Siena 38, Toledo (081 402 395/www.turchini.it). Funicular Centrale to corso Vittorio Emanuele/bus C16. **Open** *Box office* 45 mins before performances. *Performances* Nov-June 9pm (days vary; phone for details). **Tickets** €9-€12. **No credit cards.** **Map** p315 1A.

In a deconsecrated church, conductor Antonio Florio leads this group through a varied, well-executed programme of works by 17th- and 18th-century Neapolitan composers. Its base has recently extended to include small ensembles from different countries, all specialising in early and baroque music.

Venues

Bellini

Via Conte di Ruvo 14-19, Toledo (081 549 9688/ www.teatrobellini.it). Metro Cavour or Museo/bus 24, R1, R4. **Open** *Box office* Oct-May 10.30am-1.30pm, 5-8pm Mon-Fri; 10.30am-2pm Sat. *Performances* Oct-May 9pm Tue-Sat; 5.30pm Sun. **Tickets** €20-€30. **Credit** MC, V. **Map** p312 2C.

Sumptuously redecorated, Bellini stages prose performances, international musicals in English, dance groups, local musicals and concerts. Decidedly mainstream and occasionally tacky – the place to go if you want to see *Grease* in Italian.

Elicantropo

Vico Gerolomini 3, Centro storico (081 296 640/ www.teatroelicantropo.com). Metro Cavour or Museo/bus 149, CD, CS. **Open** *Box office* Oct-May 5.30-8pm daily. *Performances* Oct-May 9pm daily. **Tickets** €10-€15. **No credit cards.** **Map** p311 2C.

With only 40 seats, this tiny space in the Centro storico may be intimate, but it's also one of the best

Totò and Eduardo

Totò and Sophia Loren.

Look at the pictures on the walls of many small *trattorie* in Naples, and among the various saints and footballers you will likely see two other figures: one is a sunken-cheeked, heavily mustachioed, gloomy-looking man, not so different from many who still hang around the bars in Naples. The other is a long-chinned, crooked-nosed figure often wearing a bowler hat.

The first of these is **Eduardo de Filippo**, one of the most important Italian playwrights of the last century. His unadorned portrayals of Neapolitan life, complete with poverty and corruption, were bold innovations in social realism, and the public adored him for it.

Born in Chiaia in 1900 into a theatrical family, he left school at 13 to become a full-time actor. He wrote his first one act-play, *Farmacia di Turno*, in 1920, and in 1931 formed his own company with his sister and brother, debuting one of his best-known plays, *Natale in Casa Cupiello* (*Christmas in the Cupiello Household*). He came into his own after the war, producing some of his finest work – perhaps the best known being *Napoli Milionaria* and *Filumena Marturano*. De Filippo himself took the lead in both the

stage and film versions of *Napoli Milionaria*, playing an Italian soldier who returns from a POW camp to find his wife has made a million on the black market while his son is a thief and his daughter is about to become a single mother. *Filumena Marturano* (filmed by Vittorio De Sica in 1964 as *Matrimonio all'Italiana* with Marcello Mastroianni and Sophia Loren) tells the story of an ex-prostitute with three sons by different fathers. She manages to coerce the outwardly respectable Domenico into marrying her, and then reveals that one of her sons is his – although she doesn't tell him which one it is.

Totò's story is closely linked to Eduardo's, for a variety of very good reasons. According to local legend, a bond was forged between the two when, shortly after an attempt on Hitler's life, Totò performed a sketch impersonating a bandaged and limping Führer. Everyone laughed, but the following day he was warned that he would be arrested along with Eduardo, who had been equally critical of the regime. Totò tipped off Eduardo and they both went into hiding, returning after the war to star together as a brilliant double-act in *Napoli Milionaria*.

Born in the Sanità area of Naples in 1898 as Antonio Clemente, his mother's various remarriages eventually conferred on him the title of Antonio de Curtis, Principe de Constantinopoli. He wisely stuck with the snappier nickname: 'Totò'. A wild youth, he contracted gonorrhea from a prostitute and then tried to redeem himself by joining the army at 16. However, the prospect of being sent to the front led him to fake an epileptic fit, earning a discharge.

He soon began acting in local theatres, eventually rising to fame during the era of the *avanspettacolo* – a form of theatre that mixed gags, sketches and songs in short pieces never lasting more than 45 minutes. This variety-style theatre suited Totò well, and its influence can be seen in his later prolific film career. He made some 97 films in all, most based around his signature character of the seemingly daft, but really very wise Neapolitan who is plunged into various hilarious circumstances.

The films are not for the neophyte – the cultural references and dialect-based gags render them largely unintelligible to many non-Neapolitans (let alone non-Italians). The best introductions to his work are Vittorio De Sica's *L'Oro di Napoli* (in which he plays the jester-like *pazzariello*, usurped as head of his own family by a local Camorra boss until he eventually asserts his own dignity) or in Mario Monicelli's *I Soliti Ignoti* (known in English as *Big Deal on Madonna Street*), a crime caper in which he played a retired safe-cracker. Totò is also famous for his songs – you will inevitably hear 'Malafemmena' (Evil Woman) played by the *posteggiatori* in local restaurants.

Both Eduardo and Totò are quintessential Neapolitan figures, in that they knew how to draw on Roman farces and *commedia dell'arte* characterisation as well as modern social satire. Both mixed realism and fantasy, both used dialect for comic and poetic reasons. And their genius critiques of Italy's rigid social hierarchy and the hypocrisy that it engendered make them figures whose example has only ever really been equalled by the late Massimo Troisi (of *Il Postino* fame). Given time to get to know them, you'll find they are also very, very funny.

places to see young companies doing new pieces. Like any fringe theatre, there's always an element of risk. But when it's good, it's worth it.

Galleria Toledo

Via Concezione a Montecalvario 34, Toledo (081 425 824/www.galleriatoledo.com). Metro Montesanto/bus E2. **Open** *Box office* Sept-May 10.30am-7pm Tue-Sun. *Performances* Oct-May 8.30pm Tue-Sun. **Tickets** €12-€18. **No credit cards. Map** p314 2A.
This is a small modern theatre in the heart of the Quartieri spagnoli, providing a rare forum for new, often challenging theatre by high-standard local and international writers and companies. A favourite hangout of Enzo Moscato, it also runs a good cinema programme (*see p149*).

Mercadante

Piazza Municipio 1, Royal (081 551 3396/ www.teatrostabilenapoli.it). Bus 24, C22, C25, C57, R2. **Open** *Box office* late Sept-Apr 10.30am-1pm, 5.30-7.30pm Tue-Sun. *Performances* late Sept-Apr 9pm Wed, Fri, Sat; 5.30pm, 9pm Thur; 6pm Sun. **Tickets** €15-€30. **Credit** DC, MC, V. **Map** p315 1A.
Now the city's *teatro stabile*, this extraordinarily beautiful theatre originally opened in 1779 and, except for the occasional hiccup and worrying attempt at modernisation, it has been going strong since. It hosts some of the best actors and shows touring Italy. Veteran director Roberto de Simone occasionally does pieces here.

Le Nuvole

Viale Kennedy 26, Fuorigrotta (081 239 5653/081 239 5666/www.lenuvole.com). Metro to Cavalleggeri/ Cumana rail to Edenlandia. **Open** *Box office* 30mins before performances. *Performances* Nov-Apr 11.30am on the 2nd & 4th Sun of the mth. **Tickets** €6.50. **No credit cards.**
Inside the Edenlandia amusement park (*see p148*), the Nuvole is the only area theatre specialising in works for children. Puppets, some excellent mime and new pieces mean it's not just for kids.

Politeama

Via Monte di Dio 80, Royal & Monte Echia (081 764 5001) Bus C22. **Open** *Box office* Oct-May 10.30am-1.30pm Mon-Sat; 4.30-7.30pm on performance days. **Performances** 9pm Tue, Wed, Sat, Sun. **Tickets** €15-€30. **No credit cards. Map** p315 1A.
The large, modern Politeama is somewhat characterless, but it has good acoustics and sightlines. It hosts international music and dance as much as theatre (recent visitors have included Pina Bausch and Philip Glass) and stages chamber operas and contemporary works for Teatro di San Carlo.

Teatro Nuovo

Via Montecalvario 16, Toledo (081 425 958/ www.nuovoteatronuovo.it). Metro Montesanto/ bus E2. **Open** *Box office* from 5pm on night of performance; phone bookings 9.30am-2pm, 5-7pm Mon-Fri. *Performances* mid Oct-May 9pm Tue-Sat; 6pm Sun. **Tickets** €14; €8 under-25s. **No credit cards. Map** p314 2A.

The modern Nuovo has only been active for around 20 years, but it's built on the site of one of the city's oldest theatres. Like its rival, the Galleria Toledo just up the road, it is one of the few venues in Naples dedicated to new and international theatre. The space is unexciting, but the quality of performance is usually pretty high. There's a rapid turnover of three or four productions a month: be quick if there's something you want to see.

Teatro di San Carlo

Via San Carlo 98F, Royal (081 797 2331/ www.teatrosancarlo.it). Bus 24, C22, C25, C57. **Open** *Box office Sept-May 10am-3pm Tue-Sun; June, July 10am-3pm Tue-Fri; 1hr before performances. Performances times & days vary.* **Tickets** €15-€120. **Credit** DC, MC, V. **Map** p315 1A.

Described as a 'sultan's palace' by Stendhal, and 'as remarkable an object as any man sees in his travels' by famed 'Grand Tourist' Samuel Sharp, the original 1737 San Carlo went the way of too many opera houses: up in flames. This replacement structure, built on the same site in 1816, while not quite worthy of the rapturous descriptions its predecessor received is still an impressive building. Inside it seems as if everything that could not be lined in velvet has been gilded. But there is a method to their madness – the soft fabric helps the excellent acoustics. While solidly traditional programming gives it a rather staid image, standards here are often exceptional, and its reputation as being second only to Milan's La Scala is deserved. The orchestra and chorus are still dogged by poor teamwork; however, given the right conditions and conductor performances can be very good indeed.

Openings at San Carlo are Neapolitan high-society events (complete with the obligatory anti-fur protesters). While many go to the opera *per farsi vedere* (to be seen), chunks of the San Carlo audience are demanding opera buffs. Extremely warm in their appreciation when a performance merits it, they can be devastatingly cool when it doesn't. It's not enough, either, merely to be famous: however big a name you are, you risk being whistled (the Italian equivalent of booing) off the stage if you don't come up with the goods. Traditionalists at heart, San Carlo-goers give innovative works a rough ride. If it's not a classic, it has to be very good to avoid being rubbished. Still, an ever-increasing number of 20th-century works in recent symphonic seasons has not driven the public away.

Attempts to invigorate the programme have included a 2002 *Turandot* enlivened by David Hockney's direction and stage design. Local filmmaker Mario Martone directed a *Don Giovanni*, also in 2002, and the controversial Spanish avant-theatre group Fura del Baus found ways to liven up Debussy's *Martyrdom of St Sebastian*. German artist Anselm Kiefer designed 2003's *Elektra*.

The opera season runs from January to December, but is suspended in late July and August as the place is simply too hot. Owing to the *abbonamenti* (sub-

scription) system, in which opera-goers reserve their seats for the whole season, most of the theatre is booked out most of the time. What is left over tends to be the dregs: high up, or far off to the left of the stage. Don't despair though; good stall seats can be found (bear in mind that sightlines from many parts of the theatre are not very good, and securing central places will greatly enhance your enjoyment of the performance). There are no dinner jackets to be seen in a San Carlo audience, but 'casual' here means stylish and elegant; jeans and T-shirts are acceptable in the low-profile top-floor seats, but they may provoke hostile stares in the stalls.

The San Carlo ballet company operates year-round, providing an eclectic mixture of traditional and modern works. Standards are improving, and local composers (not to mention local rock band 24 Grana) have been commissioned to write for the company. *See also p67.*

Teatro Trianon

Piazza Calenda 9 (081 225 8285 ext 30/www.teatro trianon.it). Metro Piazza Garibaldi. **Open** *Box office Oct-June 10.30am-1.30pm, 5-8pm Mon-Fri; 10.30am-2pm Sat. Performances Oct-May 9pm Tue-Sun.* **Tickets** €10-€30. **Credit** MC, V.

Deep in the dark heart of Forcella, this refurbished cinema opened in 2003 with the explicit aim of giving a home to traditional Neapolitan theatre and song. You may not be able to follow the dialect, but this is the place to come if you've a penchant for Neapolitan kitsch.

Summer music festivals

In July and August, the lack of air-conditioning in Naples theatres makes them too hot to bear. But this doesn't mean there's no music – it just strays out of doors (and out of town) and takes up residence in some spectacular venues.

In summer 2004 the San Carlo company put on an open-air performance of *La Bohème* at the Arena Flegrea in Fuorigrotta. Tickets started at a mere €10, but the quality was as high as ever. Following this success the company has been promising to repeat the performance.

The most spectacular of all the region's outdoor summer happenings is the **Festival Musicale di Villa Rufolo** (*see p170*), which runs from June to August. Some of its events are staged in the 12th-century villa in Ravello where Wagner composed parts of *Parsifal,* and it's not difficult to see what inspired him. Other performances are held in similarly lovely venues along the Amalfi Coast. These include a surreal, spectacular, specially constructed platform above the sea in Ravello. Very occasionally, early risers may be lucky enough to catch a *concerto all'alba* (dawn concert), during which an orchestra welcomes the sunrise in a breathtaking spectacle that begins at 4am.

Pulcinella and *commedia dell'arte*

Deep in the Centro storico off via Anticaglia are the barely visible remains of a Roman theatre where it's said that Nero popped down when he fancied a laugh. This was the home of the *fabula Atellana* – bawdy, burlesque comedies based around stock characters played by masked actors. Once wildly popular, changing fashions around the first century swept them off all the stage.

In the 16th century, a form of popular theatre again radiated from Naples to the rest of Italy. This was the *commedia dell'arte* (where *arte* means not 'art' but 'trade', to distinguish the professional jugglers and mountebanks who made up its cast from the courtiers-turned-thespians in 'serious' Latin drama). Like the *fabula* tradition, the *commedia dell'arte* had stock characters, recognisable by their outfits and masks, in wild, part-scripted, part-improvised scenarios.

Each character was associated with an Italian city: Harlequin was a faithful, calamity-prone servant from Bergamo, Pantaleone a money-grubbing merchant from Venice. Naples revived one of the *fabula Atellana*'s characters – a coarse-tongued, pot-bellied, white-clad clown – and called him Pulcinella.

Pulcinella is carefree yet disillusioned, cynical yet optimistic, prone to uncontrolled laughter followed by fits of the deepest melancholy: all Neapolitan traits. He is dressed in a voluminous white smock and white trousers, with a white cone-shaped hat, and a black mask with a long hooked nose – a symbol of sexual potency. His main aim in life is to do nothing. He drinks too much and goes hungry, he falls foul of the law and retaliates with devious schemes.

The character probably originated in its modern form in the town of Acerra just outside Naples, as a clown for Carnevale celebrations. The first performer to adopt the character was probably Zanni Policiniello.

Pulcinella turned up in Britain in 1662 in puppet form as 'Punchinello'. Samuel Pepys saw a performance in Covent Garden, describing 'an Italian puppet play, that is within the rails there, which is very pretty, the best that I ever saw, and great resort of gallants.' As often happens to emigrants, that Pulcinella adopted British ways, ultimately becoming the violent and funny Mr Punch.

In the meantime, the Neapolitan Pulcinella became more respectable. By the time he was in proper theatres he'd been transformed from a clown into a grassroots philosopher, a seer of the streets, and a symbol of Naples itself. Today, Pulcinella masks can be bought on any street corner in the Centro storico, and the character is a firm (if somewhat bizarre) fixture in the Christmas *presepe* (nativity scene). Nor has the tradition died in the theatre; Roberto De Simone, Luca De Filippo, Peppe Barra and Enzo Moscato all work with the comedy and cruelty of the character.

The character is commemorated in Acerra in the Museo di Pulcinella. The museum, in a ninth-century castle, has a collection of memorabilia and an exhibition on life in the 1500s, the century of Pulcinella's birth.

Pulcinella is, all in all, the personification of Naples' many contradictions. Like his contemporaries in this beautiful, crowded, culture-packed, sustenance-starved city, Pulcinella accepts his harsh life with philosophical resignation. The greatest actors who have donned his mask have united his wild, anti-authoritarian hilarity with gut-wrenching pathos. Because laughter is a serious business in Naples.

Museo di Pulcinella

Castello Baronale di Acerra, Acerra (081 885 7249/www.pulcinellamuseo.it). **Open** 9.30am-1pm Mon-Fri; 4-6pm Mon, Wed; 10am-noon Sat, Sun. **Admission** free.

Teatro di San Carlo, a theatrical sultan's palace. *See p168.*

Musical events continue for the rest of the year in Ravello, including the **Concerti di Musica Sinfonica** (a series of symphonic concerts) in July, and the unique **Settimane Internazionali di Musica da Camera** (international series of chamber music) in September and three concerts each week throughout the winter.

The Fondazione Axel Munthe stages **Concerti al tramonto** (concerts at dusk) at the Swedish doctor/author's gorgeous Villa San Michele on the island of Capri most Fridays from June to August.

Concerti al tramonto

Fondazione Axel Munthe, Villa San Michele, Anacapri (081 837 1401/www.sanmichele.org). **Open** *Box office* June-Aug from 7pm Fri. *Performances* June-Aug 7.30pm Fri. **Tickets** €15. **No credit cards.**

Festival Musicale di Villa Rufolo

Società dei concerti di Ravello, via Trinità 3, Ravello (089 858 149/www.ravelloarts.org). **Open** *Box office* Mar-Oct 9am-1pm Mon-Sat; 4-8pm on performance days. *Performances* Mar 6.30pm Wed. Apr-Oct 9.30pm Mon, Wed, Sat. **Tickets** €20. **Credit** AmEx, DC, MC, V. Tickets can be booked online.

Sport & Fitness

Fitness is fashionable, football is essential.

'Footing' in **Mergellina**. See p174.

Sport in Naples, and throughout Italy, is a serious business. *La Gazzetta dello Sport*, with its distinctive pink pages, is the most widely read newspaper in Italy. Plenty of locals are members of private sports clubs, even though annual membership fees are pretty high. And, whatever game they play, Neapolitans inevitably wrap themselves in the trendiest sportswear, regardless of their playing ability.

Neapolitans are obsessed with football even though success has eluded them in recent years (*see p172* **Le CalcioNapoli file**), but they have better luck in other sports – in 2004 **Carpisa Posillipo** won the Italian waterpolo league, and **Pompea**, the local basketball team, ranked fifth in its league. It was also a good year for **Briganti Napoli**, the American Football club, which was promoted to a higher league.

Naples' waterside location is ideal for swimming or fishing (although the further you go out of town the cleaner the water). Facilities for other sports – particularly water sports – can be found on **Ischia** (*see p196*), **Capri** (*see p178*) and the **Amalfi** (*see p243*) and **Sorrento** (*see p228*).

Bowling

Bowling Oltremare
Viale Kennedy 12, Fuorigrotta (081 624 444/www.bowlingoltremare.it). Cumana rail to Edenlandia/bus C2, C3, C5. **Open** 10am-2am daily. **Admission** €1.70-€4. **No credit cards**.
A traditional 20-lane bowling alley next to Edenlandia funfair (*see p148*). There are also ping-pong and pool tables for hire.

Cycling

Initial impressions may suggest that anyone who gets on a bike in this city is crazy, and that's actually a pretty reasonable thought. However, for the brave, there are some wonderful cycling areas around town. The **Bosco di Capodimonte** (*see p90*) is an oasis far from the traffic and smog, although the steep climb up to the park can deter the less hardy. The hills around **Monte di Procida** on the north of the bay offer spectacular views of Ischia and Procida. As always, though, be extremely careful and don't expect drivers to extend you any courtesies.

Golf

Golfers can also try the 18-hole mini-golf links closer to the city at Camaldoli (**Minigolf Kennedy**, via Camillo Guerra, 081 587 1386). The course is open daily (5-10pm Mon-Fri, 5-11pm Sat, Sun; €4 Mon-Fri, €5 Sat, Sun). Fans of crazy golf can sink a ball into a model of Vesuvius at the course at via Terracina 228, Fuorigrotta. Opening times are erratic, and there's no phone, but it is generally open at weekends.

Volturnogolf

Via Domitiana km 35+300, Pinetamare Castelvolturno (081 509 5855/www.holiday-inn-resort.com). Bus M2. **Fees** €21 Mon-Fri; €24 Sat, Sun; club hire €14. **Credit** AmEx, DC, MC, V.
Golf is still a minority sport in Italy, and this 30-hectare course is quite far from the city, in the grounds of a Holiday Inn. In 2004 it had only nine holes, but a further nine were in the pipeline. The hotel also has two tennis courts, a swimming pool, table tennis, mountain bike hire, a gym and facilities for horseriding.

The CalcioNapoli file

The summer of 2004 was agonising for Naples' football team, **SS CalcioNapoli**, and for its six million fans worldwide. After prolonged efforts to save the club it eventually succumbed to bankruptcy, and that was the end of the matter. Well, sort of anyway. Today the city's team is called **Napoli Soccer**, and it is beginning in one of Italy's lower-level football leagues, Serie C1.

CalcioNapoli's misfortune was the culmination of years of much-criticised management, followed by a losing battle to save the club, then another to keep the new club in the higher-level Serie B, all of which dragged through the traditionally empty August courts.

This was a far cry from the dizzy heights of the late 1980s, when Argentinian superstar Diego Armando Maradona helped them win two Italian championships, one UEFA cup, and two Coppa Italia victories: a golden age that's still in the hearts of Napoli's passionate supporters.

Napoli was rarely much of a threat to the bigger teams in the league until 1984, and the arrival of Maradona for a then-record $7.5 million. Two years later, Naples won the league championship, the *scudetto*, and the Coppa Italia for good measure – and the city erupted. Apartments and buildings were festooned with banners and flags, the streets and walls were painted blue (traces of which can still be seen), and festivities continued for weeks.

Napoli seemed unstoppable. Near the end of the next season, they led the league again. Then, in the third to last game of the season, at Naples' San Paolo stadium, the team was beaten by AC Milan, amid allegations of bribery and match-fixing.

Legend has it that San Gennaro's blood failed to liquify that year (*see p78* **Blood rites**).

The team rebounded in 1988-9, winning the UEFA Cup, while Maradona and his Brazilian teammates Alemao and Careca made 1989-90 the season of Naples' second *scudetto*.

The following season saw the end of the glory years, though, as Maradona's personal problems took their toll on the team's performance. He would turn up late, or not at all, for training sessions, and was rumoured to enjoy debauched parties with unsavoury friends from the Camorra. He played his last game for Napoli on 17 March 1991 against Bari. He was disqualified for drug use shortly afterwards, and fled to Argentina to escape problems including a

Gyms

A comprehensive list of sports clubs and facilities in the city can be found on the tourist office's website: www.inaples.it.

Athena
Via dei Mille 16, Chiaia (081 407 334/www.athena. it). Metro Piazza Amedeo/bus C22, C25, C28. **Open** *Oct-Mar* 8am-10.30pm daily. *Jun-Aug* 8am-10.30pm Mon-Fri. **Admission** €10 daily. **Credit** AmEx, DC, MC, V. **Map** p315 1B.

Facilities for bodybuilding, spinning, aerobics, weights, bicycles, body-sculpt, step and some martial arts. Other attractions include Turkish baths (sauna followed by cold dip), a bar and a squash court (€9 non-members per half hour; the gym hires out rackets).

Bodyguard
Via Torrione San Martino 45, Vomero (081 558 4551). Funicular Montesanto to via Morghen, Centrale to piazzetta Fuga, Chiaia to via Cimarosa/metro Vanvitelli/bus E4, V1. **Open** 9am-11pm Mon-Fri;

---

criminal investigation into involvement in a vice ring and a paternity claim.

Naples' football fans have never forgotten him, however. There's even a **shrine** to him outside Bar Nilo on via San Biaggio a Librai on Spaccanapoli, which holds a Diego hair. CalcioNapoli's number 10 shirt was retired (although Serie C1 bureaucracy brought it back in 2004, much to fans' chagrin).

Despite herculean efforts, the 1990s saw Napoli decline into mediocrity as its financial problems mushroomed. The club was relegated to Serie B, with just one season back in Serie A before its demise. After years of diminishing returns and questionable management, Corrado Ferlaino, owner of the club for 30 years, sold a majority share to telesales mogul Giorgio Corbelli in 2002.

Corbelli's own shady dealings with his telesales company then came under scrutiny, and after a period in a Rome jail, he relinquished the club to businessman Salvatore Naldi. Attendances dropped to as low as 200 per game, and the bankruptcy lawyers were summoned.

Luciano Gaucci, owner of Serie B's Perugia, offered to rent the club for five years, insisting it should remain in Serie B. The battle dragged through the courts, with an eventual decision that the club must enter Serie C. Angry fans staged demonstrations – at one point blocking the railway station – and Gaucci withdrew.

While many bidders offered to take over Napoli, billionaire film producer Aurelio De Laurentiis offered the greatest investment and guarantees for creditors, and was granted three weeks to form a team.

As this guide went to press Napoli Soccer have yet to set the stadium on fire, although 40,000 regularly fill its stands, and season

ticket sales are higher than the combined total of the rest of Serie C1. Clearly the passion has returned to Naples.

TICKETS AND MATCHES
The season runs from September to June, and matches are usually played on alternate Sunday afternoons (although Serie A and B games are sometimes played on Saturday evenings), at the impressive 80,000 seater **Stadio San Paolo** in Fuorigrotta. Entry to the stadium is by ticket only, purchased at the Azzurro Service ticket office (*see below*) or at some Lotto sales points at *tabacchis* (*see p293*), although, for bigger matches, its easier to buy tickets from the numerous touts (scalpers) outside the stadium. Unless it's a very important game, they don't usually charge much more than face value. Prices vary, but in 2004 ranged from ¤10 for the curve (where you'll be in the thick of the passionate supporters) to ¤35 for a numbered grandstand seat. This will, of course, change if Napoli makes its way back to Serie A.

Azzurro Service
Via F Galeoata 17, Fuorigrotta (081 593 4001/www.azzurroservice.it/www.punt azzurro.com).Cumana rail to Mostra or Leopardi/metro Campi Flegrei/bus 180, 181, C2, C6, C7, C8, C9, C10, C15. **Open** 9am-12.30pm, 4-6.30pm Mon-Fri; 9am-1hr before kick-off for home games Sun. **Credit** MC, V.
Be sure to get there early for important games, as it will be mobbed.

Stadio San Paolo
Piazzale Teccio, Fuorigrotta (081 593 3223). Cumana rail to Mostra/metro Campi Flegrei/bus 180, 181, C2, C6, C7, C8, C9, C10, C15.

Arts & Entertainment

10am-7pm Sat. Closed 1wk Aug. **Admission** €8.
Credit AmEx, DC, MC, V. **Map** p314 2B.
As well as weights, bicycles, a sauna, walking and
running machines you'll also find a handy bar here.

Horseracing

Ippodromo di Agnano
*(081 735 7111/www.ippocity.it). Metro to Campi
Flegrei, then bus C2.* **Open** *summer* 8.30pm Tue-
Thur, Sat, Sun. **Admission** €3. **No credit cards**.
The race programme changes month by month, so
check the website. Sunday night meetings during
the summer are particulary fun and colourful.

Horseriding

Horse Centre Le Caselle
*Via Montagna Spaccata 519, Pianura (335 569
5678). Cumana rail to Pianura, then bus P8.*
Open *May-Sept* 9.30am-7pm daily. *Oct-Apr*
9.30am-4.30pm daily. **No credit cards**.
Be sure to telephone to check availabilty.

Jogging

Known in these parts as footing, jogging is a
popular pastime. The lungomare of via
Caracciolo, from Castel dell'Ovo (*see p64*) to
Mergellina (*see p99*) is ideal for a short run (or
for the self-explanatory fitwalking), especially
on Sunday mornings when the road is closed to
traffic. For cleaner, fresher air, Parco Virgliano
(*see p100*) in Posillipo, with its spectacular
views, and Bosco di Capodimonte (*see p90*) are
very popular. Bosco is also ideal for cyclists or a
quick game of frisbee or footie (though,
theoretically, ball games are banned).

Rollerskating

Palapartenope
*Via Barbagallo, Fuorigrotta (081 570 0008/www.pala
partenope.it). Cumana rail to Edenlandia/bus C2, C3.*
Open *Oct-June* 7pm-midnight daily. *July-Sept* 7pm midnight Fri-Sun. **Admission** €6/hr. **No credit cards**.
The *lungomare* is popular with in-line skaters, but the
real fun is to be found at the Palapartenope (which
occasionally doubles as a concert venue). The admission price includes skate hire and protective gear.

Sailing

Many small companies rent out boats, including
Jordan & Jordan (081 497 6032, www.sailing
holidays.it). Costs range from €600 to €2,000
for a weekend. Cataboat (081 853 0500/www.
cataboat.com) in Pozzuoli also charter
catamarans. If you fancy rowing in the Bay, go
down the tiny stairs on the bridge at **Castel
dell'Ovo**, where you can hire a rowing boat.

Scuba diving

Centro Sub Campi Flegrei
*Via Napoli 1, Pozzuoli (081 853 1563/www.centro
subcampiflegrei.it). Cumana rail to Gerolomini.*
There is plenty of diving on the islands and the
Amalfi coast, but an advantage of diving close
to the city is the opportunity to view the *città
sommersa* of Baia (*see p104*) at close quarters. This
company arranges dives on the Neapolitan coast or
the islands and runs courses at all level, with
English-speaking instructors available. Half a day's
diving costs €25 per person; a full day, including
lunch, is €50. PADI accredited.

Skiing

Surprising as it may seem, southern Italy has
decent ski resorts just a couple of hours' drive
from Naples. The roads to the slopes are often
clogged on winter Sundays, so travel mid-week
if you can. The most popular local resorts are
Roccaraso (www.roccaraso.net), 153 kilometres
(95 miles) from Naples and the less demanding
Campitello Matese (www.campitello.com),
145 kilometres (90 miles) from the city.

Swimming pools

Note that you need a membership card to use
the city's swimming pools.

Collana
*Via Rossini, Vomero (081 560 0907). Metro Quattro
Giornate/bus C30, C32.* **Open** *July, Aug* 10am-2pm,
3.30-8pm Mon-Sat; 9am-4pm Sun. Closed Sept-June.
Admission €4. **No credit cards**. **Map** p314 2C.
A good-sized city-owned indoor pool with access to
a sundeck. Under-12s pay half-price.

Tennis

Tennis San Domenico
*Via San Domenico 64, Vomero Alto (081 645 660).
Bus C36 from piazza Vanvitelli to Tennis San
Domenico.* **Open** 8am-10pm Mon-Fri; 8am-8pm Sat;
8am-1pm Sun. **Admission** €11 per hr per court.
No credit cards. **Map** off p314 1C.
The five floodlit clay courts. Rackets can be pro-
vided, free of charge. Gym facilities are also avail-
able (if you present a medical certificate) at €5 daily.

Yoga

Siddharta
*Via S Maria della Neve, Chiaia (081 668 426/
www.siddhartascuola.org). Metro Mergellina/bus
140, C12, C18, C19, C24, R3.* **Open** 10.30am-noon
Tue; 6.30-8pm Fri. Closed August. **Cost** €13 lesson.
No credit cards. **Map** p315 2C.
This centre offers individual lessons along with
its annual courses.

Around Naples

Features

Maps

THE LIQUEURS OF "L'EDEN"

"An old monastery, an abbot, custodian of ancient recipes, and a doctor full of passion and enthusiasm." This is how a great and sincere friendship started up in Massa Lubrense a quarter of a century ago. Along with this friendship came the legend of the King of L'Eden and the delights of his garden, shared and offered with joy to his most well-loved friends.

L'EDEN®

www.leden.it

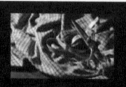

Introduction

Get out of town and explore.

The province of Naples and the region of Campania of which it is a part fall neatly into separate holiday compartments: **Capri**, **Ischia** and **Procida**; then there is **Sorrento** (and the magnificent hinterland of the Sorrentine Peninsula, though few visitors climb the hill to discover it); and the **Amalfi Coast**. And, of course, no stay in Campania is complete without a day-trip to **Pompeii** (as some two million people prove each year).

This is a very diverse region. Take its archeological sites: Pompeii is staggering but it's only part of the story. Just down the road from Italy's most-visited tourist attraction are the little-known digs and museums at **Herculaneum** (*see p215*), **Stabiae** (*see p224)* and **Boscoreale** (*see p213*). A short train ride into southern Campania brings you to the dramatic Greek temples at **Paestum** (*see p271*).

Then there are all the imposing reminders of the baroque grandeur of Naples' past. The *palazzi reali* (royal palaces) in **Caserta** (*see p275*) and the **Portici** (*p215*) were the architectural wonders of their age, seriously challenging foreign competition from Versailles and Schönbrunn.

Minor gems are to be found in **Salerno**, where a small museum charts the glorious history of its medieval Medical School (*see p270*), and in **Portici**, where the Pietrarsa railway museum (*see p215*) is an engaging tribute to Italy's first train line.

Then there's the volcanic activity – spurting steam and boiling sulphurous springs – that lurks close to the surface in Ischia and the **Campi Flegrei** (*see p102*).

There are walks too: well-kept, well-marked paths criss-cross the Sorrentine Peninsula and scale the heights of the Amalfi Coast (*see p238* **Walking country**); Capri's mountainous heart is best explored on foot (*see p194* **Island hikes**); Ischia has tracks wending through forests to the heights of **Monte Epomeo** (*see p204*); **Monte Faito** (*see p224*) and even bubbling **Vesuvius** (*see p225*) are a walker's paradise. All this, plus the buzzing, vibrant city of Naples itself, make a visit to Campania that is spent entirely by a pool look like a missed opportunity.

ACCOMMODATION

Hotel listings are given for most destinations covered in the **Around Naples** section after the sightseeing information for each town or area.

GETTING THERE & AROUND

Each chapter in the **Around Naples** section contains instructions on getting to the destinations mentioned by car, train, boat and/or bus from Naples (and from Salerno, in the case of the Amalfi Coast and Paestum). For general information on travel in Naples and Campania, *see chapter* **Directory**.

MUSEUMS & GALLERIES

Entrance to all state-owned museums is free for EU citizens of over 65 and under 18 years. Many also have reductions for EU citizens under 26 in full-time education: bring appropriate picture ID. A list of concessions for non-EU citizens whose countries have bilateral cultural agreements with Italy should be posted in each museum. The Campania Artecard can also be used at various sights in the region (*see p35* **Smart art**).

Amalfi Coast. *See p243.*

Capri

This rocky outcrop has been a pleasure island since Roman times.

Looking towards Anacapri from Capri Town.

On a cloudless day, when the sea looks too ludicrously blue to be real, and Capri's crags plunge into it in stark relief, it's easy to see why this small, jagged island has been the centre of so much drama, bewitching everyone from Roman emperors to Russian revolutionaries – and Gracie Fields.

True, the days when only Europe's poets and intellectuals flocked here in search of sun and the simple life are well and truly over. Now up to 60,000 visitors a day – most of them on day-trips from Naples or Sorrento – invade the island to spend money in cafés, designer shops and souvenir stores and to visit the island's famous Blue Grotto. Yet somehow the glamour remains. A certain air of nostalgia may have something to do with it, but the fact is that Capri's elegant beauty remains intact: lemon groves, bougainvillea-draped terraces, and wild, thorny slopes are all preserved, thanks partly to the island's rocky topography and continued use of traditional farming methods, and partly to stringent planning regulations and the protectiveness of wealthy villa owners.

Get up early to avoid the day-trippers and wander a few metres from the trodden track, and Capri will cast its spell on you; you may well find yourself agreeing with the founder of Futurism – a prescursor of Fascism – Tommaso Filippo Marinetti, when he defined Capri's cliffs as 'rebellious, tumultuous, lyrical, violent, belligerent and revolutionary'.

Traditionally, Capri town has been regarded as more chic and urbane, while Anacapri – the village furthest from the Marina Grande port, on the upland side of the escarpment that slices across the island – is thought of as more rugged, rural and down-to-earth.

This contrast was certainly more evident in the past (there wasn't even a road connecting the two until 1872) but to some extent it remains the case. Most of the luxury hotels and villas cluster around Capri town, while Anacapri is home to a working population of smallholder-farmers. But with the big tourist pull of Villa San Michele (*see p192*), Anacapri now has as many visitors as its rival, as well as its fair share of garish souvenir shops and pricey restaurants.

Around Naples

Setting themselves a world apart from their Neapolitan neighbours, both villages are proud of their perfect paths and clean, whitewashed walls, while blue-and-white ceramic signs remind visitors not to drop litter and to keep noise at a minimum.

To unlock the island's charm, bite the bullet (and Capri's inflated hotel prices) and stay overnight. By day, the Piazzetta, the heart of Capri town and one of the best places in the world to see and be seen, is a pedestrian log-jam. In the evening though, as the lights come on and the last of the day-trippers drift down to the port, the island reveals itself as one of the Mediterranean's most elegant open-air living rooms.

The best time to visit is out of season (May or October) when the weather tends to be cool enough to embark on some of the marvellous walks that the island offers (*see p194* **Island hikes**), but still warm enough to get a suntan. Between November and mid March, Capri practically closes down; only a fraction of the island's hotels stay open, and even fewer of the restaurants (the tourist offices post weekly bulletins of the survivors). For the adventurous, though – and to enjoy the island when only the native *capresi* are left – this can be a rewarding time to visit.

GOAT ISLAND

The island's name is the subject of any number of conflicting theories; the most consistent is that it is derived from *capreae* (a Romano-Italic word meaning 'island of goats'). It has been inhabited since prehistory – first by Neolithic tribes, later by the Greeks of Cumae (Cuma; *see p106*) and Neapolis (Naples). Virgil associated the place with the Teleboans, a legendary race of Greek pirates. For centuries it was more a strategic outpost than a settled community.

It was not until 29 BC that Capri was touched by mainstream history, when Octavian – soon to become the Emperor Augustus – first landed on the island. So charmed was he by its beauty that he persuaded the Greeks of Neapolis to take back the already Romanised and much larger island of Ischia and give him Capri instead, for use as a private estate. Though he never lived here, Augustus set about building villas and water cisterns, and seems to have taken an active interest in the island's culture and traditions.

TIBERIUS'S CAPRI

Augustus's successor, Tiberius, ignored the place for the first part of his reign, but while on a tour of southern Italy in AD 27, he took a boat here, and never again returned to Rome. Capri was to be his home for the last ten years of his life, and the reign he established here

– absolutist to the point of derangement – has been the subject of much historical embroidery. Suetonius, the scandalmongering author of *De Vita Caesarum* (Lives of the Caesars) depicted Tiberius as a misanthropic reprobate, who liked to watch as groups of young male and female servants had sex in front of him; in case they were at a loss, the villa was well furnished with erotic statues, paintings and Egyptian sex manuals. Evidence of torture rooms, prisons and execution chambers in all Tiberius's Capri villas testify to his other preferred form of entertainment. But Suetonius is practically our only literary source for these final years of the emperor's life, and it has been suggested by many – most notably the British writer Norman Douglas, a long-term resident of Capri – that his account is vindictive and one-sided. For Douglas, Tiberius was no monster but a bitter old recluse, happier in the company of books, works of art and astrological charts than that of human beings.

After the death of Tiberius in AD 37 the island was forgotten once more, and the 12 imperial villas gradually fell into ruin. Capri was used a couple of times as a place of exile for Roman undesirables, then came under the sway of first the Abbey of Montecassino and later of the Republic of Amalfi. Repeated Saracen attacks in the ninth and tenth centuries caused the population to move up from the main settlement of Marina Grande to the more easily defensible sites of Capri town and Anacapri. Through the Middle Ages the island followed the fortunes of Naples, passing meekly from Anjou then Aragon to Spanish rule. In the 18th century the Bourbons used Capri as a hunting reserve; the bishop of the island was known as the 'bishop of quails', as he had a right to a share of the profits on all sales of the bird.

During the Napoleonic Wars the British occupied Capri as a bastion against the French Kingdom of Naples, but some brilliant decoy tactics by a French invasion force led to the recapture of the island in the space of just two weeks in 1808.

INTELLECTUAL INVASION

Capri soon became less of a military prize and more of a magnet for artists and intellectuals once they discovered its warm Mediterranean charms. The first hotel, the Hotel Pagano (now **La Palma**, *see p188*) was opened in 1822, while the funicular was inaugurated in 1907. With a reputation as a haven for Greek and Sapphic lovers, an aura of licentiousness hung around the island where Tiberius had swung both ways with such dedication. Gay Capri's finest years were the first two decades of the 20th century, when wiry writer Norman

Around Naples

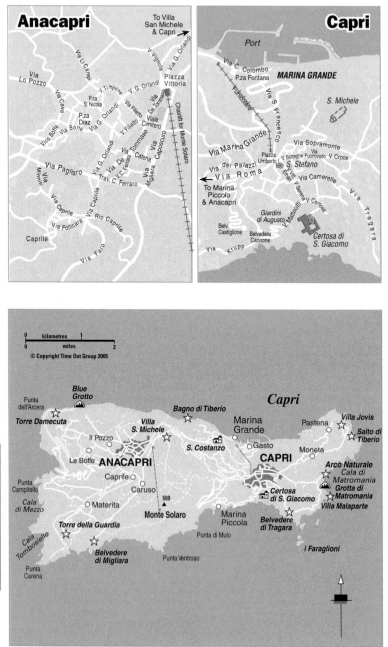

Anacapri

To Villa
San Michele
& Capri

Via Li Campi

Via
Lo Pozzo

Via G. Orlandi

V. Vignola

Via G. Orlandi

V.Timpone

P.za
S. Nicola

Piazza
Vittoria

Via Cava

Via Boffe

Via G. Orlandi

P.za
Diaz

Via Filietto

Via De Tommaso

Viale
Cimitero

Vico Boffe

Via De
Via G. Orlandi

Via Filietto

V. Catena

Chairlift for Monte Solaro

Via
Mimmiti

Via Pagliaro

Via G. Orlandi

Via De
V.C. Ferraro

Via
Migliara

Via
Caposcuro

Trav. C. Ferraro

Via Caprile

Via Caprile

Via Rio Caprile

Caprile

Via Follicara

Via Fato

Capri

Port

MARINA GRANDE

Via C. Colombo
P.za Fontana

Via S. Francesco

S. Michele

Funicolare

Via Sopramonte

Via Marina Grande

Piazza
Umberto I

V. Botteghe Fuoriovado

V. Croce

S. Stefano

Via dei Palazzi

Via Roma

V. Li

V. Matteotti

V. Camerelle

To Marina
Piccolo
& Anacapri

V. Serena

V. Certosa

Via Tragara

Giardini
di Augusto

Belv.
Castiglione

Belvedere
Cannone

Certosa di
S. Giacomo

Via Krupp

Around Naples

```
0        kilometres        1
0           miles              2
© Copyright Time Out Group 2005
```

Capri

Punta
dell'Arcera

**Blue
Grotto**

Bagno di Tiberio

**Marina
Grande**

Pastena

Villa Jovis

Torre Damecuta

**Villa
S. Michele**

Il Pozzo

S. Costanzo

Gasto

Moneta

**Salto di
Tiberio**

Le Boffe

ANACAPRI

Caprile

CAPRI

Arco Naturale
Cala di
Matromania

Punta
Campitello

Caruso

589

**Certosa
di S. Giacomo**

**Grotta di
Matromania**

Villa Malaparte

*Cala
di Mezzo*

Materita

Monte Solaro

**Marina
Piccola**

*Cala
Tombosiello*

Torre della Guardia

Punta di Mulo

**Belvedere
di Tragara**

Punta
Carena

**Belvedere
di Migliara**

Punta Ventroso

i Faraglioni

Douglas (whose *South Wind* is still the definitive Capri novel) and perfumed French aesthete Jacques Fersen helped keep island boys in pocket money. It was at around this time that various foreigners, including Fersen and Scandinavian doctor Axel Munthe (*see p190*), started building villas on the island. Writer Curzio Malaparte, a sort of Italian Ernest Hemingway, famous in the 1940s and '50s also built on the island: his brutalist red house on Punta Massullo, which he called Casa Come Me (house like me), designed by Adalberto Libera, is one of the island's more unusual landmarks. For more on Capri's artistic and intellectual past, *see p186* **Artistic licence**.

It was really only after World War II that Capri began to attract billionaires, heiresses, Hollywood stars and jetsetters. In 1949, Pucci opened a boutique here and introduced 'Capri pants', which took the world by storm.

Capri's most marketed sightseeing must is the **Blue Grotto** (*see p183*), while its most famous produce is limoncello (*see p233* **LimonHello**), most of which is now produced on the mainland in order to meet the demand. You can occasionally find the home-made version, especially in the more reputable family *trattorie*. One final word: if you want to impress the natives, get the pronunciation right. It's <u>Ca</u>-pree, not Ca-<u>pree</u>.

Capri town & around

Landing in **Marina Grande** in high season can be a stressful experience: arriving travellers have to slalom between groups of day-trippers, touts and tacky souvenir stores. The best thing to do is to take a deep breath and get out as quickly as possible, taking either the orange bus or the funicular up to Capri town, or the other orange bus to Anacapri.

Alternatively, you can take a motor launch for Capri's most famous sight and an important local industry: the **Blue Grotto** (*see p183*). The Grotto is well worth a visit despite the masses with whom you'll inevitably be sharing the experience. The iridescent quality of the blue light inside really needs to be seen to be believed. Known in Roman times, the grotto was 're-discovered' by a Polish poet called August Kopisch with the help of a local fisherman in 1826, or so the story goes.

Midway up the road linking the Marina to Capri town, the bus passes the island's non-Catholic cemetery, created in 1878 for the growing community of foreign residents. Here rest Norman Douglas and Count Fersen, among others. It is a peaceful place and a good opportunity to leave the tourist bustle behind and make a connection with Capri's nomadic, free thinking and artistic past (open 7am-1pm, 3-5pm Mon-Wed, Fri-Sun).

The funicular emerges at the far end of via Roma – Capri town's access road. Above the funicular station is a terrace with views over the Marina and the **Monte Solaro**. Here, too, is the picturesque bell tower that separates this antechamber from the Piazzetta (officially piazza Umberto I): core of the Capri experience, archetype of the perfect Mediterranean island square, and also the town's main pedestrian traffic chicane. In Capri, all roads seem to lead to the Piazzetta. There is a way to bypass it that is known to local and habitués, but most people end up crossing it, and the Piazzetta, with its four rival bars (distinguished by their colour-coded tables) is one of the best places to see and be seen. Grab a table, order a drink (see it as an investment), sit back and enjoy the show.

On the south side of the square, the main parish church of **Santo Stefano** (open 8am-8pm daily), with its play of curved roof arches, sits pretty at the top of a flight of steps. The present baroque structure was built on the site of an earlier church; inside, the intarsia marble flooring in front of the main altar comes from the **Villa Jovis** (*see p183*). Legend goes that the Madonna painting in the first chapel on the left was thrown down a cliff by invading Turks but remained intact. In front of the church is a museum, the **Museo del Centro Caprense Ignazio Cerio** (*see p183*), housing relics of Capri's pre-history and dedicated to Ignazio Cerio, the head of the Cerio dynasty, who moved here in the second half of the 19th century to become one of Capri's most important patrons (*see p186* **Artistic licence**).

To see something of the town's vernacular architecture – a warren of narrow lanes and houses that merge into one another in a play of steps and arches – take via Madre Serafina from the top of the church steps (keep to the right). This lane eventually becomes the steep via Castello, at the end of which is the Belvedere Cannone, with a magnificent view over **Marina Piccola** and the **Faraglioni** (*see p183*).

From the Piazzetta, via Vittorio Emanuele III – the closest Capri comes to a main street – descends past boutiques and limoncello outlets to the Quisisana (*see p188*), doyen of the island's luxury hotels. Continue down via Federico Serena to viale Matteotti, a curving balcony lane that opens on to an unexpectedly rural scene of olive groves, a medieval monastery and the sea.

The monastery is the **Certosa di San Giacomo** (*see p183*), reached by means of a walled avenue at the eastern end of viale Matteotti. It was established in 1371 by Count Giacomo Arcucci, powerful secretary to Queen Joan I, who became a monk here when he suddenly dropped from favour in 1386. The Carthusian brotherhood of San Giacomo owned land, grazing and hunting rights to most of the island – something that brought it into frequent conflict with the islanders. When plague broke out in Capri in 1656, the monks, instead of tending to the sick, sealed themselves off to avoid infection; the *capresi* replied by dumping the corpses of plague victims over the monastery wall. Suppressed by Napoleon in 1808, the monastery was used as a prison and military hospital. Today it is an atmospheric place, partly abandoned, partly given over to municipal uses – including a school, the town library and a museum dedicated to the lugubrious canvases of German painter and Capri resident Karl Wilhelm Diefenbach. Other rooms are used to house temporary exhibitions and conferences. The simple church has a fine 14th-century fresco on the façade above the door; among the three praying women to the left of the Virgin is Queen Joan, the monastery's co-founder. A repeatedly postponed restoration of the Certosa was due to begin in October 2004, so don't be surprised if parts of the complex are *chiuso per restauro* (closed for restoration).

At the other end of viale Matteotti, past the Luna (*see p188*), are the **Giardini di Augusto** (open dawn-dusk daily), a panoramic series of terraced gardens. These now form a municipal park, but were once part of the Capri estate of German arms manufacturer Alfred Krupp. Ironically, the gardens now boast a monument to Lenin, who stayed nearby with his friend Maxim Gorky. The **via Krupp** – a wonderful hairpin path that winds down the cliff below here to the Marina Piccola – has officially been closed for years due to the danger of rock slides, but the path itself is still in good condition, and locals just slip around the barrier. You, of course, should (not) do the same.

Capri dips

Capri's jagged and rocky coastline doesn't have many beaches as such. In fact, most of the island's so-called 'beaches' consist of slabs of cement set over a bed of rocks – and to add insult to injury you have to pay to get on to them. The prettiest bays can only be reached by boat or by expert swimmers. True, there is a patch of sand at Marina Grande, but it's way too close to the port to be a real option.

There are, though, a few good spots for a scenic dip. From Marina Grande, you can take a boat to the **Bagni di Tiberio**, a former ancient Roman settlement (081 837 7688), where there is a beach. Restaurants **La Fontelina** (081 837 0845) and **Da Luigi** (081 837 0591) are nestled on the rocks on the land beside the Faraglioni rocks and have the prettiest views. They can be reached via a steep path descending from Punta Tragara or via boat from Marina Piccola.

Marina Piccola has a beach, not to mention a couple of swanky private beach clubs – the best known is La Canzone al Mare, co-founded by British singer and Capri resident Gracie Fields in 1933. However, the central bit of beach at Marina Piccola – around the low rocky outcrop known as the Scoglio delle Sirene – is free, and a perfectly good place for a swim.

At **Punta Carena** on the Anacapri side – a 10-minute bus ride from the town – lies the

Lido del Faro (*see also p187*). Perched below the lighthouse in a little bay, it is half private club and half free beach. Get up early and you'll share the bus and the beach with *anacapresi* grandparents and their grandchildren enjoying the place before the tourists arrive.

Blue Grotto.

Back up at the Quisisana, via Camerelle heads east past elegant boutiques and bars to via Tragara, lined with upmarket hotels. This is the route of the classic Capri evening *passeggiata* (stroll): just long enough to work up an appetite for dinner, and with a great view at the end from the **Belvedere di Tragara**, which overlooks the three rock-stacks known as the **Faraglioni**. The outermost stack is home to a species of blue lizard found nowhere else in the world, discovered by Ignazio Cerio.

The paved path that descends from here offers one of the best walks on the island (*see p194* **Island hikes**), via the mysterious **Grotta Matromania** and the photogenic **Arco Naturale**. The climb is less steep if you take it from the other way around, descending to the grotto from the Arco Naturale to emerge at Punta Tragara.

The classic excursion from Capri town is the easy hike up to Tiberius's **Villa Jovis**. From the Piazzetta, via Botteghe leads to a crossroads just below the island's prettiest church – the tiny chapel of **San Michele** (open Apr-Oct 9am-7pm daily, Nov-Mar 10am-3pm daily). Beyond here, the path dawdles up past imposing villas and more humble *capresi* dwellings until the houses thin out and the going gets steep. Just before the remains of Tiberius's villa, on the right, is the **Parco Astarita**, an unassuming but scenic patch of grass underneath the pines. Nearby is the tiny medieval church of Santa Maria del Soccorso.

The best time to visit **Villa Jovis** is as soon as it opens, at 9am, before the bulk of day-trippers make their way up. Not much is left of what must have been its decadent Roman luxury, and yet the complex is still imposing in all its splendid, solitary glory. The most impressive remains are those of the huge cisterns in the centre, which guaranteed the self-sufficiency of what was in effect a miniature town; and the long, straight loggia to the north, which ends in the 330-metre (1,155-foot) Salto di Tiberio, the precipice from which the emperor was supposed to have pitched those who annoyed him. The legend may be mere embroidery, but the stunning view across to Punta della Campanella (*see p241*) on the mainland is real enough.

Blue Grotto

Open 9am-1hr before sunset daily. **Admission** €4 plus €4.30 rowing boat fee. Access by motor launch from Marina Grande at €8 per person. Departs 9.30am-4pm daily. **No credit cards.**

Certosa di San Giacomo

Viale Certosa (081 837 6218). **Open** 9am-2pm Tue-Sun. **Admission** free.

Museo del Centro Caprense Ignazio Cerio

Piazzetta Cerio 8A (081 837 6681/www.centro caprense.it. **Open** *Apr-Oct* 10am-1pm Tue, Wed, Fri, Sat; 3-7pm Thur. *Nov-Mar* 10am-noon Mon-Sat. **Admission** €2.60. **No credit cards.**

Villa Jovis

Via Tiberio (081 837 0634/www.villajovis.it). **Open** 9am-1hr before sunset daily. **Admission** €2. **No credit cards.**

Where to eat

Few places in the world can claim to have as many restaurants with such breathtaking views, but though Capri has proud culinary traditions and gave its name to the tomato, mozzarella and basil *caprese* salad) as well as tasty chocolate cake, the constant supply of day-trippers gives restaurants little incentive to strive for a higher plane. One result of this is the similarity of most menus: however delicious

San Michele Arcangelo.
See p191.

ravioli capresi (plump ravioli filled with ricotta and herbs) and *linguine ai frutti di mare* (flat spaghetti with seafood) may be, one is bound to tire of them eventually; the alternative is pizza. On the plus side, the views and the good local wine will help you deal with any culinary disappointment. The restaurants listed below, while not always exceptions to this rule, are at least reliable. *See also p186* **Pulalli**.

Most restaurants close for the winter season between November and mid March; from June to September, most are open all week.

Buca di Bacco da Serafina
Via Longano 35 (081 837 0723). **Meals served** noon-3pm, 7pm-midnight Mon, Tue, Thur-Sun. Closed Nov, mid Dec & Wed lunch Aug. **Average** €35. **Credit** AmEx, DC, MC, V.
A warm, bustling trattoria just a whistle away from the Piazzetta, with reliable (though unadventurous) local seafood cooking, good vegetable antipasti and real Neapolitan pizzas. It's also a good place to eat grilled fish without breaking the bank (if it's available, try the *pezzogna* – blue-spotted bream – a local delicacy).

La Cantinella
Viale Matteotti 8 (081 837 0616). **Meals served** *Mid Mar-mid June, Sept, Oct* noon-3.30pm, 7.30pm-midnight Mon, Wed-Sun. *Mid June-Aug* noon-3.30pm, 7.30pm-midnight daily. Closed Nov-mid Mar. **Average** €55. **Credit** AmEx, DC, MC, V.
The *caprese* offshoot of Giorgio Rosolino's chic Neapolitan eaterie (*see p113*) perches scenically next to the Villa Krupp hotel. The ambience is candlelit and romantic, dominated by pink and straw colours. The cuisine stays faithful to the mother ship, with classic pasta dishes such as *penne alla Cantinella* (pasta with aubergines, tomato and mozzarella); *secondi* are dominated by grilled fish and seafood. Antipasti and desserts are mostly good, but the cooking is neither as special, nor the ambience as unforgettable, as the prices would suggest.

La Capannina
Via Le Botteghe 12 bis (081 837 0732). **Meals served** *May-Sept* noon-2pm, 7.30pm-midnight daily. *Mid Mar, Apr, Oct, 1st wk Nov* noon-2pm, 7.30pm-midnight Mon, Tue, Thur-Sun. Closed 2nd wk Nov-mid Mar. **Average** €50. **Credit** AmEx, DC, MC, V.
The pink tablecloths and soft light create a chic, living-room atmosphere in what is one of the most consistently good, and best known, restaurants on Capri. Opened in the 1930s by the same family that runs it today, and a legendary celebrity haunt, this is the place to come for textbook renditions of Capri recipes. The *ravioli capresi* are perfect, as are the *spaghetti alle vongole*, the stuffed squid and the *linguine allo scorfano* (flat spaghetti with scorpion fish), which is a house speciality. Don't expect experimental fare, this place is strictly classics. Prices are on the high side.

Da Gemma

Via Madre Serafina 6 (081 837 0461). **Meals served** *Aug* noon-3pm, 7.30pm-midnight daily. *Sept-mid Jan, mid Feb-July* noon-3pm, 7.30pm-midnight Tue-Sun. Closed mid Jan-mid Feb. **Average** €30. **Credit** AmEx, DC, MC, V.

This Capri institution was Graham Greene's favourite restaurant when Gemma herself was still around. It's still in the same family to this day, and the food continues to be reliable (especially the rich buffet), though rarely inspiring. The old black-and-white photos of famous punters lining the walls, including some of a very young Shirley MacLaine, make fascinating, if slightly nostalgic, entertainment. Pizza is also served.

Le Grottelle

Via Arco Naturale 13 (081 837 5719). **Meals served** *Apr, Oct* noon-3pm Mon-Wed, Fri-Sun. *July, Aug* noon-3pm, 8-11pm daily. *May, June, Sept* noon-3pm, 8-11pm Mon-Wed, Fri-Sun. Closed Nov-Mar. **Average** €28. **Credit** MC, V.

On a clear night with full moon, Le Grottelle is hard to beat. On the path leading to the Arco Naturale, the restaurant is located half inside a cavern and half perched on a terrace overlooking a verdant slope and the sea. The food is earthy and reliable, but it's the sea view that makes this place so spectacular. The kitchen turns out no-nonsense *primi* such as *ravioli capresi* in tomato and basil sauce, followed by grilled fish, *pezzogna*, chicken or rabbit; good local wine is an excellent accompaniment.

Da Paolino

Via Palazzo a Mare 11 (081 837 6102). **Meals served** *Apr, May, Sept, Oct* noon-3pm, 8pm-midnight Mon, Tue, Thur-Sun. *June-Aug* 8pm-midnight daily. Closed Nov-Mar, occasional Tue. **Average** €35. **Credit** AmEx, DC, MC, V.

One of the top places in Capri to see and be seen, this long-established restaurant set in a lemon grove is five minutes' walk from the first serious bend in the road from Marina Grande to Capri town. Lemon-themed right down to the plates and waiters' vests, Da Paolino is justly famed for its antipasti and the final limoncello.

La Savardina da Edoardo

Via Lo Capo 8 (081 837 6300). **Meals served** *June-Aug* noon-3pm, 7-11pm daily. *Jan, Mar-May, Sept, Oct, Dec* noon-3pm, 7-11pm Mon, Wed-Sun. Closed Nov-Feb (except for Christmas and New Year). **Average** €25. **Credit** AmEx, MC, V.

For a change from fish – and to see where real *capresi* live – head for this rustic farm-restaurant, an appetite-building 20-minute walk from the Piazzetta up towards Villa Jovis (*see p183*). In warm weather, tables are arranged outside in an orange grove with views over country villas and smallholdings. Ingredients are almost all home-grown or raised, including the fried courgette flowers that provide such a delicious starter. The ravioli are good, as is rabbit and *parmigiana di melanzane* (aubergines baked with parmesan).

Da Tonino

Via Dentecale 12 (081 837 6718). **Meals served** noon-3pm, 7-11pm daily. Closed mid Jan-mid Mar. **Average** €30. **Credit** AmEx, DC, MC, V.

Tucked away in a tourist-free area off the road that leads to the Arco Naturale, this family-run restaurant is a rural haven. Gennaro Aprea and his dad Tonino creatively interpret the local tradition in dishes such as *caramelle nere ripiene di pesce in salsa di bianchetti, frutti mare e zucca* (cuttlefish-filled pasta 'bon bons' in a bianchetti truffle, seafood and pumpkin sauce). Meat-based *secondi* such as pigeon with pesto and pine nuts, or quail with raisins, are on offer alongside more familiar marine options – all at decent prices. The friendly Apreas are particularly proud of their wine cellar, and rightly so. Hewn out of the solid rock, it stocks some 800 labels from all over Italy and further afield.

Verginiello

Via Lo Palazzo 25 (081 837 0944). **Meals served** *Apr-Oct* noon-3.30pm, 7.30-11.30pm daily. *Dec-Mar* noon-3.30pm, 7.30-11.30pm Mon,Wed-Sun. Closed Nov. **Average** €30. **Credit** AmEx, DC, MC, V.

A decent, no-frills budget option (budget for Capri standards, that is) on a little side road off the tourist-jammed via Roma, Verginiello offers a menu of pizza and *caprese* classics, including the *pezzogna* and the ubiquitous *penne aumm aumm* (with tomatoes, aubergines and mozzarella). While the place has the look of a slightly run-down corner trattoria and sees its fair share of day-trippers, the service is friendly, the fish is fresh and the view over the Bay of Naples will aid digestion.

Villa Verde

Vico Sella Orta 6A (081 837 7024/www.villaverde-capri.com). **Meals served** *Apr-Oct* noon-3.30pm, 7.30pm-midnight daily. *Nov-Mar* noon-3.30pm, 7.30pm-midnight Tue-Sun. **Credit** AmEx, DC, MC, V. **Average** €45-€50.

Currently one of Capri's most fashionable restaurants (it has catered for the likes of Keanu Reeves and Mariah Carey), Villa Verde serves good traditional *caprese* cuisine sprinkled with other Mediterranean recipes, and pizza. The home-made *scialatielli* with *aragosta* or *frutti di mare* (square spaghetti with lobster or seafood) are delicious. The simple furnishing, the friendly staff and rural courtyard give it a homely atmosphere, but if you're on a budget don't be fooled by the down-to-earth appeal – it's more expensive than it looks.

Cafés, bars & nightlife

Capri's social hub is the legendarily glamorous Piazzetta, with its four bars complete with elegant waiters in cream-coloured jackets. Although Capri is not as exclusive as it used to be, almost everyone who's anyone has sat and sipped a drink here at least once. The oldest of the four is the **Piccolo Bar** in the corner (081 837 0325, closed Mon Nov-Mar), which is

Around Naples

good for those who like to watch rather than be watched – especially if you grab one of the window tables upstairs. Right below the church, **Bar Tiberio** (081 837 0268, closed Nov & Wed Dec-Feb) attracts locals and young people and has the best cakes and cocktail nibbles. The **Gran Caffè** (081 837 0388, closed Thur Nov-Feb) is the most elegant, while **Bar Caso** (081 837 0600, closed Tue Nov-Mar) serves good *granite* (crushed ice drinks). But basically, the differences are minimal and any of them is fine to watch the show unfold in what Norman Douglas once called 'the world's little theatre'. Alternatively, try **Pulalli** (081 837 4108, closed Tue mid Nov-mid Dec & Jan-mid Mar), once a simple locanda and now a swanky wine bar inside the clocktower overlooking the Piazzetta (food is served at lunch and dinner).

The locals have their morning coffee at the **Bar Funicolare** (closed Thur Nov-Mar) next to the cable car entrance (Piazza Diaz, 081 837 0363).

The rich and the beautiful who think the Piazzetta has lost its 'hipness', now hang out at the terrace bar of the **Grand Hotel Quisisana** (*see p188*), especially at *aperitivo* time.

For ice-cream and *granite*, try the tiny **Scialapopolo** kiosk (via Vittorio Emanuele 53, 081 837 0558, closed Nov-Mar and Wed mid Mar-June, Oct); Costanzo Spataro used to sell his ices and drinks from a barrow, but set up this little bar in 1952. His nickname 'Scialapopolo', is a contraction of '*scialare il popolo*' or 'make everyone eat and drink to their hearts' content'. The island's best cakes can be found at **Buonocore** (via Vittorio Emanuele 35, 081 837 7826, closed Tue Mar-June, Oct & all

Artistic licence

Amid the chi chi cafés and shops of modern Capri, it's easy to forget that the first foreigners who made this place their island escape (ancients aside) were artists and intellectuals in search of freedom of thought and action, as well as the good life. Between the mid 19th century and the 1960s, Capri was a magnet for artists and intellectuals of various nationalities: anarchists, socialists, proto-fascists, painters, writers and philosophers converged here to revel in the inspiring scenery, 'rustic' culture, cheap food and lodging, and – often – the charms of the handsome young *caprese* men.

Local dynasties like the Pagano and Cerio families were quick to join in, and in 1822 Giuseppe Pagano opened the island's first hotel (the Hotel Pagano, now **La Palma**, *see p188*). Ignazio Cerio arrived in Capri in the late 19th century and studied its history at length (*see p183* **Cerio Museum**). For 50 years his cosmopolitan, but slightly eccentric, son Edwin played host to the motley crowd that washed up on Capri's shores.

Among the more flamboyant foreign residents was French opium-addict Count Jacques Fersen, who left a physical mark on Capri with his distinctive 1920s **Villa Lysis**, now open to visitors. Hastily leaving Paris after a scandal involving schoolboys, Fersten set about building a villa worthy of his decadent fantasies. He lived here, over-indulging in opium and cocaine, with his young Roman lover until his death, apparently of a deliberate overdose. Other eccentrics in

this unconventional community included 'living work of art' Marchesa Casati Stampa, prone to stroll around the island with a leopard on a leash.

Political flotsam and jetsam of left and right also found their way to Capri. Following the failure of the 1905 revolution, a group of Russian exiles led by Maxim Gorky took up residence here; they even founded a 'school of propaganda and agitation'. And in 1910 Lenin paid a visit to the island.

By the 1920s founder of Futurism Filippo Tommaso Marinetti was making speeches from the balcony of Capri's town hall, railing against the past and promoting a future of technology, modern warfare, extreme nationalism and violence, and holding Futurist art shows at the Grand Hotel Quisisana with like-minded associates.

In the majority, though, were individual writers and artists: androgynous US painter Romaine Brooks lived on Capri, as did Fortunato Depero – much of his work was painted on the island. And the list goes on: DH Lawrence, Henry James, André Gide, Marguerite Yourcenar, Rainer Maria Rilke, Joseph Conrad, Alberto Moravia and Chilean poet Pablo Neruda all spent time on Capri. Neruda left a *caprese* legacy with some verses about the island in his *Versos del Capitan*, including 'El viento ne la isla'.

Villa Lysis

Via Lo Capo. **Open** 9am-noon, 3-6pm. Guided tours only. Phone tourist office (081 837 0686) to check times.

The place to see and be seen: the glamorous **Piazzetta**.

Nov-Feb, except one week over New Year);
try the famed *caprilù* lemon and almond cakes
and the *torta caprese*. **Sfizi di Pane** (via Le
Botteghe 15, 081 837 6180, closed Mon & all
Jan) looks more like a jeweller's but is Capri's
best bakery and sells slabs of pizza and *torte
rustiche* (savoury flans) to take away.

In the quieter Anacapri, holidaymakers like
to have a 'sundowner' at the scenic **Lido del
Faro** (081 837 1798, *see also p182* **Capri dips**)
at Punta Carena. For those who want to feel
like royalty, try the stunningly elegant (and
expensive) **Bar degli Artisti** in the Capri
Palace (*see p192*).

Capri nightlife revolves around hotels, bars
and restaurants. There are five or six discos
and some smooth nightclub-cum-bars – the
most famous of which is the **Taverna Anima
e Core** (via Sella Orta 39E, 081 837 6461,
closed Mon-Fri Oct, mid Nov-Mar except one
week over New Year, admission €20-€25).
Slick Italian politicians head for **Guarracino**
(via Castello 7, 081 837 0514, closed Nov-Mar
except New Year) for Neapolitan-style songs
and music. But frankly, unless toupées and
silicone are your thing, it is generally more
fun to make your own party in the Piazzetta,
or stay up late in one of the hotel bars.

Arts & entertainment

For a place that was once the destination for
many of Europe's intellectuals, there's precious
little here by way of entertainment. Cinephiles
rely on two cinemas – the **Auditorium** in Capri
town (Vico Sella Orta 3, 081 837 6926, closed
Mon, Thur, Fri Oct-Apr) and the **Apollo** in
Anacapri (via G Orlandi 103, 081 837 1169, closed
Mon-Fri Nov-Mar). Both show commercial films;

all non-Italian offerings are dubbed. The
Certosa di San Giacomo, the **Cerio
Museum** (for both, *see p183*) and a few
galleries and upmarket hotels host small
exhibitions – mainly of local artists or of former
residents, some conferences and performances.
The top hotels, especially the **Capri Palace**
(*see p192*) and the **Cesare Augustus** (*see
p192*) offer some piano bar entertainment, live
chamber music, jazz and even electronica. In
the summer, Anacapri's Piazza San Nicola
becomes the stage for free folk music (or terrible
Italian pop) fests. For updated information,
ask in the tourist office (*see p190*).

Shopping

Capri town could easily set a world record for
the biggest concentration of designer boutiques
within the smallest space: tiny prestige outlets
of Ferragamo, Gucci, Fendi, Alberta Ferretti,
Cavalli, Prada and others are all crowded along
the main shopping streets via Vittorio Emanuele
and via Camerelle. You will also find several
stores selling the famous Capri sandals so
beloved of jetsetting icons Jackie O and Sophia
Loren. The other Capri speciality is limoncello,
the 33 per cent proof lemon liqueur that, in the
past decade, has become the statutory Italian
restaurant digestivo. The island is crammed with
limoncello shops but for authenticity and high
standards head for **Limoncello di Capri** (via
Roma 79, 081 837 5561, www.limoncello.com),
which has the rights to the name and the recipe
invented around a century ago by the founding
father of limoncello, Vincenzo Canale.

Other island shop-ops revolve around
antiques, ceramics and perfumes. The limited-
production Carthusia perfumes – made locally

according to old convent recipes – are great take-home gifts. There are three shops on the island (the one on Viale Parco Augusto 2/c is the factory, the biggest is on via Camerelle 10, 081 837 5335, www.carthusia.com).

Those hankering after the old, loftier Capri of philosophers, poets and artists should stop at **La Conchiglia**, a local publisher with 70 or so titles in its catalogue (a few of which are in English translation), all dealing with aspects of the island's history or its literary denizens. It has three bookshop outlets on the island: the main one (via Camerelle 18, 081 837 8199, closed Jan or Feb) has a wide selection of secondhand books about Capri – many in English – as well as a good range of antique prints.

Where to stay

Capri teems with chic hotels but has few budget options, in a deliberate attempt to encourage the 'better' sort of tourists. Booking well in advance is always a good idea – especially in low-budget establishments or small boutique hotels. Most hotels close between the first week of November and mid March, though some reopen for a week or two over Christmas and New Year.

Casa Morgano
Via Tragara 6 (081 837 0158/fax 081 837 0681/ www.casamorgano.com). **Closed** Nov-Mar. **Rates** €240-€380 double; €390-€460 junior suite. **Credit** AmEx, DC, MC, V.
Under the same ownership as the Quisisana (*see p188*) and La Scalinatella (*see p189*), this cheerful blue-and-white hotel, which descends (like at least three others) in a series of bougainvillea-filled terraces from via Tragara, is a Capri classic, offering five-star luxury on a small scale. It has chintzy Mediterranean decor and all the usual comforts, including a good-sized pool.

Grand Hotel Quisisana
Via Camerelle 2 (081 837 0788/fax 081 837 6080/ www.quisi.com). **Closed** Nov-mid Mar. **Rates** €230-€280 single; €300-€330 double; €580-€700 junior suite. **Credit** AmEx, DC, MC, V.
This Capri institution began life in 1845 as a sanatorium, but soon transformed itself into the island's top hotel. Behind the cream-and-white neo-classical façade are two swimming pools (one inside, one outside) a shady garden, a gym and the new Quisi Spa (opened in 2004), which has a sauna, a steam room and offers a range of beauty treatments. Service is impeccable, but the decor of the bedrooms can be anonymous, and the air of refinement is sometimes disturbed by herds of conference-goers.

Luna
Viale Matteotti 3 (081 837 0433/fax 081 837 7459/ www.lunahotel.com). **Closed** Nov-Mar. **Rates** €125-€160 single; €175-€380 double; €320-€469 suite. **Credit** AmEx, DC, MC, V.

In a spectacular position overlooking the Certosa and the sea, the Luna is soberly furnished in a slightly old-fashioned style. But the cheerful colours of the common areas, the peaceful setting and magnificent views make up for any design shortcomings (make sure you ask for a room with a view, as some look on to an internal garden). The hotel is approached via a pretty walk shaded by bougainvillea and surrounded by gardens, with an Olympic-size swimming pool and a restaurant on a rocky balcony above the sea.

La Reginella
Via Matermania 36 (081 837 0500/fax 081 837 0500/www.hotelareginella.com). **Rates** €50-€95 single, €100-€190 double. **Credit** AmEx, MC, V.
This old-fashioned budget hotel on the road leading to the Arco Naturale used to be the home of the friendly Falco family, who are still running the hotel today. The terraced rooms are very basic and the place looks as if it has seen better days, but it speaks of the great Capri of old – that of writers and artists. Paintings by eccentric artist Austrian Hans Paule line the walls. Prices given are for half-board accommodation.

La Palma
Via Vittorio Emanuele 39 (081 837 0133/fax 081 837 6966/www.lapalma-capri.com). **Rates** €115-€345 double. **Credit** AmEx, DC, MC, V.
Since its opening in 1822, La Palma (formerly Hotel Pagano) has welcomed many celebrities, including Umberto Eco, Sophia Loren, Gina Lollobrigida and King Costantine of Greece. There are 74 rooms, some with jacuzzis on the panoramic terrace, and many luxuriously equipped with frescoed bathrooms. There is a roof garden where you can enjoy an aperitif before moving on to dinner in Le Relais restaurant.

Punta Tragara
Via Tragara 57 (081 837 0844/fax 081 837 7790/ www.hoteltragara.com). **Closed** Nov-Mar. **Rates** €300-€360 double; €400-€500 suite. **Credit** AmEx, DC, MC, V.
Designed by Le Corbusier in the 1920s as a private villa, this pink hotel also served as a US headquarters during World War II. It has one of best views and the most impressive exterior of any on the island, but it also wants everybody to know how exclusive it is (and does not admit children under 12). Most of the 50 rooms are small private suites, each with its own balcony overlooking the Faraglioni. There's nothing inspirational about the room decor, but the terrace bar, with its heated seawater pool, is a great place to watch the sunset.

Relais Maresca
Via Provinciale Marina Grande 284 (081 837 9619/ fax 081 837 4070/www.relaismaresca.it). **Closed** Jan, Feb. **Rates** €120-€200 double; €180-€300 superior double. **Credit** AmEx, DC, MC, V.
The bright Mediterranean decor (yellow, green or blue) and the pretty fourth-floor breakfast room compensates for this hotel's location – down in

Marina Grande, it offers a fine view of the ferry traffic and of the noisy road leading to the port. It also works a longer season than most Capri hotels, making it a good out-of-season choice.

La Scalinatella

Via Tragara 8 (081 837 0633/fax 081 837 8291/ www.scalinatella.com). **Closed** Mid Oct-Easter. **Rates** €400-€470 double; €500-€560 suite. **No credit cards.**
This boutique hotel, with its magnificent Moorish-style façade and country-house feel, is a good place for a romantic weekend – if you can afford it. The 28 rooms and suites, most with private terraces, are tastefully decorated, and there's no need to get out of the jacuzzi to make a phone call. The service is professional if occasionally rather haughty. Note that credit cards are not accepted.

La Tosca

Via Birago 5 (tel/fax 081 837 0989/www.latosca hotel.com). **Closed** Mid Nov-mid Mar. **Rates** €40-€80 single; €63-€125 double. **Credit** MC, V.
This is a small and clean one-star hotel decorated in a spare but elegant white Mediterranean style. The reasonable prices, cordial welcome and enviable position – in a quiet lane leading down to the Certosa with a view of the Faraglioni – make La Tosca a popular choice with the wallet-challenged (in Capri terms). There are only 12 rooms, so it's essential that you book ahead.

Villa Brunella

Via Tragara 24A (081 837 0122/fax 081 837 0430/www.villabrunella.it). **Closed** Nov-Mar. **Rates** €260-€290 double; €320-€390 suite. **Credit** AmEx, DC, MC, V.
This long, narrow hotel boasts one of Capri's best views. It descends the hillside on a series of terraces looking over Marina Piccola and Monte Solaro. It's bright and friendly, with a pool on the lowest level and terraces outside all the rooms. Service in Capri hotels is often distant and offhand, but Villa Brunella is a welcome exception: guests are given personal attention, and families are made to feel especially at home.

Villa Krupp

Viale Matteotti 12 (081 837 0362/fax 081 837 6489). **Closed** Nov-Mar. **Rates** €90 single (with breakfast); €120-€150 double (with breakfast). **Credit** MC, V.
Perched above the Gardens of Augustus, this white hotel with breathtaking views used to be Maxim Gorky's house. It's one of the best options in this price range, and therefore needs to be booked a fair bit in advance, especially in ever-popular July and August. It is run by a friendly elderly couple and rooms are clean and bright – many have terraces with sea views.

Villa Sarah

Via Tiberio 3A (081 837 7817/081 837 0689/fax 081 837 7215/www.villasarah.it). **Closed** Nov-Mar.

Rates €80-€125 single; €145-€190 double. **Credit** AmEx, DC, MC, V.
This light-filled Mediterranean villa off the road leading to Villa Jovis (*see p183*) offers peace and relaxation in a semi-rural setting of olive groves and vineyards. The 20 rooms are clean and simply furnished and the breakfast, served in the tranquil and verdant front courtyard, is excellent. Books about Capri are available for consultation next to the fireplace in the hall and the friendly staff will help you plan your sightseeing.

Resources

First Aid

Guardia Medica *Via Madonna delle Grazie 1, 081 837 5716.* **Open** 24hrs daily.
In a medical emergency, the Guardia Medica will arrange transport to the mainland.

Internet

Telecom Italia *Piazza Umberto I, above newsstand, 081 837 5447.* **Open** 9am-1pm, 4-8pm daily.

Police

Carabinieri *Via Provinciale Marina Grande, 081 837 0000.*

Post Office

Via Roma 50, 081 837 5829. **Open** 8am-6.30pm Mon-Fri; 8am-12.30pm Sat.

Tourist information

Azienda Autonoma di Cura, Soggiorno e Turis *Turismo Banchina del Porto, Marina Grande, 081 837 0634/www.capritourism.com.* **Open** *Apr-Sept* 8.30am-8.30pm daily. *Oct-Mar* 9am-3pm Mon-Sat.

In 2001, Capri's tourist board launched Tiberio, an audioguide available in Italian, English and German, from the island's three tourist offices (Marina Grande, Capri town, Anacapri). It's fairly easy to use, though the form of the narration – a dialogue between Tiberius and his wife Julia – sometimes gets in the way of the information. Price is €3 per day.

Azienda Autonoma di Cura, Soggiorno e Turismo *Piazza Umberto I, 081 837 0686.* **Open** *Apr-Oct* 8.30am-8.30pm Mon-Sat; 8.30am-7pm Sun. *Nov-Mar* 9am-1pm, 3.30-6.45pm Mon-Sat.

Anacapri & around

Incredibly enough for such a small island, the first road linking Capri town and Anacapri was only built in 1872. Until then, and for the most part of their history, the two villages led different lives on the opposite sides of the seismic fracture and wall of cliffs that splits the island into two.

Set on the cliff's western side at the base of Monte Solaro, the loose-knit cluster of houses forming Anacapri, or 'up-Capri', are interspersed by olive groves and vineyards. A community of farmers and artisans had already begun to form here first in Greek and then in Roman times, but it only condensed into a proper village in the late Middle Ages.

Anacapri's rural way of life and centuries of physical isolation are reflected in the proud, independent character of the *anacapresi*, who preferred to work as ships' caulkers for the king of Naples than have anything to do with the *capresi* down below.

The only means of communication between the two centres was the **Scala Fenicia**, a steep flight of steps built by Capri's first Greek settlers that leads up from Marina Grande (the island's only proper port, which the *anacapresi* were forced to use even though it was in 'enemy territory') to the tiny chapel of Sant'Antonio, just below Villa San Michele; the steepest, final stretch was formerly entered through a gate called the Porta della Differencia, designed to safeguard Anacapri's 'difference'.

When Swedish doctor Axel Munthe first walked up here in the late 19th century, overtaking the village postwoman (who couldn't read), the hostess of Anacapri's one and only inn told him that she had 'once been down to Capri' – but it hadn't impressed her much. If rural Anacapri today receives as many visitors as swish Capri town, it is largely thanks to Munthe himself. His book *The Story of San Michele* filled Cold Northerners with

longing for the 'warm South' by bringing to life the charming rustic characters of Anacapri. Translated into over 30 languages, Munthe's memoir continues to sell steadily seven decades after its original publication in 1929.

Born in 1857, Munthe first set foot on Anacapri in 1874 as a young medical student. But it was not until 15 years later – after he had become the youngest and most sought-after society doctor in Paris – that he was able to realise his dream of building the **Villa San Michele** on the edge of the Anacapri cliff, on the site of one of Tiberius's 12 Capri villas. Designed in an eclectic style that mixes Romanesque and Renaissance influences with Moorish trills, the villa and its trim gardens are studded with bits of classical statuary.

Some visitors will undoubtedly agree with writer Bruce Chatwin, who wrote in his Munthe-debunking essay *Self-love Among the Ruins* (reprinted in *Anatomy of Restlessness*) that 'in Pasadena or Beverly Hills, Munthe's creation wouldn't get more than a passing glance'. Nevertheless, the views are spectacular, and the villa and gardens are preserved with Nordic tidiness by a foundation whose members are nominated by the Swedish state. The gardens host music concerts, some timed to make the most of the summer sunset (ask at the tourist office, *see above*, for information). The ruined **Castello di Barbarossa** on the crest above – named after the Greek pirate who destroyed it – is part of the same property; it can be visited on a free guided tour each Thursday at 5pm (places are limited, bookings can be only be made a day ahead). Part of the surrounding hillside, which has a resident population of peregrine falcons, is a **World Wildlife Fund nature reserve**. Guided tours are organised at weekends between May and October; ring 081 837 1325/081 837 1401 for details.

Munthe was the first of a steady trickle of foreign residents who preferred Anacapri's quiet charm to the more glitzy delights of Capri town: writers Compton Mackenzie and Graham Greene had houses here, and Queen Victoria of Sweden had a summer villa at Caprile, just south of the town. Today the peace and quiet that attracted these escapees is challenged by the busloads of tourists that come to visit Villa San Michele and offload their euros in a slough of tacky souvenir shops; but away from this thankfully limited outbreak of bad taste – and out of season – Anacapri is a good place to see the other, more rural side of Capri, which, like most Italian islands, has always looked more to the land than to the sea for sustenance.

Gateway to the town, and setting-down point for the regular buses that connect Anacapri with Marina Grande and Capri town,

The view from the **Luna**. *See p190*.

is little piazza Vittoria. Most visitors head
straight along the souvenir-lined via
Capodimonte to Villa San Michele. From the
square, pedestrianised via G Orlandi leads
west past the tourist office into the centre
of the old town. Halfway down on the right is
the **Casa Rossa**, an antiquity-encrusted folly
built in 1876 by a former Confederate soldier,
J C MacKowen, who wrote one of the first
guides to Capri.

On the left, via San Nicola leads to piazza
San Nicola, dominated by the parish church
of **San Michele Arcangelo**. The standard
baroque façade presages a standard baroque
interior, but the latter is enlivened by a
delightful majolica floor dating from 1761.
The theme is Earthly Paradise, complete with
ostriches, camels and crocodiles. Continuing
down via G Orlandi past the baroque Santa
Sofia church you reach the pretty district
of **Le Boffe**, with its pavilion-like, round-
roofed arches.

From Anacapri, two bus routes run west
(*see p193* for transport information). One
route goes to the **Blue Grotto** (*see p183*) via
the remains of **Villa Damecuta** (ask the bus
driver to put you off by the side road to the
villa); one of Tiberius's 12 imperial villas, it
was devastated first by the volcanic rain of
Vesuvius, then by a series of depredations
by Bourbon and later French troops, and little
is left today, but it's a pretty spot, covered in
wild flowers in spring, and ideal for a picnic.
The second bus goes to the lighthouse at

Punta Carena, on the south-western tip
of the island. Just before the lighthouse (built
about a century ago), there is one of the less
crowded rocky beaches on the island (to be
avoided when the wind is blowing in from
the west). For walks from Anacapri, and for
information on the chairlift to Monte Solaro,
see p194 **Island hikes**.

San Michele Arcangelo

Piazza San Nicola, 081 837 2396. **Open** *Apr-June,
Sept, Oct* 9.30am-5pm daily. *July, Aug* 10am-7pm
daily. *Nov-Mar* 9.30am-4pm daily. **Admission** €1.
No credit cards.

Villa San Michele

*Viale Axel Munthe, 081 837 1401/www.san
michele.org.* **Open** *Mar* 9.30am-4pm daily. *Apr,
Oct* 9.30am-5pm daily. *May-Sept* 9am-6pm daily.
Nov-Feb 10.30am-3.30pm daily. **Admission** €5.
No credit cards.

Where to eat

Add'O Riccio

Grotta Azzurra (081 837 1380). **Meals served**
Mid Mar-May, mid Sept-Oct noon-3pm daily. *June-
mid Sept* noon-3pm Mon-Wed; noon-3pm, 7-10.30pm
Thur-Sun. Closed Nov-mid Mar. **Average** €35.
Credit AmEx, DC, MC, V.
Perched on a cliff just along from the Blue Grotto
in one of the island most famous, and prettiest,
spots, Add'O Riccio could easily get away with
almost anything. And yet, the fish and antifood (as
featured in a highly recommended *antipasto di
mare*) is superbly fresh and is picturesquely

arranged around a little pool at the centre of the restaurant. Pasta dishes, such as *linguine ai frutti di mare,* are well turned out and the house white wine can only serve to enhance the view.

Da Gelsomina alla Migliera

Via Migliera 72 (081 837 1499). **Meals served** *Mid May-Sept* noon-3pm, 8-10pm Mon,Wed-Sun. *Oct-Dec* noon-3pm Mon,Wed-Sun. **Closed** 3wks Jan and 2 wks Feb. **Average** €30. **Credit** AmEx, MC, V.

This oasis of peace nestled on a hilltop in the *anacaprese* countryside boasts a stunning sea view and one of the best price-quality ratios on the island. The wine is made from the produce of the surrounding vineyard; the menu revolves around fish- and meat-based local classics, such as *spaghetti alle vongole* or grilled *pezzogna,* cooked just as they should be. It's perfect for a day (or a few) out with the kids, as it also has a swimming pool (open 10am to 7pm) and seven rooms for rent. The downside is that it is located a 30-minute walk from Anacapri, but the staff will pick you up and drive you back for free if you call (which is good news if you get carried away with the great local wine).

Where to stay

Caesar Augustus

Via G Orlandi 4, 081 837 3395/fax 081 837 1444/ www.caesar-augustus.com). **Closed** Nov-Mar. **Rates** €275-€340 double; €335-€850 suite. **Credit** AmEx, MC, V.

This luxury hotel set on a cliff looking out to the Bay of Naples and Marina Piccola has the most beautiful swimming pool, and one of the best views, on the island. The pool is made of two cascade-like levels that seem to plunge into the sea below. The terraced patio and many of the rooms have the same, stupendous view. The decor is a nothing-special chintzy, though.

Capri Palace Hotel & Spa

Via Capodimonte 2B (081 978 0111/fax 081 837 3191/www.capri-palace.com). **Closed** Nov-Mar. **Rates** €170-€325 single; €265-€585 double; €525-€870 double with private pool; €615-€2,440 suite. **Credit** AmEx, DC, MC, V.

Every detail is tailored down to perfection in this soberly elegant patrician palace that has become the island's luxury hotel of choice. The white and creamy decor, the airy spaces, sea-coloured swimming pool, attentive service, tastefully decorated rooms and great food (it has an excellent, but pricey, restaurant, l'Olivo, and an unforgettable breakfast buffet) combine to create a glamorous, yet understated effect. Art-loving owner Tonino Cacace has filled the hotel with contemporary art, including paintings by De Chirico, and has created three new 'art suites'. The Bar degli Artisti is perfect for sophisticated cocktail sipping. Four rooms and two suites have their own private pools; the top suite, the Megaron, even has a private roof garden with an olive tree and a panoramic swimming pool. The

hotel also hosts the Capri Beauty Farm (also open to non-residents), complete with doctors and dieticians. The roof terrace has stupendous sea views. On a clear day, you can see Vesuvius and beyond.

Il Girasole

Via Linciano 47 (081 837 2351/fax 081 837 3880/ www.ilgirasole.com). **Closed** Nov-Mar except 1wk over New Year. **Rates** €138-€173 double; €265-€345 suite. **Credit** AmEx, MC, V.

Popular with budget travellers, this hotel is set in a rural landscape of vines and olives between Anacapri and Punta Carena (guests can be picked up at Marina Grande for €4 per piece of luggage). Rooms look out on to terraces bursting with flowering plants. There is a small swimming pool and a panoramic dining area under an awning.

San Michele

Via G Orlandi 1/5 (081 837 1427/fax 081 837 1420/www.sanmichele-capri.com). **Closed** Nov-Mar. **Rates** €83-€105 single; €140-€180 double. **Credit** AmEx, DC, MC, V.

A good choice for families, this large white hotel on the main road beneath the Villa San Michele has the island's biggest swimming pool, a semi-Olympic affair that also hosts swimming courses for local kids. The decor is old-fashioned and there is a certain amount of traffic noise from the nearby road, but the views are stunning and the welcome friendly. The minibus up from or down to Marina Grande costs extra.

Villa Eva
Via La Fabbrica 8 (tel/fax 081 837 2040/081 837 1549/www.villaeva.com). **Closed** Nov-Feb.
Rates €85-€100 double; €35-€50 apartment (per person, sleeps 5 or 8). **Credit** MC, V for stays of 3 or more nights.

Run by a guy who looks like a *caprese* Santa Claus, this excellent budget option offers a range of accommodation in extensive, verdant grounds, from double rooms in the main building to a series of self-contained chalets in the gardens. There's even a decent-sized swimming pool. Transport can be arranged to and from Marina Grande; otherwise, it's a short walk from the Capri–Blue Grotto road and bus route.

Resources

Tourist information
Azienda Autonoma di Cura, Soggiorno e Turismo *Via G Orlandi 59, 081 837 1524.* **Open** 9am-3pm Mon-Sat. Closed mid Oct-Feb.

Getting around

Beyond the bus terminus on via Roma, Capri town is closed to all forms of motorised traffic except little luggage-bearing electric trolleys, which are also licensed to carry disabled people. If you're staying in an upmarket hotel, you should be met at the quay by a porter, identified by the hotel name on his cap, who will arrange to have your luggage sent up to the hotel. Most upmarket hotels in Anacapri and some mid-range ones have their own minibuses. Otherwise, the funicular, buses and taxis are all at the end of the quay. The funicular is on the left; taxis on the right.

All public transport on the island – including the funicular from Marina Grande to Capri town, but not the Monte Solaro cable car – is covered by the Unico Capri ticket, which comes in three versions: €1.30 for a single trip, €2.10 for 60mins on the whole network (allowing you to change at Anacapri for the Blue Grotto, for example), €6.70 for a day-pass. Tickets should be bought beforehand from the terminus and shown to the driver upon boarding. If you get on at an intermediate stop, tickets can be bought from the driver. You can also obtain a rechargeable Unico Capri pre-paid card by leaving a deposit of €1.

By boat
For the **Blue Grotto** (*see p183*), take a speedboat from Marina Grande. The other popular trip is the complete circuit of the island (*giro dell'isola*) offered by a number of operators in Marina Grande. The price is about €10 per person. You can also rent small motorboats from Marina Grande or Marina Piccola (a driving licence is not required).

By bus
If you come in high season, be prepared to queue, especially if you get on at the Piazza Roma bus terminus and in Anacapri. The three main services are Marina Grande–Capri (6am-midnight), Marina Grande–Anacapri (6am-7pm, and until 10pm Marina Grande–Anacapri in connection with Caremar boats) and Capri–Anacapri (6am-2am).

Other routes, with less frequent services, are Capri–Marina Piccola, Anacapri–Grotta Azzurra (Blue Grotto) and Anacapri–Punta Carena (Faro). Ring SIPPIC (081 837 0420) for information; phone Staiano (081 837 2422, groups only) for the Blue Grotto and Punta Carena lines.

By funicular railway
Departures from the station at Marina Grande to Capri town (and vice versa) run every 15mins (6.30am-9pm Oct-Mar; 6.30am-9.30pm Apr, May; 6.30am-12.30am June-Sept). Run by SIPPIC (information 081 837 0420).

It can get crowded in high season, especially in the early evening when it's departure time for the day-trippers; if you are pressed for time and need to get to Marina Grande quickly, it is advisable to take the bus or walk (it takes 15-20 minutes, the path to go down starts next to the entrance to the funicular).

By scooter
Given the motor traffic restrictions in place and considering that Capri's narrow roads are often congested, scooters are not the best way to get around. Still, if you don't want to miss this all-Italian experience, there are a number of options. The store to rent EU-funded, eco-friendly electric scooters – imaginatively named Rent an Electric Scooter – is based at via Roma 68 (081 837 5863), the approach road to Capri town. Rental costs €15 per hr (minimum 2 hrs), including helmet; a driving licence is not required. The scooters have a range of 50km (31 miles; that's a lot on Capri), after which they have to be returned to base for recharging. You can also rent normal fuel-powered mopeds (Capri, via Marina Grande 280, 081 837 7941) and Oasi Motor, via Colombo 47, 081 837 7138).

By taxi
Capri's seven-seat, open-top taxis are unique and manufactured especially for the island. They provide a fun alternative to the overcrowded buses but will not save you much time, given the near-impossibility of overtaking on the island's narrow roads. Allow €10-€12 from the port to Capri town (can go no further than the taxi rank by the bus terminus in via Roma) and a few euros more to Anacapri. (Capri 081 837 6657, 081 837 0543; Anacapri 081 837 1175.)

Getting there

Naples newspaper *Il Mattino* publishes daily updated timetables of all bus, train, sea and air connections to and from Naples. On Capri, the tourist offices give out a free timetable, updated fortnightly, with all the sea crossings; these are also posted on the Capri tourist board website (www.capritourism.com). All the services mentioned below are daily. *See also p284* **Ferries & hydrofoils**.

By helicopter
Hollywood stars and anyone really pressed for time can take a helicopter from Naples' Capodichino airport to the heliport at Anacapri – €1,200-€1,300 per one-way flight for up to four people. Details from Cab.air (081 584 4355, www.cabair.it).

Around Naples

By sea from the Amalfi Coast

Services run Apr-Oct only. LMS (Amalfi 089 873 301; Salerno 089 234 892/089 227 979) runs hydrofoils between Salerno, Amalfi, Positano and Capri. From Positano, Consorzio Linee Marittime (089 873 301/ 081 871 483) runs hydrofoils to Capri; journey time 30mins.

By sea from Ischia

Services run Apr-Oct only. There are three hydrofoils a day (two in the morning, one in the afternoon). Both are run by Alilauro (081 991 888); crossing time 40mins.

By sea from Naples

NLG Linea Jet (081 552 7209) and Snav (081 428 5111) run hydrofoils (hourly in summer) from the central quay of Molo Beverello. Snav also runs hydrofoils from Mergellina at the western end of the bay (every 2hrs in summer). Crossing time by hydrofoil is around 40mins. Caremar (081 551 3882) also runs six daily ferries all year round from Beverello. Three of these are high-speed *traghetti veloci* (50mins); the others take 1hr 20mins. Ferries are cheaper, and they're the only option when the sea is too choppy for the hydrofoils. The last boats leave around 8.30pm (winter), 10pm (summer).

Island hikes

Few think of the Mediterranean's most stylish island as a trekker's paradise. But although space is limited, there is some fine walking to be had on the island, some of it almost Alpine in character. The following walks, at their best in spring and autumn, are classics: the first, which threads its way above the sea in the spectacular south-eastern corner of the island, is within reach of just about everyone; the second, while not nearly as difficult as it appears from afar, is for more experienced or adventurous walkers. Sunblock, a decent hat and plenty of water are essential.

I Faraglioni, Grotta Matromania & the Arco Naturale

Time 1hr. **Grade** easy.

After the stroll up to **Villa Jovis** (*see p183*), this classic round-trip is easily the best of the paved walks that depart from Capri town. From the **Belvedere di Tragara** (*see p183*), take either of the sets of steps that head downwards (they soon meet up). Passing a turn-off on the right to the Faraglioni (where there is a small rocky platform of a beach, mostly occupied by the deckchairs of a bar-restaurant), the path continues east around the wooded slopes of Monte Tuoro, with views over the rocky coast and the stunningly located **Villa Malaparte** (*see p181*). Soon after the villa the path becomes a flight of steps that lead up to the **Grotta Matromania**, a huge cavern that was long thought to be sacred to the cult of Cybele (the Mater Magna, or Great Mother); the only certain evidence of use, though, is some first-century masonry, a tribute to the Roman mania for turning anything remotely cave-like into a cute nymphaeum. The steps continue up to a junction by the Le Grottelle bar-restaurant (*see p186*). Turn right here and in another couple of minutes you will see the **Arco Naturale**, a limestone arch that was a favourite with Romantic travellers. To head back to Capri town from here, continue straight past Le Grottelle along via Matermania. Smallholdings gradually give way to houses, and soon enough you'll find yourself back in the inevitable Piazzetta.

Monte Solaro via the Passetiello

Time *up* 1hr 30mins; *down* 1hr. **Grade** *up* a tough scramble; *down* moderate.

From the panoramic terrace above Capri town's funicular station, the sheer mountain wall that divides Capri town from Anacapri looks impenetrable, aside from the road with its beetling orange buses and the crazy zigzag staircase known as the **Scala Fenicia** (*see p190*). But there is a third way up, all but invisible from down below: the **Passetiello**. Though this is nowhere near as difficult as it looks, it's rather more than a Sunday stroll: the total height gain is 350 metres (1,149 feet) and you should be prepared to put hands on rock in a couple of places. From the Piazzetta, walk down via Roma to the four-way junction known as Due Golfi. Take the road down to Marina Piccola, turning right almost immediately on to the paved lane that leads up past the side of the island's little-functioning, EU-funded hospital. A little further on, a wooden map-signpost indicates the beginning of the path proper, which is marked with red-and-white flashes (though the colour scheme has changed at least once in the past five years).

Villas and allotments soon give way to a forest of holm oak, and the going becomes steep. Above the tree-line, a tumble of rocks and Mediterranean macchia leads to a narrow gully – the **Passetiello** itself, a secret pass in the seemingly impenetrable wall of rock that separates Anacapri from Capri. French soldiers used this route to surprise the

By sea from Sorrento
Caremar (081 807 3077) and LMP Alilauro (081 878 1430, 081 807 3024) hydrofoils leave from Sorrento's Marina Piccola for the 20min crossing to Capri (at least half-hourly in summer). There are also less frequent conventional ferries.

By sea metro
The '*metro del mare*' service (which runs from mid June to early September) links the main coastal towns of the Campania region. It has six lines; Capri is on the MM4 connecting Naples's Beverello quay to Sapri via

Capri, Palinuro and Camerota. There are two boats a day, but this service saves time if you are coming from Cilento (199 446 644, www.metrodelmare.com).

By water taxi
Taxi del Mare, 081 877 3600, www.taxidelmare.it, has a fleet of smart yellow 10-seater speedboats available for hire, with driver, at a rate of €32 per nautical mile (Sorrento–Capri will set you back €256 one way). There is a minimum tariff of €256, which means that stretches shorter than 8 nautical miles will still cost you that amount.

English troops quartered down below in 1808. Once over the pass, one emerges on the ridge of **Monte Santa Maria**, with magnificent views. Follow the waymarked path that heads left (due south), just below the ridge, to the pretty hermitage of **Santa Maria a Cetrella** (erratic opening hours) founded by Dominican hermits in the 14th century.

From here, the clearly visible summit of **Monte Solaro** can be reached by taking the wide path that leads north-west to the pass of **La Crocetta**, where it joins the path up from Anacapri (*see below*). This strenuous walk can be turned into a fairly easy downhill hike by getting the bus up to Anacapri and the chairlift to the top of Monte Solaro.

Monte Solaro
Time 1hr. **Grade** easy.
The Funivia (chairlift) di Monte Solaro, runs – weather and mechanics permitting – from piazza Vittoria up to the heavily rebuilt English fort on top of Monte Solaro (589 metres/ 2,062 feet). However, away from the hottest days of summer, it is much more pleasant to make the ascent on foot, or to take the chairlift up and walk down. The marked path forks off from via Capodimonte in Anacapri, halfway between piazza Vittorio and Villa San Michele. It's a steady but not strenuous 300-metre/1,050-foot climb, past vines and through patches of forest, with good views over the western half of the island. Once over the pass of **La Crocetta** – marked by an iron cross – the scenery changes abruptly to reveal a valley of ferns and gorse that seems a continent away from the beau monde of the Piazzetta. The views from the summit, where there is a small snack bar, are vertiginous; Gustave Doré used them to make hell seem more realistic in his illustrations to Dante's *Inferno*.

Punta Carena to the Blue Grotto
Time 2hrs each way. **Grade** easy.
A new waymarked footpath, dubbed *La Passeggiata dei Fortini* ('the fortress walk') has been laid out along the little-visited west coast of the island, connecting Punta Carena with the Blue Grotto by way of three ruined Napoleonic forts. Bring swimming things, as some of the coves along the way are difficult to resist. The path is a little high to access the water, however.

Anacapri to the Blue Grotto
Time 45mins. **Grade** easy.
Away from the summer heat, one of the best ways to visit the **Blue Grotto** (*see p183*) from Anacapri is to walk down and take the bus back: from piazza Armando Diaz in Anacapri, via Cava and via Lo Pozzo lead down to a path that continues past orchards and smallholdings to the parking lot above the Blue Grotto, which is also the bus terminus. Stop for a picnic en route at the **Villa Damecuta** (*see p181*).

Anacapri to Migliara
Time 45mins. **Grade** easy.
Another good walk from Anacapri is the flat, contour-hugging stroll to Migliara. Take via Caposcuro, to the left of the Monte Solaro chairlift (*see below*), and continue along it for a couple of kilometres (it soon changes its name to via Migliara), in a landscape that is about as rural as you can get on Capri. At the end of the path, the Belvedere di Migliara affords spectacular views over the cliffs below Monte Solaro.

Funivia di Monte Solaro
Via Caposcuro 10 (081 837 1428). **Open** *Mar-Oct* 9.30am-4.30pm daily. *Nov-Feb* 9.30am-3.30pm daily. **Tickets** €6 return. **No credit cards.**

Around Naples

Ischia

Island of bubbling springs, beaches and green hills.

There are some things about Ischia that most tourists never discover, and more's the pity. Staying in the generally unattractive (though mercifully low-rise) accommodation provided in Ischia's main towns and villages, it's easy to miss the vineyards and baroque architecture in **Forio** (see p202). And most never chance upon the island's secret delights: excellent restaurants (if you know where to look); great hotels (in hidden corners); exotic gardens and the verdant forests. Not to mention the weird and wonderful antics of imprisoned Typhon.

According to mythology, a vengeful Zeus confined Typhon beneath Ischia, where he remains for eternity, occasionally struggling to get out of his prison, but mostly just sighing and crying. Typhon hasn't tried to shrug the weight off his back since 1883, but his sighs of fiery vapour and hot rivers of tears give away his presence.

Although Greeks were first to arrive on the island, in the eighth century BC, it was under Roman rule that Ischia first became famous for its thermal cure treatments. When under Neapolitan rule in the Middle Ages it suffered badly from attacks by North African Saracens. In 1301, Monte Arso erupted, forcing the inhabitants to leave the island for four years. When they returned, they crowded on to what is now the **Castello Aragonese**, the fortified rocky outcrop off Ischia Ponte (see p197). The Castello was hotly contended by the Angevins and Aragonese throughout the 14th century and, later refortified, remained a place of refuge from Saracen attack. Saracens continued to threaten the island, their last attack coming as late as 1796.

When Ischia supported the Parthenopean Republic in 1799, King Ferdinand's British allies soon overran the place. The British had more trouble ousting the French who occupied Ischia in 1806; the devastation the British wreaked in their bombardment of the Castello Aragonese can still be seen.

Today the island once desperately coveted by Saracens is overrun by luggage-toting visitors, many here for its relaxing spas.

CHURCH HOURS
Ischia's many churches tend to open at the discretion of their priests. In general, though, most can be visited from around 7am to 11am and from 5pm or 6pm to 7pm or 8pm. To be sure of getting in, go immediately before or after the Mass times (posted on the door).

To add to the excitement, many churches are known by several different names, and confusion can often ensue.

BOOKING A HOTEL
Many hotels offer only half board (meaning breakfast and dinner are included), especially during the summer months. But ask firmly for *camera con colazione* (bed and breakfast) and most will reluctantly quote you a price. You'll also find that single supplements are almost always added on if you're travelling alone.

Most Ischia hotels close for the whole winter (November to March). But a growing number are now open a couple of weeks around Christmas and New Year, and some offer limited accommodation through the winter. If you fancy a Yuletide break, it is worth phoning to see whether the hotel of your choice has decided to follow this trend.

Castello Aragonese. *See p198.*

Ischia Porto & Ponte

Once two separate towns, Ischia Porto and Ischia Ponte are now one long, colourful, hotel-, shop- and tree-filled agglomeration, stretching from the ferry port to Castello Aragonese.

The swift and complex manoeuvring of ferries and hydrofoils in the little port can distract you from the uniqueness of the harbour itself. Until 1854, this was an inland lake in an extinct volcanic crater, but while the island was under Spanish control, King Ferdinand II was sickened by the smell of its brackish waters, and so demanded that an opening be made to the sea. The 150-year celebrations of the port have brought about its restoration, but you still need to be prepared for traffic jams blocking access to the ferries on busy Sunday evenings.

Overlooking the port, the church of **Santa Maria di Portosalvo**, also built in 1854, was another of Ferdinand's good works.

East of the church, the former royal palace is now a military spa, of all things, and is reached down a driveway guarded by imposing lions on the gateposts. Across the road, another old spa, the **Antiche Terme Comunali**, now houses government offices and hosts occasional (often mediocre) art exhibitions.

On the eastern shore of the port, via Porto leads past restaurants and bars out to the point at **Punta San Pietro**, which is dominated by a dark-red underwater research station, closed to the public.

Ischia's pedestrianised main drag – via Roma, which becomes corso Vittoria Colonna – is usually packed with people. Lanes running north of via Roma lead to the town's main beach. Where corso Colonna meets via Gigante, is the church of **San Pietro** (aka Madonna delle Grazie, or Purgatorio), a baroque extravaganza with a curving façade.

Just beyond the junction with via D'Avalos, a gate off the main road leads to the unkempt but beautifully shady gardens of the **Villa Nenzi Bozzi** (open 7am-8pm daily). Looking uphill from here, the stone pines – those that haven't been sacrificed to creeping construction – are all that remains of the woods planted in the mid 19th century on the great lava flow from Monte Arso; beneath them is an entire village – **Geronda** – that was buried in the devastating 1301 eruption. The little chapel of **San Girolamo dell'Arso** (or Madonna della Pace) commemorates the disaster.

The eastern end of corso Colonna, and via Pontano, run along the **spiaggia dei Pescatori**, where fishing boats pull up among the sunbathers along an expanse of dark sand, and where there's an unimpeded view across to the Castello. The church of **Santa Maria delle Grazie e Sant'Antonio**, at the top of the steps off corso Colonna, was built in the 18th century to replace the 14th-century original.

Via Seminario is home to the **Palazzo del Vescovado** (Bishop's Palace, open 3-5pm Mon, 9.30am-noon Wed, Fri) where sarcophagi from the fourth century to the 14th century are on display. Opposite, Vicolo Marina leads to **Palazzo Malcoviti**, where much of *The Talented Mr Ripley* was shot; stark and forbidding as you approach, the palazzo hides a pretty flower-filled courtyard behind.

On via Mazzella, the 17th-century church of **Santo Spirito** (aka San Giovan Giuseppe) has a fine 18th-century marble altar. Across the road from here, the **Assunta** (aka Santa Maria della Scala) became Ischia's cathedral after its predecessor in the Castello Aragonese was bombarded by the Royal Navy in 1809. The original 13th-century church was replaced in the 17th and 18th centuries, but the 14th-century baptismal font survived, as did the Romanesque wooden crucifix, and a 14th-century painting of the Madonna in the right-hand end of the nave.

Facing the cathedral **Palazzo dell' Orologio** is home to the engaging **Museo del Mare**, where nets, tackle, photos, stamps, and a few classic posters of films shot on the island chart Ischia's relationship with the sea. Via Mazzella continues to the lovely 1432 **Ponte Aragonese** bridge, and then on to the **Castello Aragonese** (*see below*).

CASTELLO ARAGONESE

The rocky outcrop on which the Castello sits was fortified in the fifth century BC by Greeks from Syracuse in Sicily. Since then it's been used as a stronghold by Romans, Goths, Arabs and just about every other group that ruled, or tried to rule, Naples. When Monte Arso erupted in 1301, it was within the thick walls of the castle that the locals sought protection.

Alfonso of Aragon fortified the crumbling rock in the mid 15th century, adding the bridge and making the Castello into an impregnable fortress where the island's inhabitants could hole up during Saracen attacks. In the 16th century, it was home to a brilliant court centred around Vittoria Colonna, wife of Ischia's feudal chief. Beautiful, devout and learned, Vittoria made the rocky outcrop in the Mediterranean a cultural centre. Her verses were praised by the poet Ludovico Ariosto and her learning by the humanist philosopher Pietro Bembo. But it was Vittoria's profound and touchingly platonic relationship with Michelangelo that ensured her lasting fame (he may have lived in the tower that bears his name near the castle, *see p199*). 'Nature, that never made so fair a face, remained ashamed, and tears were in all eyes,' wrote Michelangelo in 1574 after watching over Vittoria on her death bed.

By the 18th century, the Castello held 2,000 families, 13 churches, and a few Poor Clare (Clarisse) nuns. A hundred years later, with the Saracen no longer a threat, the families had moved out and the castle was falling into ruin. What time didn't destroy, the British did when they bombarded the island in 1809 in a bid to oust its French occupiers. The crippled fortress was later used as a prison.

There's a lift up to the castle's higher levels, but if you're feeling energetic, take the magnificent tunnel hewn through the solid rock by King Alfonso. Paths to the Castello's various churches and viewpoints are clearly signposted.

Inside the castle, the 18th-century church of the **Immacolata** has a stark white interior built to a Greek cross plan, and holds temporary exhibitions. The convent of **Santa Maria della Consolazione** was a convenient place for families with more titles than funds to park their dowry-less younger daughters. When the nuns died, their corpses were placed sitting upright on macabre thrones in the *cimitero* beneath the convent. The living visited their

Watching over **Ischia Porto**. *See p197.*

decomposing sisters daily as a stark reminder of mortality. The nuns remained ensconced in their convent until 1809.

The **Cattedrale dell'Assunta** was erected in the castle after the 1301 eruption, but, like so many of the region's churches, it was given a heavy baroque reworking in the early 18th century. The stucco decorations that survived the British bombardment are eerily lovely. In the cathedral crypt are fragments of 14th-century frescos created by followers of Giotto.

The elegant, grey-and-white hexagonal church of **San Pietro a Pantaniello** was constructed in the mid 16th century.

The Castello is now in private ownership; the former ruler's residence at the top of the building is closed to the public.

Ischia's own private Atlantis, the Roman town of Aenaria, may lie immediately to the east. According to contemporary records, this thriving settlement sank beneath the waves some time during the second century AD. Underwater explorers have come up with a sufficient number of ancient artefacts from the zone to lend some credence to the legend.

Around the Bay of Cartaromana, the 16th-century chapel of **Sant'Anna** overlooks rocks thrusting out of the sea. Brightly decorated fishing boats and rafts from Ischia, Procida and Capri compete for a trophy in the bay on 26 July each year in a multicoloured celebration and spectacular firework display. Nearby, the solid, square **Torre Michelangelo** (open occasionally in summer for concerts) may or may not be where the great Renaissance artist stayed when attracted to Ischia by Vittoria Colonna and her court.

Castello Aragonese

081 992 834. **Open** *Mar-Nov* 9am-1hr before sunset daily; also 10 days over Christmas. **Admission** €8. **No credit cards**.

Museo del Mare

Via Giovanni da Procida 2 (081 981 124). **Open** *Nov-Jan, Mar* 10.30am-12.30pm daily. *Apr-June, Sept, Oct* 10am-12.30pm, 5-8pm daily. *July, Aug* 10.30am-12.30pm, 6.30-10pm daily. Closed Feb. **Admission** €2.58. **No credit cards**.

Where to eat & drink

Alberto a Mare

Via Cristoforo Colombo 8 (081 981 259). **Open** noon-3pm, 7-11pm daily. Closed Nov-mid Mar. **Average** €50. **Credit** AmEx, MC, V.

Sitting on a platform jutting out over the blue sea, Alberto serves imaginative versions of local favourites; the pasta with *spigola* (sea bass), almonds and tomato is excellent.

Bar Calise

Piazza degli Eroi 69 (081 991 270). **Open** *Nov-Mar* 7am-2am Mon, Tue, Thur-Sun. *Apr-Oct* 7am-2am daily. **Credit** MC, V.

The jungle at the centre of this traffic roundabout conceals one of the island's best bars, where the ice-cream's good and the cakes are great.

Da Ciccio

Piazza Antica Reggia 5 (081 991 314). **Open** *Nov-Feb* 7am-midnight Tue-Sun. *Mar-Oct* 7am-2am daily. **No credit cards**.

Ciccio makes perhaps the best ice-cream on the island. The coffee's good too, and there's an enormous selection of mouth-watering cakes.

Cocò

Piazzale Aragonese (081 981 823). **Open** *Mar, Apr, Oct-Dec* 12.30-3pm, 7.30-11pm Mon, Tue, Thur-Sun. *May-Sept* 12.30-3pm, 7.30-11pm daily. Closed Jan, Feb. **Average** €40. **Credit** AmEx, DC, MC, V.

Right at the 'mainland' end of the Ponte Aragonese, Cocò is frequented by locals who appreciate the simple seafood pasta and fish dishes.

Damiano

Via Variante Esterna (081 983 032). **Open** *Sept, Oct, Apr, May* 8pm-midnight Mon-Sat; noon-3pm, 8pm-midnight Sun. *June-Aug* 8pm-midnight Mon-Sat; 8pm-midnight Sun. Closed Nov-Mar. **Average** €45. **Credit** DC, MC, V.

Slightly overpriced, and resting on its laurels, Damiano will have to work hard to keep its place among Ischia's top restaurants. But the fish is fresh and the view is lovely. Note there's no Sunday lunch opening from June to August.

Oh! X Bacco

Via Luigi Mazzella 20 (081 991 354). **Open** *Nov-Feb* 6pm-midnight Mon, Wed; 11am-3pm, 6pm-midnight Thur-Sun. *Mar-Oct* 11am-3pm, 7pm-2am Mon, Wed-Sun. **Credit** DC, MC, V.

This wine bar serves hearty bruschette (from €4), salads, *salumeria* (charcuterie) and cheeses from all over the place. There's an excellent *menu degustazione* (taster menu) for €15.50.

Pane & Vino

Via Porto 24 (081 991 046). **Open** *Nov-mid Jan, Mar* 10am-1pm, 4.30-9.30pm Mon, Tue, Thur-Sun. *Apr-Oct* 10am-2am daily. Closed mid Jan-Feb. **Credit** MC, V.

The *pane* (bread) served here, in what is primarily a wine shop, is extraordinarily good, as are the cheeses, cold meats and the few hot dishes that change daily. Wash it all down with something from the fine range of *vino* that you can order by the glass or bottle at little more than off-the-shelf prices.

Sport

Captain Cook – Ischia Diving

Via Iasolino 106 (081 992 218/339 583 8463/www.captaincook.it). **Open** *Easter-Oct* 8.30am-1pm, 3-7.30pm daily. *Nov-Easter* by appointment. **Credit** MC, V.

Around Naples

Captain Cook organises night dives and marine nature dives for experienced divers between Ischia and Procida. A double dive costs from €62 and courses can be arranged for divers at all levels.

Tennis Lido
Via Cristoforo Colombo 2 (081 985 245). **Open** 8am-1pm, 3-9pm daily. **Admission** €12-€16 per court per hr. **No credit cards**.
These well-kept tennis courts are in a recently revamped park by Ischia Ponte's beach.

Car & scooter hire

Autonoleggio PA.AN
Via Iasolino 76 (081 982 332). **Open** *Apr-Oct* 8am-8pm daily. **Credit** MC, V.
Scooters from €25 per day.

M Balestrieri
Via Iasolino 35 (081 985 691/www.autonoleggio balestrieri.it). **Open** *Apr, May, Oct* 8am-1.30pm, 3.30-8pm daily. *June-Sept* 8am-8pm daily. *Nov-Mar* 8am-1.30pm, 3.30-8pm Mon-Sat. **Credit** MC, V.
Scooters cost from €20 a day, cars from €30. Staff can deliver hired vehicles straight to your hotel.

Where to stay

Miramare e Castello
Via Pontano 9 (081 991 333/www.miramaree castello.it). **Closed** mid Oct-mid Apr. **Rates** €114-€186 single; €164-€490 double. **Credit** AmEx, DC, MC, V.
Literally on the beach, and eyeball-to-eyeball with the Castello, the Miramare is tastefully furnished in shades of blue. Rates rise for rooms with a sea view and/or a balcony overlooking the sea. The spa centre offers weekly pampering packages from €161.

Il Monastero
Castello Aragonese 3 (081 992 435/www.castello aragonese.it). **Closed** mid Oct-Mar. **Rates** €65-€85 single; €100-€122 double. **Credit** AmEx, DC, MC, V.
Inside the Castello Aragonese, Il Monastero has one of the finest views anywhere in the world, and by Ischian standards it's cheap to stay here. The rooms could do with a facelift and there's no spa pampering, although renovations are slowly taking place under new, friendly management. Bed and breakfast only.

Il Moresco
Via E Gianturco 16 (081 981 355/www.ilmoresco.it). **Closed** mid Oct-mid Apr. **Rates** €175-€215 single; €240-€440 double; €440-€680 suite. **Credit** AmEx, DC, MC, V.
Part of a group that includes the newly restored Grand Hotel Excelsior across the road, the Moresco lives up to its name with low white Moorish-style arches and wrought-iron gratings. The gardens are delightful, it's close to the sea, there's a thermal pool in a rocky cave, and the staff are charming and informative.

La Villarosa
Via G Gigante 5 (081 991 316/www.lavillarosa.it). **Closed** Nov-Mar. **Rates** €83-€108 single; €140-€190 double. **Credit** AmEx, DC, MC, V.
Immersed in a jungly garden a close the centre, this is a homely place with comfortable nooks, family antiques in hidden corners and a fourth-floor dining room with a view over the town. There are chalets in among the greenery, plus all the usual spa treatments.

The north coast

Casamicciola Terme

Ischia's second port, Casamicciola, added *terme* (thermal spring) to its name in 1956. As far back as the first century AD, however, Pliny the Elder wrote about the town's Gurgitello spring, where water bubbles out of the earth at 80°F (27°C). Hundreds of years later, Casamicciola came up with the idea of combining thermal treatment for medical conditions and luxurious hotels.

By 1883, when the town was razed by an earthquake that killed 2,300 people, a stopover at Casamicciola was an essential part of any Grand Tour of Europe. And although a decrease in demand for spa cures has now driven many centres to shut down, there's still plenty of scope here for soaking, sweating and inhaling the waters from the natural wells and springs bubbling from verdant Monte Tabor above the town. The aim is serious cures rather than beauty pampering (*see p206* **Spa culture**).

Despite its ancient roots, most of what you see in Casamicciola today was built after the 1883 earthquake. The seafront is crowded with bars, while the desolate shell of the once-glorious **Pio Monte della Misericordia** spa dominates the central stretch; down a lane to the left of the hotel, a market (open 6am-3pm Mon-Fri) sells tacky clothes and fresh produce in the hotel's remains.

One block back from the congested coast road a warren of narrow streets features gaily painted houses. East of the Pio Monte, roads striking inland lead to corso Vittorio Emanuele, which winds uphill. Via Cretaio (left at the T-junction) heads up towards Monte Rotaro. Two kilometres (1.2 miles) along this road, on the left, there's a green metal bar across a track that leads into a volcanic crater. Thick with myrtle and huge oak trees, and criss-crossed by good walking paths, this strange depression looks pure sylvan glade. The idyll conceals a surprise, though: if you stumble across anything looking like a rabbit hole, you can put your hand inside to feel the volcanic steam the ground exhales.

Corso Vittorio Emanuele continues to piazza dei Bagni. Casamicciola's main *gurgitello* spring, below the **Terme Belliazzi** (*see p202*), has pools built by ancient Romans. Further uphill via Paradisiello leads to the huge red *municipio* (town hall) that dominates the town (it's also accessible by stairs from the town centre). The view from the square in front is stunning. The town council has also occupied Villa Bellavista, where the **Museo Civico** (*see below*) contains old photos and maps. Further up still, Casamicciola's parish church, the **Sacro Cuore** dates from 1898.

Museo Civico Villa Bellavista

Via Principessa Margherita, Casamicciola Terme (no phone). **Open** 9am-1pm Mon, Wed, Fri; 9am-1pm, 3-6pm Tue, Thur. *Guided tours* mid June-Oct 7-9pm Sat, Sun. **Admission** free.

Grand Hotel Mezzatorre. *See p202.*

Lacco Ameno

Piazza Santa Restituta and the candy-pink and white 19th-century church of the same name are the heart of this seaside town. The body of the Tunisian virgin-martyr Restituta arrived on nearby San Montano beach in the fourth century, borne (it was said) by lilies; this event is the theme for the church's artworks. Below, in the **Area Archeologica di Santa Restituta**, are the remains of a fourth-century Christian basilica, a second-century BC Roman town and some much older Greek artefacts.

Uphill from the piazza, the 18th-century **Villa Arbusto** is home to the **Museo Archeologico di Pithecusae** with its beautifully arranged artefacts. One of its prize possessions is 'Nestor's Cup', inscribed with probably the oldest writing – and the oldest transcription of a Homeric verse – in existence. The garden, and its view, are delightful.

Lacco Ameno's best-known landmark is the fungo (mushroom), sitting in the water off the seafront promenade. This piece of volcanic rock is ten metres (33 feet) tall. It is thought to have been catapulted here thousands of years ago by a rumbling Mount Epomeo.

Heading west out of town, the **Baia di San Montano** has one of the island's best beaches – follow signs to the **Negombo** spa (*see p202*) to reach the long sand crescent. There's a public end, a section for guests at the Hotel della Baia and another for those who have paid for a session at the spa.

Area Archeologica di Santa Restituta

Piazza Santa Restituta, Lacco Ameno (081 980 538). **Open** 9.30am-12.30pm, 4.30-6pm Mon-Sat; 9.30am-12.30pm Sun. Closed Nov-Mar. **Admission** €3. **No credit cards.**

Museo Archeologico di Pithecusae

Villa Arbusto, corso Angelo Rizzoli 210, Lacco Ameno (081 900 356/www.pithecusae.it). **Open** 9.30am-12.30pm, 3-7pm Tue-Sun. Sometimes closed Nov, Dec. **Admission** €5. **No credit cards.**

Where to stay & eat

You'll need your own transport or a taxi to reach the best restaurant in Casamicciola, which is around five kilometres out of town in the hills. At **Il Focolare** (via Cretaio, 081 980 604, www.trattoriailfocolare.it, closed Wed Oct-Apr, closed lunch Mon-Fri & 3wks Dec, average €35), members of the D'Ambra family use mountain resources – rabbit, snails and herbs – to create wonderful earthy dishes.

Lacco Ameno's **Albergo Regina Isabella & Royal Sporting** (piazza San Restituta 1,

Around Naples

081 994 322, www.reginaisabella.it, closed Jan-Mar, doubles €123-€518 half board per person) is a grand hotel. True, the grandeur is somewhat faded, but it's elegant nonetheless, with a pool overlooking the beach, and a glorious spa treatment centre. The **Villa Angelica** (via IV Novembre 28, 081 994 524, www.villaangelica.it, closed Nov-Mar, doubles €100-€160) is a beautiful, palm-filled hotel with a thermal pool and massage treatments.

Off the road between Lacco and Forio, the **Hotel della Baia** (via San Montano, 081 995 453, closed mid Oct-mid Apr, doubles €114-€144) is quiet, comfortable, and on one of Ischia's loveliest beaches. Further up the road, down a secluded lane, the stately **Grand Hotel Mezzatorre** (via Mezzatorre 23, 081 986 111, www.mezzatorre.it, closed Nov-Mar, doubles €290-€500) has pastel rooms with neo-classical paintings, an excellent spa and lovely views from the guestrooms.

Spas

Negombo

Via Baia di San Montano, Lacco Ameno (081 986 152/www.negombo.it). **Open** 8.30am-7pm daily. Closed mid Oct-mid Apr. **Rates** €25-€27 per day. **Credit** AmEx, DC, MC, V.

In a beautiful garden with more than 500 exotic plant species, the Negombo has thermal and sports facilities, plus access to – and deckchairs on – the pretty San Montano beach.

Terme Belliazzi

Piazza Bagni 134, Casamicciola (081 994 580/ www.termebelliazzi.it). **Open** *Apr-Oct* 7am-noon, 5-7pm Mon-Sat. Closed Nov-Mar. **No credit cards.**

This neo-classical temple to the healthy body is built over ancient Roman pools (which may be visited) and offers massages (€20-€45), a dip in the heated pool and whirlpool bath (€22) and mud treatments (€28).

Terme della Regina Isabella

Piazza San Restituta, Lacco Ameno (081 994 322/ www.reginaisabella.it). **Open** 8am-12.15pm, 5-7.30pm Mon-Sat; 8am-12.15pm Sun. Closed Jan-Mar. **Credit** AmEx, DC, MC, V.

This spa is decidedly in the grand style, with various massages ranging from €37-€93, a host of skin treatments and personal gym programmes.

Car & scooter hire

Giuseppe di Meglio

Via Tommaso Morgera 4, Casamicciola (081 980 312/www.ischia-autonoleggio.it). **Open** *Mar-Oct* 8am-1pm, 2-8pm daily. *Nov-Feb* 8am-1pm, 2-8pm Mon-Sat. **Credit** AmEx, DC, MC, V.

Right across from the ferry port, this outlet rents scooters from €25 per day, Mini-Mokes for €39 and other cars from €32.

Resources

See p207.

Forio & the West Coast

Forio

The largest town on Ischia, with around 20,000 residents, Forio has some of the island's best restaurants and most of its worst traffic jams. In times past, its problems were more severe, of course. Its exposed position left it prey to attacks by Saracen pirates, so 12 watchtowers were built along the coast. One of them, **Il Torrione**, dates from 1480 and dominates the town centre with its craggy crenellation. It's open occasionally for small exhibitions.

There are 17 churches in and around Forio, most of which were heavily reworked during the 18th century, and none of which contains outstanding artworks or observes regular opening hours.

Standing apart from the town on its headland (where Forio's youth congregates in the evening), the stark, white **Santuario della Madonna del Soccorso** would not look out of place in Spain; there are pretty majolica Stations of the Cross around the steps outside the church. In corso Umberto, a church has stood where the **Santa Maria di Loreto** is now since the 14th century; in piazza del Municipio (which has a great sea view) much of the **convento di San Francesco** is now occupied by council offices but the church can be visited. In the **Santa Maria della Grazie** (aka Visitapovere) nearby, alms were dispensed in the 17th century; in the piazza of the same name, **San Vito** is Forio's parish church.

Just north of Forio, along the road to Lacco Ameno, a sign points left to **La Mortella**, an award-winning garden that was carved out of a volcanic stone quarry. Designed by renowned British landscapist Russell Page, the garden was completed by Susana Walton – widow of the composer Sir William Walton – and here New Zealand tree ferns unfurl with a prehistoric languor, alongside heavily scented Amazon water lilies. Having arrived on the island at the end of the 1940s in search of sun, quiet and inspiration, Walton and his young Argentinian wife set about turning a wild plot of land – described by their friend Laurence Olivier as 'nothing but a quarry' – into one of southern Italy's most luxurious gardens.

The William Walton Trust, which runs the garden, also provides accommodation and coach-ing for young musicians, and organises weekend classical music concerts (included in the price of admission) from April to June, and

Luscious gardens of
La Mortella. *See p204.*

September and October. To get there, take a circular bus from Lacco Ameno to Forio, or vice versa, and ask the driver to set you down at La Mortella or take the Forio minibus straight to the door.

A few kilometres further down the lane, through typical Ischian countryside mercifully free of holiday flats, past a breathtaking belvedere, is **La Colombaia** (*see p150*). Luchino Visconti's villa is now a film foundation and cultural centre, with regular exhibitions and events.

La Mortella

Via F Calise 35, Forio (081 986 220/www.ischia.it/ lamortella). **Open** *Apr-mid Nov* 9am-7pm Tue, Thur, Sat, Sun. **Concerts** *Apr-June, Sept, Oct* 5pm Sat, Sun; arrive at least 30mins early to be sure of a seat. **Admission** €10. **No credit cards**.

Monte Epomeo & the south-west

Looming over Forio to the east, **Monte Epomeo** – Ischia's highest point at 787 metres (2,582 feet) – can be ascended by walking up via Monterone or via Bocca to one of the badly marked paths that lead through the glorious Falanga forest to the summit.

If Forio's long town beaches don't appeal, **spiaggia di Citara** to the south has another long stretch of sand, although much of it has been monopolised by the fabulous spa, **Giardini Poseidon** (*see p204*).

Sorgeto, another beach treat, can be reached from the nearby village of Panza, although it's easy to miss the flaking, half-hidden signs directing you to the beach. A series of hairpin bends, then some long flights of stairs, lead down to the rocky cove. In the eastern corner, a thermal spring gushes up between the rocks and into the sea at about 90°F (32°C). Alternatively, there is normal cold water with hot rock-pool soaking.

Where to stay & eat

Cheap beds can be found in the Forio area at the busy youth hostel **Il Gabbiano** (via Provinciale Panza 182, 081 909 422, closed Nov-Mar, rates €16 per person) right above Citara beach, and also at the pretty farm **Il Vitigno** (via Bocca 31, 081 998 307, www.ilvitigno.com, closed Nov-Mar, double €70-€90) where the restaurant (average €18) will serve delicious meals of home-grown produce to non-guests too, but only if they book.

Well south of town, the **Hotel Punta Chiarito** (via Sorgeto 51, 081 908 102, www.puntachiarito.it, double €136-€180)

is another attractive option. It perches on a spectacular peninsula jutting out into the sea between Sorgeto beach and Sant'Angelo. Rooms are pleasant, and there's a beautifully landscaped garden with a thermal pool; some rooms have kitchens.

If good hotels are a rarity in Forio, the same is not true of restaurants. Beneath the Soccorso church, **Umberto a Mare** (via Soccorso 2, 081 997 171, www.umberto amare.it, closed Jan, Feb, and Mon, Wed in Nov, Dec & Mar, average €35) has delicate pasta with squid and asparagus, or *al profumo di mare,* the freshest of fish, and a great orange sorbet. If you can't bear to leave there are ten bright rooms (doubles €100-€180). The central **Bar Stany & Elio** (via Castellaccio 77, 081 997 668, closed 2 weeks in Oct) serves some of the best ice-cream on Ischia.

Off the coast road heading south, Ischia's only Michelin-star restaurant, **Il Melograno**, (via G Mazzella 110, 081 998 450, closed Jan-mid Mar, Mon in Oct & Mon, Tue in Nov, Dec, average €55) does excellent raw seafood *antipasti* and delicious *orecchiette* pasta with clams, mussels, broccoli and chilli. The fish is fresh off the boat and the outside patio is charming.

Miles up a tortuous road leading to Monte Epomeo, **Da Peppina di Renato** (Via Bocca 42, 081 998 312, closed Dec-mid Mar, Wed in Apr, May & Oct, average €30) has great pizza and good fish, but isn't open for lunch.

Pietratorcia (via Provinciale Panza 267, 081 907 277, www.pietratorcia.it, closed mid Nov-Mar, lunch mid June-mid Sept) is one of Ischia's leading wine producers; taste the grape on a sunny terrace where *assaggi* of three different wines and a big plate of cheese and cold meats cost €12; the chef will cook full meals in the summer evenings, but only if you order in advance; open until late evening in summer.

Spas

Giardini Poseidon

Via Mazzella, spiaggia di Citara (081 908 7111/ www.giardiniposeidon.it). **Open** *May-Oct* 8.30am-7pm daily. *Apr* 9am-6.30pm daily. Closed Nov-mid Apr. **Rates** €25 per day. **Credit** AmEx, MC, V. This grand old spa is really a complex with saunas, 21 pools, jacuzzis and a long private beach – all run with firm Teutonic efficiency. Credit cards are accepted for massages and health treatments only, so bring a bit of cash with you.

Resources

See p207.

www.hotelcelestino.it, closed mid Oct-Apr, doubles €130-€240) is a reliable option in the village centre.

Lo Scoglio (via Cava Ruffano 58, 081 999 529, closed mid Nov-mid Dec, Jan-Mar, average €25) perches on a cliff overlooking Sant'Angelo, with fresh sea spray on the windows, and fresh seafood on its plates.

In the port, **La Tavernetta del Pirata** (via Sant'Angelo 77, 081 999 251, closed Jan, closed Wed in Oct, Nov) is Sant'Angelo's hippest bar, and a good place to sink an *aperitivo* or a seafood snack (served all day, average €20).

When you can't face any more seafood, **Da Pasquale** (via Sant'Angelo 79, 081 904 208, closed mid Nov-mid Mar) will stock you up with good, cheap pizza and beer, to be eaten alongside noisy crowds on long benches.

Spas

Parco Termale Aphrodite Apollon

Via Petrelle, Sant'Angelo (081 999 219/ www.aphrodite.it). **Open** *Apr-Oct* 8.30am-6pm daily. **Admission** €21 all day; €16 after 1pm. **Credit** AmEx, DC, MC, V.
Rambling over the headland east of Sant'Angelo, the sprawling Aphrodite has 12 pools, saunas, gyms and even a boat-taxi from Sant'Angelo port is included in its admission fee. There's a nude bathing area. Massages (from €30) and medical treatments are extra.

Terme di Cava Scura

Via Cava Scura, spiaggia dei Maronti, Serrara Fontana (081 905 564/www.cavascura.com). **Open** 8.30am-1.30pm, 2.30-6pm daily. Closed mid Oct-mid Apr. **No credit cards.**
Squeezed between (and hewn out of) tall cliffs at the end of a long coast walk, this is a spa for devotees. There's a natural sauna in a dingy cave, grave-like baths with steaming sulphurous water (€24), massages (€20) and thermal and beauty treatments.

Sport

Roja Diving Center

Hotel Conte, via Nazario Sauro 54, Sant'Angelo (081 999 214/338 762 0145/www.ischiadiving.it). **Open** by appointment only. **No credit cards.**
Roja does single dives from €27 and also runs training courses for groups.

Resources

Hospital

Ospedale Rizzoli *Via De Luca Antonio 20, Ischia Porto (081 983164).*

Internet

Turboplay *Via Vittoria Colonna 147, Ischia (no phone).*

Police

Carabinieri *Via Casciaro 22, Ischia (081 991 065; emergencies 112).*

Post office

Via De Luca Antonio 42, Ischia Porto (081 507 4611). **Open** 8am-6.30pm Mon-Fri; 8am-12.30pm Sat.

Tourist information

Azienda Autonoma di Cura Soggiorno e Turismo *Corso Vittoria Colonna 108 (081 507 4231/www.infoischiaprocida.it).* **Open** 9am-1.30pm, 3-7.30pm Mon-Sat.
Ischia's tourist office also has a branch by the Ischia Porto hydrofoil dock in piazzale Trieste. Opening times are erratic.

Getting around

By boat

Capitan Morgan (081 985 080, www.capitan morgan.it) organises boat trips around the island (tickets €12), and day trips to Capri (€21).

By bus

Sepsa (081 991 808) runs a highly efficient, if crowded, bus service around the island. The main routes are the *circolare sinistra,* which circles the island anticlockwise, stopping at Ischia Porto, Casamicciola, Lacco Ameno, Forio, Serrara, Fontana, Barano, returning to Ischia Porto; and the *circolare destra,* which covers the same route in a clockwise direction. The services run every 30mins, with buses every 15mins during rush hours. There are also services from Ischia Porto to Sant'Angelo (every 15mins), Giardini Poseidon at Citara (every 30mins) and Spiaggia dei Maronti via Testaccio (every 20mins). In addition, minibus services operate within Ischia Porto and Ponte, and in Forio. Tickets must be purchased before boarding; get them (along with bus maps and timetables) at the terminus in Ischia Porto, or at any *tabacchi* or newsstand. Tickets cost €1.20 (single trip), €4 (24hr), €6 (48hr), €15 (weekly) and €22 (fortnightly).

Getting there

By boat

Several boat companies, including Caremar (081 551 3882, www.caremar.it), Lauro (081 551 3352, www.lauro.it) and Traghetti Pozzuoli (081 526 7736) run regular hydrofoil and car ferry services between Ischia (from Porto and Casamicciola) and the mainland (from Naples and Pozzuoli), plus less frequent ones between Ischia Porto and Capri, Sorrento and Procida. Naples to Ischia takes about 1hr 35mins by ferry and costs around €7, depending on the company, or 45mins by hydrofoil (around €11- €14). State-subsidised Caremar is the cheapest and most crowded. Lauro also runs a hydrofoil direct to Forio. Some companies accept internet pre-bookings, but not credit card payment. There's a charge for ordering advance hydrofoil tickets, but it's worth it on crowded summer Sundays.

Around Naples

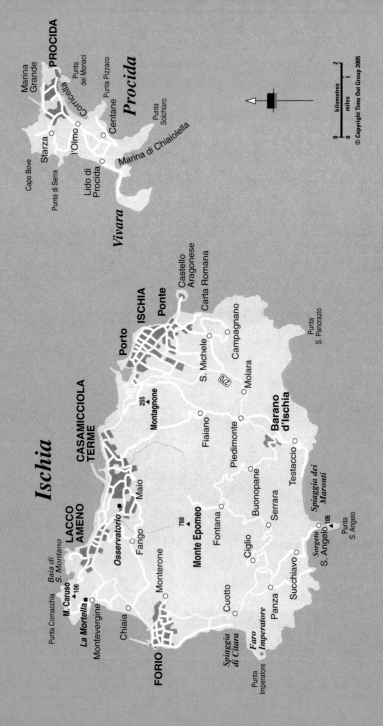

Ischia

PROCIDA

Marina Grande

PROCIDA

Capo Bove

Corricella

Punta dei Monaci

Starza

l'Olmo

Centane

Punta Pizzaco

Punta di Serra

Lido di Procida

Procida

Marina di Chiaiolella

Punta Solchiaro

Vivara

CASAMICCIOLA TERME

Porto

ISCHIA

Ponte

S. Michele

Castello Aragonese

Carta Romana

LACCO AMENO

Baia di S. Montano

Punta Comacchia

M. Caruso ▲ 106

La Mortella ■

Montevergine

Chiaia

Osservatorio ■

Fango

Maio

255 ▲ Montagnone

Campagnano

Punta S. Pancrazio

Monterone

788 ▲ Monte Epomeo

Fontana

Fiaiano

270

Molara

Piedimonte

Barano d'Ischia

FORIO

Spiaggia di Citara

Faro Imperatore ■

Punta Imperatore

Cuotto

Panza

Succhiavo

Ciglio

Serrara

Buonopane

Testaccio

Spiaggia dei Maronti

Sorgeto ○ S. Angelo

Punta S. Angelo

▲ 106

0 ... kilometres ... 1 ... 2
0 ... miles ... 1

© Copyright Time Out Group 2005

Procida

Island retreat a short hop from the city.

Procida at dusk.

One of the smallest dots in the Gulf of Naples and the most densely inhabited island in the Med, Procida barely stretches out to four square kilometres (one-and-a-half square miles), but its population explodes from a low-season 11,000 to up to 22,000 in August. And yet, even with the crowds, the island has its own particular charm.

In the past, the local economy revolved around lemon groves and the sea – Procida has produced generations of fishermen and sailors. Today, though, it's tourism that fills the coffers: smart cafés and restaurants line the harbours, and yachts tie up at gleaming Marina Grande. On the down side, cheaply built holiday homes have sprouted in the old orchards, lemons rot unpicked and in August the place really heaves. But even then there's still space to stroll through lemon groves, savour a freshly made *granita di limone* (lemon ice) or watch the day's catch being offloaded from boats: a perfect way to spend a few days' break away from the hustle of Naples.

Frequent Saracen attacks in the Middle Ages forced the villagers to flee to the highest point of the island, Terra Murata. The characteristic local architecture, with its steep staircases, arches and loggias, dates back to this period.

Procida really began to develop in the 16th century, despite continuing attacks by pirates. (In 1544, according to local legend, Barbarossa the barbarian fled the island after a miraculous vision of St Michael in the Terra Murata, but not before indulging in a little rape and pillage.) Medieval Terra Murata was fortified after 1520, but the defence mentality was already fading by then. Prosperous families from the mainland built summer homes on the island, shipbuilders constructed family *palazzi*, and the population

ventured outside the walls to make Marina Grande the centre of the fishing industry. Sailing ships were built next to the port until the end of the 19th century.

This was a favourite haunt of the Bourbon kings who, in 1744, bought the Castello d'Avalos and did the island the dubious honour of turning it into a royal hunting reserve.

Approaching Procida by ferry, the view is dominated by the formidable Castello – an Italian Alcatraz until 1986 – surrounded by the gently faded colours of the fishermen's houses, with their traditional arches and loggias.

Ferries dock in the **Marina Grande** among the fishing boats moored in front of modern cafés and restaurants. Old men sit on the edge of the wharf mending their nets. The fish stalls – all run by fishermen – open in the afternoon (4pm until the catch is sold out, Monday to Friday). They sell only what they have caught that day from the Canale di Procida: prawns, red mullet and squid, as well as the familiar *misto di paranza* (small fish and seafood caught in the fishermen's nets) for frying.

Towards the eastern end of the Marina Grande, by the church of **Santa Maria della Pietà** (1760), the steep via Vittorio Emanuele leads off to the right up into the centre of the island. Some 100 metres (350 feet) further on the left, via Principe Umberto, with its old houses (peek through open gates to see the traditional courtyards and gardens), leads to **piazza dei Martiri**. From here, catch the view of the castle and the Terra Murata above, with the enchanting fishing village of Corricella below.

The road continues steeply past the forlorn, abandoned **Castello d'Avalos**. Built in the mid 16th century, the castle belonged to the D'Avalos family until it was bought by the Bourbon kings in 1744.

From here it's not far to the **Porta di Mezz' omo** (1563), which leads into the medieval **Terra Murata** walled village. Now you're up so high that there are breathtaking views over Naples and Capri, especially from via Borgo at the top of the hill, where the **Abbazia di San Michele Arcangelo** is built on the edge of the sheer rock. Dating from the 11th century, but remodelled in the 17th-19th centuries, the abbey has a painting (1699) by Luca Giordano of Archangel Michael on its coffered ceiling. Inside the building is an 8,000-strong religious manuscript library, a museum containing religious thank-you pictures from shipwrecked sailors, an 18th-century Nativity scene, and a maze of catacombs (once the local cemetery) leading on to a secret chapel.

Procida's fascinating Good Friday *processione dei misteri* starts here at the abbey. In what was once a procession of flagellants, a life-size wooden sculpture (dating from 1754) of the dead Christ is carried under a black veil by fishermen from the Abbazia to Marina Grande. It is followed by the other *misteri* – handmade wooden models that represent religious scenes – carried by the Turchini fraternity, in white habits and turquoise capes, and by children in medieval costume.

Not far from the abbey, the ruins of the 16th-century church of **Santa Margherita Nuova** stand on the Punta dei Monaci.

From piazza dei Martiri, the little harbour at **Corricella** is reached down the Scalinata Scura steps. On the way you'll pass tiny houses massed on the rock with arches and communal entrances (some have been renovated into chic homes for weekenders). The bay, exposed to African winds, has a mild microclimate where bananas grow.

From the western end of Corricella steps lead up to via Scotti, where 18th-century buildings

have vaulted entrances leading to flowery gardens, lemon trees and terraces overlooking the sea. As you pick up via Vittorio Emanuele again, the road (unpleasant at this point, with cars and scooters screaming by) brings you to the southernmost part of the island.

From piazza Olmo, via Pizzaco leads to **Pizzaco**, where a lovely nature walk rounds a crumbling promontory with fantastic views across to Corricella and Terra Murata. The beach below – **la Chiaja** – is reached from the piazza by about 180 steps. Flagging spirits can be revived at the excellent beach trattoria **La Conchiglia** (*see p211*).

Via Giovanni da Procida leads from piazza Olmo to **Chiaiolella**, a small yacht marina, enclosed by two promontories. On the western side of the island, the kilometre of sand stretching from Chiaiolella to Ciriaccio is Procida's most fashionable (and most crowded) beach, the **Lido**. At the southern tip of the Lido, a lane leads to a bridge connecting Procida to the nature reserve of Vivara (*see p211*).

The north-east of Procida between the lighthouse on Punta di Pioppeto and Punta Serra takes you off the beaten track (even in high season), with lanes meandering through lemon groves and fantastic sea views. From piazza Olmo, via Flavio Gioia leads to a belvedere with an outstanding view over Chiaiolella, Vivara and Ischia. A short path hugs the promontory of Punta Serra, overlooking the sea. Via Flavio Gioia heads to the old cemetery and, below, is **Pozzo Vecchio** beach (café open during summer), made famous by the film *Il Postino*. The road (at this point, via Cesare Battisti) passes a restored 16th-century tower and hamlet. Via Rinaldi (left) rambles past isolated farmhouses and woodlands (taking in yet more views) to the lighthouse, from where via Faro leads back to the main road.

Piazza dei Martiri. *See p209.*

Off Procida's south-western tip and reached by footbridge, the tiny island nature reserve of **Vivara** was inhabited even before Procida: traces of Neolithic remains have been found here. Once a hunting reserve for the Bourbon kings, this is one of the most beautiful and unspoilt nature reserves in Italy. More than 150 species of birds live or migrate through here. You may spot the island's rare species of rat – it's the one walking on its hind legs.

The path from Vivara's gatehouse leads up through woodland with glimpses of the sea. An overgrown path to the right winds down to the ruins of a hamlet beside the coast. In the centre of the island is an abandoned manor house with a loggia, and an old olive press in the cellar. The path continues down to a lookout point.

Regrettably, Vivara has been closed to the public for the past several years. (Needless to say, locals are not deterred from ducking through the fence.) Restricted opening is planned for 2005. Contact the Pro Loco (*see p212*) for details.

Abbazia di San Michele Arcangelo

Via Terra Murata 89 (081 896 7612). **Open** 10am-12.45pm, 3-6pm Mon-Sat; 9.45am-12.45pm Sun. **Admission** Church free. *Museum, library & catacombs* €2. **No credit cards.**

Santa Maria della Pietà

081 896 7005. **Open** 8.30am-noon, 5-8pm Sun. The church is currently being restored, so it may be closed in the mornings.

Where to eat & drink

In recent years, the choice and quality of restaurants on Procida have improved, but prices have jumped to match, and in August and on summer weekends, queues and grumpy, overworked staff are the norm.

Among the many restaurants on the Marina Grande harbour, **Fammivento** (via Roma 39, 081 896 9020, closed Mon Sept-June, and all of Jan, Feb, average €28) offers the best value with friendly service under the beady eye of Filippo the parrot. Enormous portions of pasta are served with fresh fish and vegetables. The squid and artichokes, octopus *alla genovese* stewed with onions) is a favourite.

Locals go to **Il Cantinone** (via Roma 55-57, 081 896 8811, closed Tue Sept-Mar, and all of Jan, Feb, average €15) for the wood-fired pizza. Start with the marinated tuna or anchovies.

Bar Roma (via Roma 163, 081 896 7460, closed Tue Oct-Apr), tucked away next to the church of Santa Maria della Pietà, has great cakes. Or rub elbows with yachting types and Neapolitan intellectuals while quaffing the cocktails at **Bar del Cavaliere** (via Roma 42-3, 081 810 1074, closed Mon Oct-Mar).

Wait for the boat or just hang out at friendly **Bar Capriccio** (via Roma 99, 081 896 9506, closed Thur Oct-May), one of the few bars that offers lunchtime snacks.

Corricella's **Gorgonia** (Marina Corricella 50, 081 810 1060, closed Nov-Feb) is good for fish, vegetables and desserts. Those travelling by yacht can moor next to the restaurant.

And for a romantic evening, take a private boat ride from Corricella to family-run **La Conchiglia** on Chiaja beach (no car access, steps from via Pizzaco 10, piazza Olmo, 081 896 7602, closed mid Nov-Feb, average €25, booking necessary for boat ride) for pasta with seafood straight off the boat.

Experimental cooking inspired by local ingredients with a twist is the speciality at **La Pergola** (Via V Rinaldi 37, 081 896 9534, closed Mon Apr-July, Sept, Oct, closed Nov-Easter, average €40). Booking is advisable on summer evenings for this small garden restaurant where menus change daily according to the market – choices might include artichoke ravioli with rabbit, or fish ravioli with rocket pesto and clams.

For home cooking on the beach, lunch at **Grotte Blu** (via Roma 153, 081 896 0345, average €28; sea-front rooms also available), on the right of the port in Marina Grande. The Procida-style rabbit is delicious; takeaway snacks are good too – try a roll with mozzarella and *parmigiana di melezane* or green peppers.

Diving

Procida Diving Centre

via Marina Chiaiolella, Lido di Procida (081 896 8385/www.vacanzeaprocida.it). **Open** 9am-8pm daily. **Credit** MC, V. Diving courses and trips with expert instructors, and diving equipment hire.

Boats

The success of the long-established **Sailitalia** and the opening of the tourist port in **Marina Grande** makes Procida ideal for yacht charters.

Blue Dream

Via Ottimo 3 (081 810 0112/339 572 0874/ www.bluedreamcharter.com). Day trips, fishing and diving days and boat B&B in the Marina Grande, aboard a brand-new Beneteau.

Bluebone – Graziella Travel

For listings, see below Graziella Travel. This travel agency owns a yacht for local charters.

Ippocampo

Marina Chiaiolella, west side (081 810 1437/339 251 3525/www.ippocamposas.it). **Open** 9am-7pm daily. Closed Oct-Easter. **No credit cards.** Local *gozzi* (fishing boats) are hired for day trips (€60).

Around Naples

Sailitalia Procida

Via Roma 10 (081 896 9962/fax 081 896 9264/ www.sailitalia.it). **Open** 9.30am-1.30pm, 3.30-7.30pm Mon-Fri; 9.30am-1.30pm, 3.30-6.30pm Sat. **No credit cards**.

The most experienced charter firm in the area. Unusually, you can plan one-way trips such as Procida–Palermo at no extra cost. Skippers and crew are available on some boats. Prices range from a low-season week for four at €1,200 to a high-season crewed week on a 50ft Beneteau for €8,050.

Marina Grande

081 896 9668/335 820 3636.

The new tourist port of Marina Grande, opened in 2004 and due to be fully up and running by summer 2005, currently has mooring for 230 boats up to 18m. Prices are €40-€145/day (high season), €20-€75 (low).

Scooter hire

Autoricambi Sprint

Via Roma 28 (081 896 9435). **Open** 8.30am-1pm, 4.30-8pm Mon-Sat; 10am-noon Sun. **Credit** MC,V

A scooter is a good way to get around the island.

Travel agencies

ETP

Via Principe Umberto I, (081 896 9067/www.casa vacanza.net), **Open** Apr-Sept 9.30am-1pm, 5-8pm Mon-Sat. Oct-Mar 9.30am-1pm, 5-8pm Mon-Fri; 9.30am-1pm Sat. **Credit** AmEx, MC, V.

This offshoot of a well-established Ischia agency offers tickets and rentals.

Graziella Travel

Via Roma 117 (081 896 9594/www.isoladiprocida.it). **Open** Apr-Sept 9.30am-1pm, 4.30-8pm Mon-Sat. Oct-Mar 9.30am-1pm, 4.30-8pm Mon-Fri; 9.30am-1pm Sat. **Credit** DC, MC, V.

Offers train and plane tickets, bike hire, accommodation in fishermen's cottages, holiday flats and villas, and yacht charters. Check website for rentals.

Where to stay

Hotel accommodation is scarce so book well ahead for Easter, summer weekends and August. Another good option is to rent a fisherman's cottage through a travel agent, *see p212*, but ask for air-con and mosquito nets in summer.

Overlooking Corricella and under the Terra Murata is the romantic **La Casa sul Mare** (salita Castello 13, 081 896 8799, www.lacasasul mare.it, closed 3 weeks Jan, Feb, doubles €90-€160), housed in an 18th-century palazzo with sunny, air-con rooms and fabulous terraces overlooking the bay. Boat transfers to Chiaja beach.

In the centre of the island, near Chiaja beach, an old farmhouse (**Casa Giovanni da Procida**, via Giovanni da Procida 3, 081 896 0358, www.

casagiovannidaprocida.it, closed 6 Jan-Feb, doubles €65-€100) has been converted into a B&B with garden. The air-conditioned, split-level rooms (some are on the small side but with vaulted ceilings) are simply furnished with shower rooms. Children get an especially warm welcome.

Right by the harbour at Chiaiolella, newly-opened **La Tonnara** (via Marina Chiaiolella 51/B, 081 810 1052, double rooms €70-€135) is convenient for the sandy beach and ideal for families; its roof terrace and solarium have stunning views across Vivara to Ischia.

Resources

First aid

Guardia Medica *via Casale Annunziata 1 (081 810 1213).* **Open** 24hrs.

Police

Via Giovanni da Procida 22 (081 896 0086).

Post office

Via Libertà 72 (081 896 0711). **Open** 8am-1.30pm Mon-Fri; 8am-12.30pm Sat.

Tourist information

Pro Loco di Procida *(081 810 1968/www. procida.it).* **Open** June-Aug 9.30am-1 pm, 3-8pm daily. Sept-May 9.30am-1pm, 3-6pm daily.

Getting around

Note that during the summer there are heavy restrictions on private cars and scooters.

By bus

Buses run to all parts of the island with frequent services in July and August. Line 1 runs all year from Marina Grande to the Marina di Chiaiolella; this service operates most of the night July and Aug. Tickets cost €1 and should be bought in advance from *tabacchi* or with a surcharge from the driver.

By taxi

Marina di Chiaiolella or Marina Grande (081 896 8785); a tour around the island costs €35-€40. Taxis can also be booked on 339 485 0303.

Getting there

From Naples–Beverello

Caremar (081 551 3882/www.caremar.it) runs ferries (1hr; €4.20) and hydrofoils (35mins; €7.90).

From Naples–Beverello (and to Mergellina in summer months)

Snav (081 761 2348/081 428 5555/www.snav.it) runs hydrofoils (35mins; €8.90).

From Pozzuoli

Caremar (081 526 2711) runs ferries (35mins; €2.40); Procida Lines 2000 (081 896 0328) runs car ferries (35mins; rates vary according to size of vehicle).

Pompeii & Vesuvius

Nature and antiquity at their dramatic best.

Pompeii's **Forum**. *See p222.*

The sight of Vesuvius rising out of its plain, with the Sorrentine Peninsula to the south and Naples to the north, has always held locals and visitors spellbound. At ground level, though, the picture changes: here lie ugly urban agglomerations, home to some of Europe's highest unemployment rates. But the sprawl is a 20th-century blight and can (with a massive effort of the imagination) be ignored. The *comuni vesuviani* – the towns around Vesuvius – conceal a wealth of ancient Roman sites and lovely, elaborate 18th-century villas, all set against the backdrop of the quiescent volcano. The contrasts are striking: lava fields from the 1944 eruption lie, wild and deserted, a few miles from the busy remains of ruined streets and houses buried in a much bigger blow two millennia before; sumptuous Roman villas in quiet countryside overlook demolition-ripe 1950s tower blocks. There is no other place quite like this.

The Greeks, Oscans and then Romans all once occupied the lower slopes of Vesuvius in a variety of settlements: towns such as **Pompeii** (*see p220*) and **Herculaneum** (*see p216*), farmsteads as in **Boscoreale** (*see p220*), and villas as at **Oplontis** (*see p219*)

and **Stabiae** (*see p225*). In the 18th century, the Bourbon monarchs had the **Reggia** (royal palace; *see p215*) built in Portici; the rich and noble followed their example, building more than 120 villas between Portici and Torre del Greco in an area that became known as the *Miglio d'Oro* ('golden mile').

DIGGING DEEP

Using digging techniques that make modern archaeologists shudder in horror, the Bourbons carted off statues and frescos to be exhibited in the Reggia. Many more works of art were damaged during excavations, while others were smuggled out to private collections abroad. The sites still bear the scars of the cavalier excavation techniques; ancient villa walls had tunnels bored through them in attempts to reach the treasure within. When describing a visit to Herculaneum in the 18th century, the poet Thomas Gray wrote to his mother how 'the passage they have made with all their turnings and windings is now more than a mile long'.

With large injections of European Union funds and private sponsorship deals, the normally cash-strapped Italian cultural heritage

Around Naples

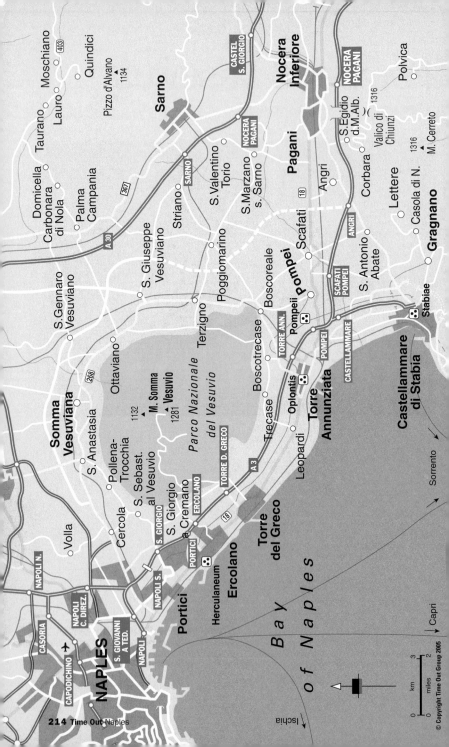

© Copyright Time Out Group 2005

ministry has been busy capitalising on the immense archaeological resources in the area: grandiose plans are afoot to divert some of the tourist traffic (1.5 million paying visitors pass through Pompeii each year) to lesser-known sites such as Stabiae; several key services at archaeological sites have been privatised, and a new area at Herculaneum was opened to a restricted public in 2003.

Some things, though, are here to stay. Ancient Herculaneum is buried beneath the modern town of Ercolano and will never be brought to light. Stray dogs still roam the streets of Pompeii, while at the entrance the old-style tour guides tout for business. In the streets of the modern *comuni vesuviani*, environmental quality is poor. The Roman satirist Juvenal complained in the second century AD of 'the swearing of drovers on narrow, winding streets', while today's visitors are plagued by noisy scooters tearing round like chainsaws on wheels.

The five key archaeological sites of *vesuviana* (Pompeii, Herculaneum, Oplontis, Stabiae and Boscoreale) can be visited on the Campania Artecard circuit (*see p35*) or on a cumulative ticket, which costs €18, is valid for three days and is available at all sites except Stabiae. Unlike the smaller sites, both Pompeii and Herculaneum now have snack-bar facilities. As of early 2005, Stabiae still had no ticket office and admission was free.

Portici

With the dubious distinction of being the most densely populated town in Europe – though the other *comuni vesuviani* can't be far behind – Portici was devastated when Vesuvius erupted in 1631. It was little more than a wasteland when Charles III, Naples' first Bourbon king, gave orders for a palace to be built here. The palace and its grounds, now surrounded by concrete on all sides, give you an idea of what the whole area looked like 200 years ago. The town was the site of over 30 villas along the *Miglio d'Oro*, and the terminus for Italy's first railway line (the old station now houses the excellent Museo Ferroviario museum).

Museo Ferroviario di Pietrarsa

Via Pietrarsa, Portici (081 472 003/ www.microsys.it/pietrarsa).
This museum was closed for restoration in 2000, and although it was due to reopen Sept 2002, it was still closed by 2005. Check to see if it is open. If it is, you can get detailed information about the museum, in English, from the reception.

The first railway on the Italian peninsula was a modest 7.4-km (4.5-mile) stretch between Naples and Portici, inaugurated with much fanfare by Naples' King Ferdinand II in 1839. The following year, a railway factory and workshops were installed in an area close to Portici called Pietrarsa ('burnt stone', aptly enough given its proximity to Vesuvius). All of the factories operated there until 1975.

The biggest – and arguably the best – railway museum in Europe, the Museo Ferroviario di Pietrarsa is a joy, even for non-railway buffs. The buildings housing the original workshops and lathes have been minimally, and tastefully, restored. Pavilion A has a wondrous display of steam locomotives, including a faithful reconstruction of the royal train used for the inaugural trip on the Portici railway in 1839. Across the gardens, Pavilion C has the full gamut of 20th-century rolling stock, and the immaculately preserved royal carriage built in 1928. Raised walkways around the carriage allow a good view of the plush upholstery and gilded ceilings. The museum's central courtyard has been made into a Mediterranean garden, including an open-air theatre used for summer concerts.

To find the museum, take the Portici exit from the A3 motorway and head down to the coast road (SS145), turning right towards Naples; the easily missed Museo Ferroviario sign is on the seaward side of the main road in the area called Croce del Lagno. Alternatively, take a mainline train from Naples' Stazione Centrale (information 848 892 021) to Pietrarsa-San Giorgio a Cremano.

Reggia di Portici & Orto Botanico

Via Università 100 (081 775 4850/www.agraria. unina.it). **Open** *Sept-July* Reggia 8.30am-7pm Mon-Fri. Orto 9am-12.30pm Mon-Sat. **Admission** free.
Designed by Antonio Medrano, the Reggia di Portici is the greatest of all the Vesuvian villas. Ferdinando Fuga worked on it, as did Luigi Vanvitelli. The Reggia's vast façade looks out across what was once its own private terraced gardens, cascading down towards the seashore. The lower of the Reggia's two buildings is separated by a square – crossed by the Strada reale delle Calabrie, the former main road joining Naples to the south – from the upper wing, which looks out towards Vesuvius. Charles and his son Ferdinand had the spoils from digs at Pompeii and Herculaneum brought here, creating a royal antiquarium of incomparable richness (although most of those former contents can now be seen at the Museo Nazionale Archeologico; *see p84*). Since 1873, the Reggia has held the Naples University Faculty of Agriculture: to visit, just wander in student-like. On the Vesuvius side of the main road is the *orto botanico* (botanical garden), an impressive collection of over 500 species of native and exotic plants, abutting the large holm oak wood where the royals used to hunt.

Ercolano & Herculaneum

While it rivals Portici for urban squalor and traffic noise, Ercolano also has some sumptuous 18th-century villas and a spectacular ancient site. But the mess here is so bad that you really could drive through the post-war construction catastrophe and never notice the splendour. But as you hurry through Ercolano, erase in your mind's eye everything built since 1945. You're left with some fishermen's huts near the shore, a once-smart late 19th-century main street, and *ville* – crumbling, dilapidated, villas behind locked rusting gates draped in the growth of runaway gardens.

Because the Reggia di Portici was home to the Bourbon court for several months each year, court hangers-on from all over the Kingdom of the Two Sicilies – anxious to be on hand when honours or cash rewards were distributed – summoned the leading architects to build luxury homes in the area. Soon the stretch of coast between Naples and Torre del Greco became known as the *Miglio d'Oro* ('golden mile').

With the absorption of Naples into the united Kingdom of Italy in 1860, the frivolous, worldly *ville* of the *Miglio d'Oro* became obsolete; the villas' owners sold them to nouveau riche Neapolitan property speculators or just left them to decay. Many were ultimately divided up into flats, while others, such as the spectacular **Villa Favorita** (*see p218*), were boarded up and abandoned for generations.

A handful have been salvaged by the Ente per le Ville Vesuviane (Board of Vesuvian Villas) and are open to the public. The Villa Favorita may have escaped the Ente's benevolent clutches,

Villa Favorita.
See p218.

but not so its lower park nor the recently restored annexe, the Palazzina del Mosaico.

In Ercolano, the *Ente Ville* has its headquarters in the stupendous **Villa Campolieto** (*see p218*). And in Ercolano, the Ente has also given a new lease of life to the lovely **Villa Ruggiero** (*see p218*).

Herculaneum (Scavi di Ercolano)

Corso Resina 6 (081 739 0963). **Open** *Apr-Oct* 8.30am-7.30pm daily; ticket office closes 6pm. *Nov-Mar* 8.30am-5pm daily; ticket office closes 3.30pm. **Admission** €10. *Audio-guide* €6.50; €10 for 2. **No credit cards**.
Letters in the text refer to map on p217.

It was described by the ancients as being *inter duos fluvios infra Vesuvium* ('between two rivers below Vesuvius'), but over the years the topography around Herculaneum has changed beyond all recognition. The rivers have disappeared, the present-day shoreline is 1km (0.6 miles) to the west, and the part of Herculaneum that has not been excavated lies as much as 25m (80ft) below the modern town of Ercolano. Descending from Ercolano, emerging from newly built tunnels leading into the site, and strolling through the ancient town, is an extraordinary experience – like entering a time capsule.

The town was probably founded by Greek settlers in the fourth century BC – although Dionysius of Halicarnassus rather implausibly attributes the foundation to Hercules on his return from Iberia. Most of what is visible today dates back no further than the second century BC. The town had a grid layout similar to its neighbour Neapolis; at the time of its destruction in AD 79, it would have had around 5,000 inhabitants. Buried swiftly in an airtight layer of solidified volcanic mud (unlike Pompeii, where volcanic ash took a while to settle and become compressed), Herculaneum has yielded organic remains allowing insights into aspects of everyday life, such as diet, clothing and furniture.

Access to the site is across from the audio-guide kiosk via an impressive ramp with fine overviews of the Roman town; from here, a tunnel leading down to the original shoreline [A] is the best place to admire the towering volcanic deposits. It was near here that 250 skeletons were discovered in the 1980s. These are believed to be the remains of inhabitants overwhelmed by the surge cloud from Vesuvius while hoping, in vain, to be rescued by sea. Most of the best-preserved houses (many with upper storeys still intact) are on either side of Cardo IV and Cardo V, perpendicular to the two *decumani* (main roads).

Near the seaward end of Cardo V, an altar and a statue base stand outside the *terme suburbane* (suburban baths) [B]; the statue, dedicated to local dignitary Nonius Balbus, is in Naples' Museo Nazionale Archeologico (*see p84*).

In Insula IV, the Casa dei Cervi (House of the Stags) [C] was a villa with a prime seafront location and gazebo. It is named after the two sculptures of deer attacked by hunting dogs found in the garden;

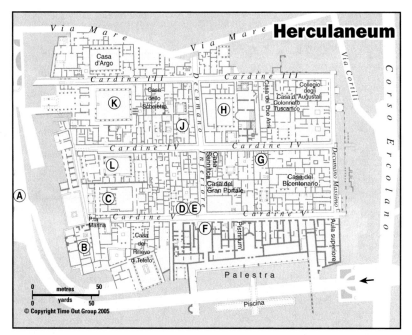

Herculaneum key

A   Original shoreline
B   Terme Suburbane
C   Casa dei Cervi
D   Taberna di Priapo
E   Thermopolia
F   Palastra
G   Casa di Nettuno e Anfitrite
H   Terme del Foro
J   Casa del Tramezzo di Legno
K   Casa dell'Albergo
L   Casa dell'Atrio a Mosaico

the ones here now are replicas. Excavated systematically in the early 20th century, Casa dei Cervi suffered less and preserved more of its upper storeys than the houses in Insula II on the north-western side of the site, excavate d 100 years before. Nearby are two shops [D & E], identifiable by their fronts, the breadth of which allowed space for folding wooden screens to partition off the shop from the street. The first [D] is the Taberna di Priapo (Priapus's Tavern), complete with waiting room, a rather tired-looking fresco in the entrance and private inner chambers. On the street corner, with amphorae set into marble counters, is one of the town's *thermopolia* [E]; these were the fast-food outlets of the ancient world, where passers-by

might have stopped off to buy garum, a fish-based sauce said to be the Viagra of the Roman era.

Where Cardo V meets the lower *decumanus* (one of the two main roads of a Roman town) there are two columns marking the entrance to the large *palaestra* (Insula Orientalis) [F], where ball games and wrestling matches would have been staged. Two sides of its rectangular peristyle are still largely buried under impressive volcanic deposits. Within this leisure complex were two *piscinae* (swimming pools or fishponds): one at the centre of the peristyle, tunnelled out of the rock, with a replica of the original bronze hydra fountain; and the other (a more recognisable pool) on the northern side, with amphorae set in its sides for fish farming.

The houses in Herculaneum are virtually all named after archaeological finds or architectural peculiarities. The Casa di Nettuno e Anfitrite (House of Neptune and Amphitrite, Insula V) [G] on Cardo IV is no exception, taking its name from the beautifully preserved mosaic adorning the wall of the secluded *nymphaeum* at the back of the house. It tells the tale of Neptune and Amphitrite – he saw her dancing with the Nereids on the island of Naxos, and spirited her away for marriage.

Just opposite are the *terme del foro* (forum baths, Insula VI) [H], with separate sections for men and women. The women's baths have the more attractive and better-preserved mosaic flooring; the male section is larger and contains an exercise area and

Around Naples

a round *frigidarium*, in addition to the mandatory *apodyterium* (changing room), *tepidarium* and *calidarium* also found in the female section next door. Note the *apodyteria* with partitioned shelves for depositing togas, and the low *podia* to use as seating space while queuing.

The Casa del Tramezzo di Legno (House of the Wooden Partition, Insula III) [J] unusually has two atria, which suggest that there were originally two houses here, joined together in the first century AD when one of the emerging class of *mercatores* (traders) perhaps bought out the patrician owner. Note the carbonised wooden screen beyond the marble *impluvium,* separating the atrium from the *tablinum,* where the *patronus,* or master of the house, conducted business with his clients.

Further down Cardo IV is the Casa dell'Albergo (House of the Hotel, Insula III) [K]. One of the largest buildings in Herculaneum, it was undergoing restoration from previous earthquake damage when it was overwhelmed by the eruption in AD 79. Note the small private baths just to the right of the main entrance, with wall decorations in second Pompeiian style. Beyond the atrium is an impressive peristyle enclosing a sunken garden. The trunk of a pear tree was found here, suggesting that the garden may have been an orchard. The pear trees have been replanted here in an attempt to recreate the original vegetation.

Outside the main site, just across the road from the bookshop and cafeteria is the Villa dei Papiri, a luxury villa 250 metres from end to end, from where a total of 87 sculptures – Roman copies of Greek originals – and over 1,000 charred but legible papyrus rolls were unearthed. Most of the papyri are the product of a lesser-known Epicurean poet and scholar called Philodemos, and not, as had been hoped, lost works of Aristotle. The wonderful statues are now in the archaeological Museum in Naples (*see p84*). The public is granted limited access to the upper floor at no extra cost, but advance reservations are required (register at www.arethusa.net).

Only part of Herculaneum is visitable at any given time, and much of the site is screened off by unsightly red plastic fencing. A list of buildings open to the public is posted in the ticket office on corso Resina.

Villa Campolieto

Corso Resina 283, Ercolano (081 732 2134/www. villevesuviane.net). **Open** *office* 9am-2pm Mon-Fri. *Villa* 10am-1pm Tue-Sun. **Admission** free.

Designed by Luigi and Carlo Vanvitelli, the Villa Campolieto was built between 1760 and 1775. The circular portico – where a summer concert season is held (check the Ente's website, above, for details) – has a sweeping view over Ercolano and down to the sea. On the first floor, a few rooms have been restored to their original state and are open to the public; even more are on view during the Villa's frequent exhibitions. For information and a list of the *ville* in the area, call in at the Ente's office on the ground floor.

Villa Favorita

House *corso Resina 291, Ercolano.* **Park** *via Gabriele D'Annunzio (081 7393 961).* **Open** *Park only* 10am-1pm Tue-Sun. **Admission** free.

Dotted with pavilions and teahouses, the Villa Favorita's lower park sweeps down towards the sea and a jetty – all that remains of a Bourbon construction that was the nearest thing Italy had to Brighton Pier. On the seaward side of the park is the recently restored Palazzina del Mosaico, now used for conferences.

Villa Ruggiero

Via A Rossi 40, Ercolano (081 732 2134). **Open** 10am-1pm Tue-Sun. **Admission** free.

This villa, set slightly back from the main road, was built in the mid 18th century for the baronial Petti family. Only the elegant courtyard is on show.

Planning permission

In 1980, a massive earthquake shook thousands of buildings to the ground in the Campania region surrounding Naples, prompting a building spree that some critics said caused more devastation than the quake itself. With utter disregard for the concept of planning permission, historic towns were transformed beyond recognition, two-storey cottages became four-level apartment blocks and fortunes were made, many of them with hastily pocketed central government funds.

But, as archaeologists and historians will tell you, there's nothing particularly new about *abusivismo edilizio* (construction without permission) in Campania. That's clear when you consider the fact that Pompeii's *terme suburbane* (suburban baths; *see p220*), were put up illegally during a building free-for-all after an earthquake in AD 62.

A combination of epigraphic and literary sources tells us that an increasingly infuriated Emperor Vespasian was eventually forced to send a tribune (named T Suedius Clemens) to enforce zoning laws. After that, several buildings appear to have been demolished, and boundary stones delimiting public areas were set in place bearing the inscription 'LPP', probably standing for locus publicus Pompeianorum ('public place of the Pompeiians').

Herculaneum. *See p215.*

Torre del Greco

Displaying much of the urban blight common to all the *comuni vesuviani*, over the centuries Torre del Greco has experienced both 'build-'em-high' post-war development and Vesuvius's eruptions. In the heart of the volcano's red-alert area, its 110,000 inhabitants blithely continue with business as usual. Besides floriculture, a major source of income is the manufacture of coral and cameos – highly prized in the East Asian market.

Skilled artists and trainees can be seen at work at the privately owned **APA Coral & Cameo Factory**, conveniently close to the Torre del Greco motorway exit. This is a fairly slick marketing operation, but negotiate your way in between large Japanese tour groups and the quality of the artistry and factory displays may persuade you to part with your euros.

The **Museo del Corallo** has fine 18th-century pieces from the Trapanese school and attractive cameos on malleable lavic stone. The museum is on the first floor of the Istituto Statale d'Arte technical college; a member of staff can show you round the locked museum.

APA Coral & Cameo Factory

Via de Nicola 1 (081 881 1155/www.giovanni apa.com). **Open** 8.30am-6.30pm daily. **Credit** AmEx, DC, MC, V.

Museo del Corallo

Piazza Luigi Palomba 6 (081 881 1360). **Open** 9am-noon Mon-Fri. **Admission** free.
Closed for renovations. Due to open in summer 2005.

Where to stay & eat

The **Hotel Marad** (via San Sebastiano 24, 081 849 2168, www.hotelmarad.it, double €120-€135), lodged between the major archaeological sites and Vesuvius, is best reached by car. This quiet, comfortable hotel has two excellent restaurants (average €26, €45).

Torre Annunziata & Oplontis

Once a thriving town where Neapolitans spent their summers lazing on black volcanic beaches, Torre Annunziata long ago lost its allure as a resort; instead it provides plenty of material for pages of the *cronaca nera* (crime news) in the local papers. The wondrous archaeological site of **Oplontis**, though, is its saving grace.

Oplontis

Via Sepolcri 1 (081 862 1755). **Open** *Apr-Oct* 8.30am-7.30pm daily; ticket office closes 6pm. *Nov-Mar* 8.30am-5pm daily; ticket office closes 3.30pm. **Admission** €5. **No credit cards.**
On the basis of an inscription on an amphora, this villa is thought to have belonged to Nero's second wife, Sabina Poppaea. The prosaically named Villa A certainly has some of the finest examples of the Pompeiian Style II of wall painting. Whether or not Poppaea really lived here and indulged in her asses' milk bath within its finely frescoed walls, she would have done better if she'd stayed with husband, Marcus Otho, rather than take up with Nero, who arranged for Otho to be posted as governor of the far-flung province of Lusitania (central Portugal). Poppaea eventually became imperial wife number two in AD 62 before – if Tacitus is to be believed – she was kicked to death by Nero while pregnant three years later.

This delightful, under-visited villa amply merits a ramble. The west wing is right up against the main road, while much more lies unexplored beneath. West of the reconstructed main atrium (room 5 – the numbers are over the doors), the walls of the *triclinium* (room 14) contain stunning illusionist motifs. The *calidarium* in the adjoining baths complex (room 8) has a delicate miniature landscape scene surmounted by a peacock in a niche at the far end; the adjacent *tepidarium* (room 18) shows off Roman baths and heating systems: the floor is raised by *suspensurae* (brick pilasters), this enables warm air to pass beneath.

Off the portico on the southern side of the site is an *oecus* or living room (room 23) with spectacular still-life frescos in Pompeiian Style II; the *cubicula* nearby (rooms 25 and 38) have frescos in the finer, less brash Style III. As you leave the warren of *cubicula*, the spaces become more grandiose, culminating at the eastern end with a large *piscina* (swimming pool) fringed, in Roman times, by oleander and lemon trees. The atmosphere of relaxation and contemplation lingers, making this a pleasant antidote to what the Latin poet Horace would have called the *profanum vulgus* down the road in Pompeii.

Around Naples

The site is close to both the Circumvesuviana railway station and the motorway exit for Torre Annunziata Nord, making a visit to the area relatively swift, painless and rewarding.

Pompei & Pompeii

To many Italians, Pompei is a place of pilgrimage. People flock here from all over the south to pay their respects to the Madonna in the large, early 20th-century *santuario* on the main square (piazza Bartolo Longo), praying for the kind of miracle that healed a girl suffering from epilepsy in 1876. Others bring their new cars to have them blessed and secure divine protection; given local driving standards and roads, this seems a wise precaution.

The sheer volume of religious and cultural tourism caught modern Pompei by surprise. Having long reaped the benefits of mass tourism and given little in return, new Pompei now has some pleasant surprises in store: once-seedy lodgings have given way to well-appointed hotels, and eating out is no longer hit-and-miss, especially if you stray from the archaeological site to the centre of town.

About three kilometres (two miles) to the north is the **Antiquarium di Boscoreale**, opened in the 1990s as a permanent exhibition on Pompeii and its environment 2,000 years ago. Reconstructions show idyllic scenes of wildlife along the river Sarno, now regrettably one of the most polluted watercourses in Italy.

Antiquarium di Boscoreale

Villa Regina, via Settetermini 15 (081 536 8796). **Open** *Apr-Oct* 8.30am-7.30pm daily; ticket office closes 6pm. *Nov-Mar* 8.30am-6.30pm daily; ticket office closes 5pm. **Admission** €5, also valid for Oplontis. **No credit cards.**
Set incongruously in the middle of a 1960s housing development, the Antiquarium documents daily life, the environment and technology in Roman times. Disparate finds ranging from fishing tackle to cages for rearing dormice (a favourite with Roman gourmets) are displayed alongside life-size photos of original mosaics and frescos from other sites and museums. In the grounds of the museum is Villa Regina, an ancient farmstead with storage capacity for 10,000 litres (2,200 gallons) of wine. The villa's vineyard has been replanted along ancient rows. The Porta Marina tourist office (*see p226*) will direct you.

Scavi di Pompeii

Via Villa dei Misteri 2 (081 857 5347). **Open** *Apr-Oct* 8.30am-7.30pm daily; ticket office closes 6pm. *Nov-Mar* 8.30am-5pm daily; ticket office closes 3.30pm. **Admission** €10. *Audio-guide* €10; €6.50 for 2. **No credit cards.**
Letters in the text refer to map on p221.
Unlike Rome, where ancient monuments have suffered millennia of weathering, re-use and pillaging,

Pompeii key

A   Porta Marina
B   Basilica
C   Forum
D   Tempio di Giove
E   Macellum
F   Terme del Foro
G   Casa del Fauno
H   Porta Ercolana
I   Villa dei Misteri
J   Terme Stabiane
K   Teatro Grande
L   Odeion
M   Casa dei Casti Amanti
N   Palaestra
O   Vineyards
P   Antifiteatro

Pompeii had the great fortune (for posterity at any rate) of being overwhelmed by the AD 79 eruption of Vesuvius. The ancient street plan is intact, the town still has its full complement of civic buildings, the houses still have their frescoed walls and – thanks to painstaking work by generations of archaeologists – we have a fairly clear picture of what life was like here 2,000 years ago.

The picture is still being completed: emergency digs during roadworks on the Naples–Salerno motorway have revealed the full extent of a frescoed leisure complex close to the Sarno river; within the site, archaeologists are still working on the Casa dei Casti Amanti (House of the Chaste Lovers); palaeobotanists, anthropologists and vulcanologists are gradually piecing together the mosaic of knowledge gleaned from latest finds.

Unfortunately, the site has seemed a bit uncared for on recent visits: audioguides come with badly photocopied maps, touts do business, the service area is in poor condition and major houses are closed for at least two part of each day.

Allow at least two hours for visiting Pompeii; it will take longer if you intend to see both the amphitheatre and the Villa dei Misteri, a good 25 minutes' hike apart. The audioguides offer two-, four- or six-hour itineraries – times that are probably underestimates if you choose to listen to the optional in-depth information supplied. From 10am until 1pm the *terme suburbane* (suburban baths; *see also p218* **Planning permission**) near the Porta Marina are open. The Casa del Menandro (House of Menander) near the theatre can be visited weekends from 2pm to 4pm. For access to these houses you have to ask for (free) coupons at the main ticket office when you buy your ticket. You will be assigned a time at each house. (The Casa dei Vettii and the *lupanare* – brothel – were closed for restoration as this guide went to press.)

There is little shade at Pompeii, so take precautions against the sun, and carry drinking water. Afternoon visits pay dividends when crowds start

Pompeii

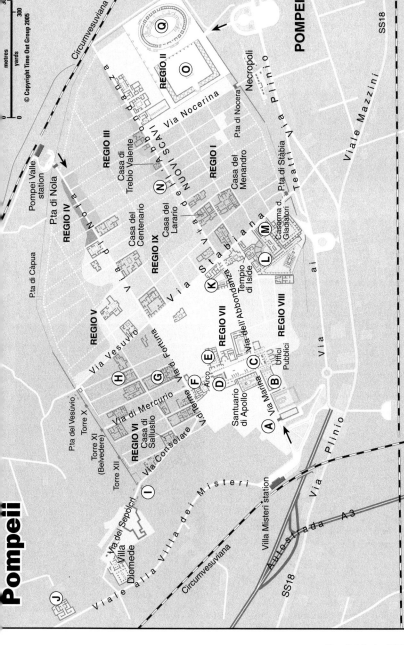

to thin out. Ask for a site map from the information office or from the audio-guide kiosk at Porta Marina. The Circumvesuviana railway station Pompei Scavi-Villa dei Misteri is opposite the main Porta Marina entrance to the site; just inside, the forum is a good place to get your bearings.

The Porta Marina [A], with its separate entrances for pedestrians (on the left) and animals and light vehicles (on the right), is near the original harbour, hence the name. (The shoreline is now much further away than in antiquity, when a canal is thought to have provided access from the sea to the town.) This gate provided the quickest way of getting to that hub of Roman life, the forum, but as the route was also the steepest, most vehicles at the time would probably have chosen one of the other seven gates leading into town.

On the right is the basilica [B], Pompeii's law court and stock exchange. These rectangular buildings ending in semicircular apses were the model for early Christian churches.

The forum [C] is a rectangular area with a colonnade surmounted by a loggia running along three sides. Plinths at the southern end indicate that there was a row of large statues here, perhaps equestrian. At the northern end is what remains of the second-century BC Tempio di Giove (Temple of Jupiter) [D] with the cone of Vesuvius behind. As Jupiter was head of the Roman pantheon, it was standard practice to dedicate a temple to him (together with Juno and Minerva) at the centre of town. The temple had already suffered severe damage in an earthquake before AD 79.

The elegant three-columned portico on the eastern side of the forum marks the entrance to the *macellum* [E], the covered meat and fish market built in early imperial times.

The *terme del foro* (forum baths) [F] are small as Roman baths go, but retain much of the original stucco decoration. Within the *calidarium* is a well-preserved marble *labrum* (fountain) with an inscription in bronze letters around the rim, recording the names of the officials (C Melissaeus Aper and M Staius Rufus) who installed it in AD 3-4, as well as its cost (5,420 sesterces). Except for a short period in early Imperial times, sexes were segregated in all Roman baths; women would have had the morning shift and men the afternoon.

Close to the baths on via della Fortuna is the Casa del Fauno (House of the Faun) [G], named after the small bronze statue in the middle of the marble *impluvium* (the original is in the Museo Nazionale Archeologico; *see p84*). One of the largest and most sophisticated houses in Pompeii, its front section is arranged around two atria rather than the usual one; behind is a peristyle with a portico of Ionic columns. Found in the *exedra* (discussion hall) at the far end of the first peristyle, flanked by two *triclinia*, was a million-tesserae mosaic (also in the Museo Nazionale Archeologico). It is thought to depict the Battle of Issus in 330 BC, fought between Alexander the Great and the Persian emperor Darius III. Artists from the Ravenna School of Mosaics

are currently involved in a long-term project to reproduce this remarkable mosaic in situ.

About 300 metres (330 yards) outside the city walls through the attractive Porta Ercolano [H], leading towards Herculaneum and Neapolis, the Villa dei Misteri (Villa of Mysteries) [I] has frescos in the *triclinium* depicting – experts believe – a young woman's initiation into the cult of Dionysus. There are ten scenes of vivid intensity, thought to have been copied by a local artist from a Hellenistic original of the fourth- or third-centuries BC. The villa was a working farm for much of its existence; the wine-making area is still visible at the northern end.

Stroll down the main street (via dell'Abbondanza) from the forum towards the amphitheatre, and the town takes on a different feel. The shops here can be identified by their broad entrances for easy access from the street. Private houses had *fauces* (narrow passages) – security was a problem in ancient Pompeii, and inhabitants went to great lengths to protect themselves and their property.

The Terme Stabiane (Stabian Baths) [J] are a much larger complex than the forum baths, with the exercise area in the middle surrounded by the male and female sections. The stuccoed vault in the men's *apodyterium* (changing room), with its images of nymphs and cupids, is particularly well preserved.

To the south is the theatre complex. The Teatro Grande [K] seats about 5,000 and – like so many theatres in the ancient world – enjoyed a stunning backdrop, in this case the Sarno river plain in the foreground and the heights of the Mons Lactarius

A beautifully preserved fresco at **Pompeii**.

Pompeii by night

During the night, the streets of ancient Pompeii were not particularly salubrious: to keep out undesirables, residents slept behind bolted and barred front doors, and any lower-floor windows that opened on to the street had iron grates or shutters. The only reason for venturing out was if you were invited to a friend's house for *cena* (dinner). In Rome, according to the Roman satirist Juvenal, going out to dinner without having made your will first was the height of carelessness. Though nocturnal rambling in Pompeii would have been quite a lot safer, entertainment still remained largely a daytime affair.

Fortunately for present-day crowds turning up for the Pompeii-by-night tour – called **Suggestioni al Foro** (information 347 346 0346, €24, €21 with Campania artecard,

see p35) – conditions for seeing Pompeii at night these days are very different.

Although the evening tour is limited to the civic and religious buildings around the forum – no houses, theatres or baths, unfortunately – the appealing combination of lighting and sound effects enhances the experience of looking round Pompeii when the daylight hordes have left.

The show runs every evening from Wednesday to Saturday in Italian (headphones are available for translation). It's in English on Wednesday at 8.30pm in winter, and 9.30pm in summer.

Site guards are on hand with torches to provide each group (maximum of 80 people) with extra light and, if short of company, you may well be adopted by one of ever-present stray dogs during your visit.

(Monti Lattari) behind. This second-century BC theatre underwent much restoration in antiquity, unlike the adjoining smaller Odeion or Theatrum Tectum [L]. The semicircular *cavea* (seating area) was truncated at both ends to facilitate the building of a permanent roof, which would have offered welcome shade to Pompeii's concert-goers in the main summer season.

North of via dell'Abbondanza, excavations continue around the Casa dei Casti Amanti (House of the Chaste Lovers) [M]. Not open to the public as this guide went to press, the house has revealed important evidence about life immediately prior to the eruption that challenges previously accepted facts. Earthquake damage from AD 62 had been repaired long before, and the inhabitants were trying to patch up cracks from recent tremors perhaps days before the AD 79 eruption; the rooms were being replastered and painted by teams of craftsmen at the very moment Vesuvius erupted. In the rapid getaway, tools were downed and plaster abandoned. The donkeys – turning the grindstone and milling wheat in the adjoining bakery – were left to their fiery fate.

West of the large *palaestra* [N] – the rectangular porticoed exercise area dating from Augustan times – are recently planted vineyards [O] that use varieties and training systems thought to have been employed in ancient times. Though the thick, scented nose of ancient Roman wine (drunk diluted) is unlikely to have appealed to modern palates, thanks to the technologically perfected processes used by the Mastroberardino winery, Villa dei Misteri 2001 was snapped up at a dizzying price tag.

By Roman standards, the *anfiteatro* (amphitheatre) [P] was small, seating about 20,000. Entertainment would probably have been limited to gladiatorial

combat, with occasional *venationes* (contests with wild animals) or *naumachiae* (mock sea-battles). Though gladiators had fairly short life expectancies – it was considered an occupation for slaves and social outcasts – records exist of the odd volunteer signing on for combat and creating quite a stir. The amphitheatre preserves a fair amount of its seating area, divided into three sections, with a series of *vomitoria* (entrances) near the top.

Where to stay & eat

Located close to the amphitheatre entrance of the Pompeii archaeological zone, the **Hotel Amleto** (via B Longo 10, 081 863 1004, www.hotelamleto.it, doubles €80-€120) has themed rooms with decor ranging from 19th-century Neapolitan to Venetian styles; the *trompe l'oeil* wall painting of the House of the Vettii in the breakfast room is guaranteed to mesmerise you. The newly opened youth hostel, **Casa del Pellegrino** (via Duca D'Aosta 4, 081 850 8644, www.hostels-aig.org, €13-€14 per person in dorms, €16.50 per person in family room) is in a low-rise Spanish-style ex-convent just off the main square; rooms open to a peaceful inner courtyard.

Il Principe (piazza B Longo 8, 081 850 5566, closed for dinner Sun, Mon, closed lunch Mon Nov-Mar, closed 3wks Aug, average €70) is one of Campania's finest restaurants, serving ancient dishes gleaned from classical authors; if you make it to dessert, try the exquisite cassata Oplontis, with honey and goat's milk ricotta.

Castellammare di Stabia & Stabiae

Famed for its spa, its shipyards and its *biscottifici* (biscuit factories), Castellammare has not only been bypassed by the coast road but has also suffered gradual industrial decline over the past 30 years. The town has recently started to exploit its archaeological heritage, though transport infrastructure and pedestrian access will have to be massively improved before ancient **Stabiae** can realise its potential as an economic mainstay for the area. Castellammare is served by rail, and has the added bonus of hydrofoil and ferry services to Capri, as well as a cable-car (*funivia*) service up **Monte Faito**.

Funivia & Monte Faito

Stazione Circumvesuviana, Castellammare di Stabia (081 7722 4444/800 053 939/www.vesuviana.it). **Open** *Apr-mid June, Sept, Oct* 9.25am-4.25pm daily. *Mid June-Aug* 7.25am-7.15pm daily. Closed Nov-Mar.

Tickets €4.65 one way; €6.71 return (€7.23 Sun, daily July, Aug). **No credit cards**.

With pleasant walks among shady beech woods, Monte Faito provides an escape from the heat in steamy summer months. An eight-minute ride on the *funivia* (cable car; leaves every 23-30mins) from the Castellammare di Stabia Circumvesuviana station whisks you up into a wood, with nerve-tingling vistas over the Bay of Naples.

Robins retreat here in summer from the coast; the distinctive calls of nuthatches can be heard as they flit from tree to tree. Plants tend to flower much later here than down on the coast; for late spring orchids, look in the clearings and in the more exposed areas below the cable-car station.

The upper *funivia* station is the start of hiking trails across to Positano (*see p246;* allow five to six hours, take good maps and water, and be prepared for lots of ups and downs); there are also low-key circular routes through the beech forest. The path from the *funivia* to the chapel of San Michele (1,278m/4,193ft above sea level) about 3km (2 miles) away, for example, climbs 170m (595ft), and you get good views of the bay for your efforts.

Saints alive Madonna dell'Arco

Easter Monday at the Santuario della Madonna dell'Arco is one of Campania's biggest religious celebrations, one of its most unusual and most passionate too. Tens of thousands of pilgrims from Naples and the surrounding villages, some bleeding from walking barefoot, converge on a sanctuary near the village of Sant'Anastasia to pay homage to an image of the Madonna there.

The cult of the Madonna dell'Arco is said to date back to Easter Monday of 1450, when a local youth playing a ball game missed a shot and, in anger, hit the nearby image of the Madonna on the cheek with the ball. The image, one of many once scattered around the countryside to protect crossroads, began to bleed. That was the first of a series of church-certified bleedings and miracles performed by the Madonna. A cult grew up around her and soon a sanctuary was built on the site. It has expanded over the years, and now includes a school, hospice, house for pilgrims and a museum.

The most hardcore pilgrims are known as *fujenti* ('those who run') because many of them run to the sanctuary. Administrators estimate that Easter draws 30,000 *fujenti* a year – a small part of the 200,000-strong crowd that surrounds the little church. The *fujenti* are dressed in white and wear a blue scarf (the traditional colour of the Virgin Mary) and a red belt. Inside the sanctuary the atmosphere is highly charged. As they reach the threshold, exhausted *fujenti* – some of them children or teenagers, some of them hysterical – approach the altar on their knees and collapse in a dramatic climax of pain and relief.

Outside the mood is lighter, and the village streets are crowded with food and souvenir stalls, and people playing music and dancing.

The museum contains the oldest collection of ex votos in Europe, including some from the 1500s. There are small models of boats presented to the Madonna by 'saved' sailors, and precious artefacts of various centuries, including objects brought by veterans of two world wars. There's even a glass case of syringes, left by former addicts 'cured' by the Madonna dell'Arco's intercession.

Santuario della Madonna dell'Arco

Near the village of Sant'Anastasia, 12km east of Naples (081 899 9225). **Open** Sanctuary *Nov-mid Apr* 6.45am-1pm, 3.30-6.30pm daily. *Mid Apr-Oct* 6.45am-1pm, 3.30-7.30pm daily. Museum *Nov-mid Apr* 4.30-6.30pm Sat; 9am-1pm, 4.30-6.30pm Sun. *Mid Apr-Oct* 5.30-7.30pm Sat; 9am-1pm, 5.30-7.30pm Sun. Also open by appointment.

Stabiae (Scavi di Castellammare)

Via Passeggiata Archeologica (081 871 4541). **Open**
Apr-Oct 8.30am-7.30pm daily; last admission 6pm.
Nov-Mar 8.30am-5pm daily; last admission 3.30pm.
Admission free.

'Ash was already falling, hotter and thicker as the
ships drew near, followed by bits of pumice and
blackened stones, charred and cracked by flames:
then suddenly they were in shallow water, and the
shore was blocked by debris from the mountain. For
a moment my uncle wondered whether to turn back,
but when the helmsman advised this he refused,
telling him that Fortune stood by the courageous
and they must make for Pomponianus at Stabiae.'

So reads Pliny the Younger's account of his
uncle's ill-fated attempt to rescue Pomponianus, a
friend living five km (three miles) south of Pompeii
at Stabiae, modern-day Castellammare di Stabia.
Pliny would not recognise today's coastline, which
extends much further out to sea than it did in AD
79. Nowadays, too, decidedly unlovely post-war
urban development rises where his uncle would
have encountered shallow water, while the seaside
settlement where Pomponianus may have lived is
perched on the bluff of a hill called Varano, almost
a kilometre (0.6 miles) inland.

Partially explored and plundered by the
Bourbons 200 years ago – and some Roman wall
paintings left behind were deliberately defaced to
enhance the value of artworks removed to adorn
the king's palaces – the archaeological site of
Stabiae fell into a state of decay when financial and
human resources were siphoned off to unearth
Pompeii during the late 18th and 19th centuries. It
was only in the 1950s that the site began to recover from centuries of neglect, although the 1980
earthquake set the work back.

Two villa complexes may be visited: Villa
Arianna and Villa San Marco, both of which can be
reached from the Passeggiata Archeologica, the
road that skirts around the south-eastern side of
Castellammare. The ground plans are complex, not
only because of the additions and extensions carried out in antiquity, but because they were
designed to fit the lie of the land. Named after a
fresco depicting King Minos's daughter Ariadne,
who helped Theseus out of the labyrinth after he
killed the Minotaur, Villa Arianna is the oldest
structure on the hill (first century BC, though renovated and extended in the first century AD).

Although the frescoed decorations are less spectacular in Villa San Marco, this would have made
for a secluded summer retreat for some Roman
magnate. The location would have been ideal:
far away from the imperial intrigues on the other
side of the Bay of Naples in Baiae, and yet reasonably close to main thoroughfares linking large
urban centres like Pompeii and Nuceria (now
Nocera). With its 30m (98ft) *natatio* (swimming
pool) flanked by four rows of plane trees enclosed
on three sides by a peristyle, this was a place for
enjoying *otium* (relaxation) to the full.

Shady **Monte Faito**. *See p224.*

Where to stay

Set in luxuriant gardens, the **Grand Hotel
La Medusa** (via Passeggiata Archeologica 5,
081 872 3383, www.italyby.com/medusa;
doubles €150-€206) is a recently renovated
fin-de-siècle villa providing the perfect antidote
for the hustle down in the *comuni vesuviani.*

Vesuvius

The question experts ask about Vesuvius is
not whether it will erupt but when. According
to the Osservatorio Vesuviano, which has
monitored its activity since 1841, it could
happen any time between 20 and 200 years

hence, and the longer it lies dormant (the last eruption was in 1944), the greater the risk. Any bleeps on the sensors that could point to an imminent eruption are closely monitored. When the volcano does blow, scientists believe, it will not be ash fallout or lava flow that pose the greatest danger, but a possible surge cloud of the kind that rolled down the mountain in AD 79 at an estimated 65-80 kilometres (40-50 miles) per hour and produced the ultimate open-air *calidarium,* reaching 400°C.

In the 13 *comuni vesuviani* around the base and on the lower slopes of the 1,281-metre (4,203-foot) volcano, 700,000 residents opt to be as blissfully unaware of this threat as their counterparts 2,000 years ago. They are not about to abandon the fertile volcanic soil; the slopes are still producing wine (Lacryma Christi, which has shaken off its downmarket reputation thanks to some state-of-the-art wineries), while the area's small cherry tomatoes or *pomodorini* (delightful on pasta) are earning tidy profits for local farmers.

Besides, there are no visible reminders of hazards, like those produced by Sicily's volcanoes. Vesuvius does not spew lava like Etna or eject ash like Stromboli. It lost its *pennacchio,* or plume of smoke, in 1944, and the lava fields created by previous eruptions are gradually being colonised by vegetation, giving the volcano a deceptively benign appearance.

Vesuvius is now a national park and a UNESCO Biosphere Reserve. But of the 200,000 visitors who trek up to the rim of its cone and peer down into the depths of the crater 200 metres (700 feet) below, few stay to enjoy the wilder side of the volcano. The park authority has begun to mark out footpaths (one of the best goes from the town of San Sebastiano al Vesuvio up to the Bourbon observatory), although much of the park is fenced off for security reasons: forest fires (often started deliberately to free up land for building purposes) have wrought considerable damage in recent years, and access to many areas is only granted for scientific purposes.

Vesuvius is at its best in May or June, when the upper slopes are awash with colour (especially the leggy broom and red valerian) and nightingales, whitethroats and blue rock thrushes are marking out their territory with prolific song. Start first thing in the morning and avoid windy days when conditions on the exposed rim can be critical.

The standard 30-minute route to the cone zigzags along a well-kept path that begins at the 'Quota 1,000' car park at the end of the road up the mountain's western flank. Although the inside of the crater itself is off-limits, there's a good view of steaming fumaroles and stratified

pyroclastic deposits on the other side of the crater rim. Fight your acrophobia and peer down into the crater; pioneer plants have moved in, and several interesting bird species.

Also on the road up the western slope of the volcano, the **Museo dell'Osservatorio Vesuviano** (*see below*) offers a broad overview of the geology of the volcano and the threats it poses, as well as some Heath Robinsonesque seismographs from the 19th century. It's housed in the old Bourbon observatory, a distinctive Pompeiian red building that has survived the ravages of at least seven eruptions.

Cratere del Vesuvio

081 777 5720/337 942 249/fax 081 739 1123. Open 9am-2hrs before sunset daily. **Admission** (including guide) €6.50. **No credit cards.**
Trips to the volcano's crater are suspended during bad weather and/or fog.

Museo dell'Osservatorio Vesuviano

081 610 8483/www.ov.ingv.it. Open 10am-1pm Sat, Sun. **Admission** free.
Look for signs to the Osservatorio at 600m (2,000ft) above sea level, just behind the Eremo Hotel.

Tourist information

Azienda Autonoma di Cura, Soggiorno e Turismo *Via Sacra 1, Pompei (081 850 7255/ www.uniplan.it/pompei/azienda).* Open *Apr-Oct* 8.30am-7pm Mon-Fri; 8.30am-3pm Sat. *Nov-Mar* 8am-3.30pm Mon-Fri; 8.30am-3pm Sat.
Ufficio di Informazione e di Accoglienza Turistica *Via IV Novembre 82, Ercolano (081 788 1243).* Open 9am-2pm Mon-Sat.
The Ercolano office will also give information on neighbouring Portici.
Ufficio di Informazione e di Accoglienza Turistica *At the Porta Marina entrance to the archaeological site, by the main ticket office (081 857 5347/www.pompeiisites.org).* Open *Apr-Oct* 8.30am-6pm daily. *Nov-Mar* 8.30am-3.30pm daily.
The tourist offices at Pompeii provide information on Torre del Greco, Torre Annunziata and Castell-ammare di Stabia.

Getting there

By bus

Circumvesuviana runs frequent services from Porto Immacolatella in Naples to **Pompei.** ANM (www.anm.it) bus 157 from piazza Municipio or 255 from piazza Carlo III go to **Ercolano.** But given the traffic hell, the train is a far better bet.
Trasporti Vesuvian (081 963 4420/081 963 4418) runs regular services up **Vesuvius.** The bus starts from piazza Anfiteatro in Pompei, stops at piazza Esedra near the motorway toll booth, and at Ercolano train station, and then winds up past the

Osservatorio and the old chairlift station, stopping in the large car park 1,000m (3,280ft) up. One-way from Pompei costs €3, from Ercolano €1.70. Check return times with driver and say if you need to stop at the Museo dell'Osservatorio.

By car

Most sites are fairly close to the nerve-tingling A3 Naples–Salerno motorway. For **Herculaneum**, take the Ercolano exit and follow the signs to Scavi di Ercolano. For **Oplontis**, exit at Torre Annunziata Nord, turning left when you hit the first main road. Follow signs to Scavi di Oplontis. For **Pompeii**, if travelling from Naples take the Pompei Ovest exit from the A3 motorway (Ancient Pompeii is beside this exit). From Salerno take the first Pompei exit.

For **Vesuvius**, from Torre del Greco or Ercolano, follow signs to Parco Nazionale del Vesuvio.

For **Boscoreale**, exit at Pompei Ovest and follow signs to the Antiquarium (or get directions from the helpful information office at Porta Marina, Pompeii).

For **Stabiae**, take the Castellammare di Stabia exit from the A3 and follow the signs to Sorrento (not Castellammare). Take the first exit (Gragnano) from the Sorrento road; the Passeggiata Archeologica starts at the junction (opposite) where the exit road meets the main Gragnano–Castellammare road.

At both Herculaneum and Pompeii you'll have to pay to park, while Stabiae and Boscoreale have free parking facilities on site.

By train

The major sites are served by the Circumvesuviana railway (081 772 2444/www.vesuviana.it). Note that for ancient Pompeii, if coming from Naples you should take the Naples–Sorrento line and get off at Pompei Scavi-Villa dei Misteri. The other Pompei station lies on a different Circumvesuviana line and is closer to the amphitheatre entrance.

Boscoreale (Boscoreale station) requires a considerable amount of legwork and is very poorly signposted, while for Stabiae (Via Nocera station, Castellammare) you need to take bus 1 Rosso from near the station.

Fares depend on distance: a one-way Zone 3 (*Fascia 3*) ticket (*biglietto di andata*) between Naples and Pompei (including travel within Naples itself) is €2.30. If you start out after 10am you can get a day pass (*biglietto giornaliero*), which is roughly equivalent to two singles. This will enable you to hop on almost all buses and trains throughout the area. Portici is in the Naples zone *Fascia 1* (€1 single, €3 for a day pass), and Ercolano in *Fascia 2* (€1.70 single, €3.50 for a day pass) along with Torre del Greco and Torre Annunziata. If travelling at weekends, get a *biglietto weekend*.

The one and only **Vesuvius**. *See p225.*

Sorrento & Around

Smooth resort on a jagged coast.

With a shore formed by a labyrinth of rocky crags and jagged cliffs, and a backdrop of lush citrus orchards, olive groves and tiny towns and villages, the Sorrentine Peninsula is an area of exceptional beauty. Viewed from Naples, the peninsula resembles an outstretched arm: a long, straight sweep of land reaching towards Capri, closing off the southern end of the Bay. The area is criss-crossed by a dense web of well-kept paths with unforgettable views.

Sorrento itself, the area's hub, was a mecca for the Grand Tourists of the 18th and 19th centuries, and it's still popular with 21st-century visitors. With its central location, facilities and decent transport links, it's a good place to start an exploration of the area.

There's a paradox about Sorrento and its surrounds: the dazzling blue sea provides a frame for all the views from the peninsula, but the sea is oddly divorced from many of the towns and villages, which have a decidedly mountainous, countryside feel to them. The narrow, winding roads leading down to the few tiny fishing villages and ports in pebbly coves are rarely even signposted. If it's a watery holiday you're after, make sure your hotel has a swimming pool, or be prepared to walk.

The area around Sorrento has been inhabited since prehistoric times, as the remains on display in museums in **Vico Equense** (*see p236*) and **Piano di Sorrento** show (*see p235*). Etruscans who moved in from the north in the sixth century BC found Greek settlers there. When the Romans routed the Greeks and the local Samnite tribes in the late fourth century BC, they made the peninsula a sought-after holiday venue, building luxury villas along the coast from **Castellammare di Stabia** (*see p224*) out to **Punta della Campanella** (*see p242*).

As the Roman Empire in the west wavered and fell, the Goths stampeded along the peninsula, razing small towns in their paths. Sorrento, on the other hand, passed formally to the control of Rome's Eastern Empire, ruled from Byzantium (Constantinople). Harried by Lombards, who had set up their southern Italian headquarters in nearby Benevento around 570, as well as by power-hungry Amalfi on the other side of the peninsula, and later by marauding Saracen pirates from north Africa, the Sorrentines fought hard to maintain independence, and they often succeeded. However, the Normans (who arrived in the

Duomo.
See p229.

12th century) were too powerful for them. The towns of the peninsula were soon absorbed into the southern Italian kingdom, their fate inextricably linked to that of Naples.

Sorrento

Sorrento only partly deserves its reputation as Eastbourne-on-the-Med. It is true that the blue-rinse brigade wanders the main streets and haunt *diners-dansants* at the priceless **Circolo dei forestieri** (Foreigners' Club – *see p231*). And the beer-and-tattoos brigade can be found crowded around English-language TV in the numerous English and Irish pubs (the places to go to for unmissable English games). But it's easy to leave the package tourists behind, and the town's largely peaceful atmosphere makes a refreshing change from chaotic Naples.

The regular grid plan of the streets stretching west from piazza Tasso is about all that is left of Greek and Roman Surrentum. The Normans destroyed much of the Roman fortifications. What remains of the town's 15th-century walls can still be seen along the traffic-clogged via degli Aranci ring road or on piazza delle Mure Vecchie. As late as the 16th century these defences were fundamental for the town (and the whole peninsula), subject as they were to attacks by Saracen pirates from across the Mediterranean. On 13 June 1558, these North African marauders sacked Sorrento, after which a chain of lookout towers, many of which are still standing, was built along the coast. There is a more complete picture of how the city looked until quite recently at the **Museo Correale di Terranova**, where 18th- and 19th-century paintings show rustic scenes around crumbling town gates, and along wild unspoilt coasts.

While Sorrentine youths congregate in the soulless modern area around piazza Lauro, older citizens and endless hordes of visitors gather in **piazza Tasso**. Bar tables cluster on the pavement, and the evening *struscio* (stroll) begins and ends here when the surrounding streets of the Centro storico are closed to traffic between 8pm and midnight daily.

A balcony on the northern side of the square offers views of the dark ravine that leads to **Marina Piccola**, the port from where ferries depart for Capri and Naples. Stairs lead down from the piazza towards the dock, which is also served by the local bus company.

Sorrento's most famous literary son, Torquato Tasso (1544-95), author of the ponderous epic poem *Gerusalemme liberata* (Jerusalem

Deliver'd), lends his name to the square and his statue looks over it. Leading out of the south-western corner, the narrow via Pietà contains **Palazzo Correale** (No.24), an early 15th-century building with an impressive door and arched windows upstairs (go into the florist's shop in the courtyard to admire the 18th-century majolica-tiled wall), and the 13th-century Palazzo Veniero (No.14) with windows framed with geometric designs in pretty coloured stone.

Via Pietà emerges on to corso Italia by the Romanesque **Duomo**. The cathedral is surrounded by a bishop's palace now occupied by church offices. From here, via Sersale leads to the remains of the Roman southern **town gate**, and to a stretch of 15th-century wall. Corso Italia heads on, lined with smart shops, past the small park and art gallery **Villa Fiorentino** (No.53) and quiet piazza Veniero before leading round the cliff towards Capo (*see p237*).

Turn right down via Tasso to reach the narrow, souvenir-shop-packed **via San Cesareo**. Here you can pick up examples of the marquetry for which Sorrento was famous in the 18th century (although it was made into furniture, rather than the music boxes now on sale) as well as bottles of the omnipresent tart, refreshing local liqueur, *limoncello*.

One block east, where via Cesareo intersects with via Giuliani, the arched **Sedile Dominova**, with its fading frescos, was one of two open-air meeting places where the local aristocracy discussed local policy in the 15th century; their coats of arms can be seen around the walls. In an ironic twist of fate, the Sedile is now the front porch of a working men's club; pensioners gather there to play cards and argue volubly about nothing in particular.

Parallel to via Cesareo, via Santa Maria delle Grazie changes name several times as it runs west towards the **Museobottega della Tarsialignea** (*see below*) inside the beautifully restored 18th-century Palazzo Pomarici Santomasi. Its private collection of *intarsio* (wooden inlay), both local and from further afield, is extensive and beautiful. It also has old paintings and photographs of Sorrento.

Several blocks to the north-east, via Veneto gives on to the **Villa Comunale**, a small but leafy park with splendid views over the Bay of Naples to Vesuvius.

By the entrance of the church of **San Francesco** stands a small 14th-century cloister (open 8am-1pm, 2-8pm daily; ring the bell if the gate is closed) with pretty ogival arches. The nearby piazza Sant'Antonino is named after Sorrento's patron saint, whose tomb can be admired in the 18th-century crypt of the **basilica of Sant'Antonino** (open 9am-noon, 5-7pm daily). Though heavily baroque-ified, the basilica has stood here since the 14th century, and occupies the site of an even earlier church. On the right side of the building an 11th-century door is surrounded by bits and pieces of Roman remains, and there's an impressive Nativity scene inside.

Via Marina Grande or narrow via Sopra le Mura lead down to the confusingly named **Marina Grande** (it's smaller than the Marina Piccola), around which was the original fishing village of Sorrento; the natural deep-water harbour of the Marina Piccola made it more convenient for ferries to dock there (thus shifting the entire focus of the town). Today it's rundown but sweet – paint is peeling off the walls of tall, grey stone houses, stray dogs sleep under the seafront benches, stray cats raid bins for fishy leftovers, kids play football in front of the tiny church of **Sant'Anna** and fishermen mend their nets leisurely. A couple of big restaurants have tried to make the place more like the rest of Sorrento; fortunately, however, it remains amiably down at heel.

If you want beaches in Sorrento, avoid the dark, volcanic sand of Marina Grande. Instead, head for a private beach (such as **Bagni Salvatore**, via Spiaggia San Francesco, 081 878 1214, open daily 9am-7pm in summer) or

Bagni della Regina Giovanna (*see p237*) where there's clean water and good snorkelling. Otherwise, ask one of the local boatmen to drop you off in some secluded bay and pick you up later; they'll usually do this for a handsome tip of about €25.

Duomo (Santi Filippo e Giacomo)
Corso Italia (081 878 2248). **Open** 7.40am-noon, 4.30-8.30pm daily.
The original Romaneque cathedral was largely rebuilt in the 15th century. Despite its Gothic appearance, the Duomo's façade is fairly modern, although the door with the Aragonese coat of arms on the right dates from the late 15th century. The three-aisled interior has 16th- and 17th-century paintings in its chapels and on the ceiling. The bishop's throne (1573) is a jigsaw of ancient marble fragments; the choir stalls are adorned with fine examples of local *intarsio* work.

Museobottega della Tarsialignea
Via San Nicola 28 (081 877 1942/www.alessandro fiorentinocollection.it). **Open** *June-Sept* 10am-1pm, 4-7.30pm Mon-Sat. *Oct-May* 10am-1pm, 3-6.30pm Mon-Sat. **Admission** €8. **Credit** AmEx, DC, MC, V.
In the mid 18th century, Sorrento became famous for its delicate *intarsio* wood furniture, avidly collected both by the Neapolitan royal family and by Grand Tourists. In addition to the excellent collection, the shop sells contemporary designers' interpretations of marquetry furniture a world away from the quaint knick-knacks you'll find in Sorrento's souvenir shops.

Museo Correale di Terranova
Via Correale 50 (081 878 1846). **Open** 9.30am-1.30pm Mon, Thur, Fri, Sun; 9.30am-1.30pm, 8-10.30pm Wed, Sat. **Admission** €6. **No credit cards**.
Alfredo and Pompeo Correale, the last male heirs to the title of Count of Terranova, left their 18th-century family villa and its collection of local art and artefacts to the town in the 1920s, and this museum was opened to hold it all. The archaeological section with finds from around the town lies on the ground floor; upstairs are views of 18th- and 19th-century Sorrento, plus examples of local furniture. Beyond the camellia garden lies a lookout point with a view across the bay.

Villa Fiorentino
Corso Italia 53 (081 533 5111). **Open** 10.30am-1pm, 6-8pm daily (6-10pm when there is an exhibition). **Admission** free.
Run by the local council, this late 19th-century villa has a small but pleasant public garden. Occasionally hosts exhibitions on local history or by local artists.

Where to eat & drink

While much of the food served in Sorrento tends to be undistinguished and undemanding, standards have risen somewhat recently. Locals still head for the surrounding hills when they fancy a good meal, but decent food can be found in the centre – albeit at a price. Places offering simple dishes or pizza (preferably with menus translated into the minimum number of languages) do exist. Bars proudly advertising 'English beer' are best avoided – unless you desperately need a fry-up.

Il Buco

Seconda Rampa, Marina Piccola 5 (081 878 2354). **Meals served** noon-3pm, 7-11.30pm Mon, Tue, Thur-Sun. **Closed** Jan. **Average** €50. **Credit** AmEx, MC, V.

The rather unpromisingly named 'Hole' is off piazza Sant'Antonino in the cellars of an old convent, with tables on the steps outside in summer. The food is nouvelle Italian (the portions may look small, but they are filling and beautifully presented) and mostly fish-based. Service is swift and courteous, and if the food is slightly overpriced, the extensive and reasonable wine list just about balances it out.

Circolo dei forestieri (Foreigners' Club)

Via Luigi di Maio 35 (081 877 3263). **Open** *Bar* 9.30am-midnight daily. *Restaurant* noon-3pm, 6pm-midnight daily. **Closed** Nov-Feb. **Credit** AmEx, DC, MC, V.

An odd institution inside the tourist office building, the Foreigners' Club seems to be a leftover from the 1950s – as are most of its clientele. Occasional bands and cabaret shows enhance the rather surreal expat atmosphere. Worth visiting for the lovely terrace.

Da Emilia

Via Marina Grande 62 (081 807 2720). **Meals served** *July, Aug* 12.30-3pm, 7.30-11pm daily. *Apr-June, Sept, Oct* 12.30-3pm, 7.30-11pm Mon, Wed-Sun. *Nov-Mar* 'for lunch when the weather's fine'. **Average** €20. **No credit cards**.

Still run by the redoubtable Signora Emilia herself, this little restaurant often has family groups gathered around its wooden tables with checked tablecloths. Food is traditional, service is brilliant. Grab a table outside and imagine Sophia Loren sashaying past.

Bar Ercolano

Piazza Tasso (081 807 2951). **Open** *Apr-Sept* 6am-1.30am Mon, Wed-Sun. *Oct-Mar* 6am-10.30pm Mon, Wed-Sun. **Closed** 5wks Jan-Feb. **No credit cards**.

An elegant spot from which to observe evening strollers. Good ice-cream, slow waiters.

Il Fauno

Piazza Tasso 13-15 (081 878 7735/www.fauno bar.it). **Open** 7am-midnight daily. **No credit cards**.

The largest and chic-est of the Centro bars, this is a great people-watching venue. Good service and a wide range of drinks and light meals.

Photo

Via Correale 19 (081 877 3686). **Open** *Mar-Sept* 10am-midnight daily. *Oct-Apr* 7pm-2am Tue-Sun.

A modern lounge-style bar and restaurant with huge comfy sofas, an airy feel, a local crowd and a cool atmosphere. Along with drinks, there are also reasonably priced light meals.

Ristorante Vittoria

Grand Hotel Excelsior Vittoria, piazza Tasso 34 (081 807 1044). **Meals served** 12.30-2pm, 7.30-10pm daily. **Closed** Jan, Feb. **Average** €50. **Credit** AmEx, DC, MC, V.

For the ultimate Grand Tour dining experience, head for the grandiose frescoed and mirrored dining room at the Excelsior Vittoria Hotel, where grave white-jacketed waiters whisk silver cloches off food that tries hard – with some degree of success – to reach standards a notch above usual hotel fare.

Sant'Antonino

Via Santa Maria delle Grazie 6 (081 877 1200). **Meals served** *Apr-mid Oct* noon-3pm, 7pm-midnight daily. *Mid Oct-Mar* noon-3pm, 7pm-midnight Tue, Thur-Sun. **Closed** Jan. **Average** €20. **Credit** AmEx, MC, V.

This unassuming trattoria serves pizza at lunch and dinner, and does a good fish barbecue on its terrace beneath the orange trees.

Piazzo Tasso. *See p229.*

Bar Villa Comunale

Villa Comunale (081 807 4090). **Open** *Mar-June, Sept, Oct* 9am-9pm daily. *July, Aug* 9am-midnight daily. **Closed** Nov-Feb. **No credit cards.**

With tables beneath the palms and pines of the Villa Comunale park, this otherwise forgettable bar is the perfect place for a traffic-free rest while appreciating the sea view from the cliff-top.

Shopping

Corso Italia is packed with clothes shops: the cheaper stores are east of piazza Tasso while the more upmarket boutiques are to the west. Via Cesareo and its continuation via Fuoro are the places for souvenirs, particularly *limoncello* (if you want to see the stuff being produced on the premises, try **Limonoro**, via San Cesareo 51, 081 807 2782) and local produce (piazza Tasso 16, 081 878 1263, www.fattoriaterranova.it). For marquetry souvenirs, try **Salvatore Gargiulo** (via Fuoro 33, 081 878 2420, www.gargiuloin laid.it), a well-established workshop where objects are made on the premises.

Arts & entertainment

Sorrento's largely tourist-centred economy rules out a truly vibrant cultural scene, and most of the city's night-time entertainment consists of strolling up and down the traffic-liberated via Cesareo, or relaxing in bars and watching others strolling.

Artis Domus

Via San Nicola 56 (081 877 2073/www.artisdomus. com). **Open** *Sept-June* 11pm-3am Sat. **Credit** MC,V.
A small stone doorway leads into the garden of a sumptuous villa where the tanned Versace-wearers of Sorrento congregate of a Saturday, when there's either live music or a disco, as well as a buffet.

Teatro Tasso

Piazza Sant'Antonino, 25 (081 807 5525/www.teatro tasso.it). **Open** *Box office* 9am-noon, 4.30-9.30pm on performance days. *Shows* mid Mar-Oct 9.30pm daily. **Tickets** *Theatre* €25. **Credit** AmEx, DC, MC, V.
Teatro Tasso's programme leans heavily towards the kind of *folkloristico* musical variety shows that require no knowledge of Italian culture. Watch out for the season of summer shows titled 'Sorrento Musical'. Cheesier than the mozzarella.

Estate Musicale Sorrentina

Chiostro della Chiesa di San Francesco (www.estatemusicalesorrentina.it).
Attempting to rival the musical summer season of neighbouring Ravello, Sorrento's summer season of classical concerts has come a long way in the last few years and can now give its rather snooty neighbour a good run for its money. Most concerts are free and of high quality. Details can be found on the website.

Fauno Notte

Piazza Tasso 1 (081 878 1021/www.faunonotte.it).
A disco throughout the year, in the summer this club gives itself over to a *tarantella* show.

Where to stay

The best of Sorrento's grand hotels are truly grand, and if your bank account is up to it, you can have a classic Grand Tourist experience. By comparison, the mid-range hotels are mediocre, and cheap places are almost non-existent. Unless otherwise stated, breakfast is included.

Campsite options in the area include the **Nube d'Argento** (via Capo 21, 081 878 1344, www.nubedargento.com, rates per person €7-€9; €5-€9.50 tent site). Further out of town, the **Santa Fortunata** (via Capo 39, 081 807 3579, www.santafortunata.com, rates per person €6-€9; €5-€6.50 tent site).

Agriturismo Marecoccola

Via Malacoccola 10 (081 533 0151/www.fattoria marecoccola.com). **Rates** €110-€150 double; €350 suite. **Credit** AmEx, MC, V.
An old stone farmhouse above Sorrento with sublime views. All meals use the farm's produce, and the owners also organise hiking expeditions.

Bellevue Syrene

Via Marina Grande 1 (081 878 1024/www.bellevue.it). **Rates** €180-€225 single; €220-€280 double; €315-€350 suite. **Credit** AmEx, DC, MC, V.
Elegant, light, airy and decorated in a tasteful if bland style, the Bellevue is built on the site of a second-century BC villa. It has been a hotel since 1820, hosting royalty, writers and many generations of the rich and famous. Rooms with a sea view cost more but are worth it – waking up to a pure blue view of sea and Mount Vesuvius is wonderful. The Lord Astor restaurant is a faithful replica of a Roman villa, but the 'Roman bath' looks suspiciously like a jacuzzi.

Grand Hotel Excelsior Vittoria

Piazza Tasso 34 (081 807 1044/www.excelsiorvittoria. com). **Rates** €252-€320 single; €295-€525 double; €520-€2,100 suite. **Credit** AmEx, DC, MC, V.
The grandest of Sorrento's grand hotels, the Vittoria has been in the hands of the Fiorentino family since 1834. The cool Pompeii-meets-art-deco corridors are in restful pastels; the rooms (not all of which have been recently decorated) have period furniture and delightful terraces overlooking the sea or the lush gardens. There's a pool and a children's playground. Low-season deals can be found on the hotel website. Caruso stayed here the week before his death; the suite where he stayed is named after him.

Hotel Regina

Via Marina Grande 10 (081 878 2722/www.hotel reginasorrento.it). **Closed** Nov-Mar. **Rates** €140-€165 double; €80-€105 per person half-board double; €118 per person single. **Credit** AmEx, DC, MC, V.

LimonHello

Whether you are heading to Sorrento by road or train, shortly after you get past Castellammare and head out towards the peninsula you will see what look like 10-foot-high cages made of wooden poles draped with dark mesh netting lining the roads. Peer through and you may just be able to make out some trees or bushes. Look more carefully and you'll see what it's all about.

Lemons.

Lemons, lemons and more lemons. Tiny little spherical green ones, regular lemon-shaped, lemon-coloured ones and huge great swollen grapefruit-sized things. To those of us who only know lemons as a yellow slice in a gin and tonic, it may seem strange that so much attention is lavished on this humble fruit, but – tourism apart – the tangy citrus is a mainstay of the Sorrentine economy.

Even a short stay in the area will introduce you to the myriad possibilities: *gelati, sorbetti* and *granite*; dressing for salads and fish; a salad in its own right (recipes are closely guarded secrets, but mostly use the white part of the lemon peel with balsamic vinegar); spaghetti sauce; any number of cakes from the simple *torta al limone* to the heavenly *delizie al limone,* and, of course – limoncello.

Adored and reviled in equal measure (on first exposure responses range from 'Mediterranean sun in a glass' to 'it tastes like sticky washing-up liquid'), the ubiquitous lemon liqueur with which you will inevitably be plied in Sorrento, Capri or Amalfi has actually only fairly recently become popular in Italy. Even a decade ago it was largely something made by southern Italian grannies and kept in a cupboard for special occasions. Then crafty people saw its marketing potential – and now, horror of horrors, there is even a Milanese company mass-producing the stuff.

A good limoncello shouldn't be too sweet and should have a fair citric bite. However, it should be smooth enough to cover up the kick of the phenomenal amount of alcohol it contains. It shouldn't be too artificially yellowy in colour, but should have a faint greenish tinge. It should always be served on the point of freezing, in tiny frosted glasses.

Should you feel adventurous, it's actually fairly easy to make. Take about a dozen small lemons that are still fairly green. Peel off only the zest of the lemons, put them in a bowl, jar or large bottle and add a litre of pure alcohol (easy to buy in Italy but harder abroad). Leave them for around two weeks – until the alcohol has taken on the colour of the zest, and the peel itself has become a pale brownish colour.

Mix a litre of water with about five or six tablespoonfuls of sugar and warm gently to make a syrup. Strain the alcohol to remove the zest, then mix it well with the sugar and water syrup. Bottle it, and leave it for at least a week. Drink. (There are, inevitably, millions of variations on this – many people swear that you should add a vanilla pod and/or a few cloves to the lemon zest).

Two warnings. First, never drink more than a couple of glasses. Limoncello may taste like ice-cream, but the mixture of sugar and alcohol can cause a fearsome hangover. Second, think twice before taking bottle-loads home with you. Somehow, when not drunk after a piece of grilled fish in a vine-covered restaurant with a view of the sea, it never tastes quite the same. Many are the bottles that have been found gathering dust at the back of a cupboard a year later.

The view from the Regina's rooftop restaurant goes some way towards compensating for the dubious colour schemes of its rooms. Clean, functional and with balconies outside almost all of them, they're just about as much as you can expect in Sorrento at these moderate prices.

Imperial Hotel Tramontano

Via Veneto 1 (081 878 2588/fax 081 807 2344/ www.tramontano.com). **Rates** €180 single; €275 double; €400-€480 suite. **Credit** AmEx, MC, V.

One of Sorrento's classic hotels, the elegant cliff-top Tramontano was a favourite of Shelley, Byron, Goethe and Ibsen (a plaque notes the fact that it was here, while 'meditating on human misery', that the Ibsen was moved to write *Ghosts*). It was also in this hotel that GB de Curtis penned the town's classic weepy ditty, 'Turna a Surriento', which you are bound to hear played ad nauseam all over town. The hotel has a pool, a lift down to the beach and a superb garden.

Bar Villa Comunale. *See p232.*

Ostello delle Sirene (Youth Hostel)

Via degli Aranci 160 (081 807 2925/fax 081 877 1371/info@hostel.it). **Rates** €16-€20 per person in dorm; €50-€60 double. **No credit cards.**
The cheapest beds in town.

Parco dei Principi

Via Rota 1 (081 878 4644/fax 081 878 3786/ www.grandhotelparcodeiprincipi.com). **Closed** Nov-Mar. **Rates** €185-€210 single; €200-€330 double; €450-€550 suite. **Credit** AmEx, DC, MC, V.
To the east of the town centre, the Parco was designed – building, furniture, fittings and all – in shades of blue and white by architect Giò Ponti in 1962. It looks like the set of a stylish 1960s Italian film. The modernist floor tiles form a different design in every room. There's a seawater pool, a sauna, a lift down the cliff to a private beach, and a lush botanical garden.

Resources

Car & scooter hire

Avis *Viale Nizza 53 (081 878 2459/www.avisauto noleggio.it).* **Open** Apr-Oct 9am-1pm, 4-8pm Mon-Sat; 9am-noon Sun. Nov-Mar 9am-1pm, 4-7pm Mon-Fri; 9am-1pm Sat. **Credit** AmEx, DC, MC, V.
Hertz *Via degli Aranci 9A (081 807 1646/fax 081 807 2521/www.hertzsorrento.com).* **Open** *Mar-Oct* 8.30am-12.30pm, 2.30-7.30pm Mon-Sat; 9am-noon, 3-8pm Sun. *Nov-Feb* 8.30am-12.30pm, 3.30-7pm Mon-Sat. **Credit** AmEx, DC, MC, V.
Sorrento Rent a Car/Rent a Scooter *Corso Italia 210A (081 878 1386/fax 081 878 5039/ www.sorrento.it).* **Open** 8am-1pm, 4-8.30pm daily. **Closed** 3wks Jan-Feb. **Credit** AmEx, DC, MC, V.

Hospital

Santa Maria della Misericordia *Corso Italia (081 533 1112).*

Police

Carabinieri *Via B Capasso (081 878 1010).*
Polizia di Stato *Vico III Rota (081 807 3101).*

Post office

Corso Italia (081 807 2828).

Tourist information

Azienda Autonoma di Cura Soggiorno e Turismo *Via Luigi di Maio 35 (081 807 4033/fax 081 877 3397/www.sorrentotourism.com).* **Open** *May, June, Sept* 8.30am-7pm Mon-Sat. *July, Aug* 8.30am-6.30pm Mon-Sat; 9am-1pm Sun. *Oct-Apr* 8.30am-2.30pm, 3.30-6.30pm Mon-Sat.
English-speaking staff will provide maps, leaflets and information on local events.

Getting around

For **Getting there***, see p241.*
Four orange bus lines serve the Sorrento area, and run from 5.30am to midnight. Line A goes from Meta to Capo di Sorrento, B from the port at Marina Piccola to the centre, C from the port at Marina Piccola to Sant'Agnello, and D between Marina Grande and the centre. Tickets (€1) from newsstands and tabacchi. Find the terminus in front of the station in piazza GB de Curtis.

East from Sorrento

Since the building and tourism boom of the 1950s and 1960s, what was once a collection of fishing and farming villages punctuated by the occasional stately holiday villa has become one big urban sprawl – albeit an extremely pretty urban sprawl. East of the town is a long, low, whitewashed conurbation of hotels there to mop up Sorrento's overflow. Many of these have pretty gardens and sports facilities that hotels in town don't have the space to offer; but if you want to be in the city centre, check the small print to avoid ending up out here.

Sant'Agnello is, administratively speaking, part of Sorrento, and its traffic-clogged main street is little more than a funnel into and out of town; as you drive through, you may not even realise it exists. More pleasant (and less congested) is the almost-coast road, which cuts past beautiful villas – many of them converted into hotels – and their flower-filled gardens just a block back from the sea.

Piano di Sorrento still retains the feel of a separate town. In the 18th-century **Villa Fondi** on the coast road, the **Museo Archeologico Georges Vallet** contains archaeological finds from the Sorrentine Peninsula: pre-Roman pottery, artefacts from necropoli and arrowheads – all beautifully

I Casali

From Vico Equense, the circular via Raffaele Bosco wends its way up (and back down) the slopes of the Sorrentine Peninsula, passing through woods and fields and the tiny villages – known as i casali – where the everyday, non-tourist-trade life of the area goes placidly on, unnoticed by visitors to the coastal resorts.

Setting out from Vico's main square, piazza Umberto I, via Roma soon becomes via Bosco, and climbs through the outskirts of town. A well-marked turn-off (via Cimitero) to the left leads to the church of **San Francesco** (opening hours erratic), a scruffy baroque affair full of plaster saints with staring eyes. Opposite the church, a path leads past Stations of the Cross set into the wall, to a vine-clad belvedere with an extraordinary view along the peninsula to Capri. On the sharp bend by the cemetery before the final climb to the church, a verdant track leads off to the sorgente di Sperlonga (Sperlonga spring, 30 minutes' easy walk). Until the coast road was built in the early 19th century, this was the only road from Castellammare di Stabia to the Sorrentine Peninsula.

Back on via Bosco, the road climbs to **Massaquano**, the unlikely location of what is perhaps the peninsula's greatest artwork. Creating a bottleneck in the main road on the right as you drive through, the chapel of **Santa Lucia** was built in 1385 and frescoed by followers of Giotto soon after. (To visit the chapel, distract the denizens of the Circolo San Luigi Gonzaga pool hall across the road from their game, and get them to locate the foot-long 14th-century key.)

Saved from imminent ruin in a recent restoration, the chapel's haunting frescos (behind the altar) show scenes from an apocryphal gospel story in which Christ returns his dead mother's soul to her (in the shape of a baby) before taking her, body and soul, into heaven; the archangel Michael slices the hands off a sacrilegious onlooker who tries to overturn Mary's bier, while saints Lucy (with the lantern) and Catherine of Alexandria (with the original catherine wheel, on which she was martyred) watch the scene from the bottom left.

On the right wall are scenes from the passion of Christ. The left wall once had a detailed cycle on the life of St Lucy, but much of this has disappeared over the centuries. The apparition of St Agatha to Lucy and the saint's intercession to stem Lucy's mother's haemorrhage are still visible.

Via Bosco continues to climb to **Moiano**, from where a hiking trail (N38) departs for Monte Faito (around two and a half hours). Beyond the village centre, a road on the left leads to the hamlet and church of **Santa Maria del Castello** (three kilometres/two miles). In the church are marble statues and paintings of saints made in Naples in the 16th and 17th centuries (the family in the house at the foot of the stairs has the key).

From the church, perched 685 metres (2,397 feet) above sea level on the crest of the peninsula, the hills fall away south to the Amalfi Coast and north to Sorrento. The view is simply breathtaking. There's a hiking trail (N33; two hours) from Santa Maria del Castello to Positano.

Back on via Bosco (either of the descents from Santa Maria del Castello will do), past the village of **Arola**, a steep, narrow road to the left leads to the remains of the 17th-century **convento dei Camaldolesi**, from where there's another superlative view down to the sea. Via Bosco then drops sharply back to reach the coast at **Seiano**.

Frequent guided walks around some of the casali are organised by local groups. Check www.massalubrense.it or the tourist offices in Sorrento or Vico for more information.

laid out, but with labels in Italian only. A tortuous track leads down to the little harbour – **Marina di Cassano** – where the beach is encroached upon by boats from one of the peninsula's few remaining economically significant fishing fleets.

Meta di Sorrento boasts the area's longest stretch of sand, the **spiaggia di Alimuri**. Until a century ago, Meta's marina moored one of Italy's largest shipping tonnages, but is now another bustling modern suburb, with more Sorrento overflow hotels, and cafés with tables out in sunny piazze. In a square on the main road, the **Madonna del Lauro** basilica (open 7am-noon, 4-7pm daily), with its low, tiled dome and neo-classical façade, was rebuilt in the 18th century but it is believed to stand on the site of a temple to Minerva.

After Meta, there is a slight lull in the urban sprawl before the village of **Seiano**, where the 16th-century chapel of **Santa Maria delle Grazie** (closed to the public) has a medieval fresco over its front door. You'll also see the 18th-century church of **San Marco** (opening times vary according to Mass), which has the highest dome on the peninsula. Both coast road and railway line then cross the breathtaking, and somewhat frightening, viaduct over the Murrano river to Vico Equense.

VICO EQUENSE

Aequana was probably discovered by the Romans, who found its steep, sunny slopes perfect for cultivating grapes, before the Goths razed it in the fifth century. (The area's wine production has since moved further up the hill to **Gragnano**, where a tasty, slightly fizzy red is still produced today.) The town of Vico Equense was resurrected in the 13th century by King Charles II of Anjou.

The privately owned **Castello Giusso** (not open to the public) looms inescapably over the town, its fanciful crenellations a 19th-century addition to the original 1284 medieval building. The Renaissance section above was added in the mid 16th century.

To the south, in via Puntamare, the church of the **Santissima Annunziata** (open 9-10.30am Mon-Sat; 9am-12.30pm Sun) overlooks a dramatic drop to the sea, making it an essential photo opportunity. The Annunziata was Vico's cathedral until the bishopric was abolished in 1799 when the last incumbent, Michel Natale, was hanged for his over-enthusiastic support of the Parthenopean Republic. His portrait is missing from the medallions of former bishops in the sacristy: instead, there's a painting of an angel with its finger raised to its lips, inviting onlookers to draw a veil of silence over Natale's unwise choice. Some Gothic arches from the original 14th-century church are in the side aisles.

Along viale Rimembranza, the baroque church of **San Ciro** (open 8.30am-noon, 4.30-7.30pm daily) has a pretty tiled dome. Nearby, in via San Ciro, the **Museo Mineralogico Campano** has a collection of some 5,000 bits of rock, including fluorescent ones that glow under ultraviolet light; there are a few chunks of meteorite and some fossils, too. Inside the town hall, a collection of artefacts from a local necropolis (seventh- to fifth-century BC) are displayed in the **Antiquarium**.

Below the town centre to the east, **Marina di Vico** (occasional buses run from Vico station) has a short pebbly beach with a handful of restaurants. To the west, on the other hand, the harbour at **Marina di Equa** allows access to long stretches of sun-worshipping space at the *spiaggie* (beaches) of Pezzolo (where ruins of a first-century AD villa are visible) and Vescovado to the east, and Calcare to the west. The imposing ruin at the far end of Calcare beach was part of a lime quarry that operated for hundreds of years, closing down in the late 19th century. There's a Saracen watchtower and lots of bars in pretty Marina di Equa, as well as one of the best restaurants in the area, the **Torre del Saracino** (*see p237*). (Finding Marina di Equa can be a problem: head out of Vico on the SS145; just beyond the far end of the railway viaduct, there's a small sign marked 'Marina di Equa' – don't blink or you'll miss it.)

Antiquarium

Casa Municipale, via Filangieri 98, Vico Equense (081 801 9111). **Open** by appointment only 8.30am-12.30pm Mon, Wed, Fri; 8.30am-12.30pm, 4-6pm Tue, Thur. **Admission** free.

Torre del Saracino.

Museo Archeologico Georges Vallet
Via Ripa di Cassano 14, Piano di Sorrento (081 808 7078). **Open** 9am-1pm, 4-7pm Tue-Sun. **Admission** €5. **No credit cards**.

Museo Mineralogico Campano
Via San Ciro 2, Vico Equense (081 801 5668). **Open** *June-Sept* 9am-1pm, 5-8pm Tue-Sat; 9am-1pm Sun. *Oct-May* 9am-1pm, 4-7pm Tue-Sat; 9am-1pm Sun. **Admission** €2. **No credit cards**.

Where to eat & drink

In Piano di Sorrento, the **Bar Villa Fondi** (via Ripa di Cassano 14, 081 534 1050, closed Mon) is an airy pavilion in the lovely cliff-top gardens surrounding the Museo Georges Vallet and overlooking the sea.

Vico Equense calls itself 'the home of pizza by the metre', thanks solely to the endeavours of **Gigino Pizza al Metro** (via Nicotera 15, 081 879 8426, average €15), a great barn of a place, popular with busloads of tourists and large Neapolitan families. Stretch-pizzas of all imaginable varieties are served here; order slices of a length to match your appetite.

In Marina di Equa, the **Torre del Saracino** (via Torretta 9, 081 802 8555, closed dinner Sun Sept-June, Mon, 29 Jan-12 Feb, average €60) more than deserves its Michelin star, offering some of the best food on this (or any) coast: the seafood antipasti is a mouth-watering selection with everything from caviar to sea urchins; the pasta for the exquisite first course is home-made, and the fish tastes as if it just left the sea. Food can be enjoyed on a beautiful patio beneath the Saracen watchtower after which the place is named.

Where to stay

Down a sharp drop off the coast road east of Vico Equense, the **Hotel Capo La Gala** (via Luigi Serio 8, 081 801 5758, www.capolagala. com, closed Nov-Mar, doubles €170) is a big cut above the generally mediocre accommodation on offer in town. Tastefully decorated rooms with balconies overhang waves crashing on to rocks below; the pool is filled with mineral-rich water from the nearby Scraio spring.

Perched above Vico in Santa Maria del Castello, off via Bosco, the **Agriturismo La Ginestra** (via Tessa 2, 081 802 3211, www.laginestra.org, doubles €80-€90 half-board, €98-€110 full-board) has simple, bright rooms in a farmhouse with spectacular views down the green slopes of the peninsula to the sea in the distance. The farm's own organically grown produce is used in the restaurant (average €25), where non-residents are welcome if they book.

Resources

Tourist information
Azienda Autonoma di Cura Soggiorno e Turismo *Via San Ciro 16, Vico Equense (081 801 5752/fax 081 879 9351/www.vicoturismo.it).* **Open** *Apr-Sept* 9am-8pm Mon-Sat; 9.30am-1.30pm Sun. *Oct-Mar* 9am-2pm, 3-5pm Mon-Sat.
Keeps a good supply of maps, including walking maps, of the area.

West from Sorrento

Heading west from Sorrento is a very good idea since ribbon development and heavy-duty tourism have yet to reach this area. Towns are hemmed in by lemon groves, and the air in spring and summer is full of the pungent perfumes of wild garlic and gorse.

The first stop out of Sorrento is the small village of **Capo di Sorrento**, where Maxim Gorky's stay at the **Villa Il Sorito** from 1924 to 1933 is commemorated by a plaque on the front wall. A little further on a high-walled path leads off the coast road to the right (north). Edged by impossibly romantic fields of lemon trees and asphodels, it goes down to what is known locally as the **Bagni della Regina Giovanna** (baths of Queen Joan). In fact, the medieval Joan had little to do with what was a sumptuous Roman villa, possibly built by Pollio Felice. The ruins that ramble across the headland, surrounding a deep, man-made seawater inlet, are much easier to interpret after a pre-emptive visit to the **Museo Archeologico Georges Vallet** in Piano

di Sorrento (*see p237*), where there's a scale model of the villa. The outcrops of brick are a good place to sit and contemplate the view up the sweep of coast to Sorrento.

Beyond Capo, a pretty road drops down to the tiny **Marina di Puolo** where there's a sandy beach (a long walk down from the car park). More citrus orchards and olive groves (nets to collect the falling fruit are stretched out between the trees from October to December, then rolled up and left between the trees in multicoloured swathes) line the winding stretch of coast road from here to the lively town of Massa Lubrense.

Walking country

It's quite possible that after climbing the steps up and down from Marina Piccola more than a couple of times, you'll want to hear no more about walking in the Sorrento area. But if you don't mind steep slopes, you can discover that the beautiful and apparently inaccessible hills around Sorrento are actually not inaccessible at all. Often invisible from the road, a network of reasonably well-kept footpaths web the area from Castellammare di Stabia to Amalfi to Punta della Campanella.

Most of the paths are colour-coded and, in general, easy to follow. Some are maintained by the Italian rambling group, Club Alpino Italiano (CAI), which marks routes with coloured paint flashes on rocks, walls, lampposts or whatever else comes to hand. Paths vary dramatically in difficulty; the further you go from habitation, the less well defined they become, and occasionally you end up cutting across someone's vineyard or olive grove.

Half-day walks and easy strolls

Sorrento is a starting point for several easy, pleasant walks. For one, take the via Capo west out of Sorrento as far as Capo di Sorrento (or get the bus a few stops), and then turn right down to the Roman Villa di Pollio Felice (*see p237*) and continue on across the wooden bridge as far as the Bagni della Regina Giovanna, where you can stop for a swim. Another walk begins by the Sorrento Palace Hotel, where you take the via Crucis steps (marked out with the Stations of the Cross). The path continues as far as Sant'Agata (*see p244*) and then on to the Deserto monastery (*see p244*). The views there from Sant'Agata are stunning – you can see all the Bay of Naples and the Gulf of Salerno (hence the town's name, Sant'Agata sui Due Golfi). Either of these walks can be done in a morning.

If you have the legs for it, carry on from Sant'Agata to the Marina di Crapolla. The path winds steeply down the hillside to a tiny pebble beach. Aside from this path, the beach is only accessible from the sea, so, when you pull off your sweaty boots and dive into the sea, you're likely to have the beach to yourself. The 12th-century church of San Pietro is just behind you, and there are some Roman walls on the beach itself.

For those who have no fear of heights yet can't face uphill hikes, take the Circumvesuviana train to Castellammare and get the *funivia* (cable car) up to the top of Monte Faito (operates April-October). It's worth the trip for the cable car alone (don't look down though); the ride can be followed by a pleasant, level stroll around the mountain's peak (after Vesuvius, the second highest in the area).

See also below **Punta della Campanella**.

Day-long walks

If you have a good long day to spare, there are a couple of dramatic coast-to-coast walks. The first goes from Puolo to Crapolla (stopping in Sant'Agata just over halfway). The climb is long and fairly relentless, though the views make it worthwhile. Slightly shorter is the walk from Marina della Lobra to Marina del Cantone. It's no less strenuous, however, but most of the ascent is done in the first hour of the walk, leaving you with a long gradual descent across the Positano side of the peninsula. Neither are recommended for those with bad knees.

More serious walkers will want to check out the **Alta via dei Monti Lattari**, which stretches from Colli di Fontanelle above Positano down to Punta Campanella. This is said to be the old shepherd's path down from the hills into Sorrento and is marked by a red and white line. It will take at least a day to walk the path; it's better to break your journey with a stopover in Massa or Sant'Agata.

The other long path in the area is the **Sentieri degli Dei** (Pathway of the Gods). There are several variations on this path: the name is given to a number of old routes that pass along the top of the ridge from Ravello and down to Sorrento. Wandering

MASSA LUBRENSE

Probably founded in its current position by the Lombards – Massa comes from the Lombard word for settlement, *mansa* – this area was known in ancient times. *Lubrense* derives from the Latin word *delubrum* or 'temple', two of which are known to have existed in the vicinity.

There's a great view across to Capri from the belvedere in **largo Vescovado**. On the other side of the square there's the haunting, crumbling façade of the former cathedral of **Santa Maria delle Grazie** (open 7am-noon, 4.30-8pm daily), which dates from the early 16th century, although it was reworked in

as it does along the pinnacle of the mountains – sometimes with a sheer descent on either side – it is easy to see how the path got its name.

Punta della Campanella

Many of the area's best walks are near, or end at, the **Punta della Campanella** national park, or 'marine reserve' as it is formally known. Opened in 2000 with the aim of protecting the date shell mollusc (*dattero del mare*) from being harvested out of existence, strong opposition from powerboat owners and property developers has not stopped the park from flourishing.

The park got its name because there was once a bell (*campanella*) here that would be rung to warn the residents when marauding pirates were sighted. The best entry points to the park are the towns of Termini or

Nerano. From Termini there is a long, gentle walk (two to three hours) that winds down to Punta della Campanella. You are only five kilometres (three miles) from Capri, and the island seems close enough to touch. There was originally a Greek temple on the tip of the peninsula, although the ruins you can see are of a second-century Roman villa and the 14th-century bell tower. From Nerano, head south to Punta Penna and Punta di Montalto, with its Napoleonic lookout tower. There is a tiny beach at Capitello on the Baia di Jeranto (*see p244*) – possibly the most spectacular swimming spot in the whole area.

Need to know

A few warnings – some of the painted colours on the signposts have faded, been removed or become contradictory due to changing paths. Don't be embarrassed to ask for directions – most people are helpful.

In spring or autumn, watch out for sudden heavy rain showers. Some of the ravine-like paths can block up with leaves, branches and other debris, while stone paths can become slippery. In summer, many of these paths have little or no shade for long stretches. Wear a hat, bring sunscreen and lots of drinking water.

Be aware, also, of Italian farmers' habit of leaving large, aggressive dogs to roam freely around what they perceive to be their land. Though they may bark, they rarely bite.

The best places for information on walks are the tourist information offices in Sorrento and Massa Lubrense (*see p234 and p241*). The owner of the Bar Orlando in Sant'Agata is also a mine of information (ask him about the legend of the smoking cat while you're there). For more information about walks, contact the local branch of the **World Wide Fund for Nature** (WWF, Corso Italia 67, Sorrento, 081 807 2533, www.wwfpenisolasorrentina.org). More information on the park is available from **Ente Parco Punta della Campanella** (viale Filangieri 40, Massa Lubrense, 081 808 9877, www.puntacampanella.org).

Around Naples

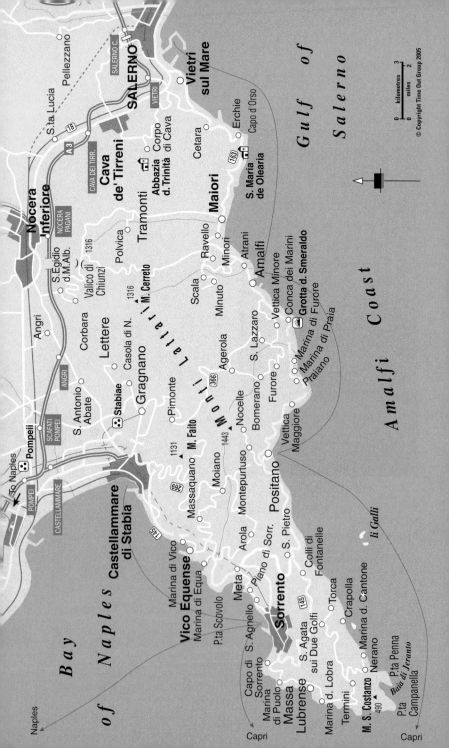

1769. The chapel of **Sant'Erasmo**, to the left of the main altar, is believed to stand above a temple to Hercules. Directly opposite the church, a road leads down to the attractive village and beach of **Marina di Lobra** (take a scenic shortcut down the first downward flight of steps right from the road; you may, however, want to hitch a lift or wait for the infrequent bus on the way back up).

Halfway down the road, the church of **Santa Maria di Lobra** (open 6.30-8am, 5-8pm daily) has a pretty yellow-and-green tiled dome, a 'miraculous' 16th-century Madonna and Child over the altar, and a cool, homely cloister with a tiled well-head (there's a door from the cloister into the church that is generally open when the church is officially shut). There was a temple here, too, probably dedicated to Minerva. The whole place has a charming lived-in feel, although only two old Franciscan monks remain in the adjoining monastery; if you feel moved to join them for a while, the **Piccolo Paradiso Hotel** (*see below*) takes bookings for a handful of simple monastery rooms.

From Massa's main square, a road north-west (soon swinging south) heads to the villages of **Santa Maria** and **Annunziata**, the latter little more than a handful of houses around a rarely open church of the same name, and the ruins of the 14th-century castello di Massa.

A well-marked walking trail goes from Massa to Annunziata. It's worth taking it not only for the walk itself, but also to see the **Villa Rossi** where Joaquin Murat holed up after the Battle of Capri and signed the capitulation that put an ignominious end to French rule in Naples.

BEYOND MASSA

The coast road out of Massa swings past the church and cemetery of **San Liberatore** (open Apr-Sept 8am-12.30pm, 4-6pm Mon, Tue, Thur-Sat; 8.30am-noon Sun; Oct-May 8.30am-12.30pm, 2.30-5pm Mon, Tue, Thur-Sat; 8.30am-noon Sun), a final resting place of incredible beauty on the edge of a cliff with Capri tantalisingly close across the bay. The little whitewashed chapel was built in 1420, although it has been heavily restored since.

In ancient times the coast road continued as far as the temple to Minerva on Punta della Campanella. Nowadays, it curves inland a couple of kilometres short of the point, to the town of **Termini**.

A nondescript place with a spectacular view, Termini is the starting point for walks around Punta della Campanella, down to the Amalfi Coast and along the crests of the peninsula. The lane that heads south opposite the church leads to the chapel of **San Costanzo** (the walk

takes around 40 minutes). The chapel is a stark white construction, rarely open; the view down towards the very tip of the peninsula at Punta della Campanella and the Baia di Jeranto immediately to the north is awe-inspiring.

From the same point, another path (grey and green stripes; 90 minutes) follows the headland out to the Saracen watchtower on **Punta della Campanella**; there are the remains of a Roman villa. The path for Punta Penna, with access to Jeranto Bay, begins in Nerano.

Where to stay & eat

Accommodation is low key in Massa Lubrense, and the family-run **Hotel La Primavera** (via IV Novembre 3G, 081 878 9125, www.laprimavera. biz, closed mid Jan-mid Feb, €74-€95 double) is no exception, but it's clean, most of the rooms have balconies, and the restaurant serves excellent, unpretentious seafood (average €28). The **Antico Francischiello da Peppino** (via Partenope 27, 081 533 9780, www.francischiello. com, closed Wed Nov-Mar, average €50) is Massa's premier restaurant, serving wonderful local cheeses as well as good, fresh, traditional seafood dishes. Staff will even come and pick you up if you're staying in Sorrento.

Il Tritone (via Massa Turro 2/A, 081 808 9046, closed Jan & Mon, average €20) is a good alternative if you don't fancy splashing out and want something simple; worth trying are the home-made *scialatielli* pasta with clams and mussels.

In Marina di Lobra, the **Piccolo Paradiso** (piazza Madonna della Lobra 5, 081 808 9534, www.piccolo-paradiso.com, closed mid Nov-Feb, doubles €43-€75 per person half-board) is a more upmarket accommodation option with a swimming pool and scuba diving arranged on request. It also handles the very simple monks' cells for rent at the monastery opposite (€28 per person B&B, *see p241* **Santa Maria di Lobra**).

Resources

Tourist information

Proloco *Viale Filangieri 11, Massa Lubrense (081 533 9021/www.massalubrense.it).* **Open** *Apr-Oct* 9.45am-1pm, 4.45-8.30pm daily. *Nov-Mar* 9.45am-1pm, 4.30-7.30pm Mon-Sat.

Getting there

From Naples airport

Autolinee Curreri Service (081 801 5420) runs six coaches in each direction daily between the airport and Sorrento (stopping at Vico Equense, Piano, Meta and Sant'Agnello); tickets cost €6 (available on the bus).

Imperial Hotel Tramontano. *See p234.*

By hydrofoil/ferry

Alilauro (081 761 1004) and Linee Marittime Partenopee (081 807 3024) run hydrofoil services between Naples (Molo Beverello) and Sorrento. Services run all year (weather permitting). €7.50 single (30mins). From May-Sept, Metro del Mare (199 446 644/www.metrodelmare.com) operates fast ferry connections from Molo Beverello or Mergellina to Sorrento with useful stops in between. €4 single (1hr).

By bus

SITA (081 808 0237/www.sita-on-line.it) covers routes from Sorrento across the peninsula to the Amalfi Coast and Salerno. Services are curtailed on Sundays and public holidays (last bus at 7pm). Get the Unico Campania Fascia 5 ticket (€3.20) if you're coming from Naples, and the Fascia 4 (€2.80) if you're coming from Salerno.

Along the Sorrento–Meta di Sorrento–Positano–Amalfi route there are hourly services from around 6.35am to 8.05pm, but smaller inland towns aren't so well connected. There are hourly services from around 6am to 11pm on the Sorrento–Massa Lubrense–Sant'Agata sui Due Golfi route, but only a few continue to Nerano, Marina di Cantone and Marina di Lobra. Check the timetables at tourist offices or (usually) attached to each bus stop itself.

By car

Head south along the A3 motorway to its end at Castellammare di Stabia. At the end of the motorway the SS145 goes south-east around the peninsula; it's tortuous and slow, but it's the only way.

Take the SS142 to pass through Vico Equense, Piano and Meta, or stay on the SS145 as it swings inland towards Sant'Agata sui Due Golfi. An unnumbered road forks east along the peninsula through Massa to Termini, before rejoining the SS145 at Sant'Agata.

Inland roads on the peninsula vary greatly in quality; all have hair-raising bends (sound your horn). These roads can get horribly traffic-filled at weekends and during the holiday season.

By train

Sorrento is the terminus of the Circumvesuviana railway (information 081 772 2444/www.vesuviana.it), which can be picked up from Naples' Piazza Garibaldi; services every 30mins in both directions. The train also stops at Vico Equense and Sant' Agnello. The last Sorrento–Naples train leaves at 10.25pm; if you miss it there's a bus at 12.15am.

A Naples–Sorrento ticket costs €3.20 and is valid for 180mins on any form of public transport between the two towns.

Around Naples

The Amalfi Coast

A cliff landscape that once made for a hard life is now home to *la dolce vita*.

There is a curious irony in the fact that the Amalfi coast, once unable to sustain its own population, forcing locals to emigrate in droves, is now a destination for the Europe's nouveau aristocracy. Bejewelled jet-setters from Eastern Europe and beyond descend its craggy cliffs each summer to admire their pedicures in an azure sea.

As hotel prices rise, the area is rapidly becoming a playground for the wealthy alone, but, thanks to its unyielding topography, it will never truly be conquered by money. Unlike St Tropez, Porto Cervo and the Mediterranean's similarly swanky ports of call, Amalfi's harbour has scant space for yachts. There is precious little flat land on which to land a helicopter, and no, absolutely no real estate at all on its coastline out of which to carve a highway. By land, all visitors must enter this terrestrial paradise by one of two points of entry – Salerno in the east, or Sorrento to the west.

The road in between is a narrow string of twists and turns. It is said there are more than 1,000 curves, but any driver will lose count after just a few of them, distracted by the sight of tour buses negotiating the hairpin bends and speed demons performing death-defying moves on the road ahead.

If you are the lucky (nerveless) passenger, on the other hand, you will be busy taking in regal views of a coastline that is unmatched anywhere in the world. Terraced gardens tumble vertically from the sky and plunge into the pastel-painted houses below. Bougainvillea and olive trees swallow up the steeples and embrace the swimming pools that cling to the face of the cliffs.

Construction here is limited by geography (cliff-hugging towns can't grow into sprawling resorts) – a big plus when it comes to retaining original charm. Fishermen still go out at night in small wooden boats to catch tomorrow's lunch. Locals still sell home-made limoncello on the beach – or the version made with strawberries called *fragolino* (not to be confused with the grape of the same name). The people's seafaring passion and close relationship with the land are genuine sentiments, not just folklore to be served up to tourists like a €24 lunch menu. Here there is true pride in the region's storied past.

It is easy to forget that the diminutive city of Amalfi was once a major maritime power,

so important that its crest sits alongside those of Venice, Genoa and Pisa on the Italian naval flag. It is often repeated that the compass was invented here (a groundless claim), and that the first set of maritime laws was passed here, which is a matter of record. Such naval ingenuity was born of the necessity to regulate Amalfi's bustling commerce and to combat the Pisans and the hordes of Saracen pirates drawn to its wealthy shores.

Indeed, the only practical way to plan an invasion of the imposing cliffs was by sea, and that remains just as true today. Hopping from town to town on a boat is much more convenient than getting around by bus or car. Even better is to walk: a well-signposted network of paths extends along the whole coast, from short village-to-village strolls to a spectacular long-distance footpath, the

Kicking back in the **Marina di Cantone**.

Alta Via dei Lattari, that follows the ridge dividing the Amalfi Coast from the Bay of Naples. Walking between two points – for example, the short hop from Ravello to Minori or Atrani – is often quicker than taking the bus. The footpath numbers in the text refer to the official CAI (Club Alpino Italiano) numbers, and should be written on markers along the way. The CAI's excellent Monti Lattari map and walking guide can be found in book and newspaper shops all over the Amalfi Coast.

West of Positano

For many visitors, Positano is the western limit of the Amalfi experience. The steep, rocky, spectacular stretch of coastline further west has few hotels or historical sites; administratively part of the province of Naples, it possesses only a sprinkling of tiny villages, most of them built well back from the shoreline, which until relatively recently were only accessible by boat. Even today the road descends to the sea in only one place, the **Marina di Cantone**.

It is the remoteness that makes the coast between Punta della Campanella (*see p239*) and Positano worth exploring, as this is what the Amalfi Coast proper must have looked like before it was discovered by mass tourism in the 1950s. The lack of roads is the walker's gain:

there are some spectacular paths down to hidden coves and wild headlands, and the western section of the **Alta Via dei Lattari** – for serious walkers only – traverses the whole coast (*see also p238* **Walking country**). Perhaps unexpectedly, this stretch also boasts some of the best restaurants on the Costiera Amalfitana.

Sant'Agata sui Due Golfi, set in a dip on the ridge dividing Sorrento from the sheer southern coast, was a favourite summer resort for well-off Neapolitan families in the 18th and 19th centuries. It doesn't look like much today, with cars vying with agricultural equipment for parking places outside the 17th-century church of **Santa Maria delle Grazie** (open 8am-1pm, 5-7pm daily), with its monumental multicoloured inlaid marble altar. But there are two very good reasons for a stopover. One is the Michelin-starred restaurant **Don Alfonso 1890** (*see p245*); the other is the convent of Il Deserto, situated a kilometre (just under a mile) north-west of town along a (badly) signposted road.

A forbidding bunker built by the Carmelite order in 1679 and now occupied by a recalcitrant closed order of Benedictine nuns, **Il Deserto** (081 878 0199) has a roof terrace with a view across the peninsula that defies description. It is ostensibly open 3-6pm daily; in fact, it's open when the nuns feel like it, and when they're prepared to slide the huge key out through the revolving barrel in their visitors' room, in exchange for a small contribution towards the upkeep of the convent.

From Sant'Agata, via Torricella leads south-east to **Torca**, a tiny village with terrific views down over the coast. From Torca, a marked footpath (No.37) leads steeply down to the **Marina di Crapolla**. Don't let the name (a corruption of the Latin for goat) put you off: this picturesque, pebbly fishing cove is well worth the scramble down and the slow climb back. On the headland to the west are the remains of a 12th-century abbey; on the beach is a ruined Roman villa. The islet of Isca, just offshore, was owned by the Neapolitan actor and playwright Eduardo de Filippo.

The road from Sant'Agata west to **Termini**, jumping-off point for **Punta della Campanella** (*see p239*), is frustratingly viewless. Beyond the hamlet of Caso, a side road on the left winds down to the pretty village of Nerano and the seaside resort of **Marina di Cantone**, which has one of the longest beaches on the southern side of the peninsula. This is not necessarily a blessing, as Cantone seems to have gone from nothing to resort without passing through the limbo of planning permission, but it's still small scale – the topography sees to that – and has a certain low-key family charm that contrasts with the sometimes excessive refinement (and often excessive prices) of resorts such as Positano.

Cantone has an excellent diving centre offering courses and guided dives, **Diving Nettuno** (via Vespucci 39, 081 808 1051, www.divingsorrento.com, closed Nov-Mar), and the resort makes a good springboard for the breathtaking natural beauty of the **Baia di Jeranto** to the west. This untouched sandy bay is reachable by either boat (shop around on Cantone beach) or by marked footpath (No.39) from the church in Nerano. East of Cantone, **Torca** can be reached in three hours along a spectacular – and strenuous – cliff-hugging section of the Alta Via dei Lattari long-distance footpath. For more on walking in this area, *see p238* **Walking country**.

East of Sant'Agata, the Nastro Azzurro road leads, in 14 nail-biting kilometres (nine miles), to **Positano**. Off the coast are three small islands that the ancients believed to be the home of the Sirens, who lured mariners on to the rocks with their song; once known as Le Sirenuse, they now have the more prosaic name of Li Galli – the cockerels. In 1925, the villa on the largest of the islands was bought by dancer and choreographer Léonide Massine; Stravinsky and Picasso were among his guests.

Over the pass of San Pietro, where the road across from Sorrento joins the Nastro Azzurro, the Amalfi Coast proper comes into view – but if you're driving, you won't be looking at the view. Even passengers may have a hard time: in 1953, John Steinbeck and his wife 'lay clutched in each other's arms, weeping hysterically', while their driver, Signor Bassani, expounded happily on the region's history.

Where to stay & eat

In Sant'Agata sui Due Golfi, the chintzy decor of **Don Alfonso 1890** (corso Sant'Agata 13, 081 878 0026, www.donalfonso.com, closed mid Jan-Feb, Mon & Tue lunch June-Sept, Mon & Tue Oct-May, average €95) may not be to everyone's taste, but there's no denying that Alfonso Iaccarino's exquisite seasonal Mediterranean cuisine deserves its two Michelin stars. Typical dishes could include lobster with fennel and aubergine, goat roasted with herbs or an unbelievably light soufflé of marrow with mozzarella and anchovy sauce. All the garden produce comes from the Iaccarino family's organic farm. Don Alfonso also has five pretty apartments (doubles €195 for bed and breakfast – and what a breakfast).

In Marina di Cantone, the **Taverna del Capitano** (piazza delle Sirene 10, 081 808 1028, www.tavernadelcapitano.it, closed Jan, Feb, Mon & Tue lunch Oct-May, average €55),

housed in a nondescript white building on the seafront, proves that appearances can be deceptive. Inside, on the ground floor, is an elegant restaurant presided over by young chef Alfonso Caputo, who does succulent things with seafood and local garden produce. Upstairs are 15 bright, airy, reasonably priced rooms (doubles €90-€130). Cantone's other hot culinary contender is **Quattro Passi** (via Vespucci 13N, 081 808 2 800, www.ristorante quattropassi.com, closed Tue dinner, Wed, 6 Nov-26 Dec, open daily mid June-mid Sept, average €60), which lies a little way back up the approach road in extensive grounds. It's an elegant place with the heart of a family restaurant and a real vocation for fine food. Starters could be monkfish ravioli or risotto with large shrimp and broom flowers, followed by freshly caught red mullet or *pezzogna* (bream) parcels with curly lettuce and pine nuts. The cellar – dug into the tufa stone and extending under the road – is a cave of oenological wonders. There are also six simple double rooms (€85) and three suites (€135), which look on to terraces of olive trees.

Resources

See p250.

Amalfi's west coast.

Getting there

See p250.

Positano

Positano is not so much a town as a cliff with houses on. Unlike its neighbour, Amalfi, it had no long, narrow river valley to expand up and shelter in; here, life is vertical and exposed. Perhaps this explains why the town has little history on show: more vulnerable to pirate raids and without the watermills that made Amalfi an industrial as well as a naval power, it kept things small and rebuildable. In the 12th and 13th centuries, Positano's merchant fleet rivalled Amalfi's, but thereafter the town declined, coming under the control of a succession of Neapolitan overlords. In the 19th century, three-quarters of the population emigrated to the United States; even today, Columbus Avenue in New York has more *positanesi* than Positano.

When John Steinbeck came here in 1953 to write an article for *Harper's Bazaar*, Positano was a secret closely guarded by the few Italian writers and painters who had discovered it. But its *dolce vita* star rose rapidly; in the mid 1960s, it was briefly more fashionable than Capri. Traces of this high tide are visible everywhere – in hotel decor, 1960s seaside postcards and above all in the town's much-touted 'fashion' shops, where the truly fashion-conscious will find slim pickings.

The dramatic topography that made life in Positano so difficult is what makes it such a tourist attraction today. It's endlessly photogenic, with stacks of colourful houses clinging to every inch of the steep terrain. Positano's vertical layout means that almost every house has a clear view over the top of the one in front; to their despair, this means decent-sized swimming pools are out of the question – at least until someone invents a vertical one. Like Capri, Positano has deliberately priced itself out of the package-tour market: of its 30 hotels, more than two-thirds are three star or above, and in high season it's well nigh impossible to find a double room for less than €100 a night, unless you have booked weeks or even months in advance.

Tourist income is used to keep the place looking spruce and clean, though the cleanliness is skin-deep, as Positano still does not have an efficient sewage treatment system: in high summer, the smell emanating from the conduit that runs through town and under the main beach is far from pleasant, and the sea can be distinctly murky.

Directions in Positano are either up or down, unless you're in a car, in which case they're round and round for hours. The SS163 coast road hugs the contours in the upper part of town,

where it goes by the name of via Marconi. From the town hall to the west, one-way viale Pasitea winds down in a series of curves to piazza dei Mulini, then changes its name to via Cristoforo Colombo and climbs again to rejoin the coast road on the eastern edge of town. These are the only roads open to traffic; in summer, the lower one is permanently clogged with cars hunting for parking spaces. A strong pair of legs will get you almost anywhere in town more quickly than a set of wheels, though if you can't face the climb there is a regular circular bus service.

From piazza dei Mulini, narrow, shop-lined via dei Mulini runs down to the beach past the parish church of **Santa Maria Assunta** (open 8am-noon, 3.30-7pm daily), with its characteristic brightly coloured majolica dome; there's a 13th-century burnished gold Madonna and Child above the main altar.

The beach, **Marina Grande**, consists of a neat stretch of fine grey pebbles with colourful fishing boats pulled up in serried ranks; to the right looking seawards is the quay for boats to Capri, Amalfi, Salerno and Naples (Metro del Mare), to the left a private section of beach. Above the quay, steps lead up to a path that winds around the side of the cliff, past the **'O Guarracino** restaurant (*see p248*) to the smaller, rockier, but very popular beach of Fornillo, in a bay guarded by two ancient watchtowers. Above Positano lie the perched villages of **Montepertuso** and **Nocella**. Until very few years ago, the road (and bus) up from Positano ended at Montepertuso. The inhabitants of Nocella either took the mule track from here, or walked straight up the 1,700 steps from Positano. Road access seems not to have spoiled Nocella, which is still a charming scatter of rustic houses with breathtaking views. And the fact that the bus now stops here (check the timetables down in piazza dei Mulini in Positano) means that one of the Amalfi Coast's great hikes is that much more accessible.

The Sentiero degli Dei (Path of the Gods, *see also p238* **Walking country**), winds up the side of a sheer cliff to the pass of Colle di Serra, from where there is an easy descent to Bomerano and Agerola (with buses to Amalfi). This spectacular hike is not particularly difficult, though some walking experience, a good head for heights and plenty of water and sunblock are essential. Allow two-and-a-half hours for the ascent to Colle di Serra.

Where to eat

La Cambusa

Piazza Vespucci 4 (089 875 432). **Meals served** *Nov, Dec, Feb, Mar* noon-4pm, 7pm-midnight Mon, Wed-Sun. *Apr-Oct* noon-4pm,

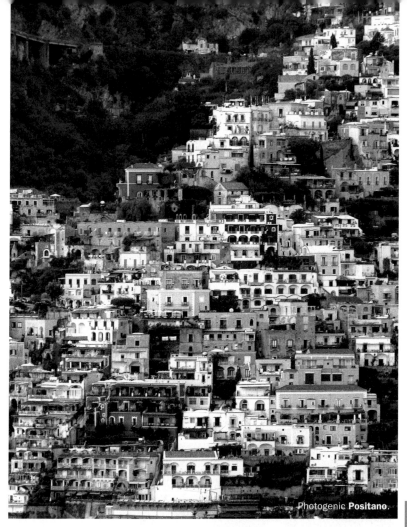
Photogenic **Positano**.

7pm-midnight daily. Closed 3wks Jan. **Average** €40. **Credit** AmEx, DC, MC, V.

Of the handful of long-established tourist restaurants down by the beach, this is one of the most reliable. It's not a bargain by any means, and service can be rather unctuous, but it offers decent seafood, and the few outside tables on a balcony above the main beach offer a prime people-watching position.

Il Capitano

Via Pasitea 119 (089 811 351/www.hotelmonte mare.it). **Meals served** noon-3pm, 7.30-10.30pm Mon,Tue, Thur-Sun; 7.30-10.30pm Wed. Closed Nov-Mar. **Average** €50. **Credit** AmEx, DC, MC, V.

Positano's best restaurant prepares classic versions of local dishes such as spaghetti with anchovies, red pepper and cherry tomatoes, and ravioli filled with lobster. Fish dishes, such as monkfish with citrus and potatoes, are excellent; the seafood antipasti are delectable. There is a fine view over the coast from the terrace, where tables are set out under a flower-decked pergola. The professional service and extensive, reasonably priced wine list give this place an edge. It pays to book, especially if you want an outside table.

Donna Rosa

Via Montepertuso 97/99 (089 811 806). **Meals served** *Aug* 7pm-11.30pm daily. *May-July, Sept, Oct* 7pm-11pm Mon, Tue; noon-4pm, 7pm-11pm Wed-Sun. *Apr, Nov, Dec* noon-4pm, 7-11pm Mon, Wed-Sun. Closed Jan-Mar. **Average** €35. **Credit** AmEx, DC, MC, V.

Perched in the village of Montepertuso, this once-simple trattoria with views over the main village square and the football pitch is now an elegant,

Around Naples

romantic restaurant. Smart *positanesi* drive up here of an evening because they know that the food is better than just about anywhere down on the coast. The pasta that goes into *primi* such as *tagliatelle verdi ai frutti di mare* (green pasta with seafood) is all home-made. Main courses and desserts (hot chocolate soufflé) are good too. Lunchtimes are generally quiet, but if you're planning to eat here on a summer evening, book at least a day in advance.

'O Guarracino

Via Positanesi d'America 12 (089 875 794). **Meals served** *Mid June-July* 12.30-3pm Mon, Wed-Sun; 7pm-midnight daily. *Aug, Sept* 12.30-3pm, 7pm-midnight daily. *Apr-mid June, Oct* 12.30-3pm, 7pm-midnight Mon, Wed-Sun. Closed Nov-Mar. **Average** €35. **Credit** AmEx, DC, MC, V.

The position is splendid – a long scenic veranda on the footpath that leads around the cliff to Fornillo beach. The decor and service are ostentatiously no-frills; so too the menu, which offers basic classics such as *linguine alla puttanesca* (pasta with olives, capers and tomatoes) or simply grilled sea bass, swordfish and seafood. There's also pizza. On summer evenings it's always packed with locals and second-homers – so book ahead.

Il Ritrovo

Via Montepertuso 77 (089 812 005/www.ilritrovo. com). **Meals served** *May-Oct* 12.30-3pm, 7pm-midnight daily. *Feb-Apr, Nov, Dec* 12.30-3pm, 7pm-midnight Mon, Tue, Thur-Sun. Closed Jan, 1wk Feb. **Average** €35. **Credit** AmEx, DC, MC, V.

Just off the main square of Montepertuso, Il Ritrovo provides a more rustic alternative to its close neighbour, Donna Rosa (*see p247*). Strings of local Furore cherry tomatoes hang from wooden beams and,

when winter sets in, a fire roars in the grate. In summer, tables fill a large wooden terrace with views back down the valley to the sea. The vegetable antipasti – all made from home-grown produce – are excellent; the pasta is mostly home-made, and there is also a good range of non-marine *secondi*, such as grilled chicken or rabbit. Ring ahead to arrange free transport from Positano in the restaurant's minibus.

Bars & nightlife

La Zagara (via dei Mulini 6, 089 875 964, www.lazagara.com, closed Nov-mid Mar) has a scenic patio with lemon trees coming up through a garish red floor and an inner *salotto* with a fireplace for cold winter days. It's utterly touristy, but the cakes, pastries and fruit sorbets are delicious. At the eastern end of the main beach, the scenic **Music on the Rocks** nightclub (Grotta dell'Incanto 51, 089 875 874/ 335 422 856, www.musiconrocks.it, closed Oct-Mar, & Mon-Thur, Sun Apr) purveys smooth piano-bar music and safe disco.

Far and away the best club on the Costiera (not that there's much competition) is the **Africana**, just west of Marina di Praia, between Positano and Amalfi (089 874 042, closed Oct-May). Hidden in its very own rocky cove, the Africana has a dance floor inside a grotto done out in wild Mondo Bongo style; in the cove below, fishermen hunt for *totani* (baby octopus) undisturbed by the driving beat. An access road leads down between the 21- and 22-kilometre milestones on the main road; otherwise, walk from Marina di Praia. When the club is open,

Hairy hairpins and breathtaking views on **Amalfi**'s coast road. *See p243.*

boats run to it from Salerno, Maiori, Minori, Amalfi and Positano; for details phone 089 811 171 (for boats from Positano), 333 795 4404 (from Amalfi), 081 852 885 (from Maiori).

Shopping

La Libreria (via Colombo 165, 089 811 077, closed mid Nov-Feb), a bookshop near the top of via Colombo, has a good selection of guidebooks, some in English; it also organises literary soirées.

Scuba diving

Divers should head to **Centro Sub Costiera Amalfitana** (via Fornillo, 089 812 148/347 378 7372, www.centrosub.it), which rents out equipment and runs courses.

Where to stay

Casa Albertina

Via della Tavolozza 3 (089 875 143/fax 089 811 540/www.casalbertina.it). **Rates** (half-board) €140-€160 single; €190-€210 per person in double. **Credit** AmEx, DC, MC, V.
Casa Albertina occupies a 12th-century building in a narrow, stepped lane about halfway up the daunting stack of houses to the west of the main beach. It offers a cool refuge from the summer heat and bustle with its white walls, ornate decorative details and old-fashioned blue- or red-themed rooms with a view. The panoramas from the restaurant terrace where breakfast and dinner are served, the relaxed atmosphere, and the helpfulness of the Cinque family, who own and run the hotel, justify the climb. However, the high-season half-board only policy is a bind, especially as the restaurant is by no means one of Positano's best. Off-season rates are significantly lower (call and haggle; you may be rewarded), and allow one to eat around. The hotel sometimes closes during January and February. Parking is €20 per day extra.

La Fenice

Via Marconi 8 (089 875 513/fax 089 811 309). **Rates** €130 double. **No credit cards**.
A sort of low-budget San Pietro (*see below*), this charming B&B sprawls up a series of verdant terraces on either side of the main coast road, on the Amalfi side of town. There are six rooms in the main villa above, with a terrace complete with a lovely view where breakfast is served and a caged mynah bird says *buon giorno* in the voice of Kevin Spacey. Another six rooms occupy a series of little *villette* below, near the pretty swimming pool (open June-Oct). From this lower section, a path descends to a small semi-private beach. Which is not at all bad for the price, though you'll need to bring wads of cash to cope with the Phoenix's 'no credit cards' policy. Between April and October, a three-night minimum stay is required.

Maria Luisa

Via Fornillo 42 (tel/fax 089 875 023). **Closed** mid Nov-Feb. **Rates** €70-€75 double. **No credit cards**.
In Positano, you get what you pay for, and this is the cheapest hotel in town. So don't expect any frills, just a simple *pensione* with bright, sea-facing rooms, on the lane down to Fornillo beach. The panoramic balcony rooms are worth the small extra outlay.

Palazzo Murat

Via dei Mulini 23 (089 875 177/fax 089 811 419/ www.palazzomurat.it). **Closed** Nov-Mar. **Rates** €190-€250 single; €220-€425 double. **Credit** AmEx, DC, MC, V.
This characterful 18th-century palazzo, right in the centre of the old town, once belonged to Joachim Murat, king of Naples and Napoleon's brother-in-law. Get a room in the old wing, if you can, which extends around two sides of a palm- and bougainvillea-filled courtyard, where classical concerts take place in late summer. The rooms here are furnished with antiques and have tiny decorative iron balconies overlooking the courtyard. In the adjacent modern wing, rooms are more mod-Med in style, but also significantly cheaper; some have balconies with sea views. In summer, breakfast is served under the arches of the entrance patio; free boat trips are also available. All in all, a perfect refuge for the latter-day Grand Tourist – especially now that the hotel restaurant, Al Palazzo, is making a bid for serious consideration.

Poseidon

Viale Pasitea 148 (089 811 111/fax 089 875 833/ www.hotelposeidonpositano.it). **Closed** Jan-Mar. **Rates** €198-€295 double; €284-€510 suite. **Credit** AmEx, DC, MC, V.
The most health-and-fitness-oriented of the town's hotels, with its own independently run Laura Elos Beauty Center, the Poseidon is set in a pretty garden just off viale Pasitea. Rooms have panoramic balconies where breakfast is served; the restaurant gives on to a large terrace, which manages to fit in a heated swimming pool and solarium. There is also a gym, a sauna and a hydromassage room; alternatively, you could just try walking up and down all those steps to the beach a couple of times. The rates are competitive for a Positano four-star. Parking costs €21 extra per day.

San Pietro

Via Laurito 2 (089 875 455/fax 089 811 449/ www.ilsanpietro.it). **Closed** Nov-Mar. **Rates** €370-€430 single; €385-€510 double; €530-€990 suite. **Credit** AmEx, DC, MC, V.
One of the most exclusive hotels anywhere in Italy, the five-star 'L' (one better than five-star) San Pietro is based around a private villa that the hotel's founder, Carlo Cinque, built on (and into) a rocky promontory 2km (1.4 miles) east of Positano. Over the years, more rooms were added, and gradually the idea of turning this remarkable feat of engineering into a hotel took shape. From the road, the only evidence of the hotel is a discreet sign and a

tiny chapel surrounded by parked cars; a lift plunges to the bright lobby, which opens out on to a hibiscus-strewn terrace. The rooms – decorated with Mediterranean tiles and friezes, and each with a jacuzzi and private balcony – spill down the hillside on 20 separate rock-hewn terraces, connected by a warren of stairways. A second lift plunges down through the cliff to the private beach, bar and what must be one of the world's most dramatically placed tennis courts. Service is attentive and professional, and breakfast sumptuous.

Le Sirenuse
Via Cristoforo Colombo 30 (089 875 066/fax 089 811 798/www.sirenuse.it). **Rates** €250-€750 single; €280-€780 double; €550-€3.300 suite. **Credit** AmEx, DC, MC, V.

The Sirenuse has almost as many fans among the international jet set as the San Pietro (*see p249*) – and it's certainly better placed for Positano shopping, dining and nightlife. Everything about the former private villa of the Marchesi Sersale is tastefully and thoughtfully done, from the majolica-covered panoramic terrace (with its pocket-sized swimming pool) to the lived-in elegance of the antique-filled rooms. There is also a well-equipped gym, and one of the few hotel restaurants in Positano – La Sponda – impressive enough to attract diners from outside (closed December to February).

Villa Franca
Viale Pasitea 318 (089 875 655/fax 089 875 735/www.villafrancahotel.it). **Closed** Nov-Mar. **Rates** €310 single; €340 double. **Credit** AmEx, DC, MC, V.

Right above the sea at the point where viale Pasitea comes closest to the cliff edge, Villa Franca is an extremely elegant, well-run hotel with bright Mediterranean decor and a profusion of plants and flowers; the pretty rooms have cream bedspreads and curtains, frescoed details and panoramic balconies. The hotel also has one of the nicest of Positano's rooftop swimming pools, with a truly magnificent view over the coast, and a new *centro benessere* (fitness centre). If you can't face the walk down or up, there is a free minibus service. Parking is €16-€18 per day extra.

Resources

First aid
Guardia Medica *via G Marconi (081 811 444).* **Open** 24hrs daily. In an emergency staff will arrange for transfer to hospital.

Internet
Pupetto Café *spiaggia Fornillo (089 875087/www. pupettocafe.com).*

Post office
via G Marconi 318 (089 811 076). **Open** 8am-1.30pm Mon-Fri; 8am-12.30pm Sat.

Tourist information
Azienda Autonoma di Soggiorno e Turismo *Via del Saracino 4 (089 875 067/fax 089 875 760/ www.aziendaturismopositano.it).* **Open** *June-Sept* 8am-2pm, 3-8pm Mon-Sat. *Oct-May* 8am-2pm Mon-Sat.

Getting around

By bus
A local bus service departs from piazza dei Mulini and does the anticlockwise circuit of via Colombo, via Marconi and viale Pasitea every 15mins between 8am and 10pm (winter) or midnight (summer). A less frequent service (roughly every 2hrs) serves the perched villages of Montepertuso and Nocella. Tickets for both of these routes cost 80¢ and can be bought on the bus.

By boat
From a booth on the quay to the right of Positano's main beach, Gennaro and Salvatore (089 811 613/ www gennaroesalvatore.it) runs boat trips to Capri, the Grotta dello Smeraldo (*see p253*) and the Li Galli islets, inclusive of meals; the company also organises night fishing trips on request.

The Lucibello brothers (089 875 032/www.luci bello.it) run similar excursions from a nearby booth; they also hire boats, canoes and pedalos.

Getting there

By car
Take the A3 motorway to Castellammare di Stabia, and follow signs to Sorrento. At Meta, 4km (2.5 miles) east of Sorrento, take the SS163; alternatively, take the slower but more scenic SS145 Nastro Azzurro route across the peninsula from the western edge of Sorrento, passing through Sant'Agata dei Due Golfi. From Salerno, take the SS163, which runs the length of the Amalfi Coast.

By bus & train
SITA (199.730.749/www.sita-on-line.it) runs one morning bus between Naples and Positano from Monday to Saturday, returning in the early evening. The rest of the time, take the Circumvesuviana railway from Naples and change at Meta, just before Sorrento, for the Sorrento–Positano–Amalfi bus. Buses to Amalfi and Sorrento from Positano stop at the top of via Colombo and at the top of viale Pasitea, outside the Bar Internazionale. Tickets can be bought from the Bar Internazionale (via Marconi 164) or the Bar-Tabacchi Collina (via Colombo 3-5).

From **Naples airport** take the Curreri (081 801 5420/www.curreriviaggi.it) bus to Sorrento (six daily) and change for SITA services (*see above*).

By boat
Hydrofoils run between Salerno, Amalfi, Positano and Capri: there are one to four per day, depending on the time of year. Amalfi–Positano shuttle services are more frequent. Between June and September, there is a direct hydrofoil link to Naples' Mergellina dock, run by Consorzio Linee Marittime (089 873 301). It is also possible to hop from

Once were warriors

With its delicate beauty and diminutive charm, it is hard to envision the Amalfi of old – 12 times its current size and boasting a powerful fleet. But from the ninth to the 11th century, the independent city was run by doges who regularly flexed their maritime muscle at Pisa, Venice and Genoa. Along with allies Naples and Gaeta, the Amalfitans protected their commerce well against their many opponents. Perhaps the coalition's most astonishing victory was the obliteration of the Saracen fleet at Ostia in 849 AD, under the direction of Pope Leo IV.

But prosperity breeds jealousy, and the Pisans were as greedy as they come. When Pisa was commissioned by the Pope to rid the coastline of the Normans in 1135, they instead took the opportunity to crush their nearest business rivals, and the Amalfi Republic was no more.

Every year, the Amalfitans get a chance at revenge during the **Regata Storica**. Each former city state provides a boat – a replica of a 12th-century craft bearing the insignia of its erstwhile republic – propelled by oarsmen in colourful medieval costume. Amalfi's boat is blue, adorned by a mermaid and with a winged horse as its figurehead. Pisa's vessel is red, with the imperial German eagle recalling the days when the Ghibelline republic swore allegiance to the Holy Roman Emperor. Genoa's ship is white, fitted with the dragon of St George. The boat from Venice is green, with the lion representing St Mark.

The contest was the brainchild of two men, one from Amalfi and one from Pisa, who thought up the race in 1956, and it has been run every year since, alternating among the competing cities.

The next race will be held in June 2005.

Positano to Naples via Capri – though this is only really worth it if you want to spend some time on the island.

From Positano to Amalfi

Until 1853, most Amalfi Coast settlements were accessible only by sea or by tortuous mountain tracks from the other side of the Sorrentine peninsula. In that year, Ferdinand II of Naples inaugurated the Strada Amalfitana, the rock-blasted coast road that connects Positano with Vietri and Salerno. Built to accommodate horse-drawn traffic, this narrow road is used today by lorries, buses, tourist coaches and swarms of private cars; it's hardly surprising

that the Amalfi Coast suffers from some of Italy's worst summer traffic jams.

East out of Positano, the road winds around steep gullies towards **Vettica Maggiore** and **Praiano**, which merge into one another on either side of the Capo Sottile promontory. Neither place has much of a centre, and both are often lumped together as Praiano. Vettica has a small beach and one of the coast's more worthwhile churches, **San Gennaro** (erratic opening hours), with colourful tiles on both dome and bell tower. The square outside the church affords good views back along the coast to Positano and beyond. Praiano proper, on the eastern side of the promontory, is a viable low-key alternative to

Positano. It has a charming seaward extension to the east – tiny **Marina di Praia**, a fishing cove consisting of a scrap of beach pinched between two high rock walls, with just enough room for a few boats, a handful of houses, a couple of bar-restaurants and a diving centre, **La Boa** (089 813 034/335 723 739, www.laboa.com). A path around the cliff to the right leads to the retro-groovy **Africana** disco (*see p248*). The jagged coastline between here and Conca dei Marini is the wildest stretch of the Costiera – nowhere more so than at the **Vallone di Furore**, a deep gully two kilometres beyond Marina di Praia. Such an unrepentantly steep river valley is called an *orrido*, or 'horrid', in Italian; its seaward opening is the nearest Italy comes to a fjord. From the viaduct over the valley – where it is virtually impossible to park – a steep footpath descends to **Marina di Furore**, an even tighter squeeze than Marina di Praia, with a few rock-hewn fishermen's huts and a scatter of boats on the narrow beach.

The buildings were recently restored with funds from the Campania region local authority, and include a bar-restaurant (*see p253*), a herbarium, a cinema archive, a cultural centre dedicated to Italy's 'painted villages' and a museum of paper-making inside an old paper mill at the head of the beach. All these bits go under the rather grand name of the **Ecomuseo**. There's no fixed timetable, so finding the buildings open can be a problem. For information, go to www.fiordodifurore.it or phone 089 830 781 or 328 881 5393.

Back on the coast road, just before Conca dei Marini, is the big tourist pull of this stretch: the **Grotta dello Smeraldo** (*see p253*). There is a car park on the road above, with a lift that plunges down to the cave, where visitors are decanted into box-like rowing boats; alternatively, various operators offer boat trips from Positano and Amalfi. Every self-respecting Mediterranean tourist destination needs its Blue (or in this case Emerald) Grotto; this one was discovered in 1932, ending Capri's 100-year grotto monopoly. Cave buffs will tell you that it is but a pale imitation of that island's Blue Grotto (*see p183*), but the translucent blue-green light that filters into the cave from an underwater crevice is pretty enough, and it's a lot cheaper than its rival. The main attractions are the crazed boatmen, who cajole their passengers into seeing Mussolini's profile in the shadow of a stalagmite.

Beyond the headland of **Capo di Conca**, the bay of Amalfi appears at last in all its glory. The sprawl of houses on the hillside to the left is **Conca dei Marini**, which once had a merchant fleet to rival those of its more muscular neighbours, Positano and Amalfi.

The upper part of the town is accessible from the Agerola road, which forks off sharply to the left just past the random collection of houses that call themselves (confusingly) **Vettica Minore**, a couple of kilometres before Amalfi. If you've had enough of the glitz and crowds of the Costiera, this road offers a worthwhile detour – though it's not a short one, and unless you want to press on to Naples, the only way back is the way you came. It begins by heading west, passing by the long, barrel-vaulted profile of the Convento di Santa Rosa.

This was formerly a house of Augustine nuns, famous as the inventors of the *torta di Santa Rosa*, a flaky pastry, blancmange and dried fruit concoction traditionally eaten on 30 August, Santa Rosa's feast day. Nowadays the abandoned convent is used as an evocative backdrop for the classical concerts of the Festival di Ravello (*see p262*).

Rising gently up through the contour lines, the road continues around the upper part of the Vallone del Furore to **Furore** itself, a rugged village that – like so many around these parts – lacks a centre. But it does have some unexpected bits of modern sculpture and murals – part of a laudable municipal attempt to make the place known for something other than being isolated – and it also produces the Amalfi coast's best wine. To sample it, head for the **Gran Furor-Divina Costiera** winery (via GB Lama 14, 089 830 348, www.granfuror.it, open 8am-6pm daily by appointment), which also goes under the name of its owner, Marisa Cuomo. From precarious vineyards on steep slopes come the grapes that go into the six wines produced here, the best of which are the white Furore Fiord'uva cru, and the red Furore Riserva. Furore also does a small trade in prickly pears – *fichi d'india* in Italian – and tiny cherry tomatoes (*pomodorini a piennolo*).

Beyond Furore, the road snakes up to the ridge in a series of intestinal curves before spilling out into the upland plain of **Agerola**, an entirely unexpected collection of agricultural settlements, cut off by the rugged terrain both from the Costiera below and from the Vesuvian plain beyond. Though the coast sells itself as a fertile Garden of Eden, it is Agerola that actually produces most of the fruit, vegetables, cheese and meat that end up in swanky Amalfi restaurants; the local mozzarella is especially famous. Its small-scale textile workshops also act as sweatshops for Positano's 'glamorous' boutiques. The only visitors that Agerola usually sees are elderly Neapolitans, who come here for the summer cool, and the occasional walker (the Alta Via dei Lattari passes along the ridge that closes the plain to the north, *see p238* **Walking country**).

The view from Positano towards Amalfi.

Grotta dello Smeraldo

1km west of Conca dei Marini on the main coast road (information from APT Amalfi/089 871 107). **Open** *Apr-Oct* 9am-4pm daily. *Nov-Mar* 10am-3pm daily. **Admission** €5. **No credit cards**.

Where to stay & eat

Hidden away off a quiet lane below the coast road in Praiano, the **Hotel Le Sirene** (via San Nicola 10, 089 874 013, www.lesirene.com, closed Nov-mid Mar, doubles €85-€100) is a simple, pretty white hotel with stone-flagged courtyard (complete with Ping-Pong table) in front and kitchen gardens behind over olive trees and kitchen gardens behind the sea. The rooftop terrace-solarium and the friendliness of the owners are two other bonuses.

On the main road out of town towards Amalfi, the **Hotel Continental** and **Villaggio Turistico La Tranquillità** (via Roma 21, 089 874 084, www.continental.praiano.it, closed Nov-Mar, doubles/bungalow €90, camping pitch for two €40) is a multi-purpose accommodation option popular with budget travellers. As well as providing scenic camping pitches under the olives for those with canvas, it also offers more conventional rooms, plus a series of bungalows immersed in greenery on a terrace above the sea, accessible via a rock-hewn staircase. It's also handily placed for the Africana disco (*see p248*).

Back in Praiano's 'main' street, the scenic **La Brace** (via Gennaro Capriglione 146, 089 874 226, closed Wed mid Dec-mid Mar, all Nov, average €35) does good, simple seafood dishes, such as spaghetti with clams, and excellent Neapolitan pizzas, cooked in a wood-fired oven. In Marina di Praia, **Alfonso a Mare** (089 874 091, www.alfonsoamare.it, closed Nov-Mar,

average €35) has a huge, covered terrace on the beach and offers simple but competent seafood.

Marina di Furore's tiny bar-restaurant **Al Monazeno** (368 451 542, closed Nov-May), run by an engineer from Watford, is one of the more unusual places to dine on the Costiera; at the foot of a cliff, overlooking an inlet, it offers bar snacks and a few more substantial dishes in the classic Amalfi tradition. On the road above, towards Positano, **La Locanda del Fiordo** (via Trasita 9/13, 089 874 813, www.lalocanda delfiordo.it, closed 3wks Jan, doubles €110-€210) is a stylish B&B with an entrance at road level and rooms (each named after an Italian screen diva) on two rock-hewn terraces below, where steps descend to the sea.

In Vettica, **Vettica House** (via Maestra dei Villaggi 92, 089 871 814, www.hostels calinatella.com) offers some of the best budget accommodation on the entire Costiera. Run by the family that owns A' Scalinatella in Atrani (*see p259*), it's a cluster of simple white-washed rooms carved into the rock above a fragrant lemon orchard. Accommodation options include hostel-style beds (from €18.50 per person) and double rooms with private bathrooms (€52-€62). Be warned though – it's a stiff climb up 270 steps (the equivalent of 12 storeys) from the nearest bus stop on the Furore/Agerola road, about 200 metres (700 feet) before the Convento di Santa Rosa (phone ahead for precise instructions on how to get here – the owner may come meet you on his scooter). The climb is torturous, but the view from the top repays your effort.

In Furore, **Hostaria da Bacco** (via GB Lama 9, 089 830 360, www.baccofurore.it, closed Nov-Feb, average €30) is run by the energetic mayor of this airy sprawl of a

Duomo di Amalfi.
See p256.

village, and draws customers up from the
coast with its refined home cooking. Local
produce (as much land- as sea-based) goes into
trademark creations such as *ferrazzuoli alla
Nannarella* – spiral pasta with swordfish,
capers and pine nuts, a dish dedicated to
actress Anna Magnani, who briefly owned
a house down in the Marina. Succulent *agerola*
cheeses are on offer, and one of the more
unusual local harvests can be sampled in the
form of *cicale di Furore* – little almond and
prickly pear cakes. The ambience is rustic,
the local wine extremely drinkable and, if
that's not enough, there's a huge selection of
grappas and other spirits to finish the meal
on a high note. If you can't face the cliff-
hugging drive back, there are also 18 simple
rooms (doubles €70-€80).

Resources

See p259 Amalfi and *p250* Positano.

Getting there

The villages can all be reached by bus or car
from Positano or Amalfi. *See p250* and *below*
respectively.

Amalfi & Atrani

Amalfi may be a pretty, lemon-fringed tourist
resort, spilling over on to the coast and lining
both sides of the steep and fertile Valle dei
Mulini, but it bears remembering that, between
the ninth and the 12th centuries, this was a
glorious maritime republic – precursor to, and

later rival of, Pisa and Genoa. In its prime, Amalfi had 70,000 inhabitants, and many more lived abroad in merchant colonies scattered around the Mediterranean from Tunis to Beirut.

On land, Amalfi's dominion extended over the whole of the Sorrentine peninsula and beyond; at sea, it had few rivals, and its navy protected the republic's independence and won battles for allies such as the Lombards and the Duchy of Naples. It was almost certainly Amalfitan sailors who introduced the compass to the Christian West from Muslim Africa at the end of the 12th century, and it was Amalfitan merchants who founded the hospice of St John in Jerusalem in 1020, which became the headquarters of the Knights Hospitallers of St John, later the Knights of Malta.

The republic survived at least nominally from 839 until the devastating Pisan raids of 1135 and 1137, though for its last 100 years it was subject to repeated periods of Norman domination. Gradually, a Venetian-style system of government was adopted, led by a doge elected by a council consisting of the male members of the town's most important families. Amalfi coined its own money and made its own laws – its maritime code, the Tavole Amalfitane, was recognised in the Mediterranean until well into the 16th century.

Mercantile prosperity continued even after the end of the republic; in the early 14th century Boccaccio wrote that Amalfi was 'full of little cities, gardens and fountains, and rich men'. But an earthquake in 1343 destroyed most of the old town, which now lies under the sea, and Amalfi never really recovered – at least not until the 19th century, when its spectacular setting and fame of former glories began to attract literary and artistic travellers from northern Europe. The **regata storica** – a ceremonial boat race between Amalfi, Pisa, Genoa and Venice – is a reminder of the town's golden age, held on the first Sunday in June (*see p251* **Once were warriors**).

On its coast side, the pretty, cream-coloured town makes a weak effort at bustling, as the port, bus terminus, bars and restaurants all jostle for room on the tiny waterfront. To the east, the grey shingle beach is crowded in summer, although prettier water is tucked away in a series of coves to the west, served by a regular circular ferry service (marked '*spiagge*') from the main quay.

Dominating the hillside to the west are the collonaded halls of the **Capuchin convent**. Founded in 1212, it was a hotel until 2004, but is now in limbo. Along corso delle Repubbliche Marinare to the east are the post office and the tourist office; just around the corner, in a palm-shaded piazza, stands the Municipio, or town

hall, where – in a room grandly referred to as the **Museo Civico** (*see p259*) – a late manuscript draft of the Tavole Amalfitane is on display. The sweep of the bay ends in a medieval watchtower that houses the **Luna Convento** restaurant (*see p259*); the hotel itself occupies a former Franciscan convent on the other side of the road.

From sea-facing piazza Flavio Gioia – dominated by a statue of Flavio himself (a man who not only didn't invent the compass, as the plaque at his feet claims, but may never even have existed), the Porta Marinara gate leads into the centre of town. Before you go under it, have a look at what remains of Amalfi's shipyard, the **Arsenale della Repubblica**, beneath an arch to the left of the gate. This was the engine room of the republic, where huge galleys with over 100 oars were built by teams of shipwrights.

The town's central piazza is dominated by the colourful **Duomo** (*see p256*), a masterpiece of the Arab-Norman style, reached – like everything in this region – by a steep staircase. The lively façade is a doubtful reconstruction of the early 13th-century original, and most of it was added after part of the church collapsed in 1861. The pretty, free-standing campanile, from 1276, is the real thing, having been tampered with very little in the course of the centuries. Underneath a lofty porch, the central bronze doors of the Duomo were cast some time before 1066 by a Syrian master and carried back by a local shipping magnate's fleet. The inscription explains that they were donated to the republic by Pantaleone di Mauro Comite, head of the Amalfitan colony in Constantinople.

The cathedral interior, recently restored to reduce some of its baroque excess, is nevertheless a disappointment in comparison with the clean, Romanesque simplicity of its close cousin in Ravello (*see p260*). Remnants of the original church furniture include the two *amboni* (pulpits) on either side of the main altar, some ancient columns and a beautiful mother-of-pearl cross – another piece of Crusader loot.

More worthwhile is the delightful **Chiostro del Paradiso**, entered (for a small fee) through a door at the left end of the porch in front of the Duomo. Built in 1266 as a burial ground for the members of Amalfi's aristocracy, this cloister, with its Moorish-style arches and central garden, is as close as one comes on the Costiera to the cosmopolitan spirit of the glory days of the maritime republic.

A door leads from the cloister into the **Cappella del Crocefisso**, the only part of the church to have survived more or less intact from the 12th century. Here, glass cases hold treasures belonging to the diocese, including a lovely 15th-century marble bas-relief known as

La Madonna della Neve, and a bejewelled mitre made for the Anjou court of Naples in 1297.

From the chapel, with its faded 14th-century frescos, stairs lead down to the crypt, dedicated to St Andrew, whose mortal remains were stolen from Constantinople in 1206. The sarcophagus that contains the saintly body oozes a miraculous fluid, which the locals call manna (*see p257* **Squeezing manna from a stone**).

With its bars and cafés, the piazza in front of the Duomo is a good place to rest, refuel and contemplate the nubile nymph splashing in the central fountain. To the north, via Genova and via Capuano lead up through an increasingly quiet residential part of town where the sound of fast-flowing water can be heard everywhere, even at the height of summer.

This deep valley – the Valle dei Mulini – was the site of some of Europe's first paper-making factories, powered by a series of watermills; one, at Palazzo Pagliara, has been turned into the **Museo della Carta** (*see below*), with photos illustrating the history and techniques of this ancient industry. Downstairs, the original vats and machinery are preserved.

The wild upper part of the Valle dei Mulini (take the road that skirts the eastern side of the valley) is well worth exploring. In its Alpine upper reaches, the valley becomes the Vallone delle Ferriere, named after the ironworks (*ferro* means iron) that – like the papermills down-stream – drew their power from the fast-moving water of the torrent.

Marked path No.25 follows the valley floor beneath high rock walls, past a riot of botany to the entrance of the **WWF riserva naturale**, which occupies the high part of the valley; from here a circuit of the valley head can be made on a scenic footpath that ends up in the village of Pontone, on the ridge between Amalfi and Atrani. A shorter but equally vertical path heads up a mere thousand or so steps from Amalfi to the village and castle of **Pogerola**, with a splendid view over the water.

In the days of the republic, **Atrani** – less than a kilometre east of Amalfi along the coast and reachable on foot via the confusing web of staircases that straggle across the hill – was the upmarket residential quarter. It was razed by the Pisans in 1187 and today feels, if anything, more workaday than its neighbour. It has a busy fishing port and some good examples of local architecture, with a maze of arches, long pedestrian tunnels, staircases and barrel-vaulted houses on different levels. Space is so tight here that the main coast road sweeps right across the centre on a viaduct whose arches separate the port from the main square, piazza Umberto I. As you walk around, keep an eye out for the full bottles of water that stand

on the thresholds of the village houses: ostensibly there to keep cats from pissing on the tiles and plants, they have a more ancient pedigree as wards against of malignant spirits.

The little church of **San Salvatore de' Bireto**, perched at the top of a flight of steps on the opposite side of the piazza, was where the investiture of Amalfi's doges took place; its name derives from the *berretto*, or ducal cap. The church has been *in restauro* for years; its bronze doors – a gift, in 1087, from the same Amalfitan merchant in Constantinople who commissioned the doors of Amalfi's Duomo – can now be seen in the parish church of **Santa Maria Maddalena** (open Sunday mornings for Mass), which rises high above the road to the east. The dome is a classically colourful example of local style; inside, the original Romanesque was swept aside in a baroque makeover, but there are some marvellous wooden statues of roasting sinners on the wall to the right of the main door.

High above the town to the west, the 13th-century church of **Santa Maria del Bando** (open only in September; ask at the town hall on via dei Dogi) perches on a narrow ledge halfway up a vertical cliff below the **Torre dello Zirro**, a medieval watchtower that the locals believe is haunted.

Duomo di Amalfi (Cattedrale di Sant'Andrea)

Piazza del Duomo (089 871 059). **Open** *Apr-June* 9am-7pm daily. *July-Sept* 9am-9pm daily. *Oct, Mar* 9.30am-5.15pm daily. *Nov-Feb* 10am-1pm, 2.30-4.30pm daily. **Admission** *Cathedral* free. *Chiostro del Paradiso* €2.50. **No credit cards**.

Museo Civico

Piazza del Municipio 6 (information from tourist office 089 871 107). **Open** 8.30am-1pm Mon, Wed, Fri; 8.30am-1pm, 2.30-5pm Tue, Thur. **Admission** free.

Museo della Carta

Palazzo Pagliara, via delle Cartiere 23 (089 830 4561/www.museodellacarta.it). **Open** *Nov-Mar* 10am-3pm Tue-Sun. *Apr-June, Oct* 10am-6pm daily. *July-Sept* 10am-8pm daily. **Admission** €3.50 (includes guided tour in English). **No credit cards**.

Where to eat

Cantina San Nicola

Salita Marino Sebaste 8 (089 830 4549). **Meals served** noon-3pm, 6pm-1am Mon-Thur, Sat, Sun. Closed 3wks Jan-Feb. **Average** €20. **Credit** AmEx, DC, MC, V.

It's well worth exploring the quiet side streets that run parallel to Amalfi's tourist-ridden main drag. Not only do they reveal a lesser-known, more ver-nacular side of the town, they also harbour some unexpected surprises, such as this wine bar, housed in the chapel of a former monastery. It fills an important niche, providing high-quality fare for those who don't necessarily want a full meal. There is a good cheese selection, including delicious *mozzarella di bufala* from the Sele plain and *scamorza* (grilled cheese) wrapped in lemon leaves. Hot dishes range from *caponata* (a sort of Sicilian ratatouille) to chickpea soup. The cellar is especially strong on Campanian wines.

La Caravella

Via Matteo Camera 12 (089 871 029/www.ristorante lacaravella.it). **Meals served** noon-2.30pm, 7.30-10.30pm Mon, Wed-Sun. Closed mid Nov-Dec. **Average** €65. **Credit** AmEx, MC, V.

Easily Amalfi's best restaurant, the Caravella hits culinary peaks. Sandwiched between the main road and the remains of the old Arsenale in two rooms without a view, it offers excellent seafood, attentive service and an extensive wine list. Try the whole-grain *panzerotti* stuffed with lobster and ricotta and covered in prawns and sauce. Don't miss the *stuzzichini della Caravella,* mouth-watering seafood antipasti. Pasta dishes such as *tagliata di pasta allo zafferano con zucca e crostacei* (pasta strips with saffron, marrow and crustaceans) are equally fine, and *secondi* such as *totano ripieno di zucchine* (flying squid stuffed with courgettes) pull out all the

stops. Keep an eye out for the day's fresh catch grilled in lemon leaves. The desserts are one step down from all this splendour; but it's a small step.

Da Gemma

Via Fra' Gerardo Sasso 10 (089 871 345). **Meals served** 12.30-2.30pm, 7.30-10.30pm Mon, Tue, Thur-Sun. Closed mid Jan-mid Feb. **Average** €45. **Credit** AmEx, DC, MC, V.

The setting of this popular Amalfi restaurant is hard to beat: a rooftop terrace high above the bustle of the main street, with views across to piazza del Duomo. Mario Grimaldi continues the tradition of good local cooking begun here by his mother Gemma, which looks mostly to the sea, but also includes a few dishes from the hinterland, such as *fettuccine alla genovese* (fettuccine in a beef and onion sauce). Lovers of *zuppa di pesce* (fish soup) will find Gemma's hard to beat. The home-made desserts include *melanzane in salsa di cioccolato* (aubergines in chocolate), a local speciality that harks back to Amalfi's days of trade with the Middle East. Book well in advance in summer.

Da Maria

Via Lorenzo d'Amalfi 14 (089 871 880). **Meals served** noon-3pm, 7-11.30pm Tue-Sun. Closed Nov. **Average** €25. **Credit** AmEx, DC, MC, V.

There are plenty of cheap *trattorie* and *pizzerie* in Amalfi. This one, just up from the piazza on the

Saints alive Squeezing manna from a stone

In Campania, miracles happen every day – or at least every week. The blood of San Gennaro (*see p78* **Blood rites**) is only the most famous example of the many vials of congealed, saintly blood across the South whose contents become liquid at regular intervals.

Another such miracle occurs every July 27 in **Ravello**, in the cathedral named after St Pantaleone. The blood of the martyr, decapitated by Roman emperor Maximillian in 325, is said to have been collected in a jar by a pious bystander. It now electrifies the faithful by allegedly turning to liquid on the anniversary of his death.

Instead of blood, the inhabitants of **Amalfi** prefer the heavenly nectar manna – and the rocky sarcophagus of their patron saint readily obliges. St Andrew was a fisherman, martyred by crucifixion under Nero around 60 AD, and subsequently venerated as a patron saint by a host of countries, from Scotland to Russia. His embalmed remains were shipped to Constantinople in 357, but, like many holy corpses once held in Byzantium,

Andrew's remains were looted during the Crusades and brought back to Italy.

Now housed in a crypt in Amalfi's Moorish-Norman-style cathedral (*see p256*), the apostle's body exudes a substance which, while termed 'manna', is actually a plant extract that is also said to be the saint's sweat. The miracle occurs twice a year: on 30 November, the anniversary of his death; and 27 June, when the saint is said to have saved the city from an attack by the dread pirate, Barbarossa. In memory of that day, when a swirling tempest foiled the pirate's plans, men in white carry a statue of the saint down to the waterfront, where it is greeted with offerings of fish.

But the real show is back at the crypt, where the faithful await an offering from the saint. The manna is greedily collected; the particularly pious drink it as it is said to have curative properties. If, on the other hand, no manna materialises, the saint is clearly upset, and bad things are bound to happen. Fortunately for the *amalfitani*, Andrew rarely lets them down.

main street, is a notch above the average, with affable (not to say extravagant) service and reliable home cooking. Don't be put off by the menu in four languages; even for simple starters such as *frutti di mare* (mixed seafood), the standards are generally high. The seafood pasta dishes are tasty and filling, and the excellent pizzas, cooked in a wood oven, are the authentic Neapolitan variety.

A Paranza

Traversa Dragone 2 (089 871 840). **Meals served** *July-mid Sept* 12.30-3pm, 7.30pm-midnight daily. *Mid Sept-June* 12.30-3pm, 7.30pm-midnight Mon, Wed-Sun. Closed 3wks Dec. **Average** €35. **Credit** AmEx, DC, MC, V.

The Proto brothers certainly know one end of an octopus from another. On the road that leads inland from Atrani's pretty main square, their friendly, relaxed seafood trattoria spreads over two plain barrel-vaulted rooms done out in white and orange. Antipasti such as *alici marinati* (anchovies marinated in oil and lemon) are a prelude to delicious home-made pasta (the *scialatielli 'a paranza* – thick, hand-made spaghetti with seafood – is especially good). Go for simple *secondi* like the *grigliata mista locale* (mixed seafood grill) or the grilled swordfish, straight off the boat. Desserts are home-made, the lemon sorbet being particularly delicious.

Bars & nightlife

Opposite the Duomo in Amalfi, the **Bar Francese** (piazza del Duomo 20, 089 871 049, closed Nov-Jan) is a good place to sit and muse on the passing of empires over a cappuccino and a copy of the *Duchess of Malfi*. In Atrani, **Bar Risacca** (piazza Umberto I 16, 089 872 866, closed Mon Oct-Mar) in the main square is the locals' favourite lounging spot; have breakfast here before heading under the arches to the beach, try the bruschetta at lunchtime, or enjoy the evening cool over a campari soda. In Amalfi, the only disco of note is **RoccoCò** (via delle Cartiere 98, 089 873 080, open daily summer, Fri & Sat Nov-Mar), a rather cheesy place some way up the valley with the occasional guest DJ. Alternatively, jump on a boat to the **Africana** (*see p248*).

Shopping

Food is the big draw in Amalfi – especially anything to do with lemons. In piazza del Duomo, **Pasticceria Andrea Pansa 1830** (piazza del Duomo 40, 089 871 065, www.pasticceriapansa.it, closed Tue) uses the local fruit in any number of inventive ways: candied lemon rind, *frolla* (a ricotta-filled pastry dome) and the sticky *delizia al limone* cakes are especially good. Almond lovers will also appreciate the delicate *paste di mandorla*. The same owners now also run the

lovely **Cioccolateria** (piazza Municipio 12, 39 089 873 291, www.andreapansa.it,). For more intoxicating treats, head for the tiny corner outlet of **Antichi Sapori d'Amalfi** (piazza del Duomo 39, 089 872 062, closed Thur), by the cathedral steps, which makes its own limoncello and fruit liqueurs (a rarity in this neck of the woods).

Paper is the other traditional industry; the best place to view and buy some of the high-quality paper still made hereabouts is **La Scuderia del Duca** (largo Cesareo Console 8, 089 872 976, www.carta-amalfi.it), a cave of wonders with a good selection of books on Amalfi and the surrounding area, some of them in English.

Where to stay

Amalfi

Vico dei Pastai 3 (089 872 440/fax 089 872 250/ www.hamalfi.it). **Rates** €60-€110 single; €100-€140 double. **Closed** mid Jan-Feb. **Credit** AmEx, MC, V.
The town's best three-star, the Amalfi gives on to a quiet lane in the old town, up a flight of steps from the main street. Though occasionally overwhelmed by British tour groups, it is affably and efficiently run. Breakfast and other meals are served on the roof terrace, and there's a pretty garden around the back. All rooms have phones and satellite TVs, and some have balconies. It's good value out of high season.

Pasticceria Andrea Pansa 1830.

Luna Convento

Via P Comite 33 (089 871 002/fax 089 871 333/
www.lunahotel.it). **Rates** €190-€230 single; €210-
€250 double; €370-€540 suite. **Credit** AmEx, DC,
MC, V.

This tastefully designed former monastery has had
its share of famous guests, including Wagner, Ibsen,
Mussolini and Tennessee Williams. The focal point
of the hotel is a delightful Byzantine cloister where
breakfast is served in summer. The pool is carved
out of the rocks beneath the Saracen tower opposite,
which houses the hotel restaurant. Rooms are bright
and comfortable, and the desk staff are helpful. Half-
board is usually obligatory.

Santa Caterina

Via Nazionale 9 (089 871 012/fax 089 871 351/
www.hotelsantacaterina.it). **Rates** €250-€640 double;
€420-€1,150 suite. **Credit** AmEx, DC, MC, V.

Location, location and location are the three best
things about the Santa Caterina, which has a whole
section of the coast to itself a kilometre west of central Amalfi, on the Positano road. Now looking better than ever after a 2002 makeover, this is not a bad
option for a luxury cocoon holiday – if you can afford
it. All rooms have terraces with sweeping views, and
the hotel is surrounded by its own terraced park, verdant with lemon trees and bougainvillea, where two
self-contained suites hide (the Romeo and Juliet is the
most spectacular). From the spacious hall, a lift takes
guests down to the private beach, pool and one of the
hotel's two restaurants; there is also a fitness club.

Hotel Luna Convento.

The original structure was destroyed by a landslide
in 1902, but don't worry – they say that the replacement was built on safer rocks.

A' Scalinatella

Piazza Umberto I 5/6, Atrani (089 871 492/
fax 089 871 930/www.hostelscalinatella.com).
Rates *hostel* €15-€21 per person; €45-€83 double
room. **No credit cards**.

The charming, laid-back village of Atrani has no
hotel as such, but it does have this budget operation
with a couple of hostel-style dormitories in a house
off the main street, and some double rooms and mini-
apartments spread all over the village. Breakfast is
served from April to September at the Scalinatella
bar in the main square, which is also where new
arrivals should check in (before 2pm if possible).
Open all year, A' Scalinatella acts as a meeting point
for backpackers and independent student travellers
otherwise poorly served on the Costiera.

Resources

Police

Via Casamare (089 871 022).

Post Office

Corso delle Repubbliche Marinare 33 (089 830 4811).
Open 8am-6.30pm Mon-Fri; 8am-12.30pm Sat.

Tourist information

Azienda Autonoma di Soggiorno e Turismo
Corso delle Repubbliche Marinare 27 (089 871
107/www.amalfitouristoffice.it). **Open** *May-Oct*
8.30am-1.30pm, 3-8pm Mon-Sat; 8.30am-12.30pm
Sun. *Nov-Apr* 8.30am-1.30pm, 3-5.12pm Mon-Fri;
8.30am-1pm Sat.

Getting around

By boat

The main quay behind the bus terminus is the
hopping off point for regular boats to the western
beaches (marked *spiagge*), which leave at least every
hour 9am-5pm daily from June to September. A
return ticket costs €3.

By bus

Amalfi's bus terminus is in piazza Gioia on the
waterfront. Local services run to Ravello, Scala and
Pogerola. Tickets can be bought from the SITA
outlet in largo Scoppetta, next to the bus terminus.

Getting there

From Naples airport

Take the Curreri bus (*see p250*) to Sorrento (six
daily) and change for the SITA bus to Amalfi.

By car

From Naples, leave the A3 motorway at the Angri
exit, just past Pompeii, and follow signs through the
urban blight to the Valico di Chiunzi pass and
Ravello. Equally scenic, but a good deal longer, is the

Around Naples

SS366 route, which crosses over from Castellammare di Stabia via Gragnano, Agerola and Furore, to emerge on the coast road 2km west of Amalfi. From Salerno, take the SS136 road along the Amalfi Coast.

By train

There is no Amalfi Coast line; the nearest station is Vietri, at the eastern limit of the Costiera, served by only a few very slow trains. It's better to go to Salerno station (40mins from Naples) and continue either by boat or SITA bus.

By bus

Throughout the day SITA buses make the cliff-top journey between Amalfi and Salerno, with curves and hairpins aplenty. For Naples, there are three main options: via Positano (one daily), via Agerola (15 daily) or via Vietri (four daily). Or, take the Circumvesuviana train from Naples and change at Meta for the Sorrento–Amalfi bus. For times and information: www.sita-on-line.it. Note that Sunday services on all these lines are infrequent.

By boat

It is possible (Apr-Oct) to hop to Amalfi from Naples via Capri, but unless you want to spend some time on the island, it is cheaper and quicker to get the regular boat from Salerno. TraVelMar (089 873 190, www.coopsantandrea.it) run ferries (Apr-Oct only) from the Molo Manfredi quay in Salerno to Amalfi via Maiori; most continue to Positano and Capri. LMS (Amalfi 089 873 301, Salerno 089 227 979, www.vola viamare.it) covers the same route by faster hydrofoils, some of which continue to Naples.

Ravello

Ravello is the aristocrat of the Amalfi Coast. Down there are the chattering sunburned masses, the traffic jams, the long queues for ice-cream. Up here, high above the sea, all is shade, gardens and serenity. Even in high season, when coach parties hit Ravello and troop dutifully around, it takes very little to leave them behind: turn a corner in the old town or, visit the lovely gardens in the early evening, and you can find yourself quite at peace. Subject through most of its early history to its more muscular neighbour Amalfi, Ravello grew rich on trade. But if Ravello's golden age was almost as florid as Amalfi's – in the 13th century it counted as many as 36,000 inhabitants – its fall from grace was even more complete and devastating.

With the end of its mercantile empire, Amalfi took to trades like fishing, paper-making and iron foundries. Its continued activity meant that its medieval centre was continually overlaid by new buildings. But in Ravello, the decline from the boom to its present population of around 2,500 was so swift that parts of the town look like a medieval Pompeii, frozen in the 14th century. Traces of the town's 15 minutes of fame are everywhere: in its delightful, treasure-packed Duomo, in the doorways of its *palazzi* with their ancient columns, in the Sicilian-Moorish exoticism of Villa Rufolo's cloisters.

Ravello's romantic ambience of decayed nobility has always attracted writers, artists and musicians, among them Wagner, Liszt, Virginia Woolf and most of the Bloomsbury group, and DH Lawrence, who wrote parts of *Lady Chatterley's Lover* here. Graham Greene stayed in Ravello while writing *The Third Man* and Gore Vidal lived here, happily grouching away in his private villa, for many years. The town's musical vocation is celebrated in a summer classical festival.

Staying overnight is the best way to tune in to Ravello's quiet, contemplative atmosphere, at its most limpid in the early morning or at sunset. But, if you can avoid it, don't drive here. the main non-residents' car park, just beneath piazza del Duomo, is expensive, even with a 50 per cent reduction for guests of any of the town's hotels; and other spaces are hard to come by. There are frequent buses from Amalfi; alternatively, Ravello is a long walk up quiet footpaths from Amalfi, Atrani or Minori.

From Atrani, the Ravello road winds up the Valle del Dragone and, doubling back on itself just before a long tunnel, enters the town at the church of **Santa Maria a Gradillo** (open 9am-1pm, 3-6pm daily; if closed ask at the Duomo), a pretty 12th-century Romanesque structure whose bell tower is a good example of the Arab-Sicilian style, and whose charming interior has been stripped of distracting ornament. The lanes that skirt the church on the right and left both end up in piazza del Duomo, the civic heart of Ravello.

The **Duomo** (*see p256*) was founded in 1086; little remains of its original façade, which was reworked in the 16th century. The real interest begins when you ascend the steps that lead up to the central bronze doors, divided into 54 bas-relief panels that tell the stories of the saints and the Passion. Barisano da Trani, who designed them in 1179, was undoubtedly influenced by the Oriental Greek style of the earlier doors at Amalfi and Atrani.

The light-filled interior was re-done, baroque style, in 1786; in the early 1980s, the courageous decision was taken to rip it all down and restore the church to something close to the state it would have reached by the late 13th century.

Halfway down the central aisle, two exquisite pulpits are arranged face-to-face, as if for a preachers' duel. The *pergamo* (high pulpit) on the right was commissioned by a scion of the local Rufolo family in 1272; six lions support the spiral columns holding up the pulpit, richly decorated with mosaics. The simple *ambone* (low pulpit) opposite was donated by

Villa Cimbrone. *See p262.*

Costantino Rogadeo, the second bishop of Ravello, in 1130. Its two cute mosaics of Jonah being swallowed by the whale (on the right) and regurgitated (on the left, with a little wave for all his fans) are symbols of the Resurrection.

To the left of the main altar is the chapel of San Pantaleone, Ravello's patron saint, with an ampoule of his blood, which is supposed to liquefy on 27 July each year and stay liquid until mid-September. The crypt contains the **Museo del Duomo**, a better-than-average collection of late imperial and medieval architectural and sculptural fragments, including a delicate marble bust of Sichelgaita della Marra – wife of the Nicola Rufolo who paid for the *pergamo* upstairs.

Both Ravello's famous villas are historical assemblages, the work of expatriate Britons who came, saw, and did a bit of gardening. **Villa Rufolo** (*see p263*), entered via the 14th-century tower to the right of the Duomo, is named after its original 13th-century owners, the Rufolo family, who amassed a fortune acting as bankers for, among others, Charles of Anjou, and are mentioned in Boccaccio's *Decameron*.

By the time Scotsman Francis Reid bought the place in 1851, the villa and its surrounding garden were little more than tumbled ruins. The house was reborn as an eclectic melange, although certain parts – especially the charming double-tiered Moorish cloister – were not tampered with too much. But it is really the gardens that draw people here with their geometric flowerbeds amid Romantic ruins. When Wagner saw them in 1880, he knew that he had found the magic garden of Klingsor, the setting for the second act of *Parsifal* (though he could hardly have guessed that one day the Pasticceria Klingsor would rise from the mystic mists in piazza del Duomo to celebrate its discovery).

In Wagner's honour, a world-class series of classical concerts is held here in the summer, along with the occasional ballet. Though collected under the **Festival di Ravello** umbrella, these performances, by prestigious Italian and international musicians and orchestras, are not so much a concentrated festival as a long season of open-air concerts, predominantly of chamber music, running from March until the beginning of November. There are also various associated sub-festivals during the year, including the **Concerti di Musica Sinfonica** (symphonic concerts) in July and the **Settimane Internazionali di Musica da Camera** (Chamber Music Week) in September. The gardens of Villa Rufolo are the main venue, but recently, two other venues have been added: the Convento di Santa Rosa in Conca dei Marini and the bay of Marina di Praia. Full details can

be found on the Ravello Concert Society website, and you can also book online (089 858 149, www.ravelloarts.org). Numbered seats cost €20 each; they can be reserved by phone, fax or email, and collected on the evening of the concert. Tickets are also sometimes available on the same day (but phone ahead to check). There is a special bus after each concert from Ravello or Conca dei Marini to all main Amalfi Coast towns and Sorrento.

The town's other garden estate, **Villa Cimbrone** (*see p263*), is a fair walk from the centre along via San Francesco, which climbs up past the reworked Gothic church and monastery of the same name, and via Santa Chiara, which does the same. But it is an enchanting place, one of the real highlights of the Amalfi Coast, and well worth the trek, even though, when you get right down to it, Villa Cimbrone is an out-and-out fake. The structure was built at the beginning of the 20th century by Lord Grimthorpe, whose also designed London's Big Ben. In its heyday in the 1920s it hosted most of the Bloomsbury group; later, the reclusive Greta Garbo and conductor Leopold Stokowski used it as their love nest.

To see inside the villa, you'll need to check in to the **Hotel Villa Cimbrone** (*see p264*), but the gardens can be admired by all. Roses, camellias and exotic plants line the lawns and walks, which are less formal than those of Villa Rufolo. There is a pretty faux-Moorish tearoom and – one of the high points of the visit – a scenic viewpoint, the **Belvedere Cimbrone**, lined with classical busts, where the view stretches along the coast for miles.

Back in piazza del Duomo, the stepped lane by the side of the tourist office leads up to via dell'Episcopio; veering to the left, this becomes via San Giovanni del Toro, site of Ravello's most upmarket hotels, and where the **Belvedere Principessa di Piemonte** provides a great (free) view over the coast to the east. Further along on the left, opposite the fabulous **Hotel Caruso** (closed for refurbishment until June 2005, *see p264*), the church of **San Giovanni del Toro** (erratic opening hours; information from the tourist office 089 857 096) conserves much of its original 12th-century appearance. Its mosaic-encrusted pulpit, built for the local Bovio family, rivals the two on show in the Duomo, with another Jonah-eating whale and deep blue-green plates of Arab workmanship embedded in the centre of mosaic circles. In a niche in the sacristy is a rare 12th-century stucco statue of Santa Caterina, with traces of the original paintwork.

If even the slow pace in Ravello is too fast, head up to **Scala**, a village perched on the opposite side of the Dragone valley. Older than

Distinctive buildings at **Atrani**. *See p265.*

either Amalfi or Ravello, and once almost as prosperous, Scala is now the sort of place where the arrival of the grocery truck is a major event. It has a fine **Duomo** dedicated to San Lorenzo (open 8am-noon, 5-7pm daily), with a good 12th-century portal and an interior that conceals a few gems beneath its baroque facelift. The wooden crucifix over the main altar dates from 1260; to the left is the Gothic tomb of the Coppola family. Note among the figures on the canopy above the tomb that of the rabbi who – according to an apocryphal gospel – had his hands lopped off when he gave the Virgin Mary's coffin a shove.

Scala is a good starting point for a number of walks. The most ambitious (No.51) takes two hours to travel via the peak of Il Castello to Casa Santa Maria dei Monti, with a magnificent view over the Sorrentine peninsula. An easier option is to continue past the Duomo to the aptly named hamlet of **Minuto** (whose name appropriately translates as 'tiny') – served by six buses a day from Amalfi and Ravello – where the road ends just above the pretty 12th-century **Chiesa dell'Annunziata** (open Sunday morning for Mass; otherwise knock on the first door on your left down the steps from the road and ask the custodian for the key). Inside are ten ancient granite columns and

very fine Byzantine frescos in the crypt. In the square in front of the church is a drinking fountain; behind this, a well-made stepped path descends in about 40 minutes to Amalfi via the little medieval village of Pontone.

Duomo di Ravello (Cattedrale di San Pantaleone)
Piazza del Duomo (089 858 311). **Open** *Church* 8.30am-1pm, 3-8pm daily. *Museum* Apr-Oct 9.30am-1pm, 3-7pm daily. Nov-Mar 9.30am-1pm, 3-7pm Sat, Sun. **Admission** €2. **No credit cards.**

Villa Cimbrone
Via Santa Chiara 26 (089 857 459). **Open** 9am-30mins before sunset daily. **Admission** €5. **No credit cards.**

Villa Rufolo
Piazza del Duomo (information from tourist office 089 857 096). **Open** 9am-30mins before sunset daily (closes 5pm on concert days). **Admission** €5. **No credit cards.**

Where to eat

Cumpà Cosimo
Via Roma 46 (089 857 156). **Meals served** *Mar-Oct* 12.30-3pm, 7.30-11pm daily. *Nov-Feb* 12.30-3pm, 7.30-11pm Tue-Sun. **Average** €30. **Credit** AmEx, DC, MC, V.
The decor and dishes are those of a simple trattoria, but the prices are in the restaurant league. Still, this is Ravello, so the people do come. Luckily, it serves five types of home-made pasta, and excellent meat-based *secondi* such as *involtini*, or *salsiccia al finocchietto in mantello di provola* (fennel-flavoured sausage covered in cheese). The ambience is unassuming but friendly, the wine drinkable.

Palazzo della Marra
Via della Marra 7-9 (089 858 302). **Meals served** *Apr-Sept* 12.30-2.30pm, 7.10pm daily. *Oct-Mar* noon-3pm, 7-10pm Mon, Wed-Sun. Closed 2wks Nov, mid Jan-Feb. **Average** €40. **Credit** AmEx, DC, MC, V.
Housed in a 12th-century palazzo, carefully restored to keep the original vaults and arches intact, the Palazzo produces creative Mediterranean cuisine. Some dishes don't quite achieve their mark, but overall it makes a good (fairly priced) attempt to go a little beyond the standard local seafood experience.

Rossellinis
Hotel Palazzo Sasso, via San Giovanni del Toro 28 (089 818 181). **Meals served** 7.30-10.30pm daily. Closed Nov-Feb. **Average** €100-€110. **Credit** AmEx, DC, MC, V.
Until this restaurant opened in 1997, Ravello was a blank on the gourmet map of the Amalfi Coast. On a typical evening, the seasonally changing menu might include a starter of scallop carpaccio with caviar, sundried tomatoes, asparagus tips and lime ice, followed by tarragon-scented *garganelli* (a local pasta) tossed in a sauce of veal fillet, cannellino

Around Naples

Ravello's lush **Villa Rufolo**. *See p263.*

beans and crispy bacon. *Secondi* are evenly divided between fish and meat, and desserts are suitably theatrical. Add the charm of candlelit tables on the panoramic terrace, professional service and excellent wines, and you have a memorable meal.

Shopping

Limoncello opportunities abound; two of the more reliable are **I Giardini di Ravello** (via Civita 14, 089 872 264, closed Sun), which also makes its own extra virgin olive oil, and **Ravello Gusti & Delizie** (via Roma 28-30, 089 857 716, closed Wed, Thur afternoon, and Jan, Feb) – a tiny shop that also has a good selection of wine and deli treats. Ceramics are the best bet for serious shoppers, although don't expect rock-bottom prices.

Where to stay

Hotel Caruso

Piazza San Giovanni Del Toro 2 (085 267 890/fax 084 267 899/www.hotelcaruso.com). Closed Nov-Mar. Closed for refurbishment until June 2005. **Rates** €420 single; €570-€680 double; €850-€1,800 suite. **Credit** AmEx, MC, V.
Along with the Hotel de Russie in Rome, the Principe di Savoia in Milan, and the Splendido in Portofino, this is one of the most talked-about names in Italian hotels.

It has a bulging guestbook of celebrity signatures, from Humphrey Bogart and Truman Capote (here to work on the 1954 classic, *Beat the Devil*), to Jackie Kennedy and Ronald Reagan. Such guests would have spent their cocktail hours on the terrace, taking in panoramic views of the coastline through Norman arches, or admiring the hotel's 18th-century frescos. Were Bogie and Capote able to pay a return visit now, they might perhaps spend their evenings checking their email on broadband, or watching their own movies on DVD players, all installed during a renovation scheduled to end in June 2005.

Hotel Rufolo

via San Francesco 1, Ravello (089 857133/fax 089 857 935/www.hotelrufolo.it). **Rates** €180-€250 double; €400-€450 suites. **Credit** AmEx, DC, MC, V.
The Rufolo is the first hotel one reaches after running the souvenir-shop gauntlet at the beginning of via San Francesco. It's a welcome relief from the coach-party crush outside, with stunning views down the coast from most of the rooms and from the garden terrace around the satisfyingly large pool. Rooms are trad but comfortable; and this is one of the few hotels in the Centro storico with its own parking spaces. D H Lawrence began writing *Lady Chatterley's Lover* here in 1926.

Hotel Villa Cimbrone

Via Santa Chiara 26 (089 857 459/fax 089 857 777/www.villacimbrone.it). **Closed** mid Nov-Feb. **Rates** €250 single; €280-€450 double; €500-€650 suite. **Credit** AmEx, MC, V.
If you want to soak up a sense of privilege, there are few better places than this, which occupies the historic main building of Ravello's famous garden. A stay here gives you the chance to stroll around the garden in peace after the paying visitors have left; and the villa itself is nearly as impressive. Many of the rooms (all recently refurbished) are museum pieces in their own right, with frescos and antique furniture. Vietri sul mare tiles add local character, while the library, with its huge stone fireplace, is simply wonderful. Just a few years ago the villa had few modern conveniences, but now there is air-conditioning, satellite TV and internet access throughout. The lack of car access still makes it difficult for some to reach, but there are few more romantic hideaways on the Amalfi coast.

Marmorata

Strada Statale S163, località Marmorata, between 32km and 33km milestones (089 877 777/fax 089 851 189/www.marmorata.it). **Rates** €185-€310 double. **Credit** AmEx, DC, MC, V.
Ravello's seaside offshoot, this is no more than a scatter of houses and is really closer to Minori than to Ravello itself. Now part of the Best Western group, the hotel of the same name occupies a former paper factory perched above the sea in a small cove. A nautical theme runs through it, up to and including the beds, which have wooden borders like sailors' bunks. There's a small pool and a private swimming platform off the rocks. Marmorata is best for those with cars.

Palazzo Sasso

Via San Giovanni del Toro 28 (089 818 181/fax 089 858 900/www.palazzosasso.com). **Closed** *Nov-Feb.* **Rates** €330-€649 double; €935-€2,090 suite. **Credit** AmEx, DC, MC, V.

This 13th-century palazzo has sweeping views over the valley and the coast. Its creamy façade is almost over-restored, but the mix of Moorish detail with Empire-style furniture works, in an airbrushed international luxury sort of way. The 44 air-conditioned rooms and suites are pleasant, and most have jacuzzis. There's also a terrace pool and the excellent Rossellinis restaurant (*see p264*).

Palumbo

Via San Giovanni del Toro 16 (089 857 244/fax 089 858 133/www.hotelpalumbo.it). **Rates** *Apr-Oct* (half-board only) €580 per person in single room; €330 per person in double room; €935 suite. *Nov-Mar* €330 single; €380 double; €460-€600 suite. **Credit** AmEx, DC, MC, V.

If you want lived-in luxury, then it's got to be the Palumbo. More atmospheric than its upstart neighbour, Palazzo Sasso, this hotel has been run by the Vuilleumier family since 1875. The 12th-century Palazzo Gonfalone that houses the hotel has ancient marble columns, traditional tiled floor, a profusion of plants and antique furniture. The inner courtyard has Moorish pointed arches, and the garden terrace where breakfast and other meals are served in summer is delightful. Each of the 18 rooms and three suites is individually decorated with antiques. The annexe across the road is cheaper (€210 per person half-board for two sharing a double room), but has a lot less atmosphere. The summer half-board requirement is a bit of a bind, especially as the Palumbo restaurant relies too much on its captive audience. The hotel also makes its own wine, bottled under the Episcopio label.

Villa Amore

Via dei Fusco 5 (tel/fax 089 857 135). **Rates** €48-€56 single; €73-€90 double. **Credit** DC, MC, V.

Ravello's best budget option, this hotel is on a quiet, stepped lane near Villa Cimbrone. Twelve clean, bright rooms, a garden with views down to the sea, and a friendly welcome from the two elderly ladies and the mynah bird who run the place add up to a real bargain. In among the threadbare sofas and pine panels are ancient columns and biforate windows. If you come with a car, some free parking spaces can be found at the bottom of via dei Fusco on via della Repubblica – but be warned, it's a steep climb.

Villa Maria

Via Santa Chiara 2 (089 857 255/fax 089 857 071/www.villamaria.it). **Rates** €145-€175 single; €175-€270 double; €385-€425 suites. **Credit** AmEx, DC, MC, V.

In this converted villa's shady garden, where meals are served in summer, tables and chairs are arranged to make the most of the view across the spectacular Dragone valley and the coast. Most rooms are light and spacious, and all are furnished with brass bedsteads and antiques. Room three is a huge suite with a terrace and panoramic views. Friendly owner Vincenzo Palumbo also runs the nearby Hotel Giordano (via Santissima Trinità 14), a modern and less atmospheric (but also cheaper) option. Guests of the Villa Maria can use Giordano's free parking spaces and heated swimming pool.

Villa San Michele

SS163, Castiglione di Ravello (tel/fax 089 872 237/www.hotel-villasanmichele.it). **Closed** Jan-mid Feb. **Rates** €100-€156 double. **Credit** AmEx, DC, MC, V.

Those who want to combine Ravello with beach access (but without maxing out their credit cards), say the San Michele is a good option. Just below the turn-off for Ravello on the main coast road, the hotel occupies a pretty white villa with blue shutters amid terraced gardens ablaze with hibiscus and bougainvillea. The rooms are pretty and light-filled, and all face the sea. Steps descend from the garden to a stone diving platform with deckchairs and beach umbrellas.

Resources

Police

Carabinieri via Casamare (089 871 022).

Post office

Via Roma 50 (081 837 5829). **Open** 8am-6.30pm Mon-Fri; 8am-12.30pm Sat.

Tourist information

Azienda Autonoma di Soggiorno e Turismo *Piazza del Duomo 10 (089 857 096/fax 089 857 977/www.ravellotime.it).* **Open** *May-Sept* 8am-8pm Mon-Sat; 9am-7pm Sun. *Oct-Apr* 8am-7pm Mon-Sat; 9am-7pm Sun.

Getting around

By bus

A SITA bus runs at least hourly (less frequently on Sundays) from piazza Flavio Gioia in Amalfi to Ravello from 7am to 10pm (25mins). In Ravello, the bus sets down and turns around just before a short road tunnel; walk through this to Villa Rufolo and piazza del Duomo. The bus then stops (and turns around again) in front of the church of Santa Maria a Gradillo, and continues to Scala, on the other side of the valley, before making the return journey to Amalfi (some services stop at Scala before Ravello). Six buses a day continue up the crest of the hill beyond Scala to San Pietro and Minuto.

Getting there

Ravello is best approached from Amalfi by bus (*see above* **Getting around**), but if you are driving, follow the signs leading you off the coast road.

This stretch of coast is often seen as little more than the inevitable traffic jam between Amalfi and Salerno, but if you have the time to explore it, you'll find that it has its charms.

Minori, three kilometres (two miles) east of Atrani (or a pleasant hour's hike from Ravello down an ancient staircase) is by no means picturesque in the Positano sense, but it is a pleasant enough place with a restaurant, **L'Arsenale** (*see p268*), which justifies a stopover. If you're heading east, this is also a rare town on the craggy Amalfi coast with a relatively flat centre, nestled between high valley walls. In the middle of a warren of houses is the **Villa Romana** (*see p268*), the only visitable archaeological site on the Costiera.

Excavations began in 1951, but were held up by a catastrophic flood in 1954 that consumed not only the villa but much of Minori and neighbouring Maiori. The property, arranged around a large *viridarium,* or courtyard garden, once belonged to a rich nobleman, as is evident from the dimensions of the structure and the traces of frescos on the walls of many of the rooms, whose style dates the building to the beginning of the first century AD. Upstairs, an antiquarium contains material found here and in two other nearby sites.

Just around the next headland, **Maiori** nestles in a flood plain that has been a continual source of danger to its inhabitants – but has also given them the space to expand. In the 11th century the town was girded with walls and used as a shipbuilding centre for the Amalfi republic. Today, it is the Costiera's only truly nondescript tourist resort, packed with modern hotels that sprang up after the 1954 flood. But, in its favour, it does have the coast's longest beach and one unexpected, historic gem of a hotel, **Casa Raffaele Conforti** (*see p268*).

From Maiori, a side road ascends the Valle di Tramonti to the Valico di Chiunzi, a pass 665 metres (2,327 feet) high (also accessible from Ravello) with amazing views across the construction-plagued Sarno plain to the menacing bulk of Vesuvius. Like Agerola (*see p252*), **Tramonti** itself is not a single village but a series of communities scattered over a fertile upland plain known for its farm produce, cheese, honey and baskets woven from branches of the chestnut trees that grow here. A cold north wind that Amalfi mariners called the *tramontana* howls out of the mountains that encircle the plain; the word has now become standard Italian verbage for a biting northerly.

The coast road east of Maiori negotiates the rocky **Monte dell'Avvocata**, providing spectacular views along the coast. A short distance beyond the 39-kilometre milepost, a path on the left leads up to the rock-hewn chapel of **Santa Maria de Olearia** (open by appointment, 089 877 452), also known as the Catacombe di Badia, one of the more unusual holy sites on the coast, and well worth a visit if you can find a place wide enough to leave the car or persuade the bus driver to set you down. Two hermits were the first to occupy this site in 973; their shrine became a Benedictine abbey, squeezed between the towering rocks, which still has some atmospheric faded frescos from the 11th century.

Beyond the little fishing cove of **Erchie**, with a pretty beach watched over by a Saracen tower (look for the access road on the eastern side of the valley, after the main road has rejoined the shore), the coast road winds along to **Cetara**, a fishing village with the by-now familiar Amalfi Coast layout: long, thin and up a narrow valley. Historically, this was the eastern limit of the Amalfi Republic, and the place still has a salty, frontier town feel to it. Of all the settlements along the coast, this is the one with the most active fishing fleet, which roams the whole Mediterranean in search of shoals, with the help of two spotter planes.

Forget limoncello: the best Amalfi Coast souvenir is a small pot of salted anchovies or an even smaller pot of *colatura di alici,* a close relative of the Roman fish sauce known as *garum,* whose recipe survives only here. With its small beach – overlooked by a medieval watchtower – and the honest, unprettified houses that line the single street, Cetara is a good place to stop to get some sense of what life must have been like here before the tourist industry moved in. Of course, another incentive is its two excellent restaurants (*see p268*).

East of Cetara, the road sticks close to the sea, passing by what is left of the massive hotel at Punta Fuenti. For years, this illegally built blot on the landscape was at the centre of a struggle between environmental pressure groups and local politicians, who feared a domino effect (and the end of lucrative backhanders) if it were shown that what went up could indeed come down. Finally, in 2000, the bulldozers moved in.

Further east, on the site of the Etruscan town of Marcina, **Vietri sul Mare** is the capital of southern Italy's handcrafted ceramics industry, and the town is clogged with shops selling the ubiquitous breakables (*see p267* **Vietri ceramics**). Although pottery has been made here since Roman times, the locals had lost their touch by the early 20th century, but then German ceramicists moved into the area and got the industry going again.

There are pretty examples of the local line in tiles on the dome of the 18th-century church of

Vietri ceramics

Keep your eyes trained on the pavement when you enter the town of Vietri sul Mare (*see p266*), and you will come across a piazza adorned with colourful tiles representing a seascape. Lift your gaze, and you'll see that the mosaic renders the scenery that is spread out before it.

The colours are bright and contrasting, with no hint of shadows. Hand-painted tiles such as these, usually with lively geometric patterns, flowers and animal motifs, are a distinctive element of Campania's architectural style – and Vietri sul Mare produces some of the best. If you're in the market for majolica tabletops or other crockery, the cheapest prices are here.

Ceramics production in Vietri began with the Romans, who scoured nearby terracotta deposits for the raw material used in making oversized urns and pots for transporting goods and liquids. By the 15th century, craftsmen had turned ceramics into an element of design. In those days, Vietri was just one of several local producers of ceramics, and one of the less important ones at that – artisans in Nocera and Salerno had better clay. But Vietri's active entrepreneurial class and its trade links with Sicily, Tuscany and Liguria allowed it to grow. By the 17th century Vietri was cranking out plates and jars on an industrial scale. The **Museo Provinciale della Ceramica** in the adjacent town of Raito traces the history of the local industry in detail. The streets of Vietri are clogged with ceramics shops. **Ceramiche Solimene** produces some of the area's best and brightest pieces; its factory, a multicoloured tile-and-glass extravaganza (*pictured, top left*), is a sight in itself.

Traditionally, the tiles featured scenes from faraway lands: exotic animals, forests, and the kind of country homes and farms that you would never find in a vertical landscape such as this. That practice disappeared with the arrival of foreign artists – Dutch and German especially – in the 1920s. These days the tiles depict local landscapes and typical scenes from Vietri, subjects attractive to the primary customers, who are now foreigners looking for souvenirs, rather than locals looking to spice up their surroundings.

Ceramiche Solimene
Via Madonna degli Angeli 7, Vietri sul Mare (089 210 243/www.solimene.com). **Open** 8am-6pm Mon-Fri; 8am-1pm, 3-6.30pm Sat. **Credit** AmEx, DC, MC, V.

Museo Provinciale della Ceramica
Torretta di Villa Guariglia, Raito (089 211 835). **Open** *May-Sept* 9am-1pm, 4-7pm Tue-Sun. *Oct-Apr* 9am-1pm, 3-6pm Tue-Sun. **Admission** free.

Around Naples

San Giovanni Battista (open 7.30-9.30am, 5.30-8.30pm daily). And the beach at **Marina di Vietri**, with its seaside bars and gelaterie, is a popular summer hangout.

Villa Romana and Antiquarium

Via Capodipiazza 28, Minori (089 852 893). **Open** 9am-1hr before sunset daily. **Admission** free.

Where to eat, drink & stay

In Minori, **L'Arsenale** (via San Giovanni a Mare 20, 089 851 418, closed 3wks Jan-Feb, closed Thur Oct-Mar, average €35) offers good-value seafood cooking. Space is tight, so book ahead, especially if you want to eat at one of the few outdoor tables. Alongside local favourites such as *scialatielli ai frutti di mare* (pasta with seafood) and *totani con le patate* (flying squid with potatoes), the friendly Proto brothers do one or two more creative dishes, such as fish tortellini with prawns and *funghi porcini*. Minori also has perhaps the best bar on the Amalfi Coast, **Bar de Riso** (piazza Cantilena 1, 089 853 618, closed Wed Sept-May), which sits on a corner between the main square and the traffic-bound Lungomare. The coffee is excellent, as are the local cakes (*sfogliatelle, babà*) and home-made ice-cream. Grab a seat outside and eat a *granita di caffé* ostentatiously while those caught in the inevitable traffic jam look on with envy.

It's not obvious from the cement-lined waterfront, but Maiori too has a historic centre, though floods and other catastrophes have pared it back a little. Just off pedestrianised corso della Regina stands a glorious remnant of a more elegant past: the **Casa Raffaele Conforti** (via Casa Mannini 10, 089 853 547, www.casaraffaeleconforti.it, doubles €86-€161, closed Nov-Mar), a small, nine-room hotel occupying the second floor of a 19th-century townhouse. Lovely frescoed ceilings, antique furniture and large gilded mirrors set the tone.

In Cetara, the **Acqua Pazza** (corso Garibaldi 38, 089 261 606, www.acquapazza.it, closed Mon Sept-May, 3wks Jan, average €30) is one of those restaurants fans like to keep quiet about. Not that the place is a snooty temple of haute cuisine, far from it – it's the freshness of the seafood, the bravura of the chef at combining them in tasty but simple ways, the friendliness of owner and frontman Gennaro Castiello and the honest prices that keep the clientele loyal. The never-ending *antipasti* are delicious (some dishes – based on raw tuna – are close to sushi) and a meal in themselves. The local speciality goes into the *linguine con colatura di alici;* and the home-made desserts are marvellous. Book well ahead, and don't show up too early for dinner:

you're likely to find that tables in this relaxed eaterie aren't even set until well after 8pm.

Back up in the main square, **San Pietro** (piazzetta San Francesco 2, 089 261 091, closed Tue, mid Sept-May & late Jan-Feb, average €30) is Cetara's other cut-price gourmet fish temple. The *antipasti misti caldi* are well worth nodding yes to: dishes such as *farro* (spelt or emmer wheat) with *colatura di alici,* courgettes with clams and prawns, follow in a seemingly endless progression. Try to leave room for excellent pasta dishes such as *tubatoni con pescatrice* (pasta with anglerfish) and make the heroic effort to swallow at least one *secondo* – perhaps the *neonati* (whitebait) in a garlic and parsley broth. Finish up with a delicious home-made dessert and mandarin liqueur. It's a little more upmarket and formal than Acqua Pazza, but all done to an equally high standard; and the *piazzetta* is a lovely place to sit outside of a summer's evening.

If you would rather take away the local goodies, head for **Sapori Cetaresi** (corso Garibaldi 44, 089 262 010) and invest in small jars of *colatura di alici* (anchovy sauce) or – to really ingratiate yourself with the rest of the people on your flight home – huge earthenware pots of salted anchovies.

Resources

Tourist information

Associazione Autonoma di Soggiorno e Tourismo *Corso Regina 73, Maiori (089 877 452/ www.aziendaturismo-maiori.it).* **Open** *Oct-Mar* 8.30am-1.30pm, 3-5pm Mon-Fri. *Apr-Sept* 9am-1.30pm, 4-7pm Mon-Sat; 9am-1pm Sun.

Circolo Turistico ACLI *Piazza Matteotti, Vietri sul Mare (089 211 285/www.comune.vietri-sul-mare.sa.it/cta).* **Open** *Nov-Apr* 10am-1pm, 5-7pm Mon-Fri; 10am-1pm Sat. *May-Oct* 9am-1pm, 5-8pm Mon-Fri; 9am-1pm Sat.

Getting there

By boat

TraVelMar (089 873 190) runs frequent summer ferry services between Maiori, Amalfi and Positano.

By bus

The regular Amalfi–Salerno SITA bus stops in all the localities mentioned here, and plenty more besides.

By car

Take the Vietri exit from the A3 motorway; from here, the SS163 coast road winds its way west.

By train

The station at Vietri sul Mare is served by only a very few very slow trains. Most of the time it's quicker to go straight to Salerno station (40mins from Naples) and continue by SITA bus.

Further Afield

Provinces beyond Naples have different and distinct appeal.

Castello di Arechi, overlooking the bay at Salerno. *See p270.*

Geography and history have combined to give each of Naples' neighbouring provinces a very different feel: the province of **Caserta** stretches from flat coastal plains high up into the craggy Apennines; **Benevento** is dominated by huge expanses of rolling farmland; while **Salerno** and its surrounding area is a scenic mix of landscapes and cultures, epitomised by the Greco-Roman site of Paestum.

Salerno

The crescent-shaped Gulf of Salerno stretches from Punta della Campanella to Punta Licosa, its northern and southernmost edges laced with rocky cliffs and beautiful coves, its central part low and flat. At the northern end of this plain lies **Salerno**.

Archaeological evidence shows that the area was settled by Etruscans as early as the sixth century BC. Its official history begins, however, in 194 BC, when the Romans founded a colony called Salernum. Fought over and occupied down the centuries by Goths and Byzantines, it came firmly under the thumb of the Germanic Lombards in 646. Despite internal power struggles and constant harrying by Saracens, the city flourished. It was the Lombard Prince Arechi, local lore relates, who founded the city's illustrious Medical School.

But it took the Normans, who conquered Salerno in 1076, to fulfil the city's real potential. The first capital of what was to become the Kingdom of Southern Italy (Palermo succeeded it in 1127), Salerno's Norman court was legendary, and its Medical School drew patients and students from all over the known world. After centuries of fluctuating fortunes, Salerno became an increasingly insignificant backwater as Naples' star rose under the Angevins and Aragonese. Only after Italian Unification in 1870 – as Naples declined – did Salerno begin to regain some of its lost vitality. During World War II, on 8 September 1943, Allied troops landed just south of the city, forcing the Germans to withdraw north; for five months in 1944, Salerno was the seat of the Italian government.

Today, it is a buzzing industrial city, with an important port. The seafront area, badly bombed during World War II, is decidedly post-war functional; the medieval heart of the old town, however, has recently undergone extensive – though controversial – restoration, much of it at the hands of Catalan Oriol Bohigas, the architect responsible for Barcelona's makeover.

Dominating the old centre, Salerno's **Duomo** – dedicated to the city's patron saint Matthew – was begun by the Norman conqueror Robert de Hauteville (known as *le Guiscard*, 'the Crafty') in 1077, in thanks for his victory over

Around Naples

the Lombards. The cathedral received a full restoration after an earthquake in the 18th century, though subsequent facelifts have revealed large sections of the glorious Romanesque original.

At the base of the imposing gateway leading into the Duomo are a sculpted lion and a lioness feeding her cub, symbols of the power and charity of the Church. The church itself has a porticoed courtyard with columns taken from ancient buildings and an ancient granite basin at its centre, a spectacular 12th-century bell tower and a room off to the right that may have been the lecture theatre of the Medical School.

Inside, through vast bronze doors cast in Constantinople in 1099, the Latin cross-plan church has three naves; in the central one are two carved and inlaid pulpits, the one on the right (with matching paschal – Easter – candlesticks) dating from the early 13th century, and the one on the left from the late 12th.

The 16th-century wooden choir stalls are preceded by sections of the 1175 mosaic-encrusted iconostasis (screen). Beside the stalls, in the left aisle, the statue of Margaret of Durres, mother of Naples' Angevin King Ladislas, dates from 1435. In the transept and choir are sections of the Duomo's original, spectacular Byzantine-inspired floor. In the cavernous baroque crypt, columns wind to form interlacing curves. Beneath the main altar lie the remains of St Matthew.

East of the Duomo, via San Michele leads to the **Museo Archeologico Provinciale**. Housed in the former abbey of San Benedetto (one of 36 religious institutions in the city), the museum's collection testifies to the extensive Etruscan influence in their southernmost outpost, as well as displaying an interesting chance find – a first-century bronze head of Apollo fished from the Gulf of Salerno in 1930.

Bustling with boutiques (most of the city's smart shops are here) and lined with medieval buildings, via dei Mercanti is the picturesque main thoroughfare of the old town. The **Museo della Scuola Medica Salernitana** is housed in the deconsecrated church of San Gregorio and illustrates the activities of Salerno's illustrious Medical School. Manuscripts, documents and illustrations are organised in eight sections, each dedicated to a branch of medieval medical knowledge, and chart the school's activities during its heyday in the 11th to 13th centuries and beyond.

Rising above the centre on Colle Bonadies, the **Castello di Arechi** (bus 19 runs infrequently uphill from piazza XIV Maggio) was part of a great Lombard defence system, with walls extending from the castle to the sea surrounding the wedge-shaped town. It's worth a look just for the spectacular view; the castle itself has been extensively restored and is used as a scenic venue for summer concerts. Opposite the café and restaurant is a museum containing ceramics and other artefacts that were found within. At the time of writing, the network of ancient footpaths linking the castle with the town was impassable in places: it's a pity the castle's restoration didn't include improved access from the town.

Castello di Arechi
Via Croce (089 227 237). **Open** 9am-1hr before sunset Tue-Sun. **Admission** free.

Duomo (Cattedrale di San Matteo)
Piazza Alfano 1 (089 231 387). **Open** 7.30am-8pm daily.

Museo Archeologico Provinciale
Via San Benedetto 28 (089 231 135). **Open** 9am-7.30pm Mon-Sat; 9am-1.30pm Sun. **Admission** free.

Museo della Scuola Medica Salernitana
Via dei Mercanti 72 (089 257 3111/089 257 3220). **Open** 9am-2.30pm Mon-Sat. **Admission** free.

Where to stay & eat

Situated right on the beach, the **Jolly Hotel** (Lungomare Trieste 1, 089 225 222, www.jolly hotels.it, doubles €122-€142) is within walking distance of the old town. Opposite the train station you'll find the comfortable **Hotel Plaza** (piazza Vittorio Veneto 42, 089 224 477, www.plazasalerno.it, doubles €95). Close to the cathedral is the atmospheric **Albergo della Gioventù** (Youth Hostel) in 17th-century premises (Via Canali, 089 234 776, www.ostello disalerno.it, doubles €36, single bed in dorm €14).

For good seafood, try **Portovecchio** (Molo Manfredi 38, 089 255 222, closed Mon, 2wks Dec, average €25). In the old town, **Pizzeria Vicolo della Neve** (vicolo della Neve 24, 089 225 705, closed lunch, Wed, average €17) serves great pizzas and delicious pasta and beans, as well as its famous *cianfotta* (a dish made with potatoes, peppers, courgettes, bacon and tomatoes).

Between the Duomo and the Villa Comunale park, **Portacatena** (via Portacatena 28-34, 089 235 899, closed Mon, dinner Sun, 2 weeks Aug, average €30) occupies an atmospheric vaulted cellar and has creative vegetable-based cuisine.

Getting around

CSTP (089 252 228/089 487 286/toll-free 800 016 659/ www.cstp.it) operates bus services around Salerno and surrounding areas. Tickets cost €0.80 for 90 mins travel, €2 for 24hrs. For €20 you can buy a 3-day pass throughout Campania (www.unicocampania.it).

Resources

Hospital
Ospedale San Giovanni *via San Leonardo, 089 671 111.*

Internet
Attendere Prego, via Roma 26.

Police
piazza Amendola, 089 613 111.

Post office
via Roma 130, 089 229970.

Tourist information
Ente Provinciali per il Turismo (EPT) *Piazza V Veneto 1 (tel/fax 089 231 432/toll-free 800 213 289/www.salernocity.com).* **Open** 9am-2pm, 3-8pm Mon-Sat.
The website is in Italian only.

Getting there

By bus
SITA (089 405 145/www.sita-on-line.it) runs regular services from piazza Municipio in Naples.

By car
Salerno is 55km (34 miles) south of Naples on the A3 motorway.

By train
There are regular services from Naples' Stazione Centrale on the Naples–Reggio–Calabria line.

Paestum

Letters in bold in the text refer to the map on p272.
The flat, straight coast road out of Salerno skirts wide sandy beaches where locals flock in summer. There are pine and eucalyptus trees, and fields full of artichokes or strawberries, depending on the season. River buffalo, whose milk is used to produce mozzarella cheese, graze on land that was once a malarial swamp around the mouth of the River Sele. It was on this fertile plain that the Allies battled against the Germans for 20 days in September 1943, eventually forcing them to withdraw north.

Paestum's ancient territory starts on the southern bank of the River Sele. The **Santuario di Hera Argiva** (accessible from both the coast road and the SS18) was built by the Greeks around 600 BC, at the same time as the city of Poseidonia-Paestum. It was a temple to Hera, goddess of women and marriage. Although the actual site consists of little more than temple foundations, a state-of-the-art learning centre, formidably called the **Museo Narrante del Santuario di Hera Argiva**, gives useful

insights (with English panels) into the cult of Hera, while displaying replicas of original finds now housed in the **Museo Archeologico Nazionale** (*see p273*) in Paestum. The **Museo Narrante** occupies an imaginatively converted farmhouse on land adjacent to the temple site.

Paestum itself – ten kilometres (six miles) south of the Santuario – is best known for its three standing Greek temples, though there are traces of continued occupation throughout ancient times, including extensive Roman building works down to the second century AD.

The town – originally named Poseidonia – was founded most probably in the early sixth century BC by Greeks from Sybaris, a Greek colony on Italy's south-eastern coast. Like almost all the other settlements in Greece and Magna Graecia (southern Italy), the colony had the basic trappings of the Greek *polis*: places of worship, a civic centre (the *agorà*), an assembly area for all male citizens (*ekklesiasterion*), and an area for exercise and games (*gymnasion*). In about 400 BC, the city appears to have been overrun by a local tribe, the Lucanians; they unwisely backed Pyrrhus, king of Epirus, in his struggle against the Romans and were eventually trounced.

In 273 BC Poseidonia became a Roman colony, and the tangible signs of Greek civic life were gradually removed: the *ekklesiasterion* was filled in and replaced by the Roman *comitium* (assembly area) to the south; the temples were left standing (the pious Romans would never have dismantled them), but were probably rededicated to other divinities; and the Roman forum replaced the Greek *agorà*, again further to the south. At some stage, the name of the town was adapted to a more Italic pronunciation, ending up as Paestum. This overlapping of civilisations can make Paestum a confusing site to visit.

To see it at its best, visit Paestum first thing in the morning or late in the afternoon after the tour buses have left. Even better, take an atmospheric evening stroll along the pedestrianised road outside the site but within easy view of the floodlit temples. There are now evening tours on Thursdays, Fridays and Saturdays in Italian (€14, €11 with artecard, for reservations call 0828 721 113, 3-6.30pm Tue-Sat).

For standard daytime visits, after passing through the impressive ancient **city walls [A]** – almost five kilometres (three miles) long and rising from five metres (16.5 feet) to 15 metres (49 feet) high – keep to the main road (SS18), which offers easy access to both the site and the museum.

At the northern end of the site lies what was previously called the **Temple of Ceres [B]**, dedicated – as archaeologists subsequently discovered from the temple's votive offerings – to

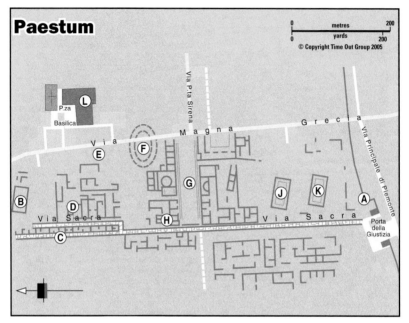

Paestum

metres 200
yards 200
© Copyright Time Out Group 2005

Via P.ta Sirena

Via Magna Grecia

Via Principale di Piemonte

P.za Basilica **[L]**

Via **[E]** **[F]**

[B]

[D]

Via Sacra

[C]

[G]

[H]

[J] **[K]** **[A]**

Via Sacra

Porta della Giustizia

the goddess Athena. This Athenaion, built in about 500 BC, was a Doric temple with some Ionic features: there was an inner colonnade with Ionic capitals, two of which are now on display in the site museum. The temple was used as a burial site in early Christian times and then succumbed to the same fate as many other Greek temples throughout the Mediterranean, being converted into a church in medieval times.

From the Athenaion a well-preserved **Roman road [C]** leads south through the site, passing the curious half-buried sixth-century shrine (*heroon*) **[D]** to Poseidon in which archaeologists unearthed some finely worked bronze vases (*hydria*) now given pride of place in the museum. Although much of the rest of the Greek area was built over in Roman times, the *ekklesiasterion* **[E]** is the one part of the Greek *agorà* that is now recognisable; most of the limestone seating is lost. Fifty metres (55 yards) further south, past Roman residential areas, the Roman civic area begins; close by stand the partially rebuilt arches of the **amphitheatre [F]**.

Begun during the first century BC, the amphitheatre was enlarged in early imperial times when an outer colonnade was added (only stubs of brick pillars are left standing). With an estimated capacity of 2,000, the amphitheatre is pint-size compared to those in Pompeii (*see*

p219), Capua (*see p278*) and Pozzuoli (*see p103*), and is unlikely to have been able to offer the whole bloodthirsty gamut of Roman entertainment. Much of it – including the Porta Libitinensis through which the hapless losers were hauled out – lies under the main road hacked through the site in the 18th century.

Close by stand the remnants of other civic buildings from Roman times, all of which were within easy reach of the Roman **forum [G]**, the hub of urban life from the third century BC onwards. The centrepiece of the *campus*, the ancient sports and leisure centre, is the third-century BC **piscina [H]** or swimming pool, which evokes the memorable diving scene in the frescoed Tomb of the Diver on display in Paestum's museum, although the tomb itself predates the piscina by as much as 200 years. The purpose of the sunken network of limestone pillars remains a mystery.

The architectural jewel of the site, 100 metres (110 yards) south of the Roman forum, is the remarkably preserved (but misnamed) **Temple of Neptune [J]**. Dedicated perhaps to Poseidon or – according to a recent theory – Apollo, the temple was built in the mid fifth century BC when the Greek colony was enjoying a period of prosperity. It employs similar techniques to those used in other contemporary Doric temples (curvature of the horizontal lines, slightly convex columns or entasis). Like the other temples in Paestum this was built with local limestone rather than the more usual marble.

The columns were originally faced with white stucco to imitate marble and perhaps mask the defects of the stone. Together with the sixth-century basilica – more accurately called the **Temple of Hera [K]** – to the south, it rises out of the Paestum plain like a mirage and continues to throw even the world-weariest of visitors into raptures.

The **museum [L]** has some excellent displays of archaic Greek sculptures from the Santuario di Hera Argiva temple (*see p271*), interesting finds from local necropolises complete with the paraphernalia for the afterlife, an extensive collection of frescoed tombs and a Roman section on the top floor. As with the site, there are several information panels in English giving minimal information.

In summer, concerts and theatrical performances (information 0828 811 016) are held close by the temples.

Museo Archeologico Nazionale
Via Magna Grecia (0828 811 023). **Open** *Site* 9am-1hr before sunset daily. *Museum* 8.45am-7pm daily. Closed 1st & 3rd Mon of the mth. **Admission** *Site* €4; *museum* €6; *both* €8.50. **No credit cards**.

Salerno's **Duomo**. *See p269.*

Museo Narrante del Santuario di Hera Argiva
Masseria Procuriali, Capaccio (0828 861 440). **Open** 9am-4pm Tue-Sat. **Admission** free.

Where to stay & eat

About two kilometres north of Paestum on the road to Capaccio Scalo, the **Azienda Agricola Seliano** (via Seliano, 0828 723 634, www.agriturismoseliano.it, half-board €55-€65 per person) occupies two remodelled 19th-century farmhouses. There's riding, a pool and cooking lessons too. It's closed from November to February, except over New Year.

In Paestum's archaeological zone, is the **Villa Rita** (via Nettuno 5, Zona Archeologica, 0828 811 081, www.hotelvillarita.it, closed Nov-mid Feb, doubles €75-€85) and the Hotel **Helios** (via Principe di Piemonte, Zona Archeologica, 0828 811 451, www.hotelheliospaestum.com, doubles €80). Both have quiet gardens.

In the midst of a welter of restaurants serving fairly dreadful tourist fare, **Nonna Scepa** (via Laura 53, Paestum, 0828 851 064, closed Thur Oct-May, average €27) stands out a mile with excellent seafood and good pizzas.

Resources

Tourist information
Azienda Automa Soggiorno e Turismo (AAST) *Via Magna Grecia 889 (0828 811 016/ fax 0828 722 322/www.infopaestum.it)*. **Open** 9am-1pm, 3-5pm Mon-Sat; 9am-1pm Sun.

Getting there

By bus
CSTP (089 252 228/089 487 286/toll-free 800 016 659) runs hourly services to Paestum from the railway station square in Salerno.

By car
The SS18 follows the coast south of Salerno. If coming direct from Naples, take the Battipaglia exit off the Salerno–Reggio–Calabria motorway.

By train
There are frequent services to Paestum on the Naples–Salerno–Reggio–Calabria line. Paestum town's main station is called Capaccio Scalo, from where infrequent buses run to the ruins; a few trains each day stop at the smaller Paestum station, which is a 10mins walk from the archaeological site.

Benevento

Despite appearances – unattractive late 20th-century development straddles hillsides and valleys around – Benevento conceals

Around Naples

Antiquity preserved at **Paestum**. *See p271.*

unexpected nuggets from its long, distinguished history. In early Roman times the area was occupied by the Oscan-speaking Samnites, a fearsome Italic hill tribe. But by the beginning of the fourth century BC the Samnites were out on a limb, and a peace treaty with Rome was finally concluded in 290 BC. The settlement where Benevento now stands was renamed Beneventum and became a Roman colony in 268 BC, reaping considerable benefits from its strategic position along the main north–south Appian Way and from its later status as a *municipium*, formally subject to Rome but governed by its own laws.

In the turbulent centuries that followed the fall of the Roman Empire, Benevento emerged as a Lombard capital whose influence extended throughout most of southern Italy. Caught in a tug of war between the Normans and the Papacy in the 11th century, it remained a papal stronghold for two centuries before it was sacked (twice) by the Swabian Frederick II.

Its subsequent history is marked by a lengthy period of papal dominion until 1799 when it was occupied by French troops who indulged in their usual pastime of purloining local artworks. Extensive damage was done during World War II, when an estimated 65 per cent of the city was turned to rubble.

Today, its plush shop windows and shiny new fleet of cars show that Benevento has resisted the urban blight often found in other towns in Campania. Landmarks are well kept, traffic is heavy but fairly well disciplined, and the surrounding countryside is generally well tended and conserved.

The major sites in the city are clustered either side of the main shopping thoroughfare, corso Garibaldi. Evidence of Benevento's early Roman heritage can be seen at the **Museo del Sannio**, tucked in behind the church of Santa Sofia. The museum has several galleries that are filled with Roman sculptures and fine marble sarcophagi from ancient settlements in the province, while the covered courtyard contains finds from the first-century Temple of Isis, one of several Egyptian deities worshipped in the area. Statues of Thoth, Horus and Anubis may seem out of place in an Italian hilltown, but eastern cults enjoyed considerable popularity at home as Rome's empire expanded and assimilated new religions. With the arrival of the Lombards in the sixth century, all traces of pagan worship were eliminated: the magic powers of Isis were demonised, perhaps giving rise to the area's reputation for witchcraft, a reputation that survives to the present day.

The museum extends into the delightful 11th-century cloister of the church of **Santa Sofia**, which has elaborately sculpted column capitals that are reminiscent – in style and quality – of medieval masterpieces such as Monreale in Sicily.

The church of Santa Sofia was founded by the Lombard Duke Arechi II in 762 AD; though restored in the 12th century, the innovative original plan – an inner hexagon of columns sur-rounded by a decagon of pillars – has survived intact. In two of the three apses behind the altar there are traces of an eighth-century fresco cycle depicting locally born St Zacharias on the left and a New Testament scene on the right.

But Benevento's real jewel – recently unveiled after a lengthy facelift – is the **Arco di Traiano**, a triumphal arch erected in 114 to celebrate the achievements of Roman emperor Trajan. Described as *'optimo'* in the inscription surmounting the arch, Trajan had restored a measure of peace and prosperity to the Empire with his military campaigns in Germany and the Danube area. Despite its location – the busy inner-city ring road passes to one side of it – the arch's sculpted friezes depicting the emperor performing various civic duties have weathered the millennia remarkably well. Floodlit at night, this is one of Campania's finest monuments.

At the western end of the town beyond the Duomo is the Teatro Romano, probably built during the reign of Commodus at the end of the second century. While much of the arcaded superstructure has been lost, other parts of the theatre have been extensively restored. With the distant backdrop of the Taburno mountain range, the theatre is an atmospheric venue for summer concerts and plays – contact the local tourist office for information.

Museo del Sannio

Piazza Santa Sofia (0824 21 818). **Open** 9am-1pm Tue-Sun. **Admission** €3. **No credit cards**.

Santa Sofia

Piazza Santa Sofia (0824 21 206). **Open** 7am-noon, 4-8pm daily.

Teatro Romano

Piazza Caio Ponzio Telesino (0824 47 213). **Open** 9am-1hr before sunset daily. **Admission** €2. **No credit cards**.

Where to stay & eat

The obvious choice in town is the well-appointed **Hotel President** (via GB Perasso 1, 0824 316 716, www.hotelpresident.8m.com, doubles €97), conveniently close to the museum. For budget accommodation, opt for one of two historic farmsteads six kilometres (four miles) north-east of Benevento on the road to Pietrelcina: **Agriturismo Le Camerelle** (contrada Camerelle, 0824 776 134, www.lecamerelle.it, doubles €50) or **Agriturismo La Francesca** (contrada La Francesca, www.agriturismo lafrancesca.it, same rates and phone number as above), both owned by the Barricelli family. La Francesca also operates a thriving restaurant (average €19) serving local produce within a pleasingly restored 17th-century farmhouse.

In Benevento itself, make for the **Corte di Bacco** (via Traiano 65, 0824 54605, closed lunch, Mon, average €20) specialising in local wines and regional fare, located conveniently close to Trajan's arch.

Resources

Hospital

Ospedale Fatebenefratelli *viale Principe di Napoli 14/A (0824 42348)*.

Police

via De Caro (0824 373 111).

Post office

viale Principe Di Napoli 62 (0824 326 911).

Tourist information

Ente Provinciale per il Turismo (EPT) *Piazza Roma 11 (0824 319 938/fax 0824 312 309/ www.eptbenevento.it)*. **Open** 8.30am-1.45pm, 3-6pm Mon-Fri; 9am-1pm Sat.

Getting there

By bus

Autoservizi FBN (0824 24961) does several daily runs from Naples (piazza Garibaldi) to Benevento, where the bus station is a 5min walk from piazza Santa Sofia.

By car

From Naples take the A1 motorway to Caserta Sud, then the traffic-laden SS7 to Benevento; or take the relatively stress-free A16 Naples–Bari motorway to the Benevento exit.

By train

There are few direct trains from Naples; you may have to change in Caserta. To avoid long waits check connections carefully. Benevento station is a good 30mins walk from the major sites, though bus 1 runs frequently between the station and the centre.

Caserta

Situated 20 kilometres (12 miles) north of Naples, Caserta was a quiet backwater until the first Bourbon king, Charles III, selected it as a peaceful residence where he could indulge his passion for hunting and at the same time avoid Naples' twin dangers of Vesuvius and marauding Saracens. Aiming at the opulence of the Palace of Versailles, he commissioned leading Neapolitan architect Luigi Vanvitelli (*see p38*) to build the Reggia, one of Italy's largest palaces. The royal project sparked a baroque property boom as trade and industry flocked to cash in on the town's new status.

In the 19th century, Caserta was an important military base. The key encounter of Italian Unification – when Giuseppe Garibaldi met King Victor Emanuel II and agreed to hand over his southern Italian conquests to the crown (*see p21*) – took place at nearby Teano in 1860. Although the economy of the town is primarily agricultural and its industry operates at little more than craft level, modern Caserta is comfortably off by southern Italian standards, and is a lively backdrop to the stately Reggia.

Begun by Vanvitelli in 1752 and finished by his son Carlo in 1774, the **Reggia** is perhaps the finest example of the Neapolitan baroque. Though construction work set off at a great rate under the enthusiastic Charles III (1731-59), it almost ground to a halt in 1759 when he returned to his native Spain to assume the crown there. It was not until the 1770s, in fact, that Charles's son Ferdinand I (1759-1825) began pushing for the work to be completed.

The palace is built around four courtyards, has 1,200 sumptuous rooms (only a fraction are open to the public; many, controversially, are occupied by the air force), 1,790 windows, and cost around six million ducats to build.

Around Naples

The **Scala d'Onore** (main staircase), with 117 steps carved from one stone block, leads up to the royal apartments. Beyond the upper octagonal hall, the **Salone degli Alabardieri** (halberd bearers) has busts of various queens, while the **Salone delle Guardie di Corpo** (bodyguards) has scenes from the lives of the Farnese family, dukes of Parma, a title that passed to King Charles through his mother Elizabetta Farnese. The bust of Ferdinand I on a mantelpiece is attributed to Antonio Canova. The next room – **Sala di Alessandro** – gets its name from the fresco depicting Alexander the Great's marriage to Roxana; the porch outside was used by the monarchs and their families for royal waves.

To the left of this room lies the suite of rooms called the **Appartamento Vecchio**, the first in the Reggia to be occupied. The first four rooms are dedicated to the seasons: *primavera* (spring) with paintings by Antonio Dominici;

estate (summer) with works by Fedele Fischetti, walls covered in San Leucio silk and a Murano glass chandelier; a dining room dedicated to *autunno* (autumn) with frescos of Bacchus and Ariadne; and *inverno* (winter).

In the private study of Ferdinand II (1830-59) the clock and vases are French and the lacquered furniture is German, but the overall effect is oriental. Behind the mirror, a private door leads to the king's bedchamber via a narrow passageway. Since this king died of a contagious disease, the contents of his bedchamber were destroyed; the furniture now on display dates from Ferdinand I's reign. Next to the bedchamber is the queen's dressing room, followed by the spacious **Sala di Ricevimento**, where the sovereigns received their guests. Beyond two large reading rooms is the **Biblioteca** (library), where a collection of more than 10,000 volumes is distributed over several rooms. The adjoining

Wine tourism

Given a wide berth by wine buffs as little as ten years ago, Campania's wines are gradually regaining their ancient reputation: Falernum from northern Campania was considered one of the great wines of the Roman Empire, extolled by first-century bon viveur Horace in his odes. Natural historian Pliny the Elder claimed wines from Campania were the healthiest, while its grape varieties were considered almost as numerous as the sands of the Libyan desert. The two thousand years from then until the very recent past saw a nosedive in quality, a massive reduction in the gene pool of grape varieties, and a trend towards artisanal production where the end-product – though lauded as *genuino* – was at best a hit-or-miss affair.

Often hitching a convenient ride with *agriturismo*, Campania's newly emerging wine market has seen exponential growth, and quality has improved enormously. An outlay of €5-€10 (€10-€15 in a restaurant) should ensure you get a bottle of very palatable Campanian wine. The southward march of the ubiquitous Sangiovese grape has been halted, and local varieties (Aglianico and Piedirosso stand out among reds, Fiano and Falanghina among whites) are now well established throughout Italy. Producers, such as Mustilli near Benevento (0823 718142, www.mustilli.com), Pietratorcia on Ischia (081 908206,www.pietratorcia.it) and Villa Matilde north of Mondragone (0823 932088, www.villamatilde.it), are increasingly opening

room contains a nativity scene with 1,200 figures crafted by 18th-century artisans and dressed in clothes made by the queen and her ladies-in-waiting; the glass display cases occupy the place where a small stage used to be, before the palace theatre was built.

To the right of the Sala di Alessandro is the suite of rooms called the **Appartamento Nuovo**. This suite was not completed until 1845. The first two rooms were probably used by court officials for routine palace business. The **Sala del trono** (throne room) was where the king received ambassadors and where balls were held; it is lit by 14 Bohemian glass and bronze lamps, and the throne is of carved and gilded wood. The private part of the suite begins with Ferdinand II's bedchamber. The adjoining bathroom and study belonged to the private apartment of Napoleon's brother-in-law Joaquin Murat, Naples' king from 1808 to 1816. His

bedchamber is in the French Empire style, with mahogany and bronze inlay furniture and his initials ostentatiously carved into the chairs. The Royal Chapel has a barrel-vaulted ceiling reminiscent of the one at Versailles.

Within the palace complex is the **Museo dell'Opera**, which contains documents and plans tracing the history of its construction.

Also designed by Luigi Vanvitelli, and modified by his son Carlo, the 120-hectare (296-acre) gardens – **Il Parco** – surrounding the royal palace are a vast expanse of manicured green, traversed by spectacular fountains and pools. Some 700 metres (765 yards) from the palace exit stands the **Fontana di Margherita**, followed by a series of long ponds, at the head of which is the **Fontana dei Delfini** (dolphin fountain). The **Fontana di Eolo** (Aeolus, god of the winds) has six tiered waterfalls; it should have been adorned with 54 statues, but only 29 were completed.

At its far end lies the **Fontana di Ceres** (goddess of fertility). The final fountain, composed of 12 mini-waterfalls, has statues of Venus and Adonis.

Beyond, the **Grande Cascata** crashes down over greenery from a height of 78 metres (255 feet), flanked by statues of Diana, and of Actaeon being turned into a stag for daring to observe the bathing goddess. The stairs on either side of the waterfall lead to the grotto, where water brought from the surrounding hills by the **Acquedotto Carolino** arrives to feed the garden's fountains; stretching for 40 kilometres (25 miles), passing through five mountains and over three bridges, the aqueduct was an amazing feat of hydraulic engineering by Vanvitelli.

Reggia di Caserta (Palazzo Reale)

Via Douet 2 (Reggia 0823 277380/Museo dell'Opera 0823 332 1400). **Open** *Reggia* 8.30am-7.30pm Tue-Sun. *Museo* 9am-1pm Tue-Sun. *Parco* 9am-2hr before sunset Tue-Sun. **Admission** *Reggia, Museo & Park* €6. *Parco only* €2. **No credit cards**.

Where to stay & eat

Caserta is not spoilt for well-appointed accommodation. Of the budget places, the **Hotel Baby** (via Verdi 41-3, 0823 328 311, doubles €52) is one of the more acceptable. Opposite the Reggia is the newly renovated **Jolly Hotel** (viale Vittorio Veneto 9, 0823 325 222, www.jollyhotels.it, doubles €134), which has disabled facilities.

Surprisingly, the self-service cafeteria in the **Reggia** (just by the entrance to the palace gardens) offers reasonable food at highly competitive prices (average €15). Of the surrounding towns, Casertavecchia offers the best chance of finding a good, atmospheric

their doors to the public, combining cellar visits, *degustazioni*, and appetising fare at moderate prices.

A plethora of *enoteche* (where wine is both sold to take away and served on the premises with a wide range of food pairings) have opened in major centres in Campania, with a quality niche being occupied in Naples by **L'ebbrezza di Noè** (vico Vetriera a Chiaia 8b/9, 081 400 104). As a general rule, *enoteche* open for sit-down clients only in the evening.

The knock-on effect in restaurants is also noticeable. Where not so long ago Chianti and other northerners reigned supreme, nowadays a serious *carta dei vini* (wine list) will often have pages of local wines to pore over.

Blending tradition with technology, the doyen of regional viticulture **Mastroberardino** (0825 614111, www.mastroberardino.com) has re-planted five vineyards in the archaeological site of Pompeii using ancient training systems and grape varieties. In 2003, a limited supply of the Villa dei Misteri red came on to the market at almost €200 a bottle. Despite the dizzy price tag, it is perhaps a wine to be drunk fairly soon – in moderation – rather than laid down. According to Pliny the Elder, wines from Pompeii gained nothing from greater maturity and were known to give a hangover lasting until noon the following day.

Around Naples

restaurant. A ten-minute drive north of the centre, **Leucio** (strada Panoramica, San Leucio, 0823 301 241, closed Mon, dinner Sun, average €30) serves outstanding food with a heavy fish bias, as well as home-made pasta, and has excellent service.

Getting there

By bus

CTP (081 504 8150/www.ctpn.it) runs frequent services from piazza Garibaldi in Naples to Caserta and Capua; the buses marked '*per autostrada*' take the motorway and get there faster.

By car

From Naples take the A1 motorway and exit at Caserta Sud.

By train

There are frequent services from Naples' Stazione Centrale (journey time 30mins). The station in Caserta is a 5mins walk from the Reggia.

Resources

Hospital

Azienda Ospedaliera San Sebastiano di Caserta *Via Palasciano (0823 231 111).*

Internet

Internet Caffè *Viale Lincoln 89/91 (0823 322 146).*

Police

Piazza Vanvitelli 5 (0823 429 111).

Post Office

via Roma 14 (0823 325319).

Tourist information

Ente Provinciale per il Turismo (EPT) *Piazza Dante (0823 321 137/fax 0823 326 300/www.casertaturismo.it).* **Open** 8.30am-5.30pm Mon-Sat.

Around Caserta

Probably founded in the eighth century, **Casertavecchia** (Old Caserta) is self-consciously picturesque, with medieval alleyways and a ruined castle; it was the seat of the counts of Caserta until the 16th century, when they moved to the plains below. Deserted during the day, the place bursts into life as its many *trattorie* open up in the evening. The 12th-century cathedral of **San Michele Arcangelo** in piazza del Duomo (the entrance is round the corner) is one of the finest examples of Romanesque architecture in the region, with an outstanding bell tower of Arabic and French influence, and an Arab-looking eight-sided dome. Ancient columns with Corinthian capitals added to compensate for height differences divide the Latin-cross interior into three aisles.

Every September, Casertavecchia is home to the popular **Settembre al Borgo** festival (information 0823 273 268/0823 322 233), with music, dance, open-air theatre and exhibitions.

Nearby is the quiet, old town of **Santa Maria Capua Vetere**; with its crumbling *palazzi*, medieval cobbles and new money, it is hard to imagine it was once the apple of the Roman imperial eye, gateway to the south and to the wealth of oriental sea trade.

Inhabited since the ninth century BC, it flourished under the Etruscans, resisted the Greeks, but fell to the Samnites. When the Romans got down to building the Appian Way in 312 BC, it led to old Capua, now Santa Maria Capua Vetere. The city supported Hannibal during the second Punic War (218-210 BC) but Roman rule was heavy-handedly reinstated after his defeat and an attempted uprising.

By that time, its trade and agricultural sectors were flourishing and its Seplasia forum (today's piazza Mazzini) was world-famous for perfume. In the first century BC, Livy described old Capua as the biggest and richest city in Italy; for Cicero it was 'a second Rome'.

In AD 465, the city was sacked by the Vandals and in 841 the Saracens arrived to finish off the job. The population took to the hills, to where modern Capua now stands. The destruction of the old city was completed by the citizens themselves, who freely pillaged building material from the ruins until as late as the 19th century. Even archaeologists happily plundered the site and sold off their booty to the highest bidder. This may explain why it took so long for the delightful **Museo Antica Capua** to claw back some of its heritage. It opened in 1995.

In piazza Matteotti, the **Duomo** (Basilica di Santa Maria Maggiore; open 8-11.30am, 5-7pm daily) was founded in 432 on the site of first-century catacombs; it was heavily remodelled in the 17th and 18th centuries.

The **Anfiteatro** is across town. There was probably an arena here in Etruscan times, and there was certainly a gladiator school in 73 BC, when Spartacus and 30 other gladiators broke down its doors in a bid for freedom, sparking the two-year Slave Revolt. The gladiators gained and trained 50,000 supporters, and conducted guerrilla warfare from hideouts on Vesuvius. Six thousand of them later decorated crosses along the Appian Way.

Successive emperors extended the amphitheatre until it was second only to Rome's Colosseum in size and crowd capacity. It featured heavily in the Empire's bread-and-circuses policy for whipping up political support and camouflaging social problems. Crowds were issued tickets with gate numbers (there were around 80 entrances). Elevators brought gladiators, animals and scenery into the arena from the underground passages. Part of the outer wall still stands. It originally consisted of four tiers of arches with Doric half-columns and busts of the gods set in the keystones. The marble facing was stripped and recycled long ago.

The newly opened **Museo del Gladiatore** at the site shows a wedge of the amphitheatre reconstructed with the aid of architectural finds, as well as an incongruous life-size model of a gladiator, complete with a commentary and sound effects (in Italian) of action in the arena.

Such an important city attracted the full gamut of religions. The ancient Persian cult of Mithras, known to the Greeks from the fifth century BC, was probably brought to the town by the gladiators, who frequently came from the east. The religion divided everything into good and evil; its all-male adherents (it was very popular among Roman soldiers) swore to combat evil. Membership was secret and there was an initiation ceremony, depicted on the walls of the **Mithraeum**; note that some of the novices are blindfolded. The Tauroctonia, which forms the centre panel on the back wall,

shows Mithras slaying a bull, the symbol of brute force and vitality. According to the Mithraic creation myth, all life forms sprang from the blood spilt when Mithras killed the bull, the only other living creature on a barren earth. The channel that runs from the altar collected the blood spilt in animal sacrifices.

On the Caserta–Santa Maria Capua Vetere road is one of the best wine and gourmet shops in Campania, **Enoteca La Botte** (via Nazionale Appia 168-180, 0823 494 040, www.enotecalbotte. it, open 4-8pm Mon, 9am-1pm, 4.30-8pm Tue-Sat).

Anfiteatro
Piazza 1 Ottobre, Santa Maria Capua Vetere (0823 798 864). **Open** 9am-1hr before sunset Tue-Sun. **Admission** *Amphitheatre, Mithraeum, Museo Antica Capua* €2.50. **No credit cards**.

Duomo (San Michele Arcangelo)
Piazza Vescovado, Casertavecchia (0823 371 318). **Open** *May-Sept* 8.30am-8pm daily. *Oct-Apr* 9am-1pm, 3.30-6pm daily.

Mithraeum
Via Morelli, Santa Maria Capua Vetere. **Open** by request 9am-4pm Tue-Sun; ask at the amphitheatre or museum. **Admission** *Amphitheatre, Mithraeum, Museo Antica Capua* €2.50. **No credit cards**.

Museo Antica Capua
Via Roberto D'Angiò 48, Santa Maria Capua Vetere (0823 844 206). **Open** 9am-7pm Tue-Sun. **Admission** *Amphitheatre, Mithraeum & museum* €2.50. **No credit cards**.

Where to eat

In Casertavecchia, **La Castellana** (via Torre 4, 0823 371 230, closed Thur dinner Oct-Mar, average €20) has good home-made pasta (try the *tris*, a taster of three different types) and game.

Resources

Tourist information
See p278 **Caserta**.

Getting there

By bus
See p278 **Caserta**.

By car
For Casertavecchia take the Caserta Nord exit from the A1 motorway; 2km (1.5 miles) north-east of town on minor road (signposted). For Santa Maria Capua Vetere, leave the A1 motorway at Caserta Nord; SS7 (via Appia) from Caserta (4.5km/3 miles).

By train
For Santa Maria Capua Vetere, there's an infrequent service from Caserta.

Medieval
Casertavecchia.
See p278.

Around Naples

Directory

Directory

Getting Around

By air

The **Aereoporto Internazionale di Napoli (Capodichino)** is 8 kms (5 miles) or 5 to 10 minutes from Stazione Centrale rail station, and 20 minutes from ferry and hydrofoil ports.

Alibus (800 639 525) runs direct bus service from outside the arrivals lounge to Stazione Centrale (on piazza Garibaldi) and piazza Municipio (near the ferry port). Buses leave every 30 minutes, from 5.55am to 11.30pm daily. Return buses leave from piazza Municipio from 6.25am to 11.55pm daily. Tickets are €3.

Local **orange bus** number 3S runs from outside arrivals to piazza Garibaldi every 15 minutes or so throughout the day. You can buy tickets (€1) at any *tabacchi* (*see p293*) and stamp them on board.

A **taxi** from the airport to central Naples should cost between €15 and €20.

If you're headed to Sorrento, **Autolinee Curreri** (081 801 5420) runs six buses daily from outside Arrivals. Tickets are €6.

Alisud
081 789 6272/081 789 6645. **Open** 9am-8pm daily. **Credit** AmEx, DC, MC, V.
Bookings for all airlines using Capodichino.

GESAC
081 789 6259/toll-free 848 888 777/www.gesac.it. **Open** 5.30am-midnight daily.
Flight and transport information.

Major airlines
Alitalia Information 848 865 643/ domestic flights 848 865 641/ international flights 848 865 642/ www.alitalia.it.
British Airways 199 712 266/ www.ba.com.
Easy Jet 848 887766/www.easy jet.com.

By bus

Most long-distance buses arrive at and depart from piazza Garibaldi. **SITA** buses serving destinations around Naples operate from the main Naples port area, piazzale dell'Immacolatella.

By train

There are three main-line **Ferrovie dello Stato-Trenitalia** (FS, the state railways) stations in Naples, the main one being the **Stazione Centrale** in piazza Garibaldi. Most FS trains come and go from here, including the very fast (**Eurostar**, **InterCity**) and very slow (local trains). Below the street-level main station there are two lower levels. On the first lower level is the ticket counter for the **Circumvesuviana** line (*see p284*). The second level down is **Piazza Garibaldi** station, which is used by regional metro lines and some long-distance services. Some of these services also stop at Naples' other big stations, **Mergellina** and **Campi Flegrei**.

For more information on rail services, *see p284*.

A single ticket, allowing up to three trips on all metropolitan transport – including one trip only on the underground railways and funiculars – costs €1 and is valid for 90 minutes. A 24-hour ticket for unlimited travel on all metropolitan public transport costs € 3. Tickets must be bought at a news-stand or *tabacchi* shop before boarding any transport. *See also p283* **Useful bus routes**.

Buses

Traffic makes bus travel in Naples a pain; you're likely to spend more time stuck in traffic jams than if you'd walked. Luckily, a dedicated bus lane along corso Umberto, makes bus travel to places between the San Carlo opera house and the Stazione Centrale viable. The bus is also indispensable when travelling to Mergellina and Posillipo (leave from Santa Lucia or the Riviera di Chiaia).

Bus services in Naples are run by **ANM** (800 639 525, 081 763 2177, www.anm.it). There is no central bus station in the city, as some services operate from piazza Garibaldi, and others from via Pisanelli, near piazza Municipio.

Electronic signs at Metro stations and bus stops give details of waiting times.

Before boarding a bus, buy tickets at any *tabacchi* (*see p293*) and then stamp them in the machines on board. Tickets cost €1 for 90 mins on local buses, the metro and funiculars.

You should enter a bus through the front or back door, and exit through the centre doors, although this rule is rarely respected. Before your stop, press one of the red buttons you'll see around to alert the driver.

Useful bus routes

Circular routes

There are four **R** routes plied by the pride of the city's new bus fleet; large and cumbersome, these buses can be guaranteed to block even the widest of streets. All four routes intersect in the via Medina/piazza Municipio area.

R1 From piazza Medaglie d'Oro (see p90) to the Museo Nazionale Archeologico (see p79), piazza Dante, piazza Carità/via Toledo (see p77), piazza Municipio (see p57) and back.

R2 From the Stazione Centrale train station along corso Umberto (see p62) to piazza Municipio and back.

R3 From Mergellina (see p93), along the Riviera di Chiaia (see p92) and the Villa Comunale to piazza Municipio, piazza Carità/via Toledo and back.

R4 From the Cardarelli hospital in the north-western suburbs, past the palace at Capodimonte (see p84), piazza Carità/via Toledo to piazza Municipio and back.

A-to-B routes

C16 Regular, reliable service running from Mergellina (see p93) along corso Vittorio Emanuele to piazza Mazzini and via Salvator Rosa (Vomero; see p85).

C18 The only direct bus running from piazza Vittoria along the seafront, through the Fuorigrotta tunnels (see p104) and into the heart of Maradonaland (see p168 **Calcio & Napoli**).

C21 Posh route starting from piazza Sannazzaro in Mergellina and running up the hill to Capo Posillipo (see p95) along via Orazio and via Petrarca.

C24 Reliable service for the well-heeled, running from Mergellina through piazza Amedeo (see p91), along via Colonna and the Villa Comunale (see p93) to piazza Vittoria.

C25 Pleasant tourist round-trip from piazza Amedeo along the Villa Comunale and seafront, past Castel dell'Ovo (see p56) into piazza Municipio, touching the end of corso Umberto at piazza Bovio; back via the San Carlo opera house (see p61) and piazza Trieste e Trento.

C27 Important but crowded route running from piazza Amedeo up via Tasso to via Manzoni, and right along snobs' alley to Capo Posillipo itself (see p95).

C28 Running into the heart of Vomero from piazza Vittoria, taking in the smart shopping street of via dei Mille, via Tasso and via Aniello Falcone along the way.

140 The only bus that runs up via Posillipo from Mergellina, this route starts at Santa Lucia opposite the Castel dell'Ovo.

Shuttle routes

E1 Skirts most sides of the Centro storico from its departure point in piazza Gesù Nuovo (see p68). Most of its stops are within easy walking distance of each other, however; the bus is useful mostly for overladen shoppers.

Metro

Naples is laced by a complex system of underground and overground railways and trams (information 800 568 866), which can be the fastest way to get around the city.

Red M signs indicate a Metro station, and tickets are the same as those used for buses. As well as being on sale at *tabacchis* (see p293), you can also purchase them at machines in every station. They cost €1 and are valid on any transport within the city for 90 minutes.

Metro Linea 1 runs from piazza Dante to piazza Vanvitelli and the hospital zone in the north-eastern suburbs (5.30am-10.30pm).

Metro Linea 2 (the underground service of the state railway) runs from piazza Garibaldi (beneath Stazione Centrale), skirting the Centro storico, to the Mergellina main-line station and the Campi Flegrei (5.38am-11.52pm).

The **Ferrovia Cumana** (081 551 3328, www.sepsa.it) runs services (above and below ground) from piazza Montesanto to Campi Flegrei (5.20am-9.40pm).

The new **Metropolitana Collinare**, started in 1993, is still gradually adding stations. The line, which includes some ingenious bits of civil engineering, runs from piazza Dante through piazza Vanvitelli then on to the suburbs.

The **Piazza Cavour** stop serves the Sanità district and the northern part of the Centro storico; **Montesanto** station is best for via Toledo and the southern part of the Centro storico; **Piazza Amedeo** station serves the Chiaia district; **Mergellina** station is ten minutes' walk from the port where hydrofoils leave for the islands.

Funiculars

The funicular railways only take you to the Vomero and back. Kids love them. Long overdue maintenenance work on the **Montesanto Funicular** means that this line will not repoen till mid-2005 at the earliest, although modernisation of the **Chiaia Funicular** is nearing completion, with a bewildering series of escalators to carry weary travellers up into the carriages.

Trains

All Italian stations now have the same phone number for information and bookings: 892 021. It operates 7am-9pm daily. To talk to an operator – who may (or may not) speak basic English – rather than coping with a recorded message in Italian, dial 1 and say *'altro'* very clearly after the initial recorded instructions.

There are three main-line **Ferrovie dello Stato-Trenitalia** (FS) stations in Naples. The main station is the Stazione Centrale in piazza Garibaldi. Most FS trains come and go from here, including the very fast (**Eurostar, InterCity**) and very slow (local trains). Below the street-level main station there are two lower levels.

On the first lower level is the ticket counter for the **Circumvesuviana** line (*see below*). Piazza Garibaldi station is on the second level down; it is used by local metro lines and long-distance services, some of which also stop at Naples' other big stations, **Mergellina** and **Campi Flegrei**.

The **Ferrovia Circumvesuviana** (081 772 2444, www.vesuviana.it) leaves from its own terminus in corso Garibaldi, south of (and accessible from) Stazione Centrale. Trains run south-east to Pompeii, Herculaneum and Sorrento (5.09am-10.42pm).

Advance tickets for main-line train services can be bought at stations or from travel agents with the Ferrovie dello Stato-Trenitalia (FS) logo. At main stations there are automatic ticket machines as well that accept all major credit cards.

Lining up for tickets can be a bit confusing if you don't speak Italian, as it's hard to tell whether you're are in the right queue: some desks sell ordinary intra-Italy tickets (*biglietti interno* or *senza supplemento*), Eurostar tickets (*Eurostar Italia*) and high-speed supplements (*supplementi rapidi*); some also do advance bookings (*prenotazioni*); and some only do advance bookings. There is a separate window for international trains (*internazionali*). If you get completely confused, the staff in the busy information office (*informazione*) at Stazione Centrale speak English.

Ticket prices are directly related to distance travelled. The slower trains (the *diretti, espressi, regionali* and *interregionali*) are much cheaper here than in northern Europe, but a system of supplements means that the faster trains – **InterCity** (IC), **EuroCity** (EC), and **Eurostar**

Italia (ES) – are closer to the European norm.

Seat bookings are obligatory (and free) on ES trains, and can be made up to 20 mins before departure. Bookings on IC and internal EC routes should be made 24 hours before departure, and cost €3 – well worth it, especially on Friday and Sunday evenings when it can be terribly crowded. If your ES, IC or EC train arrives more than 30mins late and you have a seat booking, you can claim a refund (at the booth marked *'rimborsi'*) of part of the cost of the ticket (30% of IC and EC, 50% of ES).

You must stamp your ticket – and any supplement – in the yellow machines at the head of each platform before boarding the train. Failure to do this can result in a fine. If you forget to stamp your ticket, find the inspector as soon as possible after boarding the train and have it clipped, if you fail to do so, you could face a €25 fine.

For complete schedule information (in English), and the possibilty of booking tickets by credit card, try www.trenitalia.com.

Trams

Naples' **trams** run along the shoreline from piazza Mercato through to piazza Vittoria in the Chiaia district. Work on the new express tramway running out to Fuorigrotta and beyond, started in 1990 and is still in progress, so that line stops short of the delightful trundle along the revamped Villa Comunale.

Waterways

Timetables for water transport around the Bay of Naples are published daily in *Il Mattino*, as well as on www.campania trasporti.it.

From **Molo Beverello** port (Map p313 2C) you can catch ferry and hydrofoil services to the islands, Sorrento and the Amalfi Coast. The major operators are **Alilauro** (081 761 1004, www.alilauro.it), **Caremar** (199 123 199, www.caremar.it), **MedMar** (081 551 3352, www.medmar group.it); **Navigazione Libera del Golfo** (NLG) (081 552 0763, www.navlib.it); and **SNAV** (081 428 5555, www.snav.it).

Metro del Mare (199 446 664, www.metrodelmare.com) runs a service from Molo Beverello to various points in the gulf, the Amalfi Coast and beyond.

Ferry services to Palermo, the Aeolian Islands (2-3 times weekly) and Sardinia (twice weekly) are run by **Tirrenia** (199 123 199, www.tirrenia.it). **SNAV** runs a hydrofoil service to Palermo (Apr-Oct daily). **TTT Lines** (800 915 365, www.tttlines.it) sails to Catania, Sardinia and Tunisia – all of these depart from Molo Beverello.

Mergellina
Map p315 2C.
Hydrofoil services to Capri, Ischia and Procida are run by SNAV and Alilauro (081 761 4909) from Mergellina.

Pozzuoli
Car ferries also leave for Procida and Ischia from the port of Pozzuoli, 12km (8 miles) north-west of Naples. Traghetti Pozzuoli (081 526 7736, www. traghettipozzuoli.it) and Caremar (081 551 3882, www.caremar.it).

Taxi del Mare
Cosro Italia 263, Sorrento (tollfree 800 547 500/081 877 3600/fax 081 877 3672/www.taxidelmare.it).
Open 24hrs daily. **Credit** AmEx, DC, MC, V.
These water taxis hold 10 people and will go anywhere around the Bay of Naples. Sample prices: Capri–Ischia (one way) €608; Capri–Positano–Capri €832.

Driving

EU visitors can drive on their home-country's licences; an international licence is advisable for non-EU citizens.

When driving, bear in mind the following rules, written and unwritten:
● The law requires you to wear a seat belt and to carry a hazard triangle and reflective safety jacket in your car; motorcyclists and scooter-riders must wear helmets.
● Keep your driving licence, insurance documents, vehicle registration and photo-ID documents on you at all times; if you are stopped by the police, you may be fined if you can't produce them all on the spot.
● Flashing your lights means that you will not slow down/give way.
● Neapolitans often ignore red lights, so approach any junction with caution. If traffic lights flash amber, stop and give way to the right.
● Watch out for death-defying scooters and pedestrians; the latter fully expect you to stop if they step out in front of you.
● Be patient, be flexible, maintain your cool and stay calm at all times; be prepared for anything.
● Remember: Italians drive on the right.

Reasons not to drive

There's nothing car-friendly about Naples and its surrounding area. Far from giving you the freedom to explore, motoring is more likely to give you a serious headache.
● Only vehicles with catalytic converters are allowed to circulate in the city between 8.30am and 6.30pm Mon, Wed and Fri. There's an Area Azzurra (Blue Zone) in the centre where, in theory, only residents can circulate between 7.30am and 6.30pm Mon-Fri. On many Sunday mornings (usually the first of the month) all vehicles are banned.
● In summer, traffic in and around Sorrento and on the Amalfi Coast is horrific, as tour buses wind their way

along narrow coastal roads. Local day-trippers worsen the situation at weekends: if you must drive here, stick to weekdays.
● On the islands, roads are packed in the summer. You can't take cars to Capri; you're better off using public transport or walking on Procida. Car rental companies on Ischia charge better rates than on the mainland, but you cannot take the car off the island.

Breakdown services
National motoring groups (Britain's AA or RAC and the AAA in the US) have reciprocal arrangements with the Automobile Club d'Italia (ACI), which offers breakdown assistance. If you require extensive repairs, go to a manufacturer's official dealer. Dealers are listed in the Yellow Pages under Auto; specialists are listed under *Gommista* (tyre repairs), *Marmitte* (exhaust repairs) and *Carrozzerie* (bodywork and windscreen repairs). The English Yellow Pages (*see p291*) lists garages where English is spoken.

ACI
Piazzale Tecchio 49D, Fuorigrotta (24hr emergency service 803 116/ 081 725 3811/www.aci.it). Metro Campi Flegrei/Cumana rail to Piazzale Tecchio/bus 180, 181, C2, C6, C7, C8, C9, C10, C15, CU. **Open** 8.40am-2.30pm, 3.30-5.30pm Mon-Fri; 8.40am-11.30am Sat. **No credit cards.**.

Touring Club Italia
Via C Battisti 11, Toledo (081 420 3485/fax 081 420 3477/ www.touringclub.it). Bus 24, C57, CS, E3, R1, R3, R4. **Open** 9am-7pm Mon-Fri; 9am-1pm Sat. **Credit** AmEx, DC, MC, V. **Map** p314 2A. Specialised bookshop for maps and guides, with a travel agency.

Car rental

The minimum age for renting an economy car is 21; you must be 25 years old to rent a larger-cylinder car. Most rental companies require you to be covered for both theft and collision-damage: if they don't, you should be anyway.

Consider renting a scooter, as they're excellent for getting around Ischia, Sorrento and the Amalfi Coast.

Avis

Airport (199 100 133/081 780 5790/fax 081 751 7544/ www.avisautonoleggio.it). **Open** 7.30am-11.30pm daily. **Credit** AmEx, DC, MC, V.
Branch: *Corso Novara 5, Port & University (081 284 041).* **Open** 8am-7.30pm Mon-Fri; 8.30am-1pm, 4-6pm Sat; 9am-1pm Sun. **Map** p312 2B.

Europcar

Airport (tollfree 800 014 410/081 780 5643/www.europcar.it). **Open** 8am-11.30pm daily. **Credit** AmEx, DC, MC, V.

Hertz

Airport (081 780 2971). **Open** 8am-10pm daily. **Credit** AmEx, DC, MC, V.
Branch: *Stazione Centrale (199 112 211/081 206 228/www.hertz.it).* **Open** 8am-1pm, 2-7pm Mon-Fri; 8am-noon Sat. **Map** p312 2B.

Maggiore-Budget

Airport (848 867 067/081 780 3011/ fax 081 599 1233/www.maggiore.it). **Open** 7.30am-11.30pm daily. **Credit** AmEx, DC, MC, V.
Branch: *Stazione Centrale (081 287 858).* **Open** 8am-1pm, 3-7pm Mon-Fri; 8.30am-1pm Sat. **Map** p312 2B.

Thrifty

Airport (081 780 5702/fax 081 751 5013/www.italybycar.it). **Open** 8am-11.15pm daily. **Credit** AmEx, DC, MC, V.

Parking

Blue lines on the road mean residents park free and visitors pay. The cost varies from €1.50 to €2 per hour; pay at the pay-and-display ticket machines.

Elsewhere, anything resembling a parking place is up for grabs, with some exceptions: watch out for signs saying *passo carrabile* (access at all times), *sosta vietata* (no parking) and for disabled parking spaces (marked off with yellow lines). A sign reading *zona rimozione'* (tow-away area) means 'no parking', and is valid for the length of the street it's on, or until the next tow-away sign with a red line through it. If a street or square has no cars parked in it, you can assume it's a no-parking zone. Be aware that illegal 'parking attendants' operate in many areas – they will offer to

look after your car for about €1. The safest solution is to use a pay parking area; there is a full list in the Yellow Pages under *autorimesse e parcheggi*.

Via Brin Parking

Via B Brin, Port & University (081 763 2855). Bus 3S, 194, 195, C81, C82, C89, CS/tram 4. **Open** 24hrs daily. **Rates** €1.20 for first 4hrs, 30¢ per successive hr; €16.50 for 75hrs; €30 for 150hrs. **Credit** AmEx, DC, MC, V. **Map** p313 1A.
An 800-car facility located between Stazione Centrale and the port (take the Porto exit from the ring road or motorway). Shuttle buses for the ferry port at Molo Beverello leave every 15mins.

Taxis

Taxis can be found either at signed ranks or they can be flagged down in the street. Authorised white taxis have the city's emblem on the front doors and rear licence plate, and a meter. Steer clear of any unauthorised 'taxi'.

As you set off, the metre should read €2.60. There's a €4.20 minimum charge per trip. Extra charges include: €1.60 on Sundays or holidays; €2.10 from 10pm to 7am; 50¢ per piece of luggage in the boot; 80¢ for a radio taxi call; and an additional €2.60 to or from the airport. For some of the more distant suburbs a supplement of €1 is added, while outside the city limits the amount on the metre is doubled for the return trip.

Many Neapolitan cab drivers will try to hike up the fare, so make sure the meter is switched on. If you suspect you are being ripped off, make a note of the driver's name and number from the photo ID in the cab. The more ostentatiously you do this, the more it's likely that the fare will drop to its proper level. Complaints can be lodged with the drivers' co-operative (the phone number is written on the outside of the car) or with the police (*see p292*).

The taxis listed below are generally known to be reliable. When you phone for a cab,

you'll be given a code-name (a geographic location followed by a number) and a time, as in *Bahama 69, in tre minuti* ('Bahamas 69, in three minutes'). The driver should put the meter on as you get into the taxi; a call supplement of 80¢ will be added. Most taxis accept cash only, although credit cards are slowly becoming acceptable.
Consortaxi 081 552 5252, www.consortaxi.it.
Cotana 081 570 7070.
Free Taxi 081 551 5151.
Napoli 081 556 4444
Partenope 081 556 0202.

Outside Naples

Many of Capri's taxis are vintage cars; Ischia has three-wheeled 'micro taxis'; Sorrento has horse-drawn carriages. Each has its own fare structure, although they are not always respected by operators: be prepared to bargain.

Some of the taxi companies listed above run fixed-rate one-way or return trips to Pompeii, Vesuvius, the Amalfi Coast and the Campi Flegrei, among other places. Many drivers speak English, which can make the trip a kind of guided tour. Prices are not outrageous: Naples–Pompeii–Naples, including two hours to visit Pompeii, costs €90; Naples–Positano costs €110; Naples–Lago di Averno–Cuma–Naples costs €72.

Tours

CitySightseeing Napoli (081 551 7279, www.city-sight seeing.it) offers two multilingual tours (three at week-ends) of the city in open-top double-decker buses. The buses depart every 30 mins from Piazza Municipio (beside Castel Nuovo), and you can hop on and off as you like. Tickets (valid 24 hours) cost €18 for adults, €9 for children and €54 for families of four. There is a discount of 10% for holders of the Campania Artecard (*see p35* **Smart art**).

Resources A-Z

Addresses

Addresses are written with the number following the street name, as in via Toledo 23. The number after the word '*int*' (short for *interno*) is the flat or apartment number. If you are given a '*scala*' and a '*piano*' number, then you know which staircase to take and which floor to go to.

Age restrictions

Cigarettes and alcohol cannot legally be sold to under-16s. Beer and wine can be consumed at bars from the age of 16, spirits from 18. You must be over 18 to drive and over 21 to hire a car. Anyone aged 14 or above can ride a moped or scooter with a 50cc engine; no licence is required for over-18s (this will change in July 2005 when anyone riding a moped or scooter will need a driving license to do so.

Business

The commercial sector of your embassy may be able to provide you with information and contacts, as well as trade publications, marketing reports and databases. Both the UK and US consulates have lists (not necessarily up to date) of lawyers, translators and interpreters.

The **British Chamber of Commerce for Italy** is at St Peter's English Language Centre (Riviera di Chiaia 124, Chiaia, 081 683 468). It provides support services for British and Italian businesses, as well as trading, legal and taxation information.

Conferences

Most major hotels cater for events of all sizes. If you don't wish to handle the details yourself, **GP Relazioni Pubbliche** (via San Pasquale a Chiaia 55, Chiaia, 081 401 201) will smooth the way for you.

Couriers

Reliable couriers include **DHL** (199 199 345, www.dhl.it); **Federal Express** (800 123 800, www.fedex.com); **Freccia Azzurra** (081 552 1520, www.frecciaazzurra.it); **TNT** (800 803 868, www.tntitaly.it); and **UPS** (800 877 877, www.ups.com), and **Mail Boxes, Etc** (via Bracco 57-59, Port & University, 081 580 0256), which is a one-stop centre for couriers, posting, shipping and photocopying.

Interpreters

There are many professional services available, including those of **GIC'90** (via Monte di Dio 66, Royal, 081 764 7427, www.gic90.com), **Marchilia Volini** (piazza degli Artisti 7c, Vomero, 081 578 3598) and **Giovanna Pistillo** (vico Pallonetto S Chiara 32, Centro storico, 338 760 5324).

Customs

EU citizens do not have to declare goods brought into or out of Italy for personal use, as long as they arrive from another EU country. For all visitors, there are no restrictions on the import of cameras, watches or electrical goods for personal use. Visitors are allowed to carry up to €12,500 in cash. For all non-EU citizens, the following limits apply:
- 200 cigarettes or 100 small cigars or 50 large cigars or 250g of tobacco.
- 1 litre of spirits (over 22% alcohol) or 2 litres of fortified wine (under 22% alcohol).
- 2 litres table wine.
- 50cc of perfume.

Disabled travellers

You won't see many people in wheelchairs around Naples, and those you do see are nearly always accompanied. Narrow streets make life difficult for those who can't flatten themselves against a wall to let passing vehicles by. Cobblestones turn even wheelchairs with good suspension into bone-rattlers. Where they exist, wheelchair ramps from streets to pavements are likely to be blocked by a car or motorbike.

Once off the street, you're faced with old buildings with narrow corridors, lifts that (if they exist at all) are too small for wheelchairs, and toilets perched uselessly at the top or dropped at the bottom of steep stairs.

Travel advice

For up-to-date information on travelling to a specific country – including the latest news on safety and security, health issues, local laws and customs – contact your home country government's department of foreign affairs. Most have websites packed with useful advice for would-be travellers.

Australia
www.smartraveller.gov.au

Canada
www.voyage.gc.ca
New Zealand
www.mft.govt.nz/travel

Republic of Ireland
http://foreignaffairs.gov.ie
UK
www.fco.gov.uk/travel
USA
www.state.gov/travel

Directory

That said, though, things are slowly getting better. Lifts, ramps and disabled-adapted toilets are being installed in museums, restaurants, stations and public offices, and although willingness has not always been matched by planning intelli-gence (you may be expected to levitate up a couple of steps to reach that brand-new toilet or lift), these days you're more likely to be treated like a human being rather than some noble victim of fate.

Surprisingly, Capri is one of the most wheelchair-friendly places around. A craggy island of steep cliffs and picturesque stairways, it is also car-free, and the only way to get supplies, luggage and people up and down is by small electric carts. The main paths are steep slopes, but at least there are no stairs. Getting up to the town from the port will, however, involve help up the few steps to the funicular, and Capri buses are decidedly not disabled-friendly.

Information

This useful website, with an English section, selects accessible sites throughout Italy depending on your specific needs.

SuperAbile

Toll-free 800 810 810/www.superabile.it. **Open** *Phone enquiries* 9am-7pm Mon-Fri; 9am-1pm Sat.
This group provides information on hotels, restaurants and job opportunities for the disabled throughout Italy.

Hotels & restaurants

Upmarket hotels in well-established tourist resorts cater best to special needs. Cheaper hotels and pensioni, often on the upper floors of old palazzi, can be a problem. If you have special needs, make them known when you book. Ask specific, detailed questions about the facilities; Neapolitans have a tendency to look on the bright side of life, ignoring the 'minor' barriers that could make your stay a misery.

Local by-laws require restaurants to have disabled access and toilets,

but in practice few have made the necessary alterations. If you phone ahead and ask for an appropriate table, most will do their best to help. In summer, the masses of restaurants with outdoor tables makes life easier.

Italia Per Tutti

www.italiapertutti.it.

Transport

By boat

The hydrofoil and ferry lines (*see p284* **Waterways**) have begun to adapt to make room for wheelchairs. It's a good idea to book ahead, though, to ensure that the ferry on your route is not an older model.

By bus

Naples has some city buses – 180, C12, C14, C16, C19, C25, C34, C38, R2, R3 – equipped with extra-large central doors and access ramps; inside, there's a space where a wheelchair can be secured. These buses are identifiable by the wheelchair symbol on the front and beside the bus number at bus stops. Outside the city, the situation varies from town to town; contact local tourist offices or bus companies for information.

By train

For rail travel, the Stazione Centrale has a *Direzione servizi alla clientela* (customer services office, near platform five; also accessible from outside the station by car) that can provide information for disabled travellers (081 567 2991, open 7am-9pm daily), can take reservations (at least 24 hours prior to departure) and will provide wheelchair assistance and access to most, but not all, trains. It will also arrange for staff to meet wheelchair-bound passengers at their destination. Departing passengers must be at the *Direzione servizi alla clientela* office at least 45 minutes before the train departs.

Wheelchair hire

Ortopedia Morelli

Via Costantinopoli 28/29, Toledo (081 444 281). **Open** 9am-1.30pm, 4-6.30pm Mon-Fri. **No credit cards**. This company rents wheelchairs out for €3.50 + VAT a day, and delivers all over Naples. Book at least one week in advance.

Sanitas Rosy

(081 807 3858/339 184 9819). This agency will deliver your wheelchair to your hotel in Sorrento (€6 per day). You can also request crutches (€1 per day), and prams (€1 per day). It does not accept credit cards.

Drugs

Obviously, it is illegal in Italy to buy or sell drugs, or even to give them away. If you are caught in possession of illegal drugs of any type, you will be taken before a magistrate. If you can convince the judge that the tiny quantity you were carrying was for purely personal use, then you may be let off with a fine or ordered to leave the country. Anything more than a tiny amount will push you into the criminal category, and couriering or dealing can land you in prison for up to 20 years.

Sniffer dogs are a fixture at most ports of entry into Italy; customs police will take a dim view of visitors entering with even the smallest quantities of narcotics, and are likely to allow them to stay no longer than it takes a magistrate to expel them from the country.

Electricity

Most wiring systems work on 220V. Two-pin adapter plugs can be bought at electrical shops (look for Casalinghi or Elettricità) or at airports.

Embassies & consulates

Countries with official missions to Italy have embassies in Rome; Naples has many consulates, which will provide essential documents (such as birth and death certificates) and emergency help (such as replacement passports). A full list of consulates and embassies can be found in the phone book under *Ambasciati/consolati*.

Britain

Via dei Mille 40, Chiaia (081 423 8911/fax 081 422 434/www. britain.it). Metro Piazza Amedeo/ bus C24, C25, C27, C28. **Open** 9am-12.30pm, 2-4pm Mon-Fri. Times change slightly in summer. **Map** p315 1B. For emergencies outside opening hours, phone 335 710 897.

Canada

Via G Carducci 29, Chiaia (081 401 338/fax 081 410 4210). Metro Piazza Amedeo/bus C24, C25, C27, C28. **Open** 9am-1pm Mon-Fri. **Map** p315 1B. After 1pm phone 081 407 825.

United States

Piazza della Repubblica, Mergellina (081 583 8111/fax 081 761 1869/www.usembassy.it). Metro Mergellina/bus 140, C12, C18, C19, C24, R3. **Open** 8am-1pm, 2-5pm Mon-Fri. **Map** p315 2C.

Embassies in Rome:

Australia 06 852 721.
Ireland 06 697 9121.
New Zealand 06 441 7171.
South Africa 06 852 541.

Gay & lesbian

Visiting gays are unlikely to meet hostility from anyone but members of the unpleasant conservative fringe that exists everywhere. For more info on gay and lesbian life in Naples, *see p154-56.*

ArciGay and ArciLesbica

Vico San Geronimo 17-20, Centro storico (081 552 8815/web.tiscali.it/ arcigaynapoli) Metro Dante/bus 24, C57, CS, E1, R1, R2. ArciGay **open** 5-8pm Wed, Fri; ArciLesbica **open** 5-8pm Tue, Thur, Sat. **Map** p313 1C.

Health

Emergency health care is available for all travellers through the Italian national health system and, by law, hospital casualty departments must treat all emergency cases for free. However, to avoid hassle if you're only visiting for a short time, it's worth taking out private health insurance (*see p289*).

If you require regular medication during your stay in Italy, bring adequate supplies of your drugs with you. Also, ask your GP for the chemical rather than the brand name of your medicines; they may only be available in Italy under a different name.

Both the British and US consulates (*see p288*) have lists of English-speaking doctors. For women's health, *see p297.*

Accident & emergency

The following Naples hospitals provide 24 hour emergency (*pronto soccorso*) services. For emergency treatment outside Naples see under Resources in Around Naples chapters.

Cardarelli

Via Cardarelli 9, Vomero Alto, Naples (081 747 1111). Metro Colli Aminei/bus C38, C39, C40, C41, C43, C44, C76, OF, R4. Southern Italy's largest hospital, with an ever-busy casualty department. It's not luxurious, but it gets the job done.

Santobono

Via M Fiore 6, Vomero, Naples (081 220 5111). Metro Piazza Medaglie D'Oro/bus 181, C34, C39, C41, C44, R1. **Map** p314 2B. The South's main paediatric hospital.

Contraception & abortion

Condoms are on sale near the check-out in supermarkets or over the counter at chemists. The contraceptive pill is available at pharmacies, although a doctor's prescription is required.

Abortion is legal if performed in public hospitals; health or financial hardship criteria must be proven.

Dentists

In the case of serious dental emergencies, make for the hospital casualty departments (*see p289*).

For non-emergency treatment, the English Yellow Pages (*see p291*) has a list of English-speaking dentists in the Naples area. These two dentists have English-speaking staff.

Dott Francesco Olivieri *Via Carducci 6, Chiaia (081 245 7003). Metro Piazza Amedeo/bus 140, C25, R3.* **Map** p315 B1.

Dott Massimo Palmieri *Via G Orsi 8, Vomero (081 566 3721). Metro Medaglie D'Oro/bus R1.* **Map** p314 B1.

Insurance

EU nationals are entitled to reciprocal medical care in Italy, provided they have an E111 form.

However, using an E111 condemns you to dealing with the intricacies of the Italian health bureaucracy, and for short-term visitors it's generally better to take out health cover under private travel insurance.

Non-EU citizens do not qualify for the E111's ostensibly free health care, and should take out private medical insurance before leaving home. US, Australian, New Zealand and South African citizens should check with their health insurance companies to ensure that their policies will cover them when they're abroad.

Note that emergencies are treated free in *pronto soccorso* (emergency) departments of public hospitals; *see p289.*

Medical helplines

AIDS Helpline *Toll-free 800 019 254.* **Open** 24hrs Mon-Sat; 8am-2pm Sun.
Information on tests and prevention advice. Italian only.

Alcoholics Anonymous *Via San Pasquale a Chiaia 15, Chiaia (347 544 0254/www.naplesaa.8k.com). Metro Piazza Amedeo/bus 140, C12, C18, C19, C24, C25, C27, C28, R3.* **Open** *meetings* 3.30-4.30pm Sat. **Map** p315 1B.
An English-speaking support group meets at the Anglican/Episcopal Christ Church.

Drogatel *800 196 196.* **Open** 9am-8pm Mon-Fri.
Government-run drug helpline. Italian only.

Pharmacies

Farmacias, marked by a large red or green cross, will give informal medical advice for simple ailments, and will make up prescriptions from a doctor. Over-the-counter drugs such as aspirin are more expensive in Italy than in the UK or US.

Standard opening hours are 8.30am-1pm, 4-8pm Mon-Fri; 8.30am-1pm Sat. Every pharmacy should have a list by the door indicating the nearest pharmacies that open outside normal business hours. Some levy a surcharge of €3.75 per client (but not per item) when the main shop is shut and only the late-night counter is open.

Most pharmacies sell homeopathic and veterinary medicines. All will check your height/weight/ blood pressure.

For pharmacy listings, *see p289.*

ID

Under Italian law, you are technically required to carry a photo ID at all times. However,

Directory

in reality you will only be asked to show it on rare occasions, such as when cashing traveller's cheques or checking into a hotel. Some hotels may even ask to keep your passport until you check out; you are, however, entitled to ask for your ID back at any time, and should do so if that is your only photo ID.

Insurance

For health insurance, *see p289*.

Travel insurance is always a good idea, and should you rent a car, motorcycle or moped, be sure you pay the extra charge for full insurance cover and sign the collision damage waiver.

Internet & email

Italian providers offering free internet access include Libero (www.libero.it), Caltanet (www.caltanet.it), Tiscali (www.tiscalinet.it), Kataweb (www.kataweb.com) and Fastweb (www.fastweb.it).

There are plenty of internet cafés and centres in Naples, and even small towns in the provinces and on the islands will have, at best, an internet café and, at worst, a bar with an old computer in a corner. Ask in any computer store (listed in the Yellow Pages (see p291) under Personal computers e informatica) for the nearest.

Most Italian phone lines now have sockets for RJ11 jacks (a standard telephone connector). Older lines will have sockets for large three-pin plugs. If you're lucky, you'll find there's a removable RJ11 going into the old three-pin model. If not, you may have to scour supermarkets, phone and electricity shops for an adaptor.

Clic Net
Via Toledo 393, Toledo (081 552 9370/www.clicnet.it). Metro Montesanto/bus CS, E2, R1, R4. **Open** 9.30am-9.30pm Mon-Sat. **Rates** €2 per hr. **No credit cards.** **Map** p314 2A.

Internet Bar
Piazza Bellini, Centro storico (081 295 237/www.internetbarnapoli.it). Metro Dante or Museo/bus 24, C57, CS, E1, R1. **Open** 9am-2am Mon-Sat; 8pm-2am Sun. **Rates** €3 per hr. **No credit cards. Map** p313 1C.

Dre@mer-club
via F. De Sanctis 16, Centro storico (081/4203277). Metro Dante bus 24, CS, E1, R1, R4. **Open** 10am-8pm Mon-Fri. **Rates** €1.30 per hr. **No credit cards. Map** p313 1C.

Legal advice

If you need legal advice, your first stop must be your embassy or consulate (*see p288*).

Libraries

All the libraries listed below are open to the general public. Other specialist libraries can be found in the phone book under '*Biblioteche*'.

Biblioteca Nazionale
Palazzo Reale, piazza del Plebiscito, Royal (081 781 9111/www.bnn online.it). Bus 140, C22, C25, E3, R2, R3. **Open** 8.30am-7.30pm Mon-Fri; 8.30am-1.30pm Sat. (Aug 8.30am-1.30pm Mon-Sat.) **Map** p315 1A. The National Library contains possibly the largest collection anywhere of works on southern Italian history, as well as many other collections. These include the Officina dei Papiri Ercolanese, with papyruses dating back to the ninth century BC, and the JFK American section, a lending library containing mostly American literature (both North and South). Library users and borrowers must be 16 or older and have valid ID.

Biblioteca San Francesco
Via San Francesco 13, Ravello (089 857 727). **Open** 9am-1pm, 4-6pm Mon, Wed, Fri; outside of these times, knock on the convent door at via San Francesco 9.
A vast, eclectic collection of books in myriad languages, including the library left by long-term Capri resident Gracie Fields.

Istituto Universitario Orientale
Palazzo Giusso, piazza San Giovanni Maggiore, University (081 690 9916/www.iuo.it). Bus CS, E1, R1, R2, R4. **Open** 9am-5pm Mon-Thur; 9am-1.30pm Fri. Closed 3wks Aug. **Map** p313 1C.

A decent English-language section focuses on North American literature; there are also works on and in Chinese, Japanese, Arabic, Finnish, Bulgarian and other languages. Anyone can consult; only registered students can borrow.

Lost property

If you lose anything valuable – or suspect it has been stolen – go immediately to the nearest police station (*see p292* to make a 'denuncia' (statement).

If you leave anything on a train, go to the ufficio oggetti rivenuti (081 567 4660) at platform 24 in Stazione Centrale. If you leave anything on city buses or the metro in Naples, go to the capolinea (terminus) of the route you were travelling and ask there. Failing that, try phoning the helpline (800 639 525 from Naples only, 081 763 2177 from outside Italy. Open 8.30am-6pm Mon-Fri).

For items left on SITA buses, call 081 552 2176.

The lost property office at Capodichino Airport is open 7am to midnight daily (081 789 6237 or 081 789 6765).

Luggage storage

At Naples' **Capodichino** airport, the luggage storage office is just outside arrivals. Open 24 hours, it charges €5 per bag, per day.

The luggage storage office at Naples' Stazione Centrale (081 567 2181) is open 8am-8pm daily for leaving luggage, and bags can be collected from 7am-11pm. Charges are €3.50 per item for the first five hours, and 30¢ per hour after that. There is no luggage storage at Mergellina or Campi Flegrei stations.

At Ischia Porto, the luggage storage office (081 982 061) is at the Centro servizi turistici by the ferry port; it is open 9am-9pm daily April to October. The daily rate is €12 per item weighing up to

10 kilograms (22 pounds), €14 for up to 20 kilograms (44 pounds) and €18 for up to 30 kilograms (66 pounds).

In Capri the luggage storage office (081 837 4575) is operated by the Caremar ferry company at the port in Marina Grande. It's open 9am-6.30m daily in the summer, 9am-5pm in winter, and costs €2 per item.

In Sorrento, the tourist office (see p234) may watch your bag during opening hours.

Media

Newspapers

Even if you can read Italian, Italy's newspapers can be a frustrating read. Stories tend to be long and indigestible, and very little background is provided. On the plus side, they are delightfully unsnobbish and happily blend serious news with well-written, often surreal, crime and human-interest stories.

Though most Italian papers look like national affairs, the printed press is traditionally local or regional. Naples' major daily is *Il Mattino*; the Rome-based *La Repubblica* and Milan's *Corriere della Sera* have Neapolitan sections. Sports coverage in the dailies is generally extensive, but if you're not sated try the sports rags *Corriere dello Sport*, *La Gazzetta dello Sport* and *Tuttosport*.

Foreign newspapers and magazines are easily available at newsstands in Naples, especially in touristy areas. Editions usually arrive at the kiosks the day after publication. You can find British broadsheets, tabloids and magazines, as well as the *International Herald Tribune*, which includes the four-page supplement 'Italy Daily', at kiosks in the Stazione Centrale, in piazza Municipio facing the port, and in via Calabritto off piazza dei Martiri.

Corriere della Sera
www.corriere.it.
To the centre of centre-left, this solid, serious but often dull Milan-based daily is good on crime and foreign news. Its Neapolitan insert, 'Corriere del Mezzogiorno', is worth reading, with good local entertainment listings.

Il Mattino *www.ilmattino.it*
The epitome of moderation, *Il Mattino* is firmly seated on the political fence. National news is thoroughly covered, but there's only superficial coverage of international affairs. Most of what it reports could

be overheard (with more dramatic flair) eavesdropping at a bus stop.

La Repubblica
www.repubblica.it
The centre-ish, left-ish La Repubblica is good on the Mafia and the Vatican, and comes up with the odd major scoop on its business pages. It has a fairly exhaustive Naples section.

Magazines

With naked women posing on their covers most weeks, Italy's 'news' magazines are not always distinguishable from soft porn at newsstands. But despite their appearances, *Panorama* and *Espresso* provide a high-standard round-up of the week's news. For tabloid-style scandal, try *Gente*, *Oggi* or the execrable *Novella 2000* and *Cronaca Vera*. The biggest-selling magazine of all is *Famiglia Cristiana* – everything a Christian family would want to know about current affairs and so much more.

Listings/phone book

English Yellow Pages
www.englishyellowpages.it.
The handy EYP directory lists English-speaking professionals, services, organisations and businesses in major cities in Italy. You can usually find it available or your use at consulates and hotels, or you can buy one at major bookstores (€8). The website is extremely useful.

Television

Italy has six major networks – three owned by the state broadcaster **RAI** (RAI 1, RAI 2, RAI 3) and three belonging to Prime Minister Silvio Berlusconi (Rete 4, Canale 5, Italia 1), which essentially means that all Italian TV, at the moment, is state controlled. Perhaps this relates in some way to the fact that all of the Italian channels are uniformly dreadful. You're probably better off ignoring the television in your hotel room unless it has international channels. Now might be a good time to really get into that novel you've been meaning to read.

Radio

There are three state-owned stations: **RAI-1** (89.3 and 94.1 MHz FM stereo and 1332 KHz AM); **RAI-2** (91.3 and 96.1 MHz FM stereo and 846 KHz AM); and **RAI-3** (93.3 and 98.1 MHz FM). They play classical and light music, with news bulletins hourly.

AFN *www.afneurope.army.mil*
If southern Italy gets too much for you, the American Forces Network radio programme will shoot you straight into Smalltown, USA. On 106.0FM (Z-FM) there are locally produced programmes and news, and music ranging from American contemporary and pop to country. On 107.0FM (Power Network) there are talk shows and National Public Radio news bulletins.

Radio Capital *www.capital.it.*
On 88.05 and 104.75 MHz FM. Classics and hits from the UK and US with lots of home-grown goodies thrown in. Based in Rome.

Radio Kiss Kiss Napoli
www.kisskissnapoli.it.
On 99.25 and 103.0 MHz FM. This music station plays popular hits from Italy and abroad, and broadcasts Naples' football games live.

Money

Euro coins and notes from any Eurozone country are legal tender in Italy. By law, you must be given a receipt (*scontrino fiscale*) for any transaction. Some places may try to avoid giving you a receipt for tax reasons, in which case it is your right (and according to the *guardia di finanza*, also your duty) to ask for one.

ATMs

Most banks, even in the smallest towns, have cash machines (*Bancomat*) that allow you to withdraw money with cards bearing the Eurocard, Maestro, Cirrus or Visa symbols. Your card should work in these… if the machines are turned on: in more out-of-the-way places, the ATMs are sometimes switched off at night and at weekends.

Banks

Most banks are open 8.20am-1.20pm, 2.45-3.45pm Mon-Fri. All are closed on public holidays, and work reduced hours the day before a holiday, usually closing around noon.

Credit cards

Italians still harbour a great affection for cash, although debit cards are gaining favour, and far outstripping the popularity of credit cards. Nearly all hotels of two stars and above accept at least some of the major credit cards, as do most shops.

If you lose a credit card, phone one of the emergency numbers listed below. All lines have English-speaking staff and are open 24 hours a day.

Directory

American Express 800 864 046
To speak to an operator dial 0 after the recorded message.
Diner's Club 800 864 064
Dial * twice, then dial 2 after the recorded message to speak to an operator.
Mastercard 800 870 866
Visa 800 819 014

Foreign exchange

Exchange offices (*cambio*) are plentiful at the airport, around the Stazione Centrale area, on the port side of piazza Municipio, and near all major tourist sites. Their rates are usually not as good as those offered by banks, but they are conveniently located and open much later than banks. Some city-centre branches have automatic exchange machines that will change bank notes (provided they are in good condition) from most major currencies.

Wherever you change your money, it's a good idea to bring a passport or other ID, and you will definitely need ID if you want to change travellers' cheques or withdraw money on a credit card (other than through an automatic machine).

Commission rates vary considerably: you can pay anything between nothing and €10 per each transaction. Beware of 'no commission' signs, as the rate of exchange in these places will almost certainly be terrible.

Most banks will give cash advances against a credit card, but this varies according to the bank, and increasingly, many refuse to do so if you do not have a PIN number.

Main post offices also have exchange desks. Commission is €2.58 plus 1.5% for cash transactions up to €1,032.91; traveller's cheques are not changed.

If you need to have money sent to Italy, the best method is via Thomas Cook or Western Union. There is no American Express office in Naples.
San Paolo/Banco di Napoli *Via Toledo 177/178, Toledo (081 792 4567). Bus CS, E2, R1, R4.* **Open** 8.10am-1.20pm, 2.40-3.30pm Mon-Fri. **Map** p315 1A.
Thomas Cook/MoneyGram *Airport (toll-free 800 004 488/departure lounge 081 780 1825/arrival lounge 081 780 9107).* **Open** *Departures* 5.30am-10pm daily. *Arrivals* 8am-11.30pm daily. MoneyGram levies a charge of €9.30 for up to €64, with commission rising on a scale based on the amount of the transaction. Money can be transferred to the Naples offices from any Thomas Cook or MoneyGram branch in the world.
Western Union *c/o Espresso Service, piazza Garibaldi 69, Port & University (081 207 597). Metro*

Piazza Garibaldi/bus 14, 191, 192, 194, 195, C30, C40, C58, CS, OF, R2/tram 1. **Open** 9am-7pm Mon-Fri; 9am-1pm Sat. Closed 2wks Aug. **Map** p312 2B.
Money sent from/to Western Union should arrive within the hour. Commission is paid by the sender.

Police

Naples' *polizia* aren't known for getting the job done, and any encounter may prove to be frustrating, but, should you need them, you really don't have much choice. You can report any crimes to to either the *polizia* or the *Carabinieri's Commissariati*. Stations are listed in the phone book.

Questura Centrale
Via Medina 75 (081 794 1111/ emergency 113). Bus R1, R2, R3, R4. **Map** p314 A2.
The main Polizia di Stato station.

Postal services

For postal information of any kind (in Italian), phone the central information office – 803 160 (8am-8pm Mon-Sat). After the recorded message, dial 2 if you want to talk to an operator.

Concrete improvements have been made recently in Italy's notoriously unreliable postal services, and you can now be more or less sure your letters will arrive in reasonable time (although in some southern Italian backwaters, 'reasonable' will be interpreted loosely).

Most post-boxes are red and have two slots marked '*per la città*' (for the city) and *tutte le altre destinazioni* ('for everywhere else'). Some have a blue sticker on the front for *posta prioritaria* (first class) and should, in theory, be used only for that.

Only *posta prioritaria* stamps can be used for letters sent outside the country. First-class service promises delivery in 24hrs within Italy, in three days for EU countries, and… a lot longer for the rest of the world.

A letter of 20g or less to Italy or any EU country costs 62¢, to the US 80¢, and to Australia €1. Special *posta prioritaria* stamps can be bought at post offices and *tabacchi* (*see p293*) and letters can be posted in any box, although there's more chance of them arriving within the stipulated time if they're placed in the special boxes in post offices.

Also available is the more expensive *Postacelere,* which also promises 24 hour delivery to major cities in Italy and two- to three-day delivery abroad. It is available from main post offices only, and offers you the advantage of being able to track the progress of your letter or parcel through the website.

Registered mail ('*raccomandata*') starts at €2.80. It may assure delivery but is no guarantee of speed. Private couriers (*see p287*) are quicker but considerably more expensive.

Post office
Palazzo Centrale della Posta, Piazza Matteoti, Toledo (081 790 4754). Bus 24, C57, E2, E3, R1, R3, R4. **Open** 8am-6.30pm Mon-Fri; 8am-12.30pm Sat. (Aug 8am-12.30pm Mon-Sat.) **Map** p314 2A.
This is Naples' main post office.

Queuing

Italians, and southern Italians especially, tend to have an inherent me-first attitude when driving, boarding a bus or approaching a ticket counter. If you're too polite you may just have to catch the next bus. Despite the apparent chaos, in slow lengthy lines, queue-jumpers are usually given short shrift. Hanging back deferentially, on the other hand, is taken as a clear sign of stupidity and if you're not careful the tide will sweep past you. In busy shops and bars, be aware of who is in front of you and behind you and when it's your turn, assert your rights emphatically.

Directory

Religion

You can hear the Catholic Mass in English every Sunday at 5pm at the church of **Gesù Nuovo** (*see p74*).

Anglican/Episcopal

Christ Church *via San Pasquale a Chiaia 15, Chiaia (081 411 842). Metro Piazza Amedeo/bus 140, C12, C18, C19, C24, C25, C27, C28, R3.* **Services** 10am Sun. **Map** p315 1B.
A hub for Naples' English-speaking community. The Church Hall is also used for Commonwealth Club meetings (081 640 755), American Women's Club meetings (081 560 4483), and English-speaking meetings of Alcoholics Anonymous (347 544 0254).

Baptist

Chiesa Battista *Via Foria 93, Sanità (081 287 650). Metro Piazza Cavour/bus 12, 47, 182, C51, C52.* **Services** 7pm Thur, 11am Sun. **Map** p312 2C.
There's a bilingual Italian-English service on Sundays, and on Thursdays by request.

Jewish

Comunità Ebraica *Via Santa Maria a Cappella Vecchia 31, Chiaia (081 764 3480). Metro Piazza Amedeo/bus 140, C12, C18, C19, C22, C24, C25, C27, C28, R3/tram 1, 4.* **Services** 9.30am Sat. Closed 3wks Aug. **Map** p315 1A.
For information on times and events, call the above number from 10am to noon, on Mon, Wed or Fri.

Relocation

Naples and its surrounding region is a great place to live, as long as you don't need to work. Trying to earn a living here can bring many problems, both in adjusting to southern Italian attitudes and in practical terms. If you intend to move here, you need to prove to the police that you can support yourself, or that you're in full-time education, to get a *permesso di soggiorno* (*see below*).

Documents

Having a proper job involves obtaining certain essential documents. Private agencies specialise in getting all kinds of documents if you can't face going through all the procedures yourself (look under '*Pratiche e certificati – agenzie*' in the phone book).
EU citizens employed in Italy must have the following:

Permesso di soggiorno (permit to stay)

Visitors should theoretically get a *permesso di soggiorno* (permit to stay) after eight working days in Italy; few do. You need to take your passport, three passport photos and, for non-EU citizens, a €10.33 *marca da bollo* (a tax stamp, available from *tabacchi; see p293*) and a letter from your employer, university or college – or from your spouse if they have the right to reside in Italy – to the *ufficio stranieri* (foreigners' department) of the police station at Via G Ferraris 131 (081 606 4111). Bus 3S, 191, 195. Open 8am-1pm Mon-Fri. Map p313 1A.

Codice fiscale (tax code)

This a credit card-sized piece of plastic with a number that you'll need for things as varied as opening a bank account and getting electricity for your flat. Take your passport to the nearest offshoot of the Ministero delle Finanze (for the office closest to you look for '*Agenzia delle entrate*' under *Uffici finanziari* in the phone book). It should be issued immediately. For (a limited amount of) further information consult the ministry's website at www.finanze.it.

Permesso di lavoro (work permit)

You should also have (although you may find you'll never need) a *permesso di lavoro* (work permit). This can be obtained by going to the Direzione Provinciale del Lavoro. You'll need a letter from your employer, your passport and your *permesso di soggiorno* (with photocopies).
Non-EU citizens coming to Italy to take up a prearranged job should apply for a working visa from the Italian consulate before arriving.

Certificato di residenza (residence certificate)

Certificato di residenza (residence certificate) is necessary if you want to buy a car or import your belongings without paying customs duties, but in order to get it, the tax on rubbish collection (*nettezza urbana*) must be paid for the property you reside in – which means that either you have to volunteer to pay it (and landlords renting out property but not paying taxes on the income run the risk of being discovered), or you have to persuade your landlord to do so.

Employment agencies

Adecco *Via F Crispi 52, Chiaia (081 761 8829/www.adecco.it). Metro Piazza Amedeo/bus C24, C25, C27, C28.* **Open** 9am-6.30pm Mon-Fri. **Map** p315 1B.

Manpower *Via Pessina 90, Toledo (081 564 0790/www.manpower.it). Metro Dante or Museo/bus 24, 47, CS, E1, R1, R4.* **Open** 9.30am-1pm, 3-6pm Mon-Fri. **Map** p313 1C.

Safety & security

Street crime in high in Naples. Pickpockets and bag-snatchers on foot and on scooters are particularly active in the main tourist areas and in much-frequented sites in the surrounding region. If you are a victim of any crime, go immediately to the nearest police station to report a '*scippo*'. A '*denuncia*' (written statement) of the incident will be made by or for you. You will need the *denuncia* for making an insurance claim. See also *see p292* **Police**.
To avoid being a victim take all of the usual big-city precautions:
● Attitude is crucial. Look as if you know what you're doing and where you're going.
● Don't carry a wallet in your back pocket, particularly on a bus. If you have a bag or camera with a long strap, wear it across your chest and not dangling from one shoulder.
● Keep bags closed, with your hand on them. If you stop at a pavement café or restaurant, do not leave bags or coats on the ground or draped across the back of a chair where you cannot see them.
● Hold cameras and bags on the side away from the street, so you're less likely to become the prey of a motorbike thief (*scippatore*).
● Don't pull out large wads of cash to pay for things at street stalls or in busy bars. Keep some small bills and change easily accessible.
● Don't wear expensive jewellery or watches.
● Avoid groups of noisy children. Walk past as quickly as possible, keeping a hold on your valuables. Insistent, touchy women with babies at their breast may also be after more than a coin or two.
● Crowds offer easy camouflage for pickpockets. Be especially careful when boarding buses and boats, and when entering museums.

Directory

● You will almost certainly be offered a mobile phone, video or digital camera at very attractive prices – stay away from these bargains, as you will invariably be sold a plastic toy or a block of wood.
● Only take registered, marked taxis.

Emergency numbers

Polizia di Stato (national police) 113
Carabinieri (national/military police) 112
Fire brigade 115
Ambulance 118
Car breakdown (Automobile Club d'Italia) 803 116

Smoking

Smoking is theoretically not permitted in public offices, bars, restaurants, on public transport or in taxis. For the most part, though, this law is ignored, still, times are changing and smokers will probably put out their cigarettes if you diplomatically point out the *vietato fumare* (no smoking) sign.

Tabacchi

Tabacchi or *tabaccherie*, identified by signs with a white T on a black or blue background, are the only places where you can legally buy tobacco products. They also sell stamps, phone cards, tickets for public transport, lottery tickets and the stationery that's required for dealing with Italian bureaucracy. Most *tabacchi* keep shop hours, but many are attached to bars and stay open later. Many have cigarette machines outside for when the shop is closed. These only work from 9pm to 7am.

Study

Naples' universities are the **Università Federico II** (www. unina.it), founded in 1224; the modern **Seconda Università di Napoli** (www.unina2.it); and the **Istituto Universitario Orientale** (www. iuo.it). EU citizens have the same right to study at Italian universities as Italian nationals. You will need to have your school diplomas translated and authenticated at the Italian consulate in your

own country before presenting them to the *ufficio studenti stranieri* (foreign students' department) of any university.

Centro Italiano
Vico Santa Maria dell'Aiuto 17, Centro storico (081 552 4331/fax 081 552 3023/www.centroitaliano.it). Bus 24, C57, CS, E1, E2, E3, R1, R3, R4. **Open** 9am-5pm Mon-Fri. **Map** p313 1C.
A lively language school that also offers cultural, musical and literary events, and video screenings. The school helps foreign students find temporary accommodation in Naples.

Centro Turistico Studentesco (CTS)
Via Mezzocannone 25, University (081 552 7960/fax 081 552 7975/www.cts.it). Bus CS, E1, R2. **Open** 9.30am-1.30pm, 2.30-6pm Mon-Fri; 9.30am-12.30pm Sat. **Credit** MC, V. **Map** p313 1C.
The CTS Student Travel Centre arranges discount travel tickets for students and non-students.

Telephones

All Italian phone numbers must be dialled with their area codes, even if you are phoning from within the area. All numbers in Naples and its province begin 081; this includes Pozzuoli, Ischia, Capri, Sorrento and Pompeii. It does not include Positano and Amalfi, which are in the province of Salerno, area code 089. Numbers in Caserta begin 0823 and Benevento 0824.

Naples phone numbers usually have seven digits; some of the older numbers may have six digits. If you have difficulties, check the directory (*elenco telefonico*) or ring directory enquiries (12; remain silent through the recorded message and eventually a human being will talk to you).

All numbers beginning with 800 are toll-free lines. For numbers starting 840 you'll be charged one unit only (just under 7¢ from a private Telecom phone) and 848 numbers are the same cost as a local call. For 199 numbers,

regardless of where you're calling from, the cost is two units a minute. These numbers can only be called from within Italy; some only function within one phone district.

Mobile phone numbers begin with 3; until recently they began with 03 and may still be written thus.

Public phones in Naples tend to be clustered in areas where the traffic makes it almost impossible to hear. However, as locals are addicted to their mobile phones, telephone kiosks are rarely occupied. The minimum charge for a local call is 10¢. Most public phones now only accept phone-cards (*schede telefoniche*). A few also accept major credit cards (especially at the airport or train stations).

Telecom Italia phones are silver; cards costing a variety of amounts are sold from *tabacchi* (*see p293*), some newsstands and some bars (remember to break off the perforated corner before using the card). Phone-cards have expiry dates, after which, no matter how much credit you have, you won't be able to use them.

International calls

To make an international call from Italy, dial 00, then the appropriate country code, area code (for calls to the UK or Ireland, omit the initial zero of the area code) and the individual number.

To phone Naples from abroad, dial the international code, then 39 for Italy and 081 for Naples, followed by the individual number.

To make a reverse-charge (collect) call, dial 170 for the international operator in Italy. If you are calling from a phone box, you will need to insert a coin or card, which will be refunded after your call.

Phonecards for international calls can be found in newspaper stands and *tabacchi*, especially in or near stations or ports or tourist sites. These may be issued by Telecom Italia, or by competitors such as Xenia, Europa or Planet Communi-cations. The cards can be used from any phone, public or private: dial the phone number specified on the card, then punch

in the card's PIN number. Units are subtracted as you talk.
Italian directory enquiries 12.
International operator 170.
International directory enquiries 176.
Telegrams 186.

Mobile phones

Owners of GSM phones can use them on 900, 1800 and 1900 bands, although reception can be patchy in some areas of Naples and in smaller towns in mountainous areas.

Time

Italy is one hour ahead of Greenwich Mean Time, six hours ahead of New York, and nine hours behind Sydney. The clocks are moved forward one hour in spring (*ora legale*) and back one hour (*ora solare*) in autumn, as in all EU countries.

Tipping

In Italy, tipping is discretionary, and you are quite justified in leaving nothing for service that merited nothing. However, a tip – rarely over 12% – is appreciated everywhere (and in more expensive, sophisticated eateries, it's expected). Most locals leave 10¢ or 20¢ on the counter when buying a coffee or a drink standing at a bar. The price will be much higher if you sit down at a café table and have the same thing – and your tip should be proportionately higher. It's better to tip in cash than by credit card.

Restaurants may add a service charge of 10%-15% to the bill; don't feel obliged to leave anything over this.

Rounding your fare up to the nearest euro will make a taxi driver happy; in summer beach resorts, where maids, porters and waiters work seasonally, tips are especially welcome.

Toilets

There are few public toilets in the city or outside it, and those you do find are likely to be

closed. The easiest thing is to go to a bar. Fast-food joints and some department stores can also come in handy. There are modern lavatories at or near most of the major tourist sites; most have attendants and many still require a nominal fee.

Visas

Citizens of the EU, Australia, the US, New Zealand and Canada do not need visas for stays of up to three months, after which they must apply for a *permesso di soggiorno* (*see p293*).

Water & drinking

The tap water in the city of Naples is pure spring water from the mountains, and entirely safe to drink. Most resorts around Naples also have drinkable tap water. For locals, there's no stigma attached to having *acqua non potabile* (non-drinking water); if you are in a country area, they will give you advice as to whether or not to stick to bottled water.

When to go

Naples sizzles at 30°-40° Celsius (85°-105° Farenheit) in July and August, and humidity

levels can also be high. On the islands and coast, sea breezes make the heat more bearable.

Spring and autumn are almost always warm and pleasant, with occasional heavy showers, particularly in March, April and September. March and October can be wonderful times to visit the islands, as it's extremely quiet and you stand a chance of lingering summer warmth.

From November to February, it's usually crisp with some sunshine, although there are long spells of cloudy, dreary weather. But the lack of tourists provides compensation for less than perfect weather. In December and January temperatures fall to zero, and there's a dusting of snow on Mount Vesuvius.

Festivals & events in Naples

January
La Befana *Piazza del Plebiscito.*
Map p315 1A.
The old hag who brings gifts to good children and leaves charcoal in the shoes of bad ones descends from the sky to distribute presents in piazza del Plebiscito (6 Jan).

February
Galassia Gutenberg *Mostra d'Oltremare, Fuorigrotta (081 230 3181/www.galassia.org).*
This is the largest book fair in southern Italy.

Average temperature

Month	Average high	Average low
January	12°C/54°F	4°C/39°F
February	13°C/56°F	4°C/40°F
March	15°C/59°F	5°C/42°F
April	18°C/65°F	8°C/47°F
May	23°C/73°F	12°C/54°F
June	26°C/79°F	15°C/60°F
July	29°C/84°F	18°C/64°F
August	29°C/85°F	18°C/64°F
September	26°C/79°F	15°C/59°F
October	22°C/71°F	12°C/53°F
November	17°C/63°F	8°C/46°F
December	13°C/56°F	4°C/41°F

Directory

February/March
Carnevale *081 247 1123.*
The celebration before the beginning of Lent.

March
Benvenuta Primavera *081 247 1123.*
Guided tours and theatrical 'happenings' in the squares and gardens of central Naples.

April
Settimana per la cultura *800 991 199/www.beniculturali.it.*
All of Italy's publicly owned museums are free and many open until late for this week of culture.

May
Maggio dei Monumenti
081 247 1123.
A vast calendar of free events, with access to sites that have been locked for decades, concerts and exhibitions.

May
Napoli Marathon *www.napoli marathon.it.*
Full marathon, five-kilometre fun run and a more leisurely walk.

June-September
Estate a Napoli *081 247 1123.*
Open-air films, theatre and music for 'Summer in Naples'.

July
Neapolis Festival *www.neapolis.it. Mostra d'Oltremare, Fuorigrotta.*
Local and international rock groups appear at the largest musical event in southern Italy.

July
Santa Maria del Carmine
Piazza del Carmine 2 (081 201 196). **Map** p315 1B.
The bell-tower of this church (*see p71*), is 'blown up' with fireworks on 16 July.

August
Ferragosto
The Feast of the Assumption (*Ferragosto*, 15 Aug) is celebrated all over the region; in Pozzuoli there's a competition involving shinning up a slippery pole.

September
Feast of San Gennaro
The blood of Naples' patron saint liquefies (if all goes to plan) amid frantic praying and in the presence of dignitaries in the Duomo on 19 Sept. *See p78* **Blood rites**.

December
Natale a Napoli (Christmas in Naples)
081 247 1123.
Concerts of sacred music in churches around the city.

Natale (Christmas)
Shopping frenzy in the streets around San Gregorio Armeno (*see p80*), where Neapolitans stock up on figures for their traditional Nativity scenes. Few churches are without a Christmas crib; the 18th-century examples in the Certosa-Museo di San Martino (*see p93*) and the Palazzo Reale (*see p67*) are particularly fine.

Capodanno (New Year's Eve)
Piazza del Plebiscito. **Map** p315 1A.
The New Year's Eve celebration features a packed concert of classical, traditional and rock music that lasts well into the morning, with fireworks over Castel dell'Ovo.

Festivals & events around Naples

Easter
Forio
Easter procession around town (can halt traffic for miles around).

Marina Grande
Hooded penitents carry a veiled statue of Christ through the town, accompanied by Roman centurions and hosts of little angels.

Massa Lubrense
Easter procession with hooded penitents.

Sorrento
There are processions in costume throughout the week leading up to Easter.

Vesuviana
Madonna dell'Arco. *See p224.*

April
Positano
Cartoons on the Bay (06 3749 8315/www.cartoonsbay.com), an animated film festival.

May
Salerno
Salerno Porte Aperte (089 231 432). Long-closed churches, *palazzi* and collections are open to the public.

14 May: Capri
A statue of the town's patron, San Costanzo, is carried to the sea, where procession participants are blessed.

16-18 May: Lacco Ameno
Procession and fireworks for the feast of the town's patron saint, Restituta.

Tourist information

There are three local tourist-boards in Naples, all of which provide free maps and information. For towns outside of Naples, see 'Tourist information' sections in the individual chapters in **Around Naples**.

ASST
Via San Carlo 9, Royal (081 252 5711). Bus 24, C25, C82, E3, R2, R3. **Open** 9am-1.30pm, 3-7.30pm Mon-Fri; 9am-2pm Sat, Sun. **Map** p315 1A.
Other locations: *Piazza del Gesù, Centro storico (081 552 3328/081 551 2701). Bus 24, C57, E1, R1, R4.* **Open** 9am-1.30pm, 3-7.30pm Mon-Fri; 9am-2pm Sat, Sun. **Map** p313 1C.

Ente Provinciale del Turismo (EPT)
Piazza dei Martiri 58, Chiaia (081 410 7211/fax 081 401 961). Bus 140, C12, C18, C19, C24, C25, C28, R3/tram 1, 4. **Open** 9am-2pm Mon-Fri. **Map** p315 1A.
Other locations: *Mergellina rail station (081 761 2102). Bus 140, C16, C24, R3.* **Open** 9am-6pm daily. **Map** p315 2C. *Stazione Centrale (081 206 666). Bus 14, 135, 191, 192, 194, 195, C30, C40, C58, CS, OF, R2/tram 1.* **Open** 9am-6pm daily. **Map** p312 2B.

Osservatorio Turistico-Culturale
Piazza del Plebiscito, Royal (081 247 1123/ www.inaples.it). Bus 140, C22, C25, E3, R2, R3. **Open** 9am-7pm Mon-Fri; 9am-2pm Sat. **Map** p315 1A.

May-August

Anacapri
Concerti al tramonto concert season in the Villa San Michele.

June

Amalfi
Every four years the town hosts the Regata Storica delle Antiche Repubbliche Marinare (first Sun of the month). 2005 is a Regata year.

13 June: Anacapri
Statue of the town's patron saint, Antonio di Padova, is processed around the town.

25-27 June: Amalfi
Processions and fireworks for the feast of Sant'Andrea; a statue of the saint and Amalfi's fishing fleet are blessed by local priests.

June-September

Ravello
Concerti a Villa Rufolo – classical concerts in a spectacular setting.

July

Ercolano
Festival delle Ville Vesuviane (081 732 2134/www.villevesuviane.net). Classical concerts are held in neo-classical villas.

26 July: Ischia Ponte
Fireworks and torchlit procession of boats for the feast of St Anne (www.festadisantanna.it) around the *scogli* (rocks) di Sant' Anna.

Giffoni Valle Piana
Giffoni Film Festival (089 866 363/ www.giffoniff.it). Cinema for and by children.

July-August

Minori
Jazz on the Coast (089 877 087), a series of open-air jazz concerts.

Paestum
Theatre, music and dance around the Greek temples (0828 811 016).

Positano
Procession and fireworks for the feast of the Assumption (15 Aug).

Sorrento
Classical concert season in the cloister of the church of San Francesco.

July-September

Benevento
Sannio Estate (0824 319 938) provides music and theatre in the Teatro Romano.

September

Caserta
Antiques fair in the grounds of the Reggia during the last two weeks the month.

Casertavecchia
Settembre al Borgo festival (0823 322 233). Music, dance, open-air theatre and exhibitions.

Ischia Ponte
The feast of the island's saint, Giovan Giuseppe della Croce (www.settembre sulsagrato.ischia.it), is celebrated with four days of *feste* and fireworks around the first Sun of the month.

Marina Grande
Statue of Santa Maria della Libera is carried to the sea on the Sun after 8 Sept.

Torrecuso
VinEstate, a week of wine tasting (0824 889 711).

October

Salerno
Festival Internazionale del Cinema (089 231 953/www.cinefestival salerno.it).

Sorrento
Incontri Internazionali del Cinema, a festival of feature and made-for-TV films, and cartoons.

Torre Annunziata
Procession for the feast of the town's patron saint, the Madonna della Neve (Our Lady of the Snow, 22 Oct).

December-January

Amalfi
A shining 'star' descends from Mount Tabor into the main square (24 Dec-6 Jan).

Sant'Angelo in Formis
Locals transform their village into a living Nativity scene (25 Dec).

Public holidays

On public holidays (*giorni festivi*) public offices, banks and post offices are closed. So, in theory but not always in practice, are most shops. How severely public transportation is curtailed depends on the whims of government. Christmas Day, New Year's Day, Easter Monday and 1 May are popular days for cancelling buses.
1 Jan **New Year's Day** (*Capodanno*);
6 Jan **Epiphany** (*La Befana*);
Easter Monday (*Pasquetta*);
25 Apr **Liberation Day**
(*Festa della Liberazione*);
1 May **Labour Day**
(*Festa del Lavoro*);
2 Jun **Republic Day**;
15 Aug **Feast of the Assumption** (*Ferragosto*);
1 Nov **All Saints' Day**
(*Tuttisanti*);
8 Dec **Feast of the Immaculate Conception** (*L'Immacolata*);
25 Dec **Christmas Day** (*Natale*);
26 Dec **Boxing Day** (*Santo Stefano*).
Naples shuts down entirely on 19 September, the feast of the city's patron saint, San Gennaro.

August is the holiday month and there are interminable queues on roads to holiday resorts. Many businesses, shops and restaurants close.

Women

The *maschilista* (macho) southern Italian male can be daunting for the foreign female traveller, but he is, as a rule, more bark than bite. A bit of common sense and a lot of attitude will get you out of all but the very rare worst-case scenarios.

Avoid lodging or lingering in the area around Stazione Centrale/ piazza Garibaldi; it's bad enough in the day but really horrible at night. On the other hand, you are quite safe in the Centro storico – piazza San Domenico with its strollers and strummers, while piazza Bellini with its intellectual crowd presents no greater threat than the occasional druggie. At tourist sights, there's a good chance that would-be Romeos will approach women without male companions. Perfect the art of saying 'no'. A joking tone will be much more effective than reacting in an aggressive, hurt or upset fashion.

Taxi Rosa

Consortaxi (081 552 5252/ www.consortaxi.it).
This company provides safe taxi service for single women. Call between 10pm and 6am and you will not be charged the usual 77¢ for the radio call. Your driver will see you to your door.

Health

Each district has a *Consultorio familiare* (family-planning clinic), run by the local health authority. EU citizens with an E111 form are entitled to use them, paying the same low charges as locals. Ask in any chemist's for the address of the nearest one. Queues can be interminable, but you will eventually get any advice and help you need on contraception, abortion and gynaecological care. The pill is available with a prescription. *See also p289*
Contraception & abortion.

AIED

via Cimarosa 186, Vomero (081 578 2142). Funicular Montesanto to via Morghen, Centrale to piazzetta Fuga or Chiaia to via Cimarosa/bus C28, C31, C32, C36, E4, V1. **Open** 9.30am-6.30pm Mon, Wed, Fri; 9.30am-12.30pm, 3.30-6.30pm Tue, Thur; 9.30am-12.30pm Sat. Closed 2wks Aug.
Map p314 2B.
This private clinic offers medical care, check-ups, contraceptive advice and smear tests. With a membership card (€8 for one year), check-ups cost €39 and smear tests €15.

Further Reference

The Ancients
Massie, Allan *Augustus, Tiberius, Caesar*
Popular rewrites of history.
Suetonius *De Vita Caesarum*
(Lives of the Caesars)
Ancient muck-raking by a highly biased Roman historian.
Virgil *Georgics*
Written during his stay in Naples.

Art & history
Acton, Harold *The Bourbons of Naples*
A lively historical romp focusing on the reign of Ferdinand I.
Behan, Tom *See Naples and Die: The Camorra and Organized Crime*
A vivid account of the Camorra, the criminal organisation whose influence today is as strong as ever.
Cutler, Bruce *Seeing the Darkness: Naples, 1943-1945*
An account of the liberation of the city during World War II.
Ginsborg, Paul *A History of Contemporary Italy*
Excellent introduction to the complex goings-on in post-war Italy.
Grant, Michael *Eros in Pompeii: The Erotic Art Collection of the Museum of Naples (with photographs by Antonia Mulas)*
A history of ancient Pompeii, examining all aspects of the city and its people, with emphasis on erotic imagery.
Lefkovich, Mary & Fant, Maureen *Women's Life in Greece and Rome*
A riveting collection of extracts, covering everything from ancient gynaecology to choosing a wet nurse.
Mazzoleni, Donatella *Palaces of Naples (with photographs by Mark E Smith)*
A look inside 30 of the city's estates and palaces.
Norwich, John Julius *The Normans of the South*
A colourful account of the other Norman conquest.
Palescandolo, Frank J (Translator) *The Naples of Salvatore Di Giacomo: Poems and a Play*
A collection of this Neapolitan poet's works.
Wittkower, Rudolf *Art and Architecture in Italy 1600-1750*
All you ever wanted to know about the Italian baroque.

Cuisine
Schwartz, Arthur *Naples at Table: Cooking in Campania*
A gastronomic trip through the Campania region.

Sheldon Johns, Pamela *Pizza Napoletana!*
A history of pizza, plus authentic recipes from ten of the city's pizzerias.

Fiction
Dibdin, Michael *Cosi Fan Tutti: An Aurelio Zen Mystery*
Suspense and mystery in this thriller set on the dark side of Naples.
Douglas, Norman *South Wind*
Celebration of Bacchic Mediterranean goings-on.
Sontag, Susan *The Volcano Lover*
A postmodern bodice-ripper centring on the Nelson-Hamilton trio.

Travel & biography
Casanova di Seingalt, Giacomo *The Story of My Life*
The libertine's highly coloured autobiography includes adventures in 18th-century Naples.
Goethe, Johann Wolfgang *Italian Journey*
The German poet's 18th-century travel diary; the translation by WH Auden and Elizabeth Mayer is best.
Hazzard, Shirley *Greene on Capri*
Memoirs of a post-war Capri resident's meetings with the writer.
Lewis, Norman *Naples '44*
Experiences of an intelligence officer in wartime Naples.
Munthe, Axel *The Story of San Michele*
A whimsical, self-glorifying account of the Swedish doctor's life, times and love affair with Anacapri.
Tullio, Paolo *North of Naples, South of Rome*
Life in the Comino Valley.
Walton, Susana *Behind the Façade*
Bloomsbury moves to Ischia.

Il Decameron (dir Pier Paolo Pasolini, 1970).
Pasolini used Neapolitan locations and dialects for his adaptation.
Napoli D'Altri Tempi (dir Amleto Palermi, 1938).
Composer renounces fame and fortune for his anonymity in Naples; starring Vittorio De Sica.
L'Oro di Napoli (dir Vittorio De Sica, 1954).
Featuring Sophia Loren, Eduardo de Filippo and Totò; anthology of tales depicting aspects of Neapolitan life.
Polvere Di Napoli (dir Antonio Capuano, 1998).
Update of *L'Oro di Napoli*.
Il Postino (dir Michael Radford, 1994).
Oscar-winning drama based on the life of Chilean poet Pablo Neruda.

Le Quattro Giornate di Napoli (dir Nanni Loy, 1962).
Oscar-nominated war drama.
Totò, Peppino e La... Malafemmina (dir Camillo Mastrocinque, 1956).
Classic comedy.

Almamegretta *Sanacore*
Dub and techno.
Bennato, Edoardo *Non farti cadere le braccia*
Still produces hits after 30 years.
Bennato, Eugenio *Taranta Power*
Folk songs from southern Italy.
Daniele, Pino *Terra Mia*
Melodic blues.
99 Posse *Curre curre guaglio'*
Politics, rap and hip hop.
Nuova Compagnia di Canto Popolare *Lo guarracino*
Folk outfit.
Pavarotti, Luciano *Favourite Neapolitan Songs* Includes *O' Sole Mio* along with other Neapolitan classics.
Sepe, Daniele *Spiritus Mundi*
Eclectic saxophonist.
Spaccanapoli *Lost Souls*
This group had adopted *tarantella* style to make modern music.

Culture, museums & events
www.aziendaturismonapoli.com
www.beniculturali.it
Culture Ministry site (Italian only).
www.comune.napoli.it
The Naples City Council's site.
www.ept.napoli.it
The tourist board's excellent site.
www.guidatour.it
The Chamber of Commerce's site.
www.icampiflegrei.it
www.italia.ms/campania/napoli
www.museoapertonapoli.com
Information on the excellent Open Museum Service.

Popular culture
www.antoniodecurtis.com
All about comic actor Totò.
www.napolisworld.it/napoli gentile/index.htm
Information on the city's parks.

Listings
www.campaniahotels.com
http://napoli.lanetro.it
http://napolinews.too.it
www.napolichespettacolo.it
www.napoli.com
www.nottambulando.it
www.touchnapoli.com

Glossary

Amphitheatre (*ancient*) oval open-air theatre
Apse large recess at the high-altar end of a church; adj **apsidal**
Ashlar large square-cut stones, usually used to face a building (*see also below* Rustication)
Atrium (*ancient*) courtyard
Baldacchino canopy supported by columns
Balustrade series of vertical posts and a handrail, usually as protection on the open side of a flight of stairs
Baptistry building – often eight-sided – outside church used for baptisms
Baroque artistic period from the 17th to 18th centuries, in which the decorative element became increasingly florid, culminating in Rococo (*qv*)
Barrel vault a ceiling with arches shaped like half-barrels
Basilica ancient Roman rectangular public building; rectangular Christian church
Bas-relief carving on a flat or curved surface where the figures stand out from the plane
Brunelleschi considered the first Renaissance architect, Filippo Brunelleschi (1377-1446) applied his discoveries in the field of perspective to his classical-style architectural designs
Byzantine artistic and architectural style drawing on ancient models developed in the fourth century in the Eastern empire and developed through the Middle Ages
Campanile bell tower
Capital the decorated head of a column (*see below* Orders)
Cardine (*ancient*) secondary street, usually running north–south
Caryatid supporting pillar carved in the shape of a woman
Castellated (building) decorated with battlements or turrets (*see also* Crenellations)
Cavea semicircular step-like seating area in an amphitheatre (*qv*) or theatre (*qv*)
Chapter room room in monastery where monks met for discussions
Chiaroscuro painting or drawing technique using no colours, but shades of black, white and grey
Choir area of church, usually behind the high altar, with stalls for those singing sung mass
Cippus (*ancient*) cylindrical stone or marble block standing on one end, usually as a milestone or funerary monument
Coffered (ceiling) with sunken square decorations
Colonnade row of columns supporting an entablature (*qv*) or arches

Confessio crypt (*qv*) beneath a raised altar
Crenellations battlements and/or archery holes on top of building or tower
Cupola dome-shaped roof or ceiling
Crypt vault beneath the main floor of a church
Cryptoporticus underground corridor
Decumanus (*ancient*) main road, usually running east–west
Domus (*ancient*) Roman city house
Embrasure a recess around the interior of a door or window; a hole in a wall for shooting through
Entablature section above a column or row of columns including the frieze and cornice
Ex-voto an offering given to fulfil a vow; often a small model in silver of the limb/organ/loved one to be cured as a result of prayer
Fresco painting technique in which pigment is applied to wet plaster
Gothic architectural and artistic style of the late Middle Ages (from the 12th century), using soaring, pointed arches
Greek cross (church) in the shape of a cross with arms of equal length
Hypogeum (*ancient*) underground room
Impluvium (*ancient*) cistern in the middle of a courtyard to gather rainwater funnelled into it by a sloping roof with a hole in the middle
Insula (*ancient*) city block
Intarsio technique by which patterns or pictures are made in wooden surfaces by inlaying pieces of different-coloured wood
Latin cross (church) in the shape of a cross with one arm longer than the other
Loggia gallery open on one side
Mannerism High Renaissance style of the late 16th century; characterised in painting by elongated, contorted human figures
Marquetry wooden inlay work, also known as intarsio (*qv*)
Mullioned windows made up of small panes divided by vertical bars
Narthex enclosed porch in front of a church
Nave main body of a church; the longest section of a Latin-cross church (*qv*)
Necropolis (*ancient*) literally 'city of the dead'; graveyard
Nymphaeum (*ancient*) grotto with pool and fountain dedicated to the Nymphs, female water deities; name given to ornate fountains with grottos in Renaissance architecture
Ogival (of arches, windows and so on) curving in to a point at the top
Orders classical styles of decoration for columns, the most common being

the very simple Doric, the curlicued Ionic and the leafy, frondy Corinthian
Palaestra (*ancient*) wrestling school
Palazzo large and/or important building (not necessarily a palace)
Parlatorio a convent or monastery's reception room or room for conversation
Pendentives four concave triangular sections on top of piers supporting a dome
Peristyle (*ancient*) temple or court surrounded by columns
Piazza (or **largo**) square
Pilaster square column, often with its rear side attached to a wall
Portal imposing door
Portico open space in front of a church or other building, with a roof resting on columns
Presbytery the part of a church containing the high altar
Pronaos (*ancient*) roofed temple vestibule (*qv*) with closed sides and columns in its open front
Proscenium (*ancient*) stage; arch dividing the stage from audience
Reggia royal palace
Reliquary receptacle – often highly ornate – for holding and displaying relics of saints
Rococo highly decorative style fashionable in the 18th century
Romanesque architectural style of the early Middle Ages (c500-1200), drawing on Roman and Byzantine influences
Rustication large masonry blocks, often roughly cut, with deep joints, used to face buildings (*see also above* Ashlar)
Sacristy room in church, usually off choir (*qv*), where vestments are stored
Sarcophagus (*ancient*) stone or marble coffin
Spandrel near-triangular space between the top of two adjoining arches and the ceiling or architectural feature resting above them
Stucco plaster
Succorpo similar to a crypt (*qv*), underground space beneath the apse (*qv*) of a church
Tablinium (*ancient*) private study
Tessera small piece of stone or glass used to make mosaic
Theatre (*ancient*) semicircular open-air theatre
Transept shorter arms of a Latin-cross church (*qv*)
Triclinium (*ancient*) dining room
Triumphal arch arch in front of an apse (*qv*), usually over the high altar
Trompe l'oeil decorative painting effect to make surface appear three-dimensional
Tufa volcanic stone widely used in building
Vestibule entrance hall

but Italian. In Naples... foreign-language speakers are even thinner on the ground. The exceptions to this rule are Sorrento, which is practically a British colony, and Ischia, where you can use any language you like as long as it's German.

Any attempt on your part at spoken Italian, no matter how atrocious, will be appreciated.

Italian

Italian is spelled as it is pronounced, and vice versa: learn. Grammar books will tell you that the stress falls on the penultimate syllable, but this is not a fail-safe rule: pronunciation must be learnt by trial and error.

There are two forms of address in the second person singular: *lei*, which is formal, and *tu*, which is informal. Older southern Italians will use *voi* for both.

PRONUNCIATION
Vowels
a – as in *a*sk
e – like *a* in *a*ge (closed e) or *e* in s*e*ll (open e)
i – like *ea* in *ea*st
o – as in h*o*tel (closed o) or h*o*t (open o)
u – as in b*oo*t
Consonants
c and *g* both go soft in front of *e* and *i* (becoming like *ch* and *g* in *ch*eck and *gi*raffe respectively).

Before a vowel, *h* is silent. An *h* after *c* or *g* makes them hard, no matter what vowel follows.

gl – like *lli* in mi*lli*on
gn – like *ny* in ca*ny*on
qu – as in *qu*ick
r – always rolled
s – either as in *s*oap or in ro*s*e
sc – like *sh* in *sh*ame
sch – like *sc* in *sc*out
z – can be *ds* or *tz*

Neapolitan

If your hard-learned Italian is proving inexplicably useless, don't despair: what you're hearing is probably Neapolitan dialect. It's something more than an accent but less than a language, spoken habitually between Neapolitans of all ages and classes: even other Italians don't understand a word of it.

PRONUNCIATION
Neapolitans tend to...
...leave off the ends of words, or put an English *er* sound: *buona ser'* (*buona sera*) or *librer* (*libro*, book).
...replace some *e* sounds by *ie*: *tiemp'* (*tempo*, time/weather) or *apiert'* (in Italian *aperto*, open).
...replace some words beginning *pi* by a very hard *ki* sound: *cchiu* (in Italian *più*, more).
...replace a hard *sc* (like *sk* in English) by a soft, English-style *sh*: *scusate* (excuse me) becomes a drunken-sounding *shcusate*.
...make *a* sounds longer than other Italians: *Napule* (Neapolitan for Naples) is *Naapuler*.
... turn *v* into *b*: *che volete?* (what do you want?) becomes *che bullite?*
... turn *d* into *r*: *domenica* (Sunday) becomes *rumenica*.

Other hints
Bene (well) becomes *buono* (good).
Indefinite articles: *un/uno* (a/n, masculine) become *nu*; *una* (a/n, feminine) becomes *na*: *nu gelaete* (*un gelato*, an ice-cream).
Definite articles: *il/lo* (the, masculine) become *'o*; *la* (the, feminine) becomes *'a*: *'o gelaete* (*il gelato*, ice-cream).

ENGLISH/ITALIAN/NEAPOLITAN
basics
hello/goodbye (informal) ciao
hello (informal) salve
good morning buon giorno
good evening buona sera
good night buona notte
please per favore, per piacere
thank you grazie
you're welcome prego
excuse me, sorry mi scusi (formal), scusa (informal); *shcusate* (formal and informal)
I'm sorry mi dispiace; *dishpiasher*
I don't speak Italian (very well) non parlo (molto bene) l'italiano; *non parl' buon' l'italian'*
I don't/didn't understand non capisco/non ho capito; *n'aggio capit'*
how much is (it)? quando costa?/quanto viene?
open aperto; *apierto*
closed chiuso
entrance entrata
exit uscita
where is? dov'è?; *a ro'sta?*

Transport
bus autobus
coach pullman
train treno
underground railway metropolitana (metro)
platform binario
ticket/s biglietto/biglietti

a ticket for... un biglietto per...
one way sola andata
return andata e ritorno
right destra
left sinistra

Communications
phone telefono
email posta elettronica
fax fax
stamp/s francobollo/francobolli
letter lettera
postcard cartolina

Eat, shop, sleep
See also p124 The menu.
a reservation, booking una prenotazione
I'd like to book a table for four at eight vorrei prenotare una tavola per quattro persone alle otto
breakfast/lunch/dinner colazione/pranzo/cena
the bill il conto
is service included? è compreso il servizio?
that was poor/good/(really) delicious era mediocre/buono/(davvero) ottimo
I think there's a mistake in this bill credo che il conto sia sbagliato
100g/300g/1kg/5kg of... un etto/tre etti/un kilo (or *chilo*)/cinque chili di...
more/less ancora/di meno
shoe/clothes size numero/taglia
a single/twin/double room una camera singola/doppia/matrimoniale
a room with a (sea) view una camera con vista (sul mare)

Days & nights
Monday lunedì
Tuesday martedì
Wednesday mercoledì
Thursday giovedì
Friday venerdì; *viernari*
Saturday sabato
Sunday domenica; *rumenica*
today oggi
tomorrow domani; *rimane*
see you tomorrow! a domani!
morning mattina
afternoon pomeriggio
evening sera
night notte
weekend fine settimana, weekend

Numbers
0 zero, 1 uno, 2 due, 3 tre, 4 quattro, 5 cinque, 6 sei, 7 sette, 8 otto, 9 nove, 10 dieci, 11 undici, 12 dodici, 13 tredici, 14 quattordici, 15 quindici, 16 sedici, 17 diciassette, 18 diciotto, 19 diciannove, 20 venti, 30 trenta, 40 quaranta, 50 cinquanta, 60 sessanta, 70 settanta, 80 ottanta, 90 novanta, 100 cento, 200 duecento, 1,000 mille, 2,000 duemila, 200,000 duecentomila, 1,000,000 un milione.

Index

Advertisers' Index

Please refer to the relevant page for contact details

Place of interest	▨
Railway station	▨
Park	▨
Metro station	Ⓜ Ⓜ
Metro route	▬ ▬
Archaeological site	⊡
Area name.	VOMERO
Main road	▬▬

Maps

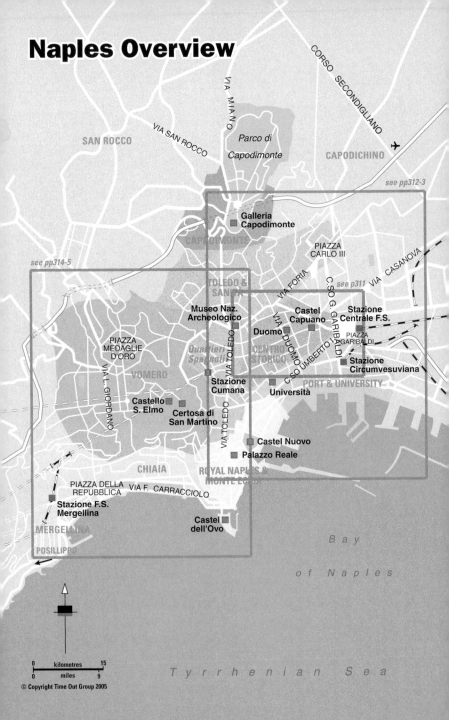

Naples Overview

CORSO SECONDIGLIANO

VIA MIANO

VIA SAN ROCCO

SAN ROCCO

Parco di Capodimonte

CAPODICHINO

see pp312-3

Galleria Capodimonte

PIAZZA CARLO III

CAPODIMONTE

see pp314-5

TOLEDO & SANITA

VIA CASANOVA

VIA FORIA

see p311

C.SO G. GARIBALDI

Museo Naz. Archeologico

Castel Capuano

Stazione Centrale F.S.

PIAZZA MEDAGLIE D'ORO

Duomo

VIA DUOMO

PIAZZA GARIBALDI

VIA L. GIORDANO

VIA TOLEDO

Quartieri Spagnoli

CENTRO STORICO

Stazione Circumvesuviana

VOMERO

Stazione Cumana

C.SO UMBERTO

Castello S. Elmo

Università

PORT & UNIVERSITY

Certosa di San Martino

VIA TOLEDO

Castel Nuovo

Palazzo Reale

CHIAIA

ROYAL NAPLES & MONTE ECHIA

PIAZZA DELLA REPUBBLICA

VIA F. CARRACCIOLO

Stazione F.S. Mergellina

Castel dell'Ovo

B a y

MERGELLINA

POSILLIPO

o f   N a p l e s

0   kilometres   15
0   miles   9

© Copyright Time Out Group 2005

T y r r h e n i a n   S e a

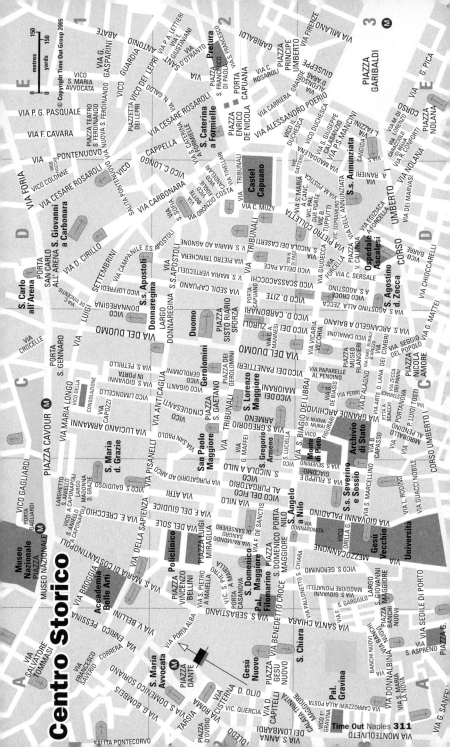

Centro Storico

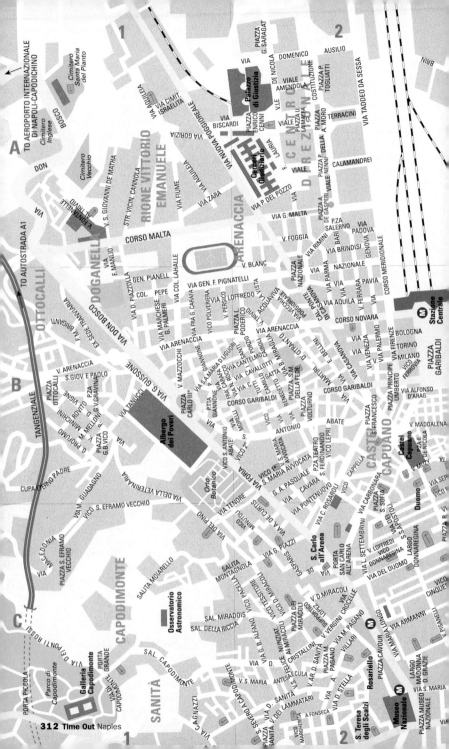

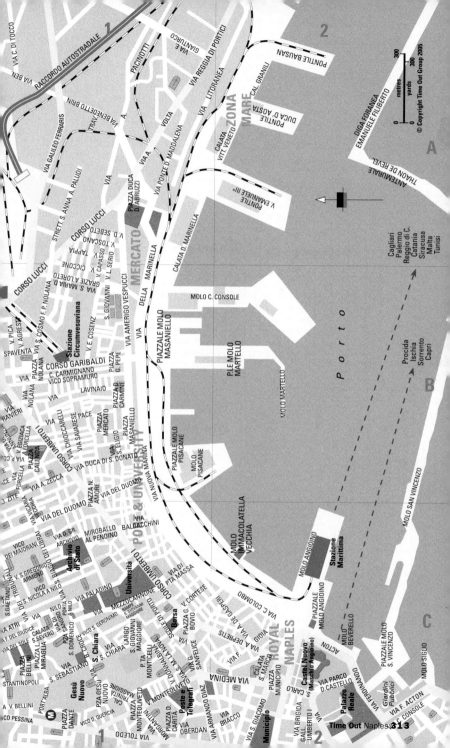

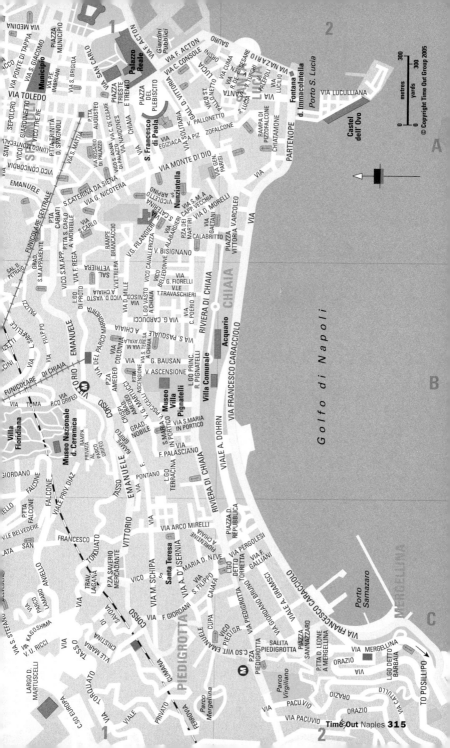

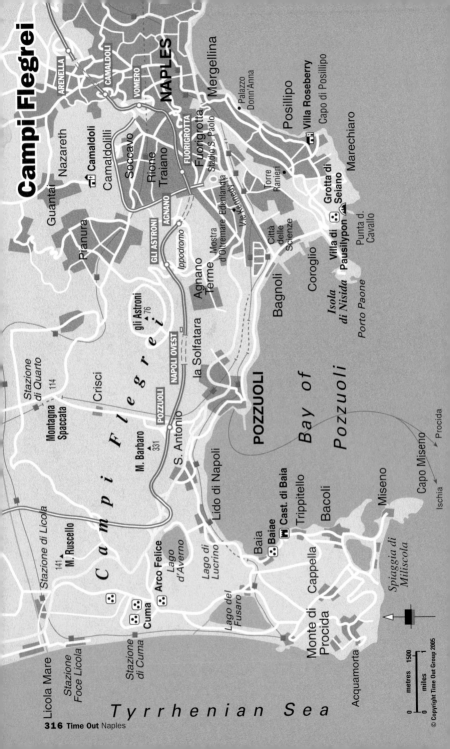

Campi Flegrei

NAPLES

ARENELLA

CAMALDOLI

VOMERO

Mergellina

Palazzo Donn'Anna

Posillipo

Villa Roseberry

Capo di Posillipo

Camaldoli

Camaldolilli

Soccavo

Rione Traiano

Stadio S. Paolo

FUORIGROTTA

Fuorigrotta

Marechiaro

Nazareth

Guantai

Torre Ranieri

Grotta di Seiano

AGNANO

Pianura

GLI ASTRONI

Ippodromo

Mostra d'Oltremare

Edenlandia

Viale Kennedy

Città delle Scienze

Villa di Pausilypon

Punta d. Cavallo

gli Astroni
▲ 76

Agnano Terme

Bagnoli

Coroglio

Isola di Nisida

Porto Paone

Stazione di Quarto

Crisci

la Solfatara

NAPOLI OVEST

POZZUOLI

Bay of

Pozzuoli

Procida

Montagna Spaccata

114

POZZUOLI

S. Antonio

Stazione di Licola

M. Barbaro
331

Campi Flegrei

Lido di Napoli

M. Ruscello
141 ▲

Capo Miseno

Ischia

Licola Mare

Stazione di Licola

Arco Felice

Lago d'Averno

Lago di Lucrino

Baia

Baiae

Cast. di Baia

Trippitello

Bacoli

Miseno

Stazione Foce Licola

Cuma

Lago del Fusaro

Monte di Procida

Cappella

Spiaggia di Miliscola

Stazione di Cuma

Acquamorta

T y r r h e n i a n   S e a

metres 1500

miles

0

0

© Copyright Time Out Group 2005

316 Time Out Naples

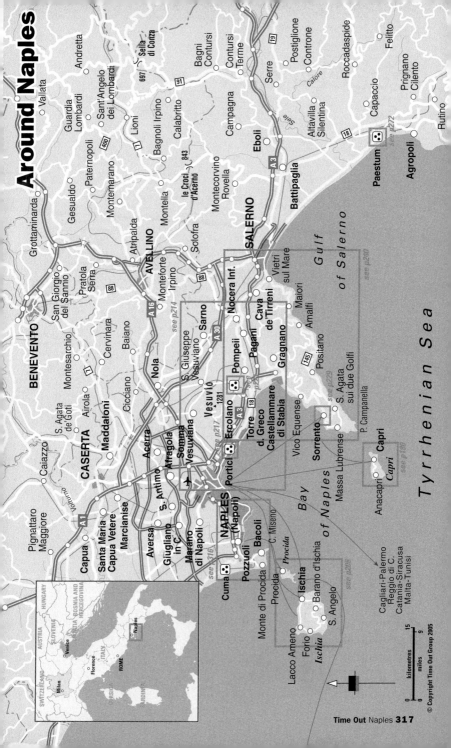

Street Index